Also by George McT. Kahin

Nationalism and Revolution in Indonesia (1952)

The United States in Vietnam (with John Lewis, 1967)

Editor

Major Governments of Asia (1958, 1963)

Governments and Politics of Southeast Asia (1959, 1964)

INTERVENTION

INTERVENTION

How America Became
Involved in Vietnam

by George McT. Kahin

Alfred A. Knopf   New York   1986

THIS IS A BORZOI BOOK
PUBLISHED BY ALFRED A. KNOPF, INC.

A portion of this work was originally published
in *Pacific Affairs*, Winter 1979–1980.

Library of Congress Cataloging-in-Publication Data

Kahin, George McTurnan.
Intervention: how America became involved in Vietnam.

1. Vietnamese Conflict, 1961–1975—United States.
2. Vietnam—Politics and government—1945–1975.
3. United States—Foreign relations—Vietnam.
4. Vietnam—Foreign relations—United States.
I. Title.
DS558.K34   1986   959.704'33'73   85–45703
ISBN 0-394-54367-X

Manufactured in the United States of America

FIRST EDITION

For Audrey

Contents

Maps will be found on pages 2, 43, and 402

Preface

In an unprecedented effort to shape and control a country's political character, the power of the United States was for some thirty years projected into Vietnam —at first indirectly through France, and then directly. Beginning a few months after the Second World War, this effort lasted until 1975; but its crucial formative period ended in mid-1966, by which time American policy was locked on course and the society of Vietnam's southern half had become fully polarized. With its focus on these first two decades, this book seeks to make understandable why and how the United States intervened in Vietnam.

Although military aspects of this involvement have been dealt with extensively, the political side has received relatively little attention, and it is with this dimension and its relationship to other aspects of American involvement that this book is principally concerned. Therefore, one of my major emphases is on the way in which changing Vietnamese political factors—both within and outside Saigon-controlled areas—impinged on and crucially affected both the military and the political aspects of American policy and its execution. I also focus on the reverse of that process, for both the changing character and magnitude of the American intervention and the shifting character of political forces in South Vietnam produced an ongoing interdependence and interaction—an often unpredictable dynamic—to which U.S. policymakers were obliged to react, albeit sometimes with disparate counsel and discordant actions.

The American effort to influence the political character of Vietnam began during France's postwar attempt to reassert control over the country, but that effort became more intense after French forces withdrew, when Washington wished to prevent the extension of communist control over additional Vietnamese territory. The building of a separate anticommunist state in southern Vietnam demanded a continuing American effort aimed at shaping the Saigon government into an instrument supportive both of U.S. strategic and geopolitical objectives and of the military policies required to attain them. This book analyzes that process, and the internal Vietnamese factors that confronted the United States and affected American policies. These factors were subject to frequent change, in large part because American efforts to control the course of Vietnamese politics, together with the physical and psychological impact of U.S. firepower, precipitated strong nationalist reactions and created new or altered political forces. An understanding of the context of American involvement requires a fuller treatment of the militant Buddhists, the National Liberation Front, and factional divisions and competition within Saigon's armed forces than has, I believe, been available in earlier studies, and this I have sought to provide.

Against this background, it should be easier to understand and evaluate the course of Vietnam's political and socioeconomic life, as well as the often divergent assessments of American policymakers and the decisions they urged. And against it, too, one should be better able to judge how well American presidents were served by their advisers. The book also concerns itself with relevant aspects of domestic American politics and the global strategic and political perspectives that heavily influenced Washington policymakers.

I have drawn on and tried to weave together three principal strands of information: the views of Vietnamese civilian and military leaders gained in interviews during half-a-dozen visits to Vietnam from 1961 to 1972; information from American officials, from several levels, who were concerned with Vietnam, as well as from a number of knowledgeable British and French officials; and some 12,000 pages of U.S. government documents declassified under the Freedom of Information Act that I was able to obtain over a ten-year period. This material substantially augments that available in the three editions of the *Pentagon Papers,* of which I have also made good use.

My first relevant interviews were with John Foster Dulles in 1950 and Ngo Dinh Diem in 1953; the most recent, with George Ball, McGeorge Bundy, and William Bundy in 1984–85. In addition, other government officials, active and retired, have been generous in the time they have given me. Among them, I would particularly like to thank Averell Harriman, Paul Kattenburg, James Thomson, Jr., and the late John Paul Vann, as well as Etienne Manac'h, formerly head of the Quai d'Orsay's Far Eastern Division, and the late Anthony Eden (Lord Avon). To William Bundy I wish also to record my gratitude for letting me read his unpublished but extensive and richly informative study of American policy toward Vietnam during 1961–65. The disinclination of Robert McNamara to be interviewed on matters pertaining to the Vietnam war explains his absence from this roster, while a similar disposition on the part of Dean Rusk accounts for the fact that I record only one discussion with him, which took place in 1965.

I have also benefited from talks with numerous active and retired civilian and military leaders of the Saigon government, and I wish to express my gratitude to them for the time they spent in helping me understand its often convoluted civilian and military politics. This book also reflects, I believe, the unusual access I had to the leadership of both the Buddhists and the NLF; and I should like to record my debt especially to three of the Buddhist leaders with whom I spent many hours of enlightening conversation—Thich Nhat Hanh, Thich Tri Quang, and the late Thich Thien Minh—as well as to two NLF leaders whom I met and who during different periods each served as that organization's secretary-general

—Nguyen Van Hieu and Tran Buu Kiem—for the open and informative discussions I had with them.

I have made considerable, and I believe discriminating, use of the uneven coverage provided by the three editions of the *Pentagon Papers,* including the rare separate volume of footnotes keyed to the Government Printing Office edition (and now deposited in Cornell University's library) which is useful in determining the quality of certain narrative sections of the *Papers.* Most of the U.S. government documents which I have utilized, however, were obtained under the Freedom of Information Act. I am fortunate that I initiated my requests for them in 1974, the beginning of a brief period when, on balance, that act was interpreted in ways that usually helped rather than hindered scholarly research. Although many important documents which I have specifically requested have not been released, a large amount of material—describing important aspects of American activities in Vietnam and areas of U.S. policymaking not covered in the *Pentagon Papers*—has been declassified and made available to me. The time consumed and frequent frustration involved in the effort to secure declassification should be evident when I note that it has averaged almost two years per document, with some taking as long as six. Under the Reagan administration, such declassification requests have usually fared much worse than under the Ford and Carter administrations; and recently one key document bearing on the removal of Diem, which President Johnson himself declassified in 1968, has been reclassified. Nevertheless, it should be emphasized that the relevant documents which have become available since the appearance of the *Pentagon Papers* illuminate numerous crucially important matters not covered there. These recently released materials are also helpful in compensating for some inaccurate or superficial coverage in the *Papers.* (Unless otherwise noted, declassified documents referred to in this study can now be found in the library of the president in office on the date of the document in question.) Having earned the dubious reputation of being the initiator of the largest number of specific requests for declassification of U.S. documents relating to Vietnam, I want to thank the many Foreign Service officers and other officials saddled with the dismal task of responding to these requests and to subsequent appeals for review of initially negative decisions.

My access to the documents was greatly expedited by assistance, well beyond the call of duty, from archivists in the Eisenhower, Kennedy, Johnson, and Truman libraries, as well as by the staff of the National Archives and Britain's Public Records Office.

Among these archivists, I should like especially to thank Megan Desnoyers, Martin Elzy, David Humphrey, Martin McGann, Martin Teasely, John Wickman, and Don Wilson. My thanks go also to Nancy Bressler of Princeton's Seeley G. Mudd Library and to Giok-po Oey, Mary Crawford, John Hickey, and Joan Smith of Cornell's John M. Echols Collection on Southeast Asia and Serials Collection.

I would like to acknowledge a special debt to three American Vietnam specialists who critically and with great care read one or more of the draft chapters of this book (all of them, Chapter IV): David Elliott, David Marr, and Gareth Porter. Two younger scholars at Cornell, Alan Epstein and Leslie Watson, gave me valuable assistance in organizing and analyzing many of the declassified documents used in this study and by offering some excellent suggestions. Thanks also go to James Coyle, Judith Ecklund, Maria Pestiau, Maureen Hoffert, and Esta Ungar, for helping assemble and order the incoming tide of documents and other materials. I alone, of course, am responsible for all interpretations and analyses in this study.

For her sensitive and accurate translation of most of the Vietnamese-language materials I have used, my deep appreciation goes to Mai Elliott. My thanks for similar translations go also to James Nach and Gareth Porter; and for most of the translations from Chinese, to Jia Qing-Guo.

Work on this book began more than ten years ago, but it would have taken several more to complete had it not been for support from the Guggenheim and Luce foundations which freed me from periods of teaching, and to both of them I am very grateful. My thanks also go to the Lyndon Baines Johnson Library for a travel/research grant, to the Rockefeller Foundation's Villa Serbelloni at Bellagio, where I began the first chapter, and to the Institute of Southeast Asian Studies in Singapore, where I completed the last draft of the book.

In the final stages of writing I had the good fortune of working with Ashbel Green of Knopf. I could not have had a more perceptive or understanding editor, and his suggestions for clarification and amplification, as well as his editing, have significantly improved this study. I am very grateful, also, to the copy-editor, Terry Zaroff, for a most excellent, thorough, and conscientious job.

Whatever clarity and felicity of language this book may have is even more attributable to my wife, Audrey. In addition to giving me her unflagging encouragement, she edited several drafts and helped ensure greater balance and objectivity; her role was also critical in helping me keep this book from running an additional hundred pages.

GEORGE McT. KAHIN
May 1985

INTERVENTION

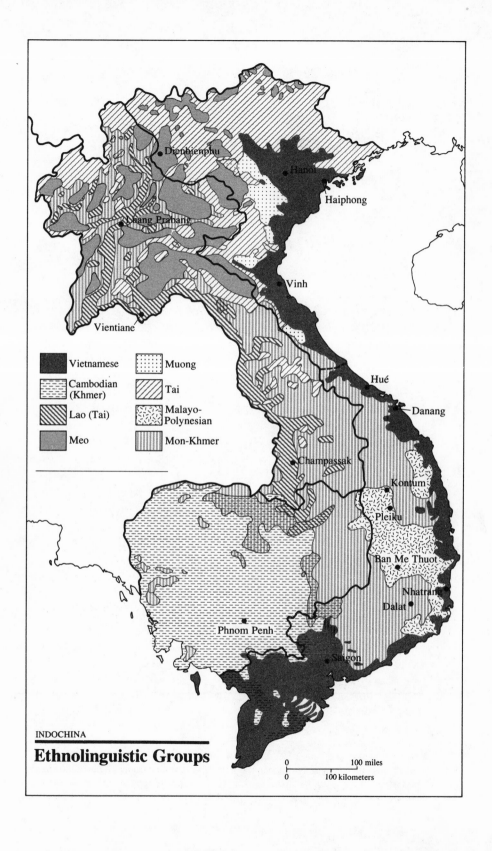

Vietnamese

Cambodian
(Khmer)

Lao (Tai)

Meo

Muong

Tai

Malayo-
Polynesian

Mon-Khmer

Dienbienphu

Hanoi

Haiphong

Luang Prabang

Vinh

Vientiane

Hué

Danang

Champassak

Kontum

Pleiku

Ban Me Thuot

Nhatrang

Dalat

Phnom Penh

Saigon

INDOCHINA

Ethnolinguistic Groups

0   100 miles

0   100 kilometers

I

The Beginnings of
American Intervention

The American policies that so heavily shaped the course of Vietnamese history for three full decades after World War II were never intrinsically Vietnamese in orientation: they were always primarily directed by considerations transcending that country. For at least the first three years after the war, because of France's position as the keystone of U.S. European policies, American priorities in Europe —not Asia—brought U.S. power indirectly, but nevertheless heavily, to bear in Vietnam. Insofar as communism was then an issue, it was primarily its potential in *France* that shaped American policy toward Vietnam. Moreover, until 1954, well after Mao Tse-tung had displaced Chiang Kai-shek on the China mainland and after the conclusion of the Korean war, Washington's policy toward France continued to have a strong influence on its approach to Vietnam, although no longer unchallengeably dominating it. Certainly the crucial factor that set in motion three decades of America's involvement in Indochina was the U.S. relationship with France.

Washington's policy toward the French-Vietnamese dispute did indeed fly in the face of an anticolonialism that was still popular in the United States in the postwar years. Even before the war ended, however, American policymakers, some of whom shared this anticolonialist sentiment, had begun to conclude that the United States had more important, countervailing interests.[1]

President Franklin D. Roosevelt's own bitterness toward French rule in Indochina stemmed not only from its harsh and exploitative character, but also from his conviction that, by their opportunistic collusion with Japan, Indochina's Vichy French officials had been responsible for the enemy's outflanking both the Philippines and Singapore.* This bitterness led to the president's initial insistence

*In an agreement of September 22, 1940, the Japanese recognized Vichy French sovereignty in Vietnam in exchange for the right to station up to twenty-five thousand troops in Tonkin (the northern third of Vietnam). A subsequent pact permitted Japanese naval units and aircraft to use naval bases and airfields all the way down to the southern tip of Vietnam beginning July 20, 1941. In December,

that France's control over its Southeast Asian colonies be replaced by a postwar United Nations trusteeship. Well before his death, however, this view had yielded before two compelling considerations, grounded in areas far distant from Indochina. First was the heavily European priority of American strategic interests, which initially required French support in the North African campaign against the Axis, and subsequently France's cooperation in the postwar economic reconstruction of Western Europe and its defense against Soviet military power. Second was the incompatibility of advocating a U.N. trusteeship for Indochina while refusing the same status for the Pacific islands that American forces had wrested from Japan. The U.S. military insisted that these islands be retained because of their strategic importance, and if Washington had continued to demand a U.N. trusteeship for France's former Southeast Asian colonies, its case for retaining control over these erstwhile Japanese territories in the Pacific would have been undercut.[2]

In the face of these considerations, Roosevelt, though still hostile to French colonialism, backed away from his earlier insistence on an international trusteeship for Indochina. A month before his death he agreed to France's retaining the area if she would simply "assume the obligations of a trustee" with the "proviso that independence was the ultimate goal."[3]

When Roosevelt died on April 12, 1945, he may have left American and French officials confused regarding U.S. policy toward Indochina,[4] but his successor soon began to clarify that policy. Within less than a month the Truman administration made clear that it recognized French sovereignty there, and top-level U.S. foreign-policy officials expressed no opposition to a return of French power. Truman did not share Roosevelt's strong anticolonial views and had apparently never been fully privy to his feelings about a resumption of French control over Indochina. Indeed, anticolonialism was a factor of marginal importance in the new administration's policies. Though it wished, like its predecessor, to hold on to the previously Japanese-controlled Pacific islands, its attitude was also determined by two other, critically important considerations. First was the immediate need to secure France's cooperation at the San Francisco Conference —where the United Nations was being established. Second, and in the long run more important, was the growing concern that U.S. opposition to French policies in Indochina might shake the precarious balance of French domestic politics to the advantage of the Communist Party, which in the 1946 elections proved to be the largest political party in France. Washington feared that, even if the communists did not turn out to be strong enough to head a Cabinet, adverse nationalistic reaction to American criticism on Indochina would make France less likely to cooperate with American plans in Europe. And here, of increasing and enduring importance, was the U.S. desire that France play a key role in the organization of Western Europe's defenses to offset Soviet military power.

---

soon after their attack on Pearl Harbor, the Japanese secured the vague but far-reaching concession of permission to utilize facilities "necessary to the pursuit of the war."

With the Communist Party able to gain a minority position in the French Cabinet, Truman-administration officials continued to be acutely anxious about the dynamics of French domestic politics for at least three years after the end of the war. Throughout this period they feared that any American pressure to grant prompt and genuine self-determination to the peoples of Indochina would risk upsetting the existing, precarious balance of political forces in France to the benefit of both the French communists and Moscow.

It is evident that Charles de Gaulle and his successors were very conscious of Washington's anxiety. They played on U.S. fears even before Roosevelt died, and quite calculatedly continued to do so throughout the Truman administration.[5] As early as mid-March 1945, when Soviet troops were pushing into Germany, de Gaulle appealed to the United States to help the French forces in Indochina, whose marriage of convenience with the Japanese had just ended. He admonished:

> What are you driving at? Do you want us to become, for example, one of the federated states under the Russian aegis? The Russians are advancing apace as you well know. When Germany falls they will be upon us. If the public here comes to realize that you are against us in Indochina there will be terrific disappointment and nobody knows to what that will lead. We do not want to become Communist; we do not want to fall into the Russian orbit, but I hope that you do not push us into it.[6]

French fears of any residuum of Roosevelt's early position on Indochina were laid to rest in early May at the U.N. Conference in San Francisco, when Secretary of State Edward Stettinius made clear to France's foreign minister that the United States had never questioned, "even by implication, French sovereignty over Indochina."[7]

There was, however, a vigorous minority opposition view within the State Department, particularly in its small, newly established Southeast Asia Division, headed by Abbot Low Moffat, which consisted of area specialists, many temporarily seconded from academic life. This group argued that acquiescence in the return of French authority in Indochina should be dependent upon assurances that France would grant its peoples an increasing measure of autonomy, leading toward self-government. The head of the department's Office of Far Eastern Affairs, John Carter Vincent, gave some support to this position, but the more influential European-oriented officials in the department opposed it. In addition to their fears of prejudicing prospects for French support in Europe and at the United Nations, many of them had little sympathy for, or understanding of, colonial nationalism, and they were thus quite unwilling to use American leverage to move France toward such goals. These officials continued to dominate American policy toward Indochina throughout the long postwar struggle France waged with Vietnamese nationalism.[8]

Opposition within the State Department was never fully overcome, but the official position that emerged in its governing policy paper of June 22, 1945,[9] tilted heavily toward the views of its European desks, with American interests in Europe decisively overriding concern for the self-determination of colonial peoples. Strikingly absent was the bold language of the Atlantic Charter's pledge that sovereign rights and self-government would be restored to all those who had been forcibly deprived of them, and nowhere was "independence" posited as a goal for the colonial areas of Asia. The United States' "chief objective" in the area was stated to be "continuing peace and security." To achieve this, it was acknowledged, it would be "probably necessary" for the peoples there to have "the largest possible measure of political freedom . . . consistent with their ability to assume the responsibility thereof." But pursuit of that objective had to accord with what was referred to as "one of the foremost policies of the United States," namely, "to maintain the unity of purpose and action of all the United Nations, especially the leading powers," France included. No suggestion was made that in its efforts "to harmonize" these objectives, the United States should apply any pressure on France. It might, however, "properly continue to state the political principle . . . that dependent peoples should be given the opportunity, if necessary after an adequate period of preparation, to achieve an increased measure of self-government." But it was reiterated that, even with respect to that politically modest goal, the United States "should avoid any course of action which would seriously impair the unity of the major United Nations" (meaning, in the case of Vietnam, Franco-American unity).

The acting secretary of state, Dean Acheson, dispelled any remaining doubts regarding U.S. policy in a series of cables to American diplomats, beginning August 30, that reiterated Stettinius's assurances regarding Washington's acknowledgment of French sovereignty over Indochina, and advised them that the "U.S. has no thought of opposing the reestablishment of French control. . . ."[10]

This general United States position toward Vietnam underwent no fundamental change throughout both Truman administrations. French sovereignty was recognized without qualification; though the United States would continue to urge France—in polite and friendly terms—to grant a significant measure of self-government to the Vietnamese, the United States would refrain from applying economic or political leverage in an attempt to push Paris toward that objective. Yet the State Department's policy paper of June 22, 1945, estimated that the French would encounter "serious difficulty" in overcoming the opposition of the nationalist Vietminh under Ho Chi Minh and in re-establishing French control, and that "an increased measure of self-government would seem essential if the Indochinese are to be reconciled to continued French control." It also noted that "Independence sentiment in the area is believed to be increasingly strong," with the Vietminh representing "some ten different native political groups," and carrying "substantial influence with between one-quarter and one-half million persons." It concluded that "the supporters of independence are neither apathetic nor supine and are willing to fight."[11]

For some two months following Japan's surrender in mid-August 1945, most of the handful of Americans in Vietnam acted in ways at odds with Washington's policy, displaying sympathy and support for the Vietnamese nationalists rather than for the French. Probably the major reason for this was an initial failure to transmit effectively the policy decisions of May–June 1945 to American OSS (Office of Strategic Services) and army personnel operating in the Indochina area. For some six months after Roosevelt's death, these men, some of whom were strongly anticolonial in outlook, therefore tended to assume that Roosevelt's earlier opposition to the return of Indochina to French control remained the fundamental basis of U.S. policy. Unaware of the increasingly European bias of Washington's global view, they naturally looked with favor upon those Vietnamese nationalists who had helped Americans fight against a common enemy. Ho Chi Minh, the leader of these anti-Japanese forces, was generally viewed as a man whose attachment to communism was overshadowed by his nationalism. Thus, Abbot Low Moffat later recalled, "I have never met an American, be he military, O.S.S., diplomat, or journalist, who did not reach the same belief: that Ho Chi Minh was first and foremost a Vietnamese nationalist."[12]

A badly ravaged postwar France possessed neither the military equipment nor the financial resources to mount a major military effort in Indochina. It was thanks to the United States that she was able to marshal the crucial elements of power which she began to apply there within a few months of the war's end. For the most part indirectly—channeling its aid through metropolitan France—the Truman administration supplied de Gaulle's postwar government and its successors with the essential means, manpower apart, for their military campaign in Vietnam.

The public position of "neutrality," whereby the United States would not "assist or participate in forceful measures for the imposition of control" by France, officially precluded the sale of armaments to the French for use in Indochina and the transport of any war materiel or troops to or from the area in U.S. ships. In fact, however, the Truman administration supported and helped finance all of these actions. The French were permitted to keep without payment the substantial armory of "Lend-Lease" equipment the United States had given de Gaulle's forces for use in the projected Allied assault on Japan's home islands. When Japan's unexpected capitulation made that campaign unnecessary, the French were free to use these arms as they saw fit, together with additional large amounts of similar U.S. equipment handed over to them in Vietnam by the British. French troops soon turned this firepower on Ho Chi Minh's Vietminh and other smaller nationalist organizations in Vietnam, and, despite protests from the Southeast Asia Division of the Department of State,* the Truman administration acquiesced.[13]

*The most this dissident State Department group could achieve was to hold up for about a month the release of ships from the Allied shipping pool requested by Paris for transporting troops to Indochina, and to get Secretary of State James Byrnes to order all U.S. insignia removed from American equipment. Like the Dutch in Indonesia, however, the French frequently neglected to observe this restriction.

Moreover, within two months of Japan's surrender, American ships in large numbers were carrying French forces to Vietnam, and Washington provided Paris with credits to help it purchase seventy-five U.S. troop transports. Thereafter the United States supplied Paris with a large quantity of modern weaponry —ostensibly for the defense of France and Western Europe, but with the understanding that a substantial part could be used for the military campaign in Indochina. Although the U.S. position officially remained that American arms could not be sold to France "in cases which appear to relate to Indochina," no such limitation was operative. In fact, the State Department acknowledged this in a secret policy statement of September 27, 1948, to the effect that U.S. arms being exported to France were "available for reshipment to Indochina or for releasing stocks from reserves to be forwarded to Indochina." As Robert Blum, a member of the U.S. Marshall Plan mission to France who subsequently (1950–53) served as chief of the U.S. mission to Vietnam, later put it, following the end of the war the United States supplied France with military equipment "for a colonial reestablishment [in Indochina] indirectly by way of Paris."[14]

At least as important to France's war effort in Indochina as the supply of military hardware was the substantial financial support that the United States provided. The first Truman administration did not grant credits specifically earmarked for her large expeditionary force in Vietnam, any more than it designated arms for that theater. But just as the United States was aware that many of its arms dispatched to France were being diverted to Vietnam, so it understood that a considerable portion of its funds being pumped into France to restore the war-shattered economy were being pumped out to maintain her expeditionary force in Indochina. It is clear that Paris could not have otherwise financed her military effort in Vietnam.[15]

This policy was not unique. In Indonesia, the only other area of Southeast Asia where indigenous nationalists mounted a major military challenge to the return of colonial power, American policy for more than three years after the war closely paralleled that in Vietnam, tilting substantially in favor of the Dutch, and for the same reasons.* But France's relatively greater importance for Washington's European objectives made American policymakers even more unwilling to contest its attempt to re-establish control over its former colony.[16]

In accepting U.S. military and financial support, France refused to accede to continued American prodding to move toward granting the substance of self-government to her Vietnamese protégés. Not until nine years after the end of World War II, when her armies in Vietnam were sustaining their ultimate defeat, did she finally do so. The French government's intransigence in this matter was not simply a consequence of often cited psychological and economic

---

*This partiality for the colonial power was not lost on the indigenous Southeast Asian populations. As a CIA assessment of November 1947 noted, "Already in Indonesia and Indochina the native population tends to regard Dutch and French efforts to reestablish their control as having been made with U.S. support. To the extent that the European Recovery [Marshall] Program enhances Dutch and French capabilities in Southeast Asia, native resentment toward the U.S. will increase."

factors, although these certainly played a role. The need to compensate for the nation's bitter humiliation in World War II through a reassertion of French "grandeur" in her overseas empire was undoubtedly important. Washington as well as Paris regarded French nationalism, smarting from the ignominy of defeat and occupation by Nazi Germany, as too sensitive to countenance any further blow to national pride, such as would attend France's forced withdrawal from Indochina, without an explosively indignant reaction. The validity of this consideration was attested to by the fact that, for more than two years after the war, the French Communist Party held back from pressing for Vietnam's independence, because it assumed that such a position would lose it votes. France's economic interests in Indochina were not extensive, of minor value in comparison with those in her North African colonies. The Bank of Indochina, the principal lobbyist for French economic interests in Vietnam, however, exerted an influence in the French Parliament heavily disproportionate both to the area's secondary economic importance, and to the number of Frenchmen with an economic stake there.[17]

More important for policymakers in Paris, however, was what they regarded as a vital strategic factor transcending Indochina and relevant to the internal political cohesion of France's overseas empire as a whole. Often known colloquially as the "ten-pin theory," this had a dynamic comparable to that of the subsequent American-coined "domino theory," but it was better grounded. According to this view, if one colony won its independence, nationalism would be encouraged elsewhere in overseas France, with the first fallen colonial tenpin striking others, which could in turn bring down the whole stand. More specifically, if Vietnam fell before the onslaught of indigenous nationalism, there would be political repercussions not merely in economically unimportant Cambodia and Laos, but in France's more valuable overseas possessions, Morocco, Tunisia, and —most important of all—Algeria, with its one million French *colons*. The currency of this theory, and the seriousness with which it was viewed in France, were given a sharp boost in early 1947 with the outbreak of a major rebellion in the rich colony of Madagascar. The French finally subdued the uprising by a ruthless application of military power, requiring a major diversion of troops en route to Vietnam, which some believed was responsible for the failure of the fall 1947 offensive to crush the Vietminh. French officials were convinced, moreover, that the leaders of the Madagascar insurrection had drawn direct inspiration from the Vietnamese nationalists.[18]

The organization of the Indochinese Communist Party in southern Vietnam (Cochin China) had been shattered in December 1940 when the French suppressed an abortive insurrection headed by the party, executing or jailing most of its leadership in that part of the country. This not only left the residual party organization stronger in the center (Annam) and strongest in the north (Tonkin), but opened the way to ascendancy within the party for less doctrinaire communist leaders, such as Ho Chi Minh. Huynh Kim Khanh, in his recent comprehensive study of Vietnamese communism, concludes that this event helped change the organization's stance. "In addition to the Party's isolation from the international Communist movement, the elimination of most of the internationalist-oriented leaders, who had complied closely with whatever line Moscow espoused, facilitated the reascendancy of leaders who had stressed the creative adaptation of Marxism-Leninism to the sociopolitical conditions of Vietnam." In this situation Ho Chi Minh—who, after playing a prominent role in the development of Vietnamese communism from the mid-1920s until 1931, but thereafter having fallen out of favor with the Comintern's leadership—could more easily emerge as the paramount leader.[19]

Leaving the Soviet Union in the winter of 1938–39, probably in a convoy of trucks carrying war materiel to Chiang Kai-shek's forces, Ho arrived in China on his way back to Vietnam. After spending time in both Yenan and Chungking, he moved to the southern frontier area, held by Chiang's Kuomintang government, and finally, in February 1941, crossed over into Vietnam. Drawing on both noncommunist and communist underground nationalist elements that had managed to survive the joint repression of the French Sureté and the Japanese Kempeitai, Ho Chi Minh and his lieutenants then began to organize a resistance movement in Vietnam directed against both the Japanese and the French. In May 1941,* under their leadership, residual elements of the prewar Indochinese Communist Party met in Vietnam, just across the border from their previous sanctuary in the southern area of Chiang Kai-shek's China, and established a national united front, the Vietnam Doc Lap Dong Minh (League for the Independence of Vietnam), better known by its abbreviation, Vietminh.[20]

Ho's ideological pragmatism was reflected in the political line that was then agreed upon. National liberation was assigned top and overriding priority, a goal to which Vietnamese communists were called upon to subordinate all other objectives. This meant that the long-planned agrarian revolution would have to await the achievement of national liberation. All social, economic, and religious groups were appealed to, to work toward the immediate goal of freeing the country from both Japanese and French domination. Pending achievement of that objective, only the properties of those landlords who collaborated with the French and Japanese (a not inconsiderable number) would be confiscated and redistributed to the peasantry. The Vietminh rapidly introduced a program with broad popular appeal which was to be carried out by locally elected people's committees: reduction of land rents and interest on loans; abolition of forced labor and of all French and Japanese taxes and their replacement by a single progressive tax; the introduction of primary education; a campaign against illiteracy; and laws protecting labor.[21]

---

*Local Kuomintang (Nationalist) Chinese authorities jailed Ho from August 1942 to September 1943, not releasing him until finally convinced that only his Vietminh cadres could provide reliable intelligence on Japanese troop strength and movements on China's southern flank in Vietnam.

On March 9, 1945, five months before Tokyo's capitulation, there was a sudden rupture of the five-year-old marriage of convenience between the Japanese and the pro-Vichy French colonial administration. Fearing an Allied invasion and suspecting that shifts in the fortunes of war would induce their French collaborators to align themselves with the Allies and de Gaulle's Free French, the Japanese army ousted and rounded up nearly all French colonial civil and military elements in Indochina (except for a minority of the military that escaped to China). The Japanese then declared Vietnam "independent" and undertook to establish a client Vietnamese administration that they hoped could take over some of the governmental functions that their Vichy French collaborators had previously exercised. The Japanese initially planned that this new "government" would be headed by Prince Cuong De, an elderly representative of the Nguyen dynasty—the imperial house that had lost its power to France half a century before—who had long resided in Japan. He was to replace Bao Dai, whom the French had appointed emperor in 1932. Ngo Dinh Diem, who had once briefly served Bao Dai, agreed to be Cuong De's prime minister, but refused to take the post when at the last minute, in March 1945, the Japanese changed their minds and decided to stick with Bao Dai. Now reconfirmed as emperor, Bao Dai found himself almost as much a figurehead under the Japanese as he had been under French rule. He and Tran Trong Kim, Japan's second choice for prime minister, soon discovered that the promise of independence was spurious, and that they would have little scope for building up an administration to replace that of the now incarcerated French. Not until July did they get the Japanese to relinquish direct administration of Hanoi, Haiphong, and Danang; and not until the day before Japan's capitulation were they given jurisdiction over Cochin China. Very quickly the Tran Trong Kim–Bao Dai regime, and the handful of nationalists from the Japanese-sponsored Dai Viet party and others who had believed the Japanese would ensconce them in real power, were discredited and, despite their goals of independence, came to be regarded by much of the populace as opportunistic accomplices, or even lackeys, of Japan.[22]

With its already well established underground organization, the Vietminh was able to take immediate advantage of the changed situation and assert a political presence in most of the void left by the removal of the French colonial administration. From its broadened base it began to operate much more effectively in the mountainous areas of the North against the now badly overextended Japanese forces, which had already withdrawn from some of their most exposed positions.

Hopeful of receiving American assistance, and expecting an ultimate U.S. invasion against Japanese forces in Vietnam, Ho Chi Minh had early in 1945 taken the initiative in contacting American OSS and military officers stationed in southwestern China, including General Claire Chennault, commander of the U.S. Fourteenth Air Force. Ho personally accompanied a downed American pilot rescued by the Vietminh to Kunming, where he turned him over to the U.S. military. On the basis of this entrée he had numerous discussions with OSS officers, emerging as their agent with the code name of "Lucius," and arrangements were made for Vietminh-OSS cooperation.[23]

By the time the first of five OSS teams arrived in northern Vietnam in May 1945, the Vietminh was in control of most of the six northernmost provinces. In the context of the United States' all-out effort to defeat Japan, it is natural that OSS operatives should have forged an *ad hoc* alliance with this group, since it was the paramount organized nationalist force in Vietnam. As did Chang Fa-k'uei, one of Chiang Kai-shek's senior South China generals, the American military and OSS officers saw Ho's communist-led nationalist coalition as the only substantial anti-Japanese force available. It alone could deliver the military help they needed: by providing accurate intelligence on the strength and movement of Japanese forces; harassing them, cutting their supply lines, and in some cases pinning down their garrisons; providing weather reports for the U.S. air force, and finding and helping downed American pilots. It made good sense for the OSS to provide Ho's poorly armed followers with a modest quantity of American small arms, radios, and medicines.[24]

When Ho Chi Minh formally established a "liberated zone" on June 4, 1945, the Vietminh controlled substantial parts of ten northern provinces—and their strength was soon to burgeon as a consequence of the first steps in their "Great August Revolution." To meet their war requirements the Japanese had forced peasants in many areas to substitute jute, hemp, and castor beans for food crops, and by late 1944 they had exacerbated food shortages through a policy of forcing the sale of rice, which they collected for their own use into huge granaries in anticipation of an Allied invasion. Adverse weather conditions in 1945 then further reduced food crops, as did the widespread flooding caused by Allied bombing of the dikes. The French and the Japanese, partly because of the disruption of transport facilities, burned surplus southern rice normally sent to central and northern Vietnam to fuel factories and power plants. In the famine that ensued, during 1944–45, it is estimated that between one and two million of the ten million inhabitants of the northern half of Vietnam died. When the famine became acute, Vietminh cadres and soldiers led hungry peasants in driving off Japanese guards and breaking open some of the granaries. More than any other action, this identified the Vietminh both as a symbol of opposition to Japan and as a champion of the peasantry. Thus, Alexander Woodside concludes, "The Vietminh, indeed, rode to power upon two slogans—'national independence' and 'destroy the paddy granaries and solve the famine,' " with the campaign to destroy the granaries and solve the famine becoming "the centerpiece of revolutionary mobilization." William Duiker notes that Truong Chinh, one of Ho's top lieutenants, held that "the focal issue" in the August Revolution was the famine, and that "Communist-led armed demonstrations in front of government granaries were the key to the development of the movement in rural areas throughout the North." And, as Christine White has observed, "The seizure of Japanese or French rice stocks and the establishment of village revolutionary government went hand in hand, while Vietminh membership increased many times over."

Indeed, most scholars agree that it was this early and very palpable championing of a famine-ravaged peasantry, together with the Vietminh's unequivocal anti-Japanese and anti-French nationalist stance, that was chiefly responsible for its rapid increase in popular backing.[25]

With Japan's collapse, the Vietminh launched a well-planned general insurrection. Its control quickly spread beyond its northern Tonkin base, and on August 12, immediately after news of Japan's surrender, it called for a general uprising to seize power throughout Vietnam. With plans for this already well under way, the response was immediate, and Vietminh cadres found themselves in the vanguard of a movement that embraced most of the country. On August 19, thousands of peasants from near Hanoi joined with city dwellers to seize power in the capital, taking over all government installations except a few that were still guarded by the Japanese.[26] With thousands of peasants marching into the royal capital of Hué and seizing government buildings unopposed, Emperor Bao Dai offered to abdicate on August 23, and a week later turned over the royal seal and other regalia to a Vietminh committee, which also accepted his offer to serve its government as a common citizen.

It was during this period that Ho Chi Minh radioed OSS headquarters:

> National Liberation Committee of VML [Vietminh League] begs U.S. authorities to inform United Nations the following. We were fighting Japs on the side of the United Nations. Now Japs surrendered. We beg United Nations to realize their solemn promise that all nationalities will be given democracy and independence. If United Nations forget their solemn promise and don't grant Indochina full independence, we will keep fighting until we get it.[27]

The Vietminh's road to power was greatly eased, and indeed made possible, by the absence of French troops and the passivity of most of the overextended Japanese forces. As early as June and July, some Japanese commanders were content to abide by a largely tacit accommodation with the Vietminh and left it pretty much alone. Shaken and demoralized by Tokyo's sudden decision to surrender to the Allies, the others soon followed suit. As long as the Vietminh did not challenge their now primarily urban concentrations of troops, Japanese commanders rarely contested its operations in the countryside.[28]

The Vietminh's main military problem at this early stage was not with Japanese units but with uncooperative elements of the armed Vietnamese auxiliaries who had served both the French and the Japanese. These included the militias of the collapsing Japanese-sponsored Bao Dai–Tran Trong Kim administration, as well as the smaller associated or autonomous elements armed by the Japanese from the Dai Viet party and Prince Cuong De's Restoration League (Phuc Quoc) in the North, and the Hoa Hao and Cao Dai religious sects in the South. Some two weeks after Japan's capitulation, the Vietminh began to encounter more serious adversaries, when the numerous and better-armed adherents of two Chinese-supported Vietnamese nationalist parties, the VNQDD (Viet Nam Quoc Dan Dang—Vietnamese Nationalist Party) and the Dong Minh Hoi (Vietnamese Revolutionary League) crossed the northern frontier in the train of the first Kuomintang Chinese occupation units.[29]*

The Vietminh moved quickly to establish additional local revolutionary committees throughout as much of the country as possible. It hoped, if possible, to pre-empt an Allied occupation, or at least to obviate the need for more than a token British and Chinese presence. The situation has been succinctly described by Moffat:

> The Vietnamese tried to take over all Vietnamese territory and disarm the Japanese before the Allies should arrive in Indochina. They were successful in establishing a working administration in . . . Tonkin and Annam, but factional dissension among various independence groups in Cochin China minimized the effectiveness of their administration [there]. . . . Nevertheless for twenty days the Provisional Vietnam Government [the Vietminh] ruled all the territory inhabited by the Vietnamese. Then the British placed the French back in power in the area they controlled south of the 16th parallel. In the north the Vietnamese remained in power by arrangement with the nationalist Chinese who were there to secure the disarming of the Japanese north of the 16th parallel.[30]

However tenuous the Vietminh's administrative hold over the South, American OSS agents were impressed by evidence of its enjoying support throughout most of the country. These Americans had established a close working relationship with the Vietminh, and it must have seemed natural for some of them to share the reviewing stand with General Vo Nguyen Giap, head of the Vietminh army, in the ceremonies in Hanoi on September 2, 1945, when Ho Chi Minh declared Vietnam's independence. Presumably the Vietminh's inclination to believe that the United States would give its independence movement at least moral support was enhanced when, in early October, General Philip Gallagher, U.S. adviser to the incoming Kuomintang Chinese occupation forces, and his American staff joined with the OSS units in Hanoi to help found the Vietnamese-American Friendship Association.[31]

Ho Chi Minh's hopes of U.S. support for his country's independence were not merely the result of the cooperative relationship that had developed between his Vietminh and American military and intelligence personnel. Like those of anticolonial nationalists in other Southeast Asian countries, his expectations had been affected by several other factors: the persistent advocacy of the principle of self-determination in the wartime broadcasts of the U.S. Office of War Information; the United States' unqualified espousal of the Atlantic Charter's provision

*The VNQDD was an underground anti-French organization established in 1927 and modeled on the Chinese Kuomintang, and the Dong Minh Hoi was the rump residuum of a Kuomintang-sponsored coalition from which the VNQDD had pulled out.

that sovereign rights and self-government would be restored to all peoples who had been forcibly deprived of them; and Washington's clear-cut promise of independence to the Philippines. Although Ho was probably not entirely sanguine about actual U.S. performance, it seemed appropriate, on the basis of these overt indications of American policy and the expectations they had aroused, for the Vietnamese band to play "The Star-Spangled Banner" at the independence celebrations, and for Ho, in proclaiming this independence, to incorporate phrases from the United States' own Declaration.[32]

With Indochina, as with Indonesia, during the early postwar period the United States was shielded from any direct confrontation over the issues raised in the struggles between nationalists and the colonial po ᵣrs. In both disputes the Truman administration was able to maintain a plausible public attitude of neutrality, in part because it channeled most of its support to the colonial armies through Paris and The Hague, rather than directly to the areas of combat in Southeast Asia. Two additional circumstances, however, also made it easier for the United States to avoid taking a partisan stand in behalf of the two colonial powers. The first of these was the roles assigned to Britain, in Indonesia and in the southern half of Indochina, and to Kuomintang China, in the northern half of Indochina, in liquidating the Japanese occupation; and the second was the noncompetitive nature of Soviet policy during this period. Both factors were also of enormous benefit to France and the Netherlands in their efforts to reassert control over these former colonies.

At the Potsdam Conference of July 1945, Admiral Louis Mountbatten's British Southeast Asia Command was given wider territorial responsibilities in order to free American forces for the anticipated invasion of Japan. In the Indochina region, Britain was now responsible for Cambodia and for Vietnam and Laos south of the sixteenth parallel, and Chiang Kai-shek's government for Vietnam and Laos north of that parallel. Britain and China, then, had the task of disarming and repatriating Japanese troops throughout Indochina and freeing all Allied prisoners and internees. The two commands confronted very different situations, for the Vietminh had a much stronger organization and popular foundation in the northern half of Vietnam than in the South. In part, this was a result of the differing character of the Japanese occupation in the two areas. Their direct control in the southern regions was not relaxed until the very eve of their surrender, whereas varying degrees of authority had been delegated to the Bao Dai–Tran Trong Kim administration in much of the North and central Vietnam from one to four months earlier.[33]

North of the sixteenth parallel, only four significant political groups contested for power with the Vietminh: the VNQDD; the Dong Minh Hoi; Prince Cuong De's followers in the Japanese-backed Phuc Quoc; and the faction-ridden Dai Viet (Greater Vietnam Party), a 1940 offshoot from the VNQDD that was soon sponsored by the Japanese Kempeitai (military police). The total membership of all four was much smaller than that of the Vietminh, and was almost exclusively urban and drawn largely from former civil servants and other petit-bourgeois elements. Moreover, the nationalist credentials of each of these groups had been sullied by dependence upon an unpopular outside power, whereas the Vietminh during this period had the advantage of being considered to have established cordial relations with the United States, the power credited with defeating Japan. The Phuc Quoc and Dai Viet groups, though genuinely aiming for independence, had grown up with largely covert—but widely known—Japanese backing, initially including only small arms, but, following Japan's March 1945 coup against the French, involving heavier weapons as well. The VNQDD and Dong Minh Hoi, though pledged to full independence from China as well as from France, had spent the last few years in South China, where they had been financed and armed by Kuomintang generals.[34]

In the South, on the other hand, there was less political homogeneity. Although the Vietminh was the strongest nationalist element, it faced competing groups with broader popular backing and/or cleaner nationalist records than its competitors in the North. Unique to the South was a vigorous Trotskyist group that had substantial backing in Saigon and no external ties. It opposed the Vietminh's efforts to negotiate with the British and, indeed, sabotaged Vietminh efforts to work out compromise arrangements with them. Rather less idealistic, but politically significant because of the arms it had received from the Japanese, was the Binh Xuyen, a group named after the village in the marshes south of Saigon that was its original headquarters. It was an amalgam of bandit gangs, some of whose members had been released by the Japanese from prison. The Binh Xuyen soon came to terms with the Kempeitai, and in pursuing various rackets either was unmolested by or cooperated with the Saigon police.[35]

More important in the South were two strongly nationalist religious organizations, the Cao Dai and the Hoa Hao, each with a substantial popular following and a small quantity of arms that the Japanese had given them. The creed of the Cao Dai, established in the late 1920s, was an eclectic synthesis of some of the world's major religions, with the Buddhist element probably strongest. It had an estimated membership of over a million, and by 1944 the Japanese were giving some three thousand of its members rudimentary military training, though no arms. The Hoa Hao, named after a village in the far-western Mekong Delta, was an unorthodox mystical sect of Theravada Buddhism founded in 1939 that by 1945 was believed to have enrolled close to a million members, mostly in the western Mekong Delta, in an organization generally regarded as much less centralized than that of the Cao Dai. Within two years of its formation, the Hoa Hao were being given a measure of protection by the Japanese against the French Sureté, and by the end of 1943 were able to deploy armed village patrols. Apparently, following the Japanese coup against the Vichy French administration of March 6, 1945, both sects received a significant increment of light arms from the Japanese. The Japanese encouraged them in their anti-French posture and their support of Prince Cuong De as emperor.[36]

In 1945, elements from both the Cao Dai and the Hoa Hao initially joined with the Vietminh in the South in an uneasy coalition, but effective cooperation proved difficult from the outset. Moreover, in part because of their resentment at the sects' collaboration with the Japanese, local Vietminh officials were sometimes heavy-handed in dealing with them. Each side occasionally resorted to brutal measures against adherents of the other. By late 1945, the Hoa Hao, "in spite of its long tradition of anti-colonialism had become more interested in fighting the Communists than the French." In sum, while there were periods of transitory rapprochement between the sects and the Vietminh, their differences remained—differences that the French deliberately moved to exploit.

On January 8, 1947, the signing of a military accord between the top Cao Dai leader and the French signaled an end to prospects for Vietminh cooperation with most of that sect. Four months later, the growing rift between the Vietminh and most of the Hoa Hao became unbridgeable when that sect's founder and leader, Huynh Phu So, was assassinated under circumstances that indicated Vietminh instigation.[37]

The Vietminh's increasing difficulties with the sects and the harsh measures it took to eliminate its Trotskyist opponents helped ensure that, though clearly the strongest nationalist group in the South, it would continue to have a narrower base of support there than in the northern and central parts of Vietnam. Moreover, as noted above, the severity of French repression following their abortive uprising in the Mekong Delta of November-December 1940 had left the communists—whether as a separate party or as a component of the Vietminh—weaker below the sixteenth parallel than they were above it. Furthermore, in 1945 the party remnants in the South appeared to be suffering from internal divisions.[38]

In pursuit of their main tasks of disarming and repatriating the Japanese and freeing Allied prisoners, British forces entering Indochina had been charged with maintaining law and order. They were also instructed to give "every assistance necessary" to the French representatives in "all matters affecting the civil population," but they had no authority to intervene politically themselves. Yet they did just that. Despite Mountbatten's admonitions that Major General Douglas Gracey, the British commander in southern Indochina, confine his operations "to those limited tasks he had been set," Gracey intervened heavily, in accordance with his own, clearly evident pro-French prejudices. His actions contrasted with those of British generals operating under roughly similar circumstances in Indonesia, who soon felt it prudent to negotiate with the revolutionary nationalists there and seek some sort of compromise between them and the Dutch. The "law and order" Gracey undertook to establish was exclusively in behalf of the French.[39]

Soon after he arrived in Saigon on September 13, Gracey presented Mountbatten and the British government with several *faits accomplis* that decisively altered the political balance in southern Vietnam. Not only did his actions strongly favor the French over the Vietminh; they also inadvertently undermined the latter's ascendancy within the fragile, disparate Vietnamese coalition that was

governing Saigon and most of the South when the first units of Gracey's British/
Indian division arrived. On September 22, he released and armed fourteen hundred French troops whom the Japanese had interned in March, helping them
stage a coup against the Vietminh administration, which he in effect outlawed.
Also contrary to Mountbatten's wishes (but later supported by the British Chiefs
of Staff), he then expanded his grant of authority beyond the Saigon area and
undertook to help the French re-establish control over as much of southern
Vietnam as possible.[40] With insufficient British and French forces to secure this
objective, or even to control Saigon effectively, Gracey relied heavily on the
assistance of the Japanese troops he had been sent to disarm. In addition to
dragooning the surrendered Japanese into carrying out extensive patrol duties in
Saigon and its surroundings, he ordered their units into offensives against the
Vietminh and other Vietnamese nationalist groups there and much farther afield,
and even, on September 27, threatened to treat Japanese officers as war criminals
if they did not cooperate. Japanese soldiers and airmen, in fact, provided much
of the military muscle marshaled by Gracey. The importance of their role in
helping the British subdue the Vietnamese nationalists and re-establishing the
French is evident in official British casualty figures for the period of most intense
conflict during Gracey's stewardship—mid-October through January 13. In this
fighting, slightly more Japanese were killed (129) than British/Indian and French
forces combined (125). A total of 1,303 Vietnamese were killed, wounded, or taken
prisoner by Japanese troops, as against 978 by British/Indian forces, and 2,357
by what some British officers referred to as the "trigger-happy" French. Though
disarming the Japanese was supposed to be a matter of top priority, eight weeks
after the arrival of his forces Gracey acknowledged that fewer than 5 percent of
these recent foes had been required to give up their arms, and a small number
of Japanese still remained for the French to deal with when the last British
soldiers departed.[41]

On October 9, after an agreement with Paris, the British government, consistent with the path blazed by this local proconsul, formally recognized the
French civil administration as the "sole authority in that part of Indochina south
of [the] 16th parallel." By the time Gracey left Saigon at the end of January, he
had managed to shoehorn over fifty thousand French troops into southern Vietnam, a figure that reached some sixty-five thousand when the last British battalions left in mid-March. And as they departed the British turned over to the
French large stocks of arms, including U.S. Lend-Lease materiel. On March 5,
1946, Mountbatten announced that Britain's control in Indochina had passed to
France. The French commander, General Jacques Philippe Leclerc, had good
reason to be grateful to Gracey, and it was appropriate that the French should
bestow on the British general the title of "Honorary Citizen of Saigon."[42]

In the northern half of Vietnam the Chinese generals faced a much stronger
and more cohesive nationalist movement, and one more decisively dominated by
the Vietminh. One of the primary political missions of the four armies dispatched
by Chiang Kai-shek, totaling at least 152,500 men, was to install their own

Vietnamese protégés in power. When Chinese troops began to cross the frontier in late August, they drove out or disarmed the local Vietminh garrisons and installed in power the VNQDD and Dong Minh Hoi elements that were in their train. But though a number of towns were so invested, the Vietminh's local support was too strong for these takeovers to stick, and in most of them the Chinese-armed Vietnamese militias were soon ousted. Political as well as economic realities soon dissuaded the Chinese generals from further pursuit of this mission, and their own self-interest inclined them to deal with Ho Chi Minh's Democratic Republic of Vietnam (DRV) as the *de facto* government. The Kuomintang forces, which were many times greater than needed to disarm the Japanese, lived off the country, ravaging the famine-stricken land above the sixteenth parallel, with loot often a greater priority than disarming the Japanese.[43]

The Chinese were not spoiling for a fight, and Ho and his lieutenants made sufficient concessions to their economic appetite and political face to keep them at bay. To placate them, and probably to broaden the Vietminh's appeal to other Vietnamese nationalists, the Indochinese Communist Party declared that it stood "ready to put the interests of the nation above class interests" and formally dissolved itself on November 11, 1945. This dissolution was in fact more a matter of political imagery than of real substance, and the party's existing organization operated quietly and effectively as the heart of the broad Vietminh coalition. Moreover, Ho Chi Minh and his top lieutenants continued to hold most of the major government positions, even though soon yielding some of apparent importance to the Vietnamese protégés of the Chinese generals. More significant in immediate political terms, Ho Chi Minh promised the Chinese that the VNQDD and Dong Minh Hoi would be guaranteed respectively fifty and twenty seats in the projected National Assembly, regardless of the votes they received in the forthcoming January national elections. Whatever the irregularities and discrepancies in these elections—held openly in the northern and central areas and clandestinely in parts of the South—most observers, William Duiker observes, concluded that they were "relatively free and the results reasonably representative of attitudes among the population." Hsiao Wen, political adviser to General Lu Han, the Chinese commander, was apparently so impressed by the Vietminh's strength in the elections that he threw his support to them. At least partly as a consequence of Chinese pressure, the VNQDD and Dong Minh Hoi now merged with the Vietminh, and in February 1946 their members took positions in Ho's Cabinet, from which, as a consequence of the same Chinese pressure, two communist ministers were concurrently dropped.[44]

In the meantime, the United States, having made clear its own recognition of French sovereignty throughout Vietnam, had, since at least the end of September 1945, been calling upon the Chinese to facilitate the recovery of power by the French. Thus, though General Gallagher had, as late as August 24, been directed by his superiors to remain politically neutral, a month later he was ordered to act in accordance with the new policy. He then undertook to influence Lu Han to help the French regain control over the northern half of Vietnam, but the

Chinese were in no hurry to comply. Not until they had extracted a broad range of lucrative concessions from France would they permit French troops' entry into the northern half of Vietnam. First the French had to agree to a double-barreled treaty, the diplomatic component of which was finally signed on February 28, 1946, although its critical implementing military agreement was not concluded until March 13.[45]

But, to be operative, any Chinese arrangement with France providing for the introduction of French troops into Vietnam required the Vietminh's acquiescence. Thus, actual execution of the Sino-French treaty was dependent upon an agreement between France and the Vietminh that would permit this, and the critical final stages of the two agreements were in fact concurrently negotiated. Reluctantly, and under duress from the Chinese, the Vietminh accepted this provision in its own treaty with France, signed March 6. Therein lay the major impact of the Chinese occupation. Without Chinese cooperation, the French would have found it very difficult to introduce their own forces at this time, and attempts to do so would have entailed significant French casualties even had the Chinese remained neutral. (And if the Chinese had supported the Vietminh, as the French commander General Leclerc then concluded, France's "reconquest of Tonkin, even partially, would have been impossible.") But, as Harold Meinheit observes, "The Chinese were now in a sense allied with the French, and China's interests were in seeing the French return and its agreement honored."[46]

If the Vietminh had not accepted the introduction of the French military presence to which Chiang Kai-shek's government had agreed, it would have risked a two-front war—not only against France, but also against the Chinese, whose last division did not leave the country until October 9, 1946. Indeed, as King Chen puts it, the Vietminh risked a "three-front battle," for as the negotiations got under way the Vietnamese nationalist protégés of the Chinese asserted a position of their own, refusing almost any concessions to the French and threatening to sabotage any agreement the Vietminh reached with them. In the face of this, Ho and General Giap put their prestige on the line to persuade the Cabinet and the newly elected assembly to accept this unpalatable provision of the Sino-French agreement of February 28, and incorporate a version of it into the Franco-Vietnamese treaty that the Vietminh signed a week later.[47]

The Franco-Vietnamese agreement of March 6, 1946, permitted a limited force of fifteen thousand metropolitan French troops to replace the Chinese in the northern half of Vietnam. The DRV was to receive these troops "amicably"; "mixed commissions" representing the French and Vietnamese commands were "to insure liaison in a spirit of friendly cooperation"; and, "in cooperation with the Vietnamese [DRV] army," these French forces were to ensure "the maintenance of public order and the security of Vietnamese territory." Each year one-fifth of these French troops were to be withdrawn, until after five years all would have left. The French moved quickly to take advantage of this provision.

Under the aegis of the Chinese, during the second half of March they sent garrisons into all the main centers north of the sixteenth parallel except the small city of Vinh. In moving into Hanoi, General Leclerc's force brought truckloads of weapons for rearming some five thousand interned French military prisoners who were to be released there.[48]

In return, France granted seemingly extensive political concessions to the Vietminh, recognizing the DRV as "a free State having its own government, parliament, army and finances and forming part of the [still to be established] Indochinese Federation and the French Union." The French also agreed to abide by the results of a plebiscite to determine whether or not Cochin China should be unified with the central and northern portions of the country.[49]

But this apparently handsome grant of extensive autonomy and at least *de facto* independence soon proved to be a sham. The French refused to carry out the plebiscite in Cochin China, which the Vietminh had been expected to win. With Cochin China, Cambodia, and Laos largely under French control and ruled by France's own protégés, the French maneuvered to construct an Indochinese federation of coequal components in which the DRV would be submerged and outvoted by three essentially puppet states. Rather than resembling the British Commonwealth, as some Vietnamese had initially hoped, the French Union turned out to be no more than an elegant façade for France's continuing domination of her overseas colonial empire. Any doubt as to Paris's aim was removed by the representation that was to be granted the colonies in the French National Assembly: out of the 627 deputies in the assembly, 544 were to be from Metropolitan France, which contained only some 40 percent of the Union's population, while Overseas France, with 60 percent of the population, would have just 83 seats.[50] As a Vietnamese official put it to me: "That means that one Frenchman is equal to at least ten Vietnamese."

The French, however, received immediate benefits from their March 6 agreement with the Hanoi government. They were able to bring their first military units into the northern half of Vietnam through the door the Chinese had pushed open for them in the Sino-French agreement of a week earlier. And once their initial complement of fifteen thousand troops had entered, the French, with Chinese acquiescence, kept that door ajar for the introduction of many more.

Soviet policy or lack of policy toward Vietnam also initially shielded the Truman administration from any straightforward confrontation with the issues involved in the Franco-Vietnamese dispute. In fact, for nearly five years after the end of the war, the United States had no need to cope with even Soviet diplomatic recognition of Ho's government. And after recognition was extended in 1950, the Soviet Union's anxiety over the course of French policy kept it from offering Hanoi much more than moral support for another four years.

Soviet priorities were no less Europe-oriented than those of the United States, and Moscow was no more responsive than Washington to the hopes of

Vietnamese nationalists. Indeed, initially the Kremlin paid almost no attention
to anticolonial liberation movements anywhere in Southeast Asia. In general, its
policies for colonial areas lagged far behind events. Until the fall of 1947 Soviet
prescriptions for colonial nationalists still centered on the outmoded twelve-year-
old Dmitrov Doctrine—a policy attuned to a collective stand against international fascism and in support of popular-front governments. Under this doctrine,
communists and other nationalists in colonial countries had been called upon to
defer their struggles for independence until fascism had been overcome. At the
end of World War II Moscow was too preoccupied with more immediate concerns to work out a new approach, and in any case its priorities were incompatible
with support for the Vietminh. Not until September 1947, after the proclamation
of the Truman Doctrine and the announcement of the Marshall Plan, did it
formulate a new policy. But the Zhdanov Doctrine then announced at the first
meeting of the Cominform was primarily concerned with Europe, and "the
colonial question was almost totally ignored."[51]

Moscow continued in its passive policy toward events in Vietnam, and not
until the spring of 1948 did it even go so far as to indicate full approval of Ho
Chi Minh's course in Vietnam.[52] Subsequently, until early 1950, Russian support
of the Vietminh was confined to sympathetic rhetoric. Only in January 1950, after
Ho's government had taken the initiative of appealing globally for diplomatic
relations—to all countries, whatever their political system—did either Moscow
or Peking even extend it recognition. Possibly Soviet tardiness in recognizing
Hanoi stemmed from Ho's evident subordination of communism to nationalism,
for he was as much an independent nationalist communist as Yugoslavia's Tito.
In any case, given its priorities in Europe, it was natural for the Kremlin to favor
the French Communist Party over a distant maverick communist named Ho Chi
Minh.

As Donald Zagoria has put it, "The most important consideration in Stalin's
decision to ignore Southeast Asia undoubtedly lay in the rich opportunity for a
Soviet political harvest in Europe." Thus, he "worked to insure that Asian
Communist aspirations would not conflict with the bright prospects of the West
European Communist Parties," and Soviet policy in Indochina from 1945 to 1947
was "dictated almost exclusively by Stalin's desire to see the French Communist
Party . . . take power in Paris and to subsequently align France and Russia in
a Soviet dominated Europe."[53]

Moscow had too great a stake in the French Communist Party's prospects
to allow these to be put at risk by pressuring it to take an unpopular anticolonial
course in Vietnam. As noted earlier, in the immediate postwar years the communists were the largest party in France. As a result of the 1946 elections they
secured several Cabinet portfolios, and their head, Maurice Thorez, was appointed deputy premier. With a good chance of emerging even stronger in subsequent elections, the party's leaders were apprehensive of losing votes if they
acquiesced in the liquidation of France's overseas empire. Thus, the communists
remained in the Cabinet and supported policies that sought to re-establish French

control over Vietnam by force. Thorez promised de Gaulle that his party would not comply with a cabled appeal for support he had received from Ho. Later, referring to the March 6 agreement with the DRV, he told Jean Sainteny, delegate of the French high commissioner in Vietnam, "If the Vietnamese do not respect the terms, we will take the necessary measures and let guns speak for us, if need be." French guns did speak at Haiphong and Hanoi, with Thorez countersigning the order for military action against the DRV, and he and other communist members of the French Cabinet continued to vote credits for supporting the war against the Vietminh as late as March 1947. For at least another year after they left the Cabinet that May, over differences in domestic economic policy, the party's posture toward Vietnam was still strongly influenced by domestic political calculations, and it moved only gradually toward voicing full support of the Vietminh. Communist-dominated labor unions continued to load ships for Indochina until December 1949, when the party finally adopted a policy of demonstrations and strikes aimed at obstructing the movement of troops and supplies to Vietnam.[54]

Ho evidently had more faith in the French Socialist Party than in the French communists, but the socialists too proved a keen disappointment. They were themselves divided over colonial policy, and the elements within the party on whom Ho apparently had pinned his hopes were unable to mount the pressure necessary to head off the coalition French government's* blatant betrayal of key provisions of the March 6 agreement. In the words of the State Department's Abbot Moffat, reporting on August 9, 1946, "The evidence suggests that the French are attempting to gain their objective by maneuvers designed to confine and weaken Viet Nam [Ho's DRV]. . . . The conclusion is inescapable that the French are endeavoring to whittle down Viet Nam [i.e., the Vietminh] and to settle the future form of organization of Indochina with those who may be expected to be amenable to French influence." While Ho was in Paris during the summer of 1946, in a last desperate attempt to salvage the agreement, the armistice it had provided disintegrated further. On June 1, the day after Ho left Vietnam, French officials there reneged on a central feature of the agreement, refusing (as noted earlier) to carry out the promised plebiscite in Cochin China, and instead setting up their own puppet administration there. The head of this "Republic of Cochin China" committed suicide four months later, upon realizing that his "government" still existed only on paper, a flimsy façade for the continuation of absolute French control. Further French violations of the agreement were followed by a series of small-scale clashes that both sides precipitated.[55]

The French premier, Georges Bidault, urged on by hawkish officials in both Paris and Vietnam, used these incidents as the pretext for abandoning negotiations and applying major military force. He authorized military action at the port of Haiphong "to teach the Vietnamese a lesson," and the local French comman-

---

*Since the end of the war in Europe, the socialists had been one of three parties in a precarious coalition government, along with the communists and the MRP (Movement Républicain Populaire).

der was ordered to make himself "complete master" of that major city. On November 23, when the Vietminh refused his order to evacuate the port, a French cruiser opened fire with its heavy guns, destroying the Vietnamese quarter and, by official French estimates, killing six thousand Vietnamese. Within a week General Morlière, the French commander, followed up this action with an ultimatum that the DRV yield to French military control the whole of the city of Haiphong, its immediate surroundings, and roads between it and Hanoi.[56]

While under heavy pressure from within the Vietminh to declare war, Ho continued to urge restraint. On December 15, after receiving no response to his personal appeal of November 27 to Premier Bidault, asking him for his ideas as to how to arrange a cessation of hostilities, Ho cabled his old acquaintance Léon Blum, head of the Socialist Party, who had then just succeeded Bidault as premier. Ho warned Blum that French colonialists were violating the March 6 agreement and suggested a detailed formula for relieving the tension. But Blum's transitional Cabinet remained in office a scant two weeks, and French officials in Vietnam and in the bureaucracy in Paris held up Ho's message for three days—until after the war had begun—with Ho not realizing it had not been delivered. In the meantime, incidents between the two sides increased. The French brought heavy concentrations of troops into Hanoi and on December 18 occupied several key Vietnamese government buildings. The next day they ordered General Giap to disarm his forces in the city. Whether or not Ho was willing to wait any longer for a response from the French socialists, he was clearly in no position to restrain the Vietminh militia, who were not about to turn in their arms. That night, following a decision made by the Central Committee of the Vietnamese Communist Party, Giap ordered a war of nationwide resistance to begin, and his forces temporarily drove French troops out of the buildings they had occupied.[57]

With their air power and heavy artillery the French soon won the battle for Hanoi, but the eight-year war for Vietnam this action initiated was to have a very different outcome. Superior firepower and air support enabled French forces to quickly seize and to hold the cities and major towns, but the Vietminh continued to dominate most of rural Vietnam. French forces, if large enough, could penetrate almost any area except some of their enemy's mountain redoubts, but as soon as they regrouped to attack elsewhere the Vietminh was usually able to reassert its authority.

The French commander, General Leclerc, soon realized that there could be no solution through military force alone. In January 1947 he stated, "Anti-Communism will be a useless tool as long as the problem of nationalism remains unsolved." That summer he secretly advised the French government, "The capital problem from now on is political. It is a question of coming to terms with an awakening xenophobic nationalism." Leclerc's report, however, was not revealed to the French Parliament for more than three years, and his successors were considerably less perceptive. Not until another year of fighting had passed did the French government's actions begin to reflect its acknowledgment of the force of Vietnamese nationalism, and the need to come to some sort of terms with it.[58]*

When the French finally realized that their effort to impose a purely military solution had failed, they attempted to establish a second channel of Vietnamese nationalism to compete with and draw support from the Vietminh. But with no other significant organized indigenous force available, the French had to create one. The very nature of anticolonialism meant, of course, that their chance of success in such an endeavor was remote. But their insistence on maintaining control ensured that the channel ran almost completely dry.

In their search for a Vietnamese collaborator, the French finally fell back on the same expedient resorted to by the Japanese some two years before. They turned to the ex-emperor Bao Dai, conveniently forgetting that he had abdicated, publicly rallied to the Vietminh, and then, at Ho's invitation, served on the DRV's advisory council for some seven months, until shortly after the March 6 agreement. He then went on a mission to Chungking, which he states was undertaken on behalf of the DRV, at the personal request of Ho, and with the object of getting Chiang Kai-shek to enforce the Chinese withdrawal from Vietnam in accordance with their agreement with the French. Bao Dai writes that, after he had talked with Chiang, he received an invitation to meet with the American plenipotentiary in China, General George C. Marshall, who ten months later would become secretary of state, but he provides only the vaguest account of their discussion. Whatever transpired in his meetings with Marshall and a number of Kuomintang officials, Bao Dai decided not to return to Hanoi. He stayed six months in China, then, under circumstances that are still not clear, flew to Hong Kong, where he was later contacted by the French and probably by American officials as well.[59] Concerning Bao Dai's strange odyssey, a future president of France, François Mitterrand, commented a few years later:

> In 1932, he ascends the throne . . . and France pays him. . . . On March 11, 1945 . . . [He] . . . collaborates with the Japanese. Japan pays and Bao Dai obeys. On August 25, 1945, he abdicates. . . . Ho Chi Minh appears the stronger [and] Bao Dai hopes that, on that side, too, pay will be forthcoming.
>
> But what can such a young republic offer? . . . This does not suit Bao Dai . . . [and he] crosses over to China. Chiang sends him back to his [Bao Dai's] habitual moneylenders, and we find him in Hong Kong, surrounded by emissaries of the United States and of the Bank of Indochina, and by the Reverend Father Vircondelet, Procurator General of the Missions Etrangères. . . .[60]

. . .

*U.S. intelligence sources estimated that in early 1947 Vietminh forces numbered about 150,-000, but "only about one-third of the troops were equipped with weapons at least the size of small arms"; and "their heavier weapons included about 50 artillery pieces, 650 automatic weapons, and 150 mortars." Facing them were "some 100,000 of the best trained and best equipped regular troops at the disposal of the French."

For three years Bao Dai remained away from Vietnam, first in Hong Kong and then on the French Riviera, acquiring the rather harsh but not altogether undeserved sobriquet of "the nightclub emperor" until, after a succession of efforts, the French managed to negotiate an agreement with him. Genuinely interested in his country's independence, he tried to exact the best terms possible, entering into a series of long discussions that culminated in the Elysée Agreement signed in Paris on March 8, 1949. In this the French agreed to "independence" for a "State of Vietnam" that he would head, which was to include all of the country —Cochin China as well as the central and northern region. Not only was Bao Dai's state to be incorporated into the French Union, with all the constraints that entailed, but even if the French had actually implemented the agreement, it provided only a very limited form of autonomy—nothing approaching real independence. So many of the substantive attributes of sovereignty were retained in French hands—defense, foreign affairs, control over French property among them—that even on paper the new "state" remained effectively dominated by Paris. Furthermore, most of the modest concessions that the French did grant were not actually carried out, and Bao Dai's government never gained the independence necessary for attracting significant nationalist support. The resurrected emperor's efforts to wrest the actual substance of independence from France were unsuccessful. His regime remained an unconvincing façade for a continuing French military rule that excluded Vietnamese from roles of political significance. Moreover, as many Vietnamese appreciated, such limited leverage as Bao Dai possessed for extracting concessions from the French derived almost entirely from the strength of the very Vietminh with whom he was supposed to be competing. David Marr has put this well: "There was a curious symbiosis, with Bao Dai having influence with the French mainly as a reflection of Vietminh power."[61]

A handful of Vietnamese—ironically, many of them from factions of the Japanese-nurtured Dai Viet party—found jobs in sectors of the enduring French colonial administration, now called the civil service of the State of Vietnam. As the result of a liberal dispensing of French funds and military positions, several Cao Dai and Hoa Hao leaders brought their paramilitary forces into Bao Dai's "Army of the State of Vietnam." Despite its new name, this was still essentially the same as the French-commanded and fundamentally mercenary army previously existing in Vietnam, and there were no real changes in the actual disposition of authority.

The French effort to divert the stream of Vietnamese nationalism away from the Vietminh and into another channel was a failure. It did, however, provide the pretext for claiming that a colonial war had been transformed into a civil war, in which France was simply supporting one of the two contestants. As the chief political adviser to the French viceroy in Indochina put it, the objective was to transfer France's own direct confrontation with the Vietminh to "the internal Annamite [Vietnamese] level." And the Truman administration soon participated in this charade, Secretary of State Acheson in particular helping to ensure that one of the most perduring myths of the Vietnam War gained popular acceptance in the United States—if not in France.[62]

. . .

In its memorandum of May 13, 1947, to U.S. diplomats in Paris, Saigon, and Hanoi, the State Department cabled, "We recognize Vietnamese will for indefinite period require French material and technical assistance and enlightened political guidance which can be provided only by [a] nation steeped like France in democratic tradition and confirmed respect [for] human liberties and worth [of the] individual." At the same time, however, it affirmed that any lasting association between the French and the Vietnamese would have to be voluntary. American officials, like their French counterparts, became increasingly aware that it was necessary to reach some sort of accommodation between French authority and Vietnamese nationalism, but, like the French, they did not want the accommodation to be with Ho's Vietminh. Most of these Americans could not accept the idea of a fusion of nationalism and communism in one movement; the prevailing view among them was that a genuine nationalist could not be a communist. While acknowledging that Ho and his lieutenants in the Vietminh had been successful in "capturing control of the nationalist movement," they could not bring themselves to see these leaders as men in whom the strength of nationalism decisively overshadowed any propensity to follow some line dictated in the Kremlin. Although the State Department's Office of Intelligence and Research was satisfied it had evidence of Moscow's control over communist organizations in other Southeast Asian countries, it acknowledged that it could discover no such evidence with respect to Vietnam. In the Cold War climate of 1946–47, however, where communism was considered a global monolith, U.S. officials could only regard Ho and the Vietminh as agents of the Kremlin—and hence enemies of the United States.[63]

With power in Vietnam almost completely polarized between France and the Vietminh, American officials saw no basis for suggesting any "practicable solution," for any solution would require coming to terms with Vietnamese nationalism, and its principal embodiment was the Vietminh. Thus, the State Department acknowledged in its September 27, 1948, policy statement on Indochina, "We are all too well aware of the unpleasant fact that Communist Ho Chi Minh is the strongest and perhaps the ablest figure in Indochina and that any suggested solution which excludes him is an expedient of uncertain outcome."[64]

In neither France nor the United States, however, was the domestic political climate conducive to actions that accorded with this reality, and those American officials who most clearly perceived it had insufficient influence to shape decisions. Those who dominated American policy formation were in varying degrees aware of the odds against success for the Bao Dai expedient, but they all hoped that the French would take the steps that might increase the chances for its success. They believed, however, that the United States had scant leverage for persuading her to relinquish the attributes of power that would have been necessary for such a venture to succeed. As this same September 1947 State Department policy paper concluded, any such effort would be "complicated by the fact that we have an immediate interest in maintaining in power a friendly French government, to assist in the furtherance of our aims in Europe. This immediate and vital interest has in consequence taken precedence over active steps looking toward the realization of our objectives in Indochina."[65]

Shortly after the Bao Dai formula had been fully elaborated in the Elysée Agreement of March 8, 1949 (and almost a year before the French Parliament finally ratified it), the head of the State Department's Division of Philippine and Southeast Asian Affairs gave a prescient evaluation of its prospects. Arguing that American officials should not be deluded into thinking that the United States had the power to underwrite the success of this experiment in nation building, he concluded that the mere fact that Bao Dai "offered at present the only possible non-Communist solution in Indochina is no reason, in view of his very dubious chances of succeeding, for committing the United States at this time to his support, as [if] in the event he turns out to be a puppet, we then must follow blindly down a dead-end alley, expending our limited resources—in money and most particularly prestige—in a fight which would be hopeless."[66]

Three months later, a State Department report prepared for the National Security Council observed that the French had been resorting to "political maneuvers with native collaborators hoping to create a puppet regime which would, with French help, dispose of the Vietminh and allow France to retain its paramountcy," and concluded that the French had been "so niggardly in those negotiations that they have thus far failed to create an effective puppet regime capable of drawing nationalist elements away from the Vietminh." For Vietnamese patriots, especially for that vast majority who lacked independent means, the effective range of political alternatives remained as narrow as before—the Vietminh or the French. And this polarization grew more pronounced as some French officials labeled all those who resisted them or opposed Bao Dai "communist." For increasing numbers of Vietnamese, that word came to connote something good—a sort of badge of honor, representing nationalism and opposition to French rule.[67]

European priorities continued to dominate the Truman administration's policy toward Vietnam. Only one of these was discordant with the main thrust of American support of the French. This was the growing uneasiness of American defense strategists, including George C. Marshall, about France's decreasing ability to meet its commitments to the North Atlantic Treaty Organization (NATO), because some of its best military units and a high percentage of its commissioned and noncommissioned officers were being drained away to Vietnam from Europe.[68] These misgivings, however, were more than offset by the emergence during 1949 of two other, initially subsidiary factors that were to rise rapidly in the next few years, which tended to complement each other and also to reinforce the policy previously dictated by European considerations. The first was the sudden collapse of Chiang Kai-shek's power in China, which by early 1950 had brought Chinese communist forces to the Vietnam frontier. The second was the growth of a globally oriented anticommunist sentiment in the United States.

Alarmed by the approach of Chinese communist troops to a border of which the Vietminh held extensive stretches, Paris embarked on a fruitless quest to secure an unqualified assurance of U.S. backing should the Chinese move across the border in support of the Vietminh. No such open-ended commitment, however, was likely to be approved by the American Congress. The administration was prepared to ask Congress to approve U.S. air and naval assistance to the French in the event of China's overt entry into the war—but not ground forces. That crucial level of the fighting would have to remain a French responsibility, with a possibility of help from Chiang Kai-shek's forces from Taiwan.[69] The Truman administration's refusal to give France any assurance of ground support undercut its ability to face down French threats to withdraw their own forces, which, however specious initially, were to become serious by 1953.

The language in the call of the 1947 Truman Doctrine for containment of communism and Soviet power was susceptible to easy extension beyond Europe to Southeast Asia and China. Since Americans now tended to regard communism and Soviet power as coterminous and global, there was no European boundary to the president's proposition that "it must be the policy of the United States to support free peoples who are resisting subjugation by armed minorities or by outside pressure." And the posture of his administration—at least its public face—was that "outside pressure" in Vietnam came not from a France backed by the United States, but from a global communism controlled and articulated from Moscow. Moreover, the "fall of China" to "global communism" gave plausibility to the concept of a domino dynamic, already foreshadowed in the Truman Doctrine. There Truman's domino parlance, except for its geographical focus on Europe and the Middle East, is not easily distinguishable from that employed in subsequent years by John Foster Dulles, Dwight Eisenhower, Dean Rusk, and John F. Kennedy with reference to Vietnam and its South and Southeast Asian context. Consonant with this perception, in mid-1949 the U.S. National Security Council, reacting to Mao's victory in China, which it termed a "grievous political defeat for us," predicted that, if Southeast Asia were also swept by communism, "we shall have suffered a major political rout the repercussions of which will be felt throughout the rest of the world, especially in the Middle East and . . . Australia." And by the end of February 1950, months before the outbreak of the Korean War, the council was regarding Indochina as a key domino in Southeast Asia, whose control by communists would lead to their dominance in Thailand and Burma, with the remainder of Southeast Asia "in grave hazard."[70]

By 1949, American domestic political calculations, which had initially been of only marginal importance to policy in Vietnam, were beginning to exert a different and stronger influence. The previous discord between strategic-cum-political priorities in Europe and the residual anticolonialist sentiments among the American public was already yielding to the harmonious and even mutually reinforcing rationales of backing a key ally in Europe against the perceived threat of Soviet power and supporting that ally in Southeast Asia in containing the same global communist power in that theater. This congruence helped prepare the ground for a domestic political factor that was soon to become one of the most powerful and enduring influences shaping American policy toward Vietnam: the charge that American officials were "soft on communism" or unwilling to make an effective effort to contain its spread into new areas of the world. This theme was given an enormous fillip by the triumph of Mao Tse-tung in China, with many Republican and some Democratic critics—both opportunistic and sincere—soon charging the Truman administration with responsibility for the "loss of China." Such allegations had begun to be made even before Senators Joseph McCarthy and Pat McCarran entered the lists. And in mid-1950 these accusations were further reinforced with the outbreak of war in Korea. Ironically, the way had been prepared by the extravagant hyperbole employed by the Truman administration in its efforts to raise public awareness of the Soviet threat to a level that would ensure acceptance of its expensive program of economic and military aid to Europe. In resorting to the rhetorical overkill in announcing his Truman Doctrine of "scaring hell out of the American people" prescribed by the chairman of the Senate Foreign Relations Committee, Arthur Vandenberg, the president had reached a threshold that Bernard Baruch characterized as "tantamount to declaration of ideological war." That approach, sustained in Truman's subsequent effort to enlist support for the Marshall Plan, helped develop public and congressional attitudes that, while serving the administration's immediate purposes in Europe, were equally applicable to Asia.[71]

Economic factors were never of paramount importance in influencing American policy toward Vietnam; indeed, except in an indirect strategic sense, they played no significant part at all. None of France's Indochina colonies had been of economic consequence to the United States, for French colonial policy —in contrast to that of Britain and the Netherlands in Southeast Asia—had kept them as French preserves from which American capital investment and trade had been almost completely excluded.[72] And during the early postwar years, while France was trying to re-establish her power in Indochina, it was evident that she did not intend to deviate significantly from that policy. Nor did American officials regard the continuation of French control over Indochina's resources as important to the viability of the French home economy—an argument so unsustainable that apparently even the most fervent supporters of French policy in Vietnam never attempted it.*

With the collapse of Chiang Kai-shek's regime on the mainland, however, Washington began to characterize France's anticolonial struggle in Vietnam as a crusade useful in helping contain the new Chinese communist state. In addition, American policy toward Japan underwent a drastic change that, in a more modest

---

*This was in sharp contrast to the attitude of some U.S. officials toward the Dutch-Indonesian dispute, where it was argued that maintenance of a colonial connection with that much richer area was necessary for the economic viability of the Netherlands.

way, bore indirectly on the Truman administration's evaluation of France's role in Vietnam. With the sudden shift in American policy from aiming to transform Japan into a disarmed "Switzerland of Asia," to making it a counterweight to communist China and the keystone of the U.S. strategic position in the western Pacific, American officials saw greater reason to strengthen the Japanese economy. Previously they had believed this to be important as insurance against the domestic appeal of local communists and the country's possible gravitation toward closer relations with the Soviet Union—a consideration that continued to be operative during the early 1950s. Soon strengthening the Japanese economy was apparently regarded as desirable also as a basis for projecting U.S. power in the Far East from Japan, as was sanctioned in the bilateral Japanese-American security treaty negotiated during 1950. To enable the Japanese economy, cut off from its prewar areas of economic exploitation in China and northern Korea, to meet both of these objectives, and to reduce the need for U.S. economic support, it was regarded as essential to provide as much compensatory access as possible to the raw materials and markets of Southeast Asia.[73]

It should be noted, however, that in this assessment it was the oil, rubber, and tin of Indonesia and the rubber, tin, and iron ore of Malaya that were crucial. Moreover, apart from the Philippines, Indonesia and Malaya were the only two Southeast Asian countries where the United States itself had significant investments and trade. Vietnam was distinctly peripheral to calculations of Southeast Asia's economic importance to either the American or the Japanese economy. Apart from the fact that the French gave little indication of abandoning their exclusive economic policies in Indochina, the area's known raw-material resources pertinent to Japan's current needs were negligible in comparison with those of these two other Southeast Asian countries. American officials did not see Vietnam itself as economically important to Japan's economy. Insofar as some of them believed it to be relevant, this was because they perceived it, like Burma, as a gate barring any southward advance by China into the more distant areas of Southeast Asia that were actually already of economic value to the United States and were regarded as potentially so for Japan.[74]

During the first postwar decade, economic factors did exert some influence on American policy toward Indochina, albeit minor in comparison with strategic and political considerations, but even that degree of influence dwindled to insignificance thereafter. Insofar as economic considerations weighted the scales of policy during this period, they focused on Europe, and on balance they probably militated more against than in favor of American support of France's effort to reassert control over Vietnam.

The refusal of the Truman administration during the Korean war to yield to General Douglas MacArthur's demand for an all-out military effort against China reflected the fact that both the JCS and the State Department continued to regard Western Europe and the containment of Soviet power there as the top American strategic priority, with the bulk of American military might husbanded for possible use in that theatre rather than in Eastern Asia. This being so, the

economic viability of France, still regarded as the keystone of American political
and strategic aims in Europe, remained crucial and clearly overshadowed concern
about Japan's access to the raw materials of Southeast Asia. For almost a decade
after World War II, it was not only the diversion of many of the best of France's
commissioned and noncommissioned officers from NATO to the debilitating
struggle in Indochina that undercut American efforts to build a Western European bastion for the containment of Soviet power. Also of great concern to those
charged with U.S. foreign policy, and likewise undercutting their efforts to build
up French power in Europe, was the parallel bleeding away of France's economic
substance—both her own and that channeled to her through the Marshall Plan
—to sustain her struggle against the Vietminh.[75]

This concern to husband French military and economic resources for bolstering the front against Soviet power in Europe remained in tension with the
Vietnam prong of Washington's relationship with Paris even after October 1949,
when the French military presence in Indochina took on new significance for
American officials as a shield against the growth of local communist strength and
any southern thrust of Mao Tse-tung's power. The tension continued right up
until the Geneva armistice of July 1954.[76]

All this is relevant not only to an effort to assess the relative weight of the
fundamentally incompatible economic factors that impinged on the shaping of the
American approach to Vietnam. It also helps explain France's enormous leverage
on American foreign-policy officials. In view of all the foregoing considerations,
the Truman administration wanted French military power to remain in Vietnam;
and Paris—for her own reasons—would not maintain an army there without a
concurrent political presence. Unwilling, and in fact unable, to take over France's
military role in Vietnam, the United States now became sensitive to a succession
of hints that France might pull out and leave her "responsibilities" there to the
United States, should Washington try to use its economic leverage to induce
political concessions to Vietnamese nationalism. This helped to ensure that the
Truman administration would support France's Bao Dai solution—with funds,
military supplies, and diplomacy—and that Washington would apply no real
pressure on Paris to grant a significant degree of autonomy.[77]

Dean Acheson, who moved from assistant secretary to secretary of state in
January 1949, was by then fully aware of the incompatibility of getting along with
France in Europe while ensuring that she yield enough attributes of sovereignty
to her protégés in Vietnam to allow them to draw away substantial nationalist
support from the Vietminh. And he was also very sensitive to the increasing
importance of anticommunism in American domestic politics. Recognizing that
the French were unlikely to move far toward granting real independence to Bao
Dai or any other anticommunist Vietnamese leader, he could see no feasible
course other than trying to compensate for this deficiency by injecting sufficient
additional American power through the French to deny victory to the Vietminh.[78]
Irrespective of whether it could ultimately succeed, the Bao Dai solution was seen
as the policy best calculated to ensure continuing French cooperation in Europe

while maintaining France's military presence on communist China's southeastern flank. It would at least buy time during which a constellation of factors more congenial to U.S. interests might emerge. In defending this policy many years later, Acheson argued:

> The result of withholding help to France would, at most, have removed the colonial power. It could not have made the resulting situation a beneficial one either for Indochina or for Southeast Asia, or in the more important effort of furthering the stability and defense of Europe. So while we may have tried to muddle through and were certainly not successful, I could not think then or later of a better course."[79]

As to the charge that American policy tended to "supplement" rather than "complement" that of the French, Acheson's retrospective response was simply "I decided, however, that having put our hand to the plow, we would not look back."[80] That was a fair description of the attitude of officials responsible for successive escalations of American intervention in Vietnam over the next two decades, and of the short institutional memory that characterized the approach to Vietnam of subsequent administrations. And one could add that the title of Acheson's memoir, *Present at the Creation,* was an appropriate caption for an era of Vietnam policy in which the United States took the first in a continuing series of steps to apply external power in the effort to control the threat of nationalism and create an artificial, externally sustained state that lacked any substantial indigenous foundation.

II

To the Brink of War
in Support of France

During 1949, after deciding to support France and her Bao Dai solution, the Truman administration progressively abandoned its earlier, circumspect and skeptical public attitude toward the resurrected emperor's political capacity and prospects. The Vietnamese people could see that their emperor still wore no clothes, but for the American public the administration dressed him in resplendent raiment. Although privately some U.S. officials continued to rate Bao Dai as they had before, it now became official policy to portray him as a leader of stature, with strong nationalist credentials, who stood a good chance of seizing the banner of nationalism from Ho Chi Minh and leading Vietnam out of the darkness of communism into the "Free World."

A full year before the French Parliament finally, in February 1950, agreed to ratify the Elysée Agreement that was to be the charter of Bao Dai's rule, the United States had taken steps toward recognition of his yet-to-be-formed government. As early as January 1949, Washington assured the French, then still in the process of negotiating with Bao Dai, that it favored setting him up as "the nationalist leader to check the Communist influence from the north that is expected to be intensified by the victory of the Communist forces in China," and that it saw him as offering "the only hope of stability in that strategically and economically impaired corner of Asia."[1]

The administration's emerging Bao Dai policy soon crystallized, and on May 10, 1949, the State Department advised its officials in Saigon that there was "no other alternative" to communist rule in Vietnam. Therefore "no effort should be spared . . . to assure [the] experiment [the] best chance of succeeding. At proper time and under proper circumstances Department will be prepared [to] do its part by extending recognition [to the] Bao Dai Government and by exploring [the] possibility of complying with any request by such a Government for U.S. arms and economic assistance." This policy statement incorporated the essential condition for such American assistance (to which lip service was consistently given, but which in practice was to be consistently waived): "Since U.S. could scarcely afford backing [a] government which would have color [of] and be likely [to suffer the] fate of, [a] puppet regime, it must first be clear that France will offer all necessary concessions to make Bao Dai solution attractive to nationalists."[2]

On June 21, 1949—still some seven months before action was taken by the French legislature—the State Department publicly endorsed Bao Dai's "new unified State of Vietnam," announcing that its emergence "should serve to hasten . . . the attainment of Vietnam's rightful place in the family of nations," with Bao Dai's efforts to unite "all truly nationalistic elements" providing "the basis for the progressive realization of the legitimate aspirations of the Vietnamese people."[3] It was thereby made very clear that the United States saw Bao Dai's putative regime as the legitimate representative of the Vietnamese people, with formal American recognition awaiting only the French Chamber of Deputies' endorsement of the Elysée Agreement. Ho Chi Minh's actually functioning government, it should be noted, had as yet received no similar promise of recognition from either Moscow or Peking.

At the end of 1949, it was evident that France was taking the final steps toward setting up Bao Dai as head of a regime claiming to represent the whole of Vietnam. Washington and London, as well as Paris, were already laying the groundwork for the regime to be recognized by as many states as possible. Not having yet received diplomatic recognition from any country, the DRV leaders felt the urgent need to break out of their isolation, and on January 14, 1950, they appealed worldwide to all governments for diplomatic recognition. Four days later, once Hanoi had recognized Mao's government (on the 15th), Peking reciprocated; and on January 30, the Soviet Union followed suit. Secretary of State Acheson reacted angrily, declaring that Soviet acknowledgment of "Ho Chi Minh's Communist movement" should remove "any illusions as to the 'nationalist' nature of Ho Chi Minh's aims and reveals Ho in his true colors as the mortal enemy of native independence in Indochina." On February 2, the French legislature ratified the Elysée Agreement, and the United States was then free to accord Bao Dai's State of Vietnam official diplomatic recognition on February 7. Soon afterward Washington persuaded numerous other countries to follow suit.[4]

The outbreak of the Korean War in mid-1950 increased the Truman administration's willingness to support France in Vietnam, and made it easier for the French to persuade Americans that both countries were fighting the same war to contain communism and Chinese power. When President Truman announced a further increase of American support for the French effort in Vietnam, concurrent with the assignment of U.S. troops to repel communist aggression in Korea, he reinforced this thesis. For many Americans, France was no longer fighting a dirty colonial war, but, rather, was America's staunch ally in barring Chinese power from moving south. And even after the mid-1953 armistice in Korea, Secretary of State John Foster Dulles publicly referred to the struggle in Vietnam as part of "a single Communist Chinese aggressive front."[5]

The Korean War also stimulated the so-called Korean analogy. Encouraged by the administration, congressmen and the public tended increasingly to see the warfare in the two countries as similar: unprovoked communist aggression leading to civil war. This analogy, which distorted the public understanding of the situation in Vietnam for many years after the fighting in Korea had ended, ignored fundamental differences between the two situations. As David Schoenbrun has observed, the Vietnamese had been fighting for years without help from Russia or China; they had not been occupied by either of these countries; there was then no dividing line between the northern and southern halves of the country as there was in Korea; Vietnam was a case of anticolonial revolution being fought throughout the whole country without a single Russian or Chinese soldier present; whereas in Korea the United States fought under a U.N. flag, in Vietnam it had associated itself with France's standard of empire, and her effort to reconquer a colony.[6]

The speciousness of the analogy was further elaborated by Senator John F. Kennedy. In a Senate speech on April 6, 1954, he pointed out that, if the situation in these two former colonies were to be equated, one would have to posit a scenario wherein the United States was helping the Japanese army in its effort to put down "the revolution of the native Koreans, even though they were Communists, and even though in taking that action we could not have the support of the non-Communist elements of the country." Nevertheless, the Korean analogue stuck, and served as a continuing justification for the American government's intervention in Vietnam.[7]

By successfully convincing Americans that the situations faced in Vietnam and Korea were similar, the administration won public approval for an expanded program of support to the French military effort in Indochina. Apart from the additional impetus provided by the outbreak of war in Korea, the administration's disposition to raise its level of financial and arms assistance for France's military effort in Indochina had already been increasing as a consequence of the rapid growth of the Vietminh's military power and the series of defeats it had administered to French forces during 1949, well before it obtained any significant quantity of arms from the new communist government in China.

In February 1950, soon after its formal recognition of Bao Dai's regime, and before the Korean War, the Truman administration introduced a new program of overt aid to the French military effort in Vietnam—initially only some $23 million—the importance of which lay at that time more in its political symbolism than its substance. At first, this only marginally supplemented the much broader channel of indirect assistance—both financial and military—via metropolitan France, which had already been in operation for four years. That major channel remained hidden, probably to avoid the public criticism that disclosure of its magnitude and covert quality might well have occasioned. Only after the Korean War began did the overt level of U.S. assistance start to become more substantial.

But throughout both Truman administrations the covert level of assistance to the French military effort in Indochina remained large.[8]

Two new components of U.S. support that assumed importance during the last year of the second Truman administration also appear to have been largely, if not completely, outside the public's purview.

The first was a program of "lending" the French military equipment specifically for use in the Indochina war, up to and including aircraft carriers, the first of which was turned over by early January 1951. In 1952, at least fifty-four U.S. C-47 transport aircraft were lent to the French for use in Indochina, along with a team of twenty-eight air force mechanics to service them. Four French fighter squadrons were able to be maintained there because the United States provided "attrition aircraft" to replace F-6Fs and F-8Fs as these planes wore out.[9]

Second, in early 1952 the "Lisbon Program" was launched, providing an initial $200 million for purchases of war materiel from French factories for use in Indochina, another $500 million for fiscal years 1952 and 1953, and $785 million in fiscal year 1954. As the U.S. Joint Chiefs of Staff historians observe, "By purchasing items in France for Indochina the United States helped alleviate the French dollar shortage, underwrote military expenditures that otherwise would have seriously damaged the French budget, and enabled France to meet her N.A.T.O. obligations more readily."[10]

The direct supply of U.S. war materiel to the French in Indochina under the Mutual Defense Assistance Program (MDAP) also began to burgeon during the last years of the second Truman administration. According to the records of the Joint Chiefs of Staff, from June 1950 through December 31, 1952, 539,847 tons of American military equipment, valued at $334.7 million, was funneled to the French through Saigon and Haiphong; the total costs for such U.S. war materiel sent during the Truman administrations to the French in Indochina amounted to $775.7 million. No breakdown of major items of equipment is available for 1952, but JCS records give the total of such items reached by the end of June 1953 (nearly all of which would have had to enter the pipeline during the Truman administration) as 302 naval vessels, 304 naval and air-force aircraft, 1,224 tanks and combat vehicles, 20,274 transport vehicles, 2,847 pieces of artillery, and 120,792 small arms and machine guns, plus ammunition for all this weaponry.[11]

Although U.S. intelligence at the beginning of 1952 credited this flood of equipment with raising the morale of French forces in Vietnam, the policy did not translate into military success; during the next two years, despite the growth in their numbers, French troops found themselves more and more on the defensive and obliged to yield control over increasing amounts of territory to the Vietminh.[12]

French officers remained at the head of Bao Dai's newly established Army of the State of Vietnam, which as a fighting force was ineffective and often an unqualified embarrassment. By May 1951, its essentially mercenary nucleus—mostly seconded from auxiliaries of the French expeditionary force—numbered 38,500. Attempts to expand it by 60,000 through obligatory military service proved a fiasco. "Little more than half of the specially selected candidates ever reported for training"; and "Of the first increment of 15,000 men only 7% could be persuaded to enlist" after their training. "The second increment of conscripts was released after only five weeks of training and the fourth increment was never summoned at all." To make matters worse, the head of a major Cao Dai component of Bao Dai's new army pulled out 2,500 of his troops in June 1951 and departed for Cambodia. Apparently his action reflected the general malaise among the former auxiliaries of the French army over their forcible incorporation into the army of a State of Vietnam that had not been given its independence and was not likely to achieve it, as well as over the curtailment of the French subsidy to the Cao Dai troops. As the Joint Chiefs of Staff historians observed, "The response to the mobilization program was scarcely an indication of popular support" for Bao Dai's Viet Nam Government or its army.[13]

The Bao Dai experiment was quite obviously not providing a pole of nationalism able to compete with the Vietminh. The "civil war" in Vietnam was still fundamentally a case of outside intervention, with France, now bolstered even more by the United States, attempting to work her military and political will against her Vietnamese opponents. And neither French promises nor Bao Dai's new trappings disguised the fact that it was still a colonial war.

The advent of the Eisenhower administration brought no discernible change in American policies toward Vietnam. Vietnam and Korea were still regarded as interdependent parts of the same dike against Chinese communist expansionism, and the new administration quickly emphasized that the United States would not abide by the prospective armistice in Korea if that freed Peking's troops to enter the Indochina conflict.[14] The need to keep French forces in Indochina continued to argue against risking pressuring Paris to give Bao Dai's regime the degree of independence believed necessary to attract significant nationalist support. The American domestic political context, and the constraints it imposed upon Vietnam policy, also remained much the same. Senators McCarthy and McCarran were now enjoying their maximum influence, and the new administration, like its predecessor, sought to avoid being attacked as "soft on communism." The effectiveness of the "loss of China" charge that they themselves had leveled in the campaign against the Democrats had made the Republicans acutely sensitive to the possibility of becoming vulnerable to similar charges in Vietnam: if millions of Americans had been persuaded that their government actually could have prevented the communists from coming to power in China, then it was plausible to assume they might also believe it had the capacity to deny Vietnam to communist control.

During the new administration's first year in office, however, the Vietnamese context of American policy underwent significant changes as the result of the rapid erosion of the French military position. Maintaining the military initiative in most areas, the Vietminh had, by the spring of 1953, extended their authority over more than two-thirds of the area of Tonkin. There the French were largely confined to the densely populated Red River Delta, a fortified enclave where their effective control, outside of Hanoi, Haiphong, and a few big towns, extended only to some eighteen hundred out of five thousand villages; control over most of the remainder was contested.[15] In the central and southern areas, the Vietminh held most of the coastal regions all the way down to the outskirts of Saigon, apart from enclaves around Hué, Danang, and a few other towns; and about half of the Mekong Delta was firmly in Vietminh hands.* By the end of the year, General Giap had driven a wedge through Laos to Thakhek on the Mekong. Aimed at forcing the French to reduce their garrisons in Vietnam to meet this threat, Giap's tactic proved successful in loosening French control over additional areas of Vietnam.

At the end of 1953 a Vietminh force that had grown to an estimated 290,000 faced a total of 517,000 troops under France's Indochina Command.† Only some 80,000 of these latter were actually Frenchmen, the remainder consisting of 20,000 members of the French Foreign Legion (at least half of whom had served in the former Nazi armies), 48,000 soldiers from France's North African colonies (particularly Senegal), and 369,000 Indochinese (preponderantly Vietnamese), including those seconded into Bao Dai's putative and embryonic French-commanded "national army." Fewer than half of the French soldiers in Vietnam were in the rank and file; approximately one-third of the cadres of France's professional regular army—including 37 percent (over 40,000) of its noncommissioned officers and 26 percent (8,209) of its regular officers—made up the remainder. The French government acknowledged that these men "represent the cadres required for at least 20 French divisions that would otherwise be at the disposal of NATO in Western Europe," and that out of the twelve French divisions actually assigned to NATO, five stood at only 75 percent of their strength. The situation remained very much as it had been a few years earlier when George C. Marshall had observed, "When we reached the problem of increasing the security of Western Europe, I found all of the French troops of any quality were all out in Indochina . . . and the one place they were not was in Western Europe."[16]

France's military expenditures in Indochina for 1952 were budgeted at 447 billion francs, leaving only 830 billion to cover all her military expenses in Europe and North Africa combined. Her deficient troop strength in Europe and inability to pay for more led Paris not only to demand greater financial assistance and more arms for Indochina from Washington, but also to balk at Washington's plans to develop NATO into a European Defense Community (EDC). This top American priority for strengthening Western Europe's defense capability called for the rearming of Germany to form a major component of the envisaged American-

---

*See the May 1953 map of the French commander in chief, General Henri Navarre, on p. 43.
†Of the French combat battalions in Indochina, eighty-four or their equivalent were in Tonkin (northern Vietnam), sixty-five in Annam (central Vietnam), forty-two in Cochin China (southern Vietnam), twelve in Cambodia, and sixty-two in Laos.

sponsored coalition. French memories of German invasion, however, were too recent for Paris to be willing to participate in such a coalition unless France could maintain a higher level of troop strength in Europe than she then commanded. Thus, although the French Cabinet had agreed to the EDC, the Chamber of Deputies held back from ratifying it. In the words of the U.S. National Security Council, "Uncertain whether she could maintain military equality with Germany while carrying the military and financial load of Indochina, France has sought to delay and postpone E.D.C. and drifted towards neutralism."[17]

By August 1953 casualties among the expeditionary force in Indochina were reported to have reached 148,000, and a year earlier France had already sustained more casualties among her officers than the total of graduates from Saint-Cyr (the French "West Point") over the previous four years. This was the final straw that brought about a shift in the French public's attitude toward the struggle in Vietnam. When, at the end of July 1953, Washington agreed to an armistice in Korea, a new French attitude began to crystallize: if the United States, unable to achieve a military solution, had moved to a negotiated settlement in Korea, why should France not do the same in Vietnam? That question was asked repeatedly in the French Parliament during the second half of 1953, with every leading candidate for premier now bidding for popular support "with some kind of promise to reduce the Indo-China commitment in some way." At the end of October, the Parliament endorsed resolutions that instructed the government to explore every possibility for negotiations.[18]

In the face of this pressure, on November 12 Premier Joseph Laniel announced that his government did "not consider the Indochinese problem as necessarily requiring a military solution," and that "if an honorable solution were in view, either on the local level or on the international level, France, I repeat, like the United States in Korea, would be happy to welcome a diplomatic solution of the conflict." Laniel's statement soon elicited a positive reaction from the DRV. Responding on November 20 to a questionnaire from a Swedish correspondent, Ho Chi Minh stated that if France wished an end to the conflict, his government was ready to study all its proposals for a cease-fire. This response gave a sharp impetus to the popular demand in France for an end to the conflict, which no government could ignore.[19]

Nevertheless, Premier Laniel believed that negotiations to end the war should not be undertaken from a position of weakness. Regarded by the State Department as "almost certainly the *last* French government which would undertake to continue the war in Indo-China," the Laniel government was willing to lead France into one final military effort that would improve her position sufficiently to risk a negotiated settlement. The Eisenhower administration approved, hoping to forestall any negotiated resolution of the conflict; for in conformity with its domino theory, this course "would mean the eventual loss to Communism not only of Indo-China but of the whole of Southeast Asia" and "make more difficult and more expensive the defense of Japan, Formosa and the Philippines," while complicating "the creation of [a] viable Japanese economy."

The administration's memo concluded, "If the French actually decided to withdraw, the U.S. would have to consider most seriously whether to take over in this area." The National Security Council determined, however, that, if the French sought "to conclude the struggle on terms likely to result in the loss of Indochina," the United States would not be able to provide sufficient ground forces to take over effectively from them (reckoned at seven divisions) without "major alterations in fiscal and budgetary policies and programs, major increases in military production and mobilization schedules, and a reversal of policy planning to reduce the size of U.S. armed forces."[20]

These were not, of course, policies that stood any chance of approval by Congress, and Secretary Dulles was aware that the American public was unlikely to accept direct military support of France. In April 1953, in the context of the Vietminh's invasion of Laos, he had also discovered that the French, supported by the British, adamantly opposed any internationalization of a Vietnam solution via the United Nations. Their attitude stemmed primarily from fear that a U.N. debate could not be confined to Indochina and would quickly involve French colonies elsewhere, especially in North Africa. Since France had a permanent veto on the Security Council, the United States could not proceed as it had in Korea, with respect to either a joint military effort or subsequent negotiation of a settlement. The Eisenhower administration, therefore, saw no feasible alternative to persuading France to stay the course in Vietnam alone. Its ability to do so, however, was undermined by its reluctance to promise American ground support if the Chinese communists intervened—a danger that the French now saw increased by the end of the fighting in Korea and the consequent release of Chinese combat forces.[21]

American naval and air power could be quickly marshaled for use against China should she intervene in Vietnam; but although plans were developed to meet this contingency, the French were admonished that congressional approval was needed to implement them. And the administration would not, and could not, assure Paris of this approval. Dulles, however, was prepared to indulge in a bit of brinkmanship to reduce chances of Chinese intervention by striking somewhat ambiguous public stances calculated to frighten Peking into believing that a move into Vietnam could beget consequences "which might not be confined to Indochina"—a phrase generally construed as meaning the projection of U.S. air power, possibly with nuclear bombs, into China.[22]

Eisenhower's initial hope that Chiang Kai-shek's troops could support the French was abandoned when he realized that this risked a countermove from the Chinese communists. Admiral Arthur Radford, chairman of the Joint Chiefs of Staff, revived the idea in early June, but neither he nor the president apparently appreciated the constraints imposed by the Vietnamese national memory of their ten-century struggle to resist a reassertion of Chinese rule. The French declined the offer, reminding the American leaders of the tensions between the Vietminh and Chiang's rapacious generals in the immediate postwar period. Chiang's troops would be "highly unwelcome," Paris pointed out, given that "some of the less pleasant aspects" of his 1945–46 occupation "had not yet been forgotten."[23]

The use of South Korean troops, also urged by Radford, was more extensively explored. Eisenhower ordered the Defense Department and the NSC Planning Board to study and report on an initial offer by Syngman Rhee to send a division of South Korean troops to relieve French forces in Laos, freeing them for deployment in Vietnam. The idea was temporarily dropped, "because U.S. public opinion would not support the maintenance of U.S. forces in Korea while R.O.K. [Republic of Korea] forces were withdrawn from Korea for action elsewhere." (An equally important reason for declining may well have been Rhee's unabashed request that—apparently as a *quid pro quo*—his own American-financed army be increased from twenty to thirty-five divisions.) Later, however, in early June 1954, when it appeared that an outcome at Geneva at all acceptable to the United States might not be reached, the proposition was raised again by Radford, with plans calling for sending to Vietnam and Laos as many as three South Korean divisions plus support troops. Though given more favorable consideration in Washington than previously, the plan was deemed "unacceptable" by the French, whom Dulles found to be "insulted at the very idea." But even after the conclusion of the Geneva Conference, the administration remained unwilling to scrap the idea.[24]

Despite persistent French requests for assurance, the United States refused to give any unconditional pledge of support against the Vietminh—whether or not Chinese troops entered Vietnam. Repeatedly during the spring of 1954, Washington advised the French that congressional approval was unlikely unless the intervention were internationalized, preferably with British participation (which the French soon found was highly unlikely), and a clear-cut promise were made to grant real independence to Bao Dai, including the freedom of his Vietnamese state to secede from the French Union. The Laniel government refused to promise any such earnest of independence, fearing to lose its majority in the French Parliament.[25]

What the Eisenhower administration concluded it could do was to meet the escalating French demands for financial aid and military supplies in order to induce them to continue fighting. Initially planning to boost U.S. support from $568 million (33 percent of total war costs) in fiscal 1953 to $1,313 million (61 percent) in 1954, Washington quickly agreed to further increases, among them $385 million to finance a major offensive by General Navarre; the final tally on U.S. contributions to the French war effort in Indochina for fiscal 1954 reached 78 percent of its total cost. This contribution constituted approximately one-third of the entire U.S. global foreign-aid program. According to records of the Joint Chiefs of Staff, the American monetary contribution to the French military effort in Indochina from the spring of 1950 to the end of June 1954 was thus brought to a total of $2,763 million, divided roughly evenly between military supplies and financial support of the French national budget earmarked for the Indochina war.[26]

The priority given to the arms build-up is indicated by the National Security

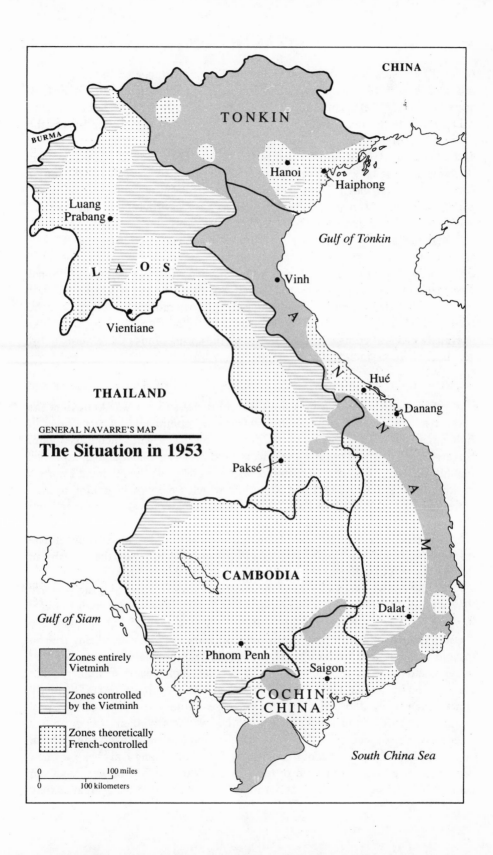

CHINA

TONKIN

Hanoi

Haiphong

Gulf of Tonkin

BURMA

Luang
Prabang

L A O S

Vinh

Vientiane

A

THAILAND

N

Hué

GENERAL NAVARRE'S MAP

Danang

The Situation in 1953

A

Paksé

M

CAMBODIA

Dalat

Gulf of Siam

Zones entirely
Vietminh

Phnom Penh

Zones controlled
by the Vietminh

Saigon

Zones theoretically
French-controlled

COCHIN
CHINA

South China Sea

0   100 miles
0   100 kilometers

Council's January 1954 assessment that "military assistance to Indochina took precedence over all allied nations and in respect to some items, even over U.S. armed forces." The magnitude of the effort is clear from figures for the U.S. MDAP aid to French forces in Indochina from mid-1950 to mid-1954: the amounts for all items increased strikingly over those reached in the last fiscal year of the Truman administration, noted earlier. The totals at the end of this four-year period were 1,880 tanks and other combat vehicles (up 50 percent), 30,887 motor and transport vehicles (up 50 percent), 5,045 artillery pieces (up 78 percent), 361,522 small arms (up 300 percent), as well as a lavish provision of ammunition. The French navy in Indochina had received 438 vessels, mostly small patrol craft and landing ships (up 44 percent), together with 70 naval aircraft; and the French air force had been provided 394 U.S. Hellcat fighters, B-26 bombers, and C-47 cargo planes. In addition, the French were supplied with considerable additional war materiel "on loan" from the United States, including a second aircraft carrier, a third light bomber squadron, and 24 C-119 transports, at least half the latter operated by Americans, apparently with pilots furnished by the CIA-operated Civil Air Transport (CAT). And by the spring of 1954 there were almost 300 U.S. air-force maintenance personnel in Vietnam.[27]

The strategy of the French in using this additional support was known as the "Navarre Plan," after General Henri Navarre, the commander of their forces in Indochina. However sanguine some of the Americans who encouraged him, Navarre knew he could not win the war. He and his government hoped, however, that his forces could go one more round, with the object of strengthening France's position for negotiations with the Vietminh, which were now beginning to look more and more inevitable to Paris. With ten more battalions from France[28] and the number of Vietnamese under his command to be increased over the next two years by some 117,000, he hoped that by mid-1955 he would be able to consolidate the eroding French position in Tonkin's Red River Delta, regain the offensive in the North, and cut the supply lines to Vietminh forces in Laos.

Thrown off stride by Giap's move into Laos at the end of 1953, the Navarre Plan was unable to develop momentum. The French commander soon found it impossible to recover the military initiative, which now lay firmly with the Vietminh; the French-directed Vietnamese auxiliary army that was being trained to hold areas cleared by the French troops was rarely able to accomplish that mission, and most of its soldiers continued to reflect a mercenary mentality rather than any fealty to Bao Dai's "state." Moreover, the Vietminh forces, formerly almost exclusively dependent on old Japanese military equipment, American weapons captured from the French, and the products of their own primitive arsenals, were now beginning to receive significant quantities of arms from China, much of it U.S. equipment acquired with the defeat of Chiang Kai-shek's armies. Within a few months of the end of the Korean War, the flow of weapons from China into Vietnam increased considerably. This became a source of great anxiety to the French, though even at its flood tide, during the siege of Dienbienphu, it was, according to Dulles's estimate, only about one-tenth of that going to Indochina from the United States.[29]

At the end of 1953, when it had become clear to Navarre that his central objective of recovering the initiative in Tonkin's Red River Delta was failing, he decided to put his chips on pinning down the Vietminh to do battle in surroundings where he believed his superior fire power and control of the air would ensure success. For this confrontation he chose the village of Dienbienphu, in a valley of northwestern Tonkin astride a major route into Laos, taking the "calculated risk" of garrisoning it with his "best units and reserves from the Tonkin Delta." Initially he had broad support for this tactic from Americans, including Eisenhower, who was now taking a direct interest in the French military effort.[30]

During the spring of 1954, the Vietminh surrounded this bastion of elite French forces, and, steadily building up their own strength around it, cut it off from reinforcement by land. Crucial to Giap's plans were the U.S. 105-mm. howitzers, of equal or larger bore than most of the French artillery, that the Chinese had handed over to him. The guns had to be broken down into many parts, then carried over newly built steep mountain trails by tens of thousands of foot soldiers and peasant porters. (The portage and the necessary road and trail work to accomplish this and supply the Vietminh forces at Dienbienphu involved more than 8 million days of labor, according to Vietminh sources.) It was several months before, in accordance with specifications of a group of Chinese technical advisers, these huge guns were emplaced in deeply dug, camouflaged positions in the hills ringing the French fortified artillery position on the valley floor. But on March 16, 1954, when the Vietminh launched its attack, the French garrison found itself outgunned as well as outnumbered, with Giap's artillery so well ensconced that it was largely impervious to French air strikes.[31]

In the meantime, the Paris government had come to hope that an international conference of the major powers might help it salvage at least a face-saving disengagement from Vietnam. Such a route appeared more feasible and increasingly attractive to Premier Laniel when the new leadership that emerged in the Kremlin after Stalin's death (in March 1953) signaled a disposition to move toward a détente with the Western powers. Over strong objections from Dulles, Laniel insisted that Indochina be added to the agenda of a conference at Geneva scheduled for late April that was to be attended by the Soviet Union and China and the major Western powers to discuss a political settlement for a still-divided Korea.

The Indochina phase of the Geneva Conference did not begin until May 8, the day after the fall of Dienbienphu. But in the preceding months France's bargaining position had already been steadily eroding as a result of Navarre's string of military reverses. Consequently, for the first time the French had become sufficiently desperate to make a clear-cut request for supportive American military intervention against the Vietminh. The Eisenhower administration shared France's alarm but was divided as to what to do. During the spring of 1954 the administration discussed a whole range of military options—including carrier-based air-delivered "tactical" atomic bombs to relieve the siege of Dienbienphu.[32]

According to General James Gavin, then chief of plans of the U.S. army staff, Admiral Radford, supported by the air force chief of staff and chief of naval operations, "was emphatically in favor of landing a force in the Haiphong-Hanoi area, even if it meant risking war with China." But the army chief of staff, General Matthew Ridgway—fresh from the experience of commanding U.S. forces in Korea—argued forcefully against such a move, and generally against ever again getting involved in a land war in Asia. He admonished that, though "American intervention in Vietnam might result in local successes," it would "constitute a dangerous diversion of limited U.S. military capabilities, and could commit our armed forces in a non-decisive theatre to the attainment of non-decisive local objectives." Undoubtedly, the main pressure not to intervene derived from vivid memories of the war that had ended less than a year before in Korea. If the approach of American ground forces to China's northeastern frontier had precipitated the massive intervention of Chinese arms, was it not likely that their introduction close to China's southeastern border would provoke a similar response? In any case, the NSC had already concluded that the chances were about even that the Chinese would intervene in the face of an impending Vietminh defeat—and the Joint Chiefs assumed that, if the Chinese did intervene in Vietnam, they might well concurrently reopen the front in Korea.[33]

In what was apparently an effort by the administration to test public opinion, Vice-President Richard Nixon made a statement on April 16 urging that American ground troops be sent to support the French if the latter could not prevail alone. But the congressional and public reaction to the trial balloon was adverse. To a president who less than a year before had won popular acclaim by ending a stale-mated war in Korea, this indication of the country's mood must have reinforced his own apparent inclination to side with Ridgway. Subsequent to the collapse of Dienbienphu, the previously divided Joint Chiefs, with Radford apparently now in full retreat, joined in Ridgway's judgment, and all then agreed that, "with reference to the Far East as a whole, Indochina is devoid of decisive military objectives and the allocation of more than token U.S. armed forces in Indochina would be a serious diversion of limited U.S. capabilities."[34] And so Ridgway, a soldier whose opinion Eisenhower respected, could fittingly write soon afterward what Lyndon Johnson's army chief of staff a decade later could not:

When the day comes for me to face my Maker and account for my actions, the thing I would be most humbly proud of was the fact that I fought against, and perhaps contributed to preventing, the carrying out of some harebrained tactical schemes which would have cost the lives of some thousands of men. To that list of tragic accidents that fortunately never happened I would add the Indochina intervention.[35]

The proposal for introducing U.S. air and naval power—as distinct from ground forces—however, enjoyed wider and more sustained support within the administration, even though it was aware that this too courted the danger of a confrontation with China.[36] During the remaining weeks before the beginning of the Indochina phase of the Geneva Conference, the question of possible American military intervention was focused on the employment of U.S. air power in the hope of saving the hard-pressed French garrison at Dienbienphu. For it was generally acknowledged that, if this now highlighted symbol of its power were overrun, France's will to fight on in Vietnam would be undermined, and the French government's position both at home and in the Geneva negotiations would be gravely weakened. It was widely anticipated that the result would be Laniel's fall and his replacement by a premier—most likely Pierre Mendès-France —who would be not just willing to make greater concessions to the DRV, but less likely to marshal support for the European Defense Community (EDC).

Once more, the most vigorous senior American proponent of intervention was Admiral Radford. He pushed hard for execution of his staff's plans, code-named Operation Vulture, for a massive American carrier-based air strike, possibly carrying tactical nuclear bombs, against Vietminh forces surrounding the residual French position at Dienbienphu. There are a number of indications that his plan may have enjoyed greater administration support than was subsequently acknowledged, for two U.S. aircraft carriers were positioned in the Tonkin Gulf within striking distance of Dienbienphu, Dulles was working on a draft constitutional resolution authorizing the president to introduce U.S. air and naval power in support of the French, and Radford himself was sufficiently confident of administration backing to give French Chief of Staff General Paul Ely the impression that such a request from France would receive "a prompt and affirmative reply."[37]

It is difficult to ascertain whether Radford was significantly out ahead of Eisenhower and Dulles, but the available record gives no indication that they criticized him for going beyond a position that was at least under serious consideration. Whatever the case, when Radford made his final pitch to secure the strike, it must have been clear to a man of Eisenhower's military experience that, in view of the accelerating deterioration of the French position at Dienbienphu and elsewhere in Vietnam, such a strike would have little real chance of being effective, even in deferring the garrison's fall, until after the conclusion of the Geneva Conference. And by the beginning of April, Admiral Radford himself had begun to acknowledge that there was no real assurance that American air strikes would be successful in saving Dienbienphu.[38]

The Joint Chiefs' study acknowledges that during the final months of this last desperate French military effort, "the United States was giving all aid short of active belligerency." But apparently the closest it came to direct participation was the dispatch of some three hundred U.S. ground-crew personnel to Vietnam to service the largely American-supplied French air force, the employment of the American air force in transporting two battalions of French paratroopers from

North Africa to Vietnam and French reinforcements from Hanoi to Dienbienphu, and the loan of U.S. planes to the French for bombing runs and napalm drops on Vietminh positions, with CIA crews flying some of the largest planes on the bombing missions.[39]

With the prospect of Dienbienphu's demise increasing daily, arguments for American intervention shifted to what could be done to stave off a more general collapse of French power in Indochina. Well before the battered remnants of the French garrison finally surrendered, President Eisenhower and Secretary Dulles looked beyond to what they perceived might be the dangerous long-term conse- quences in Southeast Asia as a whole. To lessen these, their objective was, first, to provide France with the measure of support necessary to keep her fighting until the Geneva Conference was concluded and strengthen her hand in these negotia- tions. But they also wished to open the way for administration initiatives aimed at providing for a post-Geneva Southeast Asia–wide security arrangement. Thus they sought congressional backing for a resolution providing the president with discretionary authority until June 30, 1955, "to employ the Naval and Air Forces of the United States to assist the forces which are resisting aggression in Southeast Asia, to prevent the extension and expansion of that aggression, and to protect and defend the safety and security of the United States." It should be emphasized that Dulles was seeking support for this, and not merely for a one-shot air strike to relieve the French at Dienbienphu when, together with Radford and top Defense Department officials, he met with key congressmen on April 3.[40]

Dulles argued that, if Indochina fell to communist control and nothing was done about it, "it was only a question of time until all of Southeast Asia falls along with Indonesia, thus imperiling our western island defense." The congressmen's response to his appeal was unmistakably cool and cautious. When Dulles and Radford assured them that the administration was not contemplating a commit- ment of land forces, they countered with the skeptical observation that, once the flag was committed, the use of land forces would inevitably follow. Dulles found them to be unanimous in the view that "we want no more Koreas with the United States furnishing 90% of the manpower," and that Congress would not support American military intervention in Vietnam until the administration had obtained commitments for joint action from its allies, the British in particular. These congressmen further stipulated that such American action should be conditional on France's providing a convincing earnest of real independence for the three Indochina states.[41]

Consequently, Paris's request on April 4 for an American air strike to relieve the pressure on Dienbienphu was turned down by Washington, as was an even more urgent plea on the 23rd. On this second occasion, Laniel warned that, unless Dienbienphu held, the entire political picture in France would change and it would be impossible to muster a majority in Parliament in favor of EDC. His foreign minister, Georges Bidault, further threatened that France might find it necessary to seek a cease-fire if the United States refused his government's request for an air strike. Dulles informed Britain's foreign secretary, Anthony Eden, that if his country would back an air strike he would recommend to Eisenhower that he ask Congress for its mandate for military intervention. Convinced that an air strike would be ineffective, Eden held that nothing less than "intervention on a Korean scale, if that, would have any effect in Indo-China"; that its consequences, including China's reaction, could not be predicted; and that the existence of the Soviet-Chinese military alliance had to be taken into account. With Churchill's concurrence, he refused to pledge Britain's support.[42]

In the face of this British stand, the American ambassador to Paris, Douglas Dillon, cabled that, without an air strike, the Laniel government would collapse. Britain's refusal of support having foreclosed a congressionally sanctioned intervention, he urged that this be promptly achieved by presidential executive action —a move that would bypass Congress. Dulles, however, argued against this course, stating that "The security of the United States is not directly threatened" and so "armed intervention by executive action is not warranted." Moreover, as he then observed, whatever government might succeed Laniel's could not be counted upon to welcome American military intervention. He informed the premier on April 24 that there could be no question of American military involvement without congressional authorization, and that in any case his own military advice indicated that a massive U.S. air strike would not necessarily lift the siege of Dienbienphu. Two days later Eisenhower stated to another select group of legislative leaders that, if the U.S. were to put a single combat soldier into Indochina, its "entire prestige would be at stake, not only in that area but throughout the world," and that he could not see "any reason for American ground troops to be committed in Indo-China." He cautioned, however, that, although the United States could train the people of the area to fight on the ground, it might eventually have to send its air and naval power to support them.[43]

The inability to secure British—and therefore congressional—backing for the introduction of American air power did not, however, deter Eisenhower and Dulles from trying to develop a long-term collective approach to intervention in Indochina and Southeast Asia as a whole, a course they now referred to as "United Action." But once again the British disappointed, declining to participate in any concrete steps to organize such an undertaking until the outcome of the Geneva Conference was clear. Efforts to build an organization for collective security before the conference, Eden and Churchill believed, might well destroy prospects for a successful outcome of the negotiations, and might provoke Chinese military intervention. In trying to explain London's position to key congressmen, Dulles told them that "The British, including Churchill, were almost pathological in their fear of the H-bomb" and feared participation in any Western involvement in Indochina that "might bring on H-bomb devastation" or risk "Chinese intervention and global war." Bitter at Britain's refusal to join in United Action, Eisenhower suggested to Dulles on May 19 that, when he wrote the British prime minister, "some strong note might be injected implying that the

Churchill Government was really promoting a second Munich," and that perhaps the theme of "Japan and Manchuria"* might be introduced (one that Dulles had apparently persuaded him to delete from a letter of April 4).[44]

Nevertheless, Eisenhower and Dulles still hoped to achieve a collective security arrangement before the close of the Geneva Conference—whatever its outcome—and believed that, by openly pursuing this objective, they would in any case be giving the DRV, China, and the Soviet Union sufficient pause to strengthen France's hand in the Geneva negotiations. By mid-May Eisenhower had come to agree with Dulles, Nixon, and Radford that British participation was not vital to United Action.[45] Dulles then resumed his efforts, with the objective now of enlisting the Philippines and Thailand instead—an aim that encountered greater success. Although the campaign to organize United Action was not completed before the end of the Geneva Conference, its momentum carried through into the postconference period to result finally in the Manila Pact and SEATO.

On May 8, the day the Indochina phase of the Geneva Conference opened, the French had indicated privately that they wished to discuss "comprehensively" "the political and military conditions which would enable the United States to intervene militarily in Indochina." Laniel warned that "if there was no possibility of U.S. military help at any point, the regroupment of [French] forces [necessary because of losses at Dienbienphu] would have to be much more drastic, and the first thing to be done would be the complete evacuation and abandonment to the Vietminh of the entire territories of Laos and Cambodia." Radford then advised Dulles that the only military solution "was to go to the source of Communist power in the Far East, i.e., China, and destroy that power," and that the United States would never in the future be confronted with "as clear-cut a basis for taking measures directly against China as was the case now in Indochina." Dulles, however, clearly did not agree. In responding to the French on May 11, he elaborated what were essentially the administration's previous conditions for U.S. military intervention in Indochina: "1) an invitation from the present lawful authorities [i.e., the three still French-controlled governments of Indochina]; 2) clear assurance of complete independence to Laos, Cambodia and Viet-Nam; 3) evidence of concern by the United Nations; 4) a joining in the collective effort of some of the other nations of the area; and 5) assurance that France will not itself withdraw from the battle until it is won." It was expected that U.S. forces would be "principally but not exclusively air and sea forces," and that they and forces from other participating countries would be "supplementary to, and not in substitution for, the existing forces in the area."[46]

---

*Evidently a reference to the unwillingness of the U.S. and Britain to employ force against Japan's invasion and annexation of Manchuria in 1931, a move which was eventually followed by her invasion of most of the rest of China in 1937.

As the discussions at Geneva got under way, Washington gave renewed consideration to possible military intervention on the side of the French forces in Vietnam in case the conference ended in failure. The administration still saw such a role primarily in terms of air and naval power, with the French carrying the main burden on the ground. To secure congressional approval, it was understood that this action would have to be internationalized through United Action, with at least token forces from American allies. On May 19, however, Dulles reported to Eisenhower that Congress was no more supportive of intervention than before, and that a fresh attempt to secure backing for a congressional resolution giving the president "discretionary authority" to commit U.S. military power could not even enlist support of the Republican Party's leader in the Senate, William Knowland, who, according to Dulles, "reacted strongly in opposition, saying it would amount to giving the President a blank check to commit the country to war."[47]

Eisenhower and Dulles did not immediately abandon their efforts to secure some sort of congressional mandate giving the president discretionary authority to intervene. But during June, as France's military position continued to deteriorate, they concluded that the effectiveness of any supplementary U.S. military input would be correspondingly diminished, and their inclination to support an American military intervention decreased accordingly. Presumably any remaining disposition to take such action was undermined by an intelligence estimate that "the chances were somewhat better than even" that, in response to an intervention, even if limited to air and naval power, the Chinese would take "whatever military action they thought would be required to help Vietnam." Though by June 14 the altered American stance had been made unmistakably clear to the French, it was not publicized lest France be deprived of bargaining leverage at Geneva.[48]

A U.S. National Intelligence Estimate of June 15 spelled out the precariousness of the French position in Tonkin. The Vietminh had already redeployed to the vital delta area the great bulk of its forces that had fought at Dienbienphu. Either within or near the delta it had now marshaled ninety-four infantry battalions, one artillery division, 110 district companies, and forty to fifty thousand militia, and it was regarded as already "capable of launching a major assault" against French forces there. Opposing the Vietminh was a French Union force totaling 109 battalions supported by tanks, armored cars, and artillery, but with 60 percent of infantry strength composed of battalions from Bao Dai's "Vietnamese National Army."[49]

The hopelessness of France's military and political position in Vietnam was described poignantly by General Etienne Valluy, the despondent commander of French ground forces in Indochina, in his talks with American officials in Washington during the first week of June. He reported that his troops were tired; their morale was visibly low; the effectiveness of the French commands had decreased; the French and Bao Dai's Vietnamese troops had lost confidence in one another; his mobilization was a failure; his government was discredited; and in the South there was "conflict between the Vietnamese troops [in the French command] and the population of the area," with the civilian population in general leaning more and more toward the Vietminh. The enemy's losses at Dienbienphu had been considerably smaller than the French had hoped for; their morale was high; they were building up to a strength of a hundred battalions; and within ten days their "battle-hardened divisions" would reach jump-off positions around the now shrunken French perimeter in the heart of the Tonkin Delta, with prospects for a battle for Hanoi at the end of June. If Tonkin were lost, the general admonished, the military line could not be re-established elsewhere, and neither the French nor their Vietnamese auxiliaries would continue the fight. If the United States and its allies did not underwrite the battle for Tonkin, "they would fight tomorrow without the French in Saigon and Bangkok." The U.S. Joint Chiefs of Staff History observes how seriously this assessment was taken: "From General Smith in Geneva to [the U.S.] Chargé McClintock in Saigon, there was no American who chose to contest General Valluy's estimate seriously."[50]

The French were now disabused of any expectation that American military power would succor their desperately beleaguered forces in Indochina. In addition, despite their repeated inquiries, the administration refused to give any clear-cut promise as to whether the United States would counter even an unprovoked Chinese intervention in Indochina, although in fact on June 2 it had come to a decision that in such a case it would request congressional authority to do so.[51] It is quite possible, of course, that the administration refused to commit itself on that score for fear the French might cry "Wolf!" or even provoke a Chinese riposte along the parts of the frontier still not controlled by the Vietminh.

Once the United States had turned down Paris's appeal for direct military intervention and proved unwilling to give clear-cut assurances of support in the event of a Chinese entry into the conflict,[52] the French government hardened its insistence on negotiating an end to the war. Despite American opposition, it sent a delegation to Geneva prepared to make the concessions to the Vietminh necessary to secure an armistice, though at the same time it hoped to save enough face to salvage France's honor.

To understand the nature of, and reasons for, the agreements finally reached at Geneva on July 23, 1954, it is essential to keep in mind a number of power factors outside Vietnam, as well as the military and political balance that then obtained within that country. Any close scrutiny of the Geneva Conference inevitably yields the impression that, to a remarkable degree, these external factors ensured that the negotiations were conducted over the heads of the Vietnamese.

Militarily, the Vietminh clearly dominated; it had built up such a momentum that, as was widely agreed, it could probably overrun Hanoi during the next dry season and very possibly most of the rest of French-controlled Vietnam within a year. Politically too the Vietminh was paramount; the French had utterly failed to nurture any viable indigenous opposition, and their effort to build up an alternative state under Bao Dai had become a generally acknowledged fiasco. Under Secretary of State Walter Bedell Smith informed Congress that the Vietminh already controlled three-quarters of the country and, had elections been held, Ho Chi Minh would have won 80 percent of the vote. The assessment of the British Chiefs of Staff was even less sanguine: "Virtually all of Vietnam, Laos and Cambodia," they concluded, was "under, or subject to, imminent Vietminh control."[53]

With the French public sick of what it termed the "dirty war" overseas, and the tide of domestic opinion overwhelmingly in favor of military disengagement, the Vietminh might have been expected to emerge from the Geneva Conference with an agreement reflecting its military and political superiority. But this did not happen, and the major reason was that such a resolution of the eight-year struggle would not have conformed to the self-interest of any of the major powers. A settlement that reflected the actual balance between French and Vietminh power —much less the balance of strictly indigenous Vietnamese political elements— was, for different reasons, perceived by neither the United States, China, nor the Soviet Union as being in its own interests.

France's cards in the Geneva negotiations were hardly limited to "the two of clubs and three of diamonds" of which Foreign Minister Bidault complained. The French delegation also held two aces—the threat of American military intervention, and France's ambiguous stance on EDC—and it played these with great skill. The first gave it strong leverage on Peking, some on Hanoi, and, indirectly, some on Moscow as well. The EDC card could be played against both Moscow and Washington, and was in fact of crucial importance in ensuring that a reluctant Eisenhower administration even attended the conference.

In the months leading up to Geneva, and during the conference itself, the United States and France calculatedly employed the threat of an American-led United Action to strengthen France's position vis-à-vis the Vietminh and to weaken the disposition of Peking and Moscow to support Hanoi. Dulles hoped that "the mere knowledge that multilateral talks on mutual defense were being pursued might tend to moderate communist demands at Geneva." This, he said, was "essential to give some cards to work with [there,] so as to have a chance of obtaining [an] acceptable peace." Two weeks before the conference opened, Foreign Secretary Eden proposed a similar course. The only limitation on Washington's use of this card was public opinion, which, the Eisenhower administration realized, would not respond kindly to any explicit threat of military intervention should the conference fail. As an exasperated Bedell Smith put the matter in closed session of the Senate Foreign Relations Committee, "I wish we did not have to tell them [the communists], for example, that we have no intention of putting ground soldiers into Indochina; I wish to God that we could leave that suspicion or fear in their minds . . . and the fear that we might do a lot of things that we have no intention of doing, but our public opinion becomes concerned, and it has to be reassured. . . ." But certainly by the time of the Geneva Conference all its participants were aware that, if the French were pushed too hard and the conference failed, American naval and air power might be ranged on their side in Indochina.[54]

Related to this threat of American intervention, and clearly exerting some influence on the outcome of the conference, were the "7 Points" put forward by Dulles and Eden—the maximum French concessions they would countenance if they were to "respect" agreements reached at the conference. Drafted on June 29, when it looked as if the conference might collapse, these 7 Points represented an Anglo-American move designed both to induce France to yield less and to strengthen her hand in the negotiations; but neither sponsor, especially the British, expected that France could attain them completely.[55] These points expressed what Eisenhower and Dulles saw as a minimally acceptable outcome for the conference, and, with the exception of the fourth point, they were largely achieved. They envisaged a settlement that:

1. Preserves the integrity and independence of Laos and Cambodia, and assures the withdrawal of Vietminh forces therefrom.

2. Preserves at least the southern half of Vietnam, and if possible an enclave in the delta; in this connection we would be unwilling to see the line of division of responsibility drawn further south than a line running generally west from Dong Hoi.

3. Does not impose on Laos, Cambodia, or retained Vietnam any restrictions materially impairing their capacity to maintain stable non-Communist regimes; and especially restrictions impairing their right to maintain adequate forces for internal security, to import arms and to employ foreign advisers.

4. Does not contain political provisions which would risk loss of the retained area to Communist control.

5. Does not exclude the possibility of the ultimate reunification of Vietnam by peaceful means.

6. Provides for the peaceful and humane transfer, under international supervision, of those people desiring to be moved from one zone to another of Vietnam; and

7. Provides effective machinery for international supervision of the agreement.[56]

Although unable to secure French and British agreement to "stand firmly" on this program as "a minimum acceptable solution and to see the negotiations break off and warfare resume if this position was not accepted by the Communist side," Dulles still insisted that the communists must be made aware that the "alternative is some sort of common action upon which we have all agreed."[57]

Despite its considerable leverage with France, the Eisenhower administration could not press her too hard on these objectives without jeopardizing the important existing military ties between the two countries with respect to Europe, or Washington's hopes that the French Parliament would support its top priority in Europe—the long-planned superseding of NATO by a European Defense Community that would incorporate a rearmed West Germany. Although it was now more than two years since the French executive had indicated that France would adhere to the EDC, Parliament had still to ratify it. If the United States were to abandon France at Geneva because of her unwillingness or inability to secure an agreement roughly commensurate with the 7 Points, any chance of Parliament's going along with EDC and its unpopular provision for rearming Germany would undoubtedly be lost. Thus, by withholding parliamentary action on the new defense organization until after the conclusion of the Geneva Conference, the French maintained their leverage on both Washington, which wanted EDC, and Moscow, which was desperately anxious to head off the rearmament of Germany and the integration of its forces within the U.S.–Western European alliance.[58]

Whether or not, as some suspected, the new premier Pierre Mendès-France and the Russians had reached an understanding that the French government would abandon EDC if Moscow helped ensure that France's minimum terms on Indochina were met, Parliament was clearly more likely to vote against entering that alliance with Mendès-France as premier than if the conference failed and he resigned. It would certainly be hard to maintain that Mendès-France really fought for EDC when, a month after the close of the Geneva Conference, Parliament finally debated the proposition and turned it down. In any case, the Russians presumably recognized that, if France gained an acceptable armistice at Geneva, she would be able to redeploy troops from Indochina to Europe, thereby meeting her NATO obligations and undercutting the argument that EDC, with its rearmament of Germany, was necessary.[59]

Apart from the Soviet Union's immediate concern over the fate of EDC, it probably feared that, if France were pressured too heavily at the conference, and the United States then intervened militarily in Indochina, there was a risk that the conflict might escalate into a third world war. For if the Chinese communists came into the war on the side of the Vietminh, and the United States then responded with air attacks against China, Moscow would undoubtedly be called on to honor its 1950 defense pact with Peking.[60]

Ranged against these very real concerns were no vital Soviet interests in Indochina itself, which, like the rest of Southeast Asia, was still an area of marginal importance to the Soviet Union. At the same time, Stalin's successors were then keenly interested in possibilities for pursuing détente with the United States and its allies. Consequently, as Evelyn Colbert has observed, "precisely because Indochina was a very low priority area in Moscow's global perspective, it was an ideal one in which to establish the authenticity of Soviet interest in détente."[61]

Thus, in terms of basic French, American, and British objectives, the Soviet posture at Geneva was largely cooperative and constructive—apparently significantly more so than Washington had originally expected.[62] On most of the crucial issues, Soviet Foreign Minister Vyacheslav Molotov, who alternated with British Foreign Secretary Anthony Eden as cochairman of the conference, ended up standing closer to the French position—and often even to Dulles and Eden's 7 Points—than to that of Pham Van Dong, prime minister of the DRV and its chief representative at Geneva.

China had considerably more at stake in the outcome of the Geneva Conference than any other major power save France itself. For Peking, Vietnam and Laos, both bordering on her southern flank, were of critical strategic importance. Her fears of an American threat in this area stemmed from her recent confrontation with U.S. military power in Korea and the well-publicized American plans for United Action. The Korean armistice, less than a year old, had been preceded by the Eisenhower administration's threat to carry that stalemated war to Chinese territory by means of air-delivered nuclear destruction. Peking was thus anxious to keep American power far from her southern frontiers and ensure that the DRV's demands at the conference were kept within limits that were minimally acceptable to France and therefore unlikely to precipitate an American intervention. In the view of Anthony Eden, the Chinese saw American activities in Indochina as "directed against them and not in the defense of the territories which the United States was professing to help." Consequently, "the chief Chinese opposition during the 1954 negotiations at Geneva was to any American military presence, however innocuous in itself, within any territories of the three states of Indo-China." This meant Indochina's neutralization, with China's security reinforced by continuing Vietminh control over all areas of northern Vietnam that bordered China's southern frontier. Peking's security interests could, however, be adequately served without this buffer area's being extended to the southern areas of Vietnam, which were distant from China.[63]

For other reasons too it was important to the Chinese that the conference reach a settlement agreeable to France. Peking desperately needed a period of peace to carry out its first five-year economic plan—shelved because of the Korean War—and, like Moscow, it was in the process of embarking on a policy aimed at détente with the Western powers, or "peaceful co-existence," as the Chinese termed it. Moreover, it should be kept in mind that the first five weeks of the Geneva Conference had focused on Korea, especially on the ultimately unsuccessful effort to arrive at a political solution embracing its northern and southern regimes. It is possible that Peking's desire to enlist Western support on the Korean issues, which were of extreme importance to China, may have, initially at least, suggested moderation in backing the Vietminh's objectives. China's aims at Geneva did not put her on a collision course with the French, who were pleasantly surprised at what they regarded as her moderate stance.[64]

The positions taken by China and the Soviet Union brought Dulles to report to the Senate Foreign Relations Committee that the Russians were attempting to restrain the Chinese and that "the Chinese are exercising some restraint upon Ho Chi Minh." Jean Chauvel, France's top professional diplomat at Geneva, spoke of the "Chinese-Russian moderating influence" being brought to bear on the

Vietminh, and the American diplomat who reported this went on to explain that "Chauvel has impression both Russians and Chinese give Vietminh fairly free hand to see how far they can go but when they find Vietminh demands have gone beyond limit which French can be expected to accept, they intervene." Chauvel, he said, "expressed confidence that if he were negotiating only with Russians and Chinese, he could almost certainly achieve a settlement in line with [the] provisions of [the] U.S.-U.K. aide memoire" (meaning Dulles and Eden's 7 Points).[65]

Although unprepared to make all the concessions urged by Moscow and Peking, the leadership in Hanoi was also clearly affected by its perception of a very real threat of American military intervention—possibly with nuclear weapons—if it did not meet the French partway. On the basis of contemporary official Vietnamese sources, Christine White concludes, "There is every indication that the DRV leadership did in fact take very seriously the possibility that the U.S. would replace the French on the battlefield." In a careful reading of the official DRV newspaper, *Nhan Dan*, she found that these leaders were warning as early as August 1953 "that the end of the war in Korea would lead to increased U.S. intervention in Vietnam, Laos and Cambodia . . . the ultimate goal of the U.S. being to replace France in Indochina. . . ." At the end of March 1954 an editorial in *Nhan Dan* charged that the U.S. was planning to sabotage the Geneva Conference and take over control of the war from the French. And toward the end of the conference Ho Chi Minh countered the assertions of other DRV leaders that he was making too many concessions to the French, by arguing that they "saw the French but not the Americans and failed to realize that the U.S. was replacing France as the main enemy of the Vietnamese revolution."[66]

It is clear that Peking and Moscow pressured Hanoi to make much greater concessions than its leaders felt were justified in view of its unquestionably dominant political position in Vietnam and markedly superior military positions both there and in Laos. The extent of the concessions yielded by the DRV at Geneva can readily be appreciated by comparing its opening position at the conference on May 10 with the provisions finally settled on there. Even after making broad allowances for the usual extension of negotiating positions considerably beyond actual expectations, the disparity is striking.

Central to the DRV's objectives was that a political settlement precede an armistice. The political provisions that were to precede a cease-fire would be French recognition of the sovereignty and national independence of Vietnam, Laos, and Cambodia; a regroupment followed by the withdrawal of all foreign troops from each of these countries; free general elections with a view to establishing a single national government in each of them; a mutual exchange of prisoners of war; nonprosecution of those who had collaborated with either side during the war; and recognition by all three countries of the economic and cultural interests of France, "in conformity with the principles of equality and mutual interest." In presenting these points, Prime Minister Pham Van Dong also spoke in behalf of the interests of the Vietminh-backed Pathet Lao (which controlled about half of Laos) and the Vietminh-supported Khmer Isarak (which was relatively weak and dominated considerably less of Cambodia), claiming that they represented "the great majority" of the inhabitants of these two countries and that their representatives should be seated at the conference.[67]

This was, of course, much more than the French would accept, the essentials of whose position were backed not only directly by the British and indirectly by the United States, but, in some of the most critical areas, also by Soviet Foreign Minister Molotov—and especially by the head of the Chinese delegation, Foreign Minister Chou En-lai.[68]

Under this combined pressure, the DRV then retreated by stages to a position whereby it agreed that an armistice could precede a political settlement, that pending such a settlement Vietnam could be temporarily divided into military regroupment zones for troops under French and DRV control (with Laos similarly divided for troops under French and Pathet Lao control), that Vietnam's national reunification elections could be deferred for six months, that Cambodia and Laos need not be represented at the conference by the Pathet Lao and Khmer Isarak, and that Vietminh "volunteers" would be withdrawn from the two countries.[69]

On issues relating to the Vietminh's position in Cambodia and Laos, China was especially supportive of the Western powers. Chou En-lai was prepared to deny any accommodation that favored the Vietminh-supported resistance groups in these countries, even though the Pathet Lao was actually strong and broadly based in Laos. He further made clear that China had no objections to recognizing the French-sponsored royal governments in Laos and Cambodia. Evelyn Colbert observes that "Peking was prepared to bargain away the Viet-Minh-sustained local Communist position in these countries" for assurances that U.S. bases would not be established in them. Western diplomats credited Chou En-lai with making "a major breakthrough in the negotiations by implicitly adopting the Western view that the Pathet Lao and Free Khmer forces did not represent legitimate indigenous movements" and that the Vietminh "volunteers" who sometimes encadred their units should be withdrawn along with the Vietminh battalions (two in Cambodia, ten in Laos) that had been fighting on their side. Hewing to a position so supportive of France (and acceptable to Washington), Peking effectively sabotaged the Vietminh's strong position in Laos, one that Bedell Smith himself expected would oblige the conference to leave them with control of from one-third to one-half of the country.[70]

Molotov would not completely endorse Chou's views on Laos and Cambodia, arguing that "about 50 percent" of the territory of Laos was outside the control of its French-backed government and that the Pathet Lao constituted a "substantial" resistance movement. He insisted that simple withdrawal of Vietminh forces from Laos and Cambodia was not acceptable and that "some form of de facto partition" was necessary, "in Laos, at least." In the end, however, the conference husbanded as a regroupment area for the Pathet Lao only two minor, sparsely populated Lao provinces (Phong Saly and Samneua), fronting respectively on China and the DRV, and constituting less than one-tenth of the country's area. As a consequence of Peking and Moscow's support of, or acquiescence in, the Western powers' position on Cambodia and Laos, the paramount external political influence there would continue to be that of France, not the Vietminh.[71]

The French abandoned their initial penchant for a leopard-spot pattern of regroupment areas because they feared that, if they were to hold on to Haiphong, they would have to agree to the Vietminh's retaining a comparable base in the South. The DRV finally acquiesced in the subsequent French demand for the country's temporary partition, but it stipulated that the boundary line run northwest from 13° latitude on the coast to 14° on the western border, as against French insistence on the eighteenth parallel straight across from the coast. In the long impasse over this important issue, "the French increasingly threatened the DRV with the possibility of U.S. intervention," the likelihood of which they considerably exaggerated.[72] But when the Laniel government fell on June 12 and was replaced four days later by one headed by Pierre Mendès-France, who promised to conclude the conference by July 20 or resign, the DRV refused to countenance further concessions. In this stance, however, it failed to secure the necessary Chinese and Soviet support. During the second week of July, when still-outstanding French and Vietminh differences threatened the conference, Moscow and Peking renewed pressure on Hanoi; and this was particularly heavy from the Chinese delegation. Neither of these communist powers wished to risk the volatile situation that might attend the conference's collapse. From then on, the Vietminh's residual position on basic issues was further whittled away.

The French (and the Americans) wanted to delay the all-Vietnam elections as long as possible, leaving the date unspecified, whereas the Vietminh insisted there be a fixed date for no more than six months after an armistice. Molotov suggested a compromise of one year with a precise date set, but the Chinese were agreeable to the election's being scheduled within two to two and a half years of a cease-fire (that is, sometime during 1956), with no precise date stipulated. Finally, on Molotov's initiative, a compromise was reached on this vital feature: national reunification elections to be held throughout Vietnam within two years of an armistice.[73]

The most intractable problem was drawing an east-west line between what was finally mutually agreed should be just two military regroupment zones. It was stipulated that this line was not political and was provisional—to be expunged by the nationwide elections, now scheduled definitely for July 1956. But for the intervening period control over important territory was at stake, including the old imperial capital of Hué and the major port and naval base at Danang (Tourane). Here the beleaguered French garrisons were restricted to tiny enclaves, surrounded by the Vietminh, who held an uninterrupted grip on the coastal plain and inland mountains for more than two hundred miles to the south. The Vietminh's "consequent claim to all the territory north of a line running northwest from the 13th to the 14th parallel (from Tuy Hoa on the coast through Pleiku to the Cambodian border) was far more in keeping with the actual military situation than the French demand for the partition line at the 18th parallel," or the seventeenth parallel, which Ho's government was finally obliged to accept as the demarcation line. On this point Mendès-France's elucidation of the Geneva Agreements for the French Parliament is pertinent:

> So far as the demarcation line is concerned, the enemy was asking for the thirteenth parallel; and today we have the seventeenth. Now between the thirteenth and seventeenth parallel, Tourane and Hué are located, and there are three provinces which have always shown allegiance to the Vietminh and which the Vietminh is now going to evacuate so that they may pass under our control.[74]

Chinese pressure on the Vietminh over this issue was particularly strong. Only after Chou En-lai and Ho Chi Minh met, during the first week of July, at the South China city of Nanning, where, according to a CIA report, Chou applied pressure on Ho, did the Vietminh delegation at Geneva finally accept a line along the seventeenth parallel that left the French not only Danang and Hué but also the vital Savannakhet–Quang Tri highway to the north of these cities, which linked Laos to the Vietnamese coast.[75]

As long as there was a buffer state, free of bases or military alignment with the United States, on China's southern flank, Peking was apparently little concerned whether it was 300 or 500 miles deep. This, and the emergence of neutralized, nonaligned regimes, similarly free of American military ties, in Laos, Cambodia, and the southern part of Vietnam, constituted China's top priorities at Geneva. As Bedell Smith reported to Eisenhower and a bipartisan congressional group, "What Chou really wanted was to have the Geneva Powers guarantee three little buffer countries to the south of the Tonkin Delta [the main area Peking agreed should be left under DRV control]."[76]

These Chinese objectives, along with the Soviet Union's European priorities and its desire to keep the Indochina conflict from escalating into a wider war that might test its military alliance with China, combined to produce an outcome at Geneva that was remarkably close to Dulles's minimum objectives as embodied in his British-backed 7-Point Program. Indeed, the evidence available suggests that China was prepared to go even further toward American and French objectives. A month before the Geneva Conference concluded, Chou En-lai assured the French that China recognized that there were "two governments in the territory of Vietnam," for the first time accepting "the valid existence" of Bao Dai's still largely unformed State of Vietnam. A final political settlement, he said, could be reached "by direct negotiations between the two governments"—that is, the DRV and the regime that was, in the words of the Pentagon's chronicler, "still little more than a figurehead for French authority."[77]

There is no doubt that China had been of real assistance to the DRV in supplying it with heavy artillery, antiaircraft guns, and trucks in its fight with the French, particularly at Dienbienphu. At Geneva, however, the Chinese role appears to have been on balance more damaging than helpful to the interests of Ho Chi Minh's government.

The final settlement at Geneva severely compromised DRV expectations and objectives, and the fact that the DRV did not receive concessions commensurate with its military power and political control was recognized by China and the Soviet Union as well as France, Britain, and the United States. What, then, did Ho's government actually achieve, and—international pressures apart—why did it settle for as little as it did?

Here it must be noted that the conference forged two separate but interrelated instruments. The first was a set of signed bilateral armistice agreements, agreed to on July 20, between the military commands of the DRV and France (acting on behalf of all Vietnamese in the areas it still controlled, including the Vietnamese soldiers serving under the French), as well as between the DRV command and the Franco-Laotian and Royal Khmer army commands. The second was a multinational thirteen-point Final Declaration endorsed the next day through recorded oral assent* by the DRV, France, Britain, China, and the Soviet Union. The United States did not join in this endorsement of the agreements, though it declared it would "refrain from the threat or use of force to disturb them," and "took note" of all of the declaration except for its last paragraph (that calling for consultation with other members of the conference on matters referred to them by the International Supervisory Commission). Bao Dai's representative also refused endorsement, and the delegates of the Royal Lao and Cambodian governments tacitly acknowledged or explicitly supported the declaration.[78]

The major *quid pro quo* won by the Vietminh was the assurance that the struggle for control of Vietnam would be transferred from the military to the political level, a realm in which the Vietminh leaders knew their superiority over the French and their Vietnamese collaborators was even greater than it was militarily. Thus, in exchange for regrouping their military forces to the north of the seventeenth parallel into a territory considerably smaller than the total area they actually controlled, they had the assurance that in two years they would have the opportunity of winning control over the whole country through a nationwide election that they were, with good reason, confident of winning. For the Vietminh this was the heart of the Geneva Agreements. As Eden has categorically stated, without the firm and explicit assurance of national elections aimed at reunifying the country, the Vietminh would never have agreed to the armistice. In that judgment, he has been unequivocally supported by Tran Van Do, Bao Dai's principal representative at Geneva.[79]

---

*The World Court had established, more than twenty years before, that an oral agreement, for which there is proof, between authorized representatives of countries, is legally binding. The positions registered orally by the conference participants at Geneva were officially recorded at the time and form part of the conference record.

Ho's government had ample basis for believing those elections would indeed be held. Not only were they clearly promised for a definite date in Geneva's Final Declaration, but the bilateral armistice agreement with France also stipulated that the conduct of civil administration south of the seventeenth parallel was to be the responsibility of France, "Pending the general elections which will bring about the unification of Viet Nam." Both the Vietminh and the French expected that any failure by France to carry out this central political component of the agreements could justify the Vietminh's abandonment of the essential military component—the armistice. Indeed, French officials believed that if the elections were not held, there would probably be "spontaneous rebellions" throughout the South.[80]

There was no doubt in Paris as to France's obligation to ensure "observance and enforcement" of the provisions of the Geneva Agreements in her southern area of responsibility, as stipulated in her armistice with the Vietminh. Although it was generally expected that France would stay on until the national reunifica-tion elections were held, in case she did not both the armistice agreement and her treaty of June 4, 1954, with Bao Dai's regime provided that any Vietnamese administration succeeding hers was legally bound to assume her obligations.[81]

The Final Declaration of the Geneva Conference provided that the details of the projected elections would be worked out among representatives of the French and Vietminh regroupment zones in consultations beginning July 20, 1955 (two months after completion of the military regroupment). Moreover, two im-portant conditions for the election process were stipulated in advance: they were to be conducted by "secret ballot" and "under the supervision of an international commission composed of representatives of the Member States (Canada, India, and Poland) of the International Supervisory Commission." (This commission—the body established by the armistice agreement to monitor the carrying out of its provisions—was formally designated the International Commission for Super-vision and Control, though it was usually referred to as the International Control Commission, or ICC.)

The United States opposed supervision of elections by such a commission, holding that they should be overseen by the United Nations instead. This argu-ment was somewhat disingenuous, however: American negotiators had from the outset of the conference been fully aware that both France and Britain were opposed to any U.N. supervision of the Geneva Agreements because of the precedent that "would be used against them in North Africa and elsewhere." French and British sensitivity to the possibility of adverse consequences for their interests in other areas was probably considerably heightened by an incident that occurred at this time with regard to America's ongoing intervention in Guatemala. When both Britain and France expressed reluctance to back the administration's Guatemalan policy in the U.N., a furious Eisenhower threatened retaliation by adopting a position independent of France and Britain when the issues of Egypt, Cyprus, North Africa, and the Middle East came up before the United Nations. He further warned that U.S. actions would be "entirely free without regard to their [British and French] position in relation to any such matters as any of their colonial problems." The general thrust of the president's position (though apparently not the precise words) was promptly represented to both Paris and London.[82]

It should be emphasized, because the matter has so frequently been misrepresented, that there was no provision in the Geneva Agreements stipulating that the elections were to be dependent upon the prior establishment of "fundamental freedoms and democratic institutions" in either of the two regroupment areas. As paragraph 7 of the declaration makes clear, these freedoms and institutions were the anticipated attributes of the unified Vietnamese nation that was to be established as a result of the nationwide elections.[83] Certainly it was assumed that the conditions for these elections, which the International Control Commission was to supervise, would have to be negotiated and agreed upon prior to the elections, and that is precisely why the conference provided that a year before they were held there would be consultations on this matter. Whatever pre-electoral conditions might obtain in the North, with administration south of the seventeenth parallel in French hands during this period it would be unrealistic to expect that colonial officials there would, in their eleventh hour, metamorphose into apostles of civil liberties. However, the Geneva delegates could justifiably expect both France and the Vietminh to cooperate with the ICC in trying to arrange for the pre-election consultations scheduled for mid-1955 and in supervising the actual balloting a year later.

Both the achievement of national unity and the Vietminh's political position were further protected by other provisions of the Geneva Agreements. The demarcation line separating the two military regroupment zones at the seventeenth parallel was to last only until the elections, and it was expressly stipulated that it would be "provisional and should not in any way be interpreted as constituting a political or territorial boundary." Anthony Eden later affirmed that it was not expected to become "a lasting political boundary." The armistice, then, prescribed only a military disengagement and regrouping, not a physical dismemberment of the country.[84]

During the three hundred days allotted for the regroupment of the two armies, civilians were free to relocate to either side of the seventeenth parallel, and were not obliged to follow their armed forces. Neither the political adherents of the Vietminh nor any other group or party were called upon to leave their home areas; all were to be protected against reprisals or discrimination, with the International Control Commission charged with ensuring that this and other features of the Geneva Agreements were respected. There was no provision limiting Vietminh political activity in either of the two zones; and it would, of course, have been impossible to prepare for elections if such a provision had existed.

Geneva did not leave two separate states but, rather, two contesting parties within a single national state. These two rivals—the Vietminh (the Democratic Republic of Vietnam) and the Bao Dai regime (the State of Vietnam)—each continued after Geneva, just as each had done before, to lay claim to the whole country. The difference was that whereas prior to Geneva the contending parties had sought to enforce their claim through military means, now these agreements had transferred their contest to the political level, with the resolution dependent upon the outcome of the scheduled national elections.

Finally, the Vietminh was assured that the existing balance of military power in its favor could be maintained free from outside intervention. Neither of the two regroupment zones could adhere to any military alliance, and no military base under the control of a foreign state was to be permitted in either zone. The introduction of foreign troops and military personnel into Vietnam was prohibited, as well as of all additional arms and munitions.[85]

Apart from the fundamental consideration that the French desperately wanted an armistice and that breaching another part of the agreements would prejudice its continuation (a consideration that was very much in the minds of both Paris and London), the Vietminh had other, lesser though significant, reasons for believing that the political provisions of the agreements would be respected. The International Control Commission was responsible for "supervising the proper execution by the parties of the provisions of the agreement." The commission's effectiveness was, however, limited by its composition and procedures. Its chairman was from India, and regarded as neutral; its other representatives were from Canada, regarded as favoring France, and Poland, regarded as backing the DRV. In general, the commission was to make its recommendations on the basis of a majority vote, but some of the most important questions required unanimity. This applied to "questions concerning violations, or threats of violations, which might lead to resumption of hostilities," including "violation by the armed forces of one of the parties of the regrouping zones . . . of the other party." It was provided, however, that, when the commission could not reach agreement on these issues, it was to submit majority and minority reports to the members of the conference. Likewise, the members were to be informed "if one of the parties refuses to put into effect a recommendation of the International Commission."[86] This, of course, would mean very little if the powers should later not find it in their own interests to respond to reports of the violation of Geneva's provisions; but at the time the Vietminh had little reason to believe this responsibility would not be met.

Privately, senior U.S. officials, though considering France's defeat and abandonment of North Vietnam to be damaging to American interests, clearly felt that Washington had done as well as could realistically be expected in the Geneva settlement—"the best obtainable by negotiation." And, indeed, of Dulles's 7 Points, only one had not essentially been attained: that the accord would "not contain political provisions which would risk loss of the retained area to Communist control" (the promise of elections clearly did). To have opposed the settlement, Eisenhower believed, would mean "dividing the Free World," and undoubtedly such action would not only have destroyed chances of French support for EDC, but might also have seriously prejudiced France's continuing membership in NATO. The pressures of American domestic politics, however, with the "loss of China" issue still potent and the influence of Senators McCarthy and McCarran strong, did not permit the administration to join publicly in a statement accepting provisions that included communist control of additional Asian territory. So great was this sensitivity that Dulles refused to attend the final sessions at Geneva and turned over immediate charge of the American delegation to his deputy, Walter Bedell Smith, a confidant of both the secretary and President Eisenhower. As Dulles put it to the French ambassador, it was not so much a question of what was *in* the agreement "but rather a question of making it with the Communists." Mendès-France understood these domestic political constraints and was presumably much relieved when at the last moment the United States, instead of totally disassociating itself from the accords, agreed to the diplomatically significant steps of "taking note" of them, as well as pledging not to use force to upset them.[87]

But in the course of this guardedly tacit acceptance of the accords, the United States had put some reservations into the conference's record. By explicitly disassociating itself from Article 13 of the declaration, it served notice that it was not pledged to support efforts of the International Control Commission to see that the other twelve articles were respected. By holding that the United Nations was the appropriate body to supervise the elections, it was implicitly refusing to agree with the conference's assignment of that responsibility to the commission; and in knowing full well that Britain and France would not accept the U.N. as supervisor, it was establishing some of the groundwork for later blocking elections by insisting that the U.N. was the only proper aegis under which to hold them (precisely the course that the Saigon government, with American encouragement, subsequently took). Finally, in referring to the unwillingness of Bao Dai's representative to endorse the conference's provisions, the American representative asserted the United States' adherence to the unexceptionable general proposition that "peoples are entitled to determine their own future" and that it would "not join in any arrangement which would hinder this." Unstated was the fact that from the standpoint of the administration's policy, application of this principle of self-determination in Vietnam was to be limited to Bao Dai's coterie and others willing to assume an anticommunist stance. And well before the conference ended, Dulles, with a reasonably clear vision of its outcome, had, in close consultation with Eisenhower, begun to lay the foundations of a post-Geneva policy that would circumvent some of the central features of the settlement.

III

The Establishment of a
Separate Southern State

The middle months of 1954 marked a major turning point in the American relationship with Vietnam. It was during this period that the United States made the most fundamental decision of its thirty-year involvement—the critical prerequisite to the subsequent incremental steps that culminated in President Johnson's famous escalation a decade later. Although this first major increase in American intervention was essentially political, it had important and clearly understood military implications. It was sustainable initially only by the threat of U.S. armed intervention and ultimately by its actual execution. So for the second time Washington attempted to establish an anticommunist government in Vietnam; but now it acted alone, no longer in association with France, and its effort was focused primarily on just the southern half of the country.

In this new departure the Eisenhower administration intervened directly in Vietnam, displacing France as the major external power. Rather than working through the French to support the Bao Dai regime, which claimed authority over all Vietnam, the United States took on the mission of establishing a separate noncommunist state in just the southern regroupment zone prescribed by the Geneva Agreements. The administration believed that, without the encumbrance of the old French colonial presence to undermine its nationalist legitimacy, a revamped Bao Dai regime, with Ngo Dinh Diem as its prime minister, could, if given sufficient American support, stand a good chance of competing effectively with the DRV. In addition, though their hopes on this score were apparently not so strong, senior U.S. officials thought it possible that this American-backed government would ultimately be able to absorb the North into a single anticommunist state. However unrealistic this second proposition, it was still the presidentially endorsed U.S. objective at least as late as 1958. In April of that year the National Security Council reiterated its aim to "work toward the weakening of the Communists in the North and South Viet Nam in order to bring about the eventual peaceful reunification of a free and independent Viet Nam under anti-Communist leadership."[1]

To understand this major shift in the United States' approach to Vietnam, one must assess the changed pattern of factors influencing American policy in the immediate post-Geneva period. The original, European-oriented calculations that had propelled the United States into its limited intervention in the early postwar years increasingly yielded place to considerations rooted primarily in the new ascendancy of communist power in China. Europe did still continue to exert an important influence on American Vietnam policy right through the Geneva Conference, however, because of the pivotal importance of the projected European Defense Community to Washington's Soviet containment strategy. But when the French Parliament defeated EDC soon after the close of the conference, European objectives ceased to have a significant effect on American policy toward Vietnam.

Although the French rejection of EDC only temporarily delayed German rearmament, it entailed the loss of most of France's once-formidable leverage with the United States, which had derived from Washington's uncertainty regarding French domestic politics and the extent to which France could be counted on to cooperate with American economic and military objectives in Europe. The potential of communism in France had by now dramatically ebbed, and the balance of her internal politics no longer threatened her continued presence in an American-led military alignment aimed at containing Soviet power in Europe. Indeed, the large noncommunist majority in the Chamber of Deputies saw such an alignment as clearly in their country's self-interest. The shoe was now on the other foot, for, as France began to face mounting militant nationalist pressures in her North African colonies during the fall of 1954, she badly needed American backing to maintain her ascendancy there.[2]

Other factors important to the previous American preoccupation with Vietnam were, however, still operative: the enduring myth that communism was global and monolithic; the conviction that China was expansionist; and American domestic political pressures centering on the "loss of China" syndrome, whereby all administrations feared being accused of losing additional territory to communist control. But it was, of course, against the Democrats—not Eisenhower's Republicans—that the charge of China's "loss" had been leveled. Moreover, in contrast to the American involvement in China's civil war, the congressional and public perception was thus far of primarily French, not American, responsibility for developments in Vietnam, and France stood out clearly as a lightning rod to divert attacks from the administration's record there.[3] At this stage, fear of domestic criticism, although a factor, was not fundamental to the administration's new decision for a major American involvement. It would only become an important consideration after the Eisenhower administration had publicly committed itself to sustaining a separate state free of communist control in the southern half of Vietnam.

What, then, explains the decision to intervene directly in Vietnam? To the three above-mentioned continuing determinants two new major factors had now been added. First was John Foster Dulles's retrospective analysis—subscribed to by Eisenhower—of the American failure in China, and the lessons he derived from this for policy toward Southeast Asia; and second was the inspiration he and Eisenhower drew from a set of analogies between conditions and the potential for American actions in Vietnam, and recent American and British experiences in other parts of the world.

Dulles approached the conflicts between Southeast Asian peoples and the colonial powers with certain strongly held views. Like his predecessor, Dean Acheson, he had little faith in the self-governing capacity of Southeast Asians who gained their independence from colonial powers through revolution. He was convinced that, without the involvement and guidance of the democratic West, nationalist movements in these countries would probably be drawn into communist-controlled political channels—and this, he believed, was likely even after they had attained full independence. With respect to the peoples of Indochina and Indonesia in particular, he felt that until they attained a greater degree of political maturity, the West had an ongoing obligation to help ensure that communists did not take over; and if the Western colonial powers withdrew, the United States had a responsibility to assume this burden.[4]

From Chiang Kai-shek's defeat in China, Dulles drew a lesson that he regarded as applicable to Southeast Asian countries threatened by communist power. One of the main reasons he saw for the failure of American China policy was that "The territorial integrity of China became a shibboleth. We finally got a territorially integrated China—for whose benefit? The Communists." In other words, while certainly aware of the faults of the Kuomintang regime, Dulles saw its defeat by the Chinese communists as largely attributable to American acquiescence in Chiang's shortsighted attempt to win control over the whole of China concurrently. A more effective strategy would have been to accept temporarily a loss of the country's territorial integrity, yielding part of it to communist power, while concentrating Kuomintang and American resources in order to husband as much of the mainland as possible free of Mao's control. Chiang's residual mainland territory would have provided a base for mounting a rollback of communist control.[5]

Some nine months before the beginning of the Geneva Conference on Indochina, this lesson was being applied to the situation in Indonesia. In late 1953 President Eisenhower counseled Hugh S. Cumming, his administration's first ambassador to Indonesia, that "as against a unified Indonesia which would fall to the Communists and a break up of that country into smaller segments he would prefer the latter." Dulles was more explicit, stating to the ambassador, "As between a territorially united Indonesia which is leaning and progressing towards communism and a break up of that country into racial and geographical units, I would prefer the latter as furnishing a fulcrum from which the United States could work later to help them eliminate communism in one place or another, and then in the end, if they so wish arrive back again at a united Indonesia."[6]

If Eisenhower and Dulles considered this lesson from China to have such validity for Indonesia, it must have seemed even more applicable to the situation in Vietnam.[7] In any case, their approach to Vietnam both during and after the

Geneva Conference was consistent with, and undoubtedly to a significant extent shaped by, their perception of the causes of the "failure" in China.

But why did Eisenhower and Dulles believe that the United States had the capacity to implement in Vietnam what they considered to be the logical propositions derived from their retrospective analysis of the "failure" in China? That question cannot be answered without reference to the administration's evaluation of earlier American experiences in Greece, Iran, Guatemala, and especially the Philippines, together with what was regarded as an equally relevant British experience in Malaya. Its assessment of recent developments in these countries tended to reinforce an already self-assured and assertive postwar American "can-do" hubris, inclining policymakers to believe that the success of the United States in meeting challenges from communists or other socioeconomic radicals in these other places demonstrated abilities that could be applied in Vietnam. These combined to encourage the Eisenhower administration to intervene directly in Vietnam in the belief that it could work its own political will there to achieve a solution more consistent with American interests than that provided by the Geneva Conference.

A minority of American officials perceived that conditions in Vietnam were in fact fundamentally different from these other situations. But senior policymakers continued to draw inspiration and self-assurance from these precedents until well after the Eisenhower administration had embarked on a much deeper political intervention and commitment of American prestige in Vietnam. The simplistic analogies, sometimes referred to as "models," provided by these experiences continued to inform U.S. policy throughout Kennedy's administration and during the first part of Johnson's.

In Greece, where the United States had taken over from the British in late 1947, Washington believed that the critical factor in turning the tide against a peasant-backed, communist-led insurrection had been the injection of a large amount of American money, weaponry, and a military mission incorporating some five hundred advisers. American officials thought that this intervention, which had relied heavily on forced relocation of peasants, had been decisive in shoring up a faltering anticommunist government and forcing the insurgents to abandon their struggle and fade away into the hills within two years. The belief that this American experience in Greece was pertinent to Vietnam outlasted the Eisenhower administration. It was revived repeatedly under Kennedy and Johnson, especially by Walt Rostow, but also, though less insistently, by William P. Bundy, assistant secretary of state for Far Eastern affairs under Johnson, who had been in Greece during the American campaign there and as late as 1967 was still talking about the possibility of "a Greek solution" in Vietnam.[8]

In Iran in 1953—just a year before the Eisenhower administration's major decision on Vietnam—a covert U.S. program mounted primarily by the CIA had brought down a radical, albeit noncommunist, government led by Mohammed Mossadegh that had been bent on ending foreign domination of the country's oil production, and then returned the recently ousted shah to power. The administration also took great satisfaction in the outcome of its largely covert intervention during the spring of 1954 in Guatemala. This had successfully ousted a noncommunist but radical president who had been willing to accept the support of communists as well as other political groups and been regarded as a threat to American economic interests.

Britain's experience in Malaya was at least as important as the Greek precedent. By 1953 the British were finally beginning to gain the upper hand in their effort to subdue an insurgency of some Malayan Chinese that had broken out five years previously. They attributed their success primarily to an extensive program of forced resettlement of rural Chinese, on whom their enemy was or might be reliant for food and intelligence. After 1959, when a communist-led insurgency finally re-emerged in South Vietnam, Washington saw the presumed Malayan analogy as especially relevant, and commenced to emphasize a policy of population resettlement in rural areas. The Kennedy administration was equally insistent on seeing a Malayan analogy and even more attracted to a resettlement strategy, a predilection that continued under Johnson and Nixon.

But the most influential of all these precedents was the recent example of the Philippines. During 1953–54 American officials helped secure the position of secretary of defense in the Philippines for their own candidate, Ramon Magsaysay, and they then worked successfully to ensure his election as president. While he held these positions, they cooperated effectively with him to suppress a potent communist-led, agrarian-based insurgency, the Hukbalahap. The administration believed it could achieve similar results through its own chosen political instrument six hundred miles to the east in Vietnam. And if the CIA's Colonel Edward Lansdale had been so effective in helping to organize this effort in the Philippines, why should he not be equally successful in Vietnam?[9] In January 1964 Assistant Secretary for East Asian Affairs Roger Hilsman was still looking for "a Vietnamese Magsaysay," and well into that year Secretary of Defense McNamara and Secretary of State Rusk, along with several other senior officials, were still seeing pertinent precedents in the Philippine and Malayan experiences.

The truth was that in character and context the Vietnam insurgency was only superficially akin, at best, to those in the Philippines, Malaya, and Greece. Nevertheless, the defeats of these earlier communist-led insurgencies, in combination with the heady American "successes" in Guatemala and Iran, encouraged the Eisenhower administration in its conviction that it had the capacity to work its will in determining Vietnam's political future.

Shaped primarily by Dulles, but with full support from the president, the administration's new Vietnam policy from the outset involved repudiating the two key political features of the Geneva Agreements: the stipulation that the line separating the two military zones "should not in any way be interpreted as constituting a political or territorial boundary," and the reunification elections, which had been an even more central condition for the armistice. The new policy also entailed two major positive steps by the United States. First, a mutual defense pact between it and several allies in effect treated the seventeenth parallel as a political boundary and provided in advance a measure of protection to the southern regroupment zone against attack by forces based in the North or against "internal subversion." Second, the United States displaced France's political and military presence in this area, taking over as paymaster to the Vietnamese civil servants and soldiers who had collaborated with the French and providing American training and advisers to the previously French-officered Vietnamese auxiliary component of the French expeditionary force. Still headed by Bao Dai as "chief of state," the "State of Vietnam" retained its name but was now restricted to the territory south of the seventeenth parallel. Into this area the United States pumped a massive amount of financial support, dwarfing what France had managed to provide.

These twin American efforts at an end run around some of Geneva's central provisions did not emerge fresh and full-blown after the conference. In the months preceding and during it, American policymakers had laid much of the groundwork for the two interdependent policies of building up a separate southern-Vietnamese state and protecting it from external assault and internal political opposition.

The still-unconsummated process of organizing United Action, initiated by the United States during the conference, now merged into an American-sponsored regional defense organization which was finally embodied in the Manila Pact of September 8, 1954 (ratified by the U.S. Congress February 19, 1955). In effect, the threat of an American-led anticommunist military intervention that had provided France with such useful leverage in Geneva was now spelled out with greater precision and institutionalized into a loosely structured alliance. Popularly known as SEATO (Southeast Asia Treaty Organization), it included the United States, Britain, France, Australia, and New Zealand, together with the only three Asian states Washington could induce to join—the Philippines, Thailand, and Pakistan (the last-named expecting that membership would give it leverage against India). Initially, the French were sufficiently scrupulous about Geneva's provisions for the neutralization of Indochina to resist Dulles's attempt to include Cambodia, Laos, and especially South Vietnam (where the stipulation against adherence to any military alliance was explicit) as members of SEATO. But through the device of adding a protocol to the treaty projecting an "umbrella of protection" over these three areas, Dulles was able to circumvent the impediment. The protocol stipulated that the treaty's provisions extended to Cambodia, Laos, and "the free territory under the jurisdiction of the State of Vietnam," even though they were not signatories of the treaty. Prince Sihanouk promptly repudiated Cambodia's inclusion, and with its neutralization in 1962 Laos was officially removed from jurisdiction of the protocol. Predictably, however, this protection was accepted by the French and Bao Dai for the temporary military regroupment zone south of the seventeenth parallel provided for at the Geneva

Conference, now referred to as "the free territory of Vietnam." This was made explicit in a joint Eisenhower-Diem communiqué on May 11, 1957, after U.S. officials were satisfied that Ngo Dinh Diem's authority had been sufficiently established in this half of the country.[10]

SEATO's members saw its main objective as being "to deter massive military aggression," the United States stipulating that its own involvement would be limited to cases where the aggressor was communist. Though all its signatories saw the alliance as a deterrent against a possible attack by China, the United States, France, and at least some other members regarded it as providing a similar deterrent against the possibility of an assault by Hanoi into the regroupment zone of French forces south of the seventeenth parallel.[11]

SEATO's apparently broad international base disguised a decided lack of enthusiasm on the part of some of its participants, and it was never effective as a vehicle for collective action. The formula did, however, provide subsequent American administrations with the basis for inducing Americans to believe that U.S. military involvement in Indochina had international sanction. Much more important, it provided what the executive branch came to assert was congressional authority for direct military intervention there. Indeed, SEATO's significance ultimately lay more in what came to be construed as a congressional licensing of unilateral U.S. anticommunist military intervention in Southeast Asia than in its role as a collective defense organization. This was not what the Senate had had in mind when it approved the treaty, but what happened in practice.

Nevertheless, during the decade prior to the August 1964 Tonkin Gulf Resolution, SEATO provided the major rationale for a U.S. military role in Indochina. And when, within two years, the 1964 resolution had become discredited because of a crystallization of congressional suspicion as to the circumstances surrounding its passage, SEATO once more provided the president with what was asserted to be "the legal basis" for that involvement.

For two decades SEATO was referred to as an American "commitment." Having signed the treaty, the United States was indeed committed to it. But that treaty itself did not—as successive administrations encouraged the public to believe—commit the United States to defend South Vietnam. In fact, no such pledge was made either by the members of SEATO collectively or by the United States unilaterally. The *ex post facto* presidential interpretation of SEATO that alleged it did so departed widely from the mandate actually agreed to by the U.S. Senate and did violence to its intent. Yet this interpretation gradually became the accepted conventional public perception. It was strongly enough established in the Kennedy administration to be used as justification for escalating involvement beyond the largely political and economic dimension pursued by Eisenhower to the level of direct U.S. military intervention.

Certainly, SEATO emerged as something very different from what the Senate believed it was endorsing in 1955. To appreciate this, one must scrutinize the actual provisions of the treaty and their interpretation by Dulles when he shepherded it through the Senate hearings.

There were two main components of the treaty, addressed respectively to outside aggression (para. 1, article IV) and "aggression other than by armed attack"—that is, by internal insurrection, or "subversion," as it was originally termed (para. 2, article IV). Only in cases of outside aggression could the language of the treaty be construed as providing authority for a signatory to respond with action. In such a case unanimity among SEATO members was not required, and a single member could act on its own—a possibility qualified only by the proviso that any such move had to be in accordance with the country's "constitutional processes."

With respect to situations involving insurrection, the treaty was susceptible to no such interpretation. In such instances a signatory was not empowered to act; the only stipulation was that the "parties shall consult immediately in order to agree on the measures which should be taken for the common defense." Consultation among the SEATO signatories, then, and not action—either collective or unilateral—was all that was provided for in cases of insurgency. Only if this consultation were to lead to unanimous agreement among the members of SEATO could that body make recommendations to the several signatory governments as to an appropriate course of action. But, as the Senate clearly understood when it consented to the SEATO treaty, nothing in its terms constituted any commitment or authority for the United States or any other signatory to take action in such cases. And the State Department then and later fully appreciated that unanimity among SEATO's members was required even for a recommendation.[12]

It was nevertheless the treaty's provisions covering "Communist subversion" that were later to become its chief operational feature for the architects of American Indochina policies. But when the Eisenhower administration sought Senate ratification it was this component that gave senators more pause, and because of the ambiguities in wording, they insisted on a clear-cut explication. Dulles then provided assurances that assuaged their anxiety but were disregarded by later administrations. While the Senate still had the treaty under consideration, the following exchange took place between him and Senator Theodore Green, chairman of the Senate Foreign Relations Committee:

SENATOR GREEN: Then we are obliged to help put down a revolutionary movement.

SECRETARY DULLES: No. If there is a revolutionary movement in Vietnam or in Thailand, we would consult together [with the other members of SEATO] as to what to do about it, because if that were a subversive movement that was in fact propagated by communism, it would be a very grave threat to us. But we have no undertaking to put it down; all we have is an undertaking to consult together as to what to do about it.

Dulles went on to explain that if subversion "arises or threatens, . . . we should consult together immediately [with the other SEATO members] in order to agree on measures which should be taken. That is an obligation for consultation. It is not an obligation for action." He further assured the senators that the treaty's more explicit provision covering cases of "armed aggression" where each party was permitted to respond directly "in accordance with its own constitutional processes" referred to "open and armed attack" coming from outside the treaty area and would not be used as "a subterfuge" to permit involvement in cases involving subversion. Yet that was precisely what was to happen.[13]

The senators who endorsed the SEATO treaty had not reckoned with the power of a president to define insurgency as outside aggression. By resorting to this expedient, he was able to shift to a basis of treaty authority that empowered a signatory to *act* rather than merely consult with his fellow pact members (para. 1 rather than para. 2 of article IV). The condition in the treaty stipulating that invocation of such authority be in conformity with a signatory's "constitutional processes" posed no problem to a president, as long as Congress acquiesced in his simply consulting with a few of its more amenable members. For such casuistry to succeed and the original intent of the Senate in endorsing SEATO to be defied, all that was required was an apathetic and poorly informed Congress.

If the administration's objectives and SEATO's language describing them seemed ambiguous to some senators, the administration itself was clear regarding its aims, as is evident in the internal policy statement by the National Security Council a month after the Geneva Conference concluded and shortly before the opening of the Manila [SEATO] Conference. If Theodore Green and numerous other senators who agreed to support SEATO had been privy to the administration's objectives embodied in this NSC directive, they would have been less likely to agree to that treaty.

This NSC statement specified the terms that were later incorporated into the new security treaty and spelled out their implementation and that of associated policies. It stipulated that if "a legitimate local government" required assistance "to defeat local Communist subversion or rebellion not constituting armed attack," the president should "in addition to giving all possible covert and overt support within Executive Branch authority . . . at once consider requesting Congressional authority to take appropriate action, which might if necessary and feasible include the use of U.S. military forces either locally or against the external source of such subversion or rebellion (including Communist China if determined to be the source)." Moreover, the projected Southeast Asia Treaty was not to "limit U.S. freedom to use nuclear weapons." Under the rubric of "Indochina: Political and Covert Action," the NSC called for "every possible effort, not inconsistent with the U.S. position as to the [Geneva] armistice agreements, to defeat Communist subversion and influence" to "maintain a friendly non-Communist South Vietnam and to prevent a Communist victory through all-Vietnam elections." Among other things, the United States was also to "aid emigration from North Vietnam and resettlement of peoples unwilling to remain under Communist rule" and it was to "exploit available means to make more difficult the control by the Vietminh of North Vietnam." In support of all of these policies, it was to "conduct covert operations on a large and effective scale."[14]

. . .

By granting protection in advance to Vietnam's southern regroupment zone against any attack by communist forces in the North, SEATO endowed the seventeenth parallel with the political character the Geneva Conference had prohibited and laid a foundation for recognizing a separate statehood for this southern area. This was, indeed, the administration's intention, and, five days before the conference concluded, Dulles informed an executive session of the Senate Foreign Relations Committee, "In fact the military regrouping [zones] will be apt to gradually become a live *de facto* political division. . . ."[15]

With SEATO providing the context for establishing an American-protected state in the southern half of Vietnam, the Eisenhower administration concurrently moved ahead with the second prong of its new Vietnam policy. This was the much more straightforward effort to endow that area with the attributes of governmental power, substituting a dependence on the United States for a previous dependence on France, and ensuring a leadership congenial to and shaped by the administration. This new American political venture retained the same name as its French-sponsored predecessor—the "State of Vietnam"—and Bao Dai stayed on as chief of state for some fifteen months after Geneva, thereby providing a transitional bridge. In this politically precarious period, while the French and Vietminh military forces regrouped and Paris incrementally transferred the fundamental attributes of government to the State of Vietnam, an American presence gradually replaced that of France. During this process Bao Dai, still comfortably ensconced on the French Riviera, progressively, albeit reluctantly, yielded more and more power to Ngo Dinh Diem, the Catholic leader and U.S. protégé whom he had appointed as prime minister in June 1954.

The regrouping of the French and Vietminh armies was largely completed well before the three-hundred-day maximum stipulated at Geneva. A hundred and thirty-two thousand French Union troops, probably somewhat more than half of whom were Vietnamese auxiliaries, moved south, and some 130,000–150,000 or more southern-based Vietminh soldiers, administrative cadres, and their families went north. A sizable number of the regular French forces were sent to North Africa, while the best-trained Vietnamese elements were assigned to augment Bao Dai's army,* and the remainder were demobilized.[16]

Ngo Dinh Diem told American officials that, if he could have public assurance of U.S. aid and support, from one to two million northerners could be induced to move south. Although the French commander, General Paul Ely, believed that no more than two hundred thousand northern civilians would voluntarily move to the South, he acknowledged that through "dramatic propa-

---

*Of the total of some 360,000 Vietnamese troops and militia commanded by the French, 150,000 were retained; that being the size army the U.S. was in 1955–56 prepared to approve (and fund).

ganda" a million or more might be persuaded to go. Such a propaganda campaign was indeed mounted, and approximately eight hundred thousand Vietnamese civilians, a substantial majority of them Catholics, opted to move south
of the seventeenth parallel under the provisions of the Geneva Agreements permitting civilian regroupment. An estimated two hundred thousand of these
civilians—both Catholic and non-Catholic—were civil servants who had
worked with the French, together with their dependents and those of the Vietnamese soldiers who had fought for the French. Undoubtedly they were motivated to leave because they feared reprisals or at least a dim future if they
remained. Probably most of the Catholics, however, were peasants and other
rural inhabitants who had not been employed by the French either in the civil
service or the regular armed forces. The large number who came from the
predominantly Catholic districts of Phat Diem and Bui Chu must have felt
compromised because, under French pressure, their pastors had organized them
into locally based militias to operate under French command. But whether or
not they feared Vietminh reprisals, most of these priests presumably felt they
would have greater scope to practice their religion in a noncommunist South
under a government headed by a Catholic. Altogether, about half of the northern Catholic community moved south of the seventeenth parallel, thereby more
than doubling the South's Catholic population and bringing it to approximately
a million, or about 9 percent of the total.[17]

The dramatic exodus of Catholics has often been described as their "voting
with their feet." But, as the former CIA and White House Indochina specialist
Chester Cooper has noted, "Although there was great uncertainty, even anxiety
about their fate under a Communist regime, the vast movement of Catholics to
South Vietnam was not spontaneous." He and others have observed that the
Catholic Church, as well as the Americans, French, and Diem, mounted a campaign to arouse Catholics to the dangers to freedom of worship and encouraged
the hierarchy and its adherents to move south. (Diem himself first went to Hanoi
on such a mission as early as June 30, 1954, when, of course, the city was still
garrisoned by the French.) As Cooper observes, "The slogans were hardly subtle:
'Christ has gone to the South' and 'the Virgin Mary has departed from the
North.' " Data subsequently available tends to support the late Bernard Fall in
his conclusion that "Although there is no doubt that hundreds of thousands of
Vietnamese would have fled Communist domination in any case, the mass flight
was admittedly the result of an extremely intensive, well-conducted, and, in terms
of its objective, very successful American psychological warfare operation."
Agents of Lansdale and the French along with Diem's teams were active in this,
and helped spread the word that those going south would be well treated under
a government headed by a Catholic and supported with American aid: "A water
buffalo and five acres" was a frequent promise.[18]

Probably of equal importance in helping to encourage the exodus was the
heavy barrage of black propaganda. False documents, purportedly issued by the
Vietminh, advised the population as to the introduction of forced labor and

startlingly severe strictures governing property and economic life in general in the North. According to Philippe Devillers, who had unusual access to pertinent French government documents, agents spread word that the withdrawal of anti-communist forces "was only temporary, that sooner or later Saigon, backed by the United States, would again take the offensive to liberate the North, and that the atomic bomb might then be used if China helped the Vietminh. The only way of escaping the atomic destruction intended for the Reds was to flee to the South." The deputy secretary general of the International Control Commission, B. S. N. Murti, observed, "A large number of people decided to leave because of a vague fear of atomic attack on the North. The International Commission's Teams came across a great number of people who really believed that if they remained in the North the Americans would drop atom bombs." And as a Pentagon analyst observes, "Conceivably an example of Colonel Lansdale's handiwork" was a map of Hanoi showing three concentric circles of destruction that a U.S. atomic bomb on the city would cause.[19]

Whatever the motivation of those who went south, the United States played a major role in their physical resettlement. In addition to transport provided by the French, units of the United States Seventh Fleet participated extensively, moving over 310,000 people at a cost of $93 million. In December 1954 Washington allocated an additional $282 million to pay costs of resettling them in the South, with American private charities providing several million more. The largest concentrations of those Catholics were the peasant communities settled *en bloc* with their parish priests in 203 separate villages in various areas of South Vietnam regarded by Diem and his advisers as strategically important—in a belt surrounding Saigon and in certain areas of the highlands inhabited by non-Vietnamese tribal groups.[20]

Despite this influx to the South, the Catholics still constituted less than 10 percent of the population there. But the strength of their anti-Vietminh political orientation set them apart from other religious groups, including the Buddhist majority, and commended them for inclusion in any anticommunist Vietnamese regime. The special, generally privileged position Catholics had long occupied in the French colonial regime also fitted them for a place in a political order meant to compete with the Vietminh. Most of their forebears having been converted by French missionaries, the Catholics had generally been regarded by the French as politically more reliable than other indigenous elements. Because of this and because they had enjoyed better access to Western education, they had occupied a disproportionately large number of positions in the Vietnamese auxiliary of the colonial civil service. Though a significant number of Catholics had supported the Vietminh, a majority had worked more closely with the French than had other religious groups.[21] Taken as a whole, this now much-enlarged Catholic community in the South provided for the emerging American-backed regime an important third element of support, alongside the residual Vietnamese components of the French colonial army and bureaucracy, with whose membership they often overlapped.

. . .

The actual transfer of governmental authority by France to Bao Dai was not completed until more than five months after the end of the Geneva Conference.* In consolidating the new government in the southern half of Vietnam, Bao Dai proved useful during this transitional period primarily because of his continuing influence with the soldiers and civil servants who had served the French. Bao Dai, however, was certainly not Washington's first choice to lead this government. His undoubtedly sincere efforts to secure independence from France had failed, and many of those South Vietnamese whom the administration hoped to detach from Ho's standard regarded the former emperor as a collaborator with the colonial order. He did not improve this image by remaining in France, from where he conveyed his orders to his subordinates. Nor did he have a large following among the Catholics.

In view of Washington's jaundiced assessment of Bao Dai, and the apparent ineffectiveness of his prime minister, Prince Buu Loc, it is understandable that American officials should have sought an eminent Catholic nationalist, free of any taint of collaboration with the French, to provide more effective anticommunist leadership. And in inducing Bao Dai, apparently without French approval, to appoint Ngo Dinh Diem as his prime minister in mid-May 1954, the Eisenhower administration secured a man with these attributes. Diem was probably in a better position than any other Vietnamese leader to swing the maximum number of Catholics behind the new southern regime. Furthermore, he had given advance assurances that he agreed to the U.S. proposal to take over the training of South Vietnamese armed forces.[22]

Nonetheless, at this stage American officials were by no means euphoric, and still recognized—as they were much less inclined to do a year or two later—his serious limitations. Thus, the U.S. ambassador to Paris cabled Washington on May 24, "On balance we are favorably impressed [by Diem] but only in the realization that we are prepared to accept the seemingly ridiculous prospect that this yogi-like mystic could assume the charge he is apparently about to undertake only because the standard set by his predecessor is so low." Following Diem's arrival in Saigon on June 25, the assessment of the U.S. chargé there was every bit as unenthusiastic: "Diem is a messiah without a message. His only formulated policy is to ask for immediate American assistance in every form, including refugee relief, training of troops and armed intervention. His only present emotion, other than a lively appreciation of himself, is a blind hatred for the French."[23]

Although some American officials hoped that Diem would emerge as Vietnam's Magsaysay, the only attributes he shared with the Filipino were personal

*Not until January 1, 1955, was Bao Dai's prime minister, Ngo Dinh Diem, able to proclaim the reality of independence from France, and it was another two months before France transferred control over the Vietnamese component of the French armed forces in Vietnam.

honesty, pecuniary incorruptibility, and a strong anticommunism. A mandarin aristocrat, at once arrogant and reserved and shy, Diem had scant understanding of and little rapport with the peasantry. He felt awkward, and acted so, when prevailed upon to visit rural areas, and his espousal of Catholicism appears to have made no dent in his aloofness from the populace. As Joseph Buttinger, who worked closely with him, has written, "Diem's temperament, social philosophy, and political comportment seemed to preclude all prospects of his ever becoming a popular hero. His stiff demeanor would have doomed any attempt to stir the masses by word or gesture, had he ever been persuaded of the necessity to make himself admired and loved. However, what he wanted was not love but the respect and obedience he considered his due as head of state." Moreover, except in his early years, Diem had actually had very little administrative experience. He had served ably and energetically in the French colonial administration, moving from an initial appointment as district chief in 1921, at the age of twenty, to the position of governor of a small province in 1929. Then, beginning in 1933, he was briefly the young emperor Bao Dai's secretary of the interior in the almost powerless rump Imperial Court at Hué, a position from which he resigned on principle because of French interference with his efforts to introduce reforms, and Bao Dai's unwillingness to give him sufficient backing. But for two decades thereafter he held no administrative post, nor did he show great talent as a political organizer.[24]

Diem stood out in that he had not collaborated with the French. Nevertheless, in the eyes of a significant number of Vietnamese, his nationalist credentials had been tarnished by his willingness to work with Japanese occupation authorities. For a brief period he was their leading candidate for the position of premier in the client Vietnamese government with which they planned to replace the French in March 1945. Only when, at the last minute, the Japanese abandoned their plan for replacing Bao Dai with Prince Cuong De as emperor did Diem lose interest in the premiership.[25] His claim to national leadership was further weakened by his absence from the country (he was in Europe and the United States) from August 1950 through the final years of the anti-French struggle.

At least as late as June 1953, Diem appears to have been unknown to Dulles and was unable to get an appointment with him. During that year, however, from a base in the Maryknoll order's headquarters in Lakewood, New Jersey, Diem —encouraged by several American Catholic leaders, the most prominent of whom was Francis Cardinal Spellman—was actively engaged in soliciting American backing. Acknowledging that Ho Chi Minh drew popular support because of his nationalism, he argued that Ho was succeeding primarily because Bao Dai had been so compromised by his association with the French. Only an anticommunist nationalist whose record was free of such collaboration, he argued, could draw this kind of backing away from Ho. (Diem had earlier turned down an offer of a high position in Ho's government, because he regarded the Vietminh as ultimately responsible for the murder of one of his brothers; but Ho's offer itself demonstrated that even he recognized Diem's stature as a nationalist leader.)

However dogmatic and narrow in some of his views, Diem appeared completely assured as to his own ability to provide an effective alternative to Ho. He was able to convince a growing number of influential Americans, initially including Congressman Walter Judd and Senators John F. Kennedy and Mike Mansfield—with others such as Hubert Humphrey soon to follow—that he was the man to do this. His campaign to win congressional support was undoubtedly aided by the enthusiastic backing of a remarkably effective lobby of strongly anticommunist, mostly liberal-leaning Americans, which by the fall of 1955 had been organized as the American Friends of Vietnam, and ultimately enlisted these congressmen and a good many others among its members. It is hard to measure how influential Diem's American backers initially were with Dulles and Eisenhower, but as early as February 1954, against the background of Bao Dai's acknowledged incapacity, Under Secretary of State Bedell Smith told an executive session of the Senate Foreign Relations Committee that the administration was thinking of "providing a certain religious leadership."[26]

(The American Friends of Vietnam maintained a vigorous effort to gather U.S. support for Diem until 1961, when most of its members became disillusioned with his leadership, and its activities dwindled until his overthrow. Soon after his death, however, the organization was revived and once more became a significant force for a strongly interventionist policy in Vietnam. Whereas during its early, pro-Diem period the group's activities had been sustained primarily by the generally altruistic zeal and dedication of its members, after its revival it worked increasingly closely with the New York public-relations firm representing the Saigon government. By May 1965 the American Friends of Vietnam had developed close though discreet ties with, and a considerable dependence on, the U.S. government, which helped raise private funds for it. Moreover, at least one of the publication ventures planned by the organization's national chairman was undertaken on the initiative of the White House (McGeorge Bundy's aide, Chester Cooper) in conjunction with the Pentagon-supported Historical Evaluation Research Organization, whose executive director, Colonel Trevor N. Dupuy, provided it with an editorial staff and helped arrange for its financing.[27])

Although American officials viewed Diem as the most promising candidate available to head the Saigon government, many were at first circumspect in endorsing him publicly or in offering support. This caution stemmed not only from some lingering doubts as to his qualifications but also from the extremely difficult and precarious political situation he was confronting. The administration's circumspection was clearly reflected in the qualified and conditional offer of support embodied in Eisenhower's letter to Diem of October 1, 1954, written in a hesitant tone and not actually delivered until three weeks later.[28]

Eisenhower made his pledge of aid dependent on Diem's "assurances as to the standards of performance . . . in undertaking needed reforms." American assistance was to be "combined with" Diem's own efforts to "contribute effectively toward an independent Vietnam endowed with a strong government," a government that, Eisenhower hoped, would be "so responsive to the nationalist aspirations of its people" as to attract domestic and international respect. This letter was not the all-out pledge that subsequent American presidents cited to justify their own intervention; it was, however, one of the first in a series of steps by the Eisenhower administration that, starting cautiously, were eventually to constitute a clear, positive, and virtually unqualified commitment to maintain a separate state in the southern half of Vietnam.

But during the first nine months after Geneva, this official circumspection was paralleled by the concurrent pursuit of another option, a second-track, covert policy; and any assessment of the administration's approach must focus heavily on this largely invisible level of policy. As Chester Cooper, then a top CIA official, candidly put it, "The Central Intelligence Agency was given the mission of helping Diem develop a government that would be sufficiently strong and viable to compete with and, if necessary, stand up to the Communist regime of Ho Chi Minh in the north." Appointed to head this effort was Colonel Edward Lansdale, whom Dulles reportedly asked to "Do what you did in the Philippines." During Diem's first months in office, Lansdale and a few other American agents provided him with "considerable moral support and guidance," as well as funds. Lansdale states that on the very day Diem arrived in Saigon he presented him with "notes on how to be a Prime Minister of Vietnam." He and other CIA operatives helped Diem establish dominance over the Vietnamese military forces gradually being turned over by the French, and later gave him critically important assistance in securing the adherence, neutralization, or dispersal of the armed forces of the Cao Dai, Hoa Hao, and Binh Xuyen.[29]

These successes in American covert activity, however, could not have occurred without sufficient displacement of French power. Here the U.S. leverage stemmed primarily from the degree to which both the French forces and their Vietnamese auxiliaries were dependent on American financial support. Since Washington was now substantially reducing its subvention to French troops still in Indochina, and France needed these troops to help contain the mounting nationalist insurrections against French rule in North Africa, their exodus from Vietnam took place more rapidly than either the French or the DRV had expected at the time of the signing of the Geneva Agreements. Moreover, the French desperately needed American support for their current North African policies, and only a few months before, over another issue (Guatemala), Eisenhower had made clear that he was prepared to end American support of the French in North Africa if Paris did not line up with Washington. With France critically dependent on the United States for financial support and for backing in North Africa, Premier Mendès-France was reluctant to risk antagonizing Washington by contesting American policy in Vietnam.[30]

In the face of this leverage, French efforts to replace Diem with a candidate of their own choosing, Prince Buu Hoi, were doomed to failure, despite the substantial backing he received from General Nguyen Van Hinh (commander in chief of Bao Dai's army), most of his senior officers, and most leaders of the Cao Dai and Hoa Hao. But, though he was anticommunist, Buu Hoi had previously had close contacts with Ho Chi Minh's government and favored holding national reunification elections, in the meantime introducing economic, cultural, and postal relations plus freedom of travel between the North and the South. Even American officials who had grave doubts as to Diem's abilities opposed Buu Hoi's candidacy. Diem was clearly better suited to the administration's objective of preventing possible reunification of the South with a communist North. Thus, in reporting to Paris on November 6 on "the American Government's special addiction to Diem," General Paul Ely referred to him as "the only Vietnamese politician who would absolutely never enter into contact with the Vietminh under any circumstances. . . ." In the face of French efforts to forward Buu Hoi's candidacy, Washington made clear that he, or anyone sharing his views, was unacceptable, and that unless Diem were retained as prime minister, American financial support would be terminated. In concrete terms, this meant ending the salaries of the nascent southern state's army, and most of its civil service. Consequently this effort to displace Diem collapsed.[31]

It was partly in conjunction with Buu Hoi's candidacy that Diem was presented with his first major direct challenge. This came from General Hinh, whose army had now grown substantially with the incorporation of the best-trained members of the Vietnamese component of the French Union forces. Hinh and many other senior officers had been deeply antagonized by the efforts of Diem's influential brother, Ngo Dinh Nhu, to politicize and assert control over the armed forces by infiltrating agents of his secret party, the Can Lao, into the officer corps. Since the French retained authority over all their Vietnamese military units until February 1955, Diem was initially unable to rely upon their support in his efforts to replace Hinh, who, with French backing, continued to press Buu Hoi's candidacy. Finally, on November 29, 1954, Bao Dai succumbed to American pressure and summoned Hinh to Paris to dismiss him. But it was American financial leverage applied directly on Hinh in Saigon that was crucial in bringing about his removal. Hinh had most of Bao Dai's army solidly behind him, and could easily have launched a successful move against Diem. However, as he afterward acknowledged, "The Americans let me know that if that happened, dollar help would be cut off . . . but the country cannot survive without American help." With the United States replacing France as paymaster for the armed forces, Hinh had no choice but to yield to Diem. And without the general's support, Buu Hoi stood no chance of replacing Diem as prime minister.[32]

American backing for Diem still remained reserved for a further five months. In early April 1955, Eisenhower's special ambassador, General J. Lawton Collins, sent the president a series of cables highly critical of Diem's performance and abilities. This, combined with criticism from other American quarters, brought Dulles to conclude, reluctantly, that Diem would have to go. A central criticism was Diem's provocative clumsiness in dealing with important elements of the Vietnamese armed forces, even after Hinh's dismissal, and his alienation of leaders of the large Cao Dai and Hoa Hao militias, whose support was regarded as essential if their troops were to be successfully merged into Diem's army. Diem refused to recognize the autonomy of the considerable territories these religious sects had administered (a status that the French had accepted), and he resisted their demands for additional Cabinet posts in his government. But most crucial was his refusal to take over the substantial financial subsidies to them that the French had terminated as of the end of January, and his curtailment of the military supplies that the French had also been providing. At the same time as he was confronting the sects, Diem moved against the Binh Xuyen, the small army of well-armed gangsters who, following payoffs to Bao Dai and certain corrupt French officials, had gained control of Saigon's police force, thereby obtaining lucrative monopolies of the heroin trade, gambling, and prostitution.[33]

Though American officials applauded Diem's plans to oust the Binh Xuyen, many regarded him as politically foolish and militarily reckless to move against them at the same time as he was confronting the two religious sects, possibly risking a military marriage of convenience between the sects and the Binh Xuyen. Influential U.S. officials regarded Diem's strategy—or absence thereof—in this matter as symptomatic of a lack of political realism that was critically undermining the possibility of establishing a viable state. The sects and Binh Xuyen had indeed begun forging a tactical front against Diem when he precipitated an all-out military confrontation with the Binh Xuyen on April 27.

Covert CIA operations paved the way for his actions by favorably altering the balance of military forces between him and his opponents. Large bribes had been judiciously distributed among several key military leaders of the Binh Xuyen, as well as of the Cao Dai and Hoa Hao, presumably with the help of Lansdale and other CIA operatives. Bernard Fall estimated that during March and April 1955 alone, such inducements to leaders totaled as much as $12 million. As a consequence of these bribes, and because they were persuaded that only with Diem as paymaster would the United States take over the subventions previously paid by France, a majority of the leaders of the Cao Dai—the most powerful of the dissidents—were persuaded to join Diem. Ultimately some 80 to 90 percent of the thirty thousand men in their regular army and militia were integrated into Diem's army. A majority of about nine thousand Hoa Hao soldiers were either induced to back Diem or were neutralized, with the remainder ousted from the Saigon area and on the defensive.[34]

With the cards thus reshuffled, Diem's military forces made the culminating move. Colonel Duong Van Minh, with eleven battalions of the best of the French-trained Vietnamese soldiers and three thousand of the Cao Dai's most seasoned fighters, led by Lansdale's well-bribed protégé Trinh Minh Thé, successfully drove out of Saigon that apparently substantial majority of Binh Xuyen who had not been bribed or otherwise persuaded to cooperate.[35] The operation involved heavy fighting and considerable destruction in the capital, but this military victory, together with the extensive ongoing accomplishments of bribery and integration, added up to a victory for Diem that proved decisive in securing him firm American support.

On the eve of Diem's action against the Binh Xuyen, in view of the disastrous situation that seemed to be developing, Dulles had in fact approved a cable withdrawing American support from him. The unexpected news of Diem's success caused him to cancel it.[36] Overnight, in the eyes of most American officials and much of the U.S. press, Diem was metamorphosed from a stubborn, narrow, politically maladroit failure into a wise and clever hero. He was now master of Saigon and had asserted his control over or neutralized practically all of the French-trained Vietnamese military forces, as well as the formerly French-supported Cao Dai and Hoa Hao armies. The Eisenhower administration no longer doubted that Diem was its man, and the only one capable of helping it create a new state.

Domestically, Diem drew his major support, first, from Vietnamese who had served in either the army or the bureaucracy under the French and, second, from the Catholic community in the South. Among the latter, it was the exiles from North Vietnam, now forming a majority of the South's Catholic population, who comprised the most reliable and effective element in the power base he was establishing. In the words of a Pentagon chronicler, they "provided Diem with a claque: a politically malleable, culturally distinct group, wholly distrustful of Ho Chi Minh and the DRV, dependent for subsistence on Diem's government, and attracted to Diem as a co-religionist," who were important primarily as "a source of reliable political and military cadres."[37] In organizing both his armed forces and the civilian administration, Diem showed a clear favoritism toward this group, often installing them in positions above non-Catholics who had had better training and more experience under the French.

A new piece of support came from that socioeconomic class of the South's new order that was developed and nourished by a continuous flow of heavy U.S. funding. Its centerpiece was the expanding bourgeoisie in the South, many times greater than the tiny group that France's colonial economy had sustained. An enormous umbilical cord, tapping into an American economy six thousand miles away, carried the lifeblood of a new "middle class" that South Vietnam's indigenous economic base could never have begun to support on its own. However artificial, the growth of this group effectively changed the class structure of the southern half of Vietnam.

During the entire twenty-year period it was provided, 1955–75, a massive program of U.S. economic assistance was crucial to the operation of the regimes of Diem and his successors. More than that, it conditioned a whole generation of southerners to an environment and a way of life that could not be sustained by the indigenous economic base, and which promptly collapsed once the trans-Pacific cord was cut. The rapidly growing membership of this almost exclusively urban bourgeoisie—both those who were now able to expand the modest wealth they had accumulated under the French and the much more numerous *nouveaux riches* who emerged during the American period—fully realized that their markedly enhanced economic position was fundamentally dependent on continuing U.S. support of the Saigon regime. Consequently, most of them welcomed Saigon's American connection and were disposed to give political backing to whatever government was likely to ensure its continuation. Thus, Diem and subsequent American protégés could count on substantial support from the South's new bourgeoisie.[38]

This element had already begun to grow during the Franco-Vietminh war when mounting American economic aid had permitted increasing local expenditures by the French administration and individual soldiers. Vietnamese entrepreneurs had, however, benefited less from the war's economic fallout than had the country's well-established Chinese business community. But by January 1955, American funding flowed directly to Diem, rather than through the French, and he quickly moved to direct the economy in ways that would divert the entrepreneurial activities stimulated by this aid away from Chinese channels toward the ethnic Vietnamese, especially those whom he regarded as politically supportive.[39] There was sufficient American aid for the million Chinese who lived in the South—about half of them in Saigon's sister city of Cholon—still to prosper, but much of the cream was scooped off by favored Vietnamese.

Crucial to Diem's ability to develop this new base of support was the Commercial Import Program (CIP)*—the major component of the American economic aid package. The inception of this new CIP in January 1955 coincided with France's transfer of all residual elements of authority to the Diem–Bao Dai regime, with the exception of control over the Vietnamese auxiliaries of France's expeditionary forces, which began a month later. Eighty-seven percent of the initial U.S. grant to Diem of $322.4 million in 1955 was channeled through CIP, and thereafter, from 1955 through 1961, Washington provided Diem's government with a total of $1,447 million in economic grant aid, preponderantly through the CIP. Until the end of the American presence in 1975, this program remained the heart of the American economic assistance effort.[40]

The CIP provided the means for the United States to pay most of the cost of Diem's army, police, and civil government, while at the same time inhibiting the inflation that this huge injection of dollars might otherwise have precipitated. (In addition, from 1956 through 1961 the United States contributed a total of $508 million in military grants, largely for military equipment.) The flow of CIP funds was large enough to permit Diem to accumulate a substantial dollar reserve, which by 1960 had reached $216.4 million. Of greater political importance, it relieved him of any necessity for more than a token application of the income tax, thereby winning greater support from upper-income inhabitants, though further insulating him from economic realities.[41]

If one seeks to understand the burgeoning of the Vietnamese middle class under Diem and how his political backing, and that of his successors, became so well rooted in South Vietnam's urban society, it is essential to understand the scope and operation of this program. Diem himself perceived its importance to

---

*Sometimes referred to as the Commodity Import Program.

the development of a new middle class,[42] and the American appreciation of the program's political cutting edge is indicated by the fact that when, in October 1963, Washington sought to undercut the Vietnamese business community's support of Diem's regime, it recognized that the most effective means of doing so was to suspend the Commercial Import Program.

The essential mechanism of CIP was an import subsidization scheme whereby the United States supplied dollars to the Saigon government, which sold them to local importers for South Vietnamese piasters at about half the official exchange rate. In 1955 some twenty thousand importers were given these highly prized foreign-exchange licenses, but thereafter, in order to make the process more manageable, individuals were obliged to consolidate into larger components, which reduced the numbers. Within broad guidelines agreed to by U.S. and Vietnamese officials, these privileged local importers used their bargain-rate dollars to import commodities—largely consumer goods, including a good many luxury items, and a relatively small amount of capital goods. The piasters the Saigon government garnered from these grants of American dollars went into a counterpart fund that it used to pay most of the costs of maintaining its army, police, and other civil servants. Nearly all of the remaining costs for their support derived indirectly from the customs duties levied on the imports paid by these same U.S. dollars. As John Montgomery, one of the most knowledgeable observers, pointed out, "Each Commercial Import dollar did double duty for the government of Viet-Nam: as a direct contribution from the United States, it produced thirty-five counterpart piasters . . .; in addition, customs revenue averaging eighteen piasters per dollar accrued to the government." Thereby, he concluded, "the United States supported the major part of the Vietnamese budget directly by grant aid, and a large share of the rest came from customs revenue on dollar-financed imports. . . ."[43]

The indirect consequences of CIP spread beyond inhibiting inflation by sopping up purchasing power—the major public rationale for the program. Within the U.S. government it was correctly perceived as having political consequences of great importance to building support for Diem and his successors. In the words of the head of the U.S. Aid Mission to Vietnam when the program was launched, apart from its anti-inflationary function it "served the political value of supplying the Vietnamese middle-class with goods they wanted and could afford to buy," thereby providing "a source of loyalty to Diem from the army, the civil servants and small professional people, who were able to obtain better clothes, better household furnishings and equipment, than they had before." Another American official regarded the "extravagant standard of living" made possible by CIP as helping preserve "hard-won anti-communist political gains." And a 1959 U.S. government assessment concluded that through CIP it had been possible to support "a standard of living higher than the country could maintain on its own resources," and that "a significant cutback in the standard . . . would probably create serious political problems for the government." But the program nevertheless had consequences that some

Vietnamese recognized were not altogether salutary. In the words of Dr. Phan Quang Dan, one of the regime's most widely known noncommunist critics, who was incarcerated by Diem for several years because of his outspokenness, "The U.S. Commercial Import Program—which costs us nothing—brings in on a massive scale luxury goods of all kinds, which give us an artificial society—enhanced material conditions that don't amount to anything, and no sacrifice; it brings luxury to our ruling group and middle class, and luxury means corruption."[44]

But most important of all in winning Diem and his successors' support from the middle class and in expanding its ranks was the licensing feature of CIP. The select group of firms and individuals to which the government granted the highly prized import licenses were assured such immense profits that their gratitude and political loyalty was almost automatically assured. Indeed, it would probably be fair to say that, together with the resettled Catholic refugees, the beneficiaries of these import licenses and their numerous dependents were the staunchest supporters of the emerging South Vietnamese government. From the start of the program in 1955, the exchange rate at which licensees purchased dollars was usually set at about one-half of the open market rate, so they were assured a windfall profit whether or not they had entrepreneurial acumen. Those who did not simply sold their licenses to experienced Chinese and still gained a large profit immediately. But normally the demand for consumer goods was extensive enough so that even an untutored licensee could sell his imports himself readily, with a high return.

A declassified internal U.S. governmental analysis of the CIP's operation for a typical year (1966) makes clear how much it enriched this favorite clientele of the Saigon regime. Permitted to purchase U.S. dollars for imports at the artificially low rate of 60 piasters as against a free (black) market rate of 170 to the dollar, they could not fail to make enormous profits. The report found that "35.5 billion piasters a year of windfall profits" or "over half the value of these commercial imports financed by AID [the U.S. Agency for International Development] is not now flowing to the GVN but to those who obtain import licenses of great value *gratis* (excluding 'cumshaw' to officials)." Though this premium, if reckoned at the official exchange rate, amounted to some $600 million for the year, a more conservative and realistic calculation would probably be about $209 million, the value of the piaster windfall if converted back into U.S. currency via the going black-market rate for deposit in banks abroad, an option many from this group elected to follow. Thus, the report concluded, "So long as import profiteering is permitted to continue, it means that every $1 spent by AID on CIP can result in a 100% piaster domestic profit at least for some favored importer and about 50¢ 'banked' safely in the U.S. through the black market by such political friends of the present regime in Saigon."[45]

In fact, the CIP's much-touted anti-inflationary properties became decreasingly effective as the U.S. presence in Vietnam increased, for, as the report found, "The main cause of inflation is that the GVN mostly *creates* [emphasis in original] the 34.5 billion piasters a year it is currently selling to the USG and U.S. personnel for local purchases of goods and services." With respect to the artificial exchange rate the regime as a whole benefited further from the fact that, as against the actual value of the piaster (black-market rate of 170 piasters per dollar), U.S. government purchase of Vietnamese goods and services was at a rate of 73 piasters per dollar, and for local spending U.S. civilian and military personnel could exchange a dollar for no more than 118 piasters.

But whatever its effect on inflation, there is no doubt that during its two decades of operation the Commercial Import Program, together with other elements of U.S. economic support of the Saigon regime, substantially expanded South Vietnam's middle class and helped purchase its political loyalty to both the Saigon regime and its American sponsor. And in its various ramifications it provided the means for a way of life that was as artificial as the economy upon which it rested. Overall, the United States' aid program promoted increasing dependency rather than development of an economic base supportive of the separate polity it sought to erect. As an American tax expert serving in Vietnam concluded in 1961, "American aid has built a castle on sand."[46]

By the beginning of May 1955, there was no longer any qualification in Washington's commitment to Diem. The remaining obstacle to the consolidation of a separate anticommunist southern state was the Geneva Conference's clear-cut stipulation that national reunification elections be held in mid-1956 and that consultations to prepare for them be conducted in mid-1955. Certainly some American officials acknowledged that the elections constituted a "binding commitment," and they, along with the French and British, were fearful that repudiating them would destroy the most important positive feature of the Geneva Conference—the military armistice. As the NSC reported, the French believed that "failure to hold elections would provoke a resumption of hostilities by the Vietminh in which France would be directly and involuntarily involved due to the probable presence at least of large numbers of the French Expeditionary Corps through 1955 and the first half of 1956." And American officials feared that, if a refusal to hold elections led to an end of the armistice and a renewal of Vietminh military activity, Britain and France might not support forceful U.S. action to counter it. At the SEATO meeting in February 1955, both allies made clear that this would indeed be the case.[47]

A State Department intelligence report of September 15 expected that along with Canada and India of the International Control Commission, Britain and France would "continue to press for action in sufficient conformity with the agreements so that the Communists will have no excuse for breaking the cease-fire." It warned:

If Diem is emboldened to reject or continue postponement of the elections stipulated in the Geneva Agreements, the DRV can be expected to seek its goal of unification (and control) through other means. Subject to calculation of what is feasible without stimulating U.S. military involvement the DRV would probably be prepared to use any methods necessary and would use pressures as strong as permitted by prevailing conditions in overall bloc relations with the non-communist world. . . . Should the DRV conclude that elections are unlikely in fact, it is probable that the communists will greatly increase their subversive as well as political pressures against the South. The DRV, however, would probably seek to avoid direct U.S. military intervention and would probably, therefore, choose a maximum guerrilla and subversive effort rather than direct aggression to obtain its objective of control over a unified Vietnam.[48]

As late as the Kennedy administration it was acknowledged internally that, if Diem's government did not consider itself bound by the Geneva Agreements' provision for elections, then the legal basis of a demand for Vietminh compliance with features of the accords advantageous to the U.S. and Diem, "such as respect for [the] demarcation line and ceasefire," could be called into question.[49] In short, one party to an agreement could not ignore a central provision it found unpalatable and expect the other party to adhere to provisions it disliked.

It was understood, then, that there were serious risks in supporting Diem's opposition to national elections, but the potential risks if they were held were regarded as even greater, for American intelligence sources were unanimous that Diem would lose any national election. Extensive studies by American intelligence bodies subsequent to the Geneva Conference all reinforced the conclusion that national elections could only lead to the DRV's victory. A report prepared by the State Department's Division of Research on February 1, 1955, considered that "Almost any type of election that could conceivably be held in Vietnam in 1956 would, on the basis of present trends, give the Communists a very significant if not decisive advantage." It went on to point out that the establishment of "conditions of electoral freedom . . . might operate to favor the Communists more than their opponents." Even in the South, it judged, "maximum conditions of freedom and the maximum degree of international supervision might well operate to Communist advantage and allow considerable Communist strength in the South to manifest itself at the polls." This analysis concluded that "It would appear on balance, therefore, seriously questionable whether the South should make a major issue of free political conditions in the period preceding and during whatever type of elections might finally be decided for Vietnam."[50]

The Eisenhower administration could not afford to risk elections, and it encouraged Diem in his own, understandable disposition to avoid them. That the administration was aware of the implications of this decision is clear from a State Department assessment of September 1955: "Only if Diem were to feel sufficiently assured of direct U.S. support against Communist reprisals, and if the U.S. were prepared to accept the consequences of such a development including some degree of alienation of its Western allies and Asian neutrals, would Diem be likely to persist in a position directly opposed to eventual holding of elections."[51]

The administration was prepared to give him those assurances and accept these consequences. The NSC Planning Board had concluded shortly before that, if denial of victory to Hanoi through prevention of all-Vietnam elections resulted in a renewal of hostilities, the United States had to be prepared to oppose the Vietminh "with U.S. armed forces if necessary, and feasible—consulting Congress in advance if the emergency permits—preferably in concert with the Manila Pact allies of the U.S., but if necessary alone." The United States then developed contingency plans for the immediate deployment of air and naval power in Vietnam in the event of "overt aggression by Vietminh forces." This would be followed by the "early movement of mobile U.S. [ground] forces for the purpose of conducting joint operations for tasks beyond the capabilities of South Vietnamese forces."[52]

Sure of U.S. backing, Diem now assumed a bold and confident posture in opposition to the national elections that were so central to the Geneva Agreements (and indeed he now repudiated all of its political provisions that did not suit his interests). He and his American supporters insisted that, since the Bao Dai–Diem government had not itself agreed to the accords, it was not bound by them. Furthermore, they advanced the equally specious argument that the accords had stipulated "fundamental freedoms and democratic institutions" as prerequisites to any election (rather than as their anticipated consequences, as Article 14a actually posited) and that since these conditions did not yet exist it would be impossible for any meaningful voting to take place—even if by secret ballot under the aegis of the International Control Commission, as the agreements provided.[53]

Initially American officials thought that, while avoiding the elections scheduled for mid-1956, Diem should at least make the gesture of participating in the preliminary consultations with representatives of the DRV on the plans for the conduct and supervision of the elections, which had been scheduled for mid-1955. On the basis of such consultation, it was argued, Diem's position that conditions for free elections and international supervision could not be met would appear more plausible. An unwillingness even to discuss the conditions for voting put him on weak ground for alleging in advance that it would not be fair. Moreover, the National Security Council concluded, "The over-all United States position in the world would be harmed by U.S. identification with a policy which appeared to be directed towards avoidance of elections," and "world opinion, and for that matter domestic U.S. opinion, would have difficulty in understanding why the U.S. should oppose in Vietnam the democratic procedures which the U.S. had advocated for Korea, Austria and Germany."[54] Senior American officials, however, were not disposed to pressure Diem to participate even in such preliminary consultations, and by the time the meetings were scheduled, official U.S. policy had swung behind him in his refusal to do so.

The Hanoi government had clearly not anticipated Diem's ability to repudiate this key provision of the Geneva Agreements. Along with most of the Geneva participants, it had assumed that until mid-1956 France would still be exercising sufficient authority in the South to ensure holding both the consultations and the subsequent elections. By mid-1955, however, most French troops had been sent to North Africa and the French economic and political presence had become overshadowed by that of the United States; during the three-month period before the 1956 elections were to be held, the French High Command for Vietnam was dissolved and the last French combat units were withdrawn. As was later acknowledged by Secretary of Defense Robert McNamara in a memorandum to President Johnson, "Only the U.S. presence after 1954 held the south together . . . and enabled Diem to refuse to go through with the 1954 provision calling for nationwide free elections in 1956."[55]

During 1955 and 1956 Ho and Prime Minister Pham Van Dong sent repeated requests to Diem for consultations on holding elections. But these were ignored, as were Hanoi's numerous appeals to Britain and the Soviet Union, co-chairmen of the Geneva Conference, who, Hanoi understood, shared an ongoing responsibility for seeing that the agreements were implemented. Neither Britain nor the Soviet Union and China—both of which were bent upon pursuing policies of détente with the United States—showed much interest in seeing that the political provisions of Geneva were carried out. Moscow tried to pass the buck to Paris, saying France was primarily responsible for seeing them implemented. But with the withdrawal of her troops from Vietnam, France now had little political leverage there, and she was too dependent on American economic support and political backing of her interests elsewhere in the world, particularly North Africa, to challenge the repudiation of the elections.[56]

The Soviet Union's demeanor led the State Department to conclude that it was "disinclined to risk broad policy objectives elsewhere in the world for the sake of rigid support for DRV demands." The State Department believed that Hanoi's dependence upon China and the Soviet Union for military supplies and economic support was sufficient to ensure that without their backing it would be reluctant to attack South Vietnam militarily, since this would involve "a substantial risk of U.S. (or broader Western) counteraction." Now less than two years after Geneva, Washington saw little prospect that Moscow or Peking would be inclined to provide such support. Consequently, the department concluded that Hanoi recognized its "inability to achieve a military victory against Western arms through an 'adventurist' attack unsupported by the Bloc."[57]

Moscow's unwillingness to shoulder responsibility for implementing Geneva's political provisions was evident in talks held in April-May 1956 between representatives of Britain and the Soviet Union in their capacity as ongoing co-chairmen of the conference. Soviet Foreign Minister Andrei Gromyko "did not press for either the holding of elections or the reconvening of the Geneva Conference to discuss elections within a stated period" and agreed with his British counterpart on simply "maintaining the cease-fire, and essentially the [political] status-quo for the time being." The Soviet Union demonstrated the full extent of its disengagement in January 1957, when the Eisenhower administration was attempting to line up international support in its abortive effort to secure Saigon's representation in the United Nations. It was then that Khrushchev went so far as to propose that, along with North and South Korea, Diem's State of South Vietnam and the DRV be represented in the United Nations as "two separate states," a proposal with which the Peking government concurred, even though acknowledging that it was unacceptable to Hanoi. Since the date stipulated for the national reunification elections had by then passed, this proposition appears to have signaled implicit acceptance by Moscow and Peking of Vietnam's ongoing partition. Understandably, Ho Chi Minh, "in evident surprise, violently dissented."[58]

By the beginning of 1957, then, China and the Soviet Union, as well as France and Britain, appeared content to let Vietnam remain divided, thereby increasing the Eisenhower administration's confidence that it could build a viable separate state in the southern half of the country without its additional transgressions against the Geneva Agreements being seriously challenged.[59]

If the two communist powers, the world at large, or the American public harbored any doubts as to the Eisenhower administration's commitment to its mission of building a new Vietnamese state, these were undoubtedly dispelled in May 1957, when the administration invited the man it had chosen to head this state, Ngo Dinh Diem, on a two-week state visit to the United States. Not only was he accorded the signal honor of addressing a joint session of the American Congress, but Eisenhower had him flown in the presidential plane to Washington and personally met him at the airport—an honor bestowed on only one other foreign leader in the first four years of Eisenhower's presidency.[60]

The decisive change in American policy that unfolded during the years immediately following the Geneva Conference was by no means inevitable; certainly it was not something the Eisenhower administration unwittingly backed into. It was a positive, calculated step into a direct and much deeper involvement than the earlier attempts to work through France. Moreover, this step was taken at a time when the United States had a clear option to avoid any direct commitment. Indeed, the Geneva Agreements offered the United States a broad avenue leading away from even the limited and indirect intervention it had pursued during the previous decade. The capitulation recognized at Geneva was, after all, generally viewed as French, not American, entailing responsibilities that were basically French. Instead of seizing on this clear option, the administration had moved assertively into a much more fundamental phase of intervention, and in doing so staked American honor and prestige on a policy that, once undertaken, was difficult to reverse.

IV

Diem and the Rise
of the NLF

Eighteen months after Ngo Dinh Diem had been appointed prime minister, the
Eisenhower administration was congratulating itself on its success in consolidating his leadership of a separate anticommunist state. Its increased confidence in
this venture was nicely reflected in a National Security Council progress report
at the end of December 1955. "U.S. support," this stated, "made it possible for
Prime Minister Diem to continue in office, to consolidate his position, and to
stimulate international sympathy and support for Free Vietnam . . . induced
French and British acceptance of Diem . . . effectively disposed of pressures for
undesirable alternative governments." It had "assisted Diem in beginning to
consolidate his position internally, in guaranteeing his independence from the
French," and helped him "avoid international pressures for face-to-face consultations with the Viet Minh on all Vietnam elections." The report concluded that
"U.S. actions during the period were largely responsible for the survival of a
government in Free Vietnam with a will and capability to resist accommodation
to the Viet Minh." With all this achieved, the National Security Council looked
forward to the "implementation of reforms and some long-range planning in U.S.
programs."[1]

But the reforms that American officials hoped would broaden and strengthen
Diem's popular base went largely unimplemented. He was dogmatically attached
to an imperial tradition which required his subjects to give unquestioning obedience to his rule, sanctioned in his mind by right of the office he held. Never was
he able to accept the idea, which numerous U.S. officials tried to instill in him,
that he needed to consult and interact with his subjects in order to know what
was best for them. Despite occasional lip service to democratic ideas to placate
these anxious officials, he remained intent on building power in accordance with
his own autocratic disposition. In his unceasing effort to do so he self-righteously
followed a highly authoritarian route, marked by heavy and often indiscriminate
repression, thus narrowing the regime's popular base that American policy
sought to expand.

Having secured the backing of the army, civil service, Catholics, and most of the rapidly increasing bourgeoisie—and assured of the American funding necessary to permit the continued subsidies that were a fundamental condition for the backing of all these groups—Diem felt strong enough to manage the society of South Vietnam according to his and his brother's predilections. Sheltered behind the Franco-Vietminh armistice agreement, and confident of American support if Hanoi breached it, Diem moved rapidly and ruthlessly to consolidate his political authority.

Once Washington officials had accepted Diem over rival claimants and settled him in office, they found it difficult to oppose his wishes or to pressure him into following American prescriptions for good governance. The absolute dependence of Diem's state on the American treasury, together with his ongoing need for U.S. military backing, would appear to have given the American government enormous leverage in shaping the character and course of his regime. But the United States saw no prospect of finding a suitable replacement for him who would share its anticommunist goals, oppose national reunification elections, and could at the same time command even the modest indigenous support given to Diem.

Along with his astute brother, Ngo Dinh Nhu, with whom he increasingly shared power, Diem quickly sensed that U.S. officials saw him as indispensable to their objective of building and sustaining a separate anticommunist state. The two men assessed Washington's commitment to this goal as being strong enough to give them considerable leverage in dealing with it. Diem's period of residence in the United States had occurred during the height of McCarthyism, and he had developed some understanding of the importance of anticommunism in American domestic politics and the relevance of the "loss of China" issue to the Eisenhower administration's anticommunist stance in Vietnam;[2] some Americans who worked with him presumably tutored him further in these matters. In any case, his vital economic and military reliance on the United States tended to be offset significantly by the dependence of the administration in Washington on his survival, measured not only in its perceived global strategic requirements and ideological commitment, but also in terms of domestic American political calculations. From this dependency sprang the apt and much-quoted characterization by journalist Homer Bigart of American policy during most of Diem's governance: "Sink or Swim with Ngo Dinh Diem." The tacit conditionality of American assistance expressed in Eisenhower's October 1954 letter to Diem was soon forgotten, and American expectations that aid would be "met by performance on the part of the Government of Vietnam in undertaking needed reforms" became muted, and were largely disregarded by Diem.

American officials continued to hope that Diem would broaden his political base, but this did not occur despite their exhortation and the enormous public-relations effort made in his behalf in Vietnam by the United States Information Service. Though for most of his nine years in power Diem was favorably treated in much of the American press, particularly the Luce publications (*Time* and *Life*), and publicly praised by many officials, internal U.S. government memo-

randa soon took a more realistic view. As early as July 1956 the NSC's National
Coordinating Board referred to the autocratic nature of Diem's regime and saw
its "continued trend toward centralized authority" as resulting in the "alienation
of potential supporters."[3] Thanks to the weight of American backing, however,
it was another four years before the repressiveness of Diem's rule precipitated a
strong enough political reaction, running across most of the South Vietnamese
political spectrum, to challenge him seriously.

Diem's political style was manifest early on. Knowing that the United States
stood fully behind him, he defied Bao Dai's orders for changes in the army's top
leadership and soon took steps to remove the emperor from his position as chief
of state. While Bao Dai remained in France, Diem laid the groundwork for a
referendum, mounting a scurrilous campaign of abuse and vilification against him
in the government-controlled press and radio. During the voting on October 23,
1955, the police watched over the polling places and the ballots were counted by
Diem's officials, without supervision. The referendum offered the populace two
choices: "I support the deposition of Bao Dai and recognize Ngo Dinh Diem as
the Chief of State of Vietnam with the mission of installing a democratic regime,"
or "I do not support the deposition of Bao Dai and do not recognize Ngo Dinh
Diem as Chief of State with the mission of installing a democratic regime."
Moreover, the ballot paper pictured Diem "among a group of modern young
people against a propitious red background," while Bao Dai "was portrayed in
old-fashioned robes against an unlucky green background," gimmicks for which
Lansdale took credit. Since he was almost assured a majority, Diem was urged
by his U.S. advisers to be content with a creditable 60 percent of the vote. He
insisted, however, that a much higher figure would look better. Through extensive
fraud, whereby many of the electoral districts reported thousands more pro-Diem
votes than there were voters (with some 450,000 registered voters in the Saigon-
Cholon area casting 605,025 votes), Diem announced that he had won 98.2
percent of the total.[4]

In order to placate American officials, Diem was willing to permit some of
the trappings of democratic government, but he had no interest in its substance.
Thus, in 1956 he countenanced the "election" of a powerless National Assembly
that was publicly referred to as the "legislative arm" of his government. But, as
Robert Scigliano pointed out, it never dared oppose Diem on important legislation, and its deputies' area of initiative was confined to "minor subjects" such as
"the regulation of pharmacists, rules governing the bar, and their own internal
rules."[5]

Real power, indeed "total and complete authority," remained lodged with
Diem and his immediate family—his brothers Ngo Dinh Thuc, the Catholic
archbishop of Hué and primate of Vietnam; Ngo Dinh Can, based in Hué and
in effect "political and governmental plenipotentiary in Central Vietnam"; and
Ngo Dinh Nhu, who along with his wife became increasingly influential with
Diem. Several other family members held lesser but still important positions. The
family's principal instrument of rule was its own tightly held covert political

apparatus, the Can Lao party. This and another public adjunct of the brothers' rule, the National Revolutionary Movement, were both formed, as a 1956 State Department intelligence report observed, "to support Diem and [are] dominated by members of his family." These organs, the report perceived, controlled the National Assembly and were "likely to dominate Vietnamese political life during the coming year." And certainly the Can Lao, with its tentacles reaching deep into the officer corps and police as well as into every important corner of the central bureaucracy and local administrations, did dominate the political life of the country until Diem's death seven years later. Whether or not, as Lansdale later reported, the Can Lao was "largely the brain child of a highly-respected senior American Foreign Service professional" and "promoted by the U.S. State Department," he was not far wrong in charging that it helped "promote a fascist state." Though providing the sinews of what was indeed a ruthlessly authoritarian political order, it appears to have escaped public criticism by American officials.[6]

The Diem regime moved, publicly as well as covertly, to eliminate or stifle all opposition. Despite the Geneva Agreements' prohibition against political reprisal, it quickly targeted the most visible of large numbers of Vietminh sympathizers in the South. The magnitude of this operation can be sensed when it is noted that French sources estimated that at the time of the Geneva armistice, 60 to 90 percent of the villages there, apart from those in Cao Dai and Hoa Hao areas, were controlled by the Vietminh.[7]

In mid-1955, soon after the last Vietminh army units had been regrouped to the North, Diem launched an anticommunist denunciation campaign in which his administration dragooned the population into mass meetings to inform against Vietminh members and sympathizers. One object was to classify the peasants into categories according to the extent of their connection with the Vietminh. This "thoroughly terrified the Vietnamese peasants and detracted significantly from the regime's popularity." In May 1956, after only ten months of the campaign, its head announced that more than 94,000 former Vietminh cadres had "rallied to the government," with an additional 5,613 having surrendered. Full figures were never released on the considerable number who were executed, jailed, or sent to concentration camps, euphemistically called "re-education camps." But in the spring of 1956, Diem's secretary of state for information acknowledged that 15,000 to 20,000 had been detained in these camps. And the Ministry of Information itself admitted that a total of 48,250 were jailed between 1954 and 1960. More indicative of the actual scale of the problem and its exploitation was the February 1959 report that, in the single province of An Xuyen, a five-week campaign had resulted in the surrender of 8,125 communist agents and the denunciation of 9,806 other agents, and 29,978 sympathizers; or the subsequent report of a new governor in another province who on taking office found 1,200 political prisoners "held in the local jail without evidence by the head of security, who used this method to extort money from the local peasantry." The International Control Commission found itself powerless to halt these actions.[8]

In January 1956, Diem introduced his Ordinance No. 6, under which his officials were given virtually a free hand to eliminate opposition. Until that indefinite time when "order and security" were fully restored, anyone considered a danger "to the defense of the state and public order" was to be imprisoned or put under house arrest. The consequences of this escalation in repression were described a little over a year later in *Life,* which was generally supportive of Diem:

> Behind a façade of photographs, flags and slogans there is a grim structure of decrees, political prisons, concentration camps, milder "re-education centers," secret police. Presidential "Ordinance No. 6" signed and issued by Diem in January, 1956, provides that "individuals considered dangerous to national defense and common security" may be confined by executive order in "a concentration camp." . . . Only known or suspected Communists who have threatened or violated public security since July, 1954, are supposed to be arrested and "re-educated" under these decrees. But many non-Communists have also been detained. The whole machinery of security has been used to discourage active opposition of any kind from any source.[9]

Although Diem's repression fell most heavily on the peasantry, some of the urban population also suffered. Indeed, he used his continuing purge as a pretext to strike all across the political spectrum at those he regarded as politically unreliable. In the words of Philippe Devillers, "This repression was in theory aimed at the Communists. In fact it affected all those, and they were many—democrats, socialists, liberals, adherents of the sects—who were bold enough to express their disagreement with the line of policy adopted by the ruling oligarchy." William Henderson, writing for *Foreign Affairs* in January 1957, effectively characterized a pattern that was to last until the end of Diem's governance:

> South Vietnam is today a quasi-police state characterized by arbitrary arrests and imprisonment, strict censorship of the press and the absence of an effective political opposition. . . . All the techniques of political and psychological warfare, as well as pacification campaigns involving extensive military operations, have been brought to bear against the underground.

It is pertinent to note, as has Joseph Buttinger, initially one of Diem's closest American confidants, with respect to this early period in which "thousands of Communists as well as non-Communist sympathizers of the Vietminh were killed and many more thrown into prisons and concentration camps," that "all of this happened more than two years before the Communists began to commit acts of terror against local government officials."[10]

The high tide in the campaign of repression began with Diem's promulgation of Law 10/59 on May 6, 1959. This went well beyond that of January 1956 and legalized many measures that had been operative since then. Under the new law, within three days of a charge special military courts were to sentence to death —usually through guillotining—with no right of appeal, "whoever commits or attempts to commit . . . crimes with the aim of sabotage, or of infringing upon the security of the State" as well as "whoever belongs to an organization designed to help or to perpetrate [these] crimes." The scope for retribution was every bit as broad in the economic field. Here the death sentence was to be meted out to anyone "who intentionally proclaims or spreads by any means unauthorized news about prices, or rumors contrary to truth, or distorts the truth concerning the present or future situation of markets in the country or abroad, susceptible of provoking economic or financial perturbations in the country." This license was broad enough to be used against anyone who annoyed the regime or whom it suspected of disloyalty, and just the threat of its application was sufficient to terrorize most critics into silence.[11]

Other measures also helped alienate peasants from Diem's regime. By degrees in mid-1956 he abolished elections for village councils, apparently because he feared the Vietminh would win, and replaced them, as well as municipal councils, with officials appointed by his provincial governors upon approval by the minister of the interior. With this, the partial autonomy that the villages had retained even under French rule was eliminated in favor of a centralized administration that was usually out of touch with their problems.[12]

This impingement of central authority was the more oppressive because so many of the newly appointed local officials were outsiders, a high proportion being recently arrived Catholics from the North. "Having no roots in the South, these men were sufficiently dependent upon Diem for him to be reasonably assured of their personal loyalty to him as well as of their anticommunism." But their lack of experience in this largely non-Catholic region left them with little understanding of its particular social and economic problems. Most of the government's information and civic-action agents were also northern Catholics, "strangers who spoke a different dialect and practiced a different religion." As Robert Scigliano concluded, throughout much of the South the Diem regime "assumed the aspect of a carpetbag government in its disproportion of Northerners and Centralists, in the ease of access to high positions granted officials from the Hué area, and in its Catholicism."[13] (Hué was the former imperial city in the center —Annam—where both Diem and his father had served.) And not only did these outsiders lack legitimacy in terms of customary local criteria, but many were oppressive and corrupt as well.

Another widespread cause of peasant alienation was Diem's approach to land tenure and rent. Landlords, who had sat out the colonial war under French protection in Saigon and other cities, were supported in repossessing lands that the Vietminh had turned over to their peasant cultivators. The 25-percent maximum rent that Diem now prescribed could hardly be expected to find favor with these peasants. Courts established to settle landlord-tenant disputes were dominated by landlords and officials friendly to them, and the minister of agrarian affairs was one of the biggest landlords in the country, so the tenant could expect little help when, as usually happened, a higher rent was in fact charged.[14]

When, after continued prodding by U.S. officials, Diem finally introduced a program of land distribution, it was far less in scope and actual practice than they had proposed. In implementation it was so emasculated and rigged in favor of landlords that it usually inflamed rather than assuaged peasant hostility. When this "agrarian reform" program finally got under way in 1958, it was restricted to rice-growing lands, but even here landlords—including absentee owners—were permitted to retain up to 284 acres—an enormous amount in regions where land was so fertile and rewarding. Through relatives, many held on to much more. Moreover, in cases where properties in excess of this figure were actually relinquished, the peasant had to pay in full. By the end of 1962, only about 10 percent of the more than one million tenant households had obtained title to land; of the lands that were redistributed more than 60 percent of the acreage came from French estates, for whose purchase France provided Diem the funds.[15]

Diem also managed to antagonize many of the ethnically non-Vietnamese tribal groups that occupied over half of South Vietnam, largely the interior upland areas to the north of Saigon. Under French rule these Montagnards had been permitted to retain their cultural identities, and been given considerable administrative autonomy. And though French estates had occupied some of their lands, the area as a whole had been denied to settlement by ethnic Vietnamese. Beginning in 1955, however, Diem undertook to impose Vietnamese culture on these groups and to integrate them directly into his administration. He followed this with a program of population transfer that was initiated in 1957, whereby some 210,000 ethnic Vietnamese from the coast and Catholic peasants from the North were resettled in fortified villages on lands regarded by the Montagnards as their own and as vital to their slash-and-burn pattern of agriculture. Two years later, the forcible regrouping of many Montagnard communities began. The traumatic impact of these policies can be better appreciated when it is understood that collectively the inland tribal groups had a population only a little more than three times that of these intruders. They were further alienated from the Saigon government by the fact that, in contrast to Diem's policy of annexing tribal lands, the Vietminh had previously turned back the areas occupied by French-owned estates to the Montagnards. Furthermore, the Vietminh had usually tried to win the support of these upland peoples, whereas Diem's officials adopted the traditional Vietnamese air of superiority toward them, referring to them as "savages" and seeing Saigon's mission as one of assimilating these "inferior" peoples into Vietnamese culture. All of this generated an antagonism against the regime that ultimately erupted in many localized armed rebellions, the first major one occurring in early 1958. As a Pentagon chronicler concluded, the Saigon government "provided the tribes with a cause and focused discontent against Diem," and "thus facilitated rather than hindered the subsequent subversion of the tribes by the Viet Cong."[16]

Forced resettlement of the rural population was not confined to the Montagnards. Beginning in February 1959, Diem took the first of a series of steps to relocate lowland-dwelling ethnic Vietnamese peasants in fortified concentrations where they could be both more easily controlled and better insulated from contact with ex-Vietminh and others who resisted Saigon's authority. In July, he commenced what was to become a long-term program of rural population concentration into what were called "agrovilles." Theoretically designed to provide a range of new social services and other amenities to the two to three thousand peasants who were required to live in them, these fortified concentrations became ongoing symbols of peasant hatred for Diem's government. Rarely did the promised amenities materialize, and the peasant who participated had usually been "compelled to abandon his old homestead with its ancestral tomb, small garden, and fruit and shade trees, for a desolate plot of ground in a strange place, which was usually a long walk from the agroville." He had to build his new house out of materials from the one he had been obliged to abandon, and, except for the offer of a loan, the only help he received from the government was a grant equal to about $5.50.[17] Although nowhere near the five hundred thousand peasants originally targeted for this program actually participated, most of those who did were mortally alienated from the regime. Not until late 1961 did the government realize how counterproductive the effort was, and halt it in favor of a strategic hamlet program. Under the new program, populations were usually not obliged to relocate far from their existing fields and homes, though they were often forced to move and rebuild their dwellings inside a fortified enclosure. This naturally antagonized many. Ironically, a considerable number of the peasants packed inside the barbed wire encircling these hamlets were not uncommitted fence-sitters but already strongly sympathetic toward the gathering anti-Diem insurgency, so that the barbed wire did not insulate the two elements from each other.

The central part played by Diem's newly appointed village chiefs in his programs, combined with their fearsome role in his communist denunciation campaign, ensured that many became the focal point for peasant resentment. Consequently, well before the southern Vietminh turned to militant tactics against Diem's government, angry peasants in several areas had killed some of the most hated of these village heads. Later, Vietminh leaders recognized that selective assassination of the most brutal and corrupt village officials could win peasant support[18]—though in some cases they appreciated the value of leaving the most despised officials in place, since this guaranteed recruits.

In the urban areas of the South, Diem's governance rested less heavily on the population than in the countryside. Although in Saigon and other cities there were 20-to-25-percent unemployment rates and extensive slum areas, the expanding middle class for the most part enjoyed a continuing prosperity, thanks to the sustained flow of American aid. The marked improvement in their economic position helped mute their discontent with political repression. But even among those so economically advantaged, the constant spying by Can Lao agents and the arbitrary and sometimes capricious nature of many arrests created considerable malaise. With regard to both civil and military appointments as well as economic opportunities, Diem's blatant discrimination in favor of Catholics—especially those from the central and the northern areas—became a source of increasingly widespread grievance. The Can Lao and its security apparatus were controlled by Catholics. Diem's school for senior civil servants was run by the Catholic Church and was presided over by his brother, Archbishop Thuc. The school indoctrinated its pupils into his family's official creed of Personalism, an eclectic compound of largely Catholic doctrine elaborated by Ngo Dinh Nhu. If civil servants and army officers were not already convinced that "at least nominal conversion to Catholicism" helped ensure advancement, they presumably were when, in 1959, Diem formally dedicated South Vietnam—with a population over 90 percent non-Catholic—to the Virgin Mary.[19]

With the infusion of U.S. economic aid largely absorbed in the cities and towns, and rarely penetrating in any significant measure beyond them, the growing antagonism to Diem in the rural areas was not buffered by the enhanced prosperity enjoyed by many town dwellers. Diem's dependence on American power was so evident that the animus against his government soon extended to the United States. In the words of one of the Pentagon chroniclers, "For many Vietnamese peasants, the war of Resistance against French–Bao Dai rule never ended; France was merely replaced by the U.S., and Bao Dai's mantle was transferred to Ngo Dinh Diem." Consequently, when Vietminh resistance in the South was rekindled in 1958–59 its "opprobrium catchword 'My-Diem' (American-Diem) thus recaptured the nationalist mystique of the First Indochina War, and combined the natural xenophobia of the rural Vietnamese with their mounting dislike of Diem." By 1961, Robert Scigliano could write, "So deeply has the My-Diem (American-Diem) relationship been established in the minds of the peasants that Vietnamese government officials have been addressed, with all respect, as 'My-Diem' by peasants doing business with them."[20]

In the face of the widespread peasant discontent ignited by Diem's policies, it is remarkable that it took so long for a full-blown insurgency to develop in the South. For more than four years after the Geneva Conference, nearly all southern Communist Party (Lao Dong*) leaders and most ex-Vietminh cadres in the South hung back from providing the peasantry with leadership or an organizational channel, and it took another two years before Hanoi agreed to support the level of all-out insurgency that it had sanctioned against the French. This gave Diem a substantial period of reprieve from rural Vietnam's reaction to his governance. It is evident, as we shall see, that this insulation from peasant-based insurrection would have lasted even longer if the initial balance of opinion within Hanoi's

*The Vietnam Lao Dong, or "Worker's" Party, was the name given in March 1951 to the reconstituted Vietnamese Communist Party that had been officially dissolved on November 11, 1945, but which had nevertheless remained functionally very much alive and expanded its membership.

leadership had held sway. The tide of discontent among the Vietminh's many former peasant adherents, however, ultimately became too strong to contain. If they were to maintain their local authority, the residual southern cadre of the Vietminh were obliged to accommodate to local demands for a more militant stand against Diem. The pressure in turn of these cadres on Hanoi, together with the lobby of impatient southerners who had regrouped in the North after Geneva (who did not begin to trickle south before late 1959), ultimately helped shift the weight of opinion within the party leadership to reflect more fully the local and national needs as perceived by these southerners. If Hanoi were not to lose its authority over many of these cadres, and its influence among former adherents of the Vietminh generally, it had to bring its priorities more into line with the demands of its beleaguered adherents in the South for a more militant policy there. This is not to say that the top party leadership would not on its own ultimately have shifted to such a stance, but there is little doubt that such pressure considerably accelerated that shift.

During the first post-Geneva years, armed opposition to Diem came primarily from remaining elements of the Hoa Hao, Cao Dai, and Binh Xuyen, along with the recently formed, but generally smaller, forces from the Dai Viet and VNQDD parties that Diem had outlawed. The most numerous and tenacious were the Hoa Hao, who maintained as many as eight battalions in the field against Diem until mid-1958, and two until 1962.[21] Although some ex-Vietminh in the South occasionally encouraged and provided limited logistical assistance to some of these dissident groups, the large majority eschewed military activities, at least until the escalation of Diem's repression in early 1959.

From mid-1954 through mid-1956, the ex-Vietminh who remained in the South limited their activities to nonviolent political action, because of the same expectations as their compatriots in the North—that the elections promised by Geneva would indeed be held. Consequently, their major focus was on preparing for the elections, despite the mounting harassment and hounding by Diem's officials. Their shock and bitterness were great when this central *quid pro quo* of the armistice did not materialize. Some turned away from a Hanoi that felt obliged, by the unexpectedly early withdrawal of France and lack of backing from Moscow and Peking, to acquiesce at least temporarily in this denial of national elections. Of those who turned away, a few joined in with the Hoa Hao or Cao Dai insurgents, others tried to disengage from any political activity, and a few took the risk of trying to work out an accommodation with the Diem regime. What appears to have been the large majority, however, for another two years at least, remained aligned with the position of their compatriots in Hanoi, whose leadership had successfully brought them through the long ordeal with France. A great many of those who had fought the French under the banner of the Vietminh in the South had relatives or friends in the North,[22]* and for them that

---

*The preponderant majority of the southern Vietminh who went north after Geneva left their families behind.

struggle had served to reinforce an already strong sense of national unity. They were no more disposed than their counterparts in the North to be cut off from those on the other side of the seventeenth parallel with whom they had close personal ties. Men and women who had been through a long and arduous struggle for independence could not be expected to adjust to Washington's design of continuing division.

Nor, of course, was this concept of a single all-embracing nation limited to southerners who were ex-Vietminh. It was shared by most of the Vietnamese who were obliged to live under the authority of Diem's administration. But this pervasive sentiment was something that American policymakers were usually unwilling to look squarely in the face. And even less were they disposed to acknowledge it publicly and testify that Vietnam was a country that had known at least ten centuries of strong national identity and had last been unified more than half a century before Italy or Germany had first known nationhood. Instead, the Eisenhower administration and its successors sought to rationalize their policies at home by advancing for an American audience the myth that those Vietnamese who happened to dwell below the seventeenth parallel had their own sense of nationhood and patriotism, distinct from whatever sentiments were possessed by those living under the communist regime in the North. In fact, however, even for Diem and his coterie, as for southerners in general, the idea that Vietnam should remain divided was quite incompatible with their own nationalist feelings. Adherence to the principle of a unified Vietnam was common to almost all Vietnamese; where they differed was under what authority it should be reunited.

This deep substratum of an all-embracing Vietnamese nationalism must be kept in mind in any assessments of the political phenomena that rested on and were conditioned by it. Those who had been the Vietminh's adherents in the South continued to see Ho Chi Minh as the legitimate standard-bearer of an all-Vietnam nationalism. They were certainly not, however, all blind to the fact that the DRV and the Lao Dong that led it were fallible—both the party headquarters in Hanoi and its local organization and leadership in the South—especially with respect to the needs of those who were obliged to cope directly with the power of Ngo Dinh Diem and his American backers. Living in the South and usually having their most immediate dependents there as well, some southern ex-Vietminh felt better qualified than their compatriots in the North to appraise and design the appropriate response to the local pressures that impinged on them. Appreciation of this makes more understandable the differences and tensions that sometimes developed between the southern Lao Dong together with a broad spectrum of former Vietminh adherents in the South on the one hand, and party leaders in the North on the other.[23] These tensions, and the views and circumstances that produced them, need to be appreciated if one is to understand the establishment and policies of the National Liberation Front of South Vietnam.

An early and fundamental cause of tension was the sometimes differing assessments of political factors operative in the South, particularly of the endurance and resilience of beleaguered ex-Vietminh elements in the face of Diem's mounting repression, and the point at which and extent to which they would have to abandon a primarily political effort and take up arms if they were not to be crushed. The other side of that equation was how long the strategy of rebuilding, and then expanding, the war-shattered economy of the North should receive priority over reunification of the country. At first it had been widely believed that, even though the reunification election had been denied, Diem's government would soon collapse because of a lack of legitimacy and its own ineptitude and alienation of the population. But neither Hanoi nor the southern ex-Vietminh had reckoned on the vast scale of the American support that compensated for these deficiencies. It became increasingly clear that Diem could not be dislodged through efforts at the political level alone and that the eroding membership of the ex-Vietminh would sooner or later have to resort to military measures if they were to survive. It was, however, also appreciated that this might well precipitate a greater American intervention, one that might easily engulf both North and South. That was hardly a welcome prospect for the war-weary Vietnamese population, which had just been so badly bled and battered by eight years of war with France. It was, moreover, clear that the global priorities of neither Moscow nor Peking were compatible with any such resumption of the war in Vietnam. They could not be counted upon to sustain their substantial contributions to the rebuilding and then the expanding of the North's economic base if the DRV countenanced precipitating a conflict that risked a direct American military involvement—for that might easily destroy much of the economy, while also jeopardizing efforts of these two powers to achieve détente with the United States.[24]

It must be remembered that the area above the seventeenth parallel was the part of the country that had been most heavily fought over during the war with France, and the destruction of its transportation infrastructure, as well as of canals, dikes, granaries, and other essential adjuncts of its agricultural base, had left much of its population on the verge of starvation. Agrarian recovery in the North was further set back during 1955–56 by the temporary chaos in some districts caused by clumsy, heavy-handed, and often very harsh efforts at agrarian reform. In numerous cases, implementation of the program was much too reliant on doctrinaire cadres from outside the villages, who were untutored in local political and socioeconomic realities and often gave too much scope to committees dominated by very poor peasants—many with long-festering grievances against rich peasants and landlords, whether or not they had supported the struggle against the French. As a consequence, a considerable number of these wealthier peasants were dispossessed of their lands and executed or jailed. Estimates of those who suffered these fates vary widely; but whatever the number, the impact was very serious, and was economically as well as politically damaging to the DRV.[25] The extent of this damage can be gathered from the government's public acknowledgment of major errors in General Vo Nguyen Giap's speech of October 19, 1956, and from the fact that Truong Chinh, the party secretary general, who was regarded as bearing major responsibility for the program, was obliged to resign along with the ministers of agriculture and interior. (As part of the effort to rectify these mistakes and repair the damage, Ho Chi Minh assumed Truong Chinh's position as secretary general.) The disruptive economic consequences must have reinforced the party leaders' belief that they needed more time to strengthen the economy of the North before it would be ready to serve as an effective base for liberating the South from Diem's rule.

The necessity for strengthening the country north of the seventeenth parallel in order to challenge successfully an American-backed regime in the South was not lost on party leaders and cadres. And the force of this proposition was enhanced as the United States increased material support of Diem's regime. It was not simply that the massive amount of war materiel previously given the French by the United States provided a precedent for what it might be expected to do for Diem. Beyond that, the Lao Dong leadership was acutely concerned that any widespread armed resistance to Diem might precipitate direct U.S. military intervention in his behalf. And in weighing this possibility, older party leaders—whether active in the North or South now—could not easily forget the abortive uprising of November 1940, when poor preparation and a grossly adverse balance of fire power had resulted in the destruction of most of the communist organization in the South.

But the logic of this cautionary approach soon began to erode, particularly after the deadline for reunification elections had passed. Patience was increasingly difficult to maintain for those who saw Diem's mounting repression directly threatening their families and friends. Moreover, there was a whole new generation, whose restiveness in the face of Diem's policies was relatively unaffected by memories of the 1940 fiasco.

In the fall of 1956, in the face of the escalating restlessness, there was, in the words of Jeffrey Race, "an urgent need for a clear policy to restore faith among those members who saw the [Lao Dong] Party as drifting, on the defensive, with no plan and no hope for the future." To meet this need, Le Duan, a member of the party's Central Committee and, as head of its Nam Bo (Cochin China) Regional Committee, its senior representative in the South, prepared a lengthy document entitled "The Path of the Revolution in the South." This major policy review, notes Carlyle Thayer, "settled for a time the arguments over North-South priorities and whether or not revolutionary violence and/or armed force should be employed. . . ." Widely circulated among party members in the South in December, this directive described "a new long-range strategy to achieve national reunification to replace the 'two-year' strategy" that had rested on the expectation that reunification would come through either elections or the collapse of Diem's government. It was to stand as Hanoi's policy for approximately two years, until pressure from, and deviant actions by, southern non-party adherents and also some southern party leaders finally left it both outmoded and irrelevant.[26]

In the context of the changed circumstances, this new prescription attempted to provide the party's supporters with scope to play a meaningful role. It began by ascribing the failure to reunify the country under the Geneva Agreements to "the American imperialist invaders and the feudalist dictator Ngo Dinh Diem." It proceeded, as Race observes, to "forthrightly acknowledge the war weariness of the southerners (which it called their desire for peace) as well as the severe weakening of the Party's forces in the South, owing to the regroupment to the North under the Geneva Accords, defections, and suppression activities by the Diem authorities." But it provided no option for armed action, and "directed that the conflict was to be carried on by means of political activity. . . ." Stating that the Vietnamese people were determined not to permit the "imperialists and feudalists" to prolong the division of the country, it affirmed that they were also determined not to permit them "to provoke war."[27]

There was not even a hint that southerners could expect support from Hanoi's armed forces, and the party and its adherents in the South were considered too weak to act militarily by themselves; to attempt that route would be a serious strategic error and court total destruction. "In order to cope with the situation created by the U.S. and Diem" and "to liberate the Southern people from the imperialist-feudalist yoke," the Lao Dong Central Committee prescribed "three main tasks." It is notable that the first listed was "Firmly consolidate the North," and that this was followed by "Strongly push the Southern revolutionary movement." Winning "the sympathy and support" of other peoples stood third. The document went on to explain, "The North at present must be the firm and strong base to serve as rear area for the revolutionary movement to liberate the South. That is why we must firmly consolidate the North." Implicit in this position, and undoubtedly the intent of the top party leadership, was the idea that, once the North had been sufficiently strengthened and international factors were sufficiently propitious, it could move to support a more militant policy in the South.[28]

The central question for the beleaguered southern party cadres was how soon the struggle against Diem's regime could be moved from a primarily political to a primarily military level. But certainly the party's December 1956 directive was no call to arms. In its essentials, the guidance it provided was little different from the call for peaceful political struggle that the party had given for the two post-Geneva years, which it had expected would lead to a national reunification election. Assurances in "The Path of the Revolution in the South" that, because of lack of popular support, the Diem regime could not survive for long and that as a consequence of its "cruel repression and exploitation . . . the people's revolutionary movement definitely will rise up" were not likely to engender much hope among southerners who themselves were in the process of being hounded by Diem's agents. And ex-Vietminh supporters, already badly frightened by Diem's escalating repression, could not be expected to take much comfort from such pontifications as "A revolutionary movement struggling according to a peaceful line means that it takes the political forces of the people as the base rather than using people's armed forces to struggle with the existing government to achieve their revolutionary objective." Nor could being told that the Twentieth Congress of the Communist Party of the Soviet Union had determined that "The revolutionary movement in many countries at present can develop peacefully" have provided much solace for those in the South whose friends and family members had already been executed or jailed while trying to prepare for elections. This December document admonished that "a large number of cadres" who had "responsibility for guiding the revolutionary movement" had "not yet firmly grasped the political line of the party" or "the method of political struggle"; but, apart from urging them to get closer to and work along with the people to develop as broad a backing as possible, it did not tell them how to proceed. For those who sought to extract from the directive specific suggestions as to how to implement a policy of "peaceful struggle," there was no real guidance. Many ex-Vietminh must have heard a rather hollow ring in the directive's peroration: "Only the peaceful struggle line can create the strong political forces in order to defeat the scheme of war provocation and the cruel policy of U.S.-Diem."[29]

Despite Diem's mounting repression during 1957–58, the only departure from the line of peaceful political struggle, which the party encouraged in order to ensure survival of the residual Vietminh organization, was the arming of propaganda teams for self-protection and the assassination of particular local officials. These killings were already under way, a consequence of spontaneous local reaction to particularly brutal and corrupt officials, and the party's willingness to support the activity presumably helped maintain sagging morale among its adherents. By about mid-1957 the actions had developed into what was known as the "extermination of traitors" program, involving the selective kidnapping or execution of such local officials and Can Lao cadres of the Saigon government by special armed groups of Lao Dong cadres. As Carlyle Thayer points out, estimates of the numbers involved vary widely, and apparently the only available breakdown of Saigon's reports on this to the International Control Commission covered the period from 1957 to July 1959, during which Saigon claimed there had been a total of 174 such executions, including 10 soldiers, 28 civil guards, 65 village officials, and 59 civilians. Though these assassinations presumably deterred some of Diem's local officials from arresting or executing party cadres, the scale was too limited to halt anti-Vietminh reprisals by the Saigon regime.[30]

Many ex-Vietminh felt the party's actions to protect them were entirely inadequate, and between 1957 and 1959 they began to exert increasing pressure on it to go beyond the "extermination of traitors" program. Progressively, sometimes with the help of local party cadres, they began to take their own initiatives against the Diem regime. Even before the party called for an extension of its peaceful-struggle line in the December 1956 directive, some former Vietminh had clearly already embarked upon local initiatives. Subsequently, during 1957–58, "many voices among the masses appealed to the Party to establish a program of armed resistance against the enemy." The leadership of the Nam Bo Regional Committee of the party still hesitated to authorize this, primarily because of a "fear of violating the Party line." However, "in several areas the Party members on their own initiative organized armed struggle against the enemy."[31]

A retrospective Hanoi account by Ta Xuan Linh acknowledged that in a number of areas, in the face of Diem's repression, "patriots and former resistance cadre" had found it impossible "to limit themselves to peaceful methods of struggle expressed in purely political forms," and that, in order to avoid being wiped out, they were obliged, especially in the Mekong Delta, to form "self-defense teams." Subsequently, from "the end of 1955 to 1956, as Diem stepped up his 'denounce the Communists campaign,' " these elements were forced to flee "to former resistance bases such as the Plain of Reeds [southwest of Saigon], the U Minh jungle," and old bases (Resistance Zones D and C) that had been used against the French to the northeast of Saigon. There, cornered by Diem's troops, "they had to organize self-defense together with the local population," and "in their fight for survival the first units of the Liberation Army took shape. . . ." This account goes on to state that when, at the end of 1956, some armed elements of the Cao Dai and Hoa Hao joined with residual Binh Xuyen and some dissident Catholics to form a joint anti-Diem command, a number of former Vietminh cadres helped them reorganize and train. At the end of 1958, with the strength of the dissident religious sects eroded to about two battalions, a coordinating command was established in western Cochin China between their general staff and local "armed forces of the people"—presumably ex-Vietminh. Later, according to Ta Xuan Linh, "many officers and troops of the religious sects became cadres of the Liberation Army."[32]

During 1957–58, small insurgent groups contested some of the thrusts of Saigon's military sweeps and occasionally attacked outposts.[33] It is difficult to distinguish which of these actions were undertaken on the initiative of ex-Vietminh independent of any consultation with party leaders, which with the encouragement of local party cadres, and which with the sanction of party leaders at the provincial or regional level. Whatever the case, the central party leadership's admonition against armed struggle notwithstanding, numerous local party cadres and some southern party leaders—provincial and regional—increasingly concluded that organized armed efforts were a necessary adjunct of the political struggle against Diem and essential for their own sheer survival. Disagreement with the Central Committee in Hanoi on this issue—which presumably was itself sometimes divided—was not confined to the district or provincial levels, but sometimes reached up to the regional leadership.

One of the major breaches in the dike erected by the party's directive to contain the level of struggle against Diem was made by some of the old Montagnard allies of the Vietminh, whose antagonism toward Saigon had increased because of its repression and discriminatory policies. Carlyle Thayer observes that "the sporadic and ever-increasing independent attacks by tribal minorities" against Diem's government during 1957–58 "preceded the Party's ability to control, let alone direct" them. This put heavy pressure on the local party leadership to depart from Hanoi's directive and shape policy in accordance with the reality of these local initiatives. If local leaders had not done so, it is clear that the party would have lost any prospect of maintaining, much less increasing, its influence with some of the major tribal groups. In the face of this pressure, the party's regional leadership for the northern half of South Vietnam (the area referred to as Trung Bo), "took the initiative of gradually changing the local movement into a combined political and military struggle." It decided to test this new strategy in certain parts of Quang Ngai and Ninh Thuan provinces, and "accordingly sometime around March-April 1958 . . . the Party's most senior official in Trung Bo gave the order to prepare for the first armed uprising in Tra Bong district of Quang Ngai." In July 1958 a congress of party cadres and representatives of three of the tribes met "to discuss the waging of all possible forms of resistance" to Diem's regime. But it was not only among the tribes of the Central Highlands that the Central Committee's line could not be held. Farther south too, sporadic small-scale offensive actions against the Saigon regime's military outposts and bases developed during the second half of 1958.[34]

Hanoi, however, continued to hang back from any change. Its concerns were not limited to restraining southerners from escalating a fundamentally political to an armed confrontation with a Saigon regime backed by American power. It appears also to have been worried lest the repression by Diem precipitate a southern response involving radical socioeconomic policies that would alienate existing and potential supporters among landowners and the urban middle class, a development that might in turn have helped Washington justify greater American intervention in support of Diem. One clear indication of this was Hanoi's reaction to broadcasts throughout 1958 and early 1959 from a radio transmitter in South Vietnam that billed itself as the "Voice of the South Vietnam Liberation Front." Almost certainly a "black operation" mounted by Diem's government with the likely help of American agents, its provocative broadcasts were such as to oblige Hanoi's own radio to respond to what, in Carlyle Thayer's words, it regarded as "a psywar operation designed to push the revolutionary forces 'prematurely into action.'" Had it not done so, presumably some of the ex-Vietminh opposition to Diem might have been encouraged to follow militant tactics and socially radical policies that could have narrowed the anti-Diem base in the South. Hanoi, on the other hand, was looking to expand this base, even to "the upper classes of the South Vietnam administration and army." Thus, it felt obliged to denounce the broadcasts' theme that socialism in the South should be striven for along with the struggle for national reunification, and also to counter the impression conveyed by the broadcasts that the forces of individual production—among the peasantry as well as the bourgeoisie—were to be eliminated.[35]

Hanoi's continuing passivity in the face of Diem's mounting pressure against the ex-Vietminh and its adherents in the South caused bitterness among southerners that remained vivid more than two decades later. Thus General Tran Van Tra, who emerged as one of the foremost leaders of the southern resistance, later referred to what he termed "the grievous naivete of the 1954–1959 period," and wrote, "In my heart I still mourn the many comrades who fell in battle—with weapons in hand but not daring to fire—during that period, and mourn the many local movements that were drowned in blood."[36]

By the beginning of 1959, the Diem regime's repression against ex-Vietminh had increased to a point where, in the words of Jeffrey Race, the party "had no choice" but to change policy: "it was then or never." The Central Committee faced disagreement with its southern branch; it was already losing influence over some southerners, and further delay would cause greater loss among those who were still active, assuming Diem's officials did not first liquidate them. By way of illustration, Race cites a captured high-ranking Long An province party official: "Party members were angry at the Central Committee, and demanded armed action"; its southern branch "demanded of the Central Committee a reasonable policy in dealing with the southern [Diem] regime, in order to preserve the existence of the southern organization. If not, it would be completely destroyed."[37]

These attitudes generated pressures that presumably help explain the signal departure from the Central Committee's line that was sanctioned by one of the party's interzone committees in the South in the summer of 1958. In this case, for this particular mountainous area of "the western parts of the lowland provinces in Interzone 5 and the Central Highlands," the local committee authorized the combination of "limited armed struggle with political struggle," and the development of a base area wherein "armed and semi-armed forces" would have the missions of "self-defense, protection of the bases, and protection of cadres."[38]

In the face of this situation, the Fifteenth Plenum of the party's Central Committee was convened in Hanoi in January 1959. Its decision clearly went only partway in meeting the demands of impatient southerners and basically provided for the same formula pioneered some six months earlier by the Interzone Committee in the Central Highlands. But this new directive was explicit in limiting the scope of military activity. Such activity was to be secondary and subordinate to political struggle. "The political struggle form," it stated, "is the principal form, but because enemy forces are determined to submerge the revolution in blood and flames . . . to a certain extent there will be formed self-defense and armed propaganda forces in order to support the political struggle." "In substance," as Race observes, "the new policy called for the limited formation throughout the South of armed units, according to the slogan 'political struggle mixed to the right degree with armed struggle' "—an approach whose principal purposes were to "preserve the physical existence of the party, to support the political struggle, and to partially cripple the [Saigon] government apparatus at the lowest level in the rural areas."[39]

The Lao Dong's new directive, then, while providing for an escalation in the use of force, was still no call for revolution. It very clearly stopped short of sanctioning a program aimed at the direct overthrow of Diem's regime—even though so many of the party's southern adherents pressed for this. Moreover, only with its Politburo meeting of May 1959 did the party's January decision emerge as an actual operational directive with the necessary guidelines for implementation. And after this there was a further delay, for the guidelines were not even transmitted to the provincial level in the South until December. In March 1959, the Politburo of the Central Committee appears to have implicitly sanctioned the initiative taken some eight months before by the local Interzone Committee in establishing a base in the Central Highlands. Now, evidently building on that move, it officially set forth the mission of "endeavoring to develop the Central Highlands into the main revolutionary base in the South." But this was an isolated departure from the more moderate formulation of the Fifteenth Plenum, which continued to govern the Central Committee's prescription for the rest of the South.[40]

It is evident, however, that by the summer and early fall of 1959, local party members were already taking actions that went beyond the new guidelines established by the Fifteenth Plenum. Diem's introduction of his Law 10 in May 1959, whereby members of the party were executed by beheading, clearly provided a sharp spur to independent initiatives by those who were threatened. In effect, while the new Lao Dong directive was still being discussed and during the time when it was making its way into the rural areas of the South, southerners were already blazing a trail to a higher level of struggle against Diem's regime. This was evident in the rash of sizable peasant uprisings during the summer and early fall of 1959. Race states that during the last six months of 1959 the party in Long An province "reorganized and rearmed a number of province main force battalions and began to rebuild traditional base areas" there and in adjacent areas. In June, according to the account of Ta Xuan Linh, a provincial-level committee in Nam Bo issued an appeal to the peasantry to rise against Diem's "coercive organizations" in that area; this was followed in October by a rising in Tay Ninh province. On July 8, U.S. sources reported an attack against the ARVN (Army of the Republic of Vietnam) military base at Bien Hoa, close to Saigon, in which two U.S. military advisers were killed and one wounded. William Duiker states that, in response to a province-level party directive, an uprising broke out in Quang Ngai at the end of August, where, according to DRV sources, sixteen villages with a total population of more than fifteen thousand were declared "completely liberated"; the rebellion spread to three adjacent districts. On September 26, a unit identified as the Second Liberation Battalion successfully ambushed two companies of the Twenty-third Division of the ARVN and captured most of their weapons. (It was with this incident, David Halberstam observes, that the enemy came to be referred to—by both U.S. officials and Diem—as "Viet Cong," or Vietcong, a pejorative shorthand for "Vietnamese communist.")[41]

The decisions regarding the South that were approved by the top leadership of the Lao Dong had been, Race observes, "apparently only stop-gap moves intended to catch up with events which had in fact overtaken the Party in the South." Events continued to overtake it. One that forcibly illustrated a further

escalation in militancy was the successful uprising in the Mekong Delta's Ben Tre
(Kien Hoa) province, commencing January 17, 1960. Led by a remarkable woman,
Nguyen Thi Dinh, who later became deputy commander of the armed forces of
the NLF, this was regarded as the resistance's first "concentrated uprising" and
embraced three entire districts. As Mai Elliott has written in the introduction to
her translation of Madame Dinh's vivid account, it was launched "without the
support of armed units and practically bare-handed." Beginning with just four
old rifles, a few home-made mortars, 162 troops, and the support of eighteen
village committees, the Ben Tre uprising snowballed into a widely backed movement that initially captured enough weapons from government outposts to equip
a full company. With the confidence and momentum gained in this, Saigon
countersweeps were parried, and a second uprising, in September, went well
beyond the party's 1959 guidelines. Madame Dinh's followers substantially expanded the area they controlled. According to her probably somewhat exaggerated estimate, some 70 percent of the province's villages were liberated, with
Diem's troops obliged to evacuate over a hundred posts and watchtowers, and
with about seventeen hundred assorted weapons seized. And, significantly, following in the footsteps of the Vietminh, over sixty-three thousand acres of rice
fields were returned to peasants.[42]

The Ben Tre uprising was important not merely because of its substantive
achievements, but because of the country-wide example it set. With most of the
province's party leaders executed or jailed, and most of the Vietminh's old "grass-
roots revolutionary bases" destroyed, its remaining cadres had demonstrated
what good leadership and imaginative tactics could achieve. Equally important,
the uprising constituted an example of local cadres acting successfully on their
own initiative when it was impossible to contact upper-echelon party leaders for
approval. At the same time, this bold initiative illustrated the limited capacity of
top party leaders in Hanoi to channel and prescribe limitations on the scope and
timing of actions by ex-Vietminh insurgents in the South. For whereas it might
be argued that the January phase of the Ben Tre uprising was within the limits
of the new guidelines of the Central Committee's January-May 1959 dispensation,
its second, September phase considerably exceeded them. And certainly that was
the case with the attack of January 25, 1960, launched by a full battalion of what
was now called the Liberation Army, apparently in coordination with a battalion
from the religious sects—a total force of three to five hundred men—against a
regimental army base of the Saigon government north of Tay Ninh. This major
post was overrun, with serious ARVN casualties and many weapons captured by
the attackers.[43]

That the impatient former Vietminh and some of the party leaders in the
South were unwilling to be confined within the bounds stipulated by the top party
leadership, and insisted on bypassing its line on the political as well as the military
level to move on to a broad offensive against Diem's government, was made still
clearer a few weeks later. Meeting in March 1960, "former resistance fighters,"
including "leaders and members of the Vietminh," "cadres and members of state

organizations during the resistance," and, among others, representatives of the Buddhists, Cao Dai, Catholics, and Hoa Hao, as well as "individuals not adhering to any party," issued a declaration that reflected the climax of their frustrations and impatience with Hanoi's long insistence upon a primarily political struggle. Reviewing their six years of suffering at the hands of what they referred to as "the American-Diemists," they accused them of having "declared open war." They appealed to all classes of the population to struggle against this repression, called upon former resistance fighters and all the people of South Vietnam "to struggle to put an end" to the Diem regime and to liberate the South "from submission to America, eliminate all U.S. bases . . . expel American military advisers and not accept any form of American interference." To replace Diem, a broad coalition government was to be formed, composed of representatives of different political inclinations and all parts of society, which would rigorously apply the terms of the Geneva Agreements and enter into discussions with North Vietnam in order to effect the country's peaceful reunification. In its fundamentals, this call to militant action and the political platform proposed was similar to that advanced nine months later, when, in the face of continuing pressures by southerners, the party leadership in Hanoi formally subscribed to these ideas.[44]

Initially, however, Hanoi's Central Committee was unwilling to endorse the level of military struggle and political objectives demanded by these southerners. On the heels of their proclamation, and apparently in direct response to it and the escalation of military activity, the Regional Committee for the South on March 28, 1960, issued a long, detailed critique that was sent to local party chapters. Acknowledging that "the masses are enthusiastic," that they believed that "the time has come to launch the insurrection" and were "impatient and extremely adventurous," it blamed this on their lack of understanding of party policy. It noted that "a number of Party headquarters have committed errors, some of which are critical," admonished that some members did not understand the balance of forces, and cautioned: "We have not yet reached the stage of direct revolution; that is to say, we have not yet reached the period of direct overthrow of the American-Diem government in order to put government in the hands of the people. In this period of contention, we should do our utmost to build up, preserve, and expand our grass root organization—generally speaking we should maintain the people's movement under legal cover, we cannot as yet wipe out the government's machinery; we can only chip it and damage it, etc. We are doing our utmost to push our struggle movement strongly forward to evolve from the contention [tug-of-war] phase to the direct revolution phase. In order to do so we need time."[45]

The top party leadership apparently feared that too great an increase in the level of military activity against the Diem regime risked provoking direct American intervention, and it is very clear that the leaders wanted to ensure that warfare in the South not engulf the North. All this was either implicit or explicit in the April 10 speech by Le Duan, the southerner who had recently been appointed first secretary. He acknowledged that, though the "American imperialists are established only in the South," the contradiction between them and the Vietnamese was not confined to that part of Vietnam but was "common to the whole country." Though northerners would "never neglect their task with regard to one half of their country which was not yet liberated," under existing circumstances, "when the possibility exists to maintain a lasting peace in the world . . . we can and must guide and restrict within the South the solving of the contradiction between imperialism and the colonies in our country." He argued that "the U.S.-Diem clique" was "irretrievably doomed," and that, if peace could be maintained, the clique would "rapidly decay." Consequently, he concluded that "if peace is maintained [that is, presumably, if militant actions against Diem did not escalate to a point where they precipitated an American military intervention], the revolution forces will enjoy necessary conditions to develop strongly. Hence, to maintain peace is a revolutionary slogan." This statement was prominent among the indications that brought Donald Zagoria to observe that "as of mid-1960, on the eve of the formation of the NLF, Hanoi was doing its best to contain the Southern resistance movement and was warning against adventurism."[46]

The tide of insurgency in the South did not abate, however, and it is evident that for southerners the line taken in the Declaration of the Former Resistance Fighters had greater appeal than the more restrained course prescribed by this spokesman for the party's Central Committee. If Hanoi was not to be left behind and lose more influence with southern activists, it would clearly have to adjust its policies further to the initiatives they had taken and accommodate to the momentum of their movement. That it felt obliged to do so was indicated in Le Duan's report on behalf of the Central Committee to the Third Lao Dong Party Congress, held in Hanoi on September 5–10, 1960, and in the resolutions of that congress. Abandoning the socialist economic development of the North as the overriding priority, the Central Committee and the congress that ratified its recommendations resolved that in the present stage of the Vietnamese revolution there were now two "strategic tasks." Though the first was "to carry out the socialist revolution in the North," "closely related to it" was a second: "to liberate the South from the rule of the American imperialists and their henchmen [and] achieve national reunification and complete independence and freedom throughout the country." Socialist development was to be regarded as "the most decisive task for the development of the whole Vietnamese revolution for the cause of national reunification," but the southerners were now finally encouraged to take direct action aimed at overthrowing the Diem regime. The resolution stated:

> In the completion of the national people's democratic revolution throughout the country, and the achievement of national reunification, our compatriots in the South have the task of directly overthrowing the rule of the American imperialists and their agents in order to liberate south Viet Nam. . . . The immediate task of the revolution in the South is to achieve the unity of the whole people, to fight resolutely against the aggressive and war-mongering U.S. imperialists, to overthrow the dictatorial ruling Ngo

Dinh Diem clique, lackeys of the U.S. imperialists, to form a national
democratic coalition government in south Viet Nam, to win national independence and . . . to achieve national reunification.

In attaining this objective, southerners were called upon to establish "a broad
National United Front directed against the U.S. and Diem." Based on a "worker-
peasant alliance," this front was to "rally all the patriotic classes and sections of
the people, the majority and minority nationalities, all patriotic parties and
religious groupings, together with all individuals inclined to oppose the U.S. and
Diem."[47]

It was not until the end of January 1961, however, that the Politburo of the
Central Committee "met to concretize the resolution of the Third Party Congress
regarding the direction and immediate missions and tasks of the revolution in the
South." This resulted in a directive on January 31, 1961, which provided that in
general the new policy was to "step up the political struggle while also stepping
up the armed struggle until it is on a par with the political struggle, and attack
the enemy both politically and militarily." At the same time it stipulated that the
ratio should be adapted to the characteristics of different areas: "In the jungle-
and-mountain area, stress military struggle. In the lowland area, military and
political struggle may be at equal levels. In the urban areas, stress the political
struggle."[48]

Some six weeks before, however, on December 20, 1960, the southerners had
met in "War Zone D," about 37 miles north of Saigon, to establish the National
Front for the Liberation of South Vietnam (usually referred to as the National
Liberation Front, or NLF) along the lines called for in the Third Party Congress
and the earlier Declaration of the Former Resistance Fighters. For reasons that
are still not clear, Hanoi did not publicly announce formation of the NLF until
January 29, 1961, several days after it had been reported by radio and newspapers
in Saigon and Phnom Penh, and this at a time when the Lao Dong's Politburo
was still discussing how to "concretize" the resolution of the September Party
Congress.[49]

The NLF's ten-point program called for the overthrow of Diem's government. This "disguised colonial regime of the U.S. imperialists" was to be replaced
by a national assembly elected on the basis of universal suffrage and "a broad
national democratic coalition administration" including representatives "of all
strata of people, political parties, religious communities and patriotic personalities." A wide range of progressive social and economic measures, including
agrarian reform and autonomy for minorities, were to be introduced. American
military advisers were to leave and all foreign military bases were to be eliminated,
with "the property of the U.S. imperialists and the ruling clique, their stooges,"
to be confiscated and nationalized. But leniency was to be observed toward "those
who had before collaborated with the U.S.-Diem clique and committed crimes
against the people but have now repented and serve the people."[50]

The program assumed a period of separate governance for the South before its reunification with the North. South Vietnam was to follow a neutral foreign policy whereby it would "refrain from joining any bloc or military alliance" and would "establish diplomatic relations with all countries irrespective of political regime." The new southern government and Hanoi would "negotiate and under-take not to spread propaganda to divide the peoples or in favor of war" and would not use "military force against each other." They would "carry out economic and cultural exchanges" so as to "ensure the people of both zones freedom of move-ment and trade and the right of mutual visits and correspondence." Reunification was to be "gradual" and by peaceful means, through negotiations and discussions.

On February 15, 1961, at a conference in War Zone D presided over by Tran Nam Hung, head of the NLF's newly established military commission, all "liber-ation armed forces" in the South were brought together under a unified com-mand, the "People's Liberation Armed Forces" or "Liberation Army of South Vietnam." A year later (February 16, 1962) the NLF held its first congress, which elected a Central Committee and, as its president, Nguyen Huu Tho, a lawyer educated in France and reported to have been jailed by the French in Saigon from 1950 to 1952 and by Diem from 1958 until his escape from prison in 1961.[51]

The appeal of the NLF was broad, and so was its leadership. Carlyle Thayer found its early leaders to be "long-time VWP [Lao Dong] cadres who had been active in the south, members of the sect forces, former non-Party members of the Resistance, and non-Communist opponents of the Diem regime." Douglas Pike concluded that "Many of the original participants in the NLF had turned to it because they had been denied participation in South Vietnam's political process even in the role of loyal opposition [to Diem]." He states that "Members of the original NLF, and its most ardent supporters in the early years, were drawn from the ranks of the Viet Minh Communists; the Cao Dai and Hoa Hao sects; a scattering of minority group members primarily ethnic Cambodians and monta-gnards; idealistic youths recruited from the universities and polytechnic schools; representatives of farmers' organizations from parts of the Mekong delta where serious land tenure problems existed; leaders of small political parties or groups . . . ; intellectuals who had broken with the GVN [Saigon] . . . ; military deserters; refugees of various sorts from the Diem government. . . ." Soon they were joined by increasing numbers of southerners who had gone north during the immediate post-Geneva period and now infiltrated back into the South across the seventeenth parallel, or via Laos along a route whose construction had been authorized by the Central Committee at the end of May 1959. (Initially only a footpath, this route through the Laotian border area adjacent to Vietnam was later, in its more developed stages, known as the Ho Chi Minh Trail.)[52]

Alongside the existing residual Lao Dong organization, the front provided a new party-approved channel for those opposed to and by Diem. It gained legitimacy because it was regarded as part of a continuum of the same Vietminh that had just driven out the French colonialists; because it stood in opposition to their American successors and the repressive Vietnamese regime they had set up; because it insisted that Vietnam was one nation and its division should end;

and because it championed land reform and other progressive social and economic programs.

Though the existing party apparatus in much of the rural South remained the principal conduit for peasant opposition to the Saigon regime, the NLF was able to tap into previously unorganized rural areas as well as to marshal elements from the increasingly restive urban population. It provided scope—and in some cases positions of leadership—to large numbers of noncommunists who, while not wishing to join the party as such, supported its nationalist goals and desired to work in cooperation with it against Diem and for an ultimate reunification of Vietnam. The NLF was thus an organization through which the Lao Dong could establish liaison to work cooperatively with previously fragmented dissident southern urban elements and rural-based groups not already incorporated into the party, including substantial elements of the Cao Dai and Hoa Hao. In many rural areas, however, the NLF appears to have played a secondary role, and it was primarily the existing, if often badly damaged, party apparatus itself that dealt with the peasantry. There, according to David Elliott, to the extent that grass-roots opinion was polled and taken into account, it came through party channels: village to district to province to region to COSVN (Central Office for South Vietnam, an institution whose formation was explicitly anticipated and authorized by the Lao Dong constitution of September 1960).[53]

The NLF's position on interim southern autonomy and reunification was elaborated in its program of January 17, 1962. This stipulated: "The reunification of the Fatherland will be solved step by step on the basis of the aspirations and interests of all sections of the people of South Vietnam as well as the people of North Vietnam, on the principles of freedom and democracy, negotiations and agreement between the two sides." In the meantime, after South Vietnam's independence had been secured, its government would "establish diplomatic relations with all countries without distinction of political system." It would enter into no external military alliances, but hoped to get "unconditional" economic and technical assistance from countries with diverse political systems. The program observed that the experiences of "peaceful and neutral Cambodia" testified to this possibility. Affirming its intention of struggling for the formation of "a peace and neutrality zone comprising Cambodia, Laos and South Vietnam," it "warmly welcomed" the initiative of Cambodia's Prince Norodom Sihanouk in establishing such a zone. It warned, however, that "if the U.S. imperialists and their agents obdurately go further and further into a bloody military adventure of aggression," the NLF would if necessary exercise "their legitimate and effective right" to appeal to North Vietnam and to other governments "the world over, irrespective of political system," for material and manpower support.[54]

The major powers' neutralization of Laos and provision for a coalition government there in mid-1962 appears to have reinforced the NLF's advocacy of a similar solution for South Vietnam. On July 20, it called for an international agreement to be "quickly concluded to enable the powers from different camps to guarantee respect for the sovereignty, independence, territorial integrity and neutrality of South Vietnam," which it stated was ready to form "a neutral zone together with Cambodia and Laos." This neutral zone did not include North Vietnam; there is some indication that officials there may have had some reservations regarding the NLF's emphasis on neutrality, but were prepared to accept this as a necessary transitional stage en route to ultimate reunification. The NLF appears to have regarded the sort of coalition government then being set up in Laos as a model for South Vietnam. The NLF's formula for coalition provided scope for elements from Diem's government to be represented in a transitional coalition regime that was to precede and provide for "free general elections" that were to endow South Vietnam with a democratic national assembly.[55]

This emphasis on coalition government, gradualness of reunification, and a separate, neutral foreign policy for the South pending its completion was not transitory.* This platform was reaffirmed by the NLF in its statement of November 8, 1963, shortly after Diem's assassination, and, according to Pike, again on December 20, 1964. These features remained prominent in the major NLF statement of May 8, 1969. The same emphasis was clearly evident in discussions I had as late as 1967 and 1969 with two senior NLF officials—both of whom had served as its secretary general.[56]

A full exposition of the NLF's position on reunification was given me in August 1967 by Nguyen Van Hieu, who had served as its secretary general during the crucial period 1961–63.[57] He stated:

> Reunification is a basic aim of the NLF, but the character of the reunification and the amount of time necessary to undertake it are not clear. Certainly, it is not something that could be carried out in two or three years, but might well take ten years. In the first place, the differences between the two Vietnams are so great that it will take a long time to accommodate the differences. The North is a socialist system and the South is an economic system still based upon private property. It will take a long time to shave down the differences between the two systems. The first objective must be a normalization of relations, certainly involving commerce between the two parties.

Asked whether the process of accommodation between the two Vietnams would eventuate in a unitary, a federal, or a confederal state, he replied that this was not clear, and would have to be worked out step by step over a long period of time: "It might eventuate in two separate economies, and it might eventuate in two separate governments." The NLF remained "strongly in favor of a neutralization of South Vietnam, but since North Vietnam is a socialist state it could not be neutralist."

In elucidating the NLF's position on cooperation with other groups, Nguyen

---

*Clearly NLF leaders did not envisage the rapid reunification that in fact finally was effected in 1975–76, or the very different context within which the NLF was then obliged to operate.

Van Hieu said it was willing to cooperate "in a common action program and work parallel with representative groups which shared at least some of its objectives, and for this it is not necessary for them to join the NLF." It would be possible, he said, to work toward existing common goals with the politically organized Buddhists, for instance, without having to create an organizational linkage with them. "Such common action programs could, for instance, be in any of the areas relating to the five basic goals of the NLF, for some of these goals are shared by such representative groups still standing outside of the NLF. These goals are five: peace, independence, democracy, neutrality, reunification."

The establishment within the NLF on January 1, 1962, of a People's Revolutionary Party (PRP), an avowedly communist component that was apparently a reorganized successor of part of the existing southern Lao Dong membership, may, as some analysts suggest, have reflected an effort by leaders in Hanoi to exert greater control over the front. Whether or not the party felt this was necessary, Etienne Manac'h, head of the Asian department at the Quai d'Orsay and one of France's best-informed Vietnam specialists, observed as late as September 1968 in referring to the PRP, that even this communist central core of the NLF was "rooted in the South and attuned to the needs and expectations there." It must be understood, he said, that "the polycentric nature of contemporary world communism" was a phenomenon operative to a significant extent even within Vietnam, and it clearly affected the character of the PRP and its relationship with Hanoi. Hanoi and the NLF had similar objectives, including an overarching common nationalism, but the communist leaders within the PRP could not maintain a position of effective leadership within the NLF, if they were unresponsive to the views of the southerners.[58]

Between the NLF as a whole and the Lao Dong's Central Committee in Hanoi there was much the same dynamic of interaction as had earlier operated between the Central Committee and southern party leaders whose front-line position in the struggle against Diem's regime had sometimes brought them to perceive issues and priorities differently than did those sitting in Hanoi. Presumably to ensure as broad a measure of southern support as possible, the Central Committee acquiesced in allowing the NLF's leaders a limited degree of autonomy. This would account for some differences in their views and stances, while not, however, invalidating their essential unity on all questions of fundamental importance. In any event, the appearance of some independence of position vis-à-vis Hanoi was certainly desirable in the interests of enlisting the support of broader sectors of noncommunist opposition to the Saigon government.

The extent to which the NLF had autonomy from the Central Committee of the Lao Dong in Hanoi is, and will probably long remain, difficult to establish. The two partook of the same nationalism, with expulsion of the American presence and ultimate reunification the goal of both, and they were linked together by the same communist party. But, however one assesses it, there were recurring indications of significant, though apparently largely tactical and never really fundamental, differences between them over how the struggle in the South was to be conducted, how neutral a transitional southern NLF regime should be, how long it should remain autonomous before unification was effected, and the approach to and terms for a negotiated settlement. The introduction of U.S. ground combat forces in March 1965 appears initially to have elicited somewhat dissimilar negotiating stances from the NLF and Hanoi. Lack of full congruity in either the steps toward reunification or the approach to a negotiated settlement with the United States were still noticeable when I talked with NLF leaders in 1967, 1969, 1970, and 1972. Although it can be argued that some of these differences may have been nothing more than mutually agreed-upon tactics useful in furthering common goals, it is evident that at times the differences were genuine.[59]

Whatever degree of autonomy leaders of the NLF may have had, that organization was tied in with the Lao Dong and in the most fundamental sense was subordinate to its Central Committee in Hanoi. Beyond that, however, as David Elliott observes, it is evident that within the Central Committee itself differences arose over policy, strategy, and tactics, with some members (such as Le Duan) reflecting positions closer to those of the southern insurgents than others. From time to time, moreover, there seem to have been divisions within the NLF (which Pike believes to have been especially pronounced following the overthrow of Diem, particularly in late 1964 and early 1965).[60] Ultimately, however, all major issues appear to have been contained in party channels and resolved by the Central Committee. But it must be emphasized that the party's leaders, whether in the South or in Hanoi, had to remain responsive to the views of Diem's southern opponents—both the ex-Vietminh and its recent allies—or risk forfeiting the party's capacity to channel and control the energies of these front-line elements. If the leadership was not sufficiently responsive, it faced a repetition of the years 1956–59, when it was obliged to follow in the wake of southern initiatives and adjust its own policies accordingly. And despite the predominant position of the party, it did not have the leverage—assuming it had wished to use it—to force southerners to call off an insurgency that they themselves had begun and which they saw as crucial to their own future.

During the war it was never in the interests of either the American proponents of intervention nor officials in Hanoi to admit the extent of southern initiative in mounting the armed struggle against Diem and the role this played in the formation of the NLF. This has remained the case since the war, for acknowledgment of it clearly undermines the case of current American apologists for intervention, just as it earlier did that of those officials who actually shaped that policy. And for a postwar Hanoi government whose unexpectedly rapid and rough political and economic reunification of North and South has been attended by the shunting aside or demotion of many of the most prominent and dedicated leaders of the old NLF, it is apparently expedient to gloss over both the degree of their contribution to the struggle against American power and the extent of revolutionary initiatives taken by the southern ex-Vietminh. Since reunification of the country in 1975, the party's Central Committee appears to have concluded that history will read better if its own revolutionary role in the South during the first six post-Geneva years is inflated.[61] It is ironic that on this score there is to-day such a striking convergence between revisionists in the United States and Vietnam.

For American administrations from Eisenhower onward to have acknowledged the fundamentally southern roots of the insurgency and the extent to which southerners took the initiatives that led to Hanoi's establishment of the NLF would have exposed the speciousness of a major rationale for intervention—"aggression from the North"—and also the unpopularity of Diem and subsequent U.S.-supported regimes. But, in fact, as was the case with France, the United States in its military and political intervention was not combating an equivalent, externally based intrusion by another non-Vietnamese power. Initially what it confronted was an indigenous opposition that Washington's own protégé had provoked among the southern population he sought to rule. From 1960 on, the United States faced an even more widely aroused southern opposition augmented by a growing stream of returning southerners—individuals or small groups—who had been regrouped in the North after the Geneva Conference. Then, after the sharp escalation of American fire power in early 1965, Washington faced this same opposition now buttressed by the support of actual military units of northerners from above the seventeenth parallel—units, it should be noted, that were Viet-namese, not Chinese or Russian. Nevertheless, the thesis that the war in the South was precipitated by outside aggression became an official article of faith and a perennially useful argument for justifying the military involvement of successive American administrations in Vietnam.[62]

Despite a continuing skepticism among some American officials, the over-whelming majority accepted the official dogma that the NLF and the southern insurgents in general were passive, unquestioning puppets of Hanoi—simple extensions of its power that lacked genuine southern foundations or will of their own.[63] That assumption was least questioned and most doggedly held by the U.S. military. For them, as well as most civilian presidential advisers, this conventional wisdom made easier the formulation of simple, tidy calculations as to the effec-tiveness of applying American power in Vietnam. It led to two premises: first, that control over the insurgency in the South was to be achieved through primarily military means; second, that American bombing of the North could be success-fully applied to induce Hanoi to pressure southern insurgents to stop fighting. Thereby was born the belief that air power projected against the North would provide effective leverage in bringing Hanoi to end, or at least substantially reduce, the level of military activity being mounted in the South against Ameri-can-backed Saigon regimes. This apart, it must be reiterated that to question this officially perceived character of the southern insurgency was to undermine the concept of "aggression from the North" upon which rested a central rationale for American military intervention.

V

The Decline
of Diem's Regime

During 1960, Laos heavily overshadowed Vietnam as the area in Southeast Asia
of greatest concern to the Eisenhower administration. Even though Ngo Dinh
Diem's position began to erode seriously, senior American officials paid Vietnam
relatively little heed. Moreover, not until the early months of Eisenhower's last
year did the top U.S. military leadership and its Military Assistance Advisory
Group in Saigon (MAAG) even begin to recognize that to cope with insurgent
guerrilla activity in Vietnam they should move away from their fixation on
providing Diem with an army organized along American lines with the principal
mission of blocking a possible North Vietnamese attack across the seventeenth
parallel. In tardy acknowledgment that the most immediate security threat to
Diem in fact came from an increasing southern insurgency, a counterinsurgency
plan was prepared between April and December, but was still largely unimplemented when Eisenhower left office.[1]

Equally aware of the rising tide of rebellion in the rural areas and Diem's
inability to contain it, the American ambassador to Saigon, Elbridge Durbrow,
showed much greater sensitivity than MAAG to the social and political conditions that were fueling the insurgency. His report to Washington of March 7,
1960, pointed out that contributing to the "considerable dissatisfaction which the
VC [Viet Cong] can play on in rural areas" were the growth in unpaid forced
labor involved in the agroville program, "improper actions by local officials such
as torture, extortion and corruption," and "fear of officials and members of the
semi-covert Can Lao Party." The embassy was also beginning to recognize the
counterproductivity of the harsh measures taken by Diem's Can Lao apparatus
in urban areas. This was brought into focus on April 26, when eighteen of Saigon's
most prominent anticommunists—ten of them former ministers of Diem's or Bao
Dai's Cabinet—issued a public statement of criticism, which became known as
the Caravelle Manifesto (after the name of the hotel where they met). The
manifesto referred to Diem's "anti-democratic elections," to "continuous arrests
[that] fill the jails and prisons to the rafters," and charged that "effective power"
had been "concentrated in fact in the hands of an irresponsible member of the

'family' [Ngo Dinh Nhu] from whom emanate all orders." Unreported in the thoroughly intimidated Vietnamese press, this protest was of little immediate concern to Diem; he was too contemptuous to bother arresting the group until six months later, when he concluded that some of its members had encouraged unrest within his military establishment.[2]

As early as August, American officials were becoming alarmed by discontent among the army's officer corps. A State Department intelligence report attributed this to "worsening of internal security, the promotion of incompetent officers and Diem's direct interference in army operations . . . his political favoritism, inadequate delegation of authority, and the influence of the Can Lao." The report also observed that "criticism of Diem's leadership in official circles" (that is, within his own government) had reached a level "unprecedented since he consolidated his authority in 1956," and was especially focused on Ngo Dinh Nhu and his wife. It reported that "some officials have meditated a coup with army support to oust the Nhus and their lieutenants and, if necessary, Diem himself." The paper did not hold such an attempt as being likely yet, but warned that, if criticism of them grew and internal security and peasant discontent worsened, "an early coup attempt" could not be ruled out. Prospects for this "would be enhanced," it concluded, "if Diem continued to remain uncompromising and if the opposition felt that the United States would not be unsympathetic to a coup or that U.S.-Vietnamese relations would not be seriously damaged."[3]

Criticism of Diem did continue to grow, internal security and peasant discontent did worsen, and Diem did remain uncompromising. And certainly a number of South Vietnamese army officers concluded that the United States would not be unsympathetic to a coup aimed at ousting the Nhus and their retainers from the government and reducing Diem's powers. Initially, however, Ambassador Durbrow, with the State Department's encouragement, sought a less violent course. He tried to persuade Diem of the importance of removing this unpopular and widely feared pair from government, suggesting that Nhu be appointed to a high-ranking ambassadorship, and urged Diem to undertake a broad range of reforms, including "altering the nature of the Can Lao Party." But, having come to rely heavily on Nhu, Diem refused to countenance any diminishment in his governmental role or any change in the character of the organization that was his brother's principal instrument of power. The ambassador expressed his mounting exasperation with Diem's rejection of American advice at the end of a September 16 cable to Washington: "If Diem's position in country continues deteriorate . . . it may become necessary for US government to begin consideration alternative courses of action and leaders in order achieve our objective."[4]

The coup of November 11–12, 1960, against Diem's regime very nearly succeeded. If there had been fuller agreement among the military officers who carried it out, it probably would have. But with power within their grasp, differences among the dissident officers and their civilian associates[5] gave Diem the additional time he needed to summon loyal troops from the Mekong Delta. Although all the rebels wanted at least to oust the Nhus and clip Diem's wings, some wanted to go further and kill the Nhus, rather than send them abroad on the face-saving ambassadorial assignment favored by the U.S. embassy. And there was considerable support for ousting Diem completely from the government. The rebels also differed in their attitude toward the U.S. embassy, which kept in contact with them and sought to minimize bloodshed and avoid further fracturing of army unity, and was apparently anxious to maintain Diem in a position of symbolic, if diminished, power.

In speculating about prospects for a coup, the State Department intelligence report of August 29 concluded that "Should a coup materialize the immediate and principal objective would probably be to oust the Nhus and their entourage and then leave Diem with the alternative of either continuing in office with reduced power or resigning." This was indeed the formula on which the rebels ultimately compromised. Ngo Dinh Nhu, his wife, and their retainers were to be ousted from government (whether or not they would have been executed is not clear), and Diem's political role severely reduced, with army officers or their civilian associates encircling and containing him in the new government.[6]

The major thrust of the rebels' power came from the elite parachute regiment under the command of Colonel Nguyen Chanh Thi, and from a marine battalion led by Lieutenant Colonel Pham Van Lieu. The top coup leader, and principal military tactician, was Colonel Duong Van Dong, a former airborne officer, now without a command, who may have forced Thi to participate in order to ensure that the parachutists went along. These forces struck early in the morning of November 11, surrounding Diem's palace and taking over the army headquarters, radio station, and airport. As the rebels closed in around the palace, Diem's guard fought back, but it was soon clear that Dong could tighten the ring and take the palace at will. Saigon Radio announced the success of the "revolution," the overthrow of the regime, the surrender of Diem and "his clique," and the establishment of a "Revolutionary Council" acting on behalf of the armed forces. With the only significant body of troops upon whom Diem could count headquartered at My Tho, some fifty miles from Saigon, and with the American embassy urging him to negotiate and compromise with the rebels, he felt obliged to do so. He did have the advantage of the lack of full agreement among his opponents. Whereas apparently Dong and a number of other officers favored launching a final attack and overrunning the palace and its inmates, Thi, although just as anxious to eliminate the Nhus, wanted to keep Diem on in a figurehead capacity. Wishing to retain American sympathy, and urged by the U.S. embassy to avoid bloodshed and negotiate, those rebels who inclined toward compromise apparently supported Thi, and a negotiated settlement was finally agreed upon.[7]

In the meantime, the rebels had been able to induce the aging, semiretired chief of staff of the armed forces, General Le Van Ty, to relay their demands to Diem. Just after noon on November 11, some nine hours after the coup had been launched, Ty announced over the radio that he had conferred with Diem, who had agreed to the "dissolution of the present government" and, "with agreement of the Revolutionary Council," had entrusted army officers with the responsibility of forming "a provisional military government." Subsequently, the rebels broadcast a recorded statement they had exacted from Diem, reiterating his agreement and his willingness to "coordinate with the Revolutionary Council to establish a coalition government."[8]

While negotiating these apparently far-reaching concessions, Diem was in fact playing for time. In taking advantage of the hours spent in the negotiations he was assisted by Major General Nguyen Khanh, the army's acting chief of staff, who had managed to slip through rebel lines into the palace. Diem's disposition to negotiate rather than capitulate was also reinforced by Nhu and Madame Nhu. While the rebels were occupied in discussing the composition of the military government, Diem was in contact with one of his most trusted senior officers, Colonel Tran Thien Khiem, a Catholic with close ties to Diem's elder brother, the bishop of Vinh Long. As commander of the Fifth Military Region in the Mekong Delta, Khiem was able to gather a substantial force—seven battalions and, most important of all, one of the army's largest tank units. On the second day of the coup attempt, Khiem's tanks suddenly appeared in Saigon and encircled the paratroopers surrounding Diem's palace, thus shifting the balance of active forces away from the rebels. The officers of many of the units in the capital, who had held a benignly pro-rebel, wait-and-see attitude, now found it expedient to declare for Diem. The coup attempt quickly collapsed, and Colonels Dong, Thi, Lieu, and fifteen other leaders flew to safety in Cambodia, where they remained in exile for three years—until other officers mounted a more successful coup against Diem.

For Diem and his brothers, this aborted but nearly successful coup was something of a watershed in their attitude toward, and relations with, the United States. Because they had reason to believe that some American officials had encouraged the effort, the event remained a vivid memory that often strengthened their suspicions of U.S. intentions. Whereas prior to the coup Diem had generally believed he had Washington's unqualified support, after it his trust in the United States was undermined. Among some of his confidants, he now frequently compared himself to Syngman Rhee, the Korean leader once unstintingly supported by the United States, whose removal in 1960 by a coup of military officers the Vietnamese leader saw as having been American-inspired.[9]

This Korean analogy was very much in the minds of the rebels as well. As Colonel Pham Van Lieu later explained to me, "We had no worry about getting continued American assistance if we were successful; we felt we could count on it, just like Park did when he overthrew Rhee." Whether or not Durbrow's CIA critic, Brigadier General Edward Lansdale, was correct in his charge that "At the most critical moment of the coup, the U.S. Ambassador urged Diem to give in to rebel demands to avoid bloodshed," the very fact that the embassy had urged negotiations with the rebels signified for Diem that it had "equated" them with his regime. For him this alone was indicative of American perfidy and encouragement to his opponents; but he claimed to have concrete proof as well.[10]

Whatever the depth of American involvement, the events of November 11–12 served to exacerbate the fissures and bitterness within the mission in Saigon—especially between Durbrow and MAAG, which had long been severely critical of the ambassador's efforts to pressure Diem to make reforms. And for Washington, at least, it highlighted Lansdale, circling like a hawk around their conflict, severely critical of the ambassador and unabashedly out to get his job. Of more lasting importance, the coup attempt registered the fragility of Diem's regime, and the severe tensions within it, especially between its top leaders and much of the senior officer corps.[11]

John F. Kennedy assumed the presidency on January 20, 1961, with much the same world view and set of assumptions about Vietnam as the Eisenhower administration. This was also true of most of his advisers. Despite growing evidence of serious strain between Moscow and Peking, the forces of communism were regarded as an interlocked threat that had to be met by the United States on a global basis. Nearly all American officials still perceived Vietnamese communism as one of the fronts of contest with the Soviet Union and China—critically dependent on these two major communist powers rather than drawing most of its strength from a fundamentally autonomous national foundation. And in terms of American national interest, Vietnam remained a "domino" whose fall would undermine and topple noncommunist regimes in neighboring states. Kennedy and his advisers appeared to be every bit as confident as the Eisenhower administration had been of their ability to engage in social engineering abroad and to shape foreign polities in conformity with their own perception of America's national interest. They tended to draw inspiration from the same examples as Eisenhower and Dulles—the perceived "American successes" in Greece, Guatemala, Iran, and the Philippines, plus that of Britain in Malaya. Although Kennedy usually viewed the phenomenon of nonaligned neutralism in less Manichaean terms and with more sympathetic understanding than these two predecessors,[12] he was no less rigid regarding Vietnam. As a senator he had closely followed Eisenhower's post-Geneva Vietnam policy and never indicated opposition to it. He had also, of course, been one of Diem's earliest and most important champions. There is no indication that he ever questioned Eisenhower's objective of maintaining Vietnam's partition and sustaining a separate, anticommunist state in its southern half. Not suffering a "defeat" in Vietnam meant for Kennedy continuing with that policy, and he did so, despite his growing awareness that the Diem regime was unpopular, fragile, and lacking in any substantial foundation.

There were, however, notable differences in the context within which the new president approached Vietnam. His extravagant campaign rhetoric had portended a tough worldwide anticommunist stance, and any likelihood of his soon moderating this militancy was offset by both the circumstances of his election and the existing domestic political climate. Especially important was his initial feeling of political insecurity, arising mainly from the very narrow margin by which he had defeated Richard Nixon in the election. This seems to have left him particularly sensitive to Nixon's unwarranted charge that he was soft on communism. He had also been hoist with the petard of his own campaign charges that the Eisenhower administration had been weak and ineffective in dealing with the communist powers, and his assertions that it had permitted a missile gap with the Soviet Union which did not in fact exist. Throughout most of his first year in office he felt himself to be in Eisenhower's shadow and measured against him, remaining acutely sensitive to the possibility of criticism from his predecessor. Stephen Pelz, in his study of Kennedy's 1961 decisions on Vietnam, observes, "Just before leaving office Eisenhower warned Kennedy that he and the Republicans would hold the new President responsible for any retreat in Southeast Asia." Kennedy's sensitivity was undoubtedly heightened in May 1961, when Eisenhower announced that he and his former Cabinet would maintain a continuing review of Kennedy's policies. The legacy of McCarthyism and McCarranism remained strong, and the "loss of China" issue still dogged the Democratic Party. So powerful had the China lobby and its Committee of One Million become that, even after the Sino-Soviet split had widened and become well known, Kennedy refused to consider moving toward recognition of the Chinese communist government until after he had been safely reelected.[13]

The humiliating defeat of the American-supported Bay of Pigs invasion of Cuba on April 17, 1961 (according to plans set in motion by the Eisenhower administration), served to strengthen Kennedy's conviction that he had to demonstrate toughness toward communism elsewhere. The most immediate "elsewhere" was Laos, which, in his January 19 briefing of the incoming president, Eisenhower had singled out as the most important front on which to contest communist power. Laos, Eisenhower stated, was the "cork in the bottle," and its loss would be the beginning of the loss of most of the Far East. When Kennedy asked him which he would prefer, "coalition with the Communists to form a government in Laos or intervening through SEATO," the outgoing president pointed to General Marshall's ill-fated effort to follow a coalition policy in China and urged intervention via SEATO or, if that were not feasible, "unilateral intervention on the part of the United States" as "a last desperate effort to save Laos." Eisenhower's secretary of defense, Thomas Gates, assured Kennedy "we could handle the military situation successfully if we did intervene." (It was at this same meeting that Eisenhower advocated U.S. support of "guerrilla operations" in Cuba, even if this involved the United States publicly, and stated that Washington could not let Castro's government go on.)[14]

The Eisenhower administration had already been funding the antineutralist right-wing Lao government it had ensconced in power at a higher per-capita level of U.S. economic aid than that received by any other country. Moreover, there was no effective internal military organization to which American military power could be effectively linked. With this flabby, immensely corrupt, narrow-based regime in Laos in the process of collapse even as he took office, Kennedy came perilously close to ordering American combat units to intervene there, and might well have done so had not the Joint Chiefs of Staff, themselves hesitant about such a venture, advised him that the effort could not achieve success without at least sixty thousand troops and permission to use atomic weapons if Chinese forces intervened. A force of that size, Kennedy found, could not be constituted "without taking troops from the defense of Europe where the crisis over Berlin was becoming increasingly acute." In what his military aide described as "stunned silence," he discovered that the U.S. strategic reserve was so low that if as few as ten thousand men were deployed from it, there would be practically no such forces left to meet other contingencies. Kennedy's disposition to send a large combat force into Laos was probably dealt the *coup de grâce* in the Bay of Pigs disaster in mid-April, in which he had made the mistake of relying on confident assurances from the sort of activists who were urging military intervention in Laos.[15]

From the legacy of Eisenhower's Laotian policies and his own initial disposition to continue them, Kennedy was rescued—temporarily at least—by a Cambodian initiative, soon supported by Britain and the Soviet Union, for a negotiated settlement among the communists, neutralists, and American-supported military that were contending for power in Laos. A cease-fire among them was announced May 3, 1961, but from then on and throughout the thirteen months of negotiations that followed, it was evident that the only compromise with any chance of success was one wherein the procommunist Pathet Lao and the neutralist faction were given positions reasonably commensurate with their actual power. This meant a neutralized Laos, led by a coalition government under a neutralist prime minister, but in which the Pathet Lao shared power.

Given the realities obtaining, an effort at negotiated settlement was clearly the only feasible route, but by taking this course Kennedy opened himself up to the charge of a second defeat (following the Bay of Pigs fiasco) in the face of communist power. For a still-insecure president, who felt Khrushchev looking over one shoulder and Eisenhower the other, this was an uncomfortable situation. He viewed Khrushchev's January 6, 1961, speech in support of wars of national liberation as basically a challenge to the United States rather than primarily a response to Peking's competitive claim to be the natural champion of Third World revolutionaries. In the face of it, Kennedy believed that politically he could not afford a third charge of retreat before communist power. He confided to Walt Rostow that Eisenhower had been able to deflect domestic political criticism for communist success in Vietnam in 1954 by blaming the French, but that he had no such recourse. To this aide and others he made clear that he could not afford the domestic political consequences of a defeat in Vietnam.[16] At the very beginning of his presidency he identified Vietnam as one of the four major crisis areas for the United States, and with the U.S. military much more supportive of intervention there than in Laos, he concluded that it was in Vietnam that he would have to take a strong stand, in the name of preventing new additions to what he perceived as a globally integrated communist camp.

There is no indication that Kennedy considered negotiating a compromise political settlement in Vietnam even during his early months in office, and, once under fire for doing so in Laos, he was even less inclined to take that approach to its neighbor. Apparently none of the senior advisers he brought with him to Washington differed with him, except Chester Bowles, his under secretary of state, whom he fired on Thanksgiving Day 1961, presumably in part because of his attitudes on Southeast Asia. When the Laos agreement began to break down, within less than a year after it was drawn up, any possibility that Kennedy would even explore a negotiated compromise in Vietnam was foreclosed.[17]

Thus, from the early months of his presidency Kennedy sought a military solution in Vietnam, and he soon began to militarize the direct American intervention that Eisenhower had initiated. Militarization, in the sense of American involvement in combat, was incremental, but it was not accidental; despite initial public assurances to the contrary, it was quite calculated. While resisting pressures from the U.S. military and most of his senior civilian advisers for the introduction of American ground combat units into Vietnam, Kennedy apparently had few reservations about having U.S.-piloted helicopters and American military advisers go into combat, and soon ordered this. The Eisenhower administration had been willing to breach the political elements of the Geneva settlement almost as soon as they were agreed to, but had largely abided by its military stipulations, even to the extent of limiting the number of American advisers to the 685 prescribed at Geneva.[18] Kennedy was prepared to scuttle some of Geneva's key military provisions as well, and by the time of his death over sixteen thousand U.S. military advisers were in Vietnam, many assigned to accompany (and sometimes actually to lead) South Vietnamese troops into combat. He might have gone further and introduced ground combat units had Diem been willing to accept this and had the administration not feared, as did Diem, that this might spark a riposte by Hanoi across the seventeenth parallel, with the additional possibility of China's involvement. In any case, by establishing a substantial American military presence in Vietnam, Kennedy took a major step ahead in intervention and, by moving to the level of direct military involvement, commenced a process that narrowed his options and those of his successors.

On January 28, 1961, only a week after his inauguration, Kennedy called a small meeting of his top advisers in his office, to discuss Vietnam. At the urging of Rostow, he had just read a report prepared by General Lansdale ten days earlier, following a two-week trip to Vietnam for the outgoing administration. The president opened the meeting by thanking Lansdale for his memorandum and stating that it "for the first time gave him a sense of the danger and urgency of the problem in Viet-Nam."[19]

Since Lansdale's memorandum had clearly registered forcefully with Kennedy, its main points should be noted. It was a bleak assessment. Nineteen sixty-one would be "a fateful year," and, the way things were going, the Saigon government would probably "be able to do no more than postpone eventual defeat." If the communists won in South Vietnam, "the remainder of Southeast Asia will be easy pickings for our enemy, because the toughest local forces on our side will be gone." It would be "a major blow to U.S. prestige and influence, not only in Asia but throughout the world, since the world believes that [South] Vietnam has remained free only through U.S. help." If it were to remain free, there had to be changes in the U.S. attitude and a new spirit among the Vietnamese. Ambassador Durbrow could no longer see the woods for the trees, and Diem's government believed he had "sympathized strongly with the coup leaders of II November." He should, then, be transferred immediately, to be replaced by an American (Lansdale apparently had himself in mind) "with marked leadership talents" who could "influence Asians through understanding them sympathetically. . . ." Above all, Lansdale stipulated, the new ambassador should be able to work with Diem, who was "still the only Vietnamese with executive ability and the required determination to be an effective President." Diem's opponents, however, believed the United States would look favorably upon their staging a successful coup, and it was important to realize that he had been badly shaken by the mid-November coup attempt and felt that many Americans held him in contempt.

During the January 28 meeting, Lansdale continued to speak in Diem's behalf and against the U.S. embassy in Saigon. Diem, he said, felt confidence in the CIA and MAAG, but believed "there are Americans in the Foreign Service who are very close to those who tried to kill him on November II." It is not clear to what extent Kennedy accepted this extravagant call to sympathize with Diem, but it does appear that Lansdale helped predispose him to question the wisdom of applying heavy pressure on Diem, and to favor replacing Durbrow with an ambassador less likely to do so. The president apparently came very close to appointing Lansdale as Durbrow's replacement, but then backed off in the face of opposition from elements in the State Department and some in the Pentagon, for whom Secretary Robert McNamara was spokesman. Instead, he picked Frederick E. Nolting, a man known for his gentle manner who was prepared to get along cordially with Diem. The new ambassador took over from Durbrow in early May.[20]

Broad support at the January 28 meeting was given to the counterinsurgency plan drafted during the last months of the Eisenhower administration. Introduced by the outgoing assistant secretary of state for the Far East, Graham Parsons, as a plan for reversing the course of events in Vietnam, this called for an outlay of $41.1 million to fund an increase of Diem's armed forces from 150,000 to 170,000 and to improve the quality of his Civil Guard. In response to Kennedy's question whether this would really permit "a shift from the defense to the offense" and whether the situation was not "basically one of politics and morale," Lansdale replied that "a maximum American effort could frustrate a definitive [communist] effort in 1961 and move over into the offensive in 1962." The proposed increment of twenty thousand men, he assured, "could significantly affect the margin in the field for counterguerrilla operations." Two days later the president approved the funds requested for this increase.[21]

During this meeting Kennedy reiterated his desire to mount guerrilla operations inside North Vietnam itself, regarding this as a means of raising the morale of Diem's regime. To his question "How do we get operations in the north; how do we get moving?" came the reply that "the funding problem would be difficult" since "the emergency fund was low," with some $71 million having already been committed to Vietnam and Laos. Evidently that problem was not intractable, for three months later he authorized the dispatch of Vietnamese agents to North Vietnam, and the formation of "networks of resistance, covert bases and teams for sabotage and light harassment" there, with American "civilian air crews" authorized to fly the necessary planes for these operations. At the same time, he authorized an increase of a hundred U.S. regular military personnel and four hundred U.S. Special Forces (Green Berets) in South Vietnam beyond the existing Geneva ceiling. As the January 28 meeting ended, the president bracketed Vietnam together with the Congo, Cuba, and Laos as "the four crisis areas" confronting the United States and called for a "Viet-Nam task force set up like the Cuba task force."[22]

The new president; his personal military adviser, General Maxwell Taylor; and his principal adviser on Vietnam, Walt Rostow, placed much heavier emphasis on counterinsurgency strategy than had the previous administration, and this was to become one of the hallmarks of Kennedy's Vietnam involvement. His early persuasion of its potential significance helps explain the alacrity with which he breached the Geneva ceilings on U.S. military personnel during his first year in office and sent American military advisers into combat with Vietnamese units. No one was more impatient to get the program started than Rostow, who, just two months into the new administration, urged the president to act. "We must somehow bring to bear our unexploited counter-guerrilla assets on the Viet-Nam problem: armed helicopters; other Research and Development possibilities; our Special Forces units. It is somehow wrong to be developing these capabilities but not applying them in a crucially active theater. In Knute Rockne's old phrase, we are not saving them for the Junior Prom."[23]

With Kennedy's enthusiastic support, an enormous crash program was soon under way to train U.S. military personnel for counterinsurgency operations. Its promoters, however, showed little understanding of the social and political forces that nourished these insurgencies, as certainly instanced by the training program for the military advisers who were sent to Southeast Asia. As Paul Kattenburg, for a time head of Kennedy's Vietnam task force, later wrote, the proponents of this counterinsurgency school found it impossible to term those who were opposing Diem "revolutionaries," for that would imply that the United States was promoting counterrevolution. "Accordingly, the United States coined the obfuscating word counterinsurgency, a disingenuous expression conveying the very confusion in which U.S. thinking was floundering." He went on to explain: "The general American perception of the guerrillas in the early sixties was extremely vague and largely erroneous; both among our military and our civilians, particularly those who supervised or managed these operations in Washington. . . . U.S. counterinsurgency did not view the guerrillas as men and women of the villages themselves." Rather, "the guerrillas were viewed as clearly alien and distinct elements, who intruded suddenly and after long forced marches from secure rear bases equipped by China and Russia upon peaceful rice-growing villages which they would then terrorize mercilessly." "Hardly ever," he concludes, "did a U.S. counterinsurgency expert conceive that the guerrillas in Vietnam, for all their misbehavior, could be perceived as champions of national independence, whether or not they were communists."[24]

This program was one that Kennedy needed no persuasion to embark upon, but he was soon under heavy pressure to do considerably more. By early May, failure of the Cuban invasion and his agreement to accept talks on Laos had provoked "Republican criticism which questioned his courage and competence." With Richard Nixon declaring that he must be willing to risk war on a small scale in order to avoid war on a larger scale, and Republican leaders in Congress publicly charging him with defeat in Laos, the new president sought a contrasting and compensating scenario of militancy in Vietnam. His desire to do so was apparently strengthened by the perception of key politicians that the credibility of American power and leadership had suffered during his Geneva summit meeting with Khrushchev at the beginning of June.[25]

Kennedy's disposition to act forcefully was presumably increased by a report by his Vietnam task force submitted at the end of April, to the effect that 58 percent of Vietnam was "under some degree of Communist control, ranging from harassment and night raids to almost complete [Hanoi] administration jurisdiction." Rejecting Chester Bowles's argument that further support to Diem be contingent on his first carrying out badly needed political, administrative, and economic reforms, Kennedy decided to follow Lansdale's advice that support be increased without such conditions.[26]

Though the rapid expansion of American counterinsurgency capacity remained embedded as an important feature of Kennedy's approach to Vietnam, U.S. military leaders consistently argued that the dispatch of Green Berets would be quite insufficient. On May 10, 1961, the JCS formally recommended that "U.S. [regular] forces should be deployed immediately to South Vietnam." Such action, they contended, should be taken "primarily to prevent the Vietnamese from being subjected to the same situation as presently exists in Laos," and that it would, among other things, "provide a visible deterrent to potential North Vietnam and/or Chinese Communist action" and "release Vietnamese forces from advanced and static defense positions to permit their fuller commitment to counterinsurgency actions." They urged that President Diem "be encouraged to request" the immediate dispatch of these American forces.[27]

Kennedy's attraction to this course of action became clear in the new instructions he gave to Vice President Johnson. Already planning to visit Saigon to reassure Diem of U.S. confidence in him as "a man of great stature" and allay his anxiety over the administration's willingness to negotiate a settlement in Laos, Johnson was now also charged with asking Diem whether he wanted American combat troops and a bilateral defense treaty with the United States.[28]

When the vice president raised these suggestions on May 12, Diem proved

unreceptive to either proposal. Ambassador Nolting cabled that Diem had declined U.S. combat troops (except in a case of overt aggression) "for a number
of reasons which seem to us soundly based," and reported the embassy's opposition to a defense treaty. Such an arrangement, Nolting observed, would constitute
a direct violation of the Geneva Agreements, and might provoke the International
Control Commission, set up at Geneva, into withdrawing from Vietnam, "taking
with it such deterrent as it offers against DRV direct aggression." Certainly either
troops or treaty would have constituted a frontal violation of the Geneva Agreements and could be seen as courting the prospect of some North Vietnamese
retaliatory moves. The CIA reported, moreover, that Diem feared that the presence of large American forces would "automatically diminish his power and
independence" and increase the risk of his being ousted. As a Pentagon analyst
concluded, "The larger the American military presence in the country, the more
Diem would have to worry about American ability and temptation to encourage
a coup" if he "incurred American displeasure." If Diem was actually that suspicious, Johnson must be credited with doing a magnificent job of reassurance when
he publicly referred to him as "the Winston Churchill of Southeast Asia." But
the vice president's substantive recommendations to Kennedy on Vietnam were
much more modest than his rhetorical flourishes. He concluded that better man-
agement of the U.S. military aid program and an increase of $50 million in
military and economic assistance would be sufficient to sustain Diem's regime.
American combat troops, he warned, were neither required nor desirable; if
introduced, they would revive anticolonial emotions, to Diem's detriment.[29]

During September, the Kennedy administration received disquieting reports
of sharply mounting insurgent attacks that threatened to overrun most of the
rural Mekong Delta. CIA intelligence estimated that insurgent armed forces had
grown from four thousand in April 1960 to about sixteen thousand, of whom 80
to 90 percent were local recruits and 10 to 20 percent former Vietminh who had
gone north in 1954–55 after the Geneva Conference and had recently infiltrated
back via mountain trails through southern Laos. The CIA had identified no
communist-bloc equipment, the Viet Cong's arms being locally manufactured by
village-level "arsenals" or of U.S. or French origin. But they apparently now had
a new source of modern U.S. equipment; Diem's forces had "lost" over three
thousand small arms "during combat" in 1960. Most alarming, however, was the
level of the attacks; the insurgents were able to mount three during September
in units of over a thousand men, on one occasion briefly capturing a provincial
capital only fifty-five miles from Saigon. Symptomatic of the extent and rapidity
of the deterioration in security was Diem's reconsideration of the offer of a
bilateral defense treaty with the United States, something the Kennedy administration now felt it prudent to avoid. All this precipitated a major reassessment
of policy, which led in mid-November to the first of the administration's two most
important decisions on Vietnam.[30]

On October 5, in the face of these alarming developments, Walt Rostow
proposed placing a U.S.-led twenty-five-thousand-man SEATO border-patrol

force in South Vietnam to guard the Laos frontier and the seventeenth parallel against the infiltration of men and weapons from the North. This, he argued, would release some of Diem's forces "from border patrol to pursuit of the guerrillas within the country"; "provide a restraint on Hanoi," which would understand it could not send its army across the seventeenth parallel "without immediately engaging the U.S."; permit the United States to put pressure on Diem "to organize his military effort more efficiently"; and give Washington "some bargaining position with the Russians for a settlement in Vietnam," leading to "a deal for Diem not unlike the deal which the Russians are trying to negotiate for Ulbricht; that is a de facto recognition that the country is split. . . ."[31]

The JCS quickly demolished the logic of Rostow's proposal, pointing out that, being deployed over several hundred miles, his border force could be attacked piecemeal or bypassed at the Viet Cong's own choice; in any case, it might reduce but "could not stop infiltration of men and material."[32]

Although Kennedy's reaction to Rostow's proposal is not clear, he quickly agreed with its final suggestion that "Generals Taylor and Lansdale take a good, hard look at Viet-Nam on the ground, soon." In a meeting with his advisers on October 11, the president authorized such a mission, to be headed by Taylor and including Rostow representing the White House, Lansdale the JCS and Sterling Cottrell the State Department. Kennedy charged this two-week mission with looking into both the political and the military feasibility of (a) "military intervention" by U.S. combat forces; (b) stationing "fewer combat forces" than under (a) and "with a more limited objective than dealing with the Viet Cong," i.e., merely establishing a U.S. "presence" in Vietnam; and (c) "other alternatives in lieu" of combat forces.[33] At this same meeting Kennedy directed the State Department's William Jorden to draft a White Paper that, in the words of a senior department official, "was to demonstrate wholesale violation of the 1954 Accords by the other side, thus supporting whatever counter-breach of the Accords might emerge in the President's own decisions."

Arriving in Saigon on October 18, just as Diem announced that increasing insurgent pressure necessitated proclamation of a state of emergency, Taylor's mission found Diem nevertheless opposed to the introduction of U.S. combat troops, as long as Hanoi's army did not attack across the border. But Diem did want a bilateral treaty, "a formal commitment by the United States to Vietnam" —something the administration now backed away from—and he wanted substantially increased financial support and equipment to enlarge and strengthen his own forces, as well as American-piloted planes and helicopters, but not U.S. ground combat units.[34]

Taylor's group managed, however, to devise a formula for the introduction of American ground combat troops that they stated was acceptable to Diem. This was a variant of earlier speculations by Lansdale, the JCS, and the head of MAAG, General Lionel C. McGarr, that Diem might be prevailed upon to accept U.S. ground combat forces under the guise of a training mission. The proposal embodying this calculation called for bringing in some eight thousand U.S. troops as a "logistical task force," with the ostensible aim of relieving and repairing extensive flood damage just suffered in areas of the Mekong, which, it so happened, were precisely those of greatest Viet Cong strength. It is not at all clear that Diem—any more than the American public—understood the true nature and implications of the core of the proposal enclosed by this attractive humanitarian offer, but in any case, on balance, the record indicates he was not inclined to accept U.S. ground combat forces—even such a well-camouflaged presence as Taylor proposed.[35]

However Diem may have understood this proposition, it is clear that humanitarian relief was to be the means, not the end. In Taylor's cables to Kennedy en route to Washington and in the full report he submitted on November 3, the long-term combat role of the task force was very prominent. In fact, he spoke of its having "a dual mission, initially help to the flood area and subsequently use in any other area of SVN where its resources can be used effectively to give tangible support in the struggle against the Viet Cong." More specifically, the task force would conduct such combat operations as were necessary for the security of the area in which it was stationed (its area of initial deployment being one of the major Viet Cong base areas) and would act as "an advance party of such additional forces as may be introduced. . . ." Taylor acknowledged that "if the first contingent is not enough to accomplish the necessary results, it will be difficult to resist the pressure to reinforce," and "if the ultimate result sought is the closing of the frontiers and the clean up of the insurgents within South Vietnam, there is no limit to our possible commitment (unless we attack the source in Hanoi)." But he downgraded the possibility that the course he advocated might back the United States into a major Asian war, asserting that North Vietnam was "extremely vulnerable to conventional bombing," a weakness that, he said, should be exploited diplomatically in convincing Hanoi to "lay off" South Vietnam. He concluded that "the introduction of a U.S. military task force without delay offers definitely more advantages than it creates risks and difficulties," even though, as he acknowledged, this would require drawing on forces from the strategic reserve and compensating increases in the fiscal 1963 budget.[36]

In addition to the introduction of these ground combat troops, Taylor recommended that the United States help improve the training and equipment of Diem's Civil Guard and Self-Defense Corps and raise his army's level of mobility by providing "considerably more helicopters and light aviation" and organizing a border ranger force. In supporting these efforts, the United States would supply not only equipment but also "military units and personnel to do those tasks which the Armed Forces of Vietnam cannot perform in time." These would include air reconnaissance, additional airlift, "special intelligence and air-ground support techniques."[37]

To solve the problem of Diem's administrative ineffectiveness and his army's lack of offensive spirit, Taylor and Rostow (who helped him draft this report) had a simple answer: There was to be a shift in the American role in Vietnam, from advice "to limited partnership and working collaboration" with Diem's government. "A U.S. operating presence at many working levels" would be used "for forcing the Vietnamese to get their house in order." The two men showed little understanding of either the political character of Diem's regime or of the dynamics behind the insurgency, and, in the words of the Pentagon historian, their view was "consistent with Rostow's emphasis before and since on the Viet Cong problem as a pretty straightforward case of external aggression." The United States should tell Moscow to "use its influence with Ho Chi Minh to call his dogs off, mind his business, and feed his people." They acknowledged no acceptance of the view already gaining favor among numerous middle-ranking State Department officials that Diem might not be able to overcome the insurgency even if infiltration were largely cut off. In the opinion of these two presidential fact-finders, Hanoi had launched the guerrilla campaign of 1960–61 "because of Diem's increasing success in stabilizing his rule and moving his country forward in the several preceding years."[38]

In sending out his most hawkish advisers, Kennedy presumably expected them to come up with hawkish recommendations, and that is clearly what he got. But this was not the only advice he received; indeed, he was fortunate in obtaining a much broader range of options from his advisers than Lyndon Johnson ever would. Though the JCS, McGeorge Bundy, Robert McNamara, and William P. Bundy had initially taken positions that appeared to be generally consistent with the Taylor-Rostow recommendations, a number of other senior civilian advisers expressed very different views. Dean Rusk argued against sending in ground forces to support Diem and, warning that the United States should not make a "major commitment [of] American prestige to a losing horse," urged that special attention be given to the question of Diem's willingness to take the measures necessary "to give us something worth supporting." George Ball (then under secretary of state for economic affairs), Chester Bowles, Averell Harriman (who was then ambassador at large and was about to become assistant secretary in charge of Far Eastern affairs), and Kennedy's confidant, John Kenneth Galbraith (ambassador to India) all opposed sending in combat forces and staking American prestige on Diem, of whose regime they were heavily critical. Bowles had for several months urged the neutralization of South Vietnam as part of a belt including Laos, Cambodia, Thailand, Burma, and Malaya. Harriman, in a personal memorandum to Kennedy of November 11, proposed a negotiated settlement "built on the foundation of the 1954 Geneva Accords." He suggested that if the ICC or "some substitute mechanism for observation and enforcement" could be "strengthened and modernized," the United States "might be prepared to adhere to the Accords as revised." Such a revision would allow for the temporary division of Vietnam, during which there would be a cessation of hostilities, with trade and economic relations between North and South, and "eventual reunification [would] be sought only through peaceful means," which would not preclude "a restudy of the possibility of elections. . . ." Harriman warned that the best any international settlement could do would be to buy time and that, if Diem's regime continued to be "repressive, dictatorial and unpopular," South Vietnam would not long remain independent. There is no way of knowing whether Harriman was aware how strikingly close in several respects his prescription was to that being advanced by the NLF. Whatever the case, the president clearly read Harriman's memorandum before making his mid-November decision on Vietnam policy.[39]

It was soon evident that Kennedy had decided against both negotiations and the dispatch of ground combat forces. On November 11, probably at his urging, McNamara and Rusk jointly produced a memorandum recommending the sort of middle-range course that, after hearing the spectrum of advice from his advisers, he had decided on. The decision Kennedy made, which was to describe the broad outlines of American policy for almost two years, was essentially the one outlined in this Rusk-McNamara memorandum. The only major item excluded from Kennedy's final policy was a statement committing the United States to the objective of preventing the fall of South Vietnam to communism. The new set of policies, as embodied in a National Security Council meeting of November 15 and an NSC action memorandum signed November 22, was headed "First Phase of Vietnam Program," which, of course, left open the possibility that the president might at a later stage move on to a threshold of deeper intervention, involving the introduction of ground combat units as urged by Taylor and his supporters. But such forces were never sent during Kennedy's period in office.[40]

Although it did not go as far as Taylor's report had urged, this major decision did nevertheless substantially escalate America's intervention in Vietnam. In a memorandum to Rusk and McNamara of November 14, the day before the NSC meeting that was to discuss and formally endorse his new policies, the president, in exactly the same words as (and evidently borrowing from) Rostow's critique of negotiations submitted to him earlier on the 14th, explained his opposition to exploring a negotiated settlement and Harriman's proposal in particular.

> If we postpone action in Vietnam to engage in talks with the Communists, we can surely count on a major crisis of nerve in Viet-Nam and throughout Southeast Asia. The image of U.S. unwillingness to confront Communism —induced by the Laos performance—will be regarded as definitely confirmed. There will be panic and disarray. . . . If we negotiate now—while infiltration continues—we shall in fact be judged weaker than in Laos; for in that case we at least first insisted on a cease-fire.

The "gut issue," the president asserted, "is not whether Diem is or is not a good ruler," but whether the United States would "continue to accept the systematic infiltration of men from outside and the operation from outside of a guerrilla war against him. . . ." For Kennedy to define the situation in this way, of course, undercut the possibility of any realistic basis for a negotiated solution. And his announcement that the United States would itself now breach the Geneva Agree-

ments further reduced that possibility. He was "mindful of the danger of escalation and war," but asserted—again using Rostow's wording—that the United
States would show strength and determination and that when it had done so
before elsewhere in the world it had "come home free."[41]

In the decision Kennedy finally reached on November 15, three things stand
out. He turned his back on the route toward a negotiated settlement; he refused
to sanction the sending of U.S. ground combat forces to Vietnam, even if he had
not closed the door on the possibility of such action later; and he was unwilling
to make the clear-cut commitment to prevent the fall of South Vietnam to
communism that the JCS and most of his civilian advisers had expected. He
avoided this commitment even though McNamara and Rusk had advised that
such a loss would "destroy SEATO," "undermine the credibility of American
commitments elsewhere," and "stimulate bitter domestic controversies in the
United States and would be seized upon to divide the country and harass the
Administration."[42] By holding back from this commitment, he avoided becoming
completely locked in and saved some room for maneuver.

But apart from the dispatch of ground combat elements, Kennedy provided
for the other main military components in Taylor's package—funding to maintain increased levels of South Vietnamese armed forces, their equipment and
training; and substantial increments in the number of U.S. military advisers,
military technicians, and American-piloted helicopters and transport and reconnaissance planes, along with their maintenance personnel.

The administration assumed that this major rise in support would provide leverage for getting Diem to introduce the reforms regarded as necessary
to strengthen his faltering regime. Thus, it stipulated: "A crucial element in
USG[overnment] willingness to move forward is concrete demonstration by
Diem that he is now prepared to work in an orderly way on his subordinates and
broaden the political base of his regime." But Diem would not have this. When
Ambassador Nolting sought to extract the *quid pro quo* the administration expected for its enhanced support, Diem argued that Taylor's proposal for an
administrative partnership would weaken his leadership and give Vietnamese
communists "a monopoly on nationalism." American expectations that he would
broaden his government and introduce reforms were also rebuffed. To open up
his government was, he said, "putting the cart before the horse; security had to
come first." As for social and political reforms, he insisted, as he had earlier in
the year, that this would also have to await the prior establishment of full security
and that the answer to the insurgency was essentially military, not political.[43] This
view, it should be noted, was consistent with that held by some U.S. civilian and
most military officials in Vietnam, including General Paul Harkins, now appointed by Kennedy to head the enlarged MAAG mission and a newly established U.S. Military Assistance Command, Vietnam (MACV). Moreover, the
administration's public-relations effort to enlist the support of its allies and the
American public for its expanding intervention in Vietnam could only reinforce
Diem's assumption that Washington's commitment to his regime was so strong

that it could not easily renege on its promises of increased financial and military support.

Release in early December of the administration's long-aborning White Paper, *A Threat to the Peace: North Viet-Nam's Effort to Conquer South Viet-Nam,* describing the insurgency's central dynamic as an intrusion from outside the South manipulated from Hanoi rather than a southern-based reaction to Diem's repression, was meant to serve as a rationale for U.S. intervention. At the same time, however, it helped reinforce Diem's argument that reform in the South was unnecessary, since the insurgency was activated from outside. Consequently, as David Halberstam described it, the Diem regime "became more convinced than ever that it had its ally in a corner, that it could do anything it wanted, that continued support would be guaranteed because of the Communist threat and that after the commitment was made, the United States could not suddenly admit it had made a vast mistake." Both Nolting and Harkins were convinced that Diem was the only possible instrument for American policy, and that to press for reforms would be self-defeating. At the beginning of June 1962, Washington abandoned its hope to induce Diem to make any significant improvements in his governance, and instructed the American mission in Saigon "to get along with President Ngo Dinh Diem's regime, come hell or high water and forget about political reforms." That prescription would continue to characterize the Kennedy administration's approach for a full year more.[44]

On December 11, 1961, there arrived in Saigon the first contingent of the augmented U.S. military support Kennedy had approved—two army helicopter companies, with pilots and maintenance crews, numbering some four hundred men. They were on schedule, despite Diem's failure to provide any *quid pro quo* by way of administrative reorganization or reforms. This set an enduring precedent. The helicopters were soon followed by the establishment of MACV and a rapid influx of U.S. military advisers. By the end of 1961, MAAG strength alone had reached 2,067, nearly three times the level authorized by the Geneva Agreements, and by April 1962 it stood at thirty-four hundred. By the end of 1962 there were over eleven thousand U.S. military personnel in Vietnam.[45]

Faced with the palpable breach of the Geneva Agreements represented by the arrival of the U.S. helicopter companies, the ICC mission met to discuss whether there was any point in trying to continue with its assignment of monitoring the accords. Some six months later, on June 2, 1962, while concluding that fundamental provisions of the Geneva Agreements had been violated by both parties, the ICC pointed out that the establishment of MACV "as well as the introduction of a large number of U.S. military personnel beyond the stated strength of the MAAG (Military Assistance Advisory Group), amounts to a factual military alliance" (prohibited under Article 19 of the agreement).[46]

These well-armed U.S. helicopter companies, and more that soon followed, first of all provided Diem's troops with a new mobility, enabling them to leapfrog and surround NLF military detachments. They—along with American copilots, who were officially supposed to be training Vietnamese to fly American fixed-wing aircraft on strafing and bombing runs—also increasingly participated directly in combat against the Viet Cong. As early as March 1962 such involvement during training missions had become so commonplace that CINCPAC (Commander in Chief Pacific), noting that the State Department "waffles and evades," urged that General Harkins be permitted to acknowledge publicly that "on some of these training sorties, the aircraft deliver ordnance on actual Viet Cong targets." During 1962 this practice became widespread, and as a consequence an enormous amount of American-directed firepower was loosed against the Viet Cong. In addition, Kennedy authorized air-delivered napalm (ignited jellied gasoline that burns deep into the flesh) and herbicidal defoliation, the only limitation on their use being that Vietnamese pilots were supposed to be at the controls when these substances were employed.[47]

All this combined to change the character of the war drastically for the forces of the NLF. Pushed off balance, they were, through much of 1962, unable to cope effectively with the awesome helicopters and even more terrifying napalm. Roger Hilsman, initially Kennedy's director of intelligence in the State Department and then his assistant secretary of state for the Far East, has described the "fantastic mobility" the helicopters gave the ARVN and their impact on the NLF's troops. "Roaring in over the treetops, they were a terrifying sight to the superstitious Viet Cong peasants," who in the first months "simply turned and ran—and, flushed from their foxholes and hiding places, and running in the open, they were easy targets." General Harkins joined Diem and Nhu in his enthusiasm for the effectiveness of napalm, and, when asked about its political consequences where villages were hit, responded that it "really puts the fear of God into the Viet Cong . . . and that is what counts." The Kennedy administration assumed the tide of battle had turned decisively against the insurgents, and it was lulled into an optimism that lasted until the beginning of 1963.[48]

Another major element in the new U.S.-Saigon strategy, the highly touted strategic hamlet program, was considerably less successful, though initially it was not so perceived. The effort was embraced with particular fervor by Kennedy's counterinsurgency enthusiasts, who saw it as "the principal operational vehicle" by which that doctrine "was to be translated into reality." Inspired by British success in combating insurgency in Malaya through large-scale agrarian resettlement, the program evidenced little appreciation of the very different political and social conditions in Vietnam. During 1962 and 1963 American officials gave heavy support to this solution, described by McNamara as "the backbone of President Diem's program for countering subversion directed against his state."[49]

In theory, strategic hamlets were to protect and insulate the peasantry from the NLF militarily, economically, and politically, thereby denying its forces manpower, food, and intelligence. In accordance with the Malayan model, the peasant was to be compensated for the discomfort of forced relocation through an extensive array of social services, fertilizer, and other agricultural support. In practice, however, the strategic hamlets were an only slightly modified form of Diem's badly discredited agrovilles. Though its units were smaller than agrovilles and enclosed peasants in barbed-wire, semifortified agglomerations that were usually less distant from their fields, the system displayed most of the same characteristics. Many peasant households—sometimes whole villages—were uprooted from their land and permitted access to it or newly assigned fields only between curfews. The many peasants who were forced to move had to tear down their houses and rebuild them with the old materials within the new compounds, receiving scant assistance from the government to compensate them for their considerable losses. Usually few or none of the promised social services ever materialized, and a large part of the funds—originating from U.S. sources—that were supposed to provide for them clung to the pockets of Diem's officials. By concentrating the peasantry, the system could much more easily impose compliance with forced-labor regulations, regarded by Diem as an effective means of taxation. Indeed, Diem and his brother Nhu, who ran the program, appeared more interested in developing control of the peasantry than in winning its support against the NLF.[50]

Understandably, most of the peasants dragooned into the strategic hamlet program bitterly resented it and were further alienated from Diem's government. The first U.S. operation in support of the program, in March 1962, should have indicated to American policymakers (as it did to some U.S. officials on the scene) how ineffective it was likely to be in combating the NLF. Only seventy out of 205 families scattered through half a dozen settlements could be persuaded to volunteer for resettlement; the remaining 135 were herded forcibly from their homes into the new concentration. It was then discovered that, out of the 205 families, there were only 120 males of an age to bear arms, "indicating very clearly that a large number had gone over to the VC [Viet Cong]." As David Halberstam concluded, "the strategic hamlet program . . . never separated the guerrillas from their source of greatest strength: young men."[51]

Although some U.S. officials in the field soon appreciated that most strategic hamlets were ineffective in insulating peasants either militarily or politically from the Viet Cong, the officially received wisdom in both the upper reaches of the U.S. mission and in Washington was that, on balance, the program was a success—and a validation of the administration's counterinsurgency policy. Despite persistent local criticism of Nhu's handling of it, American support for the program continued. As early as September 1962, Nhu claimed—with considerable exaggeration—that 3,225 of 11,316 projected strategic hamlets, incorporating 33 percent (4,322,034) of South Vietnam's population, had been completed; at the end of June 1963, it was claimed that the program had been extended to embrace 7,205 hamlets and two-thirds of the populace. The seemingly steady progress on this front contributed to the Kennedy administration's sense that the situation in Vietnam was under control and improving.[52]

· · ·

What was clearly not under control was the administration's relationship with the American press, and particularly some of the U.S. correspondents in Vietnam. During most of 1962 and 1963, much of their reporting was discordant with the administration's apparent complacency over the military and political situation and its efforts to disguise the combat roles of U.S. military advisers and pilots. The reporters, perceiving the many weaknesses, repression, and rampant corruption of Diem's regime, refused to "get on the team" and mute their criticism. As a consequence, their relations with some American officials became as tense and antagonistic as with Diem's. "The root of the problem," John Mecklin, public-affairs officer in the U.S. embassy, later wrote, "was the fact that much of what the newsmen took to be lies was exactly what the Mission believed, and was reporting to Washington." Though this was partly true, there were certainly instances of conscious deception by some officials, undertaken to meet their own and/or Washington's prejudices and expectations, and it was this that produced the bitterest disputes. Diem's expulsion of François Sully of *Newsweek,* one of the most seasoned and knowledgeable correspondents, was hardly displeasing to the embassy. The president's own exasperation with negative reporting was exposed in late 1962 in his clumsy effort to silence David Halberstam by trying—unsuccessfully—to get *The New York Times* to recall him. The administration's representations to NBC, however, proved more effective, and the head of the Pentagon's public-affairs office was able to assure Kennedy that the network had been persuaded that it would be "against the interest of the United States" to show its coverage of "rough treatment by South Vietnamese soldiers to Viet-Cong prisoners, with a United States Army captain appearing in the sequence." NBC's news director undertook to withhold this film's scheduled appearance on the Huntley-Brinkley show, and to keep it on the shelf so far as any other programs were concerned.[53]

If any event should have shattered the administration's complacency and induced it to give greater credence to the correspondents and less to the reporting of MACV and its Saigon embassy, it was the battle of Ap Bac in the Mekong Delta in early January 1963. There, only fifty miles from Saigon, a Viet Cong battalion was surrounded by an ARVN force more than four times its size, equipped with armored personnel carriers and artillery, and supported by U.S. planes and helicopters. After losing sixty-one dead, of whom three were American advisers, and over a hundred wounded, with five American helicopters shot down and nine more damaged, Saigon's forces broke off the engagement and opened up a large hole so that the enemy battalion could withdraw. The correspondents' regard for MACV's probity was hardly enhanced when, in a press conference, General Harkins described the battle as "a victory" for Saigon because "we took the objective"—a piece of territory from which the enemy had departed twenty-seven hours before. And certainly their skepticism was not assuaged when, two weeks after the battle, President Kennedy indicated in his State of the Union address that the military struggle in Vietnam was going favorably, or when McNamara echoed this two weeks later before the House Armed Services Committee. As Chester Cooper observed, Ap Bac seemed for the administration to be nothing more than "an embarrassing trough in an upward-moving curve of government progress." After all, the strategic hamlet program was a centerpiece of Kennedy's Vietnam strategy, and its rapid expansion was continuing. Throughout the first half of 1963, Harkins, upon whom McNamara so heavily relied, continued to report successes for Diem's campaign against the Viet Cong, frequently about as far from reality as his assessment of Ap Bac. Prepared to accept the reports that Diem and ARVN officers made, and intolerant of the conflicting information that a significant minority of U.S. military advisers provided, Harkins and MACV in general were so convinced that the tide of battle was flowing inexorably against the Viet Cong that in mid-January 1963 they initiated a plan for gradually phasing out the American military presence in Vietnam, though this was first to be expanded by a further 35 percent, to a total of 16,732 men, on October 31. The JCS approved the plan on March 6, and two months later, following McNamara's endorsement, directed that "As a matter of urgency a plan for the withdrawal of about 1,000 U.S. troops before the end of the year should be developed based upon the assumption that the progress of the counterinsurgency campaign would warrant such a move."[54]

In the face of this planning and the Pentagon's acceptance of Harkins's Alice-in-Wonderland reporting, it is perhaps understandable that Secretary Rusk assured the American public on March 8 that the struggle against the NLF was "turning an important corner" and that Saigon's forces "clearly have the initiative in most areas of the country." More difficult to understand, especially in view of Ambassador Nolting's current, if very much belated, disenchantment with Diem's progress on other fronts, was the secretary's speech of April 22, in which he spoke of a "steady movement [in South Vietnam] toward a constitutional system resting upon popular consent."[55]

But despite this public posture of complacent optimism, internal reports told a different story of U.S. officials' relations with Diem. The rapid build-up in American military and civil advisory strength had already begun to alarm Diem and Nhu, and they did not welcome the increase by over one-third in U.S. military personnel that MAAG and Washington projected by October. Diem found it particularly galling that the additional thousands of these Americans were expected to hold the same "privileged semi-diplomatic status" that obtained when there were only a few hundred. It was not merely the rapid increase in the size of the U.S. presence but also the impatient assertiveness of many of its members that alarmed him. This quality was later nicely depicted by a U.S. marine officer with considerable experience in Vietnam. Referring to the relationship of U.S. advisers and the ARVN, he wrote, "The U.S. 'arrogance of power' was manifested in an attitude which as much as said, 'Get out of the way, I'd rather do it myself.' "[56]

The CIA reported that by mid-April 1963 "a considerable amount of tension had developed between the Government of Vietnam and the U.S. Government," with both Diem and Nhu concerned about "recent 'infringements' of Vietnamese sovereignty." The report cited MAAG as "a violator" in this, but singled out the U.S. Special Forces as "the main irritant." It also warned that "Diem is allowing additional time for further blunders and, after building a strong case, he plans to confront Ambassador Nolting and US MACV chief General Harkins with irrefutable evidence of U.S. responsibility, demanding a reduction in the number of U.S. personnel in South Vietnam on the basis that the force is too large and unmanageable."[57]

This dispute had become the most salient in a range of differences causing increasing acrimony between Washington and Diem. More than anything else, Diem's insistence that the number of U.S. military advisers be reduced—not increased, as the Americans were planning—appears to have been the precipitating factor in changing the balance of opinion regarding Diem within the U.S. embassy. The shift taking place within the Saigon mission was unmistakable in Nolting's cable to Washington of April 6, where there was little trace of his previous acquiescent indulgence of Diem. He reported that Diem was now repudiating the concept of an "expanded and deepened U.S. advisory effort, civil and military," and using this as a basis for rejecting the counterinsurgency fund agreed to in December 1961 on the Taylor report's recommendation. The ambassador acknowledged that the "number and zeal" of some American advisers had reached a point where there were in fact similarities with the "protectorate situation" that Diem alleged had developed. Nevertheless, he argued that "without [a] massive advisory effort" progress would not have occurred, and that progress could not be maintained if drastic reductions were now made in their numbers, especially "in [the] provinces and with smaller military formations . . . precisely the areas" where Diem found them most objectionable. Nolting also reported that "there is grave risk that [the] strategic hamlet program will founder" because of Diem's refusal to grant it more than one-third of the local currency generated by the U.S. Commodity Import Program that was supposed to be assigned for that purpose.[58]

In the face of all this intransigence, the ambassador reported that he saw no alternative but to take actions "designed to convince Diem that we mean business." To get this message across, he suggested "we would quietly hold up approval of military budget support level and any new allocations of funds." But he saw risks in such action: (a) it might lead to retaliatory action by Diem and a "descending spiral" of relations; and (b) it "might light [a] coup fuse." The ambassador warned: "We continue to have no grounds to believe that coup would bring to power a government more likely to win the war than Diem. On contrary, we think a coup, either accomplished or abortive, would weaken chances of preserving independence of SVN."

Although there is no indication that either Kennedy or senior U.S. officials were as yet considering promoting a coup, they were always aware of the possibility that elements in the armed forces might repeat their November 1960 effort.[59] For their part, convinced that this effort had had the backing of some Americans and at least the sympathy of the ambassador, Diem and Nhu remained alert for indications that the U.S. mission, as well as their own military officers, might consider another attempt. Diem—who continued to insist that he first approve all major troop movements—saw repeated American efforts to improve the ARVN's effectiveness by giving its commanders greater freedom from his meddling as undercutting a system of control vital for his protection against another coup attempt. In fact, the U.S. military strongly opposed any move against Diem, but he himself did not know that.

Undoubtedly Nolting's April 6 report sharply increased the Kennedy administration's concern over Vietnam. The near metamorphosis in the attitude of the ambassador, who had been one of Diem's most ardent and sympathetic champions, inevitably crystallized the mounting criticism within the administration regarding the United States' increasingly assertive Vietnamese protégé.

VI

The Overthrow of Diem

During the early months of 1963, with an agreement—however fragile—reached on a Laotian cease-fire and neutralization, and with the Cuban missile crisis and Berlin confrontation now behind him, President Kennedy had more opportunity to focus on Vietnam. Any reluctance to confront the issue was presumably overcome by the arresting report he received from Mike Mansfield, majority leader in the Senate, who was highly respected in Congress for his knowledge of Asia. Mansfield, at Kennedy's request, had led three other senators on a trip to Vietnam in December 1962, and after talking privately with the president on his return, he released their report to the public in late February. Had Kennedy been disposed to change course in Vietnam, he could have used this well-publicized assessment as a foundation upon which to build a new policy.[1]

The senators warned that the struggle there was fast becoming an "American war" that could not be justified by existing U.S. security interests in the area. Observing that in Vietnam "all the current difficulties existed in 1955," but that seven years and "$2 billion of U.S. aid later . . . substantially the same difficulties remain, if indeed, they have not been compounded," their report found Diem's regime "less, not more, stable, than it was at the outset" and "more removed from, rather than closer to, the achievement of popularly responsible and responsive government." The intensification of American support to Diem's government already threatened to render the conflict with the NLF "of greater concern and greater responsibility to the United States than it is to the Government and people of South Vietnam." Pursuit of this course "could involve an expenditure of American lives and resources on a scale which would bear little relationship to the interest of the United States or, indeed, to the interests of the people of Vietnam." What further effort might be needed for the survival of South Vietnam had to come from the Saigon government and its people, they argued, and if it was not forthcoming, "the United States can reduce its commitment or abandon it entirely. . . ."

The door Mansfield and his three Senate colleagues opened let in a blast of genuinely fresh air, but for Kennedy it was politically chilling. According to the account of Kenneth O'Donnell, one of Kennedy's closest confidants, who was present in the spring of 1963 during a follow-up discussion with Mansfield, the president stated that he had been having serious second thoughts about the senator's argument and now agreed on the need for a complete military withdrawal from Vietnam. "But," Kennedy cautioned, "I can't do it until 1965—after I'm reelected." O'Donnell states that "President Kennedy felt, and Mansfield agreed with him, that if he announced a total withdrawal of American military personnel from Vietnam before the 1964 election, there would be a wild conservative outcry against returning him to the Presidency for a second term." This domestic political rationale was strikingly similar to the one that underlay Kennedy's reluctance to move toward recognition of the communist government of China. He could scarcely forget the very narrow margin by which he had defeated Nixon, and may well have wondered whether he would have been successful had he not been as hawkishly anticommunist as his rival. After Mansfield had left, the president said, "If I tried to pull out completely now from Vietnam we would have another Joe McCarthy red scare on our hands, but I can do it after I'm reelected. So we had better make damned sure that I *am* reelected."[2]

Kennedy may have believed that, everything else being roughly equal in Vietnam two years hence, a potentially strengthened domestic political base would have permitted disengagement. But was there any real likelihood that the situation in Vietnam would have been that similar? During the remaining seven months before he died, Kennedy deepened American military and political intervention in Vietnam. If he had kept to his central objective of sustaining a separate, anticommunist South Vietnamese state, could he have succeeded without further Americanization of the war? Given the direction and momentum of his policies as of November 1963, is it more than wishful thinking to assume that the situation in Vietnam and the extent of American involvement there would have been significantly different for him at the end of January 1965 from the way it was for Lyndon Johnson when, on that date, he emerged with his own electoral mandate? The evidence available from Kennedy's Vietnam record suggests that the circumstances would probably have been about the same.

If Kennedy had been looking for a face-saving and domestically defensible way out of Vietnam, Diem and Nhu presented it to him during the summer of 1963 with their attacks on the Buddhists. The American news media gave extensive coverage to the viciousness and stunning political gaucherie that marked this campaign, presenting to the American public a clear-cut issue of heavy religious persecution. Considerable sectors of American opinion that previously had been apathetic about any negative reporting on the Diem regime were now outraged. Suddenly public criticism of America's Vietnamese ward crystallized, providing Kennedy with an avenue for disengagement that risked considerably less domestic political damage than ever before. But the president ignored the opportunity and chose instead to respond by dramatically escalating American political involvement in a way designed at least to sustain the existing level of military intervention and ensure a more effective prosecution of the war. More specifically, rather than letting the public outrage at the actions of Diem and Nhu serve as a plausible excuse for disengaging the U.S. from Vietnam, he chose to continue on the same road by replacing these leaders with others, whom he hoped would prove more amenable to American tutelage and more effective in fighting the insurgents. This second major decision by Kennedy on Vietnam locked the United States even more firmly on its course, and willed a deepened involvement to a successor served by the same advisers he had chosen—men unlikely to change that course because to a considerable degree their reputations had come to ride on the Vietnam policies they and Kennedy had jointly fashioned.

Constituting a large majority of South Vietnam's people, the Buddhists inevitably resented being ruled by a Catholic minority that accounted for no more than a tenth of the population. The widespread belief among officials that at least nominal conversion to Catholicism was a requirement for advancement fueled this resentment. The situation had generated an increasing self-consciousness among many southern Buddhists, and during the late 1950s and early 1960s there was a consequent revitalization and expansion of their monastic and lay organizations. The largest and best-organized of these was the General Association of Buddhists of Vietnam. Under Thich* Thien Khiet, its president and superior bonze, and Mai Tho Truyen, secretary general of its lay membership, this organization emerged as the generally acknowledged spokesman for the interests of the majority of some five thousand pagodas and the Buddhist lay groups in the South. In the first months of 1963 the association still seemed to reflect the low-posture societal stance of the Theravada (Hinayana) branch of Buddhism dominant in the Mekong Delta, with its emphasis on personal salvation, rather than the greater concern with service to society in the Mahayana variant dominant in Hué and the northern provinces of South Vietnam as well as among those Buddhists from north of the seventeenth parallel who had moved south after Geneva. The harsh and provocative actions of Diem's government during mid-1963, however, led to a shift in the Buddhist leadership. Mahayana monks progressively assumed prominent positions—clerical and lay—in a Buddhist community whose political consciousness had been aroused as never before in the twentieth century. The Buddhists could no longer remain politically quiescent, in the face of the arrogant, inept, and ultimately brutal repression against them ordered by Diem's brothers Ngo Dinh Nhu and Ngo Dinh Can. (By September, Nhu had grown so powerful that State Department intelligence regarded him as exercising "an overriding and immutable influence on Diem"—a somewhat exaggerated characterization, but nevertheless close to the truth.[3])

The initial provocation came at the celebration of Buddha's birthday on May 8 in Hué, when provincial officials were ordered to enforce an old ban, heretofore largely ignored, on the display of religious flags. (The incident closely followed ceremonies honoring another of Diem's brothers, Ngo Dinh Thuc, archbishop of

---

*"Thich" is an honorific for Buddhist monks, akin to "reverend."

Hué, during which Vatican flags had been prominently flown.) Disregarding the
ban, the local Buddhists raised their flags and held a scheduled mass meeting in
commemoration of Buddha's birth. When local officials were unable to disperse
the crowd, the Catholic deputy province chief ordered his troops to fire. Nine
people, including children, were killed, and others injured. Rather than taking
action to remedy the situation, Diem insisted the carnage had been caused by a
Viet Cong hand grenade, and refused to retreat from that assertion even when
films were produced showing government troops firing on the crowd.[4]

The symbolism of discrimination and repression provided by this incident
radicalized the Buddhists and propelled less moderate monks into positions of
leadership. It marked the beginning of a period of increased political importance
for them and their followers that was to endure until their savage repression by
Nguyen Cao Ky's government three years later. It also exacerbated the tensions,
bitterness, and distrust between the Kennedy administration and the Saigon
regime. During the summer of 1963 the burgeoning and heavily reported Buddhist
crisis shattered American public illusions about Diem, which had been nourished
over the previous eight years by the Eisenhower and Kennedy administrations.
As a consequence, there was a sharp increase in the U.S. domestic political price
that Kennedy had to pay for his support of Diem.[5]

Over ten thousand people participated in a protest demonstration in Hué on
May 10. This was followed by a manifesto of monks demanding legal equality with
the Catholic Church, an end to arrests, greater freedom to practice their faith,
and indemnification of the families of victims of the May 8 shootings. In the face
of the Buddhist challenge, Diem remained obdurate. Many politically active
Buddhists were charged with being communist agents and jailed, as were a
number of leaders from the increasingly supportive urban student groups. The
June 11 self-immolation of a monk, Thich Quang Duc, in protest against Diem's
intransigence focused a spotlight of shocked American and international concern
on the regime's treatment of the Buddhists. Rising American pressure finally led
Diem to sign an agreement with Thich Thien Khiet on June 16, rescinding laws
that discriminated in favor of Catholics against Buddhists, and promising to end
special privileges to the Catholic Church and harassment and arbitrary police
activity against the Buddhists.[6]

Diem's government, however, took little more than token measures to implement this agreement, and continued its persecution and arrests. Diem accepted
the explanation given by the Nhus that the Buddhist problem was basically
created by NLF agents—a conclusion directly contrary to that reached by American intelligence. As State Department intelligence reported, Diem "consistently
held that the entire crisis was provoked for personal or political gain" by a
"Communist-influenced" leadership. He remained, according to this report,
"greatly influenced by Ngo Dinh Nhu and Madame Nhu who in effect have
become the principal architects and spokesmen of policy on this issue," with the
Diem family "confident that it could eventually discredit the Buddhist leadership
and reduce the protest movement to minimal proportions."[7] Madame Nhu pub-

licly ridiculed the further suicides of Buddhist monks by burning as "barbecues," a statement widely disseminated by the American news media.

In the succeeding weeks, the gap between the Buddhists and the Diem regime widened, with thousands of middle-class university and high-school students rallying to the Buddhist side and much of the urban population regarding the monks as welcome symbols of opposition to a widely hated family government. All this encouraged restive army officers to speculate seriously about mounting a coup. On July 4 Kennedy was informed by Assistant Secretary of State Roger Hilsman that, no matter what Diem did, "there will be coup attempts against him over the next four months." On July 10 a U.S. Special National Intelligence Estimate concluded that, if Diem did nothing more to implement his June 16 agreement with Thich Thien Khiet, there was a great likelihood of more Buddhist demonstrations, with the possibility of a noncommunist coup attempt "better than even." A regime brought to power by such a coup might be initially less effective against the Viet Cong, but, "given continued support from the US, could provide reasonably effective leadership for the government and the war effort." It is not clear to what extent this line of thinking was shared by some CIA agents and U.S. military advisers in close contact with senior ARVN officers, but on July 11, Ngo Dinh Nhu, aware that elements in the military were discussing coup prospects, called in senior generals to frighten them out of any such move by warning them about the efficiency of his own anticoup intelligence.[8]

By this time, even American officials such as General Harkins who were still convinced that there was no alternative to keeping Diem in power had begun to conclude that Nhu, his wife, and Archbishop Can should be forced out of the government, if not out of Vietnam. Though Nolting himself now shared this view, Kennedy and a number of his advisers had already concluded that the ambassador would have to be replaced by someone who could be counted on to carry out a tougher policy toward Diem, one calculated to ensure better cooperation from him on the military front and move him to compromise sufficiently with the Buddhists to reduce the threats to internal political stability. Though Harkins and other senior military officials still assured Kennedy that the war against the NLF's forces was going well, it was generally agreed that political events within the Saigon-controlled areas could easily undermine that effort. Moreover, if heavy U.S. pressure were to be applied on Diem, the president apparently wanted to make certain that this did not lead to a political backlash from the Republican Party. Under these circumstances and with the future of South Vietnam less predictable than ever, it made sense to appoint, as his new ambassador, Henry Cabot Lodge, an eminent Republican who had been Nixon's running mate in 1960 and whose party connections now were useful at a time when Vietnam was beginning to emerge as an important national issue.[9]

On June 27 Kennedy announced that Lodge would replace Nolting as ambassador in September, but the continuing adverse developments in Vietnam caused him to take the post earlier, as soon as he completed a course in counterinsurgency. It is not clear whether, as Nolting was inclined to believe, before Lodge departed for Saigon Kennedy "entrusted him with the mission of disentangling the United States from Diem," for no record of the discussions between the two is available. But certainly Lodge's actions from the outset of his stewardship in Saigon suggest that the president had indeed urged him to be much tougher with Diem than Nolting ever had been, and at least to try to rid Diem and South Vietnam of the Nhus unless they moderated their attitude toward the Buddhists. On his arrival, according to CIA head John McCone, the new ambassador gave "the clear impression that he was under instructions from President Kennedy and that unless Diem got rid of his brother, Nhu, and made a complete reversal in the way the government was being run, Lodge should use his influence to bring about a change in the top leadership." Subsequent cables between Kennedy and Lodge indicate that the new ambassador had no reason to feel he could not count on strong presidential backing or that he was being kept on a short leash.[10]

On August 14, eight days before Lodge's arrival in Saigon, Nolting had returned for a last meeting with Diem where, in what he described as "tough talk," he got him to promise an end to repression against the Buddhists and publicly to repudiate Madame Nhu's denunciation of them. Diem, however, failed to follow through on either pledge. Indeed, the U.S. intelligence community acknowledged that American pressures on Diem to moderate his anti-Buddhist stance had further antagonized him and the Nhus, and sharpened their "uneasiness about the extent of the U.S. involvement in South Vietnam." Observing that they already believed that "the extensive US presence" in South Vietnam was "setting in motion political forces which could eventually threaten Diem's political primacy," this intelligence report concluded that the Ngo family bitterly resented U.S. interference in their dispute with the Buddhists and may well have felt the demonstrations "were at least indirectly due to the U.S. presence." Consequently, American intelligence expected that Diem would further pressure the United States to reduce its presence.[11]

In assessing the extent of his leverage, Diem was possibly encouraged by Kennedy's July 17 news conference, in which he emphasized his unqualified determination that the United States remain in Vietnam: "We are not going to withdraw from that effort [maintenance of South Vietnam's national independence]. In my opinion, for us to withdraw from that effort would mean a collapse not only of South Vietnam, but Southeast Asia. So we are going to stay there." There is no indication here of making American support contingent upon Diem's "assurances as to the standards of performance . . . in undertaking needed reforms," such as Eisenhower stipulated in offering Diem support in October 1954. Though Eisenhower's administration had not in fact insisted that this condition be fulfilled, Kennedy might have been able to deal with Diem and Nhu somewhat more effectively if he had introduced such a caveat into his public statements and cited his predecessor with approval in the process, thus undercutting potential Republican attacks. By not even hinting at any condition, he undoubtedly reinforced Diem's assumption that he himself was indispensable to Kennedy's stated Southeast Asian objectives.[12]

There could have been no more blatant repudiation of Diem's promise to Nolting to end the Buddhist repression than the violent actions unleashed by order of Ngo Dinh Nhu on the night of August 21. Diem's praetorian guard, the U.S.-trained and funded Special Forces, together with the combat police, invaded and ransacked pagodas in Saigon, Hué, and other cities throughout South Vietnam, forcefully ousting the monks and arresting 1,420 of them. The assaults were often brutal; several monks were killed and some thirty injured. Outrage at this action was not limited to Diem's opponents in South Vietnam. The foreign minister, Vu Van Mau, the ambassador to Washington, and the observer at the U.N. (the latter two Madame Nhu's father and mother) resigned in protest. The Kennedy administration was stunned. Believing for several days, as Nhu encouraged it to, that the army (rather than just the Special Forces and police) had carried out the raid, it was alarmed as to the continued reliability of "the predominantly Buddhist composition of the armed forces" if further Buddhist suicides or demonstrations were attempted.[13] The "downward spiral" that Nolting had seen as the alternative to a coup appeared to be well under way.

Coup planning had in fact been in train for some two months, evidently encouraged by the ongoing soundings of American agents intent on learning its nature and prospects.[14] But, despite a growing awareness among the military that popular support for the Buddhists and American criticism of Diem's government were both increasing, the surveillance of Nhu's far-reaching Can Lao intelligence apparatus was effective enough to deter most dissident officers from making moves that risked his suspicion and retribution. Because of Diem's long-established policy of divide-and-rule in the armed forces, its leaders lacked the coherence necessary to allow effective coordination in planning a coup. Many officers feared that a colleague bent on discussing coup possibilities with them might be a double agent or a stalking horse for Nhu.

One plot, identified by American intelligence as early as the end of June, was led by Dr. Tran Kim Tuyen, Diem's disaffected national intelligence chief, and enlisted support from Colonel Do Mau, director of the Military Security Service, Colonel Pham Ngoc Thao and some junior army officers and members of the Secret Police. By July 8, Lieutenant General Tran Van Don had reportedly informed a CIA agent in Saigon that there was support for a coup among all but a couple of generals. Though such an assessment exaggerated the degree of even tentative commitment at this point among the senior officers, the extent of disaffection among them was sufficiently widespread to provoke Nhu to give them a warning on July 11. His threats appear to have been effective in temporarily intimidating almost all the dissident officer corps except Colonel Do Mau and Lieutenant Colonel Pham Ngoc Thao, neither of whom the senior officers trusted. (The flamboyant Colonel Thao—once a Vietminh battalion commander, subsequently unusually effective in containing the NLF in his province, and at this time inspector of the strategic hamlet program for all South Vietnam—was regarded by some officers as possibly a double or triple agent, with ties to the United States and possibly to Nhu and the communists as well.) Their prospects were, however, much reduced when Nhu's suspicions led him to oust Dr. Tuyen from his pivotal intelligence position and send him off to the insignificant position of consul general in Cairo.[15]

Some of the ten senior generals who successfully proposed a declaration of martial law to Diem and Nhu on August 20 may well have seen this move as helping to prepare the ground for a coup. Their ostensible purpose was to empower the army to force several thousand monks to leave Saigon and return to their own provinces. While arguing that martial law would reduce tensions in the capital, a proposition to which Diem readily subscribed, some of them may have intended at the same time—under the provisions of this military code—to establish the scope and conditions for their own, more effective interaction in organizing a coup. Whether or not Nhu appreciated this, he apparently quickly perceived that martial law provided an opportunity both to crush the Buddhists and to discredit the army leadership in a way bound to undermine popular support for any coup effort they might mount.[16]

Since martial law had been imposed the previous day, it was easy for Nhu on August 21 to make the army, rather than his police and Special Forces (many of whom were clad in regular army uniforms), appear responsible for launching the pagoda raids. Moreover, the brutality of the crackdown led to such consternation and confusion in Saigon that General Ton That Dinh, a senior officer upon whom Diem relied, could easily push through martial-law regulations in his critically pivotal Third Corps command (embracing Saigon), with a vigor that threw coup planning more off balance.[17]

It appears likely that Nhu and Diem would have been able to handle dissidence within the armed forces and the generally heightened popular disaffection had the pagoda raids not further intensified the antagonism of both Buddhist army officers and U.S. officials toward their regime. But Nhu and Diem's advantage was temporary, for the raids soon drove dissident officers and U.S. officials closer together.

Realizing the threat posed by this emerging alignment, Nhu embarked upon a dramatically new course that, whatever his calculations, ensured that the alliance would be cemented and the combined opposition to him and Diem all the greater. A rapprochement with both the NLF and Hanoi was the possibility that Nhu now opened up. Initially this appears to have been pursued discreetly, but by mid-September, in American eyes, he was discussing the prospect brazenly.[18] Assiduous efforts over some eight years under the Freedom of Information Act have been of no avail in securing declassification of the many existing internal documents that could shed more light on this affair. It is consequently difficult to ascertain whether Nhu was simply attempting to gain new leverage on the Kennedy administration—which seems likely to have been the case at first—or whether he seriously intended to see through the defiantly independent course of action indicated by his calculated leaks to American officials. Continued classification of these documents also makes it hard to gauge whether or not some of the American officials most hostile to Nhu and Diem exaggerated or misrepresented Nhu's actions in this matter in order to press their case with Kennedy that the Diem regime should be ousted. Whatever Nhu's intention, his assertion of independence seems to have provided him with psychological compensation for his keen resentment at what he and Diem viewed as increasingly arrogant and harassing pressure from American officials to act in accordance with their prescriptions. In making what appears likely to have been an ultimately serious effort at accommodation with his communist enemies, Nhu perhaps understood the relevance of the currents of domestic American politics less well than his brother, or possibly his anger had simply pressed him past the limits of caution. After the many statements from Kennedy and his colleagues about South Vietnam's importance in containing the spread of communist power, their domestic political opponents could have seized on reports of Nhu's intentions to make the administration look hopelessly incompetent. Even if Nhu's plans were not actually executed, greater publicity regarding them could have provided Kennedy's critics with highly embarrassing ammunition. In any case, there is little doubt that Nhu's stratagem increased the administration's resolve to oust him and his equally controversial wife.

Although it is plausible to assume that initially Nhu's talk of discussions with the NLF and Hanoi was designed simply to secure leverage with the United States, he may have concluded, when U.S. hostility toward him had clearly risen to a new level, that his only way to survive would be through an accommodation with these Vietnamese opponents. Such an assessment would undoubtedly have been strengthened once the United States began to withdraw critical elements of support from the Diem regime, especially its funding of the Commodity Import Program and of Nhu's own private army. But to this day it is unclear how far Nhu would actually have gone toward a rapprochement, and the extent to which Diem was willing to back him. A CIA intelligence memorandum, prepared more than two years after their death, took note of the allegations that Nhu had certain channels to the NLF, stating that he himself acknowledged them but had asserted they were simply a means of keeping tabs on the enemy, and concluded that "speculation that hostility between the U.S. and the Diem regime was prompting Diem and Nhu to consider a deal with the North has never been proven." Later, however, Lucien Conein, who had been the key CIA agent in Vietnam, stated that in early 1963 Nhu had told him that "he was dealing with the people of North Vietnam, negotiating behind the backs of his own generals. If he told this to me, the Generals knew of this also and they considered this as a danger because what in the devil were they fighting for if the Central government was negotiating behind their backs."[19] Long after the event, Diem's vice president, Nguyen Ngoc Tho, was still unsure of Diem and Nhu's aims, stating:

> The real reason why the Diem regime looked for some political compromise
> was that it had lost the people's support by its dictatorial oppression and

was under strong pressure from the United States. In a word, Diem tried to negotiate with the enemy to counterbalance the U.S. pressure, or else he made the appearance of doing so in order to worry the United States.[20]

Two men with very different perspectives—Paul Kattenburg, head of the Kennedy administration's Vietnam interdepartmental working group in 1963, and Gene Gregory, then editor of the Diem-supported *Times of Vietnam* and possibly Nhu's closest American confidant—believe that, in suggesting a rapprochement, Nhu's calculation was simply to develop leverage with the United States. On the other hand, General Tran Van Don, a principal leader of the group that ultimately toppled Diem, states, "Nhu was really serious about contact with Hanoi and had some talks with intermediaries envisaging two coexisting but cooperative regimes: a Communist North and a non-Communist South."[21]

On the basis of their research, both Geoffrey Warner and Georges Chaffard concluded that Nhu was serious at least in exploring possibilities for a cease-fire. In April 1963, Roger Lalouette, the French ambassador to Saigon, learned that Nhu was advising Diem to establish secret contacts with the NLF. Such steps were taken through intermediaries, and, via Lalouette and Mieczyslaw Maneli, Polish delegate to the ICC, contact was also made with Hanoi. Apparently Nhu believed that, once Diem ordered American military advisers to withdraw, Hanoi would respect South Vietnam's neutrality. There were reports that, as a guarantee of his goodwill, Nhu was prepared to send two of his children to reside in Hanoi for a year.[22]

Chaffard cites Ho Chi Minh's interview with a left-wing Australian journalist, Wilfred Burchett, broadcast in mid-August 1963, as indicative of Hanoi's interest in a negotiated settlement. With the withdrawal of the foreign interventionists, Ho stated, a cease-fire could be negotiated between Diem's forces and those of the NLF; but this could not be a trick to permit the Saigon dictatorship to consolidate its position and would serve to create the conditions "permitting the people to elect freely and democratically a government of their choice. Between that government and that of the DRV, agreements could be negotiated." Nhu's essential objective, Chaffard states, was to obtain Hanoi's neutrality toward affairs in the South. He had never lost faith in the strategic hamlet program, and, according to Chaffard, believed that a crash effort to expand it could so cut the population off from the NLF and strengthen the government's political control over the countryside that Diem would be in a position to risk an election in which the NLF would compete.[23]

Nhu's flirtation with the Vietnamese communists, serious or not, caused American officials enough concern so they listened to even the most radical arguments for ousting him and Diem. At the end of August, Roger Hilsman argued for ousting both brothers, and against the Pentagon's plea that one final effort be made to persuade Diem to get rid of Nhu. Observing that Diem and Nhu had previously demonstrated a capacity for "irrational acts," Hilsman took the position that "they were now facing a truly desperate situation—the end of their regime and perhaps the end of their family." If the United States now presented Diem with an ultimatum to drop Nhu, the brothers "might institute a blood bath of both Vietnamese and Americans. Diem and Nhu might even appeal to Communist North Vietnam to intervene with their divisions." Dean Rusk shared Hilsman's concern that the Diem regime might respond to "a real sanction, such as a threatened withdrawal of our support," by calling for Hanoi's assistance in expelling the Americans. It is impossible to determine whether Hilsman's lurid scenario was more widely shared within the administration. But even if it were not, Nhu's contacts with the NLF and Hanoi appear to have been sufficiently palpable to some U.S. officials to steel their resolve that he, and perhaps Diem, should be forced out.[24]

Aware of American fears of a Nhu-Diem accommodation with the enemy, Saigon's generals concluded that Washington was all the more likely to support a move to oust them. Thus, when Major General Nguyen Khanh approached the CIA on August 25, requesting some indication of the U.S. position should a coup occur, he presented as his rationale the likely imminence of an accommodation between Nhu and the communists.[25]

On August 23, two days after the pagoda raids, Major General Tran Van Don, whom Diem had just appointed commander of the ARVN, had a long discussion with Lucien Conein, a friend of many years' standing. Since Don had just been named to an important new position, Conein may well have taken the initiative in arranging the meeting. This also appears likely from the way he posed his questions. Conein's fourteen-page cabled report of their extensive discussion, which reached Washington on the morning of August 24, probably helped crystallize the thinking of a number of officials in Washington.[26] The revealing account also contradicts some of the interpretations of events, especially regarding the army's innocence in the crackdown on the Buddhists, that the generals subsequently presented to American officials.

Certainly Don's account undermines subsequent claims that he and some of his military colleagues had been the champions of the Buddhists and their student supporters. In talking with Conein, he made clear that the pagoda raids had been in line with the advice he and the other nine generals had given Diem when they met with him on the 20th and proposed the introduction of martial law in order to force many of the monks back to the provinces. Don deplored the brutality with which the raids had been conducted, claiming not to have known that the police and Special Forces would attack. But while criticizing the U.S. "Voice of America" for implicating the army in the raids, he conceded that in fact the army had been deeply involved. Army reinforcements had been brought into Saigon to occupy "strategic points" there only hours before the raids were launched, and, according to Conein, Don was "very proud of the fact that the generals had been able to maintain secrecy prior to initiation of this operation." He had worried about the ability of some of the Buddhists to activate crowds and said "the generals feared that if the Buddhist leaders assembled a large enough crowd they could order a march toward Gia Long Palace and the army would not stop them." With 1,420 monks now under detention, Don wanted to carry out "his original plan to screen all the bonzes and return them to their provinces and pagodas." The previous midnight (August 22), he and Generals Ton That Dinh and Tran Thien Khiem had gone to Nhu to recommend that all schools in Saigon be closed, because they had information there would be student demonstrations beginning August 23. Nhu, he said, had concurred, but was overridden by Diem. (Demonstrations by large numbers of university and secondary students protesting incarceration of the monks did in fact commence on that date and resulted in massive arrests.)

It is evident from Don's answers that the CIA agent kept probing concerning coup prospects. He reported that Don "acknowledged that within the military there was no one who could replace Diem," that he did not want a civilian exile brought in to replace him, and that he preferred Diem to Nhu. It would be "practically impossible," he said, to oust the Nhus while leaving Diem, because of Diem's reliance on and attachment to them. Although Diem did not always follow Nhu's advice, he depended on him as his "thinker" as well as adviser, and Madame Nhu served as his "platonic wife." Don explained that Diem never had sexual relations with any woman, but that toward him Madame Nhu was "charming, talks to him, relieves his tension, argues with him, needles him and, like a Vietnamese wife, she is dominant in the household." She used her privileged position with the president "to make him say yes when he wants to say no."

As to coup prospects, Don indicated to Conein that the declaration of martial law was a first phase, but that the secret of future phases was not his to tell. He claimed that, except for some of the younger officers, who criticized him for the action against the Buddhists, he had the support of the generals. Conein received the impression, however, that Don was "not the man behind the whole thing," only "the figurehead" responsible for the first phase.

In response to Conein's more specific questions, Don asserted that General Nguyen Khanh was "100% with him"—certainly a considerable exaggeration— and, more plausibly, that he also had the support of Generals Duong Van Minh, Tran Van Minh, Do Cao Tri, Tran Thien Khiem, and Le Van Kim. With regard to the chain of command in Saigon and its surroundings, he explained that, although General Ton That Dinh was military governor of Saigon/Cholon, he had no authority over the Special Forces, led by Colonel Le Quang Tung (whose "guts" Don hated), who executed only orders coming from Diem or Nhu.

Conein concluded, "It seems Don himself feels he does not have the power of enough influence over the generals to overthrow the president." It was his strong impression that "General Don is not completely aware of everything that is going on around him. . . . He appears not to know what to do next. He is completely controlled by events and reacts rather than plans next moves."[27]

On the same day that Conein saw Don, Major General Le Van Kim told Rufus Phillips, assistant director of USOM (the embassy's economic arm) in charge of its Rural Affairs program, that the United States must make a maximum effort to separate the Nhus from Diem and get the Nhus out of the country. If the United States would take a clear stand against the couple and support army action to remove Nhu from the government, the army (with the exception of Colonel Tung) could be expected to support such action and be able to carry it through. A similar American stand with the army against the Nhus was urged on Phillips the next morning by Nguyen Dinh Thuan, Diem's secretary of state. Conceding that it would be difficult to split the Nhus from Diem, he nevertheless felt that the United States should attempt this. The United States had to exercise leadership and be very firm; otherwise chaos was likely to result. Under no circumstances should it acquiesce in what the Nhus had done.[28]

Reports of these contacts with Don, Kim, and Thuan, of course, went to Washington as well as to Lodge, who did not arrive in Saigon until August 22. When Washington apparently queried him regarding coup prospects, the ambassador's initial response was negative. He cabled that, in view of the loyalty to Diem of troop commanders in the Saigon area and the absence of cohesive military opposition to the regime, American support for a coup attempt would be "a shot in the dark."[29]

If, as Conein reported, General Don did not know "what to do next," he and a number of other key generals were soon left in no doubt as to the Kennedy administration's prescriptions. The State Department's instructions, endorsed by the president, were cabled to Lodge on August 24[30] with the request that their central points be conveyed to the generals. Those points should have increased the willingness of the most hesitant of these officers to act. Constituting the opening salvo in the administration's frontal assault to bring down the Diem regime, these instructions gave Lodge a wide latitude for action, which, despite subsequent spasmodic urgings of caution, was never rescinded.

After acknowledging that Nhu had maneuvered himself into a commanding position, they read: "U.S. Government cannot tolerate situation in which power lies in Nhu's hands." Diem was to be given a chance to rid himself of Nhu and his coterie and replace them with the "best military and political personalities available"; but if he remained "obdurate and refuses, then we must face possibility that Diem himself cannot be preserved." The ambassador was instructed to tell "key military leaders" that the United States would find it impossible to continue support of the South Vietnamese government "militarily and economically" unless action was immediately taken to redress earlier moves against the Buddhists, a step "which we recognize requires removal of Nhus from the scene." Further encouragement for the military to take action was provided in the authority given Lodge to "tell appropriate military commanders we will give them direct support in any interim period of breakdown [of the] central government mechanism." As an initial signal of support, the "Voice of America" was to broadcast a statement removing the taint on the generals left by the pagoda raids and placing the blame squarely on Nhu. But initiatives were not to depend on the generals alone. Concurrently, Lodge and his team were instructed to "urgently examine all possible alternative leadership and make detailed plans as to how we might bring about Diem's replacement if this should become necessary."[31]

The ambassador promptly endorsed these instructions, but asked that they be modified so as to forgo any approach to Diem: any chance of his meeting the demands would be nil, and to approach him would be to alert Nhu and give him, with his control of combat troops in the Saigon area, the opportunity to thwart American plans for action by the dissident generals. "Therefore," Lodge urged, "propose we go straight to the Generals with our demands without informing Diem. We would tell them we [are] prepared to have Diem without Nhu but it is in effect up to them whether to keep him."[32] This willingness to give the generals leave to oust Diem as well as Nhu gives credence to the conclusion subsequently reached by a senior embassy official that "Lodge never made any real effort to split Nhu from Diem and that he arrived on the scene with the opinion, which he managed to obscure from most of us, that the only solution to the political problems of Vietnam was to get rid of Diem."

Although Lodge informed Washington that Harkins concurred in his message, when the general learned of this he reported that Lodge had "volunteered" his agreement. Nothing in the available record contradicts Harkins's subsequent claim that, though he supported ousting the Nhus, he never agreed to the removal of Diem. His belief that it was possible to eliminate the Nhus without at the same time removing Diem from power represented a difference in view not confined to the U.S. mission. It quickly surfaced in Washington as well, where it became clear that McNamara, Taylor, and John McCone held views similar to Harkins's and believed that they should have been more fully and directly consulted in the drafting of instructions as important as those contained in the August 24 cable. The generals in Saigon soon sensed the existence of such a cleavage. Already distrustful of Harkins, apparently because of his personal intervention to dissuade Diem's top aide, Nguyen Dinh Thuan, from resigning in protest over repression of the Buddhists, they now concluded that either he or the CIA's station chief, John Richardson, had alerted Nhu to the revived coup planning.[33]

Initially, however, several of the antiregime military leaders were encouraged by what Lodge conveyed to them of his new instructions from Washington. The Pham Ngoc Thao–Do Mau group, enrolling the backing of a significant number of junior officers, but apparently able to count on the initial support of only a few marine battalions and some other small units stationed in Saigon, planned to move during the last week of August. According to a subsequent CIA report, they "came close to precipitating a coup" and "might have succeeded if their plans had not alarmed and been overtaken" by a larger group beginning to form under the leadership of Lieutenant General Duong Van Minh. Presumably one of Conein's most difficult tasks was to convince Pham Ngoc Thao's group to abandon their separate course and work with, and subordinate to, General Minh's organization, a goal attained only on August 30.[34]

An apparently more promising effort, and one evidently more favored by American officials, was headed by Major General Nguyen Khanh, commander of II Corps (the Second Corps area), with its southern border some eighty miles north of Saigon.* On August 25 he was in the capital asking an American agent what position the United States would take if a coup were mounted to forestall a move by Nhu to arrive at an accommodation with Hanoi. Having thus moved out in front, Khanh was naturally one of the two generals CIA agents contacted the following day, when Lodge asked them to convey Washington's instructions to other "appropriate military commanders." The other general selected for this purpose was Tran Thien Khiem, chief of staff of the Joint General Staff, an official who, like Don, Kim, and Minh—and in contrast to Khanh—had no direct command of any troops. However, Khiem too appears to have already embarked on some discreet coup planning and, like Khanh, had already been in touch with CIA agents.[35]

After receiving an almost verbatim account from Conein of Washington's new instructions to Lodge, Khiem passed them on to a group of generals led by Lieutenant General Duong Van Minh, military adviser to Diem and the ranking senior officer, then reported back that the generals were in accord with these points and had agreed that a coup would take place within one week. Khiem was said to recognize (presumably on being queried by Conein) that before a coup could be launched, it would be necessary to neutralize Generals Cao and Dinh, respectively commanders of the IV and III Corps, as well as Colonel Tung, commander of the Saigon-based Special Forces. He told Conein that Minh was under surveillance and should not be contacted by U.S. agents, and that Don approved of the plot but was too exposed to risk participation. General Le Van Kim, subsequently regarded as "the brains" behind this coup group, was said to be in charge of planning for a provisional government that would emerge with Minh as president.[36]

Concurrently, the CIA was making contact with General Khanh at his headquarters in Pleiku through another agent, a move of which Conein apprised Khiem.[37] It is understandable that Khanh was sought out: as one of the four corps commanders, he had direct command of a sizable body of combat troops. To get them from his base in II Corps to Saigon, however, he would have to pass through III Corps territory, commanded by General Ton That Dinh, an officer regarded as staunchly loyal to Diem. It is not clear whether or not Khanh had liaison with the Pham Ngoc Thao–Do Mau group. Initially he did keep in contact with General Don, whom he regarded as having close ties with American officials.

Khanh states that in the period preceding a coup planned for the end of August, the CIA assigned a liaison officer to stay with him in his headquarters. He says that shortly before the coup was scheduled, Don informed him that the plan was off and came up to Pleiku to explain that someone had tipped off Nhu regarding its imminence and that the latter was prepared for it. (Don, subsequently Khanh's bitter rival, has confirmed this account.) Like Don and others

*A map showing the location of II Corps will be found on page 402.

in Minh's group, Khanh believed that either Harkins or Richardson, or both, had alerted Nhu to the plans.[38]

It is not clear how much Nhu actually knew of the coup preparations, but the generals' resolve was further undercut by apparent U.S. indecisiveness. The same "Voice of America" broadcast in the Vietnamese language that asserted that Nhu's secret police and Special Forces, not the generals, were responsible for the pagoda raids, had mistakenly reported that "the U.S. may sharply reduce its aid to Vietnam unless President Diem gets rid of secret police officials responsible for the attacks." For the dissident generals, this was tangible evidence that the United States meant to encourage them and publicly distance itself from the Diem regime. Lodge, who was within a few hours of presenting his credentials to Diem, was furious. He pointed out that the threat to cut aid might trigger a violent reaction from Nhu, and he insisted the "Voice" broadcast a State Department denial of any decision to cut aid. This retraction came as a very cold shower to the temporarily elated generals and, as Hilsman acknowledges, confirmed "their natural inclination to proceed very, very slowly, if at all. . . ."[39]

Thus, at the very time that McNamara, Taylor, and McCone were beginning to express new doubts as to the wisdom of encouraging a coup that risked ousting Diem as well as the Nhus, the leading generals themselves were also becoming more cautious about participating in one. The generals knew that it was impossible to separate the Nhus from Diem, and that Diem would never acquiesce in the Nhus' removal. Indeed, most of them feared that even if, through some reversal of perceived reality, Diem yielded to pressures to oust the Nhus, his vindictiveness would be remorseless toward the generals who had supported this action. Moreover, they now knew that Nhu was aware of their plans for a major coup attempt.[40]

Growing doubt and uncertainty in Washington and Saigon precipitated a top-level conference on the evening of August 27 between Kennedy and his senior advisers.[41] Although important sections of the account of this meeting have been withheld, enough has been declassified to illuminate the views of several of the participants and some of the advice the president was getting.

The seriousness with which the situation was regarded is indicated by Rusk's suggestion, in opening the session, that "for the immediate future it might be necessary to have daily meetings with the President and carry on an exercise comparable to that done by the NSC Executive Committee for Cuba." He then asked William Colby, identified as "the Vietnam expert from CIA," for a report. Colby stated "that [name sanitized, but clearly designating Conein] had interviewed two Vietnamese generals yesterday. One general said the situation for a coup was favorable and forecast that one would take place within a week. The second general gave what was described as a jumpy answer [sanitized]. . . . Secretary Rusk commented that Lodge hasn't come to grips with the problem of Vietnam in his talks with Diem and Nhu. He may be waiting to see what the Vietnamese generals are going to do. . . ."

Nolting, having just yielded place to Lodge as ambassador, now did most of the talking, making statements supportive of those unwilling to risk ousting Diem in the process of removing the Nhus. He said, "The Vietnamese generals haven't the guts of Diem or Nhu. They will not be a unified group but will be badly split. They do not have real leadership and they do not control the predominant military force in the country." Following a sanitized paragraph, the report continues: "In response to the President's question as to why the peasants were not upset by Diem's attack on the Buddhists," he replied that "the Buddhists were not organized as a religion as we have in the West. The Buddhist church in Vietnam is not a real force." When Kennedy asked "whether Diem had ever explained to us why he had not kept his promises to us," Nolting defended him, saying that he had tried to keep his promises but just hadn't made the necessary effort to carry them out.

Later in the discussion Rusk

> suggested that the group turn its attention to a list of contingencies which might face us in Vietnam. He listed two. What would our position be if some generals attempted a coup and were defeated by Diem? [Four lines sanitized.] Ambassador Nolting replied that military support for a coup did not exist. There might be such support if the U.S. said that the Vietnamese must get rid of Diem and Nhu. A larger number of generals would rally to a coup aimed at ousting Nhu. Most of the generals would be reluctant to oust Diem. Diem and Nhu were Siamese twins who could not be forced apart. If the generals move against Nhu, Diem would go down with him in the palace, or, if he escaped, return to Saigon to resist the rebel generals. Or Diem might quit the fight and leave the country. . . . It would be impossible to engineer a separation of the two men—the only possible way would be to persuade Diem to send Nhu abroad. Ambassador Nolting recalled that the circle had nearly been completed in a three-year period. Ambassador Durbrow had told Diem three years ago that Nhu must go. Diem refused to accept the suggestion and Durbrow was removed from Vietnam. (The President recognized the irony of this situation by smiling.) Ambassador Nolting said we should not fight the internal situation in Vietnam too hard. . . .

Kennedy then asked whether Nolting agreed that Diem's actions during the last few months would prevent him from carrying forward the war against the communists. He replied that

> we should take it slow and easy over the next several weeks. It is possible that the brutal surgical operation [i.e., against the Buddhists] may succeed as Diem and Nhu have predicted. We will take our lumps because of the actions of Diem and Nhu, but if they succeed, we will have preserved a base for the fight against the Viet Cong. If the smouldering resentment of the Vietnamese people grows and begins to show up in the Vietnamese military units to such an extent that the war effort is blocked, then we have an

entirely different problem of creating an acceptable political base. [One and a half pages deleted.]

Rusk was clearly not fully persuaded by Nolting's argument and concluded that "we should make clear to our officials in Saigon that we are not changing their existing directive [i.e., as contained in the August 24 cable] on which they had already proceeded to take numerous actions." [Final four lines deleted.] This was evidently in line with Kennedy's view, for he did not order the directive changed.

Unsure as to how firmly the U.S. government supported a coup, General Minh told Conein that the generals would remain cautious until they had clear evidence that the United States would not betray them. Minh insisted on a "token of U.S. determination to support the coup group" and urged that this be a severance of economic aid. As an immediate earnest of U.S. support, Lodge had Rufus Phillips of USOM confirm to General Le Van Kim that, in his talks with Minh, Conein was indeed speaking for the ambassador. Lodge then authorized the local CIA to assist in the tactical planning for a coup. The agency promptly provided the coup leaders with "sensitive information including a detailed plan and an armaments inventory for Camp Longthanh, a secret installation of the loyalist Special Forces commanded by Col. Le Quang Tung." Lodge appealed to Washington for authority to do more: "We are launched on a course," he cabled, "from which there is no respectable turning back: the overthrow of the Diem government. . . . U.S. prestige is already publicly committed to this end in large measure and will become more so as the facts leak out. . . . There is no possibility, in my view, that the war can be won under a Diem administration." Though Harkins, Lodge acknowledged, still believed that he should ask Diem to get rid of the Nhus before the generals' action got underway, he himself was convinced that such a course had no chance of success, would be regarded by the generals as "a sign of American indecision and delay," and was too risky. The American role, Lodge emphasized, was essential: "The chance of bringing off a Generals' coup depends on them to some extent; but it depends at least as much on us. . . . We should proceed to make all-out effort to get Generals to move promptly." This, he said, required that the administration order Harkins to repeat personally to the generals the prescriptions contained in the August 24 cable, previously relayed to them by Conein and other CIA officers. In Lodge's opinion, this would establish their authenticity (and would, presumably, at the same time dispel the generals' belief that Harkins opposed a coup). He argued that if after this the generals were still unsure of Washington's commitment and insisted on a public statement that all U.S. aid to Vietnam through Diem was going to be stopped, this should be done, but on the express understanding that their coup would start at the same time.[42]

Kennedy promptly met Lodge's request. The president was evidently banking on a coup, yet on the same day sent a strictly private message to Lodge pledging his support but urging him to disengage should prospects for the coup's success become poor. "We will do all that we can to help you conclude this operation successfully," he cabled, but cautioned—perhaps with the Bay of Pigs fiasco in mind—"I know from experience that failure is more destructive than an appearance of indecision. . . . When we go we must go to win, but it will be better to change our minds than fail."[43]

In view of the uncertain balance of forces in the Saigon area at this time, a coup attempt might easily have failed unless the United States was prepared to provide sufficient back-up. To ensure that the coup forces would prevail, Roger Hilsman argued that the administration had to stand ready to provide it. He outlined measures to be taken in order to meet various contingencies. Not only should the United States be ready to send in its forces if the coup attempt precipitated physical pressure by Diem's government against American personnel and their dependents in Vietnam. It should, if necessary, carry out "military measures to prevent any loyalist forces outside Saigon from rallying to Diem's support," such as interdicting transportation by blowing up bridges. It should if needed help the coup group "capture and remove promptly from Vietnam any members of the Ngo family outside Saigon, including Can and Thuc who are normally in Hué." Diem and the Nhus were to surrender unconditionally. If captured alive, they were to be banished abroad, but Diem was to be treated "as the generals wish." If the coup forces did not initially prevail, and hostilities in Saigon continued, "we should bring in U.S. combat forces to assist the coup group to achieve victory."[44]

The continuing refusal of U.S. government agencies to yield to Freedom of Information Act requests to declassify the pertinent documents makes it impossible to determine how the president reacted to Hilsman's recommendations, especially whether he envisaged the use of U.S. combat troops if they were necessary to ensure that the coup group prevailed against forces loyal to Diem. Whatever the case, Kennedy was clearly concerned about the dangers to which Americans, especially those in the capital, might be exposed. He secretly ordered marines sent in from Okinawa to be positioned offshore from Saigon for use in evacuating the several thousand American civilians and military dependents if the coup provoked heavy fighting or retaliatory actions against U.S. personnel. Even if these forces had gone ashore with the limited mission of protecting American lives, their mere presence would undoubtedly have exerted an influence on the way fence-sitting generals would jump. And in the face of fighting between opposing South Vietnamese military elements, it might have proved very difficult for the marines to have protected and removed Americans without being caught up in combat with forces loyal to Diem.[45]

When Harkins, in conformity with Kennedy's instructions, talked with General Khiem a day after receiving them, it was too late. Misgivings regarding the extent and firmness of U.S. backing, and fear that Nhu had been alerted to the imminence of a coup, had led some of the conspirators to hesitate, and undermined the cohesion necessary to risk action when the balance of military forces was still uncertain. Central to all calculations regarding that balance was the stance of General Ton That Dinh, military commander of the Third Corps area, which included Saigon. Given the certainty that the Special Forces battalions of Colonel Le Quang Tung would defend Nhu as well as Diem, it was vital that Dinh and his substantial command at least be neutralized. Trusted by Diem and presumed to be loyal to him, Dinh was assessed by the U.S. military as an aggressive but impetuous and unpredictable commander.[46] He had left both American and Vietnamese plotters uncertain as to the way he would lean once the chips were down. For all these reasons, General Minh and his key supporters decided to call off the coup.

The sudden and clearly unexpected collapse of the coup left American policy in disarray. Lodge appears to have lost his assurance as to what should be done. Except for granting political asylum in his embassy to three monks— including Tri Quang, a Buddhist political leader for whom he had great regard —he immediately pulled in his horns. He now retreated to a policy of semi-accommodation with Nhu, a stance that disregarded the latter's undoubted knowledge of American complicity in the aborted coup and his now fully crystallized conviction that the United States was intent on removing him. On August 31 the ambassador cabled Washington the marvelously unrealistic proposal that an arrangement be worked out calling not only for Nhu's wife and brother Archbishop Thuc to leave the country but also for Nhu's functions to be limited entirely to running the strategic hamlet program, while Diem would be expected to liberate the incarcerated students and monks and repair the desecrated pagodas.[47]

That Kennedy's senior advisers accepted Lodge's recommendations so uncritically in their post-mortem meeting of August 31 says much about the limitations of their understanding of Vietnamese realities.[48] Dean Rusk, who chaired the session in the president's absence, set its tone, indicating that he was now aligned with Harkins, McNamara, McCone, Taylor, Vice President Johnson, and others who had opposed a coup. Asking at the outset "What in the situation led us to think well of a coup," and referring to Lodge's most recent cable, Rusk said he was himself reluctant to start off now by saying Nhu had to go, and asked if "anyone present had any doubt in his mind but that the coup was off."

The only person to accept this challenge was Paul Kattenburg of the State Department. Responding that he did have some doubts, he stated that on two counts the administration had not sent the generals a clear enough message: (a) the repudiation of the "Voice of America" broadcast on withdrawal of aid; and (b) Harkins's failure to carry out his instructions to communicate with the generals. Convinced that the Diem regime was incapable of meaningful internal reform, Kattenburg pointed out that until two days earlier Lodge had held that if the administration tried to live with the current Saigon regime, the United States would be thrown out of Vietnam within six months or a year. When challenged by Taylor, Kattenburg explained that "As the people see we are losing the war, they will gradually go to the other side and we will be obliged to leave."

At the present juncture, he held, "It would be better for us to make the decision to get out honorably."

Rusk promptly took direct issue with his junior officer's interpretation of the negative role Harkins had played in the coup planning, and stated that the firm basis of U.S. policy should be "that we will not pull out of Vietnam until the war is won, and that we will not run a coup." McNamara and Vice-President Johnson voiced solid agreement.

On September 2 President Kennedy, in a well-publicized television interview with Walter Cronkite, expressed disagreement with those who urged withdrawal from Vietnam, but nevertheless stated that he did not think the Diem regime would be able to regain popular support without "changes in policy and perhaps with personnel" (generally understood to mean the Nhus). In another television interview a week later, this time with Chet Huntley and David Brinkley, he underscored his insistence that there would be no withdrawal by attesting to his belief in the "domino theory," whereby "if South Vietnam went," the way would be open for "a guerrilla assault on Malaya," and it would "give the impression that the wave of the future in Southeast Asia was China and the Communists." Neither of Kennedy's statements left room for any policy approximating Kattenburg's proposal of an honorable withdrawal. Among senior administration officials apparently only Robert Kennedy, the attorney general, was prepared to consider that possibility. According to Roger Hilsman, at an NSC meeting on September 6 the president's brother said that no one seemed to have enough information to answer the basic question of whether a communist takeover could be resisted by any South Vietnamese government. "If it could not, now was the time to get out of Vietnam entirely, without waiting. If the answer was that it could, but not with a Diem-Nhu government as it was now constituted, we owed it to the people resisting Communism in Vietnam to give Lodge enough sanctions to bring changes that would permit successful resistance." This, and perhaps, as Roger Hilsman argues, his desire to keep the JCS and McNamara aboard in case he decided to impose sanctions against the Diem government, induced Kennedy's sudden decision to dispatch that same day another fact-finding mission to Vietnam. Its two leaders, marine-corps Major General Victor Krulak and Joseph Mendenhall, a senior State Department official, returned on September 10 after a three-day visit to present the National Security Council, with the president attending, such diametrically opposed assessments of the military and political situation—Krulak strongly positive and Mendenhall strongly negative—as to prompt Kennedy to quip, "You both did visit the same country, didn't you?"[49]

At this meeting statements by Rufus Phillips, currently head of AID's Rural Assistance Program, who had served in Vietnam from 1954 to 1956 with Lansdale, had the effect of supporting Mendenhall's bleak assessment. He emphasized that the deterioration was true not only in the cities but in rural South Vietnam as well, where in the Fourth Corps area the strategic hamlet program was collapsing. Arguing that the United States could not acquiesce in the actions Nhu had taken or continue to work with him, he held that there was a chance of saving Diem's regime by splitting Nhu from Diem and that General Lansdale was the only American with sufficient influence with Diem to accomplish this. Kennedy did not act upon the plea that Lansdale be sent back to Vietnam, but on another matter Phillips appears to have planted an idea that soon took root in the president's calculations. Responding to Kennedy's question as to what else he would recommend, he urged a cut-off of U.S. aid to Colonel Tung and his Special Forces, the elite Saigon-based unit loyal to Diem and Nhu, which Nhu had just directed to carry out the savage raid against the Buddhist pagodas.[50]

Neither at this NSC meeting nor from the mission in Saigon could Kennedy find anything like a consensus on Vietnam policy. And over the central issue of whether or not the United States could continue to work with Nhu the split was so deep as to militate heavily against the creation of fresh American initiatives. Although Nhu was conscious of these divisions, he was keenly aware that only two weeks before, Washington had encouraged coup-planning aimed at his ouster. Moreover, he had just learned that Senator Frank Church, with the administration's quiet approbation, was about to introduce a resolution (which materialized on September 12), condemning repression of the Buddhists and calling for an end to American aid to Diem's government unless this ceased.

In the face of this, Nhu, as unsure of the administration's central and ultimate strategy as it was of his, made a tactical move apparently designed to placate Washington and reduce its criticism sufficiently to give him time and scope to work out his own plans. With Diem's agreement—and strong encouragement from the Vatican—their controversial brother Ngo Dinh Thuc, archbishop of Hué, was prevailed upon to take an extended trip abroad. Also with Diem's concurrence, Nhu accepted Lodge's invitation that Madame Nhu should make a "good-will" tour abroad; she departed soon after Thuc on September 9. (Kennedy had hoped to keep her out of the United States, but after a month in Europe she got her way and, believing she could influence American policy in favor of her husband and Diem, was soon frenetically active in lobbying and speechmaking. But her truculent criticism of Washington's policy, castigation of the press, and reference to U.S. officers as "little soldiers of fortune" did more to undermine than strengthen Diem's cause.) Nhu was, however, adamant in refusing to accept Lodge's counsel that he confine his own activities to administering the strategic hamlet program; he was not about to give up any of his broad array of powers—nor did Diem want him to.

Frustrated in his efforts to secure Nhu's further compliance, Lodge then began to explore ways by which suspension of American economic aid could be used to undermine and remove the Diem-Nhu leadership. He cabled Washington on September 11 that by continuing to follow a "wait and see" approach, "we insure that when and if we decide that we cannot win with the present regime, we shall have even less to work with in terms of opposition [to Diem] than we have now. . . . There is thus the real possibility of the situation getting out of hand in such a way that only the Communists will be in a position to act." Consequently, he urged that the administration act immediately: "if there are effective sanctions which we can apply, we should apply them in order to force a drastic change in government."[51] In the wake of the fiasco of the aborted end-of-August coup, however, both Lodge and Hilsman had apparently, for the time being, lost some of their influence with Kennedy, and now those officials who opposed a change in government were closing ranks more effectively than before.

It seems probable that the administration would have turned its back on Lodge's revived militancy and settled on a more moderate policy within the parameters he and Rusk had recommended just ten days before—no coup and an effort to reach some sort of compromise accommodation with the Diem regime—if a new and extraneous factor had now not jarringly intruded. This was the abrupt revival of the temporarily subsided fear that Nhu was seriously trying to reach an agreement with the NLF and Hanoi. In the aftermath of the aborted August coup and Nhu's awareness of the American involvement in it, the original supposition that he was merely using this exercise as a limited ploy to obtain leverage on the U.S. now suddenly began to yield place to grave concern lest in the face of additional U.S. pressure he, and perhaps Diem too, might now be genuinely intent on carrying through such a rapprochement.

On September 15, Thomas L. Hughes, director of the State Department's Office of Intelligence and Research, informed Rusk, "Nhu has claimed privately that should United States aid be cut he would seek help elsewhere. Should that fail, Nhu asserts he would negotiate a settlement with Hanoi. Nhu has convinced both Vietnamese and foreign observers that such a prospect is likely. Reports that Nhu is already in contact with Hanoi are so credible and widespread as eventually to undermine morale in the army and bureaucracy, regardless of their current accuracy."[52]

The next day Rusk received a memorandum from Hilsman concluding that it was futile to pursue a "Reconciliation Track" with Diem and Nhu, and that Nhu has "already decided on an adventure." Its minimum goal, he said, would be "sharply to reduce the American presence in those key positions which have political significance in the provinces and strategic hamlet program and to avoid any meaningful concessions that would go against his Mandarin, 'personalist' vision of the future of Viet-Nam." His maximum goal would be "a deal with North Vietnam for a truce in the war, a complete removal of the US presence, and a 'neutralist' or 'Titoist' but still separate South Viet-Nam."[53]

The CIA's Chester Cooper cogently articulated the mounting concern and increased acceptance of the plausibility of such a rapprochement in a memorandum he prepared for John McCone on September 19. The memorandum was precipitated by public attention to an article on Nhu's contacts with Hanoi, written by Joseph Alsop, one of the country's leading columnists and a man who followed events in Vietnam with particular interest. Pointing out that Nhu now "acknowledges contacts with the North and has dropped transparent hints that the GVN would not necessarily refuse to consider overtures from Hanoi," Cooper went on to analyze why this might indeed be serious. Despite the brothers' antipathy toward the Hanoi regime, he argued, "it would be quite in character for Nhu—and Diem—to seek some measure of maneuverability vis-à-vis the US to avoid being boxed between two unacceptable alternatives: abject surrender to US demands or a loss of all political power. . . . We believe that if Nhu and Diem feel themselves soon to be faced with such extreme alternatives, they might well be moved to cast about for some sort of agreement with Hanoi. Diem would be less likely to accept an arrangement with Hanoi than his brother, but circumstances are now more propitious than before for Nhu to argue this course." Cooper observed that, though Diem and Nhu would not accept unification with the North, they might seek a rapprochement with it simply on the basis of a cease-fire, in return for which "they might seriously entertain the certain minimum DRV demand for the removal of US forces. . . . Hanoi might be willing to consider something less than reunification, particularly if it thought its aims could thereby be achieved more quickly and cheaply than by continuing a campaign of armed insurgency." He warned that this assessment was based on the assumption that Diem and Nhu, "although operating under tremendous pressures, remain essentially rational." If, however, as some observers felt, they no longer were, he concluded that "the likelihood of Nhu endeavoring to seek an accommodation with Hanoi must be assessed considerably higher: and to a somewhat lesser extent the same would have to be said of Diem."[54]

With the administration's now mounting fear that Diem's regime might actually come to terms with Hanoi and the NLF, planning for the possible deployment of U.S. combat forces was revived in anticipation of a range of contingencies that seemed more plausible than before. This was evident in the "Action Plan" apparently prepared for the NSC meeting of September 17. In its section on "Nhu-Diem Tactics and Moves and U.S. Responses in Connection with U.S. Pressure Plan for Nhu Removal," the question of American reactions to blackmail pressure was addressed in considerable detail. If the Diem regime went so far as to contrive "spontaneous" mob actions against U.S. installations wherein "our premises are invaded and a number of Americans seriously harmed, we should intervene with U.S. combat forces at least in the Saigon-Cholon area but probably also in Hué, Danang, and Nha Trang. We should establish beachheads at these points and put into effect political contingencies—i.e. change of leadership." But if, even without any such violence, the Diem regime, in conjunction with "moves towards France and/or DRV [Hanoi]," demanded an American withdrawal from Vietnam, Washington was to be prepared to "intervene with U.S. forces if necessary to protect Americans." Apparently their protection was also being considered as providing a possible basis for intervention, as was stated in the very next sentence: "Recovery of U.S.-supplied equipment and material could also serve as a pretext for the intervention of U.S. forces."[55]

With concern rising that Nhu was seriously preparing to deal with Hanoi, and both Washington and the U.S. Saigon mission still badly divided over policy, Kennedy now insisted, over Lodge's and Hilsman's objections, that another, but higher-level, fact-finding mission be sent to South Vietnam. McNamara and Maxwell Taylor, now chairman of the Joint Chiefs of Staff, headed this group, which visited the country from September 23 to October 2. In Arthur Schlesinger's view, Kennedy was already supporting the position of Lodge, Harriman, Hilsman, and Forrestal that it was necessary to apply the pressure of economic sanctions on the Diem-Nhu leadership, and was calculating that McNamara, if exposed to the situation there and to Lodge's arguments, would drop his opposition to that strategy. (Presumably Kennedy hoped that Taylor could also be brought aboard.) In this expectation he was correct, and McNamara and Taylor returned as advocates.[56]

Although nothing has been released bearing on any assessment by the McNamara-Taylor team of Nhu's Hanoi *démarche,* the full text of their long formal report to the president is available.[57] It was marvelously optimistic with respect to the military situation, but replete with ambiguity and inconsistency with regard to political assessments—no doubt because of the impossibility of finding any firm common ground between the widely different perceptions of the camps led by Harkins and Lodge. While acknowledging the growing differences between these two men, the report accepted Harkins's incredible statements that "the military campaign has made great progress and continues to progress," and that the strategic hamlet program was "sound in concept and generally effective in execution." So euphoric were McNamara and Taylor about the military situation that they recommended announcing plans to withdraw a thousand American military personnel by the end of the year and assured the president that, by carrying out a program to train Vietnamese for essential functions at present performed by U.S. troops, it should be possible to withdraw "the bulk of U.S. personnel" by the end of 1965.

McNamara and Taylor found "no solid evidence of the possibility of a successful coup" and recommended that "at this time, no initiative should be taken to encourage actively a change in government." Their ambivalence was indicated, however, by their counsel to let "the present impression stand that the U.S. would not be averse to a change of government," and for the United States "urgently to identify and build contacts with an alternative leadership if and when it appears." While concluding that prospects for "an early spontaneous" coup attempt were not high, they acknowledged that "obviously, clear and explicit U.S. support could make a great difference to the chances for a coup." Perhaps their coolness toward a change in government stemmed from their conclusion that prospects for a replacement regime's being an improvement appeared to be about "50–50," and that a successor government would be dominated by military officers apt to be as repressive as Diem, more corrupt, and at least as xenophobic.

Between the three alternatives of "reconciliation" with the Diem regime, "selective pressures" against it, or "organizing a coup," McNamara and Taylor advocated the middle course, estimating that this level, "or indeed any level," of pressure would fail to induce Diem to remove Nhu, but that it would provide a better chance that Diem would "at least be deterred from resuming large scale oppressions." They recommended that the president continue to withhold the small fraction ($18.5 million) of the year's U.S. Commodity Import and PL 480 (U.S. agricultural products) programs not already in the pipeline, and hold up payments of funds earmarked for two major, well-advertised AID projects—Saigon-Cholon Waterworks and Saigon Electric Power. McNamara and Taylor recognized that the regime would be insulated for five to six months from any serious material effect from these suspensions, because of the amount already in the CIP pipeline and Saigon's cushion of some $160 million in foreign-exchange reserves left over from previous U.S. economic infusions. Nevertheless, they estimated that an announcement of these continuing suspensions would have a significant psychological effect and would also be useful in demonstrating to Congress and the world that the United States disapproved of Diem's policies. (An internal administration memorandum of mid-September had predicted that with such a move "the psychological effect upon the Saigon business community would be profound."[58]) Of more direct relevance to the Vietnamese military, and to the potential balance of forces in Saigon, was their recommendation that Washington threaten to cut off both CIA and MAP (Military Assistance Program) support to Colonel Tung's battalions of Special Forces unless they were withdrawn from Nhu's control, placed directly under the Joint General Staff, and committed to field operations outside Saigon, including those in Laos and North Vietnam, for which they had been trained. Whether or not Kennedy's two senior military advisers realized it, the selective pressures they recommended, and which the president approved on October 5, persuaded the wavering generals that the United States was indeed encouraging them to act against Diem and Nhu.

In the meantime, however, these dissident generals had, like Lodge, lowered their sights, and, citing growing NLF strength, had urged Diem to give military men posts in his Cabinet—Defense, Interior, Psychological Warfare, and Education. They continued nevertheless, via General Khiem, to maintain contact with Conein and other CIA agents, registering their concern about Nhu's moves toward a possible reconciliation between North and South and generally trying to plumb American intentions. Finally, on September 26, Khiem reported that Minh, though directing that communications be kept open with the American community, had stated that no coup would be mounted until after Diem had an opportunity to respond to the army's demand for Cabinet posts.[59]

During October, General Don began to supplant Khiem as the generals' principal intermediary with the CIA. Minh suspected that Khiem had played a double role in August, and by October 8 Khiem's CIA contact believed he was getting "cold feet" and "wanting to take [a] bystander role if any coup attempts [were] still being planned." On October 2 Don informed Conein that Minh wished to meet with him three days later to discuss "a specific plan," a request that Lodge approved. Minh then insisted to Conein that "he must know [the] American Government's position with respect to a change in the Government of Vietnam within the very near future." If this were not done, he warned, the NLF would win, since the government had lost the support of the people. He insisted that there was an urgent need for the United States to clarify its position, because many junior officers—presumably the group led by Colonels Pham Ngoc Thao and Do Mau—were working on coup plans of their own, which could be abortive and a "catastrophe." For Minh and the other generals to proceed with their own plans, they needed assurances that the U.S. government would not attempt to thwart their coup. He made clear that he did not expect any specific American support for this effort, but added emphatically that, if he and his generals were then to win the war, they would need the United States to support them with military and economic aid at the same level it had been providing Diem ($1.5 million per day, he said). He then outlined three possible plans. The easiest to accomplish, he said, would be to leave Diem as president (with much-reduced powers), but to assassinate Nhu and another brother, Ngo Dinh Can. The other two plans called for military action against key forces loyal to Diem and Nhu in Saigon, reckoned at 5,500 elite troops. Minh apparently did not spell out the fact that both these alternatives depended on neutralizing General Ton That Dinh and his formidable command—an objective that in fact had not yet been secured. Nor was Minh sure of General Khiem's loyalty; to check on this he asked Conein for copies of plans of the Special Forces complex at Camp Longthanh, which he could compare with those Khiem had given him after purportedly receiving them from the CIA.[60]

Lacking authority to comment on Minh's proposals, Conein passed them directly to the CIA's director in Washington as well as to Lodge. Referring to them, the CIA's Saigon station chief, John Richardson, cabled McCone that he had recommended to Lodge that the United States not set itself "irrevocably against the assassination plot [of Nhu and Can] since the other two alternatives mean either a bloodbath or a protracted struggle which could rip the army and the country apart." McCone responded somewhat ambiguously, suggesting that, though he opposed assassinating Diem, he did not completely rule out such a fate for these other brothers. "We certainly cannot be in the position of stimulating, approving, or supporting assassination, but on the other hand we are in no way responsible for stopping every such threat. . . . We certainly would not favor assassination of Diem." The agency was interested in knowing of any assassination plans, but it should maintain a "hands off" approach, and Richardson's recommendation that Lodge not irrevocably oppose an assassination plan should be withdrawn.[61]

On October 5 it was announced that Richardson was being replaced as CIA station chief and immediately returning to Washington. McCone has stated that it was because of "some sharp differences in opinion" with Lodge that Richardson was recalled, but it is evident that by this time he at least supported the ambassador's policy of ousting the Nhus. The dissident generals, however, had always regarded Richardson as especially close to and supportive of Nhu, and clearly had no inkling of his change of heart. Consequently, as was apparently Lodge's intention when he insisted on Richardson's recall, the generals regarded this move as an important and premeditated indication that Washington was encouraging them to act against the regime, or at least, as Hilsman puts it, that the United States was determined "not to cooperate with a government that continued to leave Nhu in a position of predominance."[62]

Two more moves that were quite calculatedly meant to be signals also carried great weight with the generals. Conein conveyed the official American response to Minh's fundamental question: the United States would not thwart a coup attempt, nor would it encourage one, but would hope to be informed about it. It was presumably on this occasion or soon afterward that he assured Minh that Washington would not deny economic or military assistance to a new regime if it appeared "capable of increasing effectiveness of military effort, ensuring popular support to win war and improving working relations with the United States." Diem's regime was aware of, and had publicized, Washington's decision to continue its freeze on CIP economic subventions, another clear indication to the generals—indeed, the specific signal Minh had requested in August as an earnest of American intent. Equally important, the generals were advised (soon after the event) that on October 17 Diem had been informed that all funding (MAP and CIA) for his Special Forces would be cut off, unless the three companies responsible for the pagoda raids were placed under control of the Joint General Staff (headed by Don) and transferred to the field.[63]

The generals needed no further encouragement, and they renewed their planning for a coup against Diem and Nhu. The first essential step was to persuade Colonel Pham Ngoc Thao and his group of younger officers to abandon their inadequate preparations for a coup set for October 24 and get them to join the revived central effort led by General Minh. Conein and other CIA agents labored to help the generals accomplish this, and Don gives Conein major credit for their success.[64]

Now finally working at least roughly in tandem, the dissident officers confronted one major obstacle—the balance of military forces. The ratio of troops loyal to Diem to those supporting a coup remained uncertain and right up to the last week of October was not favorable for a coup's success. This situation can be better grasped with reference to the geographical pattern of South Vietnam's four military regions ("corps areas") and the leanings of their commanders. Ultimately General Do Cao Tri, head of I Corps, the northernmost command, was induced to go along with the coup, but his forces were too distant to affect its outcome. Although General Khanh, commander of II Corps, had been in the forefront in preparing the August attempt, he had now retired from the field of active planning, and Minh and his lieutenants did not fully trust him. In any event, the southern boundary of his far-flung corps area was nearly eighty miles north of Saigon and connected by poor roads, so it was clear that his troops could not be effectively marshaled soon enough to affect coup prospects significantly. The Third Corps area was the most crucial command, for it surrounded Saigon itself. Its commander, General Ton That Dinh, although he had given Diem and Nhu no reason to doubt his total loyalty, appeared to Minh and Don as now possibly open to their arguments in favor of a coup. The Fourth Corps area stretched from about thirty miles south of Saigon through the delta all the way to the southern tip of the country, and its commander, General Huynh Van Cao, was absolutely loyal to the regime and considered completely undetachable from it. Cao's significance for coup prospects was greater than Khanh's and second only to Dinh's, for between his headquarters at My Tho and Saigon there was an excellent surfaced highway over which his substantial motorized units could move rapidly once they were ferried across the Mekong. With Diem and Nhu able to call on the loyal soldiers of Colonel Thao's Special Forces battalions and three large presidential-guard battalions, it was absolutely essential for the dissidents either to neutralize or to win over both Dinh and Cao.

Dinh eventually emerged as the key to success, and without his support of the coup and active participation in it, the effort would have proved futile. His troops were central both in keeping Cao's three divisions south of the Mekong —and out of the capital—and in outmaneuvering and then overwhelming the proregime forces based in the Saigon area. The task of enlisting him in the coup group's ranks was assigned to General Don, by now the plotters' principal liaison with the Americans. Although Don's assurances to Dinh that Washington fully backed a coup were essential in securing his support, it needed more than these to bring him aboard. In the effort to achieve this, Diem was inadvertently helpful.[65]

Dinh, who was at least nominally a Buddhist, states that his disaffection from Diem and Nhu began when students and several members of his family severely criticized him for his role as martial-law military governor of Saigon at the time the pagodas were raided and during the subsequent repression of students and monks. He was further alienated when, as spokesman for the military group that had earlier requested martial law, he asked Diem to end it, have the Nhus leave the country, and select four of his military colleagues for Cabinet posts. Diem did announce the end of martial law on September 15, but he made no mention of Nhu's departing or of Cabinet posts for the military. Don and other colleagues then persuaded Dinh to return to query the president about the status of their other proposals, and suggest that he himself would be the appropriate choice for minister of the interior. Dinh was jolted when Diem responded brusquely, "You are too greedy!" and ordered him to leave Saigon for a vacation at the mountain resort of Dalat. "I felt like a squeezed lemon," Dinh told me. Thereafter his bitterness grew. General Don, in the words of his approved biographer for this period, now "used psychology to strike at General Dinh's sensitive points." The briefer account in the *Pentagon Papers* is consistent with this, observing that "the plotting generals decided that they would play on his vanity and egoism to win him over to their side. . . . Dinh was an easy prey to Don's suggestion that Nhu had played him for a fool, but that he was really a national hero. . . ." However effective Don's psychological maneuvers were in bringing Dinh into the coup camp, it is clear that Diem's own tactless and arrogant demeanor was crucial in the process. Diem soon recalled Dinh to Saigon to deal with Dinh's aide, Colonel Nguyen Huu Co, who was suspected of plotting against the regime. Dinh states that this summons further antagonized him, for he felt that the president called on him only when he needed help. "I began to conclude that if I wanted to stop the coup I'd have to kill most of the generals." At this point Conein urged his neutrality. By the end of the third week of October, Dinh was fully committed to Minh's coup, and thus plans for its implementation could proceed. From his pivotal position as III Corps commander, Dinh became its central Vietnamese actor.[66]

The most important remaining problem was to prevent forces of General Huynh Van Cao's IV Corps from moving up to Saigon in support of Diem. That objective was partly realized when Dinh and Khiem persuaded Diem to transfer to Dinh's command, effective at midnight on October 31, the Fourth Corps's Seventh Division, a move requiring a change in divisional commanders. Assuming Dinh to be on their side, Diem and Nhu saw the transfer as beneficial, ensuring that this division, now positioned closer to Saigon, would provide additional protection against the major coup effort they now believed was imminent. Unknown to them, Dinh sent his deputy, Colonel Nguyen Huu Co, to My Tho to take command of the division. Through some adroit maneuvering, Co arrived there on the morning of November 1, in time to utilize some units of the Seventh Division in the task of moving all ferries in the area to the north bank of the Mekong. Consequently, when the coup commenced that afternoon, General Cao's Ninth and Twenty-first divisions (headquartered farther south and southeast at Sa Dec and Soc Trang) had no means of crossing the river.[67]

Equally crucial for the conspirators was to get Colonel Tung's Special Forces out of Saigon. To comprehend how they accomplished this, it is necessary to understand the plan Nhu was making in anticipation of a coup. His two-phase stratagem, calculated to preempt the generals' action against the regime and expose their leaders, involved, first, staging a small fake coup. Nhu and Diem were to flee ostentatiously to a haven at Cape Saint Jacques, on the coast, and the Nhu-sponsored coup would take over in Saigon, with the aim of flushing out the real opposition, who would not wish to be left behind by enterprising nonentities. Within forty-eight hours the second stage of Nhu's plan would commence: General Dinh's Fifth Division, headquartered just outside the capital at Bien Hoa, and other units of his III Corps command would close in on the city and net the coup leaders, including both the dissident generals and Colonel Thao's junior officers.[68] Nhu had informed Dinh of this plan, and, ostensibly to facilitate its opening phase, Dinh ordered the Special Forces out of the city. Dinh states that he persuaded Nhu to turn over their command to him so that he could post a substantial portion of them as a defensive perimeter around Saigon to prevent potential allies of the generals (presumably Khanh's II Corps forces) from coming to their rescue. In fact, however, Dinh positioned them so that they could stop General Cao's troops from rescuing Diem and Nhu, should these IV Corps units succeed in crossing the Mekong.

Apparently Nhu saw merit in getting the Special Forces out of Saigon, primarily to help induce his opponents to strike and show themselves.[69] Whatever the calculation, the central point is that Nhu, confident that General Dinh was in his camp, turned over to him command of what was essentially the regime's praetorian guard. This dramatic realignment in the balance of forces in the Saigon area meant that Diem and Nhu were suddenly heavily outgunned and caught very much off balance when, in the early afternoon of November 1, 1963, the generals finally launched their coup.

Throughout the preceding days and on the day of the coup itself, its leaders maintained close contact, through Conein, with Ambassador Lodge and, via him, with Washington. Indeed, during most of the time the coup was being carried out, Conein was seated in its headquarters, provided with a telephone through which he could keep in touch with Lodge.

But during the preceding ten days, liaison and rapport were not always smooth, largely because of Lodge's dispute with Harkins, who, until the end, though acquiescing in Nhu's ouster, insisted on keeping Diem. This continuing division in Saigon was mirrored in Washington, where Harkins's position enjoyed support from the Pentagon, including both McNamara and Taylor, as well as from McCone and much of the upper echelon of the CIA, while senior officials at the State Department (including a somewhat reluctant Rusk) and most White House staff members concerned with foreign policy believed that Diem too would have to be ousted. Harkins's dogged opposition to any move against Diem nearly intimidated the generals into a second retreat. In a conversation with Don on October 22, Harkins managed to convince the generals of his opposition to a coup and led them to assume that this view might be dominant among American policymakers. This, coupled with Harkins's previous intervention with Secretary of State Thuan, persuaded Lodge to cut the general out of future coup planning.[70]

Seriously upset by Harkins's attitude, the generals sent Don to seek reassurance from Conein that the United States would not thwart a coup, and this reassurance was forthcoming. But, as Hedrick Smith observes, the incident not only fueled the generals' suspicion of Harkins; it also "revived doubts about the coup" in the Kennedy administration. By opposing Diem's ouster right up to the last, Harkins reinforced the reservations of his Washington supporters, helping destroy any hopes of a consensus on the issue within the administration.[71]

Thus put on the defensive, Lodge was not always the most effective exponent of his own position. There is something of hypocrisy in his long cable to McGeorge Bundy of October 25, arguing against thwarting a coup:

> We should remember that this [a coup] is the only way in which the people in Vietnam can possibly get a change in government. Whenever we thwart attempts at a coup, as we have done in the past, we are incurring very long lasting resentments, we are assuming an undue responsibility for keeping the incumbents in office, and in general are setting ourselves in judgment over the affairs of Vietnam.[72]

These remarks do not seem to have allayed the doubts that Harkins and his supporters had been arousing in Kennedy's mind, doubts that were reflected in the president's directives that no coup be attempted unless it was certain of success, that planning for it be stopped if a positive outcome were in question, and that, in any case, plausible denial of official U.S. involvement be assured. A cable McGeorge Bundy sent on Kennedy's behalf jointly to Lodge and Harkins just after receiving Lodge's October 25 cable expressed these concerns:

> We are particularly concerned about hazard that an unsuccessful coup, however carefully we avoid direct engagement, will be laid at our door by public opinion almost everywhere. Therefore, while sharing your view that we should not be in a position of thwarting coup, we would like to have option of judging and warning on any plan with poor prospects of success. We recognize that this is large order, but the President wants you to know of our concern.

Revealing as to the White House's approach—and also suggesting that hypocrisy was no exclusive preserve of Lodge's—was the candid concluding sentence of a draft of Bundy's cable, deleted before his message was sent: "The difficulty is of course that we want to be able to judge these plans without accepting responsibility for them; the impossible takes a little longer."[73]

Yielding to the continued reservations being expressed by Washington, Lodge, in his first meeting with Diem since the McNamara-Taylor mission, made a final effort on October 27 to induce him to carry out reforms, and reported that he had been completely rebuffed. This effort did nothing to appease Harkins, who was now aware of the degree to which the ambassador, Conein, and the Vietnamese coup planners had bypassed him. His opposition to them and to a coup seemed to harden, as was manifest in a series of angry cables he sent to Taylor on October 30. Here he asserted that Don was giving him very different information from what he was providing Conein, and "either lying or playing both ends against the middle." He complained that Lodge had cut him out of several messages to Washington and been "forwarding military reports and evaluations without consulting me." Still opposing any coup against Diem, he asserted, "Clearly there are no generals qualified to take over in my opinion. . . . After all, rightly or wrongly, we have backed Diem for eight long hard years. To me it seems incongruous now to get him down, kick him around, and get rid of him."[74]

Apparently believing that its attitude toward the coup group could "still have decisive effect on its decisions," the White House instructed Lodge to restrain the generals from launching a coup unless there was "clearly a high prospect for success." At the same time, however, it advised him that "once a coup under responsible leadership has begun it is in the interests of the U.S. Government that it should succeed." The administration continued to worry about the outcome and possible threat to American lives if the coup were unsuccessful or if it succeeded only after prolonged fighting. This is indicated by its October 30 cables to Lodge and Admiral Harry D. Felt (CINCPAC), which authorized U.S. authorities to provide asylum to coup plotters "to whom there is any express or implied obligation" in the event of "imminent or actual failure of [the] coup," and for the positioning of U.S. marines just over the sea horizon from Saigon, with another unit standing by to be flown in from Okinawa if necessary.[75] Nevertheless, Lodge insisted that the United States had in effect already committed itself, and any effort to halt the generals' action would only betray them to Diem and Nhu. Because pertinent cable traffic between Washington and Saigon for October 31 and November 1 is still classified and unreleased, the possibility cannot be completely ruled out that the Kennedy administration might have tried to stop the coup at the eleventh hour. But in the light of available circumstantial evidence, this seems most unlikely. By the end of October, Lodge was undoubtedly correct: the United States had been so supportive of the generals' coup planning for so long that it could not have stopped a coup now without risking the lives of these officers.

On the morning of November 1, General Dinh's Fifth Division, under Colonel Nguyen Van Thieu, and marine and airborne units led by their junior officers, began to converge on Saigon. By this time the balance of forces was heavily in favor of the dissident generals, and possible reinforcements from Cao's Fourth Corps area had been cut off at the Mekong. The coup was scheduled to start at one-thirty that afternoon. Caught off guard, Nhu apparently believed that these unusual troop movements in Saigon were simply preparatory to his own counter-coup. During these morning hours Diem was kept occupied and unaware of some of the crucial prepositioning of forces by an official call paid him by Admiral Felt, a man known in Washington for his insistence that a strong stand be taken against the Nhus.[76] This visit has never been explained in American accounts of the coup, which the admiral must have been aware was imminent in view of the cables he had received on the positioning of American marines in his command.

Felt arrived at 10:00 a.m., accompanied by Lodge, to pay what was later described as a "courtesy call" on Diem. At the end of Felt's visit, Diem drew the ambassador aside and indicated "he wanted to talk to Lodge about what it was the U.S. wanted him to do." They talked privately for another twenty minutes. There is no further clue as to their discussions in any of the documents that have been released, but this joint visit may have had more significance than generally credited. According to Pham Van Tuy, while Diem was closeted with these two top-level VIPs, none of his subordinates dared to burst into the room to report on the many unusual troop movements taking place in Saigon. Pham Van Tuy (and, presumably, Tran Van Don, who approved the account) alleged that Felt's visit with Diem was "a stratagem of the hairy-handed ones [the Americans] aimed at distracting the eyes of President Diem and preventing precise, quick decisions on his part." Whether or not this assertion is correct, Diem was clearly preoccupied for some two and a half hours during the crucial period in which the coup forces were being positioned in Saigon.[77]

After seeing Felt off at the airport at 1:30 p.m., General Don arrived at a prearranged meeting at his officers' club. Assembled there for lunch since noon, on the pretext of redrawing geographical areas of military responsibility, were most of South Vietnam's generals and other key officers. (A notable exception was Captain Ho Tan Quyen, chief of naval operations and a strong Diem loyalist, whose assassination the plotters had arranged shortly before.) Armed soldiers suddenly moved to guard the exits and circulated throughout the assembly room, and the coup was announced. All present were invited to join and to record their adherence on a tape that was to be broadcast as soon as the radio station had been captured. Understandably, the fence-sitters and even some pro-Diemists felt constrained to go along with the coup's backers. The few who refused were placed under armed guard. Among them was Colonel Tung, head of the Special Forces, whom Nhu had been vainly trying to reach. With a pistol pointed at his head, Tung was ushered to the telephone to order his chief of staff to assemble his remaining troops unarmed on their parade ground, and himself to report immediately to the JGS headquarters. Not long after this, Tung was taken outside, shot, and quickly buried.[78]

At one-forty-five Don telephoned General Joseph G. Stilwell, Jr., of Harkins's staff, upon whom he knew he could rely. He asked the general to order all U.S. military advisers to remain neutral and to inform Washington that the coup was under way. Within about half an hour Roger Hilsman and others in Washington received this message. Mistrusting Harkins, Don had quite calculatedly bypassed him.[79] Since Don had made no mention of a coup to him when they had seen Admiral Felt off at the airport shortly before, Harkins continued to assure Washington that there would be none. On being apprised later of what had happened, Harkins was furious, and he never forgave Don and the other coup leaders for this loss of face and credit with the administration.

Shortly after Don's call to Stilwell, Conein arrived at the JGS headquarters and from then on gave the embassy (and Washington) an almost blow-by-blow account of the course of the coup. Presumably it was in accordance with Lodge's anticipatory request to Washington of October 30, for funds "with which to buy off potential opposition" that Conein brought money with him.[80]

During the afternoon and evening, Dinh's Fifth Division, led by Colonel Nguyen Van Thieu, together with smaller units headed by Colonel Pham Ngoc Thao, supported by artillery, tanks, and air power, moved against the presidential palace and soon overwhelmed the three battalions of palace guards, the only substantial pro-Diem combat force left in Saigon. Diem telephoned Lodge at 4:30 p.m., telling him that some military units were in rebellion and stating, "I want to know what is the attitude of the U.S.?" The response of the ambassador, who must have been receiving Conein's reports from coup headquarters for the previous two hours, was disingenuous, to say the least, and must have been a chilling shower for Diem: "I do not feel well enough informed to be able to tell you. I have heard the shooting, but am not acquainted with all the facts. Also, it is 4:30 a.m. in Washington and the U.S. Government cannot possibly have a view." Lodge went on to express concern for Diem's safety and said he had heard a report that the coup leaders "offer you and your brother safe conduct out of the country if you resign. Had you heard this?"[81] From that brief statement, Diem would have had no trouble in construing the U.S. attitude toward the ongoing coup.

After a series of frantic phone calls to various military headquarters, Diem and Nhu were soon aware that the only combat troops in the Saigon area upon whom they could count were the palace-guard battalions. The generals flatly rejected an invitation to parley at the palace, remembering all too well how that ruse had led to the failure of the coup attempt three years before. Promising the brothers safe conduct out of the country if they resigned office and surrendered, they threatened to bring the palace under air and ground attack if the brothers refused. Presumably still hoping that, if they could gain additional time, succor might come from forces outside Dinh's Third Corps area, Diem and Nhu refused. But apparently by 4:00 p.m. General Khanh had already telephoned his support to the coup headquarters.[82] It was also soon evident that the coup enjoyed backing farther north, in the First Corps area, where a third brother, Ngo Dinh Can, had fled to the American consulate for refuge. And finally it became clear that the most loyal of the commanders, General Cao, had lost control of the Seventh Division to Colonel Co and could not get his other two divisions across the Mekong.

At about 9:00 p.m., artillery opened up against the palace. The palace-guard units put up a spirited defense that was not broken until after General Dinh ordered an infantry and tank assault. At about 6:30 a.m. on November 2, Colonel Pham Ngoc Thao led a group of marines into the smoking palace, but Diem and Nhu had long since escaped. From a house in Cholon, Diem ordered the guards to cease fire, and he called coup headquarters with an offer to surrender in exchange for a guarantee of safe conduct to the airport and out of Vietnam. Minh agreed to these terms, ordering a small detail of men to pick up the brothers and bring them to coup headquarters. Controversy still surrounds the nature of Minh's orders and the question of whether or not the generals voted beforehand as to the fate to be accorded the brothers—a safe ride to the airport, or execution. As they were being driven to headquarters in the rear of an armored personnel carrier, Diem and Nhu were both shot at close range. Whether the killing had been agreed to in advance by only a few, or all, of the generals assembled at the headquarters, it is certain that several of the coup leaders had worried about their own fates should Diem or Nhu somehow later manage to make a comeback.[83]

A wide spectrum of accounts agree that most of the South Vietnamese people enthusiastically welcomed the overthrow of the Diem regime. President Kennedy was reportedly shocked and perturbed by the murders of the two brothers, but as Peer da Silva, the new CIA station chief, later wrote, these were "not altogether illogical consequences" of his administration's positions and policies.[84]

In any case, Kennedy was generous in his praise of Lodge's role. On November 6 he cabled him:

Your own leadership in pulling together and directing the whole American operation in South Vietnam in recent months has been of the greatest importance, and you should know that this achievement is recognized here throughout the government. . . . As you say, while this was a Vietnamese effort, our actions made it clear that we wanted improvements, and when these were not forthcoming from the Diem Government, we necessarily faced and accepted the possibility that our position might encourage a change of government. We thus have a responsibility to help this new government to be effective in every way that we can, and in these first weeks we may have more influence and chance to be helpful than at any time in recent years. . . . With renewed appreciation for a fine job.[85]

The President had certainly wanted to see Diem and Nhu removed from power, and he ordered full support to the generals who had overthrown them. Lodge and Rusk promptly established a close working relationship with the new government, headed by General Duong Van Minh. The day after the coup the ambassador assured the new leaders of the immediate restoration of U.S. economic aid and of the forthcoming diplomatic recognition, which was formally extended on November 8, three days after the composition of the new government was announced.[86]

VII

"The Pentagon's Coup"

Diem's replacement by a junta headed by General Duong Van Minh did not
provide the solution that the Kennedy administration had confidently assumed
would result from such a change. The new leaders' base of indigenous support
was considerably broader than Diem's, but in order to retain it they were obliged
to pursue policies less in tune with American objectives than Diem's and Nhu's
had been, and they were less disposed to countenance the continuation of a major
U.S. presence while trying to achieve their goals. Within less than two months
after General Minh's group took power on November 1, 1963, senior Washington
policymakers had become deeply disappointed at their unresponsiveness to U.S.
prescriptions in the military field. But even more alarming was the possibility that
they might negotiate a "neutralist" solution involving an end to the fighting and
a compromise agreement with the National Liberation Front. Such an agreement
would, of course, have meant an end to the United States' military and political
role in Vietnam.

    Anxious to effect as smooth a transition as possible, Minh and his colleagues
took no reprisals against the members of the previous Cabinet, and appointed
Diem's vice-president, Nguyen Ngoc Tho, as prime minister. Respected for having opposed Diem's oppressive policies against the Buddhists, Tho was widely
regarded as an able and experienced administrator. Minh acknowledged that he
himself lacked this skill, and was prepared to rely heavily on Tho in matters of
finance as well as administration. The new Cabinet was made up largely of
civilians, but the generals occupied two powerful positions: Ton That Dinh was
minister of the interior and Tran Van Don was minister of defense. Concurrently
these two officers were still serving, respectively, as commander of III Corps and
chief of staff of the armed forces. Overarching the Cabinet, as the major repository
of power in the new government, was the Military Revolutionary Council
(MRC), made up of twelve generals, with Minh as chairman, Don and Dinh as
first and second deputy chairmen, and General Le Van Kim as general secretary,
as well as member for foreign affairs. Included in this council were three former
colonels elevated by Minh to brigadier general for their active roles during the
coup: Do Mau, Nguyen Huu Co, and Nguyen Van Thieu.[1]

    So anxious had American policymakers been to get rid of Diem that they had made little effort to understand the actual aspirations of the military leaders with whom they cooperated in his overthrow. As William Bundy, soon to be assistant secretary of state for Far Eastern affairs, aptly observed later, "Actually no one on our side knew what the new people were thinking at all. It was a fantastic vacuum of information. Our requirements were really very simple—we wanted any government which would continue to fight."[2] Even regarding that fundamental criterion, however, the Minh government shortly disappointed American officials. The administration had been misled by its own wishful thinking, its scanty knowledge of the political views of Minh and his key lieutenants, and an inability to appreciate how profound and widespread was the desire for an end to the fighting among South Vietnamese and how effectively this feeling was being channeled by many recently politicized Buddhist monks.

Certainly the political consequences of Diem's overthrow and the new possibilities this opened up had been interpreted very differently in Washington and Saigon. The advisers whom Lyndon Johnson inherited following Kennedy's assassination on November 22 initially continued to assume that, run by military men, the new government would be implacably anticommunist and adamantly opposed to any compromise with the NLF and Hanoi, and would provide a more aggressive military challenge to the NLF. These men also expected that the new leadership in Saigon would accept greater American direction of the fighting, and some of them, especially among the military, believed the way would be opened for the bombing of North Vietnam. During the course of the next three months, however, the Johnson administration discovered that these expectations were far off base.

The key members of the new government's MRC—Generals Minh, Don, Dinh, and Kim—together with Prime Minister Tho, wanted to move as rapidly as possible towards transferring the struggle for power in the South from the military to the political level. And they believed that a reformed South Vietnamese government with a substantially expanded popular base could compete successfully with the NLF on the political level. They were convinced they could not win a military decision on their own, and they did not want the United States to attempt to do so for them. They saw the ouster of Diem and Nhu as an opportunity to expand Saigon's popular support and offer fresh possibilities for settling outstanding issues through peaceful means. They looked toward a negotiated agreement among the Vietnamese parties themselves, without American intervention. The NLF's rapid growth, they were certain, was due primarily to its having become the symbol of opposition to the Diem regime. Now the NLF was, in their view, deprived of its major focus of opposition and, indeed, for many of its adherents, much of its *raison d'être.* They saw it as preponderantly noncommunist in membership and heavily dependent upon the Cao Dai and Hoa Hao religious sects, along with other elements that had also rallied to its standard primarily because it had been the only effective channel of opposition to Diem.[3] Thus, Minh and his chief lieutenants concluded that the diminishing of the NLF's backing and political potential meant that the new government now had scope for building a popular base strong enough to negotiate with the NLF on favorable terms. Such an effort, they believed, would win the support of many Buddhists.

In its efforts to broaden its political foundations, the Minh government was an immediate beneficiary of its relationship with the Buddhists. Most of this largest religious community of South Vietnam—many of whose members had become aroused and politically conscious as a consequence of Diem's repression —would naturally tend to support the new Saigon leadership that had over-thrown him. Minh and several of his top officers were themselves from Buddhist families, and their regime's rapport with the Buddhist leaders was evident from the outset. Moreover, their policies helped ensure the continuation of Buddhist backing, giving the monks much greater freedom to organize than they had previously enjoyed. On its first day in office, Minh's government freed the monks whom Diem had incarcerated, and permitted the immediate re-establishment of the Committee for the Defense of Buddhism, which he had banned. It encouraged the holding of a four-day Buddhist reunification congress in Saigon beginning December 30, which brought together into a single organization the main streams of Vietnamese Buddhism, including the Theravada (Hinayana) as well as the more activist Mahayana elements. From this congress issued a new, broadly based organization, the United Buddhist Association of Vietnam (sometimes referred to as the United Buddhist Church). Although this group never com-pletely overcame divisions among leaders of the Buddhist community—based upon personality as well as policy—it helped keep Buddhism a political force with much of the thrust and leverage it had developed in opposing Diem.[4]

The new and broader social concerns of both monks and lay members was voiced by Thich Tam Chau in the major address on December 30, inaugurating the congress:

> The experiences of recent months have shown us that social events can deeply influence the religious life, because Buddhists are at the same time the citizens of the country. If we want Buddhism to be a spiritual and moral foundation of the social structure, the principal mission of Vietnamese Buddhists must be to consolidate the Buddhist ranks. This organization does not aim to dominate, but to guide, educate, and aid disciples to fulfill their social duties. What are those social duties? They are the practice of Buddhist doctrine in daily life, the propagation of this doctrine to the people around them. In other words, the Buddhists have to participate in social and cultural activities. The reorganization of Buddhist ranks aims only to create favorable conditions for their activities.

As the head of the political section of the American embassy observed, "This was a most explicit statement of the intention to use Buddhist influence to affect social conditions."[5]

This influence was soon felt, and was steadily nourished by the gathering antiwar sentiment that had now become widespread within the Buddhist community, many of whose leaders soon became responsive to the appeal of a neutralist solution for South Vietnam.[6]

Along with his closest associates, Minh tended to regard Huynh Tan Phat, Nguyen Huu Tho, and other NLF leaders as "former bourgeois colleagues" whose political views had not greatly changed since their departure from Saigon only a few years before. On basic issues, Saigon's new leaders did not see the divergence in viewpoint between the NLF leaders and themselves as wide enough to militate seriously against arriving at a mutually acceptable compromise. Minh himself subsequently insisted in private that he and his group were noncommunist rather than anticommunist and emphasized, "You must understand the distinction, because it is an important one." His prime minister, Nguyen Ngoc Tho, outlined the new leadership's plans to me in these words:

> The strategy of the new government was first to consolidate itself with the Cao Dai, Hoa Hao, Cambodian minority, etc., and then to try to bring over the NLF out of opposition and into support of what would be termed a government of reconciliation. At this time the NLF was overwhelmingly noncommunist, with the PRP [People's Revolutionary Party—its avowedly communist component] still having no dominance and, indeed, only in a minor position within the organization. The effort envisaged was to try to bring over first the most detachable elements within the NLF—particularly elements of religious sects.
>
> The second step envisaged was for the launching of a government of reconciliation, which would be one wherein all elements of the NLF would be welcome to participate in an electoral process. The NLF was then sufficiently free of Hanoi's control to have made this process quite possible. We would have striven for a neutral government—not a government without an army, but one without foreign troops or bases and one whose neutrality in international affairs would incline towards the West.

He was not talking of a coalition between his government and the NLF, it should be noted, but rather, of an open political process whereby it would compete politically—not militarily—for representation in a new all–South Vietnam government. With such a government in place, he concluded, "We thought that the best solution for both South and North Vietnam would be to establish a relationship of peaceful coexistence between Saigon and Hanoi." Wryly, Tho concluded, "Unfortunately, there were leaks of our plans, and it is apparent that the American government got wind of them."

Minh and Tran Van Don described the junta's plans to me in terms that were essentially similar, though somewhat less detailed. Whether or not they were correct, they and other leaders of the Minh government believed there were good prospects for reaching a mutually satisfactory compromise with the NLF. Since they had numerous friends and relatives, including Minh's brother, who belonged to that organization, contact was not difficult. Only a week after the overthrow of Diem and Nhu, the NLF put forth a conciliatory manifesto calling upon the new government for negotiations to reach a cease-fire, free general elections, and the subsequent formation of a coalition government "composed of representatives of all forces, parties, tendencies and strata of the South Vietnamese people." It made clear, as it had previously, its view that reunification with the North was to be regarded as neither immediate nor automatic, but something to be realized "step by step on a voluntary basis, with consideration [given] to the characteristics of each zone, with equality, and without annexation of one zone by another." In the meantime, it called for an "independent" South Vietnam that would carry out a policy of neutrality, not adhere to any military bloc or permit any foreign country to establish troops or bases there, and which would stand "ready to form together with the kingdom of Cambodia and Laos a neutral zone on the Indochinese peninsula." (Note North Vietnam's exclusion.) Throughout the period when the Minh government held office, the NLF continued to urge this course. It appears to have matched its level of military activity to its conciliatory political stance: the head of the CIA reported on December 21 that the tempo of its military actions had slowed down, with a steadily decreasing number of incidents.[7]

American officials, of course, were not privy to the Minh government's hopes for a negotiated settlement, nor apparently did they suspect it of even considering such a course until well into January 1964. Considerably before this, however, their high expectations for greater military aggressiveness by Saigon's forces were already being disappointed. Not only was there no recoupment of the extensive areas yielded to the NLF during the last year of Diem's rule, but there were actually further territorial losses. Although some U.S. officials saw this as an inevitable initial consequence of the widespread shake-up in local administration caused by the sudden replacement of so many Diemist officials, others ascribed it to the new government's reluctance to carry out offensive military actions.[8]

General Paul Harkins had been opposed to the ouster of Diem, as had his superior, Lieutenant General Maxwell Taylor, and CIA director John McCone.[9] From the outset, Harkins and his staff were every bit as cool toward Minh's government as it was toward them. Its unwillingness to assume a more aggressive military stance now drove the American military to outright opposition and gave them ammunition for securing wider administration support for their views. Ultimately, this contributed to the disaffection of even those U.S. officials who had most opposed Diem and had initially most strongly supported the new government.

But the new Saigon leadership's belief that the top priority was to shift the contest for power from the military to the political level, and its immediate plans for attracting uncommitted rural elements and the outer circle of the NLF, were quite incompatible even with the level of military activity carried out under the Diem regime, much less with the increased effort now urged by Washington. Nor, of course, they realized, could an emphasis on military offensives provide a suitable context for the negotiations into which they hoped soon to enter with the NLF.

The time was now propitious, the Minh government believed, to launch a major effort to attract a large part of the NLF's noncommunist following to its side through a positive rural-welfare program involving decentralized governance to encourage local initiative. The leaders insisted upon embarking on a new approach that would permit peasants to remain in their scattered homes, close to their ancestral graves and free to organize their own local defense units, relying on their own self-interest and in accordance with local circumstances. Minh and his colleagues believed that such a program, administered through locally rooted leaders (rather than the alien northern Catholic administrators that Diem had relied on so widely), was more likely to win peasant allegiance than the U.S.-backed "pacification" effort, with its emphasis on aggressive military activity and population control through the barbed-wire-enclosed strategic hamlets.

The Minh government was thus unwilling to reconstitute the many strategic hamlets that had been torn apart by internal pressures or overrun by the forces of the NLF. It planned to move soon on a program for dismantling strategic hamlets in the Mekong Delta and within three years to complete this process throughout South Vietnam. By early January, the Minh government's rural-welfare system had been introduced as a pilot project in strategic Long An province, where by the end of Diem's governance most of the strategic hamlets had ceased to function. Taking advantage of the fact that this was Minh's home area, that he was very popular there, and that some of the new local officials were members of his family, the Saigon government appeared to be making significant progress in establishing its control. This success strengthened its conviction that the new approach should supersede the strategic hamlet system. General Le Van Kim, who was in charge of designing and administering the program and who regarded it as still in an exploratory and uncompleted stage, would brook no interference by U.S. officials—military or civilian—refusing to permit any of them to participate in the planning process. This decreased the possibility of persuading American officials of the program's virtues, and Kim's attitude understandably aroused suspicion among them, nourishing their belief that the new government was uncooperative. Minh expected that, through its new rural program, his government could initially draw away at least 30 percent of the NLF membership, and more later. Indeed, before the end of 1963 a significant number of its Hoa Hao and Cao Dai adherents had already rallied to Saigon.[10]*

There were other, more critical issues on which the Minh government also refused to go along with Washington's expectations and stood firm against some

---

*In commenting on the new government's efforts to reach understandings with the Hoa Hao and Cao Dai, John McCone observed, "The arrangements could substantially improve the security of the Cambodian border, relieve GVN troops in Hoa Hao and Cao Dai provinces, provide information on VC concentrations and activities, and have a significant psychological impact on the population. The success of the détente arrangements will bear significantly on the future of the GVN."

of the Pentagon's most urgent recommendations. Of these, probably the most important was the U.S. military's plans for bombing the North. The prescription advocated by the Joint Chiefs called for the "aerial bombardment of key North Vietnam targets, using U.S. resources under Vietnamese cover, and with the Vietnamese openly assuming responsibility for the actions." Though it was finally formulated as an official recommendation on January 22, 1964, planning for it had been under way for some time. According to leaders of Minh's government, the matter had been a major focus of Secretary McNamara during his visit to Vietnam on December 19–20, and for approximately a month before that both Harkins and Lodge had raised it frequently. Upon returning to Washington, McNamara, according to Hilsman, "recommended that a committee lay the groundwork for a future decision to bomb the north." Thus, the available record indicates that some American officials were seeking the new leadership's backing for bombing the North well before President Johnson agreed to this. Perhaps they hoped that if they were able to assure the president of Saigon's support for the proposal, the arguments of the Joint Chiefs and Walt Rostow would be strengthened. The Saigon leaders, however, quickly rebuffed these efforts. They became increasingly antagonized by the persistence with which they allege Harkins and his military colleagues urged bombing and sought to undermine their opposition to it. According to them, he also ordered U.S. military advisers to approach the four Vietnamese army corps commanders and other high officers and press them in favor of such bombing.[11]

Minh and other senior members of the Military Revolutionary Council insisted that the NLF was still under southern direction, and that, even if Hanoi's influence within it were dominant, bombing the North would not, as the Americans argued, provide leverage for the struggle in the South. They also emphasized that such an action might well provoke Hanoi into launching a ground-force advance across the seventeenth parallel that could not be contained by Saigon's forces. Furthermore, the MRC's top leadership believed that such bombing would cost it popular support in the South. A senior South Vietnamese general, Nguyen Van Chuan, has provided an account of a major confrontation that arose over the bombing issue during a meeting of McNamara, Harkins, and Lodge with Generals Minh, Don, and Le Van Kim.

> The Americans said it was necessary to bomb North Vietnam. The Armed Forces Council represented at this meeting by Minh openly disagreed with this American policy. . . . General Minh mentioned two reasons: (1) bombing North Vietnam would not produce good military results; on the contrary it would do more harm to innocent Vietnamese; (2) by such bombing we would lose the just cause because we had [thus far] held that we were fighting a defensive war and had ascribed the role of aggressor to the communists [accusing them] of sending troops to the South, committing crimes in the South, etc. If we bombed the North we would bring war to the North and we would lose our legitimate cause.[12]

At this time opposition to bombing North Vietnam appears to have been fairly widespread among members of the Saigon officer corps, and it is significant that as much as five months later McNamara reported that even General Khanh, then regarded as the most cooperative and hawkish instrument of U.S. policy, emphasized that he was not yet ready for a move against the North, and that any such action would require an American promise of protection against any reprisal.[13]

The Minh leadership also opposed any greater American role in directing South Vietnamese army operations and refused to accept persistent proposals for increasing the number of U.S. military and civilian advisers, especially the introduction of the military down into the district and subsector levels. More than that, they called for pulling the advisers out of their existing positions with battalions and permitting them no role below the level of regiment. Any increased American presence, Minh and his lieutenants believed, would have serious adverse political consequences, robbing their government of legitimacy in the eyes of the population and undercutting its nationalist credentials at precisely the time it had an opportunity to develop them. Aware of the stigma of foreign dependency attached to the previous government, they wished to decrease the visibility of Americans, rather than give them the greater public prominence that these programs would inevitably entail.

The Minh government's spirited opposition to expanding the role of American advisers is reflected in an account of a top-level meeting held with U.S. officials on January 10, 1964.

General Kim [Le Van Kim, secretary general of the MRC] stressed the extreme undesirability of Americans going into districts and villages. It would play into the hand of the VC and make the Vietnamese officials look like lackeys. There would be a colonial flavor to the whole pacification effort. Minh added that even in the worst and clumsiest days of the French they never went into the villages or districts. Others present went on to add that they thought the USIS [United States Information Service] should carry out its work strictly hand-in-hand with the province chief. When Lodge pointed out that most of the USIS teams were Vietnamese, Minh said, "Yes, but they are considered the same as Vietnamese who worked for the Japanese and the same as the Vietnamese who drive for Americans and break traffic laws."[14]

In response to this stand, the Joint Chiefs cabled CINCPAC on January 14, 1964, that McNamara was "seriously concerned regarding . . . Minh's assertion that no advisors are desired beyond the regimental level. The Secretary considers, and JCS agree, that this would be an unacceptable rearward step." McNamara, the JCS, and the State Department then prepared a cable of guidance, which was dispatched to Lodge three days later, stating, "We deem it essential to retain advisors down to sector and battalion level as we now have them, and consider establishment of subsector advisors as highly desirable improvement from our viewpoint."[15]

The Minh government nevertheless remained adamant on this issue, refusing to yield to the continuing pressures. Their recalcitrance extended to having U.S. funds channeled directly to local levels of administration, thus bypassing Saigon, and they also protested U.S. economic affairs (ICA) officers' dealing directly with the Cao Dai and Hoa Hao. "We simply cannot govern this country if this kind of conduct continues," Minh complained to embassy officials. Similarly, the new government withstood U.S. attempts to assume an expanded role within Saigon's security apparatus, which it believed was already encumbered by too many American advisers. The consequent tension came to a head when General Mai Huu Xuan, concurrently head of the national police and mayor of Saigon, became so infuriated by persistent American pressure and continuing lectures that he was reported to have ordered the top U.S. adviser out of his office, admonishing, "If you Americans can't protect your own President from assassination, why should we follow your advice with respect to our own internal security?"[16]

Nor were relations between Minh and Lodge smoothed by what the Vietnamese leaders reported to be the ambassador's patronizing insistence that he do for Minh what he had previously done for Eisenhower. Claiming to have tutored Eisenhower to become an effective politician, Lodge found the Vietnamese leader too proud to accept his insistent offer of similar assistance. He was also disappointed by Minh's unwillingness to meet him regularly once a week to discuss governmental policy and actions. (Minh did agree to numerous sessions with Lodge, but refused to do so as often as the ambassador wished.)[17]

Of more fundamental concern to President Johnson and his senior advisers than the differences over these various issues, however, was the antiwar pressure from within South Vietnam, which they feared might impel the new government toward an accommodation with the NLF. The administration's growing apprehension on this score was fueled by several international developments. Among the most important of these were French President de Gaulle's well-publicized and continuing offer, first broached on August 29, 1963, to cooperate with the people of Vietnam in an effort to unify their country in peace, free of outside influences; Prince Sihanouk's proposals in September and November for the neutralization of Cambodia, and his call for a federation of neutralized Indochinese states, including South Vietnam—a move in line with the NLF's statement of November 8, and which it specifically endorsed on December 13. Nor were these initiatives without outside support. Two days after the NLF's November 8 proposal, *The New York Times* editorialized that "a negotiated settlement and 'neutralization' of Vietnam are not to be ruled out" and that the time had come to try to restore the Geneva Agreements by negotiations. Senate Majority Leader Mike Mansfield strongly supported neutralization. He argued to Johnson that the basic observations and conclusions he had urged on Kennedy and the

Senate a year before remained valid. Warning him of the danger of massive costs to the American people of ever-deepening involvement in Vietnam and urging him to follow Eisenhower's example in Korea of making peace rather than pursuing the war, Mansfield made clear his support of Sihanouk's neutralization proposal.[18]

Even if the question of neutralization were confined to Cambodia, however, most senior administration officials feared that the discussion might also raise hopes in Vietnam. Thus, Lodge reported that the proposed conference on Cambodian neutralization would be "disastrous:" "It is inconceivable to me that a conference like this could do other than foment and encourage neutralism which is always present in varying degrees here in South Vietnam. . . . Any encouragement of neutralism must impair the war effort."[19]

One can understand the alarm of the officials who had helped Kennedy fashion the Vietnam policies that Lyndon Johnson had inherited. The neutralization being discussed by de Gaulle, Sihanouk, and the NLF called for an end to all external military ties and any foreign military presence; yet, following the removal of the United States' military and political presence from Vietnam, no Saigon government could hope to resist popular pressures for an end to the fighting and negotiation of a compromise political settlement with the NLF. With that the whole rationale for U.S. intervention would, of course, collapse. Presidential advisers who had so vigorously championed an interventionist policy under Kennedy had reason to fear that their own credibility and careers would be open to heavy attack at home, for such an outcome would provide the clearest demonstration of the error and futility of their past recommendations. And there could also be serious domestic political repercussions damaging to the administration as a whole.

Mansfield's appeal was undercut by all, or nearly all, of the president's senior advisers. On January 6 McGeorge Bundy privately delivered to Johnson a blistering attack on the senator's advocacy of neutralization. "To move in that direction," he admonished, would mean:

a) A rapid collapse of anti-Communist forces in South Vietnam, and a unification of the whole country on Communist terms.
b) Neutrality in Thailand, and increased influence for Hanoi and Peking.
c) Collapse of the anti-Communist position in Laos.
d) Heavy pressure on Malaya and Malaysia [sic].
e) A shift toward neutrality in Japan and the Philippines.
f) Blows to U.S. prestige in South Korea and Taiwan which would require compensating increases in American commitment there—or else further retreat.

If all this was not enough to dissuade the president, Bundy then moved his argument into the domestic political arena, declaring that for the United States to move toward neutralization would be regarded as a "betrayal" by "all anti-

Communist Vietnamese," and warning Johnson, "There are enough of them to lose us an election."[20] For an inexperienced president, still unsure of his own grasp of foreign policy, who could vividly recall the sharp cutting edge of the "loss of China" issue in American domestic politics, this hyperbolic exegesis must have been a heavy counterweight to any tendency to follow the advice of even so respected a senator as Mansfield.

If this was not sufficient, Walt Rostow's apocalyptic scenario a few days later probably was. Rostow, who had been chairman of the State Department's Planning Council for over a year, began his memorandum with the statement "Three forces are converging which might produce the greatest setback to US interest on the world scene in many years." The first of these was "the rise in South Vietnam of a popular mood spreading into the bureaucracy and the armed forces, that neither the South Vietnam government nor the U.S. has a viable concept for winning the war and that a neutralized South Vietnam is the only way out." Concurrent with this, he said, were "a spread of neutralist thought and feeling in Thailand as well as Cambodia" and "De Gaulle's campaign both to encourage neutralist feeling in Southeast Asia and bring about the Chinese Communist entrance into the UN." Finding it doubtful that actions taken within South Vietnam could retrieve the situation or hold off "a definite crisis" before the end of 1964, he called for "a direct political-military showdown with Hanoi over the question of its direct operation of the war in South Vietnam including infiltration of men and supplies."[21]

Protean terms at best, "neutralism" and "neutralization" often took on ambiguous meanings as Americans and Vietnamese applied them to Vietnam. But in the most fundamental sense, the Vietnamese used these words to signify a situation in which they themselves, without any foreign intervention, could work out their own internal settlement. The most immediate attraction was, naturally, peace; thus a CIA report on this period concluded that for "many rural inhabitants" neutralism meant simply "an end to the war."[22] But beyond that, much of the population—urban and rural—realized that this goal could be achieved only through a political settlement reflecting compromise by both Saigon and the NLF. Minh and the other top government leaders were intent on trying this route. Thus, although they publicly opposed de Gaulle's and Sihanouk's neutralization proposals, they were at the same time attracted to precisely the sort of domestic political reordering that U.S. officials expected would be the inevitable consequence of a neutralist foreign policy.

Despite General Minh's public stand against neutralism, there was nevertheless, as Hedrick Smith reported, "widespread speculation in the Saigon press and in intellectual circles that neutralist politicians might be given a role in the Government . . . even rumors of neutralist sentiment within the military junta." Symptomatic of the U.S. embassy's alarm was its mid-December report to Washington that the minister of security in Minh's government, General Ton That Dinh, "is so concerned over Sihanouk's conference proposal that he is considering how to accommodate himself to a neutral solution for Vietnam." In response, the

State Department cabled, "As precautionary measure it seems to us useful to make special effort to reassure Dinh and others who may also be concerned. Nothing is further from USG mind than 'neutral solution for Vietnam.' We intend to win."[23]

In accounting for the "real reasons" for the overthrow of the Minh government, General Tran Van Don, its minister of defense, was on the right track when he later wrote, "Our problems apparently started with American Secretary of Defense McNamara during his visit to Saigon. . . ."[24] Following a brief trip to Vietnam in December, McNamara and John McCone both reported to President Johnson in highly adverse and alarmist tones.

McNamara criticized ineffective direction of military operations, the absence of "realistic pacification plans," and there being "no clear concept on how to reshape or conduct the strategic hamlet program." He concluded that the Viet Cong had made great progress since the coup, with the only exception to the "gloomy southern picture" being "the possible adherence to the government of the Cao Dai and Hoa Hao sects." But it was evident that his primary worry was the prospect of neutralization. To this concern he addressed the entire two-sentence summary of his report: "The situation is very disturbing. Current trends, unless reversed in the next 2–3 months, will lead to neutralization at best and more likely to a Communist-controlled state." Both McNamara's alarm and the possibility of deeper American intervention came through clearly in the final sentence of the main body of his report: "We should watch the situation very carefully, running scared, hoping for the best, but preparing for more forceful moves if the situation does not show early signs of improvement."[25]

McCone reported that sanguine assessments of the drift of the war during Diem's last year had been "grossly in error," and that the new government was facing "a far greater problem . . . in arresting the unfavorable trend and recovering the situation than was thought." Acknowledging the military and political benefits to be expected from the understanding Minh appeared to be reaching with the Hoa Hao and Cao Dai, he concluded that "the future of the war remains in doubt," with "more reasons to doubt the future of the effort under present programs . . . than there are reasons to be optimistic about the future of our cause in South Vietnam." Indicative of his lack of confidence in the new leadership were his plans for "dispatching to Saigon a number of our 'old Vietnamese hands' for temporary duty to assist in developing the necessary covert resources of native case officers and agents to inform us concerning the effectiveness of the MRC and the public acceptance of the new government."[26]

With the administration increasingly fearful that Saigon might yield to pressures for a neutralist solution, Johnson's advisers prevailed upon him to throw his own weight against such a move, and, accordingly, in his 1964 New Year's message to Minh he strongly attacked neutralism as "another name for a Communist takeover." But the neutralist tide did not abate, and American disillusionment with the military policies and performance of Minh's government mounted.[27] During January it became even more evident that the military and political objectives of the Johnson administration differed more fundamentally from those of the Saigon regime than they had from Diem's. Major opposition to the Minh government spread from the Defense Department and the CIA to such people as Roger Hilsman and Ambassador Lodge himself; both of these leading proponents of the ouster of Diem's regime eventually withdrew their support from its successor.

The coup against Diem originally left U.S. policymakers in disarray. There was a deepened cleavage between Lodge and coup proponents in the State Department on the one hand, and Harkins, Taylor, and McNamara on the other. Because of President Kennedy's support, those favoring the coup had prevailed, but with the American president's death a scant three weeks afterward, the scales were no longer heavily weighted in their favor. For though Lyndon Johnson emphasized the continuity between his and Kennedy's policies, he had been among those opposed to Diem's removal. The influence of the Pentagon on U.S.-Vietnam policy now increased. So did its disposition to take Vietnam initiatives of its own. Although at first an exultant Lodge appeared to have secured unquestioned dominance at the Saigon end of American policymaking, his influence and that of other U.S. officials who had backed the coup waned as it gradually became clear that Diem's military successors were no more tractable than he had been, and were bent on policies that departed further from U.S. aims than his had.

From the outset Harkins's relations were cold and tense with the new government, which knew he had opposed the coup. As the CIA reported, the new leadership saw him "as a symbol of the old order," and in general made clear that they would "not look for advice from the U.S. military." Lacking effective influence with the new government, Harkins found his position weakened vis-à-vis Lodge's. If, prior to the ouster of Diem, these two men had appeared to be estranged members of a team, thereafter they hardly seemed to be on the same team. Thus, McNamara in his report to President Johnson of December 21, 1963, stated: "The Country Team is the second major weakness [that is, after the Minh government]. It lacks leadership and is not working to a common plan. . . . Above all Lodge has virtually no official contact with Harkins. Lodge sends in reports with major military implications without showing them to Harkins." Resenting his subordinate position, his retirement no more than six months away, and presumably aware that Lodge would like to have him replaced even earlier, Harkins perhaps understandably became interested in initiatives that would bypass the ambassador and be detrimental to the Minh government.[28]

The tensions within the American country team in Saigon, however, were exceeded by those within the South Vietnamese military establishment. Some officers who had supported the coup against Diem were dissatisfied because they felt insufficiently rewarded under Minh. Others, who had been members of rival military alignments opposed to Diem, were worried about the new government's transfers, designed to break up their groups. Most concerned were the officers who had been closest to Diem. Several were cashiered or demoted in the early days of the new government, and others were fearful of becoming the next to go. Although Minh's junta proceeded cautiously in hopes of avoiding preemptive actions by insecure officers, its public program against corruption brought increasing anxiety to senior Diemist military men who were vulnerable to this charge. In assessing this situation, a CIA appraisal of December 7 concluded that "however desirable and perhaps even necessary" was the "threatened purge of corrupt elements from the ranks of the military establishment from a long term point of view . . . in the short term" it could be expected to have a "disruptive effect on the solidarity of the military establishment."[29]

This was indeed the case, and at least two important backers of the coming coup against Minh were officers immediately threatened by the anticorruption drive. Major General Le Van Nghiem, commander of the Special Forces and once II Corps commander under Diem, was now scheduled for replacement "as soon as the Executive Committee [of Minh's MRC] had consolidated its position." And General Duong Ngoc Lam, commander of the Civil Guard, was aware that he was slated for investigation on charges that he had profited heavily from misuse of military funds.[30]

Among the senior officers conspicuously missing from the new ruling group was Major General Nguyen Khanh: the coup leaders had waited so long for his support they could not trust him entirely. He was too strong for them to risk cashiering or demoting, but they promptly moved him from his command of II Corps (close to Saigon) to the more distant First Corps area in the north. Unlike the key members of the new government, Khanh maintained good relations with the U.S. military and was on close terms with Harkins in particular. In looking for ways to discredit the Minh government, he soon found allies in Major General Tran Thien Khiem, chief of staff, and General Nguyen Van Thieu, Fifth Division commander, both of whom felt the new regime had not sufficiently rewarded them for their support of the coup.[31]

Disaffection of these elements alone would have been unlikely to pose a serious threat to the Minh government, had the balance of power among the Saigon military factions not been decisively altered by a number of moves pushed through by the U.S. military. As one chronicler in the *Pentagon Papers* notes, "U.S. pressure induced the GVN to break up the palace guard and to move coup protection Ranger units out into the countryside. . . ." Of greater importance, following persistent pressure by Harkins and the Defense Department, who argued that he could not effectively discharge concurrently the responsibilities of two major positions (minister of security and III Corps commander), General Ton That Dinh was on January 5 relieved of his command of the vital III Corps —embracing Saigon and the provinces around it. The officer that the U.S. military approved as his successor, Major General Tran Thien Khiem, played a pivotal role in the events that followed, and Dinh was undoubtedly correct in later perceiving his replacement by Khiem as "a prelude to the coup" that unseated the Minh regime. As General Don has observed, this change in command was essential to the prospects of the plotters, for with it they acquired the major armed units needed to carry out their coup. With these in hand, they were finally able to lay concrete plans for their move. Certainly Khiem and his two Catholic division commanders—Brigadier Generals Nguyen Van Thieu and Lam Van Phat—provided the dissidents with their essential power base.[32]

Whether or not General Khanh was less central than Khiem in the first phases of the coup's planning, as some have concluded, he was deeply involved in later stages, was the principal Vietnamese figure directing it, and headed the government that displaced Minh's. (Khiem was initially to occupy the number-two position in Khanh's government.) Khanh's emergence as the conspirators' top leader may have been partly a consequence of the belief, as the account of Le Tu Hong puts it, that Khiem, a Catholic, "did not dare to carry out a coup d'état himself out of fear that the Buddhists would react strongly against him and accuse him of trying to re-establish the Ngo regime." It presumably also resulted from the fact that the American military held Khanh in high esteem, regarding him as abler than Khiem and just as likely to work in concert with U.S. interests. He was known to have close relations with Harkins, who considered him "the strongest of all corps commanders." According to a CIA assessment, he had been "consistently favorable to U.S. programs and advice."[33]

Having risen to the rank of lieutenant colonel under the French, Khanh had subsequently distinguished himself in suppressing the coup against Diem in 1960. Diem had rewarded him with a series of promotions, culminating in his appointment as commander of the II Corps in December 1962. Though Khanh had been one of the major organizers of the abortive anti-Diem coup plans of August 1963, those who led the successful November coup were initially unsure of his backing. Khanh finally made clear his support for them, but he was aware that the Minh government did not completely trust him. The CIA noted his feeling of insecurity and reported that his motivation in supporting the coup against Minh derived in part from reports that he was being considered for a post abroad, which would have removed him from influence on local developments.[34]

The ultimate objective of the anti-Minh conspirators was obscured by their early, relatively open focus on removing Nguyen Ngoc Tho from the prime-ministership—a move backed by a growing number within the government's twelve-man MRC and ultimately not contested by its top leaders, except for Minh himself. The plotters' apparent preoccupation with Tho explains in part why the generals who dominated the MRC—Minh, Don, Dinh, and Kim—were taken by surprise when they themselves became the target. But a more important reason was their misreading of the U.S. position. In view of what had happened to Diem, they understood very clearly the absolute necessity of retaining American backing for their government, but repeated assurances from Ambassador Lodge and President Johnson's supportive private and public communications convinced them that this remained firm. Thus, the president, in his confidential memorandum to Lodge, instructed him to assure Minh, when he met with him on January

1, 1964, that he had "the complete support of the United States as *the* leader of Vietnam" (emphasis in original). Minh's government, however, and apparently Lodge as well, underestimated the extent of Harkins's antagonism toward it, and presumably that of his superiors, Maxwell Taylor and Robert McNamara.[35]

The principal Vietnamese actors on both sides of the confrontation—General Khanh himself, as well as Generals Minh, Don, and Dinh, together with their prime minister, Tho—have testified that the United States was decisively involved in the coup of January 30, 1964, and all affirm that it would not have taken place without American backing. Their accounts are basically consistent and corroborative, and are strongly supported by the contemporary official U.S. government documents bearing on this period that have been released. When the available contemporary documentation is added to data from interviews, the press, and other sources, a fairly clear picture emerges of events leading up to the coup.[36]

Khanh and Khiem began lining up support in the first days of January 1964. Encouragement from Harkins appears to have been an early element in the process, and, according to Don and Dinh, was critical in persuading the officers in command of several key units to back the coup. The most important supporters Khanh and Khiem recruited were a group of officers who were closely associated with the southern faction of the conservative nationalist Dai Viet party. Most of them were Catholic and had held important positions under Diem. Prominent among them were two of General Khiem's top subordinates—Brigadier General Nguyen Van Thieu, commander of the Fifth Division, and General Lam Van Phat, commander of the Seventh Division—plus General Le Van Nghiem, commander of Special Forces; General Duong Ngoc Lam, commander of the Civil Guard; and finally—though joining only at the eleventh hour—Colonel Duong Hieu Nghia, acting head of the armored command. Among the conspirators the principal liaison roles appear to have been played by Generals Nghiem and Do Mau, who had served as chief of the Military Security Service under Diem and was now assumed to be under control in the largely powerless position of minister of information in Minh's government.[37]

In justifying their plans against the government, the conspirators first spread the rumor, and finally leveled a formal charge, that Minh, Don, and Kim were "pro-French and pro-neutralist."[38] They built upon the fact that Minh's government had encouraged several anti-Diem officers to return from their exile in France, citing their repatriation as evidence that Minh and his top associates were pro-French and receptive to de Gaulle's neutralization plans. Two events in January helped give plausibility to this accusation. First was a statement made by General Don at a Bangkok press conference during a trip that he and General Dinh had made at the invitation of the Thai army. Responding to a question concerning de Gaulle's plan, Don said that he was not against neutralization but that it should not be confined to the South and should cover the North as well. Second was a dinner Don gave for two visiting Gaullist deputies from the French National Assembly to which he invited Generals Dinh, Kim, and Xuan. Don and

Dinh both state that de Gaulle's neutralization plan was not discussed there, but the conspirators alleged that it had been.

These two episodes presumably provided part of the basis for the report by Giovanni D'Orlandi, the Italian ambassador to South Vietnam, forwarded by Lodge to Washington on January 20. This alleged that Don and Dinh were potential leaders of a group that might accept de Gaulle's neutralization formula. At the time Lodge commented that the embassy had no hard evidence that either of the two was flirting with neutralization, but just after the January 30 coup, he cabled Washington that he had had some second thoughts about the matter. He now referred to D'Orlandi as "one of the shrewdest men here," and observed that Don and Kim, the junta's secretary general, "had never at any time foresworn the possibility of a neutral solution at what might seem to them the proper time." Although acknowledging that they had been working effectively in the effort against the Viet Cong, Lodge observed, "But none of us had ever discussed what the next step would be after the Government of Vietnam had reached a position of strength. Perhaps they did favor the French neutrality solution at that time."[39]

As a final step in his rumor campaign, Khanh, through his U.S. adviser Colonel Jasper Wilson, informed Lodge that he had come into possession of certain documents. According to Khanh, these proved that Generals Don, Kim, and Xuan were "pro-French, pro-neutralist," and about to stage a coup, after which they would announce South Vietnam's neutralization. He asserted that in their planning they were in touch with Minh. If the plot were not immediately crushed, Khanh warned, it stood a fair chance of success, because a "neutralist platform might strike [a] responsive chord among junior officers." In addition, Khanh and his supporters spread rumors—actually not altogether unfounded— that leading members of the Minh government were preparing to come to an agreement with the NLF.[40] Khanh and his associates never produced these documents or other evidence to substantiate their allegations. But, given the existing U.S. alarm over the strength of neutralist sentiment in the South, the charge came at a propitious time. The strategy—whether conceived by dissident Vietnamese officers or certain Americans—was effective in providing a sufficiently plausible rationale for the Johnson administration to accept what Khanh described as his own "pre-emptive coup."

Some members of the American military were not only privy to the coup's planning but also involved in its implementation. As the military adviser to General Khanh, Colonel Jasper Wilson, according to both Khanh and recently declassified U.S. records, provided a crucial liaison between the coup's top leader and Harkins.

Khanh states that in the early morning of January 28, the other coup leaders in Saigon dispatched General Duong Van Duc to Danang to alert him that plans for the coup were ready and that he was expected in the capital the next day to lead it. To check that Duc's assurances of U.S. backing were correct, Khanh sent Wilson to Saigon that same day. Wilson called him back by a prearranged code around three o'clock that afternoon and assured him that neither the embassy nor MACV had any objections and that the action could be gotten under way.[41]

Harkins, in a cable to Taylor sent just after the coup had been completed on January 30, reported that two days before, at about 3:00 P.M., Wilson had come to see him at the request of General Khanh to check on whether the United States would back a pre-emptive "counter-coup" against individuals who "planned to seize control and immediately announce a position of neutralization." Harkins states he ordered Wilson to go to Lodge and relate his story, and then, according to this cable, he himself decided to go on what he refers to as "a fieldtrip."[42]

One problem that could hardly have escaped Harkins's attention on this trip was the disposition of the armored units in the Saigon area. Support from Colonel Duong Hieu Nghia, one of the most powerful of the Dai Viet military leaders, was pivotal to the success of the coup. Being a friend and an appointee of Minh, Nghia upset plans by balking at General Thieu's order to move all armored units out of Saigon to Thieu's Fifth Infantry Division headquarters at Bien Hoa. As a CIA cable stated, "Nghia suspected that Thieu was plotting against Major General Duong Van Minh and informed Thieu that the armored vehicles could not be moved. . . . Nghia also announced his support for General Minh." This unexpected development appears to have arisen around the time Harkins left on his "fieldtrip," and one of his top priorities was probably to induce Nghia to go along with the coup plans—at least to back the removal of Minh's most important supporters, Generals Don, Dinh, Kim, and Xuan. Whatever the case, this CIA report continues, "By January 29, however, Nghia apparently had switched his support to Thieu," who had secured "operational control of both the armored and the Marine Corps on that date"—an expected temporary change in command that was presumably central to the coup's timing.[43]

Harkins returned to Saigon on January 29, checked in with Lodge, and was told of Wilson's latest meeting with Khanh. He states that at 2:15 A.M. on January 30, Lodge sent an aide to alert him that "H-Hour" would be at 4:00 A.M., that Khanh would pick him up at 3:15, and that coup headquarters would be at the airborne brigade's command post.[44]

Wilson reported the coup's progress at frequent intervals to Lodge, who quickly relayed the information to Washington. The following eight cables from Lodge to the Department of State on January 30 are instructive.

5:00 A.M.: Colonel Wilson, MAAG Adviser with Khanh, reports from command post airborne brigade at 0435 [that] operation is on schedule and that JGS compound has been secured.

5:42 A.M.: At 0525 Wilson reports everything still on schedule.

6:00 A.M.: At 0550 Wilson reports General Xuan, Security Chief and Saigon Mayor, being detained at Airborne CP. Khanh plans move CP to JGS compound. Wilson will accompany.

6:20 A.M.: At 0610 Wilson reports that General Khiem now present at Airborne CP with Khanh. General Don has been picked up and is under detention. General Kim's house is surrounded. . . . General Big Minh's home also surrounded.

6:45 A.M.: At 0625 Wilson reports that General Nguyen Huu Co, IV Corps, now present in JGS compound with Khanh and Khiem. . . . Wilson instructed to inform Generals Khanh and Khiem that Ambassador Lodge strongly advises all possible efforts be made to avoid bloodshed. Khanh has expressed desire to see Lodge later today.

7:45 A.M.: At 0735 Wilson reports Big Minh on his way to JGS compound under custody. Khanh reportedly states Minh will be offered "figurehead position" if he agrees to denounce neutralism and aligns himself with Khanh's group and their objectives.

9:00 A.M.: At 0840 Wilson reports that Big Minh has arrived at JGS compound. General Thieu (5th Division) and General Do Mau have come in and joined General Khanh. . . . Atmosphere at JGS is described like an election headquarters after a victory.

9:14 A.M.: At 0855 Wilson reports . . . Khanh states he will turn to American Ambassador and rely upon him heavily for political assistance.

Colonel Nghia and his armor supported Khanh's actions against Generals Dinh, Don, Kim, and Xuan, but refused to countenance Minh's arrest, interposing his tanks to protect Minh from General Duong Ngoc Lam's Home Guard units which carried out the arrests of the four other top generals. Thus, although Minh was briefly taken into custody for his own protection from some of Khanh's more belligerent backers, he was never arrested and sent to a place of detention outside of Saigon, as were the other four. This accorded well with American plans: though Lodge and the State Department were ready to see Don, Dinh, Kim, and Xuan go, they wished Minh to stay on in the government Khanh was about to form, as a symbol of continuity. The well-planned coup had been carried out with efficiency and dispatch. Except for Minh's aide, Major Nguyen Van Nhung, widely believed to have been the executioner of Diem and Nhu, there were apparently no casualties.[45]

General Nguyen Van Chuan, a high-ranking officer present at the coup leaders' headquarters, has published an account of his impressions. He states that, having been invited by Khiem to the Joint General Staff headquarters early in the morning of January 30, "I saw General Khanh, General Khiem, and a number of officers . . . about 15 to 20 people. . . . Among them were a number of senior officers who had been given a leave of absence without pay after the November 1, 1963 coup. . . ." Chuan says that Khanh, who chaired the meeting, charged that Minh's government was "neutralist, pro-Communist and pro-French" as well as incompetent. "Even at that point," he observes, "they didn't know what to call the coup d'état to make it sound all right; it was only a while later that they thought of the term 'rectification.' " He recalled that "the thing that stood out at the meeting was the presence of the American colonel who was General Khanh's adviser; during the meeting the colonel telephoned Harkins regularly every five minutes." Finally, Chuan says, Khanh turned the meeting over to Khiem, saying as he left that he had to go see General Harkins.[46]

In commenting on the American role, Chuan stated that when he arrived at Khanh's headquarters on the morning of the coup, "I noticed the heavy involvement of the Harkins group. . . . I had the immediate feeling that this action was not being carried out independently," but "was directed by foreigners." He concluded, "It was precisely because [Minh's] Armed Forces had opposed American wishes" for a "plan requiring a U.S. presence and in particular the establishment of an American base in Vietnam" that "the Americans had reason to push for the 'rectification.' "[47]

After the anti-Minh coup South Vietnamese officers often referred to it as either "Harkins's Revenge" or "The Pentagon's Coup." On the basis of the facts available, it is highly unlikely that Harkins and his immediate subordinate Wilson could have been so freewheeling and autonomous of the Pentagon that Taylor and McNamara were unaware of their plans and did not give them advance approval. Although it is understandable that some ARVN officers would tend to personalize the coup, seeing it as Harkins's retaliation against those who had opposed and humiliated him in the ousting of Diem, the base of U.S. involvement in the overthrow of Minh's government almost certainly had to stretch beyond Harkins into the offices of his superiors in the Pentagon. With respect, then, to the crucial dimension of American involvement in this episode, the most apposite term would seem to be "the Pentagon's coup." As Khanh later put it in commenting on Harkins's and the Pentagon's opposition to the overthrow of Diem and on their attitude in the coup Khanh headed three months later against Minh, "Maybe in the coup of January 30, 1964, the U.S. Army had come to conclude that it too should have the capacity to bring about a coup." Official U.S. statements, however, disclaimed any American responsibility and indicated that the Johnson administration was taken by surprise. Even five years after the event, a *Pentagon Papers* chronicler who dealt with this period maintained that the coup "came as an almost complete surprise to the [U.S.] Saigon mission and to Washington."[48]

Whether or not the U.S. military took the initiative in laying plans for the coup, they were at least privy to them well in advance and certainly encouraged particular Vietnamese officers in their execution. The available data indicate that the major channel of intervention was through MACV, the U.S. military command in Saigon. Harkins and Wilson played key roles. Although the CIA was evidently *au courant* with the final stages of the planning, insufficient data have been declassified to establish whether or not it played an early role. It appears, however, that Lodge was not brought into the act until after preparations were well advanced, and that he and the State Department had either little or no advance knowledge of the plans. Otherwise, it is difficult to understand Under Secretary of State Ball's cable to Lodge apparently only a few hours after the ambassador had informed him that a coup had been launched.[49]

> We have so little info on motivations and other factors involved in current crisis that we leave to your judgment how to handle. Meantime we trust you will make very clear that we had nothing to do with coup. If you consider it advisable and possible there would seem to us to be merit in preserving Minh as head of Government since he appears to have best potentialities for rallying support of people.[50]

But even Lodge had learned of the plans at least a day before the plotters seized the surprised General Minh and the leading members of his government. Whatever their varying depths of involvement,[51] neither the military mission nor Lodge was willing to warn the South Vietnamese government to which they were accredited, and which they officially supported, of the plot to overthrow it.

It is unclear whether the State Department was keen about the political change that had been brought about, but it had little choice except to go along. If it had any doubts, these were presumably diminished by a CIA situation report from Saigon dispatched just after it was clear that the coup had succeeded: "It is safe to say that Khanh's group will be essentially pro-American, anti-communist and anti-neutralist in general orientation." And, given a policy of maintaining leadership in the hands of the senior Vietnamese military, there appeared to be no other candidate, for, as Harkins cabled Taylor, "One thing is for sure with this coup. We've gone through all the eligible general officers."[52]

VIII

The Rise and Decline
of General Khanh

In General Khanh the Johnson administration believed it had found the appropriate instrument for advancing its Vietnam policy. Immediately accepting the displacement of Minh's government, Washington pledged support to Khanh's even before it was actually formed. Despite the continued detention of Minh's top colleagues, the State Department engaged in the sophistry that no change in government had taken place, and thus Khanh needed no new diplomatic recognition from the United States. On January 31, 1964, following instructions from Secretary Rusk, the embassy's deputy chief of mission worked with Khanh's new Foreign Ministry to draft a text for a press conference later that day describing the coup as a simple "change in the Chairmanship and composition of the Military Revolutionary Council."[1]

While the coup was still in progress, Khanh had made clear that he was eager to turn to Ambassador Lodge for political advice, and restated this when the two met just after the coup's success. He went even further the next day, saying that he regarded the United States as a country he could trust, and requesting the ambassador's judgment as to the sort of government he should form and who would make a good premier. The administration clearly appreciated Khanh's attitude; Rusk suggested that the general himself occupy the position of premier, in addition to that of chairman of the Military Revolutionary Council (MRC), and on February 2, President Johnson sent him a warm and supportive handwritten note.[2]

Khanh rewarded the officers who had supported him with positions in his Cabinet as well as in his revamped Military Revolutionary Council. He designated General Do Mau second vice-premier, and General Tran Thien Khiem minister of defense. For several other seemingly important Cabinet posts he chose civilian members of the Dai Viet party, for, although that once Japanese-sponsored elitist group had never been able to attract popular support, some of the important officers who had backed the coup—Khiem and Thieu among them— were associated with the party. Thus, from the Dai Viets Khanh appointed Dr. Phan Huy Quat as foreign minister, Ha Thuc Ky as minister of the interior, and

Nguyen Ton Hoan, whom he had called back from an anti-Diemist exile in Paris, as first vice-premier.[3]

Within the armed forces Khanh undertook to broaden his base of support by promoting certain young colonels, in the process creating the new rank of "aspirant brigadier general." Those he appointed to this position included the commander of the navy, Chung Tang Cang, Nguyen Cao Ky, head of the air force; Le Nguyen Khang, commander of the marines; Cao Van Vien, commander of the airborne brigade (and soon to be appointed armed-forces chief of staff), and Nguyen Chanh Thi, commander-designate of I Corps. They and Ton That Xung, commander-designate of the regional forces, who was promoted to full brigadier general, were collectively referred to by the embassy as the "Young Turks." Any resentment among the armed forces' rank and file at the coup against the popular General Minh was presumably diminished by Khanh's move to increase the pay of all privates and corporals by 20 percent—an action encouraged by American officials and paid for by the United States—and his agreement to retain the older general as figurehead chief of state. Though he would have preferred to keep Minh under arrest along with his ousted colleagues far away from Saigon in Dalat, Khanh yielded to American advice and freed him, associating him with the new government as a means of symbolizing to the outside world a political unity and continuity that actually did not exist. He described to U.S. officials the unhappy Minh's actual powerlessness with a nice precision: he would be "exactly like the King of England," but on a "provisional basis."[4]

In his cooperativeness and tractability, Khanh stood in sharp contrast to the leaders he had displaced, and by the end of February Lodge's cables to Washington had become euphoric in praising him: "I continue to be favorably impressed by him. He is invariably good humored, intelligent, unruffled and quickly comprehending. He is really very much more able than the Minh, Don, Kim group and, of course, he is so far above Diem and Nhu that there is no comparison."[5]

With the U.S. military having helped Khanh to power, it was predictable that Secretary of Defense McNamara would be supportive. On March 16, a few days after returning from a visit to South Vietnam, he reported to the president that, despite the "uncertain viability of the Khanh government . . . we have found many reasons for encouragement" in its performance; it was "highly responsive to U.S. advice, and with a good grasp of the basic elements in rooting out the Viet Cong." He felt that there was "a sufficiently strong chance of Khanh's really taking hold in the next few months for us to devote all possible energy and resources to his support." As the first two points of the "basic U.S. posture," McNamara recommended that "the U.S. at all levels must continue to make it emphatically clear that we are prepared to furnish assistance and support for as long as it takes to bring the insurgency under control"; and "the U.S. at all levels should continue to make it clear that we fully support the Khanh government and are totally opposed to any further coups." He also successfully recommended funding an expansion of the South Vietnamese armed forces, and increasing the pay for their military and paramilitary personnel, additional military equipment, and the enlargement of the civil administrative cadre.[6]

During the first half of 1964, Khanh continued to please American officials with his cooperative attitude. He reversed Minh's policy of restricting the penetration of U.S. military advisers into the lower levels of the armed forces and the civil administration, and he was immediately receptive to General William Westmoreland's request that the number of U.S. military advisers be augmented at battalion level, as well as in most districts. As Peter Grose of *The New York Times* reported, the United States "became involved in the Vietnamese government at all levels," and "American captains went into the field as advisers to local authorities in the districts on the lowest rung of the central government's administrative ladder." Khanh continued asking for Lodge's advice in political matters, meeting with him in planning sessions three times weekly or more. And later in early July, when General Maxwell Taylor replaced Lodge as ambassador,* Khanh indicated a similar desire to work cooperatively with him, urging in their first meeting that the United States not merely advise his government but also participate in making and implementing plans.[7]

From early February, Khanh sanctioned and began to participate in a U.S.-designed and -directed covert action program (OPLAN 34-A) that air-dropped Vietnamese and "third country" (presumably mostly Nationalist Chinese) personnel on sabotage missions into North Vietnam that were "designed to result in substantial destruction, economic loss, and harassment," but which encountered only limited success and high casualty rates. In close consultation with the U.S. embassy, he drafted decrees covering both civil and military mobilization that accorded with McNamara's recommendations, and he promptly accepted Johnson's request that Americans be allowed to "assist on a crash basis in the development of civil administrative services" in "partially pacified" areas. Moreover, Khanh himself took the initiative in asking for American experts in the fields of finance, economics, foreign affairs, and press relations to be assigned to him personally, saying to Lodge on April 30, "We Vietnamese want the Americans to be responsible with us and not merely be advisers." (Lodge in his cable noted, "He stressed the words 'with us.' ") Delighted by this request, the ambassador referred to it as "a real breakthrough." His cable to the president the following day praised "the energetic and intelligent way" Khanh was "going about his business, and his eagerness to accept American advice and help." He concluded, "I doubt if anywhere in the world the United States has a better relationship with a chief of state than exists here."[8]

To protect this "asset" the United States made a heavy and sustained effort to shore up General Khanh's position; and it continued this even after American officials began to develop serious doubts about his reliability and effectiveness. At the end of April, President Johnson emphasized to Lodge the unstinting nature of U.S. support, cabling him: "In our effort to help the Vietnamese to help

---

*Lodge suddenly resigned in June to support Governor William Scranton's bid for the Republican presidential nomination.

themselves, we must not let any arbitrary limits on budget, or manpower, or procedures stand in our way. . . . You must have whatever you need to help the Vietnamese do the job, and I assure you that I will act at once to eliminate obstacles or restraints wherever they may appear." Washington now provided funds and equipment to expand South Vietnamese military forces by 144,000 men —half for the regular army and half for the paramilitary forces. Military and economic assistance programs to South Vietnam were substantially augmented, and in June the number of military advisers was increased by more than four thousand to a total of twenty-two thousand. By September, total U.S. aid had increased to almost $2 million per day.[9]

To help sustain Khanh, American officials were instructed to remain continuously on the alert for signs of any coup planning, and to make clear that the United States firmly backed him and was absolutely opposed to any attempt to oust him. With the Buddhists remaining the major political force in the areas controlled by Saigon, it is understandable that American officials feared that another coup "would probably have a neutralist flavor." Plots against Khanh were reported by U.S. intelligence as early as the first week of February, continuing intermittently throughout the year, and American officials consistently undertook to discourage those involved.[10]

Recognizing that Khanh was not so attractive to the public as Minh, American officials launched a public-relations effort to build up his image. In March, McNamara toured the country with the new leader to give visible emphasis to the warmth of American regard and unstinting support for him. It is doubtful, however, that these barnstorming displays of camaraderie helped Khanh's image, for McNamara towered over the squat and unprepossessing general, and the picture of the large and avuncular American beaming benignly down on this little protégé, or grasping his hand and lifting it up—some feared that the rest of Khanh's body might follow—in a symbol of joint victory, looked awkward, if not plainly ridiculous, to many Vietnamese if not to Americans. Nor was the Vietnamese view of the United States much improved by the secretary's efforts to raise their morale by exhorting them with what he believed were appropriate Vietnamese phrases. He never mastered the important tonal nuances in the few words he tried to use, and the meaning he managed to convey was sometimes startlingly different from what he intended, provoking no little mirth among his audience.

Lodge was apparently sensitive to the tactlessness of these performances and how much of an affront they might be to Vietnamese nationalist pride. Soon after McNamara's departure, he called on Khanh to tell him that he was well aware that the general "must not appear at any time to be under undue American influence," and that he "would always be sympathetic to any gesture he might feel like making to show that this was not the case." The ambassador took it upon himself to tutor Khanh in the mysteries of public relations, telling him he had been responsible for the success of Eisenhower's election campaign and that he could do as well for Khanh. In order to help Khanh develop greater rapport with his people, Lodge prevailed upon him to broadcast a series of what, in the parlance of Franklin Roosevelt, he called "fire-side chats." The ambassador ordered the head of the Saigon office of the U.S. Information Agency (USIA) to give top priority to preparing these talks, a program he regarded "as utterly fundamental." Carl Rowan, the Washington head of USIA, chaired a meeting of U.S. information officials in Honolulu at the beginning of June that was highly enthusiastic about this program. Lodge's remark to the meeting that South Vietnam lacked "dynamic or inspired leadership" was used by Rowan in a memorandum to President Johnson to stress that "nothing is more important than to exert every effort to make the present leadership *appear* [emphasis in original] to be inspired leadership. The group recommends that Ambassador Lodge continue to press Premier Khanh vigorously to make fire-side chats on a regular basis." The USIA did not leave all such innovative steps to Lodge. In his final recommendation to the president, Rowan stated that "other more sophisticated propaganda steps can be taken," and urged that "an effort be made to find a Vietnamese who can write a GVN [Government of Vietnam] version of 'God Bless America.' "[11]

Whatever this all-out public-relations effort might accomplish in making Khanh more acceptable in the areas controlled by Saigon, it was evident that it could do little to weaken the appeal of the NLF—or "Viet Cong," as U.S. and Saigon officials insisted on calling it. McNamara expressed his alarm at the continuing expansion of its popular base in a report to the president on March 16, some six weeks after Khanh had been installed in office. "The situation," he said, "has unquestionably been growing worse," and "in the last 90 days the weakening of the government's position has been particularly noticeable." He estimated that "in terms of government control of the countryside, about 40% of the territory is under Viet Cong control or predominant influence," that "in 22 of the 43 provinces the Viet Cong control 50% or more of the land area," and in five of these 90 percent. In the areas still administered by Saigon, he reported, "Large groups of the population are now showing signs of apathy and indifference. . . . The ARVN and paramilitary desertion rates . . . are high and increasing. . . . Draft dodging is high while the Viet Cong are recruiting energetically and effectively. . . . The morale of the hamlet militia and of the Self Defense Corps, on which the security of the hamlets depends, is poor and falling."[12]

John McCone took an even more dismal view. He found the recommendations in McNamara's report inadequate—"too little and too late." Indicative of his heightened concern was his suggestion that "two or possibly three divisions" from Chiang Kai-shek's army on Taiwan be sent into the southern tip of the Mekong Delta "in order to give impetus and support to the hard-pressed ARVN effort in that area." Although "several hundred" Taiwanese military and paramilitary personnel already constituted the "largest third country contingent in Vietnam," their presence and mostly covert operations had been kept secret, and the administration feared that any great increase in their numbers could not be disguised and would constitute a dangerous provocation for Peking.[13] Instead, it was to be the South Korean government that, commencing in early January 1965, and following enormous financial and other inducements, would constitute the source of most of the third-country troops that McCone and others pressed for.

Despite substantially increased U.S. military and economic backing, Khanh was never able to establish anything like a viable political base; nor could he even maintain what little cohesion his regime had initially enjoyed. It grew progressively weaker—both internally and vis-à-vis the NLF. He leaned ever more heavily upon the United States, and, in view of the Johnson administration's objectives, U.S. officials could see no option but to continue giving him full support. The position in which the administration found itself is aptly put by one of the more discerning writers in the *Pentagon Papers:* "The situation in Vietnam had so developed, by this time, that . . . the success of our programs . . . and indeed of our whole policy there, with which we had publicly and repeatedly associated our national prestige—depended upon the stability of the GVN. . . . We were therefore almost as dependent upon Khanh as he was beholden to us." Thus, American "resources and prestige" were required "to perpetuate a regime that we knew was only one faction—opposed by other factions—and without any broad base of popular support."[14]

Displacing Minh with Khanh had not stemmed the growth of antiwar and neutralist sentiment in the Saigon-controlled areas, which profoundly worried McNamara. In the face of this and Khanh's evident weakness, he argued in his March 16 memorandum that the United States would have to eschew any negotiated settlement involving Vietnam's neutralization and a withdrawal of the American military presence, for this "would simply mean a Communist takeover in South Vietnam." In driving this point home to the president, he observed:

> Only the U.S. presence after 1954 held the South together under far more favorable circumstances, and enabled Diem to refuse to go through with the 1954 provision calling for nationwide "free" elections in 1956. Even talking about a U.S. withdrawal would undermine any chance of keeping a non-Communist government in South Vietnam, and the rug would be pulled before the negotiations had gone far.

Lyndon Johnson's concern over McNamara's estimate of the strength of neutralist feeling in South Vietnam was reflected in his March 20 cable to Lodge, who was instructed to explain in Saigon that his mission was "precisely for the purpose of knocking down the idea of neutralization wherever it rears its ugly head and that on this point I think that nothing is more important than to stop neutralist talk wherever we can by whatever means we can."[15]

Responding to the now increased pressure from the Joint Chiefs of Staff for strong overt U.S. military action against North Vietnam, McNamara had suggested in his March 16 report that later, "if the Khanh government takes hold vigorously —inspiring confidence, whether or not noteworthy progress has been made—or if we get hard information of significantly stepped-up VC arms supply from the North, we may wish to mount new and significant pressures against North Vietnam. We should start preparation for such a capability now." He noted, however, that Khanh was reluctant to see an escalation against the North beyond the existing covert level of operations until such time as his "rear-area security" had been established. Evidently appreciating Khanh's reservations, McNamara proposed that, before any program of air bombardment against the North could be undertaken, it would first be necessary to provide "additional air defense for South Vietnam and to ready U.S. forces in the Pacific for possible escalation." In preparing the capability to exert "graduated military pressure" against Hanoi, the American objective, "while being cast in terms of eliminating North Vietnamese control and direction of the insurgency," would, he said, "in practical terms be directed towards collapsing the morale and self-assurance of the Vietcong . . . and bolstering the morale of the Khanh regime." That young government, concluded the secretary, "needs the reinforcement of some significant success against the North," and without this the campaign against the Vietcong might not be "sufficient to stem the tide," even with the expanded U.S. assistance he was urging.[16]

For the present, however, McNamara—unlike Lodge and the JCS—was unwilling to launch any overt escalation against the North. As he explained, "Unless and until the Khanh government has established its position, and preferably is making significant progress in the South, an overt extension of operations in the North carries the risk of being mounted from an extremely weak base which might at any moment collapse and leave the posture of political confrontation worsened rather than improved." Thus, on March 20, three days after a meeting of the National Security Council in which McNamara's report and recommendations had been approved, Johnson cabled Lodge, "Judgment is reserved for the present on overt military action [against North Vietnam]. . . . We share General Khanh's judgment that the immediate and essential task is to strengthen the southern base. For this reason our planning for action against the North is on a contingency basis at present, and immediate problem in this area is to develop the strongest possible military and political base for possible later action."[17]

In response to the call of Lodge and Harkins for carrying out a program of reprisal bombing against the North whenever the Viet Cong mounted major actions in the South, William P. Bundy (who had been released by McNamara from his position of assistant secretary of defense for international security affairs to become assistant secretary of state for Far Eastern affairs) emphasized in a cable that all planning on escalating American military involvement was "on a contingency basis and does not reflect any policy decisions yet taken by the President." He cautioned that "there would be serious domestic problems in moving directly to overt US military action, and even more basically if we are to focus the objective where it belongs, on North Vietnam." Before the administration "considered moving to overt US action," there would first have to be "a progression of actions" that would put Khanh and his government in the forefront. Moreover, there was concern that bombing of the North might provoke "drastic" North Vietnamese and Chinese communist reactions. Any further planning on escalating the U.S. military involvement would have to await the outcome of a "comprehensive National Intelligence Estimate" that would refine existing estimates of Hanoi's and Peking's reactions, "so that we can properly advise the President, at the right time, just what the real risks are and what it would take to deal with them from a military standpoint."[18]

Johnson's abiding preoccupation with the possibilities of a military riposte from Hanoi, and possibly Peking as well, was to remain as a brake on the escalatory penchant of the JCS and his more hawkish civilian advisers. Besides, the president judged the South Vietnamese government as too fragile to withstand the serious counterthrust on the ground that North Vietnam might unleash if it were bombed. This widely shared assessment provided Johnson with his most effective argument against the JCS and the civilian proponents of escalation: he and Rusk could argue that it was unrealistic to bomb the North unless South Vietnam had first been made strong enough politically and militarily to withstand such an assault. Nevertheless, McNamara, on his mid-March trip to Saigon, carried papers on the implications of direct U.S. military action against North Vietnam, and he discussed this matter with Lodge and Harkins.[19]

Whether or not Khanh was brought into these discussions, he knew well before this (as had his predecessor General Minh) that Lodge and the U.S. military advocated an escalation of American military intervention involving a bombing campaign against North Vietnam. Although at first reluctant to endorse such action, Khanh presumably sensed that it was in his interest to support the plans of these powerful advocates. Even though an air war against the North had not yet become official U.S. policy, this astute general surely appreciated that by supporting what the Minh government had refused to support, he could help ensure the continued backing of these influential Saigon-based Americans. He could scarcely fail to realize that their need for his support on the bombing issue gave him additional leverage in securing their assistance in his own efforts to exert effective control over military rivals and dissident Saigon political elements.

When the army chief of staff, General Earle G. Wheeler, visited Saigon in mid-April, Khanh informed him he had concluded it was inevitable that the war would have to be carried against the North. Wheeler apparently did not discourage him, and on May 4 Khanh asked Lodge if the United States was prepared to carry out a program of tit-for-tat bombings against the North each time insurgents in the South mounted major attacks against his forces. Such reprisals against the North, he believed, would be equivalent to an outright declaration of war, and would permit him to meet the long-standing U.S. prescription that he order national mobilization and put South Vietnam on a "war footing." This would also provide him with the excuse to declare some sort of martial law, suspend all civil rights, and rid his government of "politicians"—just as Lincoln had done "in your civil war." To offset a possible North Vietnamese ground reaction to the bombing, Khanh called for a contingent of ten thousand U.S.

Special Forces to cover the entire Cambodian-Laotian border. Lodge reported that Khanh would have liked a larger American force, but told him that an army corps of U.S. Special Forces could do in Asia what an army group could accomplish in Europe, and that "one American can make soldiers out of 10 Orientals."[20]

McNamara still had reservations about retaliatory bombing, as was indicated by a brief prepared for him by his staff prior to his May 12 meeting with Khanh in Saigon. Khanh's suggestion that U.S. ground forces be deployed along the northern border "would hardly make any contribution to the type of counter insurgency" in which he was engaged, and "such a deployment of forces would make the U.S. look ridiculously impotent because we could expect that a continuing rate of incidents would take place behind these forces and in spite of their presence." While the U.S. did not rule out the use of force against North Vietnam, such action would have to be "supplementary to and not a substitute for successful counterinsurgency in the South." It was the secretary's position that "at this time" it was not necessary for Khanh to begin threatening Hanoi with "specific retaliatory military action" against its "interference in South Vietnam." More important "at this stage" was that he "systematically and aggressively demonstrate to the world that the subversion in the South is directed from Hanoi." McNamara went on to observe that "Too much of the world's population, including that of the U.S. has the impression that this is a 'civil war' and a spontaneous uprising in the South. Khanh and his ministers must make it indelibly clear that the action is directed and controlled from the North. . . . He should realize that his own propaganda position throughout the world is weak and that the US alone cannot compensate for this weakness." This exhortation must have seemed a little incongruous to those who attended the NSC meeting of May 15, just after McNamara's return from Vietnam, for in this top-secret discussion he acknowledged that out of fourteen million South Vietnamese, Khanh controlled only eight million (of whom about a quarter were in Saigon) and that 90–95 percent of the Viet Cong forces were recruited in South Vietnam "with only cadres being sent from North Vietnam." (And these, of course, were largely returnees who had left the South in 1954.)[21]

Rusk continued to advise Lodge of the need for "a sound structure of support" in the South and "genuine progress" there before action should be taken against the North. His exasperation with the Saigon government's lack of performance was clear in a cable in which he asked:

Is there any way we can shake the main body of leadership by the scruff of the neck and insist that they put aside all bickering and lesser differences in order to concentrate upon the defeat of the Viet Cong? . . . Can we find some way by which General Khanh can convince larger segments of the people that they have a stake in the success of his leadership against the Viet Cong? Can we devise further incentives to enlist the full cooperation of people both in the cities and in the countryside to pursue the struggle as one in which they are personally involved? . . . Somehow we must change

the pace at which people move and I suspect that this can only be done with
a pervasive intrusion of Americans into their affairs.[22]

Lodge had initially been well ahead of the president's Washington-based
civilian advisers on the issue of military escalation, but one of the most influential
of them now drew abreast. On May 25, National Security Adviser McGeorge
Bundy took the critical step beyond McNamara's contingency planning and
brought himself into closer alignment with Lodge and the U.S. military leadership. Restating a theme advanced some three months before by Walt Rostow,
Bundy recommended to the president that he now make a decision to use "selected and carefully graduated military force against North Vietnam."[23]

During McNamara's mid-May visit to Saigon, Khanh had made a point that
was later—despite the strong initial skepticism of senior U.S. officials—to emerge
as one of the most important American rationales for bombing the North. When
reminded that two months earlier he had counseled deferring an attack on North
Vietnam until a stabler base had been established in the South, Khanh acknowledged the weakness of his government but said that an attack on the North was
the best way to cure it: drawing such clear lines of battle would, he said, engage
his people's hearts in an all-out effort. He elaborated on this theme two weeks
later in talks with Rusk, pressing hard for the U.S. to extend the war and stating
that without this it could not be won. When Rusk asked how South Vietnam
would react if North Vietnam or China attacked, Khanh replied that this would
strengthen South Vietnamese "national unity and faith in victory." and mobilize
"patriotic reactions in face of [a] more clearcut external threat." Rusk emphasized that the "U.S. would never again get involved in a land war in Asia limited
to conventional forces" and that "this meant that if escalation brought about a
major Chinese attack it would also involve use of nuclear arms," a course that
many free-world leaders would oppose. To this Khanh replied that he had no
quarrel with American use of nuclear arms and that "one must use the force one
had; if [the] Chinese used masses of humanity, we would use superior fire power."
Rusk refused to give Khanh any commitment on bombing, telling him that only
the president could make that decision, but he was clearly not successful in
dampening Khanh's enthusiasm for such a move.[24]

At an administration conference in Honolulu at the beginning of June, Lodge
joined the JCS (but with their chief, General Taylor, dissenting) in urging bombing attacks against the North. They also pressed for an American commitment,
which the Vietnamese would interpret as "a willingness to raise the military ante
and eschew negotiations begun from a position of political weakness." Among
that majority of the president's senior advisers the question of pressures against
North Vietnam remained, however, in the words of the *Pentagon Papers* analyst,
"theoretically moot"—with a consensus appearing to emerge which acknowledged that, though such actions might have to be resorted to sooner or later, the
U.S. domestic political framework needed preparation before they could recommend to the president any "binding commitments to serious action."[25]

Undeterred by this cautious consensus, Lodge took matters into his own hands, and clearly buoyed Khanh's expectations that Washington was preparing to increase its level of military intervention. For when he returned to Saigon on June 4, the ambassador went directly from the airport to talk with him and hint that in the immediate future the U.S. government would prepare American public opinion for actions against North Vietnam. Khanh of course had no way of knowing that Lodge's militant views were still well ahead of administration policy. The ambassador's hint appears to have emboldened Khanh to lay plans for a major government reorganization along authoritarian lines, calculated to increase his own power substantially. Lodge, however, apparently felt that such a move was premature and might so destabilize Saigon's political life as to undercut efforts of some within the administration to secure a congressional resolution that would give Johnson greater scope and freedom in conducting policy in Southeast Asia. On June 12 he cabled the State Department that he had cautioned Khanh "that preparatory work was going on in Washington affecting Vietnam" (about which "he already knew," but about which the embassy could "not give him any details") that "must not rpt not be upset by news of more changes in Vietnam which would give a further impression of instability." Khanh, he reported, had given him assurances that his projected reorganization of government would not take place until "after we have done what we needed to do in the U.S."[26]

Though the president's advisers had still not reached a consensus on what policy to recommend regarding moves against the North, an effort was made through a Canadian diplomatic intermediary, Blair Seaborn, to warn Hanoi against supporting the Viet Cong's effort in the South. According to Wallace J. Thies, Seaborn met in Hanoi with Premier Pham Van Dong on June 18 and informed him that the United States regarded his regime as fully controlling the Viet Cong and "held Hanoi responsible for the war in the South." As a consequence, he warned, American patience was growing thin, and he conveyed, on behalf of Washington, "the explicit threat that if the conflict should escalate, the 'greatest devastation' would result for the North." In what Thies describes as an obvious attempt to lend credibility to Seaborn's message, the administration, on the day of this meeting, released congressional testimony by William Bundy asserting that "the US was determined to drive the Communists out of South Vietnam, even if that meant 'attacking countries to the North.' "[27]

On the basis of his scrutiny of the relevant documents, Thies concludes that in replying through Seaborn to Washington, "Pham Van Dong was apparently trying to sketch out a solution allowing the U.S. a face-saving exit from the war." The premier insisted that "a just solution" required an American withdrawal from Indochina, and that "the affairs of the south must be arranged by the people of the south," with the NLF, representing "the broad wishes of the people," playing a major role. Though claiming that the NLF's program was the best possible for the South, he acknowledged that it did not represent all South Vietnamese, and maintained there was no reason to fear its takeover of a coalition government if one were established there. The South should have a neutrality akin to Cambodia's; there was no hurry about reunification, this being a matter for negotiation "without military pressures," between North and South.[28]

With Johnson's administration as intent as Kennedy's and Eisenhower's on maintaining southern Vietnam as a separate anticommunist state, there remained, of course, a fundamental incompatibility between the U.S. position and that sketched out by Pham Van Dong. And the president's advisers did not wish him even to explore possibilities for a negotiated settlement until the Saigon government's position in the South was much stronger—solid enough to maintain its separation from the state led by Pham Van Dong and Ho Chi Minh without an injection of U.S. military power.

In the meantime, pressures on Johnson for escalating U.S. military intervention in Vietnam had mounted. These stemmed not only from the JCS and internal Pentagon innuendos that considerations of domestic political expediency were causing the administration to drag its feet on bombing: now impinging with increasing force were the hawkish views of Senator Barry Goldwater, soon to become the Republican Party's candidate for president. Ultimately Goldwater antagonized many voters by statements which aroused twin fears—that as president he might either risk a nuclear conflict with the Soviet Union or involve the United States in a full-fledged war in Vietnam; and by the time elections were held in November, his seemingly reckless demeanor had greatly advantaged Johnson. But in the early months of the campaign, his attacks on Vietnam policy undoubtedly served to weaken any inclination within the administration to compromise in Vietnam, for fear of thereby exposing itself to charges of wavering in the contest with world communism.[29]

The potential impact of Republican criticism became even more minatory when Lodge left his post as ambassador to join the Republican campaign, for it was evident that he was now in a position to further his own advocacy of bombing North Vietnam more effectively than he had found possible from within the administration. In view of the converging pressures from the U.S. military and the Republican leadership, one can better appreciate why, in appointing Lodge's successor, the president did not pick McGeorge Bundy—who appears to have really wanted the position—or any other civilian adviser. In view of Lyndon Johnson's abiding preoccupation with "keeping the J.C.S. aboard," so that the military would not become a focus of opposition to his Vietnam policy that his political foes could exploit, it is understandable that he appointed the chairman of the JCS, General Maxwell Taylor, as his new ambassador. (The importance attached to the Saigon post was underscored by Johnson's appointment, for the first time, of a deputy ambassador, a position he filled with U. Alexis Johnson, a former under secretary of state who had also been ambassador to Thailand.)[30]

There was some unhappiness among senior U.S. officials when, on July 19, Khanh broke his promise to remain publicly silent on the bombing issue and, at what he termed a "Unification Rally," called for a "March to the North," stating that his government, and by implication the United States, could no longer "remain indifferent before the firm determination of all the people who are considering the push northward." Presumably even less welcome was the still more bellicose statement made by air-force commander Nguyen Cao Ky two days later, apparently with Khanh's concurrence. After first putting into the record the open secret that planes had for some time (actually three years) been ferrying combat teams on sabotage missions "inside North Vietnam," Khanh's erratic colleague went on to announce that his pilots were being trained to fly jets on bombing attacks. "We are ready," he said; "we could go this afternoon; I cannot assure you that all of North Vietnam would be destroyed, but Hanoi would certainly. . . ."[31]

Taylor protested to Khanh at what appeared to be a move to force the United States' hand, and reportedly reprimanded Ky for making his provocative statements. Khanh's response was that bombing had been an American idea in the first place, and that the only basic policy differences were about timing and what to announce publicly. In conclusion, he bluntly asserted that, even if the idea of a "March to the North" was not American policy, it was now South Vietnamese policy.[32]

However awkward the administration may have found these statements, Taylor argued for tolerance and patience. The embassy tended to see Khanh as emboldened by Goldwater's nomination, which he regarded as signifying support in the United States for attacks on North Vietnam; and it viewed the general's public statements as a desperate effort to keep his foundering regime afloat—an endeavor it very much wanted to see succeed. But in South Vietnam there was clearly no tide of support for war against the North, and, as one of the chroniclers of the *Pentagon Papers* observes, "Taylor feared the GVN [Khanh's government] might get tired and want to negotiate if they could not get the U.S. more involved."[33]

Although Khanh himself had given no indication of being attracted to a neutralist solution, the administration was at this time especially worried about such a prospect, because of the renewed international pressures that had begun to build up along with fears of a major escalation in the war. These first came into focus on July 8, when U.N. Secretary General U Thant publicly called for "the political and diplomatic method of negotiations" as "the only sensible alternative" to an escalated military conflict. Immediately after Khanh's and Ky's saber-rattling announcements, President de Gaulle endorsed U Thant's initiative, and soon afterward Moscow and Peking, as well as Phnom Penh, Hanoi, and the NLF, indicated that they supported the secretary general's proposal for a reconvened Geneva Conference to negotiate an end to the fighting in both Laos and Vietnam.[34]

American officials, however, were convinced that any such conference would end in a demand for the withdrawal of U.S. troops, or at least in the establishment of a neutralist government in Saigon which would soon call for this. Moreover, they believed that U.S. agreement to such a conference would in itself so undermine Saigon's hawks and encourage the Buddhists and other advocates of peace as to ensure the collapse of Khanh's government. This, in turn, would pave the way for a leadership bent upon a compromise political settlement with the NLF. The reputations of the administration's top officials and their often self-serving perception of what constituted American global prestige were at stake. Particularly on the eve of an election against a Republican Party that had so persistently attacked the Democrats as responsible for the "loss of China" to communist control, the Johnson administration was loath to accept negotiations that would have left it vulnerable to the charge of compromise with communism in Vietnam. The president promptly and uncompromisingly rejected the call for negotiations, announcing on July 25, "We do not believe in a conference called to ratify terror." Khanh promptly followed suit, his foreign minister terming the proposals "prejudicial to the fight that Vietnam leads in the vanguard of the free world against aggression imposed upon it by the Communist international." The administration's rejection of negotiations—and the weakness of the Saigon government—were underlined just three days later with the president's announcement that the size of its military mission in South Vietnam would be increased by nearly a third, from sixteen to twenty-one thousand.[35]

Khanh's public call for extending the war to the North clearly did not stem the erosion his government was suffering as a result of the political antagonisms swirling around it. He remained under increasing pressure from right-wing Catholic military and political leaders, especially those associated with the small but vociferous factions of the Dai Viet, who now resented the fact that their positions in the Cabinet lacked any real authority. This pressure reached a new intensity in mid-July, when the two most powerful Catholic officers—General Khiem, minister of defense, and General Thieu, army chief of staff—called for General Minh's ouster from his primarily symbolic role as chief of state. Although Khanh himself wished to be rid of this popular general, he dared not remove him for fear of antagonizing Taylor and other influential American officials, who, besides wanting to sustain for an American audience the fiction that there had been continuity in government since the coup against Diem, also considered Minh the only general for whom the populace had some real respect. Indeed, only five weeks earlier both Rusk and Lodge had urged upon Khanh "the full enlistment of General Minh's reputation and popularity in support of the war effort."[36]

Khanh knew, therefore, that the Americans would have little sympathy with the Dai Viet demands. On July 24 he asked Taylor for a public declaration of American support for his government, and for U.S. pressure to be exerted to dissuade the Catholic generals from trying to displace him. Taylor promptly granted both requests. Khanh played his cards so adroitly that the administration now began to have second thoughts about retaining Minh. Rusk cabled Taylor:

As part of the problem of making clear our full support for Khanh, we have been concerned that he may have the feeling that USG in part has been pressuring him to maintain Minh's position and go easy with Dalat generals [Minh's top associates in his ousted government, still being held under arrest in Dalat]. While we have always felt that Minh's position could be useful in enlisting public support, we believe this aspect may now be secondary to crucial need reinforce Khanh's position in every possible way. Accordingly, you may in your discretion sound Khanh out whether he wishes us dissociate ourselves further from Minh and whether he needs our support in taking tough line against Dalat or other generals.[37]

Taylor contended that such measures alone would not strengthen Khanh sufficiently. He told Washington that the "major pressures" on Khanh and a "sense of frustration and desire for some action particularly strong among [the] generals (though perhaps not widespread in [the] people as a whole)," made it "essential to Khanh's position and our relationship with him" that discussions be continued with him concerning action against Hanoi. Rusk responded that the ambassador was authorized to discuss this possibility with him "in a more concrete manner in [a] small select joint group," but that "our objective should be to provide [a] channel for frustration of Khanh and [the] generals without committing USG to action. . . ."[38]

Soon after this the State Department authorized Taylor to tell Khanh in confidence that the U.S. government "had considered attacks on North Vietnam that might begin, for example, if the pressure from dissident South Vietnamese factions became too great." Implicitly, if not explicitly, then, Khanh was apparently alerted to the possibility of something like the Tonkin Gulf bombing "retaliation" about a week before that event occurred. Presumably it was this knowledge that brought him to discuss with Taylor on July 27 his plans for declaring a "state of emergency."[39] (The rationale for such a declaration was, of course, that it would be needed as a consequence of extension of the war to the North and in order to face a possible military response to this from Hanoi.) The conviction that bombing the North would strengthen the morale of the faltering Saigon government and its resolve to continue fighting the Viet Cong was clearly a major factor underlying the administration's August 4 Tonkin Gulf air strike and the congressional resolution that accompanied it.

Since at least early June, some of the president's advisers, led by McGeorge Bundy, had been moving toward a consensus in favor of a congressional resolution that would give a psychological boost to Saigon's military leadership while providing greater flexibility and scope for the exercise of American military power in Southeast Asia, encompassing the possibility of air action against the North. It was Bundy's position that within the framework of SEATO the president could "plausibly move troops even into Vietnam, Thailand and Laos," but that for air or ground action against North Vietnam a congressional resolution would be necessary. Playing a major role in shaping this resolution were Bundy; his brother William; Michael Forrestal, then a senior aide of McGeorge Bundy and about to be appointed head of a White House Interdepartmental Coordinating Committee on Vietnam; and William Sullivan, chairman of the Interdepartmental Vietnam Working Group. On June 10, they met and prepared a memorandum that McGeorge Bundy sent to McNamara and Rusk for a discussion with them five days later on the desirability of recommending to the president that he seek a congressional resolution on Southeast Asia.[40]

McGeorge Bundy sent a long memorandum by Sullivan as part of his brief to McNamara and Rusk. This forcefully argued that a resolution would be of critical importance in stemming Saigon's political and military deterioration. It emphasized that both Westmoreland and Lodge looked toward an American "commitment which the Vietnamese would interpret as a willingness to raise the military ante and eschew negotiations begun from a position of weakness." Sullivan held that "an act of irreversible commitment by the United States" would be a means for providing Saigon with "a confident sense of victory." Or, as one of the chroniclers in the *Pentagon Papers* so aptly characterized Sullivan's view, "No level of mere aid, advice and support short of full [U.S.] participation" could be expected to compensate for Khanh's lack of leadership, and he would remain "discouraged and defeated until he was given full assurance of victory," something he would not be able to feel "until the U.S. committed itself to full participation in the struggle, even to the extent of co-belligerency. If the U.S. could commit itself in this way, the U.S. determination would somehow be transfused into the GVN."[41]

Forrestal argued in a similar vein. Registering his complete agreement with Sullivan's paper, he stated, "The political balance in both civilian and military leadership in Saigon is becoming increasingly fragile, partly because of worries about our intention and determination. . . . I still think that our major danger is a political upheaval in Saigon. . . . That is why, on balance, I would recommend a Congressional resolution, if we can possibly get it. . . ." William Bundy, too, strongly urged a congressional resolution, arguing that "the situation in South Viet-Nam—*without* [emphasis in original] necessarily any dramatic [adverse] event—could deteriorate to the point where we had to consider at least beginning stronger actions to the north in order to put greater pressure on Hanoi and lift morale in South Viet-Nam." A congressional resolution would be the best way of demonstrating U.S. "firmness" and providing "complete flexibility in the hands of the Executive in the coming political months." In view of the impending Republican convention, timing was important, he pointed out, and urged that the resolution precede it, optimally during the week of June 22.[42]

But it is evident that the president was still not willing to go so far. Thus, for their meeting of June 15 he instructed his advisers to limit their discussion to measures the administration could take without major military operations against North Vietnam and without the empowerment of a congressional resolution.[43]

The record as to what further counsel Johnson received from his advisers on the question of a congressional resolution is unavailable. His continuing concern with the matter is, however, evident in his request to Rusk on June 22 on the legal basis for sending U.S. forces to Vietnam. In response, the secretary pointed out that SEATO had never yet been invoked with respect to Vietnam, "since it is difficult to characterize North Vietnamese actions in South Viet-Nam as 'armed attack' within the meaning of the Southeast Asia Treaty and the U.N. Charter"; yet he then drew the incongruous, and unexplained, conclusion that the "existence of the Treaty [itself] lends support to the President's action in sending American forces to Vietnam." But, Rusk pointed out, "the legislative history of the Treaty and Protocol [i.e., the Eisenhower administration's explanation to the Senate] indicates, however, an understanding that if the treaty were formally invoked as a basis for United States military action, or if organized United States forces were committed to combat on a substantial scale, the President would act through Congress. . . ."[44] Thus, the president had been advised that, if he were to move militarily against the North, he could do so under authority of SEATO, providing he acted with congressional backing and in response to actions by Hanoi that could be regarded as "armed attack." The logical deduction, then, was that to trigger this process all that was required was an incident that could be construed as an armed attack.

An alleged—and ultimately unsubstantiated—North Vietnamese torpedo-boat attack against the U.S. destroyers *Maddox* and *Turner Joy* in the Tonkin Gulf on August 4 paved the way for a congressional resolution and provided the excuse for a one-day, sixty-four-sortie air attack, against North Vietnamese naval bases and oil-storage facilities. This was two days after an actually verified but unsuccessful attack by North Vietnamese torpedo boats on an American destroyer (hit by a single bullet) in response to clearly provocative U.S.-supported covert OPLAN 34-A" bombardments against the North Vietnamese coast during the previous few days by Saigon's navy. By its own tortuous and disingenuous description of these events and their governing context, the Pentagon and its spokesman in this affair, Robert McNamara, played the central role in securing the congressional resolution.[45]

Whether Johnson as well as the legislative branch was misinformed is still not clear, but the resolution he requested on August 7 won an almost unanimous endorsement from a Congress that had been badly misled. With the House voting 416 to 0 in favor and only two senators (Wayne Morse and Ernest Gruening) opposed, Congress passed a resolution authorizing the president to "take all necessary measures to repel any armed attack against the forces of the United States and to prevent further aggression" and to "take all necessary steps, including the use of armed force, to assist any member or protocol state of the Southeast Asia Collective Defense Treaty requesting assistance in defense of its freedom." Johnson was thus given enormous latitude for initiative whenever it seemed appropriate.[46]

Although many important government documents bearing on the Tonkin Gulf affair have still not been declassified, a few of the most crucial cables, together with statements by some of those directly involved, have become available. These make clear that centrally important information was withheld from Congress at the time it responded to the request for a presidential resolution. By the end of 1984 there was enough evidence to establish that no North Vietnamese attack took place on August 4. What is still not known, and cannot be until more documents are released or some of the president's top advisers speak more candidly than they have, is whether the president as well as Congress was misled.[47]

Three years after the incident, middle-ranking Pentagon officials leaked information to the Senate Foreign Relations Committee that, with statements by various crew members of the two U.S. destroyers, convinced Senator J. William Fulbright that the national interest required a full-fledged investigation. The evidence presented to the hearings before his committee held on February 20, 1968, corroborated the committee members' rising misgivings. Their suspicions were further strengthened when they discovered that on the day after a navy commander orally conveyed important information to them, he was "picked up and sent to a psychiatric ward." Nor were they reassured when McNamara's deputy was willing to show Fulbright only very briefly a cable he asserted was conclusive proof of a second attack, and refused to permit committee staff members to see the cable at all, on the ground that their top-secret clearance was not high enough.[48]

Notable among the senators' findings in these new hearings was that North Vietnam's August 2 attack followed some very real provocation. McNamara had been considerably less than candid in stating, during the August 1964 discussion of the administration's request for a congressional resolution, "Our Navy played absolutely no part in, was not associated with, was not aware of, any South Vietnamese action, if there were any. I want to make that very clear to you. The *Maddox* was operating in international waters, was carrying out a routine patrol of the type we carry out all over the world at all times. It was not informed of, was not aware of, had no knowledge of, and so far as I know today has [had] no knowledge of any possible South Vietnamese actions in connection with the two islands, as Senator Morse referred to." Whether McNamara also told the president this, we do not know. In 1968, under intensive questioning by Senators Fulbright, Morse, Albert Gore, Eugene McCarthy, and Claiborne Pell, McNamara was unable to provide a credible defense against convincing evidence they had recently obtained that the August 2 attack came directly on the heels of a South Vietnamese naval bombardment of two North Vietnamese offshore islands carried out as part of the clandestine U.S. Operation Plan 34 Alpha (OPLAN 34-A). The *Maddox* had been in the same general area, conducting what was termed a "DeSoto patrol" involving electronic espionage (stimulating enemy radar installations so that their locations could be pinpointed). Thus, it could hardly be argued that the ship was on a routine patrol in international waters. It was logical to assume, they concluded, that the North Vietnamese saw the provocative presence of the U.S. destroyers on August 2 as tied in with the immediately preceding and following bombardment by the South Vietnamese navy—whose ships had been provided by the United States, and which it was logical for Hanoi to regard as under U.S. control. It was with respect to this that Senator Pell produced a note that "the North Vietnamese sent to the International Control Commission, on the 31st of July objecting to the 34A operations, calling it a violation of the sovereignty and territorial integrity of the DRV, and referring to them as acts of the Americans and the Southern [Vietnamese] Administrations." To that straightforward piece of evidence McNamara could offer no rebuttal.

McNamara was particularly unconvincing when the senators confronted him with the fact that in the 1964 hearings they had been denied knowledge that some fifteen hours before the alleged North Vietnamese attack of August 4, "the Maddox sent a message to the commander of the 7th Fleet stating that evaluation of information from various sources indicated that the North Vietnamese considered the patrol [of the two American destroyers] directly involved with the South Vietnam attacks on North Vietnam." To the incredulous senators McNamara responded that "Captain John J. Herrick, the man who wrote the cable and who in 1968 was still on active duty in the Navy, testifies today he can recall no information that would have supported the conclusion. . . ."

Yet more evidence indicating that the August 2 attack was not unprovoked surfaced more than a decade later with the declassification of a cable sent by Rusk to Taylor on August 3 (just after the first attack on the *Maddox*). Its last paragraph read, "We believe that present Op Plan 34 A activities are beginning to rattle Hanoi, and Maddox incident is directly related to their efforts to resist these activities. We have no intention of yielding to pressure."

Also in the February 1968 review, it became clear that the senators had been denied another important piece of information in the first Tonkin hearing: that on August 4 Herrick, after believing his ship and the accompanying destroyer *Turner Joy* had been under attack (largely, it later developed, because of the inept use of sonar equipment), had finally become skeptical that there had been a second attack and had radioed CINCPAC "Entire action leaves many doubts except for apparent attempted ambush at the beginning [as reported by the *Turner Joy*]. Suggest thorough reconnaissance in daylight by aircraft." Soon afterward, following intensive questioning of crew members, he radioed: "Review of action makes many reported contacts and torpedos fired appear very doubtful. . . . Freak weather effects and overeager sonarmen may have accounted for many reports. No actual sightings by Maddox. Suggest complete evaluation before any further action."

After the senators raised this matter in 1968, the following exchange took place between McNamara and Fulbright.

MCNAMARA: I don't believe Commander Herrick in his cable stated that he had doubt that the attack took place. He questioned certain details of the attack. . . . Secondly, his doubts we resolved that afternoon before the retaliatory action was taken.

FULBRIGHT: I think he went much further than that. He advised you not to do anything until it had been reevaluated. . . . It is a very strong statement.

MCNAMARA: Nothing was done until it was reevaluated.

FULBRIGHT: He says "Suggest complete reevaluation before any further action." Now that is a very strong recommendation from a man on the scene in charge of the operation. . . . If I had had notice of this particular cable in 1964 I think I would have had enough sense to raise a warning sign. . . . Both committees, except for the Senator from Oregon [Morse], unanimously accepted your testimony then as the whole story, and I must say this raises very serious questions about how you make decisions to go to war.

Despite their strong suspicions, the senators were unable in this 1968 review to establish fully that there had been no second attack. And on this point McNamara remained adamant. When pressed, he adduced what he termed "unimpeachable evidence" that there had been a second attack, by pointing to intercepts of North Vietnamese radio flashes that had not been shown the Foreign Relations Committee members in 1964 and which he now refused to release to the committee because of its high security classification. As noted above, Fulbright was able to get only a cursory look at them, and the expert members of the committee staff, already cleared for top-secret material, were not permitted even this. After the 1968 hearing it developed that these intercepts from North Vietnamese Naval Headquarters almost certainly were an account of the August 2 attack that had been delayed in transmission; the deputy director of the National Security Agency informed Fulbright's committee in 1972 that he had no doubt that these intercepts referred to the first attack.[49]

Not until 1984, when a number of the carrier-based pilots assigned to accompany the destroyers began to speak up, did "unimpeachable" proof emerge that there never had been any second attack. The final clincher came when Vice Admiral James B. Stockdale presented his account of what had happened in the October 7, 1984, Washington *Post*. He was the navy commander in charge of the flight from the carrier *Ticonderoga* that on August 2 had driven off the three North Vietnamese PT boats which had attacked the *Maddox* (sinking one and damaging two of the PT boats) and who two days later had flown supporting cover for the two destroyers on the night the second attack was supposed to have occurred. (He was subsequently shot down over North Vietnam, where he remained a prisoner of war for eight years. Then, a much-decorated war hero, he was promoted to the rank of vice admiral for his services to the country.) His vivid account of what happened on the night of August 4 is a telling one.[50]

I had assigned myself the job of pouncer, of staying right over the Maddox and Joy, of leaving the big picture to somebody else while I maneuvered close to the water, unencumbered by a wingman, lights off, trying to find whatever boat the destroyers were talking about and blast it immediately.

I had the best seat in the house from which to detect boats—if there were any. I didn't have to look through surface haze and spray like the destroyers did, and yet I could see the destroyers' every move vividly. Time and again I flew right over the Maddox and the Joy, throttled back, lights out, like a near-silent stalking owl, conserving fuel at a 250-knot loiter speed. I could roll over and look right up the two churning phosphorescent destroyer wakes and see their decks heaving in chopping seas, spray coming over their bows as they maneuvered and kept the airwaves full of course-change signals. There must have been 20 knots of surface wind down there.

When the destroyers were convinced they had some battle action going, I zigged and zagged and fired where they fired unless it looked like I might get caught in their shot patterns or unless they had told me to fire somewhere else. The edges of the black hole I was flying in were still periodically lit by flashes of lightning—but no wakes or dark shapes other than those of the destroyers were ever visible to me.

On his return to the *Ticonderoga,* Stockdale was asked, "Did you see any boats?" and replied "Not a one. No boats, no wakes, no ricochets off boats, no boat impacts, no torpedo wakes—nothing but black sea and American firepower." He was then shown a just-completed log of radio messages received from the *Maddox.* Noting with relief that, after several hours of alarms, Captain Herrick had urged a complete reevaluation before any further action was taken, he said to himself, "At least there's a commodore up there in the Gulf who has the guts to blow the whistle on a screw-up, and take the heat to set the record straight."

Awakened the next morning to lead an air strike against North Vietnam as a reprisal for "last night's attack on the destroyers," he writes, "I felt like I had been doused with ice-water. How do I get in touch with the president? He's going off half-cocked."

Five days later, Stockdale writes, he was visited by the deputy assistant secretary of defense for international security affairs, Alvin Friedman, and McNamara's special assistant, Jack Stempler. They had a question for him: "Were there any f——in' boats out there the other night or not?"

At the National Security Council session on August 4, the president, as was frequently the case in his meetings with this group, had apparently already made up his mind on the actions to be taken. The record of that meeting (finally released in December 1980) is nevertheless informative as to the positions of some of his senior advisers, as well as suggestive of what may have been his own lack of some pertinent information.[51]

> SECRETARY MCNAMARA: The North Vietnamese PT boats have continued their attacks on the two U.S. destroyers in international waters in the Gulf of Tonkin. No enemy aircraft was involved. Our efforts to learn the exact situation and protect the Patrol have been complicated by a very low ceiling. One of the two destroyers was fired on by automatic weapons and was lit up by searchlights.

> SECRETARY RUSK: An immediate and direct reaction by us is necessary. The unprovoked attack on the high seas is an act of war for all practical purposes. We have been trying to get a signal to Hanoi and Peking. Our response to this attack may be that signal. We are informing NATO, SEATO, and the UN. As an indication of Hanoi's intentions, this second attack was a more serious decision for the North Vietnamese than the decision to make the first attack.

> SECRETARY MCNAMARA: We have agreed to air strikes on two bases in the north of North Vietnam and two base complexes in the south of North Vietnam. A fifth target has been deleted because it is close to Communist China. In addition, any North Vietnamese PT boats and Swatows found off Vietnam outside the three-mile limit will be attacked as part of an armed reconnaissance program. (The execute order as actually sent is attached— JCS 7720.)

> CIA DIRECTOR MCCONE: The proposed U.S. reprisals will result in a sharp North Vietnamese military reaction, but such actions would not represent a deliberate decision to provoke or accept a major escalation of the Vietnamese war. (The text of Mr. McCone's estimate of probable North Vietnamese and Chinese Communist reactions to our reprisal is attached.)

> THE PRESIDENT: Do they want a war by attacking our ships in the middle of the Gulf of Tonkin?

> [In the August 2 attack, the *Maddox* had been under orders to go to eight miles off the mainland and four miles off the two coastal islands of Hon Me and Hon Nieu. Shortly before the alleged August 4 attack, it and the *Turner Joy* paralleled the mainland up to a distance of sixteen miles and passed within thirteen miles of the two islands before turning east into the Gulf of Tonkin, where, some sixty miles from the coast, they reported being attacked.]

> DIRECTOR MCCONE: No. The North Vietnamese are reacting defensively to our attacks on their off-shore islands. They are responding out of pride and on the basis of defense considerations. The attack is a signal to us that the North Vietnamese have the will and determination to continue the war. They are raising the ante.

[On the nights of July 30 and 31, South Vietnamese naval vessels operating under the U.S.-directed OPLAN 34-A had bombarded the two offshore islands. On the nights of August 3 and 4 (shortly before the alleged attack on the U.S. destroyers), they bombarded the North Vietnam mainland coast (the Rhon River area and the Vinh Son radar facility—quite possibly one that the destroyer's electronic surveillance had activated and located.)]

THE PRESIDENT: Are we going to react to their shooting at our ships over 40 miles from their shores? If yes, we should do more than merely return the fire of the attacking ships. If this is so, then the question involves no more than the number of North Vietnamese targets to be attacked.

USIA DIRECTOR ROWAN: Do we know for a fact that the North Vietnamese provocation took place? Can we nail down exactly what happened? We must be prepared to be accused of fabricating the incident.

SECRETARY McNAMARA: We will know definitely in the morning.
[Two lines sanitized.]

SECRETARY RUSK: We should ask the Congressional leaders whether we should seek a Congressional resolution. (The draft resolution read by Secretary Rusk is attached.) This short and clear draft is similar to the Mid-East resolution.

SECRETARY McNAMARA: In addition to the air strikes, we plan to send major U.S. reinforcements into the area. These include ships, men and planes. (A detailed listing of these forces is attached.)

A draft statement for the President was revised. It is to be made public by the President as soon as the U.S. attack planes are over target.

It should, then, be no longer in dispute that Congress was denied very important information necessary to a sound judgment as to whether it should endorse either an air strike against North Vietnam or the Tonkin Gulf Resolution. Whether the root cause of this lay with the navy, the Defense Intelligence Agency, McNamara, or some combination of the three is not likely to be established until more of the pertinent government documents have been released. Nor, until that happens, will it be possible to determine whether some of this information was kept from the president. But his response to the Pentagon's subsequent Tonkin Gulf alarm, in mid-September, does suggest that this may have been the case, a possibility that warrants further investigation whenever the relevant cables and memoranda are declassified.

The Tonkin Gulf Resolution and the bombing strikes against North Vietnam that accompanied it also, of course, had their domestic political uses for the administration. It is widely agreed that the administration's handling of this situation undercut some of Senator Goldwater's appeal to the hawks, while at the same time giving an impression of strength tempered by restraint that appealed to moderate elements within the electorate. The Republican candidate felt obliged to give full support to the president's actions: "We cannot allow the American flag to be shot at anywhere on earth if we are to retain our respect and prestige."[52]

It is important, however, to note a fact pointed out by Eric Goldman: although, even in the post–Tonkin Gulf phase of electioneering, "the overwhelming impact of the LBJ campaign remarks on Vietnam was that he fully intended to stay out of a shooting war," the president usually spoke with sufficient ambiguity as not to foreclose that option completely. He was against American combat intervention, but he did not intend to let South Vietnam be "swallowed up by Communist conquest." This ambiguity is amply demonstrated in one of his most-quoted campaign speeches (Manchester, New Hampshire, September 28), which contains three of what Goldman terms "escape-hatch clauses" (here rendered in italics):[53]

> Some of our people—Mr. Nixon, Mr. Rockefeller, Mr. Scranton, and Mr. Goldwater—have all, at some time or other, suggested the possible wisdom of going north in Vietnam. Well, now, before you start attacking someone and you launch a big offensive, you better give some consideration to how you are going to protect what you have. And when a brigadier general can walk down the streets of Saigon, as they did the other day, and take over the police station, the radio station, and the government without firing a shot, I don't know how much offensive we are prepared to launch.
>
> As far as I am concerned, I want to be very cautious and careful, and use it *only as a last resort,* when I start dropping bombs around that are likely to involve American boys in a war in Asia with 700 million Chinese.
>
> So *just for the moment* I have not thought we were ready for American boys to do the fighting for Asian boys. What I have been trying to do, with the situation that I found, was to get the boys in Vietnam to do their own fighting with our advice and with our equipment. . . . We are not going north and drop bombs *at this stage of the game,* and we are not going south and run out and leave it for the Communists to take over.
>
> Now we have lost 190 American lives, and to each one of those 190 families this is a major war. . . . I often wake up in the night and think about how many I could lose if I made a misstep.
>
> When we retaliated in the Tonkin Gulf, we dropped bombs on their nests where they had their PT boats housed, and we dropped them within thirty-five miles of the Chinese border. I don't know what you would think if they started dropping them thirty-five miles from your border, but I think that is something you have to take into consideration.
>
> So . . . we are going to continue to try to get them to save their own freedom. . . . We think that losing 190 lives in the period that we have been out there is bad. But it is not like 190,000 that we might lose the first month if we escalated that war.
>
> . . . We are trying somehow to evolve a way, as we have in some other places, where the North Vietnamese and the Chinese Communists will

finally, after getting worn down, conclude that they will leave their neighbors alone. And if they do, we will come home tomorrow.

It is not any problem to start a war. . . . I know some folks that I think could start one mighty easy. But it is a pretty difficult problem for us to prevent one, and that is what we are trying to do.

Khanh did not reap the internal political benefits that both he and the Johnson administration had expected him to receive from the U.S. air strike against the North and the accompanying resolution. There occurred no lasting boost in morale for even the most warlike members of the Saigon military establishment, and, except among that small coterie, the loosing of American bombs against compatriots and relatives in the North was not popular among southerners. In the view of American officials, Khanh did seem to have secured at least one advantage: a plausible basis for increasing and consolidating his power. But his efforts to achieve this were soon frustrated.[54]

The American fear, shared by numerous ARVN officers, that the Tonkin Gulf air strike might incite military reprisals from the North provided Khanh with the excuse to decree a state of emergency that gave him and his subordinates on the Military Revolutionary Council what the CIA characterized as "all but absolute power." Hanoi did not retaliate against the strike, but, as Peter Grose reported in *The New York Times,* upon being armed with this new authority Khanh—"evidently urged and certainly supported" by the U.S. embassy and his American military advisers— severely curtailed civil liberties, imposed stricter censorship, and then moved to reduce Dai Viet representation in his Cabinet and to oust Minh as chief of state. Minh's removal was to be managed through the introduction of a new constitution ("The Vungtau Charter"), drafted in consultation with American officials, that eliminated his position and at the same time gave Khanh the new post of president, while he also remained chairman of the MRC. However, worried about the adverse effects on American opinion of too extensive a reorganization of the Saigon government, Washington prevailed upon Khanh to eliminate some of the most provocative elements of his constitution (such as his effort to scrap any promise of elections), and not to drop his foreign minister, Phan Huy Quat, or his finance minister, Nguyen Xuan Oanh, both of whom were regarded as being pro-American and as having made good impressions in the United States.[55]

Apart from this, however, U.S. officials endorsed Khanh's assumption of greater power. But neither they nor he was prepared for the explosive reaction when he announced his assumption of the presidency on August 16, promulgated his new constitution, and sharply curtailed remaining civil liberties. The protest demonstrations made abundantly clear that the bombing of the North and the congressional resolution that had emboldened Khanh had not induced the greater political solidarity anticipated by Johnson's advisers. The symbols of American power and commitment inherent in these actions evidently exerted no countervailing influence against the almost immediate protest, spearheaded by Buddhist and student activists, against Khanh's political moves.[56]

On August 24, as the Buddhists and their student allies led massive demonstrations against him and while pro-Dai Viet Catholic generals maneuvered for a coup, Khanh sought out three of the most influential monks—Tri Quang, Tam Chau, and Thien Minh—in the hopes of ending Buddhist opposition. As their price they demanded, among other things, that he abolish his new constitution, establish a civilian government, assure full freedom of religion and expression, and schedule free elections by November 1, 1965. Khanh was gauche enough to tell them that he would first have to consult the Americans, and news of this acknowledged subservience quickly circulated around Saigon. Predictably, the mounting street demonstrations against Khanh took on a more anti-American tone. He panicked, and at 1:00 A.M. on the night of August 25, routed Taylor and Alexis Johnson out of bed for advice. They counseled him to accept the Buddhist demands "in principle, but otherwise to be tough and not to knuckle under to any minority." Khanh, however, publicly backed down, announcing that he would revise the new constitution, reduce press censorship, rectify local abuses, and permit orderly demonstrations.[57]

Yet these halfway concessions satisfied neither the Buddhists nor the students, and the demonstrations became increasingly uncontrolled. Trying to placate a crowd of some twenty-five thousand gathered outside his office, Khanh made an obsequious and undignified address from the top of a car, denying that he wanted to be a dictator, and shouted, "Down with military dictatorship." When the crowd still refused to disperse, he discreetly withdrew to his military headquarters.[58]

Khanh and the top MRC officers then retreated, in the face of the power marshaled by the Buddhists. A clearly alarmed General Westmoreland cabled Washington that in a confrontational meeting with these officers the Buddhists made demands that "were in effect an ultimatum," and that Khanh and his military colleagues capitulated. Moreover, Westmoreland emphasized that the spokesman for the Buddhist monks, Tri Quang, "had not repeat had not agreed to denounce the Communists." His overall assessment was that the Buddhists had been "remarkably successful in political action tactics of divide and conquer" and that though the army continued to be "the key power factor, it is, at the moment, effectively neutralized. . . ." He warned that, although it was likely that the MRC would continue in its support of Khanh, Tri Quang's groups would probably "successively and successfully press demands on Khanh enroute to a still indeterminate final objective." In concurrent reports, the CIA saw Tri Quang as determined to become the government's éminence grise, found "overtones of anti-American sentiment" surfacing in some of these demonstrations, pointed out that "war weariness and a desire for a quick solution to the long struggle against the Viet Cong may be an important factor underlying the current agitation," and warned that "the confused situation is extremely vulnerable to exploitation by the Communists and by the proponents of a negotiated settlement." Moreover, according to the CIA, a member of Khanh's Cabinet, Le Van Hoach, who was reportedly in contact with the NLF to try to obtain the release of American prisoners, was also thought to believe that many of the NLF were "non-Communist nationalists who could be won over to the government in a negotiated settlement of the war." Noting that Taylor had mentioned to Khanh that he was aware of the minister's contacts with the NLF, but that this Cabinet member was apparently maintaining his self-professed relations with it, the CIA concluded: "This could indicate that Khanh wishes to maintain this channel to Viet Cong thinking for reasons of his own."[59]

Mounting demonstrations against Khanh in Saigon and Danang, along with indications that he was about to abdicate, thoroughly alarmed American officials. Taylor and Westmoreland recommended that as a precautionary measure a special U.S. landing force be positioned just out of sight of land midway between the two restive cities. Westmoreland sought to reassure Khanh and strengthen his hand against rival officers by promising him that henceforward U.S. military advisers throughout South Vietnam would remain on the alert to advise him of any unusual troop movements that might be indicative of a coup. But despite this sentry duty in Khanh's behalf, rivals within the armed forces continued to plan his ouster, and were finally deterred only by American intervention. Testifying to the critical nature of U.S. support at this juncture, Taylor later observed, "In the face of a buzzsaw of Buddhist Institute and student opposition to the Charter Khanh completely caved in. . . . In the two-day meeting of the Military Revolutionary Council which followed, it was only our solid and unconditional support that kept Khanh from being swept out by his fellow officers."[60]

The need for such American intervention to maintain Khanh in power made it even clearer that the Tonkin Gulf bombing and congressional resolution had not induced unity among the Vietnamese military. On the contrary, they appeared to feel that there was even less need for solidarity; as a CIA analysis of just a week after this observed, "Many officers feel that the U.S. is now fully committed, and that more of the burden of carrying on the war will now pass to the U.S."[61] This was hardly the "psychological lift" and increased dedication to fighting the Viet Cong that the JCS and most of the president's civilian advisers had predicted.

Even though the embassy had made clear to the feuding officers of the MRC that for the United States it was "Khanh all the way," the MRC was unable to reach a consensus as to who should head the government. In the face of this impasse, the embassy pressed hard for what was officially regarded as a "compromise" solution. Khanh was to share power in a "troika" with his still-popular rival General Minh and the pro–Dai Viet Catholic leader, General Tran Thien Khiem—Khanh's partner in ousting Minh's government just seven months before, but now his bitter rival as well as Minh's. Under the aegis of this clearly incompatible triumvirate, Khanh was to serve as a "caretaker" prime minister until elections were held, as had been promised the Buddhists. This interim formula created more tensions within the officer corps than it moderated; it never took hold, the military were soon split worse than ever, and the elections were not held. Although reporting that the troika's members privately acknowledged that the arrangement was "mere window dressing and not intended to solve anything," Taylor opposed abandoning this stopgap measure until Khanh had laid careful groundwork for subsequent, U.S.-approved changes in political structure. He cautioned Khanh against trying to establish any form of all-civilian rule —the Buddhists might well have been able to exert a dominant influence— arguing that such a government would be too weak and tend toward neutralism. Scarcely sanguine about what might emerge, Taylor cautioned Washington, "We should not delude ourselves that we can put together any combination of personalities that will add up to a really effective government."[62]

Seeing no South Vietnamese candidate more likely than Khanh to provide a cooperative political base, Taylor continued to work hard to shore up his precarious position and "return him to a position of responsibility and authority."[63] Through intensive lobbying among senior officers, the U.S. mission helped salvage some of his power and buy him a little more time. Assured at least temporarily of support from the Buddhist leaders whom he had just appeased, and confident of a still-unqualified American backing, Khanh was able largely to ignore the two other members of a triumvirate that now existed essentially on paper, and continue to exercise on his own most of what little authority still remained with the Saigon government.

The weakness of Khanh's position and the conditional nature of his Buddhist support were starkly laid out in a contemporary CIA assessment: "Buddhist leaders have declared that Khanh is personally acceptable as head of the government, but only if he divorces himself from the military and civilian elements deemed by the Buddhists to be remnants of the Diem regime's control organ, the Can Lao Party. On the other hand, much of Khanh's real power within the MRC and over key armed forces units is dependent upon officers objectionable to the Buddhists."[64] To complicate matters for him, while most of those whom the Buddhists opposed were ex–Can Lao Catholics, others constituted part of the membership of the "Young Turk" faction—that privileged group whose loyalty Khanh had so recently sought to purchase by rapid promotion from colonel to brigadier general.

Initially at least, the Young Turks found it expedient to back Khanh in his mutually hostile maneuvering with the ex–Can Lao Dai Viet Catholic officers (earlier his allies in the coup against Minh but now his most bitter opponents), who were supported by the cautious General Thieu, and the controversial Catholic Colonel Pham Ngoc Thao. Khanh was thus able to head off a Dai Viet coup that had been set for September 2. But the reprieve was brief, ending as soon as he moved to redress the seesawing power balance within the military by rehabilitating the Dai Viet officers' long-standing opponents, the four "Dalat generals" (the top lieutenants of Minh whom Khanh had put under house arrest in Dalat in February 1964). Khanh's plans to incorporate them into his power base and replace Khiem as minister of defense with either himself or the Dalat General Tran Van Don alienated some of the most powerful Young Turks, as well as further antagonizing the Dai Viet Catholics. If anything more was needed to light the Dai Viet fuse, it was the threat implied in Khanh's announcement that "several" unnamed generals "would be leaving South Vietnam" along with his former deputy prime minister, the prominent civilian Dai Viet leader Nguyen Ton Hoan.[65]

When these Dai Viet and other Catholic officers finally, on September 13, launched their major coup attempt against Khanh, the Young Turks at first refused to support him. American intelligence reported that the coup leaders were primarily men who felt their positions threatened or who had been antagonized by Khanh's "capitulation to the Buddhists" and his efforts to rehabilitate the Dalat generals. They were headed by Generals Duong Van Duc (scheduled soon to be relieved as IV Corps commander) and Lam Van Phat (until recently Khanh's minister of the interior), together with Colonel Duong Huu Nghia, a Dai Viet commander of a major armored unit, and that most persistent of plotters, Colonel Pham Ngoc Thao. In organizing their effort, the rebels were assisted by Defense Minister Khiem. In addition they appear initially to have enjoyed the encouragement and tacit support of General Thieu and some of the Young Turks. Employing about seven battalions from Duc's command and some armored elements, the coup forces seized many key points in Saigon, and General Phat announced over Saigon Radio that Khanh had been deposed and he and Duc had taken over.[66]

Khanh, who was in Dalat when the coup forces struck, requested that U.S. marines be sent in to rescue him and that Westmoreland help him with a "counter plan." No marines were actually sent ashore, but some were stationed off Saigon and Danang, just out of sight of land, "in position for rapid reaction if required." American officials worked hard to salvage Khanh's situation. At his request, before the rebels could consolidate their hold on Saigon, the "Voice of America" went on the air to emphasize that the United States backed him and not the coup leaders. More decisive for the outcome was the fact that Westmoreland and American military advisers made an all-out effort in applying sustained pressure on commanders of some of the units upon whom the coup leaders most counted, and persuaded them to disengage their forces and get out of Saigon. The critical watershed seems to have come with Westmoreland's confrontation with Duc, the most important of the coup leaders. In cabling his description of this encounter to Washington, the American commander stated that he "in no uncertain terms . . . informed him [Duc] that MACV, the U.S. Mission, and the U.S. Government did not support in any way his move, [and] advised that he get his troops moved out of town [Saigon] immediately. He said he understood and thanked me. He seemed to be a shaky and insecure young man." It was evident that the coup leaders had underestimated the firmness of Khanh's United States backing, and when American efforts induced a rapid erosion of their supporting troops, the rebels had no option but to give up.[67]

During its first hours, the coup attempt had been favored by the stance of some of the Young Turks as well as that of Khiem and Thieu. Air Marshal Nguyen Cao Ky and General Nguyen Chanh Thi, the I Corps commander, appeared to be sitting on the fence (along with the generals commanding II and III Corps) and did not throw their weight against the rebels until the coup effort was well under way and American opposition to the coup—or at least to its success—was clear. Perhaps, as one knowledgeable Vietnamese source states, Phat's triumphant broadcast over Saigon Radio led them to conclude that they had been double-crossed and could not expect major positions in a new regime. In any case, Ky, at least, had sufficiently close relations with the U.S. military mission so that he would have soon been apprised of American opposition to the coup. But there was also considerable speculation in Vietnamese circles that he and Thi might have calculated that, by rallying to Khanh only after his fate was in the balance, they could reduce his power and increase their leverage with him.[68]

Khanh had good reason to believe that General Khiem, his most vocal opponent in the MRC, had been an instigator of the coup, and he insisted that this rival should be gotten out of the country. Here the State Department and Taylor supported Khanh and obligingly smoothed the way by agreeing to Khiem's appointment as ambassador to the United States, where Pham Ngoc Thao soon joined him as press attaché. Coping with Khanh's ongoing feud with Minh—who had remained neutral during the coup attempt—proved more difficult for U.S. officials. By the end of October, however, McNamara and Rusk had joined Taylor in concluding that the United States should not support Minh in his efforts to become chief of state, that American interests would best be served if Khanh "comes out on top." To get Minh out of Vietnam, while preserving some of his "face," the U.S. government and Khanh arranged for him to be sent abroad on a very expensive American-financed "good will tour."[69]

The elimination of Minh, Khiem, and the defeated coup generals enhanced the relative strength of the Young Turks within the military establishment, and their leverage with Khanh became all the greater. To offset them and restore the balance, Khanh saw to it that the military court acquitted two of the coup generals, Duc and Phat, while releasing and calling back to military duties the four Dalat generals, who were still under detention. Now admitting that there was in fact no evidence of these officers having supported any French-inspired neutralist plot, Khanh sought to restore them to military duties; on November 14 he named General Tran Van Don as deputy chief of staff, and subsequently appointed General Ton That Dinh as Don's assistant. The Young Turks, however, understood quite well the motives behind these moves, and the tension between them and Khanh increased.[70]

In the face of the Young Turks' mounting threat, Khanh began to worry that his alliance with the United States was not in itself sufficient to maintain his position. Though he continued to have some success in keeping these assertive younger officers from uniting effectively against him, he concluded that in the long run he could not survive without buttressing from an additional quarter. So, in what was strictly a marriage of convenience, he turned to the only large and organized noncommunist political force in South Vietnam—the Buddhists. He thus gained additional leverage against military rivals, more room for political maneuver, and essential support in a number of crises; but his embarking on this strategy constituted something of a watershed in his relations with the United States and the beginning of the erosion of its absolutely essential backing.

Initially, neither Taylor nor most Washington officials favored yielding to the Buddhists' demand for "civilianizing" the government, fearing that a regime not dominated by the military would be less likely to prosecute the war actively and more susceptible to neutralist pressures. But the broad popular backing the Buddhists clearly still enjoyed—along with the recurrent demonstrations by students and other civilian elements—made it seem prudent for a civilian government to be established. Thus, working with Taylor and other U.S. officials, Khanh undertook to map out a new political system. Essentially, this called for yielding to the Buddhists on the issue of civilian government while keeping their sympathizers out of key positions within such a government. A militantly anticommunist and antineutralist civilian administration was set up, with a Cabinet made up of nonparty professional men and civil servants free from significant Buddhist influence, while Khanh continued to head the military establishment. But though he was to stand as much as possible in the background, American officials expected that overall he would have major political influence and ultimate authority in the new government.

A key feature of the new system was a seventeen-member High National Council installed on September 26, made up of generally respected elderly civilians.[71] Among the council's tasks were writing a new provisional constitution and assuming some of the functions of an interim legislature, pending the elections that Khanh and the MRC had promised the Buddhists. Of most immediate importance, the council was to select a chief of state, who would in turn designate a new prime minister. With U.S. concurrence, on October 24 the council chose as chief of state Phan Khac Suu, an elderly and respected but rather ineffective political leader with Cao Dai connections. With the embassy's agreement, Suu promptly appointed as his prime minister a former mayor of Saigon, Tran Van Huong—a man favored by the embassy but from the outset unacceptable to the Buddhists.

Though the fragility of Khanh's wavering support among the unstable South Vietnamese military factions was very disturbing to American officials, they were even more anxious about his relationship with the Buddhists. The military's total dependence on the United States for their salaries and equipment gave American officials considerable power in dealing with its officers. The Buddhists, on the other hand, were in no way dependent, their authority being grounded in broad popular opposition to the war and their ability to identify with and speak for a powerful current of nationalism that rebelled at the American tutelage acquiesced in by the top military leaders. Alarm at the implications of Khanh's rapprochement with the Buddhist leaders was already reflected in reports to Washington in late August, just after his capitulation to their demands. The CIA station chief in Saigon then cabled that Khanh had "in effect put his government completely in the hands of Tri Quang, and by so doing has similarly bound over to Tri Quang's safe keeping our own government's equity, commitment, and policy in this country." He went on to observe that in view of Tri Quang's "belief that Catholicism is a greater threat to Vietnam than Communism, and his fuzzy thinking on neutralism, his accession to real power even behind [the] scenes would jeopardize U.S. interests and objectives in Vietnam."[72]

A more dispassionate report by the CIA's Board of National Intelligence Estimates two weeks later concluded that "at present the odds are against the emergence of a stable government capable of effectively prosecuting the war in Vietnam," and that "the longer the present unstable situation lasts, the more difficult it will be to form a government which can preserve even the appearance of unity and determination." It cautioned that "in such circumstances, neutralist sentiment would almost certainly increase, together with the danger that a loosely organized coalition would emerge which could take advantage of frustration and war weariness to seek a neutralist solution." The possibility of such a development must have seemed all the more real when the next day a CIA report from Saigon stated that Khanh (however serious he may have been) intended to ask Tri Quang to form a government if by November 1 other civilians had not succeeded in doing so.[73]

Khanh's growing reliance on the Buddhists was a matter of mounting worry for American officials, for they had become increasingly suspicious of the monks' ultimate political goals. Among Americans in both Washington and Saigon, the belief became more and more widespread that the formidable mass backing obtained by the Buddhist leaders was basically dependent upon their espousal of neutralist goals—an end to the fighting and a negotiated peace with the NLF, followed by a coalition government. The belief was in fact well founded, and only the Buddhists' emphasis on immediate tactics—their efforts to influence the existing government's policies on less controversial matters, such as the promise of elections, greater freedom of expression, and the ousting of Prime Minister Huong—deflected attention away from these longer-range objectives. A CIA report of September 19, however, had foreshadowed a developing consensus within the American official community on the ultimate aims of the Buddhists. Referring to Tri Quang, probably then the most influential of the Buddhist leaders, it stated that though "at the present time" he was not to be regarded as "a Communist or a conscious Viet Cong agent . . . he is capable of allying himself with the Communists at any time such an alliance strikes him as advantageous for his own political ambitions and religious objectives—two causes he almost certainly views as one." It described Tri Quang as "a fanatic nationalist, undoubtedly anxious to see the U.S. out of Vietnam at the earliest possible moment," and correctly concluded: "Consequently, some negotiated or neutralist solution which would expedite the U.S. departure must have considerable appeal in his eyes."[74]

American concern over Khanh's tactical alliance with the Buddhists did not lead to any precipitate withdrawal of support from the general—U.S. officials saw no better-qualified leader—and, indeed, at the end of November, Westmoreland reported that he had dissuaded Ky from carrying out plans for a coup.[75] During the fall of 1964 this backing had become considerably less enthusiastic and much more circumspect than earlier in the year. It was not, however, until Khanh's highly publicized row with Taylor, toward the end of December, that some U.S. officials began seriously to look for a replacement—a task made more difficult because the field of even remotely acceptable candidates was drastically narrowed by the ambassador's almost simultaneous showdown with the Young Turks.

IX

Escalation
and Political Viability

The Tonkin Gulf Resolution and accompanying air strike against the North had clearly not produced the anticipated effect in South Vietnam. Despite the predictions of their proponents in Washington, these measures failed to induce greater political cohesion in the faltering Saigon regime; they had not brought it to carry out a more aggressive campaign against the Viet Cong; and they had not offset the tidal flow of war weariness and neutralist sentiment among southerners. Indeed, during the weeks following the Tonkin actions, quite the opposite obtained on all fronts. Khanh's government was close to collapse; its military commanders became increasingly intent on shifting responsibility for the fighting to the United States; antiwar sentiment and support for a neutralist solution grew; and only an alchemist could have found any upsurge of morale within the regime.

Some presidential advisers were now disposed to pause, take closer stock of political realities in the South, and re-evaluate their options. Others, however, remained confident in their original belief that greater U.S. military intervention would yield positive psychological and political results in the South. The formula was fundamentally correct, they insisted: that it had failed thus far was due to an insufficient component of military force. The Tonkin Gulf Resolution could not be expected to affect the political situation in the South unless that resolution was fleshed out with something more than a single day of air strikes against the North. Ongoing, palpable indications of American resolve were needed.

Thus, three weeks after Tonkin, the Joint Chiefs pushed for "an accelerated program of actions" against the North, arguing that "only significant military pressures on the DRV are likely to provide [Saigon] the relief and psychological boost necessary for attainment of the requisite governmental stability and viability." They criticized Maxwell Taylor for warning a week earlier that the U.S. should not commit itself to exerting added pressure against the North until after Khanh had stabilized his government and substantially improved his own military situation. More generally, they disagreed with his proposition that the United States "should be slow to get deeply involved until we have a better feel for the quality of our ally," for, they asserted, "The United States is already deeply involved." Ignoring Taylor's caveat—"We should not get involved militarily with North Vietnam and possibly China if our base in South Vietnam is insecure and Khanh's army is tied down everywhere by the VC insurgency"— they reiterated the June 2 recommendation made by all their members except Taylor that military actions be taken against the North "with the objective of destroying, as necessary, the DRV will and capabilities to continue support of insurgent forces" in the South and in Laos.[1]

Whereas the Joint Chiefs still focused on bombardment of the North, McGeorge Bundy privately urged the president to inject major U.S. ground combat forces into the South. He pointed out that existing contingency plans were "more to heighten morale and to show our strength of purpose than to accomplish anything very specific in a military sense" and that Robert McNamara, for reasons that he did not understand, was strongly opposed even to "landing a limited number of Marines to guard specific installations." Noting that "a still more drastic possibility which no one is discussing is the use of substantial U.S. armed forces in operations against the Viet Cong," Bundy concluded, "It seems to me at least possible that a couple of brigade-size units put in to do specific jobs about six weeks from now might be good medicine everywhere."[2] Clearly Johnson was unwilling to endorse Bundy's suggestion, for, instead of accepting it or the JCS's proposal, he ordered Taylor to return from Vietnam for a full review of policy.

The popular opposition against Khanh at the end of August, and the continuing tensions both among the military and religious leaders and between them and Khanh, brought Ambassador Taylor to amend his previous political assessment. On the eve of his return to Washington, he urged that the administration drop the idea of relying on promises of pressures on the North to act as leverage to improve Saigon's military performance, and lower its sights to the hope that these promises would simply raise Saigon's morale sufficiently to maintain its war effort. "We now have a better feel for the quality of our ally and for what we can expect from him in terms of ability to govern. Only the emergence of an exceptional leader could improve the situation, and no George Washington is in sight." As a consequence, Taylor observed, "we can and must anticipate for the future an instrument of government which will have definite limits of performance," which "at best . . . might be capable of maintaining a holding operation against the Viet Cong" and would "look increasingly to the United States to take the major responsibility for prying the Viet Cong and the North Vietnamese off the backs of the South Vietnamese population." The local politicians, he concluded with evident bitterness, "feel today that the political hassle is their appropriate arena" and that "the conflict with the VC belongs to the Americans."[3]

Taylor's analysis reflected the most fundamental and perdurable political problem faced by the United States in South Vietnam. Optimally, the administration sought a political base in South Vietnam, strong enough and stable enough to ensure that most of the area would be kept free from communist control, with at least enough of this territory (Saigon included) conserved to allow the basing of sufficient U.S. military power to compensate for the weakness of the South Vietnamese regime. However, to provide strength and stability for Saigon required a Vietnamese leadership with a much wider popular base than any yet had been able to enjoy. Consequently, the abiding problem for American officials was that the more broadly based and responsible to public opinion a Saigon government became, the less disposed it would be to continue with the fighting, and the greater the popular pressure it would be under to negotiate a neutralist political settlement incompatible with any continuing U.S. presence.

Thus, Taylor now perceived that the worst outcome would be a government that would "continue to seek a broadened consensus," an amalgam that "may be expected in due course to become susceptible to an accommodation with the liberation front." He concluded, "We may, therefore, expect to find ourselves faced with a choice of (A) passively watching the development of a popular front, knowing that this may in due course require the U.S. to leave Vietnam in failure; or (B) actively assuming increased responsibility for the outcome following a time-schedule consistent with our estimate of the limited viability of any South Vietnamese government." In view of U.S. "total world responsibilities and the significance of Vietnam in relation to them," he argued, there was no choice but to accept course (B), with "escalating pressures" on the North to begin around December 1; for "if we leave Vietnam with our tail between our legs, the consequences of this defeat in the rest of Asia, Africa, and Latin America would be disastrous."[4]

Having read Taylor's alarming report, Johnson and his top advisers met with him in Washington on September 9. McGeorge Bundy's Memorandum for the Record of this meeting does not refer to Bundy's own views or provide any hint of the relatively bellicose policy he had privately recommended to the president, but it does help considerably to clarify the ideas then held by several other top advisers and by Johnson himself.[5] The air-force and marine-corps chiefs held that, unless "extensive U.S. air strikes against North Vietnam" were promptly carried out, the situation in the South would continue to deteriorate. General Earle Wheeler, Taylor's successor as chairman of the JCS, and the army and navy representatives on that body, however, agreed with the ambassador "that it was important not to overstrain the currently weakened GVN by drastic action in the immediate future." Postponing any such move was supported by McNamara, Rusk, and McCone, with the latter admonishing that a sustained air assault might also trigger reprisals by communist China. In opposing attacks for the present, Rusk noted that a decision to mount them could be taken at any time—"at 5 minutes' notice"—and that meanwhile the United States might be helped by the deepening Sino-Soviet split, which, as it grew more severe, might result in "real inhibitions upon adventures by Peking and Hanoi in Southeast Asia."

It was evident that Johnson was heavily preoccupied with the weakness of the Saigon regime. Responding to his question whether the United States could not stop the internal feuding, Taylor explained that this was very difficult with a group of men "who turn off their hearing aids" in the face of appeals to the public welfare. "These people," he said, "simply do not have the sense of responsibility for the public interest to which we were accustomed and regularly estimated matters in terms of their own personal gains and losses." When Johnson asked him to compare the people's affection for Khanh and Diem, Taylor replied that the South Vietnamese cared for neither.

The CIA, McCone warned, was disturbed by the prospect that the "internal movement toward negotiations might be increasing and that there was some sign of anti-American feeling in South Vietnam." "It could happen," he said, that "the President would find that the purposes originally set forth in Eisenhower's 1954 letter [to Ngo Dinh Diem] were no longer supported by the people of South Vietnam themselves." McCone endorsed McNamara's emphasis on the importance of "politico-economic action in the urban areas . . . to lower the level of student and Buddhist pressure and increase the political base of support for the GVN." For such a program, McNamara argued, money should be no object. Rusk agreed, stating that winning would be worth any amount, and citing the example of the American role in the anticommunist struggle in Greece during the late 1940s, which he said "worked out at $50,000 a guerrilla."

When Taylor then emphasized that in the long run the current American effort in Vietnam was insufficient and that "sooner or later" the United States would have to act more forcefully against the North, though now was not the best time, the president asked "if anyone doubted whether it was worth all this effort." The response was a veritable fusillade from Taylor and Wheeler, supported by McCone and Rusk. Taylor said that, in terms of its "overall position in the area and in the world," Washington could not afford to let Hanoi win. Wheeler "supported him most forcefully, reporting the unanimous view of the Joint Chiefs that if we should lose in South Vietnam, we would lose Southeast Asia," and that "country after country on the periphery would give way and look toward Communist China as the rising power of the area." McCone concurred with this view, as did Rusk, "with considerable force."

Johnson observed that "the proper answer to those advocating immediate and extensive action against the North was that we should not do this until our side could defend itself in the streets of Saigon." The reason for waiting was that "with a weak and wobbly situation it would be unwise to attack until we could stabilize our base." He concluded by asking Wheeler "to explain to his colleagues in the JCS that we would be ready to do more when we had a base," observing that he "did not wish to enter the patient in a 10-round bout, when he was in no shape to hold out for one round," and that "We should get him ready to face 3 or 4 rounds at least."

Johnson's caution was further reflected in the National Security Action Memorandum that he approved the next day. There he agreed that the United States "should be prepared to respond as appropriate against the DRV in the event of any attack on U.S. units" or any "special" North Vietnamese/Viet Cong action against South Vietnam. But any such decision was to be "governed by a prevailing judgement that the first order of business at present is to take actions which will help to strengthen the fabric of the Government of South Vietnam; to the extent that the situation permits, such action should precede larger decisions." It should be emphasized that this was no more than an agreement in principle that the United States would make the necessary preparations to escalate if and when the president found it appropriate. The decision did not expressly prescribe bombing, nor was it a green light for future air strikes.[6] Johnson was almost immediately given additional justification for his policy just three days after this decision, when Saigon erupted in September 13's major coup attempt against Khanh.

A test of Johnson's resolve came when the JCS mounted a strongly focused effort to get him to order reprisal air strikes in retaliation for what they insisted had been another Tonkin Gulf attack against a U.S. navy vessel on September 18. Skeptical from the outset, he "made it clear that he was not interested in rapid escalation on so frail evidence and with a very fragile government in South Vietnam." On the advice of Rusk and McNamara, he was initially willing to go so far as to authorize "preparatory orders" for a strike. But then, resentful at "having his hand forced" by provocative leaks from the military, and finally discovering that "evidence of actual hostile attack [was] thin to non-existent," he canceled even these orders. Evidently wishing to avoid further incidents of this nature, he suspended the provocative DeSoto patrols by U.S. destroyers, which were not resumed for almost five months. And, following a major attack on November 1 against the large U.S. air base at Bien Hoa (only about twelve miles from Saigon), in which four Americans were killed, the president refused to meet the urgent request from the JCS and Taylor that he order retaliatory bombing of the North.[7]

Lyndon Johnson's insistence on holding to the prerequisite of a strengthened political base in the South cannot be discounted as merely a calculation for advantage in his campaign for re-election: he held on doggedly to this condition for three months beyond his defeat of Senator Goldwater.

Johnson's victory at the polls in November 1964 was so overwhelming that, in its wake, his scope for taking major new initiatives in Vietnam was much greater than either he or Kennedy had previously enjoyed. James Thomson saw this as providing the "last and most important opportunity that was lost" for disengaging the United States from Vietnam on acceptable terms. He concluded that, had Johnson been "more confident in foreign affairs, had he been more deeply informed on Vietnam and Southeast Asia, and had he raised some hard questions that unanimity [on the part of his advisers] had submerged, this President could have used the largest electoral mandate in history to deescalate in Vietnam, in the clear expectation that at the worst a neutralist government would come to power in Saigon and politely invite us out."[8]

Although the strength of Johnson's position would have permitted him to take this course, it was ruled out by all of his senior advisers. Insofar as they did discuss with him the question of negotiations, they did so critically, admonishing that these were not to be considered for the present, and could not realistically even be explored until after the ratio of military power in South Vietnam had been drastically altered in favor of the Saigon government. Given the balance at the time, negotiations were regarded as tantamount to capitulation; even discussion of the matter was likely to be disastrous to the morale of the American protégés in Saigon. The advisers argued that any hint that the United States was disposed to move in such a direction would seriously risk collapse of the now tottering political edifice that it had built with such effort. In the wake of this, a neutralist, peace-oriented Saigon government would probably come to power and would insist upon negotiating a settlement on its own terms. As Paul Warnke, then a senior Pentagon legal specialist, later observed in critical vein: "For the United States to 'compromise' and permit the indigenous forces of Vietnam to work their own way would be to condone the demise of the anti-Communist regime we had supported in Saigon for twenty years."[9]

By the early fall of 1964 George Ball—who as under secretary of state had earlier been largely absorbed by European matters—had become alarmed at the increasingly interventionist stance of the president's advisers and their constant denigration of negotiations. He believed that, as matters then stood with respect to negotiations, "the administration really didn't have anything to say to the Vietnamese communists except for the modalities of their capitulation." If it were serious about negotiations, the United States, he argued, would have to lower its sights and be prepared for a compromise solution. As for the proposition that negotiations would so shake the Saigon regime as to risk its collapse, he felt that this simply demonstrated the regime wasn't worth supporting. "My own position," Ball later recalled, "was that we should give it sixty days to shape up and if it didn't we should invoke Eisenhower's 1954 letter [with its clear conditionality of support] and get out. If it showed it wasn't worth our support, I didn't mind if it did collapse." He sought to warn Johnson of the danger and fruitlessness of an escalation in U.S. military involvement and alert him to possible courses and outcomes of negotiations.[10]

To this end, Ball prepared an extensive memorandum for McGeorge Bundy, McNamara, and Rusk, assuming that after they had discussed it Bundy would pass it on to Johnson.[11] (Though Ball himself had direct access to the president, he felt that in cases where he so strongly disagreed with these advisers, he should as a matter of courtesy first acquaint them with his ideas.) He recognized that these three were adamantly opposed to his ideas on negotiations, but he regarded the president as more open-minded than they on matters pertaining to Vietnam. He therefore hoped that the views contained in this October 5 memorandum would at least persuade Johnson that there were options to explore beyond the narrow range being presented by his senior advisers. Ball felt it especially important that the president be aware that there were possible negotiating processes and outcomes compatible with U.S. global prestige. Present policy, he pointed out, "has been justified primarily on political grounds . . . defended on the proposition that America cannot afford to promote a settlement in South Viet-Nam without first demonstrating the superiority of its own military power—or, in other words, giving the North Vietnamese a bloody nose." "What I am urging," he concluded, "is that our Southeast Asian policy be looked at in all its aspects and in the light of our total world situation. It is essential that this be done before we commit military forces to a line of action that could put events in the saddle and destroy our freedom to choose the policies that are at once the most effective and the most prudent."

Of several frameworks for achieving a negotiated settlement, Ball favored "a localized negotiation between a neutralist South Viet-Nam Government and the National Liberation Front." The United States would set the process in motion by emphatically reiterating to the South Vietnamese and to foreign governments [and presumably the American public] that it intended to remain in South Viet-nam only so long as the South Vietnamese wished its help. At the same time, Washington could serve notice on the Saigon government that "we are determined to continue the struggle . . . *only* if they achieve a unity of purpose in Saigon, clearly express that unity, and create a government free from factionalism and capable of carrying on the affairs of the country." There would probably be "a strong tendency in Saigon to regard this as a warning of ultimate United States disengagement," and this notice would encourage the organization of a neutralist government and "almost certainly accelerate existing covert probing of the possibilities of a deal with Viet Cong elements."

The United States would not immediately press for negotiations and would encourage "a period of ambiguity" and delay that "would permit the various sectors of Vietnamese opinion to adjust to the possibility of a political solution. Such a period would also permit the personalities who might otherwise be the victims of retaliation to make their own personal arrangements." A cease-fire would be prerequisite to negotiations between Saigon and the NLF, and as part of the settlement U.S. forces would have to be withdrawn, perhaps by phases. A settlement worked out within South Vietnam "would mean the incorporation of National Liberation Front elements in the governmental base. But that government would also include elements drawn from the religious sects, the Army, and other factors of Vietnamese life. The result might well be an uneasy coalition in which the Communists would presumably be the most aggressive and dominant component. But the full effect of a Communist takeover would be diffused and postponed for a substantial period of time."

Though seeing an ultimate takeover by the communists as possible, Ball hoped that a solution more palatable to the United States might be achieved if other powers could be brought in to provide a guarantee of South Vietnam's continued neutralization—something for which he wanted the administration to begin planning immediately. But even if this had not been possible, the "diffused" and "postponed" takeover he postulated would undoubtedly have been preferable for the NLF, as well as for other elements in the South, to the abrupt and traumatic takeover by Hanoi that occurred in 1975, after animosities had been nourished and intensified by nearly a decade of the escalated American military intervention that Ball's colleagues soon induced Johnson to support.

There was, then, another important option that could have been presented to the president. But although McGeorge Bundy, McNamara, and Rusk all read Ball's brief, none chose to send it on to Johnson for the major review of policy he had requested for December 1. (It was only with the help of William Moyers of the White House staff that the memorandum finally reached the president, more than a month later.) Indeed, no negotiating option was prepared for the president, and his advisers continued to warn against consideration of one—at least until such time as the military balance had shifted decisively in favor of Saigon, a change they had already begun to conclude could not come about without the injection of additional U.S. fire power.

This was not the only instance when Johnson was denied the opportunity to consider possibilities for negotiations. U Thant was convinced after his talks with Johnson and Rusk on August 6 that the president had encouraged him to arrange direct and secret bilateral discussions with Hanoi.[12]

Within a month, via a senior Soviet U.N. official, U Thant had contacted Ho Chi Minh and obtained his approval for such talks. The weight of available evidence, however, indicates that Johnson was apprised of neither this nor U Thant's follow-up effort in December until after he made his decision to escalate in February 1965. James Thomson states, "In February 1965 McGeorge Bundy sent a note to me which indicated the President never knew about the Stevenson/U Thant negotiation effort." William Bundy agrees that Johnson did not know about the U Thant initiative until later. Although he headed the task force charged with preparation of the set of policy alternatives that were vetted and passed on to the president by his senior advisers, William Bundy states that even he was not informed of the initiative until late December 1964 or early January 1965.[13]

In early September 1964, the U.N. secretary general secured Hanoi's agreement to direct bilateral talks with the United States, stipulating that they be private—a major U.S. concern—and without Peking's knowledge (apparently a major Hanoi concern). He passed this word to U.N. Ambassador Adlai Stevenson but was advised that such talks should be postponed until after the election. On November 23–24 Rusk and Stevenson discussed U Thant's September initiative and "possible venues" for such a meeting. The next day Rusk asked Stevenson to ascertain "U Thant's thinking and what reaction he had had from Hanoi." Stevenson reported back to Rusk that U Thant had learned via the Soviets that Hanoi's response was "very affirmative." Two days later Stevenson reported to Rusk that U Thant was exploring the possibility of Rangoon as a place for talks between the American ambassador and North Vietnam's consul general, a Vietnamese of some stature. Soon afterward the secretary general reported to Rusk via Stevenson that General Ne Win, head of the Burmese government, had given his permission for such a meeting. But Rusk evidently authorized no reply. A month later U Thant contacted Stevenson again to inform him that Hanoi was "ready and willing" to enter into discussions with the United States and asked what the American position was. He was informed the matter was being given "serious consideration," but there was no further American response. (Stevenson later told Assistant Secretary of State Harlan Cleveland that "Washington's response was always: 'There may be a time . . . but not now.' ") Rusk was clearly not supportive of a follow-up, and McNamara was "flatly opposed" to U Thant's proposal, stating that the Saigon government would have to be told and that negotiations would have a devastating effect on it. On February 13, U Thant informed Stevenson's deputy, Charles Yost, that despite his "positive" response from Hanoi, he was still awaiting Washington's answer to what he regarded as "quite specific proposals."[14]

Finally, alarmed by the resumption of U.S. reprisal bombings against North Vietnam, and feeling pressure from restive U.N. delegations worried over the course of events, U Thant publicly appealed on February 16 for negotiation via a reconvened Geneva Conference on Vietnam. But this attempt too, despite positive reactions from Moscow as well as Hanoi, Washington rebuffed.[15]

The administration's continuing failure to respond to U Thant's efforts and to let the American public know of the possibility for a negotiated end to the war brought an embittered secretary general to state publicly on February 24:

> I am sure the great American people, if only they knew the true facts and background to the developments in South Viet-Nam, will agree with me that further bloodshed is unnecessary. And that the political and diplomatic methods of discussions and negotiations alone can create conditions which will enable the United States to withdraw gracefully from that part of the world. As you know, in times of war and of hostilities the first casualty is the truth.[16]

Administration officials were furious and the next day publicly denied that U Thant or anyone else had presented "meaningful proposals" for negotiating a peaceful settlement. Moreover, the administration continued to preclude any possibility for such negotiations by insisting that the continued existence of the southern half of Vietnam as a separate state was nonnegotiable; no one, Dean Rusk stated, would be allowed to conduct any negotiations until Hanoi had agreed to respect the independence and national security of South Vietnam. On February 27 Stevenson officially informed U Thant that, since this condition had not been met, his proposal for talks with Hanoi was rejected, and told him privately that his public statement of the 24th had caused "consternation" in Washington and "created very serious doubts" as to whether it was any longer possible to have confidential exchanges with him "on matters of vital concern to the United States."[17] This official rejection came two weeks after Johnson had finally agreed to his advisers' recommendation to escalate from reprisal bombing to a sustained bombing campaign, and a day before he announced this program publicly.

It was not until after the die had been cast—not until March 9, 1965, after the United States had mounted its sustained air war against the North and landed the first U.S. ground forces in Vietnam—that *The New York Times* reported U Thant's 1964 efforts. (The next day a U.N. spokesman publicly announced Washington's negative response.) And it was not until eight months after the *Times's* disclosure that the State Department's spokesman, Robert McCloskey, reversed repeated denials and acknowledged that the administration had indeed rejected U Thant's proposals. Deprecating the significance of this move, he stated that Dean Rusk's "antennae is [sic] sensitive" and that if Hanoi was "prepared for serious talks . . . the Secretary of State said that he would recognize it when it came." *The New York Times* later editorialized, "This comment reminds one of the ancient Roman practice of drawing auspices from the flight or the entrails of birds. It would be a shuddering thought that the fate of nations and thousands of young Americans depended on Dean Rusk's antenna. Yet this is what Mr. McCloskey indicated."[18] Nor, of course, did he mention that the president's advisers failed to inform him of U Thant's pre-February peace efforts until after he had already committed himself to a major military escalation.

During the fall of 1964, as the political substance and military capacity of the South Vietnamese government eroded ever more rapidly, it had become starkly evident to Johnson's advisers that the policies they had been shaping ever since John F. Kennedy assumed the presidency had failed. However, since their own reputations were so closely bound up with these policies, it was difficult for them to call for a shift from a military to a political track. Even if more attuned to American interests, such a move would have exposed their own previous counsel and very possibly been costly to their tenure in the administration. On the other hand, moving to a policy of heavier and geographically expanded military intervention would be perceived by the American Congress and public as having consistency and continuity and would not—at least until after a failure of this further escalation—disclose the erroneous nature of the assumptions and perceptions upon which interventionism rested. Moreover, though only a few presidential advisers—largely among the military—believed that such an escalation would succeed, most, if not all, of the others apparently concluded that it had at least some chance of doing so. It was usually not difficult for these men to equate the U.S. national interest with their own reputations. Or, as Robert Gallucci so aptly put it, "Using the phrase, 'protecting our commitment,' to explain American presence in Viet-Nam may be as pertinent in its application to individual actors as it is to the nation as a whole."[19]

During the last months of 1964 these advisers became increasingly convinced that a major escalation of the U.S. military effort in Vietnam was necessary, and they believed that Johnson's newly established electoral strength gave him the authority to order this. James Thomson perceived that although the president had instructed his chief advisers to prepare as wide a range of Vietnam options as possible for him for postelection consideration and decision, explicitly requesting that "all options be laid out," in counseling him they presented such a narrow set of choices—"precluding any real Presidential choice among viable options" —that, whatever his own inclinations, he was virtually locked into a program for bombing the North.[20]

The civilian advisers envisaged a bombing program less extreme than that advocated by the Joint Chiefs, but as extensive as seemed feasible without broadening the war enough to jeopardize U.S. global interests seriously. Most of them had become convinced that a bombing so intense and widespread as to destroy the North Vietnamese government would be certain to provoke a massive retaliation, in which Hanoi's units—which as yet had not appeared in the South—would flood across the seventeenth parallel in numbers that would quickly overwhelm Saigon's forces. They feared too that it could bring China into the war—a possibility that was taken very seriously throughout the course of the Johnson administration. Moreover, some argued that an unlimited bombing campaign would leave Hanoi with no further assets to protect, thus depriving the United States of any leverage to induce it to pressure the NLF to cease military opposition to Saigon. Or, in Taylor's vivid parlance, it was important not to "kill the hostage" by destroying North Vietnamese assets inside the "Hanoi do-nut."[21]

In the aftermath of Johnson's re-election, a National Security Council Working Group held frequent sessions, chaired by William Bundy, and hammered out a set of narrow options. These were discussed in a series of meetings toward the end of the month with the president's senior civilian and military advisers, including Ambassador Taylor. It was from this interaction that the narrowly circumscribed range of possibilities finally presented to the president for his decision emerged. The JCS's representative played a strong role within the working group, insisting that compromise solutions and rationalizations for withdrawal be downgraded. This representative also challenged an assessment of the intelligence community (and William Bundy and John McNaughton) that "the basic elements of Communist strength in South Vietnam remain indigenous," and its view that, even if American bombing severely damaged North Vietnam, Hanoi could continue to support a reduced level of Viet Cong activity while remaining confident of greater staying power than the United States in a contest of attrition. Within the group and among the president's senior advisers, the persistence of the JCS in insisting that the bombing would be physically and psychologically effective appears to have either convinced or worn down most of the waverers. And when Taylor, the former JCS chairman, returned to Washington in late November, he provided these views of the military spokesmen with additional support. He argued, "with considerable impact," that bombing the North would improve the morale and confidence of the Saigon government and would "drive the DRV out of its reinforcing role and obtain its cooperation in bringing an end to the Viet Cong insurgency." The Joint Chiefs were, however, unsuccessful in winning a consensus in favor of sending U.S. ground forces to Vietnam, for although McGeorge Bundy, McCone, and Rusk favored the idea, Taylor stood with McNamara in opposing this.[22]

The penultimate revision of the NSC Working Group's position paper— "Courses of Action in Southeast Asia"—drafted on November 21 by William Bundy and Assistant Secretary of Defense for International Security Affairs John McNaughton, constituted, together with a subsequent memorandum and oral presentation by Taylor, the fundamental basis for discussions by the president's advisers in arriving at their recommendations for him. The working group forwarded just three broad options.

Option A was "to continue present policies indefinitely," including intensifying existing covert forms of action against North Vietnam and in Laos, but with the additional element of U.S. reprisal actions against North Vietnam for any "spectacular attack by the VC within South Vietnam, particularly but not solely an attack involving U.S. forces or installations."

Option B called for the most dramatic escalation: "a systematic program of military pressures against the north, with increasing pressure actions to be continued at a fairly rapid pace and without interruption until we achieve our present stated objectives." It was evident that the working group preferred Option B, stating that it "probably stands a greater chance than either of the other two of attaining our objectives vis-à-vis Hanoi and a settlement in Vietnam";[23] the group acknowledged, however, that this course courted "considerably higher risks of major military conflict with Hanoi and possibly Communist China."

Option C stipulated slower-paced and more cautious, but still substantial, escalation. It provided for "graduated military moves against infiltration targets, first in Laos and then in the DRV [North Vietnam], and then against other targets in North Vietnam," giving the impression of "a steady deliberate approach . . . designed to give the US the option at any time to proceed or not, to escalate or not, and to quicken the pace or not." It hedged on the question of possible U.S. ground-force deployment in the South—reflecting the continuing lack of consensus among the president's advisers—stipulating that this would not be required unless Hanoi "threatened a ground move to the south." Certainly Option C was not presented as likely to produce any spectacular results. The working group assessed it as "more controlled and less risky of major military action than Option B . . . and more likely than Option A to achieve at least part of our objectives, and even if it ended in the loss of South Vietnam, our having taken strong measures would still leave us a good deal better off than under Option A with respect to the confidence and ability to stand firm of the nations in the next line of defense in Asia."[24]

Essentially, then, these three options were variations of escalated military action; no option focused on a negotiated settlement. Any future possibility of negotiations was to be resisted, as the narrative in the *Pentagon Papers* assessed

these recommendations, "until the North had agreed in advance" to U.S. conditions, and in effect negotiations were to be excluded in the short run under
Options B and C because these preconditions were "entirely unrealistic," reflecting a "policy climate in Washington" that "simply was not receptive to any
suggestion that U.S. goals might have to be compromised." Indeed, the favored
Option B called for Washington to take "a totally inflexible position on negotiating."[25]

William Bundy pulled together "the issues" raised in the working group's
draft and associated papers for a November 24–25 meeting with McGeorge
Bundy, Ball, McCone, McNamara, Rusk, and Wheeler. In this, their last discussion prior to meeting with Taylor on the 27th to give final shape to the options
to be presented to the president, they hammered out what their rapporteur,
William Bundy, captioned "The consensus or majority view of key issues discussed at this meeting, pending discussion with Ambassador Taylor." This memorandum, along with McGeorge Bundy's appended handwritten explanatory
notes and observations of one of the Pentagon chroniclers, provides some interesting glimpses of divisions within the group. It should be noted that the group
defined "consensus" as incorporating no more than a single dissenting opinion.[26]

There was such a consensus that, if Hanoi terminated its efforts in the South,
the security situation there could be handled in time "if the government could
maintain itself." It was expected that the situation in South Vietnam "would
deteriorate further under Option A, even with reprisals, but that there was a
significant chance that the actions proposed under Option B or Option C would
improve GVN performance and make possible an improvement in the security
situation." (On this George Ball registered doubt.) There was also a consensus
that "any negotiating outcome" under Option A "was likely to be clearly worse
than under Option C or Option B." A further agreement was reached that "it was
not true," as the draft paper had stated, that Option B "has the best chance of
attaining our full objectives." (Here McGeorge Bundy's notes indicate that his
brother William as well as the chairman of the JCS, General Wheeler, dissented.)

Views were "divided" as to "whether Option B was—as stated in the draft
position paper—significantly more likely to lead to a major escalation than Option C." No firm conclusion could be reached as to whether, under Option C, U.S.
"ground forces should be introduced into South Vietnam at an early stage."
McCone supported Wheeler's advocacy of ground forces, at least in the Saigon
area, and McGeorge Bundy and Rusk argued for the pre-emptive effect of placing
them in northern South Vietnam "against any land action" (presumably by North
Vietnam). McNamara was opposed to sending ground forces unless under an "air
umbrella," and Ball argued that "air is better because it avoids French dilemma."
It was agreed that the issue of ground forces should be raised with Taylor.

A consensus was reached that "the requirement of Option C—maintaining
military pressure and a credible threat of major action while at the same time
being prepared to negotiate—could in practice be carried out. The difficulties and
domestic pressures were noted, but it was felt that continuing military actions

could handle such pressures and also pressures for premature negotiations or concessions." The general mood vis-à-vis negotiations appears to have been captured in McGeorge Bundy's scribbled comment: "no hurry."

The final step in shaping the recommendations for the president was to reconcile these views of his Washington-based advisers with those of Taylor. With his stature still undiminished by his stewardship in Saigon, Taylor then had major influence on Vietnam policy. Before returning to Washington, he set forth his views in a comprehensive briefing that, together with the working group's "Course of Action in Southeast Asia" draft, provided the main backdrop to these discussions.[27]

Taylor focused on the growing strength of the NLF and the lack of a political base in South Vietnam from which to project American power. He sensed a "mounting feeling of war weariness and hopelessness which pervade South Vietnam" and saw no "truly national spirit." It was impossible, he said, "to foresee a stable and effective government under any name in anything like the near future." Lacking such a foundation upon which to base American power, the U.S. effort remained "a spinning wheel unable to transmit impulsion to the machinery of the GVN."

Like so many other American officials, Taylor was unable to understand the nature of Vietnamese nationalism and the extent to which, for such a large part of the population, that tidal political force ran against American efforts to sustain a client regime in South Vietnam. "The ability of the Viet-Cong continuously to rebuild their units and to make good their losses is one of the mysteries of this guerrilla war," he marveled. "We still find no plausible explanation of the continued strength of the Viet Cong. . . . Not only do the Viet Cong units have the recuperative power of the phoenix, but they have an amazing ability to maintain morale." Moreover, in addition to threatening to partition the country by a drive to the sea, they were demonstrating "new or newly expanded tactics . . . against important targets [and] economic strangulation of limited areas."

In view of all this, Taylor concluded, "we are playing a losing game." To change the situation the United States had to do three things: "first, establish an adequate government in SVN; second, improve the conduct of the counter insurgency campaign; and, finally, persuade or force the DRV to stop its aid to the Viet Cong and to use its directive powers to make the Viet Cong desist from their efforts to overthrow the government of South Vietnam."

As to the first object, Taylor stated:

It is hard to visualize our being willing to make added outlays of resources and to run increasing political risks without an allied government which, at least, can speak for its own people, can maintain law and order in the principal cities, can provide local protection for the vital military bases and installations, can raise and support armed forces, and can gear its efforts to those of the United States. Anything less than this would hardly be a government at all, and under such circumstances, the United States Government might do better to carry forward the war on a purely unilateral basis.

But "even after establishing some reasonably satisfactory government and effecting some improvement in the counterinsurgency program," he added, "we will not succeed in the end unless we drive the DRV out of its reinforcing role and obtain its cooperation in bringing an end to the Viet Cong insurgency."

Predicting that American efforts to strengthen and stabilize the Saigon government would probably prove inadequate, Taylor urged that the United States raise the Saigon leadership's morale and restore its confidence by increasing the level of covert operations against North Vietnam by sea and air and engaging in reprisal bombings against the North "to repay outrageous acts of the Viet Cong in South Vietnam, such as the attack on Bien Hoa." But before making a final decision on bombing the North, the United States should sound out General Khanh and Prime Minister Huong as to their views, for they would be taking on "risks as great [as] or greater than ours," but it "should make every effort to get them to ask our help in expanding the war," something he expected they would urge "with enthusiasm." If the Saigon government maintained and proved itself, then Washington should be prepared to embark on "a methodical program of mounting air attacks in order to accomplish our pressure objectives vis-à-vis the DRV," a program that "in its final forms . . . could extend to the destruction of all important fixed targets in North Vietnam and to the interdiction of movement on all lines of communication."

Taylor acknowledged, however, that all these actions might not be sufficient "to hold the present government upright," and that the United States would then have to try "a new approach." Although it was "premature to say exactly what these new measures should be," Washington should in any case "be prepared for emergency military action against the North if only to shore up a collapsing situation." As for negotiations, Taylor counseled, the initiative would have to come from Hanoi. To underscore this last point, he emphasized in his closing lines, "Whatever the course of events . . . do not enter into negotiations until the DRV is hurting."

The meeting between Taylor and the president's top Washington advisers on November 27 again focused on the unsatisfactory performance of the Saigon government and on actions the United States might take to induce improvement.[28] There was a consensus that, if that government collapsed or told the United States to get out, it would be hard to visualize staying on, and it was agreed that "the choice must certainly be avoided if at all possible." Taylor noted that "neutralism," as it existed in Saigon, "appeared to mean throwing the internal political situation open and thus inviting Communist participation." This discussion led to the opinion that "neutralism either in the sense of no more external assistance or in the sense of a free political system could not be maintained" until after the

Viet Cong had been defeated. That acknowledgment was not, of course, consistent with what the Congress and public were being told, but it did say much about the real nature of the Saigon regime that they were being asked to support and about the administration's approach to the principle of self-determination in Vietnam.

Taylor reported that Westmoreland was more optimistic than he about the military situation and inclined to wait six months in order to have a firmer South Vietnamese base to undergird a greater U.S. military input. McNamara disagreed with this position, while Taylor stated that he himself did not believe the United States could count on the situation's holding together for as long as six months, and that something must be done sooner. There was agreement with Taylor's view that stronger U.S. action "would definitely have a favorable effect on GVN and South Vietnamese performance and morale," but that there was no certainty that this would really be enough to improve the situation. Indeed, improvement in the government was regarded as so unlikely that to achieve any amelioration the United States "should move into some parts of [Option] C soon," for its "strengthening effect" could "at least buy time, possibly measured in years." Thus, it was urged that over the next two months Washington "adopt a program of Option A plus the first stages of Option C." Taylor appears to have strengthened the existing preference for Option C and buttressed the position of the advocates of air power against the North, as against those urging an injection of U.S. ground combat forces into the South.

In forwarding the three options to the president the next day, McGeorge Bundy informed him, "Many of the working group feel that a decision to carry out the immediate program should be accompanied by a decision—in principle —to adopt Option C unless circumstances change, with the date of initiation left open." He also pointed out Taylor's recommendation that the United States be prepared to move clearly into Option C "after a period of weeks . . . if the Vietnamese Government holds together but Hanoi is still tough."[29]

In this simplistic calculus presented by the president's advisers there was no trace of the genre of thinking that characterized Ball's sidetracked memorandum, nor was there any negotiating option. All negotiation was to be eschewed until the United States had won—that is, until Hanoi had brought the insurgency in the South to a halt and accepted a secure, noncommunist South Vietnamese state. As James Thomson later put it, "The advisers so effectively converged on one single option—juxtaposed against two other phony options (in effect blowing up the world, or scuttle-and-run)—the President was confronted with unanimity for bombing the North from all his trusted counsellors." This plan was presented to him as a means of raising the political morale and military aggressiveness of the Saigon regime, while decreasing those qualities among the Viet Cong, and inducing Hanoi not only to end its support of its southern comrades but to pressure them into laying down their arms. In looking back on this period, U. Alexis Johnson, who was then Taylor's deputy and a proponent of bombing, observed, "I don't feel that at this decision point we were able to present the President, in

a clear cut fashion, the alternatives. . . . I don't think we served the President
well."[30]

The president's long meeting with his top advisers on December 1 reduced the
working group's three options to two: Option B was discarded. From then on,
A and C were referred to respectively as Phase I and Phase II of a potentially
two-stage program. Clearly dominating the president's approach throughout the
meeting was his preoccupation with the weakness of the Saigon government. The
recently declassified handwritten account of the December 1 proceedings by
McNamara's deputy John McNaughton provides the clearest available entree
into Lyndon Johnson's cast of mind at this critical juncture in the evolution of
U.S. policy. Punctuating the entire long discourse were the president's interjec-
tions, such as "Most essential is a stable government. . . . Basic to everything is
stability. . . . No point in hitting North if South not together. . . . What can we
do? . . . Why not say: 'This is it!'? Not send Johnson City boy out to die if they
acting as they are. . . . Purpose of the meeting: to pull stable government together.
. . . If need be create a new Diem, so when [we] tell Wheeler to slap we can slap
back." When Taylor responded that he doubted Hanoi would slap back, the
president rejoined, "Didn't MacArthur say the same." The president's reluctance
to "slap" Hanoi was vividly illustrated in such comments as not wanting "to send
widow woman to slap Jack Dempsey" and that the Saigon regime should be
"hesitant to sock neighbor if it [Saigon] had a temperature of 104 degrees." Want
to get [it] well first." His exasperation with the Saigon regime, evident in such
remarks as "How [can] 34,000 [Viet Cong] lick 200,000 [Saigon's regular
army]?," was surely exacerbated by Taylor's remark that the Saigon "politicos
had come to think [the] VC is [a] US problem. . . ." As for the Saigon army, the
president wondered, "Have we oversold them on the necessity of [our] being a
power in the Pacific; are they drunk on Alsop [one of the most hawkish U.S.
columnists]?" As to the persistent political schism in Saigon, he asked if the Pope
might not be able to "straighten it out with the Catholics," and was told by John
McCone that this had already been tried, apparently through the State Department. Referring to the Buddhists, the president observed that the "C.I.A. sees no
way to work with them," and urged, "Let's get a thinker to work on that
problem." With respect to the need for a more solid base in South Vietnam before
any reprisal bombings of the North were undertaken, he said he wanted to give
Taylor "one last chance," but if there proved to be "more of the same" divisions
there, then "I'll be talking to you, General."[31]

Although the chroniclers of the *Pentagon Papers* were aware they lacked all
the necessary documents on the December 1 meeting, subsequently declassified
papers confirm the general accuracy of their reconstruction of the president's
decisions then and in the week following. Certainly they were correct in concluding that the program approved by Johnson "did not constitute a significant
departure from the actions authorized" by him in the National Security Action

Memorandum of September 9, and that, though "the concept of possible future operations against North Vietnam" was made "more concrete . . . it is clear that the President did not make any commitment at this point to expand the war through future operations against North Vietnam." Moreover, it was abundantly evident that he was not prepared to commit himself to any explicit program, nor be bound within the narrow perimeters of action presented by his advisers. Thus, on December 7, when he registered his approval of the December 2 position paper stemming from the discussion of the previous day, he referred to this as "guidance for our work in this field in coming months, subject to such amendment and further development as I may approve from time to time."[32]

Johnson stipulated that he was prepared to endorse Phase I and Phase II only in principle, and that he would approve implementation of neither until certain strict conditions were met by the Saigon government. Consequently, his advisers, who were pressing for escalation, now found themselves up against a major obstacle. For Lyndon Johnson insisted that a fundamental prerequisite be met before he would approve escalation to either level. This was spelled out clearly in his December 3 instruction to Taylor: "There are certain minimum criteria of performance in South Vietnam which must be met before new measures against North Vietnam would be either justified or practicable." He insisted that, "at a minimum, the government should be able to speak for and to its people. . . . It should be capable of maintaining law and order in the principal centers of population, make plans for the conduct of operations and insure their effective execution by military and police forces completely responsible to its authority." And, finally, the Saigon government "must have the means to cope with the enemy reactions which must be expected to result from any change in the pattern of our operations." Action against North Vietnam, the president admonished, could be only "contributory, not central" to the campaign against the Viet Cong; blocking Hanoi's support of its forces would "not in itself" end the war against them. "Even if the aid of North Vietnam for the VC should end," it would be necessary to have "a stable, effective government" in Saigon if a successful campaign were to be conducted against the Viet Cong. "We should not incur the risks which are inherent in such an expansion of hostilities [against North Vietnam] until there is a government in Saigon capable of handling the serious problems involved in such an expansion. . . ."[33]

To give point to his insistence that the Saigon regime had to shape up before the United States would consider attacks against North Vietnam, the president posited eight specific objectives, progress toward which could serve as criteria for measuring governmental effectiveness.

> 1. Improve the use of manpower for military and pacification purposes.
> 2. Bring the armed forces and police to authorized strength and maximize their effectiveness.
> 3. Replace incompetent officials and commanders. Freeze the competent in place for extended periods of service.

4. Clarify and strengthen the police powers of arrest, detention and interrogation of VC suspects.

5. Clarify and strengthen the authority of provincial chiefs.

6. Make demonstrable progress in the Hop Tac operation around Saigon. [The still-unrealized plan aimed at clearing Viet Cong forces from areas immediately adjacent to Saigon.]

7. Broaden and intensify the civic action program using both military and civilian resources to produce tangible evidence of the desire of the government to help the hamlets and villages.

8. Carry out a sanitary clean-up of Saigon.[34]

While progress was "being made toward these goals by a government of growing effectiveness," the United States would be willing, Johnson said, "to strike harder at the infiltration routes in Laos and at sea," operations that constituted "the first phase of military pressures to reduce infiltration and to warn the DRV of the risks it is running." The December 2 position paper, on which these instructions to Taylor were based, was consistent with this plan: though authorizing the intensification of existing U.S. covert programs aimed at infiltration routes through Laos for a thirty-day period, it gave no such firm commitment to the more drastic step in Phase I of bombing "one or more selected targets" in the North "as reprisals against any major or spectacular VietCong action in the South." This was described as something the United States might "possibly" do, but there was no promise that such an action would actually be carried out. If, following a Phase I period of unspecified length, Washington should decide to embark on further actions, the position paper provided that "if the GVN improves its effectiveness to an acceptable degree and Hanoi does not yield on acceptable terms, the U.S. is prepared—at a time to be determined—to enter into a second phase program in support of the GVN and RLG [Royal Lao government], of graduated military pressures directed systematically against the DRV." In short, if the Saigon regime went a sufficient distance to meet the president's political and military prerequisites, and then, in negotiations reflecting that regime's strengthened position, Hanoi refused to meet Washington's minimal terms, the United States would be prepared sometime thereafter to escalate to Phase II.[35]

The message that Taylor conveyed to Saigon's political and military leaders from President Johnson was very clear: there would be no U.S. military intervention against Hanoi until they demonstrated qualities they had thus far been unable to attain—political cohesion, governmental stability, and effectiveness in their own campaign against the Viet Cong. In particular, Taylor was requested "to bring home to all groups in South Vietnam the paramount importance of national unity," and to point out that "it is a matter of the greatest difficulty" for the administration "to require great sacrifices of American citizens when reports

from Saigon repeatedly give evidence of heedless self interest and short sighted-
ness among all major groups in South Vietnam."[36]

Taylor appears to have been confident that, if Saigon's leaders believed the
United States was prepared to assume a major role in the war in return for their
improved political and military performance, this improvement would in fact
become manifest even before Washington had actually ordered an escalation.
Moreover, when he returned to Saigon in early December, Taylor brought another inducement with him. He was authorized to make a more explicit promise
—also tied to such improved performance—to pay for an increase of Saigon's
armed forces by 100,000 men, bringing their total strength to 660,000. This
measure was, of course, bound to add to the scope for promotions and to the
patronage available to senior officers, and was believed to be so much in their
self-interest as to encourage their greater cooperation with U.S. policies.[37]

Soon after Taylor's return to Saigon, however, his expectations of fostering
order and stability among the various contending civilian and military factions
were abruptly thwarted, and Johnson was given further justification for insisting
that his conditions be met prior to any escalation. The first blow came from the
politically organized Buddhists, who were now clearly out to topple the recently
installed civilian Prime Minister Tran Van Huong, whom they regarded as opposed to their objectives and simply another in a series of American creations.[38]*

Intensification of the Buddhist campaign to oust Huong led participants in
a further top-level meeting in Washington to single out relations between the
Buddhists and the GVN, and between the Buddhists and the United States, as
"the problem of immediate priority." By December 16 Taylor was cabling Washington that the Buddhists were out to unseat Huong, "in full knowledge" that
this was "contrary to [the] U.S. position." He offered no prescription for ending
their opposition and took a dim view of McGeorge Bundy and Chester Cooper's
suggestion that Washington try to buy off the Buddhists "by funneling unofficial
aid to the Buddhist leadership for their adherents at the village and hamlet level.
. . ." The monks were "intent," Taylor responded, "on a confrontation with the
GVN," and would not be swayed by efforts at direct persuasion by the United
States. On Bundy's memo apprising the president of this difference in counsel,
Johnson scrawled, "What is Taylor's alternative? Get him to do something." But
the frustrated ambassador could offer no solution, and apparently the only fresh
idea he was able to come up with was that the State Department arrange for
Tibet's exiled Dalai Lama, his brother, or other Buddhist leaders from other
countries to visit Vietnam "to educate Vietnamese bonzes on the perils of communism and their civil responsibilities."[39]

The second and most devastating blow to Taylor's hopes—and reputation
—came from the still badly factionalized Saigon military. For, despite his briefing
to Khanh and other senior officers on the new American inducements for political

---

*Huong had not been Khanh's choice, but in any case Khanh remained de facto the major power
in the government.

solidarity and better military performance, internecine warfare among the officer corps mounted and spilled over into Saigon's political life with a force that shattered what little coherence still existed. The precipitating factor in this denouement was the refusal of the largely powerless civilian legislative body, the High National Council, to yield to the Young Turks' insistence that it pass a law requiring the immediate retirement of nine generals and thirty other officers with more than twenty-five years of service. This politically motivated measure, opposed by the U.S. embassy, was directed primarily against General Minh, the Dalat generals, and several other rivals whom the younger officers feared might make a comeback that would undercut their newly won power. Exasperated by the council's show of independence, the Young Turks, Khanh, and most, if not all, of the rest of the Military Council (MRC) abolished the High National Council on December 20, arresting eight of its most influential members along with at least ten other civilian officials and political leaders. To consolidate their position, they replaced the MRC with a new Armed Forces Council (AFC)—a sort of revamped MRC in which they had greater representation. The Buddhists had not supported these moves, but since the Huong government had been seriously weakened by the pressures they had already brought to bear against it, the rickety civilian government appeared about to collapse.[40]

Taylor cabled Washington that a "naked military fist" had "crumpled [the] carefully woven fabric of civilian government," and that the action would be "immediately and understandably interpreted by all the world as another military coup, setting back all that had been accomplished since last August." It was, he stated, an "inescapable conclusion that if a group of military officers could issue decisions abolishing one of the three fundamental organs of the governmental structure . . . and carry out military arrests of civilians, that group of military officers has clearly set themselves above and beyond the structure of government in Vietnam." The unhappy ambassador reported that the generals had "felt no reluctance in acting without consulting with U.S. representatives and in disregarding our advice on important matters. . . . Perhaps most serious of all is the deliberate disregard of the message which I brought from Washington and personally transmitted to most of these generals that continued and increased U.S. aid for S.V.N. depended upon governmental stability and evidence of national unity."[41]

Furious at the Young Turks' intervention, Taylor summoned three of their top leaders—Rear Admiral Cang, chief of naval operations; Air Vice Marshal Ky, head of the air force; and General Thi, commander of I Corps—along with their ally General Thieu, commander of IV Corps, to a meeting at the embassy in which he scolded them roundly. He opened with a reminder of their discussion just after his return from Washington, when he had raised the possibility of American escalation and an expansion of the Saigon military establishment, and now admonished, "I made it clear that all the military plans which I know you would like to carry out are dependent on government stability. Now you have made a real mess. We cannot carry you forever if you do things like this." He charged that their dissolution of the High National Council had been "totally illegal" and constituted "a military coup that has destroyed the government-making process." After wringing an acknowledgment that Khanh had, with their full support, directed the dissolution of the council, Taylor left them with what he presumably believed was a sufficiently strong warning to induce them to adhere more closely to American objectives: "I have real troubles on the U.S. side. I don't know whether we will continue to support you after this."[42]

But Taylor's threat had little cutting edge with these officers, for most of them were convinced that the United States was already far too committed to withdraw its support, and was as dependent on them as they were on it. Washington's public rhetoric, and the American and global audiences to which it was addressed, had, of course, made it difficult for them to conclude differently. They were, moreover, highly incensed at the way Taylor had lectured them; Khanh was astute enough to capitalize on their sense of outrage, and the latent anti-Americanism that this confrontation had brought to the surface, to repair his own badly strained relations with these powerful spokesmen for the Young Turks.[43]

Ignoring Taylor's urgent request to delay any public announcement of the decisions he and the Young Turks had taken, Khanh promptly called a press conference to proclaim the dissolution of the High National Council, referring to this move as Decision No. 1 of the AFC, and thereby also indicating its displacement of the MRC. By this action Khanh, in the view of both Taylor and Washington, had "thrown down the gauntlet." The exasperated ambassador's smoldering antagonism toward Khanh ignited, and on the following day (December 21) he told him to resign and leave the country. However, Taylor inadvertently strengthened Khanh's hand the next day, walking into a skillfully laid trap. Unknown to him, Khanh was taping the telephone conversation in which Taylor not only confirmed that he wanted Khanh to leave, but blundered into discussing "travel arrangements" for other, unidentified Vietnamese generals who the wily commander in chief had assured him also desired to go. Khanh thus had "proof" that he could use to convince some of his military colleagues that Taylor wanted to oust them too. Now that Taylor appeared to be threatening some of the Young Turks, it was all the easier for Khanh to rally the whole group behind him. He calculatedly fed the anti-Taylor and anti-American sentiment the ambassador's confrontation with the Young Turks had aroused, and their sense of outrage rose. An extreme case was General Nguyen Chanh Thi, one of the most powerful of the Young Turks, whom the CIA reported to have declared privately that, if the United States tried to push him too far, he would "blow up everything" by the end of the week. "I will kill Phan Khac Suu, Tran Van Huong and Nguyen Khanh and put an end to all this. Then we will see what happens."[44]

Rusk's expectation that Prime Minister Huong and the military would "unite on dumping Khanh," and his endorsement of Westmoreland's suggestion that Huong's position be strengthened by giving him the credit for dismissing Khanh, were a bit premature. Equally ill-informed was the speculation of these two Americans that Thieu or Ky (who had become increasingly close to Westmoreland) might replace Khanh as commander in chief. Despite Taylor's urgings that Huong stand up to the military, the prime minister showed no desire for such a heroic role and prudently accepted their actions, arguing that it was essential to maintain army support if he was resist pressures from the Buddhists, which he saw as the gravest threat to his position.[45]

On December 22, Khanh issued an order of the day to the armed forces in which he pointedly warned against foreign intervention in Vietnamese affairs and, though pledging continued support of Huong and the chief of state, Suu, reserved the armed forces' right to change the government if they thought things were getting out of hand. The next day Khanh and most of the senior Vietnamese officers decided to have Huong and Suu declare Taylor *persona non grata* and officially request the U.S. government to withdraw him as its representative. If Huong refused to go along, these officers planned to hold a press conference the next day at which they would release a letter providing "detailed accounts of Ambassador Taylor's meetings with the four Vietnamese generals on 20 December as well as his 21 December ultimatum to General Khanh." But the embassy informed Huong and Khanh that Rusk had cabled that to declare the American ambassador *persona non grata* "would make it virtually impossible for the USG to continue [to] support [the] GVN effort." Khanh then persuaded the Young Turks to follow a more moderate course of action. The letter was not released, and although Khanh publicly charged the ambassador with abusing his power and insulting the generals, he stopped short of a *persona non grata* declaration.[46]

In a background briefing to American correspondents, Taylor charged that Khanh had taken an anti-U.S. line because he knew that he no longer had U.S. support. He said there was no indication of principle in Khanh's entire makeup, and accused him of having whipped up anti-American feelings among the Young Turks in order to gain their support against the United States. Khanh, he concluded, would have to go. The embassy's concern with the evident boiling up of anti-American sentiment was reflected in Westmoreland's request to CINCPAC on the 24th: "In view of the current unstable political situation . . . and the possibility that this situation could lead to anti-American activities of unknown intensity, request Marine Landing Force now off Cap Varella be positioned out of sight of land off Cap St. Jacques soonest." (Cape Saint Jacques was as close to Saigon as it could feasibly be positioned.) Back-up units at Subic Bay in the Philippines were put on twelve-hour notice.[47]

By the end of December 1964, then, it had become abundantly evident that the political situation in Saigon was continuing to deteriorate—moving further away from, rather than toward, the conditions that the president had posited as prerequisites for launching even a Phase I reprisal bombing. If there were doubts that Johnson was determined to stick to his conditions, they must have been dispelled with his denial of requests from both Taylor and the U.S. military that he order a bombing strike against the North. This was to be in retaliation for the Christmas Eve bombing, in the "very heart of [the] most heavily guarded section of Saigon," of the Brinks U.S. officers' billet, in which two Americans were killed and thirty-eight others plus thirteen Vietnamese injured. Military leaders and some civilian advisers (not including McNamara and Rusk) saw this as a flagrant example of the sort of provocation that was supposed to justify Phase I retaliatory air attacks. The president's refusal to bomb the North dramatically illustrated how far the political situation in Saigon fell short of the prerequisites he had set. Neither the American public nor international opinion, he concluded, was likely to believe that the NLF, rather than one of the Saigon factions, was actually responsible for the Brinks incident; indeed, it was several days before the administration itself concluded that the NLF was actually behind it. "In view of the overall confusion in Saigon," the State Department cabled Taylor, reprisal bombing against the North would be certain to elicit a "strong reaction in US opinion and internationally" that the administration was "trying to shoot its way out of an internal [Saigonese] political crisis."[48]

X

Bombing the North
Will Save the South

Lyndon Johnson's unwillingness to permit the war's extension to the North unless and until the Saigon government demonstrated greater political viability and military effectiveness posed a major problem for his civilian and military advisers who favored escalation. They saw their efforts seriously undercut by the continuing political disruption in Saigon resulting from the actions of Khanh and the Young Turks, as well as the Buddhists, in the month following Maxwell Taylor's return from Washington on December 6, 1964. Clearly one of the president's stipulated prerequisites to any bombing campaign against the North had not been met: there had been no increase in the political viability of the Saigon regime.

Once it was established that the Viet Cong actually was responsible for the December 24 Brinks attack, however, there were still problems with the president's other prerequisite: improvement in Saigon's military capability. Indeed, for the president, the weakness of ARVN-U.S. security disclosed by this attack, constituted an additional caveat against bombing: the belief that such a course would precipitate a "strong Communist reaction if not by air [retaliation by Hanoi's air force] at least by a concentrated VC effort against Americans" in the South. With so many American dependents now living there, he was all the more reluctant to run this risk.[1]

Nevertheless, though Johnson remained skeptical that bombing the North would save the South, this Viet Cong attack on a U.S. installation in the center of Saigon did serve to undermine his previous reluctance to introduce ground combat troops into South Vietnam. Against a background of nearly a year of ARVN military defeats, the Brinks attack appeared to heighten his fears that the Saigon army's decline would accelerate unless its forces were reinforced on the ground by U.S. soldiers. And thus, in the same December 30 cable to Taylor in which he explained his refusal to respond to the attack with a reprisal bombing of the North (and affirmed that he had "never felt that this war will be won from the air"), he told him he was now "ready to look with great favor on an American effort directed at the guerrillas and aimed to stiffen the aggressiveness of [South]

Vietnamese military units up and down the line." To accompany this, he indicated he would authorize "a larger and stronger use of Rangers and Special Forces and Marines, or other appropriate military strength on the ground and on the scene" if Taylor and Westmoreland recommended such a course. This did not mean dispatch of additional U.S. troops to Vietnam, but simply authority for fuller and less restrictive use of American ground elements already there, or, as William Bundy put it, "Take what you need of what you've got." The sense of the cable, according to McGeorge Bundy, was "I'm unwilling to agree to a program of bombing the North to save the South, because that won't work; but I'm prepared to be helpful by permitting use of US ground forces now already available on the scene in Vietnam if you wish to use them in combat to strengthen ARVN."[2]

Still opposed to the use of U.S. ground combat troops, Taylor continued to press hard for a Phase II sustained bombing campaign as the only way to bring political coherence to the Saigon regime. Without that he doubted there was time to salvage the situation and develop a better government than Khanh's. The alternative to carrying on in this unsatisfactory situation would be for the United States to "disengage from the present intimacy of relationship with the GVN, withdrawing the bulk of our advisers and turning over [to the Saigon government] a maximum number of functions now performed by Americans," while continuing sufficient economic support and military supplies to keep the GVN operating at current levels and at the same time carrying on responsibility for its air and maritime defense. "By this means we might hope somewhat to disengage ourselves from an unreliable ally and give the GVN the chance to walk on its own legs and be responsible for its own stumbles. The hope would be that having to accept full responsibility SVN would rise to the challenge and 'pull up its political socks.' "

That course might have had a rational allure for Lyndon Johnson, but Taylor went on to warn, "The danger is that, panicked by what could be interpreted as abandonment, the leaders here would rush to compete with each other in making a deal with the National Liberation Front." Yet even this danger, he assured the president, "could be offset if at the time we were engaged in reprisal attacks [Phase I] or had initiated Phase II operations against [the] DRV."

Bombing the North, then, was the magical missing ingredient that could bring the administration success in Vietnam, and Taylor concluded his long argument with an appeal that the United States should eagerly seize the occasion of the next major Viet Cong attack to make a reprisal attack against the North, so as "to dampen down further major terrorist acts, to signal Hanoi, and, most importantly, to inject some life into the dejected spirits in SVN." Moreover, this "could be the needed stimulant to lift the GVN into a posture of desireable readiness for initiation of Phase II operations," without which he saw "slight chance of moving toward a successful solution."[3]

To both the president and Taylor it was evident that the Saigon government could no longer be regarded as a satisfactory instrument of American policy, in either military or political terms. Moreover, the actions of Khanh, the Young Turks, and the Buddhists had revealed beyond a shadow of doubt that there was a glaring absence of either the political cohesion and stability or improved military effectiveness that Johnson continued to demand before any bombing campaign against North Vietnam could be launched. As long as the president held to this precondition, plans for such an escalation had to be shelved. Not for another six weeks, under mounting pressure by three of his most influential advisers—McGeorge Bundy, Robert McNamara, and Maxwell Taylor—did Lyndon Johnson abandon his position.

Suddenly, only ten days after the Brinks attack, the question was no longer one of improving the ARVN's military effectiveness, but simply trying to keep it from total collapse. The imminence of this possibility fueled the arguments of proponents of increased U.S. military intervention—whether they advocated an air war against the North, ground combat troops for the South, or both.

The precariousness of the ARVN's situation became progressively more evident during January and February 1965 as a consequence of a series of disastrous military engagements, a further decline in its morale, a mounting level of desertion, and exhaustion of the army's entire strategic reserve. This perception crystallized in the first week of January with the stunning defeat at Binh Gia, about forty miles southeast of Saigon, of two of the ARVN's best battalions, together with supporting armored and mechanized forces, by less numerous and relatively poorly armed Viet Cong forces—despite a major U.S. airlift of reinforcements and a swarm of armed American-piloted helicopters ordered into battle in support of the ARVN units. The magnitude and implications of this significant defeat were not fully divulged to the American public, though some diligent correspondents sensed its seriousness. A secret memorandum of January 5 to McGeorge Bundy from JCS chairman Earle G. Wheeler reported that in this battle there had been 445 Vietnamese and 16 American casualties, as against 132 Viet Cong (only 32 of which were confirmed by body count), and that 4 of the 124 U.S. helicopters engaged there had been shot down.[4]

The day after Wheeler's alarming report on the Binh Gia disaster, Taylor sent the president an assessment of the situation in South Vietnam that was gloomier and more apocalyptic than any previous analysis. Referring to "continued political turmoil, irresponsibility and division within the armed forces, lethargy in the pacification program, some anti-U.S. feeling that could grow, signs of mounting terrorism by VC directly at US personnel, and deepening discouragement and loss of morale," he warned that, unless these conditions and trends were reversed, "we are likely soon to face a number of unpleasant developments ranging from anti-American demonstrations . . . to the ultimate installation of a hostile government which will ask us to leave while it seeks accommodation with the National Liberation Front and Hanoi." Equally discouraging was a report prepared on the same day by William Bundy (even before he had been given a copy of Taylor's), stating that the continuing crisis and the Binh Gia military defeat had had "a sharp discouraging effect," with Saigon's morale now "very shaky indeed." His prognosis closely paralleled Taylor's. He expected that the situation was "now likely to come apart more rapidly than we had expected in November" and that "the most likely form of coming apart would be a government of key groups starting to negotiate covertly with the Liberation Front or Hanoi, perhaps not asking in the first instance that we get out, but with that necessarily following at a fairly early stage." This might lead to a communist Vietnam that asserted its own independence from Peking, but that outcome "would be regarded in Asia . . . as just as humiliating as any other form."[5]

Taylor saw the causes of this situation as "lack of stable government, inadequate security against the VC and nation-wide war-weariness." Among the basic factors responsible for the turmoil were "chronic factionalism . . . absence of national spirit and motivation," and "lack of cohesion in the social structure. . . ." Americans, he admonished, could not change these factors in any fundamental way and could only recognize their existence and adjust plans and expectations accordingly. In the existing governmental crisis, an American effort to salvage Prime Minister Huong would probably leave him "pretty much under military domination." If the government were still to be controlled by Khanh, "we will have to do hard soul-searching to decide whether to try to get along with him again after previous failures or to refuse to support him and take the consequences —which might entail ultimate withdrawal." If the United States was able to "mislay" Khanh and set up another officer as chief of state, it might have "a fresh option worth trying."

But whatever the outcome, "whether a jerry-built civilian government under military domination or a brand new military government, it will not get far," the ambassador said, "unless a new factor is added which will contribute to coalescing the political factions around and within the government and thus bolster its position." As for that "new factor," the "only one which offers any chance of the needed success in the available time" that would help "pull the government together, stimulate pacification and raise the morale" was, he reiterated, a Phase II "program of graduated air attacks against the will of the DRV." Referring to the president's thesis that "this guerrilla war cannot be won from the air," Taylor assured him that he was in entire agreement "if we are thinking in terms of the physical destruction of the enemy," but that the bombing would be designed "to bring pressure on the will of the chiefs of the DRV. As practical men, they cannot wish to see the fruits of ten years of labor destroyed by slowly escalating air attacks."

At the same time, Taylor continued to argue against the introduction of U.S. ground combat units into the South, which, he pointed out, would "change the basis of our conduct of the war." Moreover, he was clearly unenthusiastic about strengthening the U.S. input on the ground through an increase in military advisers, pointing out that their number had grown by 42 percent during the past year and would reach 23,700 by February 1. When these were added to the 750 civilian advisers, he concluded, "We believe that our capability to stiffen further by advisory means, is very limited; indeed, we have probably reached about the saturation point."

Assuring the president that he had shared his feeling that "a stable government in Saigon" that was "able to speak for and to its people" should be a prerequisite to our undertaking offensive action against the DRV, Taylor then argued that, for the purpose of justifying a simple Phase I reprisal bombing, "the stability of the GVN (or lack thereof) at the time appears to us to have much less importance than in the case of the deliberate initiation of Phase II bombing." Phase I retaliatory bombing, with presidential approval for each strike, would in itself "not only signal Hanoi but would give the local morale a much needed shot in the arm and should dampen VC enthusiasm for terrorism especially against Americans and thus aid in protecting our people." The boost to the Saigon regime provided by retaliatory strikes would, he argued, be enhanced by "the earnest of our intent" of joint planning with its officials "in contemplation of Phase II." In resolving the ongoing political crisis in the capital it would be of great assistance, Taylor held, "if I were authorized to state explicitly to GVN leaders that we are prepared to initiate Phase II operations in case the new government meets or shows reasonable promise of meeting your criteria." This, then, would be "a conditional commitment that if, in the U.S. judgment, the GVN reaches a certain level of performance, the USG will join in an escalating campaign against the DRV." "Hopefully, by such action we could improve the government, unify the armed forces to some degree, and thereupon move into the Phase II program without which we see little chance of breaking out of the present downward spiral."

Having laid out this prospectus, Taylor requested presidential authority to carry out the joint planning and conditional pledge of escalation to a Phase II sustained bombing campaign "in order to establish as soon as possible a government meeting the minimum criteria for justifying the extension of air strikes against the DRV in accordance with the Phase II concept." In the meantime, he urged, "I would hope that, regardless of GVN performance in respect to the criteria" the president had established as preconditions, he would stand "ready at any time" to approve Phase I reprisal strikes. Thus was launched the first major assault against Lyndon Johnson's reluctance to expand the war to the North. The president held to his position for another month, until after McGeorge Bundy and McNamara had thrown their weight behind Taylor's convoluted rationale for escalation.

Johnson registered agreement with the ambassador's thesis that the "strength and clarity of U.S. commitment and determination are of major importance in political and even military balance in SVN." He was now "inclined to adopt a policy of prompt and clear reprisal," but, challenging Taylor's judgment, he continued to insist that before any such air strikes were launched there be a "prompt and orderly evacuation of all U.S. dependents." In each case the strikes should be carried out only on approval of both the president and whoever was "chief executive" of the Saigon government, against targets in the "southern spectrum" of the DRV, within twenty-four hours of a provocation, "unless circumstances of atrocity sharply modify normal presumption of VC guilt." (Here the president was evidently thinking of the initial reaction to the Brinks attack, and trying to ensure that an action perpetrated by an element of the Saigon military would not provide an excuse for bombing the North.)

But as for a Phase II sustained program of bombing, Johnson stuck doggedly to his conditions. In planning with the top leaders of the Saigon government for this contingency, Taylor was to make it "very clear" that decisions would depend not only on the "experience in reprisal actions," but also on "joint efforts to achieve political stability." "My decisions on Phase II," the president emphasized, "will necessarily be affected by performance in earlier activities." For Johnson, "political unity" remained a basic issue, and in the final paragraph of this cable, he referred to it as "the enormous problem" Taylor faced and advised him, "I am considering whether to send someone for further discussions with you on this subject."[6]

Johnson compromised with Taylor regarding the removal of American dependents. In the draft of a cable discussed with Rusk on January 13 he agreed that this had to be undertaken "in such a way as to avoid stimulation of unmanageable rumors and reports of a change in U.S. policy in SVN." But he appears to have remained adamant about Phase II, admonishing Taylor, "It is not possible for me to make any commitment on Phase II actions going beyond our guidance of December 3. The criteria which you have set out are highly pertinent and relevant to my eventual decision but are not the only factors which must be considered."[7]

Evidently still on the defensive concerning the effectiveness of Phase II, Taylor acknowledged:

> While in our own minds it is necessary to recognize that the DRV probably does not have full control over all VC in SVN, at least to the extent of being able to bring about the surrender of all VC, we should frame our demands on the DRV in terms of the DRV "bringing about a cessation of VC armed insurgency," leaving it to the DRV to plead its lack of control. Such a formulation gives us most flexibility in determining at the time what we feel is an acceptable degree of compliance by the DRV. In the absence of a substantial cessation of VC activity in SVN it also gives us maximum flexibility in determining the extent of our continued assistance to the GVN, or the carrying out of any offers we make to the DRV, or as until the VC insurgency has ceased we could point to the DRV failure to meet our conditions.[8]

The CIA had somewhat greater reservations as to Hanoi's ability to curb the Viet Cong. Though judging the insurgency in the South to be "heavily dependent on Ho Chi Minh's government," it concluded that "the VC nonetheless has substantial capabilities independent of Hanoi," and that, though the latter could achieve a "substantial stand-down . . . nonetheless, the insurgency in South Vietnam has a momentum of its own, and some VC action would probably continue, though at reduced levels."[9]

But no matter how strongly Taylor and the JCS urged that escalation could pressure Hanoi to pressure the Viet Cong to reduce its actions against the Saigon regime, their argument remained vitiated not only by the president's abiding skepticism, but also by the character of the Saigon regime. It was all very well to argue that such a bold step against the North would raise Saigon's morale and strengthen its leadership, but it was not an easy matter for Taylor, the JCS, and some others who believed this to accept that as matters stood Khanh would be the beneficiary and remain as the agent through whom the United States would have to work. Of more immediate concern was the question whether it would be feasible, indeed safe, to conduct such a major escalation in military intervention in conjunction with a Saigon government headed by him. Should the success of such a major departure in U.S. policy be dependent upon the cooperation of a leader who had proved to be so unpredictable and unreliable?

Doubts and divisions among the president's advisers on these questions militated against a consensus as to whether it was feasible to escalate, even though most believed that the rapidity of the political and military disintegration of South Vietnam now required this remedy. During January and early February this uncertainty appeared to ease the pressures on the president to authorize the major increase in U.S. military intervention that a sustained bombing program against the North would constitute. Among his senior advisers, the polar opposites in this lack of consensus concerning General Khanh were McGeorge Bundy, the general's most stalwart defender in Washington, and Ambassador Taylor, his now implacable enemy.

In the meantime, Khanh was helped in his efforts to remain in power by the realization of proponents of bombing in Washington that his precipitate ouster would reinforce the image of political chaos in Saigon. Having concluded even before the end of 1964 that Taylor was working to remove him, Khanh continued to maneuver with great skill to stay in power. Although the ambassador's relations with the Young Turk officers soon began to thaw, and though their attitude toward Khanh hardened, Taylor still could not find sufficient leverage to bring down the man whom both Saigon and Washington saw as his adversary. Nor could he come up with a more promising candidate to replace him. Bitter as he was with Khanh's conduct, the ambassador initially went along with other administration officials and acknowledged that for the time being they had no other course than to work with Khanh "as best we can" unless the administration were to "virtually disengage from an in-country military and economic role."[10]

Taylor's criticism of Khanh found considerable sympathy in the State Department, where his view that the Vietnamese leader should be "dumped" was shared by Rusk, but where it was hoped that further perceptible political chaos could be avoided, so that, when Khanh was ousted, it should "appear as much as possible to be the result of decision of his colleagues and not ours." Rusk advised the ambassador to isolate Khanh "perhaps by working on Young Turks and other generals." There was, however, little immediate scope for such efforts, for on the key issues these officers stood very close to Khanh. This had just been made abundantly clear in Westmoreland's December 24 report, "Attitude of the Generals," based on conversations of U.S. military advisers attached to the Young Turks. The report found that it was "of little moment" to these Vietnamese officers if the actions they took were illegal, and that they regarded it as the "duty and responsibility of the Vietnamese military establishment to move to correct defects in . . . the government," with "military force, as embodied in the Armed Forces Council," as the "ultimate authority." Westmoreland concluded that "for the moment at least, there is no alternative to Khanh as Commander-in-Chief; indeed his position has been strengthened, albeit temporarily, in the last few days."[11]

This consensus and the mounting belief in Saigon that Khanh would probably soon remove the recently appointed American-supported prime minister, Tran Van Huong, were reflected in Rusk's January 11 cable to Taylor. Though aware that the "eclipse of any form of meaningful civilian government in Saigon will create awkward and even serious problems for the Embassy," Rusk acknowledged that if Khanh's government "had some degree of popular support, would get on with the war, and was ready to work genuinely with U.S. . . . we might well have to swallow our pride and work with it. Hence our only short-term guidance would be to avoid to extent possible action that commits us one way or the other."[12]

By threatening to withhold U.S. funds earmarked for a major expansion of Saigon's military budget, Taylor was able to pressure Khanh and the Young Turks to agree to a compromise. In order to secure release of the money, the generals undertook to free the jailed members of the High National Council, speed convening of a constitutional convention, continue backing Huong as prime minister, and increase military draft calls. In Taylor's opinion, the substantial military-aid funds would give him the leverage to prevent a government dominated by Khanh, and "for the immediate future" contain his ambitions "within the framework of increased military participation in the government." The ambassador thus prevailed upon Prime Minister Huong on January 19 to add four of the Young Turk officers to his Cabinet—General Nguyen Van Thieu as second deputy prime minister, General Nguyen Cao Ky as minister of youth and sports, General Linh Quang Vien as minister of psychological warfare, and General Tran Van Minh as minister of the armed forces, a portfolio previously held by Huong himself. With this Cabinet reshuffle achieved, Taylor agreed to release the funds required for increasing the total strength of the South Vietnamese armed forces from 560,000 to 660,000 men.[13]

But these moves, particularly the expansion of the armed forces and the increased level of the draft, fanned the embers of Buddhist and student opposition into a roaring blaze. Introduction of the Young Turks' representatives into Huong's Cabinet did not, as had been hoped, strengthen him sufficiently to cow the Buddhists. Nor were the military even in accord as to whether, or how much, force should be used against the huge anti-Huong demonstrations, led by Buddhists and students, that now exploded not only in Saigon, but also in Dalat, Nhatrang, Hué, and Danang. Indeed, in the last two cities General Thi, I Corps commander, with Khanh's apparent concurrence, was initially permissive if not supportive toward these protests. Accusing Taylor of having imposed the new government on South Vietnam, and the prime minister of being his lackey, the Buddhist leaders asserted the Vietnamese people's right to democratic self-determination and demanded that Washington recall the ambassador. They regarded Huong with his altered Cabinet as no more responsive to their own objectives than previously, and they mounted a fresh effort to drive him from office. As pro-Buddhist demonstrators surged through the streets, this campaign took on increasingly bitter anti-American overtones. In Saigon the United States Information Service Library was sacked, and in Hué several thousand students overran the U.S. Information Service building and demanded the withdrawal of Ambassador Taylor.[14]

Providing as it did the only effective nongovernmental outlet of expression in the areas of the South still controlled by Saigon, the Buddhists' organization inevitably constituted the main channel for nationalist expression there. Their leaders were in tune with the increasingly widespread popular opposition to the war and the mounting fear of an imminent American-instigated escalation; it was thus natural that this protest would now take on an increasingly anti-American character. Since Khanh could no longer rely on support from the United States, his only chance for survival lay in coming to terms with the Buddhists. Their leaders' abiding mistrust of him made this alliance a precarious one, but it did provide him with a short-term political base from which to compete with the U.S. mission for the allegiance of at least the non-Catholic members of the officer corps.

With Taylor in opposition, it was vital to Khanh's political survival to resuscitate the tactical alliance with the Buddhist leaders that he had previously used to offset the power of rival military officers. Since the U.S. choice for prime minister was Huong, whom the Buddhists had long opposed (for what they regarded as his unquestioning subservience to the American presence), Khanh had little to lose in allying with them to oust him. Buddhist opposition to Huong was so fierce, Taylor reported, that Khanh had developed great respect for their strength, and though he and Tri Quang were "mutually suspicious of one another, they may well succeed in arranging [a] marriage of convenience directed at Huong." As predicted, on January 22 an arrangement—or "treaty," as the embassy now referred to it—was arrived at between Khanh and the Buddhists. This tactical alliance, however shaky, immediately strengthened Khanh's hand. Deputy Ambassador Alexis Johnson reported that he found Khanh "deeply impressed" by the Buddhists' political strength and "the support that this can give him in returning to power."[15]

American officials were also impressed—and worried and baffled—by the

Buddhists. McGeorge Bundy told Johnson that they constituted "the central problem," and assured him that he was pressing for "a new and more imaginative combined effort" in dealing with them. Since neither he nor other senior officials had previously showed much understanding of the character and objectives of the Buddhist leaders, it was perhaps predictable that no such effort emerged—nor could it, in view of the fundamental incompatibility of objectives. But the administration's desperation and helplessness is suggested by the fact that Bundy's assistant Chester Cooper was assigned to "consulting with psychiatrists" who had "studied Buddhist psychology" in order to gain "some insights into how to communicate with Buddhists."[16]

With the assurance of at least short-term Buddhist backing, provided he took the necessary measures to oust Huong, Khanh's authority among the Young Turks was temporarily enhanced. His maneuver left the U.S. mission confused and uncertain. Despite their increasingly close contact with Ky and Thieu, American officials were not clear as to the balance of power among the most influential military leaders and whether enough of them could be lined up to remove Khanh efficiently and without adverse publicity and a possibly heavy Buddhist reaction. Moreover, as Alexis Johnson cabled Washington on January 26, the day before Huong's ouster, "Our problem here is to walk a very tight line and avoid Khanh's efforts to establish the impression that his rift with the U.S.G[overnment] is so far healed that he has again become our chosen instrument, while at [the] same time not giving any basis for charges that we are implicated in and seeking to encourage a coup against Khanh."[17] The mission's problem, it should be noted, was further complicated by the opposition among several influential people in Washington to a coup against Khanh: they were convinced that, despite his deficiencies, he was the best leader available for American purposes. Taylor's desire to oust him, they believed, stemmed too much from personal pique—the affront to his own pride from Khanh's offensive actions and unflattering words.

Only some three weeks after the Armed Forces Council had entered into a covenant with Taylor to support Prime Minister Huong and his still predominantly civilian government, members of the embassy awoke on January 27 to find that the Saigon military had found it expedient to betray the agreement. With Buddhist backing and support from the Young Turks and the rest of the military council, Khanh presented the Americans with the *fait accompli* of Huong's ouster, and a mandate from Khanh's military colleagues for him to take charge of the government and resolve the crisis.[18]

Khanh was, however, to savor increased authority for just twenty-three days, during which this astute opportunist sought to cling to power by straddling two incompatible positions—attempting to please both the Buddhists and the Americans. While discreetly demonstrating his support for the Buddhist-led peace movement—ultimately by covertly exploring possibilities for an accommodation with the NLF—he was privately assuring American officials that they could count upon him to support fundamental U.S. objectives, even assuring them that he favored American military escalation, which the Buddhists so strongly opposed. If U.S. officials, now increasingly panicked by the mounting popular demand for peace, had not ultimately gotten wind of Khanh's overture to the NLF, he might have managed to stay on longer: despite his role in ousting Huong, his acceptance of U.S. plans to bomb the North made him useful to proponents of this program. The president's national security adviser appears to have been Khanh's most ardent supporter. The day after Huong had been ousted from office, McGeorge Bundy cabled the outraged Taylor that, with respect to the president's goal of stable government, "we now wonder whether this requirement is either realistic or necessary." (His use of "we" is puzzling, for all available evidence points to Johnson's continued adherence to his original position.) Bundy further cabled on February 1, "If a Khanh-controlled government has some staying power and is reasonably effective, I think we're probably stuck with it."[19]

With Bundy still supporting Khanh, Taylor was unable to get the green light he sought from Washington for mounting a coup. Thus, despite the ambassador's ongoing efforts to encourage various Saigon officers to take such an action, he still could not offer them the full assurances of Washington's support that might have given these men the necessary courage.

But Khanh was not the only or the biggest problem faced by the U.S. mission. There had now emerged what a CIA study for the U.S. Intelligence Board referred to as a "shift in the alignment of fundamental political forces" that was leading to "a social and political revolution," wherein power was now passing from "an elite of French-educated and predominantly Catholic mandarin types" to "a much more 'Vietnamese,' militantly nationalistic and potentially xenophobic group of which the political bonzes, the students and certain young generals are prime examples." This was marked by an upsurge of Buddhist power: they were now "strong enough to make unworkable any set of political arrangements their leaders care to oppose." The widely supported Buddhist movement was regarded as deriving its political strength "primarily from the fact that 'Buddhism' has become the rallying point for emotionally charged though inchoate revolutionary aspirations." It was to be expected that the now aroused "extreme nationalist sentiments" and their "xenophobic and anti-US overtones" would set "severe limits on the degree to which the US can influence Vietnamese actions." Moreover, the report concluded, "The chances have increased that nationalist sentiments, in combination with war weariness and frustrations will take a pro-neutralist turn which the Communists would certainly endeavor to fan and exploit. On the other hand, however, a vigorous nationalism identified with an indigenously devised government reflecting local political realities will be an essential ingredient for any dynamic and successful counterinsurgency effort."[20]

The central problem was, of course, that such a Saigon government would not have followed policies compatible with Washington's. If it were indeed "indigenously devised" and actually reflected "local political realities" it would by definition be a government that would be independent of U.S. control and would respond to the broadly based popular desire for an end to the fighting and a peaceful settlement with the NLF.

Taylor acknowledged that the mass of South Vietnamese wanted peace, and it was the now enhanced capacity of the Buddhist monks to provide a channel for this sentiment that most alarmed U.S. officials. This concern dominated Taylor's cables during the last days of January. He warned Washington that the victory of the Buddhists and their dependent ally General Khanh had put the monks in a position of "increased prestige and influence in [the] country," whereby they "could create an atmosphere conducive to pressures for a negotiated settlement." The State Department responded by requesting Taylor's "estimate of possible actions we might take or approaches we might make to keep situation from moving towards atmosphere conducive to pressures for 'negotiated settlement.' "[21] Taylor had a prescription, but in the face of the president's views, it required an altered rationale for American military intervention.

Following his inauguration, Lyndon Johnson still hung back from authorizing any bombing of the North—either retaliatory attacks or a sustained program. With nearly all of his senior advisers defecting to a pro-escalation position almost as ardent as that of the Joint Chiefs, Johnson was left with only Dean Rusk to support his stipulation that any such program remain conditional on the political improvement and stability of the Saigon regime; even Rusk soon came to abandon this position. Yet Khanh's ouster of Prime Minister Huong and the visibly rising influence and power of the Buddhists must have given the president additional pause.

Beyond the administration's embarrassment at the political chaos in Saigon, then, was its gathering alarm at the possibility that Buddhist leaders could channel the mounting tide of antiwar sentiment in South Vietnam into the creation of a government that would demand a cease-fire, a negotiated settlement with the NLF, and ultimately the departure of the Americans. This prospect seemed very real in early 1965.[22] However awkward it was to request public support for an escalating U.S. intervention in behalf of the existing Saigon government, it would be patently absurd to expect such support for a peace-oriented, neutralist government that wanted the United States to leave.

The deterioration of the Saigon regime's military position had now reached a point where General Westmoreland urgently requested authority to use U.S. jet aircraft against Viet Cong forces in South Vietnam, arguing that because of the political disorder in Saigon, Danang, and Hué, combined with the ARVN's lack of reserves and the decline in discipline and efficiency in the South Vietnamese air force, only such action could hold back the Viet Cong. After this proposal had been endorsed by CINCPAC, the JCS, McNaughton, and McNamara, the president quickly approved it. (Largely unnoticed by the American news media, this major escalatory decision had immense physical consequences for the people and land of Vietnam, especially when, on June 18, Westmoreland secured authority for the regular employment of B-52 bombers against targets in the

South.)[23] Nevertheless, the president continued to resist pressures for the use of U.S. air power against the North.

Lyndon Johnson's key civilian advisers were almost all (with Rusk for a while remaining the exception) chipping away at his determination that Saigon must first demonstrate it had "cleaned up its own back yard." In pressing the president to change his position, the advisers abandoned their earlier argument that political cohesion in Saigon would be strengthened and its army's morale heightened by the mere promise of a future American bombing campaign. Since this was patently not the case, they now turned the old philosophy on its head, and what had been the rationale against bombing now became the rationale for it. Their earlier military-political equation was reversed so that no such improvement could be expected until after a sustained bombing campaign against the North had actually been launched. Without such a tangible earnest of American commitment—so their new argument ran—the United States would face the imminent prospect of a neutralist government in Saigon that would form a coalition with the NLF and ask the United States to leave.[24]

Fear of such a development was increasingly widespread within the top levels of the administration in the early weeks of 1965, as the military collapse of the ARVN accelerated along with its political factionalism, accompanied by a dramatic growth in the popular following and political power of the militant Buddhists in Saigon, Danang, Hué, and other major cities and towns in the northern and central areas of South Vietnam. Vice-President Hubert Humphrey, for one, discounted the need for continued agonizing over whether to escalate. "I'm convinced," he said, "that we don't have to worry about this because, before this bombing can be undertaken, there will be a neutralist government in Saigon and we will be invited out."[25]

The further political disintegration illustrated by Khanh's abrupt removal of Huong led McGeorge Bundy to enlist McNamara's support in a major effort to convince Johnson that his preconditions for bombing the North must now be abandoned if the Saigon regime were to be saved. On January 26, upon hearing that Khanh's coup was about to take place, Bundy so advised the president and then requested that in their meeting the next morning they discuss the proposition that "this back-and-forth in the government in Saigon is a symptom, not a root cause of our problem." Promising to have a paper developed for discussion, he made clear that he wished to have this be "a very private discussion of the basic situation in Vietnam," with the only other person present being Robert McNamara, who by now advocated bombing the North. The long memorandum that Bundy prepared for this meeting had been approved by McNamara, with the only other copy going to Rusk. It argued against the president's continuing restraint and prerequisites for escalation. In forceful and alarmist terms, Bundy explained that he and McNamara were both "now pretty well convinced that our current policy can only lead to disastrous defeat." He acknowledged that the president had made it "very plain that wider action against the Communists will not take place until we can get such a [stable] government." But efforts since then to meet this condition had been unsuccessful, and he and McNamara were persuaded that there was "no real hope of success in this area unless and until our policy and priorities change." The administration's unwillingness to employ greater American power was, he said, undermining the morale of anticommunists in the South.[26]

> The underlying difficulties in Saigon arise from the spreading conviction there that the future is without hope for anti-Communists. More and more the good men are covering their flanks and avoiding executive responsibility for firm anti-Communist policy. Our best friends have become somewhat discouraged by our own inactivity in the face of major attacks on our own installations. The Vietnamese know just as well as we do that the Viet Cong are gaining in the countryside. Meanwhile, they see the enormous power of the United States withheld, and they get little sense of firm and active U.S. policy. They feel that we are unwilling to take serious risks.

Declaring that "all of this is outrageous, in the light of all that we have done and all that we are ready to do if they will only pull up their socks," Bundy warned that "the uncertainty and lack of direction" pervading these Vietnamese "are also increasingly visible among our own people, even the most loyal and determined." Referring to the president's stipulation in his "basic directive" that the U.S. would "not go further until there is a stable government," he went on to admonish: "No one has much hope that there is going to be a stable government while we sit still. . . . The result is that we are pinned into a policy of first aid to squabbling politicos and passive reaction to events we do not try to control." The president's national security adviser ended this ominous introduction to his brief with the statement "Bob [McNamara] and I believe that the worst course of action is to continue in this essentially passive role which can only lead to eventual defeat and an invitation to get out in humiliating circumstances."

Again, speaking for himself and McNamara, Bundy proceeded to tell the president that he had just two alternatives: "The *first* is to use our military power in the Far East and to force a change of Communist policy. The *second* is to deploy all our resources along a track of negotiation, aimed at salvaging what little can be preserved with no major addition to our present military risks." He made clear they both favored the first course, but made a brief bow toward open-mindedness in calling upon Johnson to study both alternatives carefully and stating that other programs should be argued out before him. Declaring that he and McNamara had previously backed the president's "unwillingness in earlier months, to move out of the middle course," and acknowledging that Rusk still supported the "middle course," Bundy concluded that for himself and the secretary of defense such a policy was no longer possible. "We both agree that every effort should still be made to improve our operations on the ground and to prop up the authorities in South Vietnam as best we can. But we are both convinced that none of this is enough, and that the time has come for harder choices." Both

Bundy and McNamara must have known Lyndon Johnson well enough to appreciate how little attracted he would be to a course that would at best end in simply "salvaging what little can be preserved," with a prospect of "eventual defeat and an invitation to get out in humiliating circumstances." And so the president who had asked his advisers for a full range of options was now given just two, and these were couched in loaded terms.

Vigorously reinforcing Bundy and McNamara's arguments was the long report Maxwell Taylor submitted on February 2, "Stability of Government in Relation to Initiation of Phase II." The U.S. mission, he began, was unanimous in supporting one basic conclusion—the United States was losing in South Vietnam and would have to "change course or suffer defeat." Recalling that the mission had often commented on "the necessity for some minimal government in SVN precedent to opening the air operations we call Phase II," he observed that "until the end of 1964, I had hopes that U.S. agreement to Phase II operations might be used as a carrot to incite GVN leaders to better efforts in the governmental field, but that hope has been disappointed." Indeed, there had been "a progressive lowering of the standards of governmental performance considered a prerequisite for Phase II." Now "the Mission view . . . had been tempered by the sad experiences of the preceding months and a growing realization that we would probably never have in the foreseeable future a stable government. . . ." Consequently, "the rock bottom criterion . . . asks only for a government to exist and to have the strength of voice able to ask for U.S. help." As long as a chief of government maintained the backing of the armed forces and "a voice strong enough to reach the U.S.," he could do most of the essential governmental tasks for a short time, "until military success against the North has provided a national stimulus translatable into improvement of government." In the meantime, Taylor warned, "only the initiation of Phase II operations offers the slightest hope of providing a means of attacking . . . with a chance of success" the main problems besetting the Saigon regime. "We should not delay longer waiting for a stable government that may never come—unless eventually as the outgrowth of victory."[27]

Thus far, Taylor was in full accord with and strongly reinforcing the arguments Bundy and McNamara had advanced to Johnson. The last two sentences of his February 2 brief, however, departed from Bundy's position. Though the latter was content to work with Khanh, Taylor was not. Nor was he prepared to see the United States escalate to Phase II while Khanh still dominated South Vietnam's armed forces and remained the paramount political leader. In the ambassador's view, if "Huong had been supported by loyal armed forces, that combination would have been enough to warrant starting air operations," but lacking this, "our objective now should be to put together quickly some combination at least as good." Thus another backer of bombing was needed to occupy the prime minister's office, and some more reliable and tractable advocate than Khanh was required to represent the armed forces in this matter.

But on the central issues Taylor was in full accord with Bundy and

McNamara: the old equation had to be revised so that the United States no longer need have an actual government in place in South Vietnam from which to project its power; it would be sufficient to have a base made up of the South Vietnamese armed forces alone; and if an actual political base were ever to emerge it would come about as the consequence of the favorable psychological atmosphere that bombing the North would induce among the South Vietnamese. Taylor wished to hold off on air strikes until the Khanh regime was replaced by another military leadership, but all three of these presidential advisers now pressed for moving to Phase II as soon as possible.

George Ball has nicely summed up the new rationale for carrying the war to the North.

> I have always marveled at the way ingenious men can, when they wish, turn logic upside down, and I was not surprised when my colleagues interpreted the crumbling of the South Vietnamese government, the Viet Cong's increasing success, and a series of defeats of South Vietnamese units not as proving that we should cut our losses and get out, but rather that we must promptly begin bombing to stiffen the resolve of the corrupt South Vietnamese government. It was classical bureaucratic casuistry. A faulty rationalization was improvised to obscure the painful reality that America could arrest the galloping deterioration of its position only by the surgery of extrication. Gifted dialecticians carried the charade one step further, arguing that we were principally responsible for Saigon's low morale, since Ambassador Taylor had upset Saigon's politicians by demanding that the government shape up in a manner it had no intention of doing. We must, they argued, commit our power and prestige even more intensely to stop the South Vietnamese government from falling completely apart, negotiating covertly with the Liberation Front or Hanoi, and ultimately asking us to leave. It was Catch 22 and the quintessence of black humor. Almost alone, the President seemed to recognize and reject this inversion of logic.[28]

Despite the arguments for bombing, Johnson was evidently still not convinced. According to James Thomson—and the accuracy of his recollection has been attested to by William Bundy—"The sense in the White House was that the President did not want to do this, and this was one reason for the McGeorge Bundy mission—his felt need for a final determination shows his reluctance." Chester Cooper, the Bundy aide who accompanied him on this mission, later wrote that on the eve of their departure "the Administration seemed to be on dead center and the President was caught between McNamara's pleas for new initiatives and Rusk's reluctance to take any important new steps until the political situation in Saigon could be put in some semblance of order." Consequently, states Cooper, "The President agreed to send a high-level working group including members of his own staff to Saigon . . . for a fresh look. Out of such an examination, he felt, would come recommendations either to move ahead in new and more vigorous ways to gain the initiative against the Viet Cong or to proceed down a path of disengagement." Prior to the Bundy mission, Cooper concluded, "The option of disengagement, or at least the possibility of a serious consideration of disengagement or a scaling down, was a live one."[29]

Annoyed by McGeorge Bundy's unstinting support of Khanh and apparently believing that if the national security adviser ever actually visited Vietnam he might develop a more realistic grasp of Saigon's politics, Taylor had earlier suggested to Johnson that it would be useful to send Bundy for a visit. The president had agreed to dispatch someone to look into "the enormous problem" of Saigon's "political unity." On January 27 he decided to send Bundy. Since the president accepted Taylor's advice that Bundy's trip be deferred until "the shape of [the] new [post–January-27-coup] government became more clear," the departure was delayed until February 3. Hours before Bundy boarded his plane, a cable from Taylor, presumably referring to his own support for a coup against Khanh, warned him, "You may be arriving just in time to witness some very important governmental developments. . . . We may give you an interesting time," and chided, "In any case you will find as a specific item high on our agenda: can the U.S. do business with a Khanh government? We shall expect you to defend the affirmative as we will be on the side of the negative."[30]

When his plane left for Saigon, Bundy was hardly a detached, impartial referee. He had for many months clearly favored a major American military escalation in Vietnam. As early as May 25, 1964, he had recommended to the president that he "use selected and carefully graduated military force against North Vietnam," and his commitment was certainly evident three months later when, in the face of McNamara's reluctance to send in marines to guard U.S. installations, he had privately suggested to Johnson that he send in "a couple of brigade-size" U.S. ground forces for "operations against the Viet Cong."[31] Moreover, the small group that accompanied Bundy to Saigon was made up of men, including John McNaughton, who shared the national security adviser's views on the need for a sustained bombing program.

At 2:00 A.M. on February 7, the fourth and last day of Bundy's stay in Vietnam, a company of Viet Cong soldiers launched an attack against a laxly guarded U.S. helicopter base and advisers' barracks at Pleiku in the Central Highlands. Eight Americans were killed, 126 wounded, ten U.S. planes destroyed, and numerous others damaged. This was one, and by no means the largest, of ten Viet Cong attacks launched that day, following the termination of a unilateral Viet Cong seven-day Tet (New Year) cease-fire. It did not produce as many military casualties as two battalion-sized attacks in an adjacent province, but it did result in by far the largest number of Americans killed and wounded of any incident in the conflict thus far. And, in contrast to the Brinks attack of December

24, this time there was no doubt that the Viet Cong were responsible. Bundy promptly joined other advocates of bombing in insisting that the Pleiku assault constituted the type of credible, clear-cut provocation cited by the president as a possible trigger for a one-shot American retaliatory air strike against the North. While checking intermittently by "secure phone" with Bundy in Saigon, Johnson then presided over a meeting of the National Security Council in Washington, attended by all the advisers save Rusk. Except for the Senate majority leader, Mike Mansfield, the entire group supported a retaliatory air strike by 132 carrier-based U.S. jets against four different barracks complexes inside North Vietnam.* Less than fourteen hours after the Pleiku attack, U.S. planes were over North Vietnam. Phase I (code-named "Flaming Dart"), the retaliatory bombing campaign, had begun.[32]

For some of the president's advisers, the Pleiku attack did not come as a great surprise—nor should it have, as McGeorge Bundy later implied in his remark "Pleikus are streetcars." In other words, you could expect one to come along presently, and you were ready to board it as soon as it did. But it was propitiously timed for him and others to persuade Johnson to adopt a policy of Tonkin Gulf–type reprisals. Bundy had good reason to expect one of these "streetcars" during his visit to Vietnam. Not only was it usual for the Viet Cong to launch heavy attacks just after the termination of Tet cease-fires, but U.S. intelligence reports had indicated one was to be expected against an American installation during Bundy's visit. The reason given by Allen S. Whiting, then the State Department's director of research and analysis for the Far East, for later referring to the post-Pleiku air raids against the North as "ostensibly" in response to the February 7 Viet Cong attack, bears directly on this question. "Actually," he states, "the raids were preplanned on the basis of the author's forecast that a Communist assault would be mounted against an American installation during the visit of McGeorge Bundy, special assistant for National Security Affairs." (Bundy, however, has recently said that he cannot recall being told this.) Also pertinent to this preplanning was the "unanswered" question reported by the *New York Times* White House correspondent Charles Mohr as to why all three of the normally widely dispersed attack carriers of the Seventh Fleet (from which the U.S. planes were launched) were concentrated near the coast of North Vietnam shortly before the reprisal bombing. The Pleiku pretext came on schedule; so did the reprisal bombing, or, as Whiting later observed, "The weekend events followed according to prediction and plan."[33]

Another aspect of the timing of Bundy's trip has never been fully explained, though at the time it occasioned no little concern, at least from second-echelon officials in the State Department: he departed for Saigon knowing that on the same day Soviet Prime Minister Alexei Kosygin was leaving on a state visit to Hanoi. If Bundy's trip could be deferred a couple of days till the administration

---

*Mansfield wryly observed, "It appears that the local populace is not with us, else the Viet Cong could not have carried out the attack."

saw how Khanh would shape up his post-coup government, one may well ask why
it was not postponed for a few days more until Kosygin had left North Vietnam.
And since the scheduled resumption of the provocative DeSoto destroyer patrols
along North Vietnam's coast were deferred until after Kosygin's visit, it seems
incongruous that the much more provocative bombing should not have been
deferred as well. Given the expectation that the Viet Cong would launch an attack
against a major U.S. military installation during Bundy's visit, it is evident that
the awaited occasion for a reprisal bombing of North Vietnam would thus occur
while the Soviet leader was there. There had been agreement among the president's advisers that for any reprisal bombing to be seen as such, it should follow
as soon as possible after the Viet Cong attack for which it signaled retribution.
But there was no such consensus that such bombing should take place while the
prime minister of the Soviet Union was making his first visit to Hanoi. Ball,
Mansfield, and the ambassador to Moscow, Llewellyn Thompson, all urged—
unsuccessfully—that the post-Pleiku strike be deferred until after Kosygin had
left North Vietnam; Thompson pointed out that otherwise the Soviet government
would "almost certainly think we had chosen this moment to bomb in order to
humiliate Moscow." It is difficult to believe that other members of an American
administration so obsessed with assessing Vietnam policy in terms of their own
country's international prestige could not have had some appreciation of Kosygin's sensitivity for his own and Moscow's world image. Particularly was this so
in view of their knowledge of the then well developed Sino-Soviet dispute and the
intense competition between the two major communist powers to win ideological
and political backing from other communist states such as North Vietnam.

The administration's calculations in this matter are not clear, but presumably they must be interpreted against the immediate background of a convergence
of pressures for a negotiated settlement, emanating from both within and outside
Vietnam. Concomitant with the clearly discernible surge of an internal South
Vietnamese neutralist tide, now effectively channeled by the Buddhists, were
increasingly strong voices within the United Nations, which in a few days would
be formally articulated by U Thant in an appeal to move the Vietnam crisis "from
the field of battle to the conference table," whether inside or outside the United
Nations, involving a revival of the Geneva Conference. President Charles de
Gaulle had revived his long-standing call for such a solution in early January and,
encouraged by Hanoi, was to press for this again on February 10.

The Soviet Union too was moving in this direction. After some three years'
lapse of interest in Vietnam under Khrushchev, the new Brezhnev-Kosygin leadership had been showing greater concern, and in November had pledged a new
aid program for 1965. As the CIA's Office of Current Intelligence observed, "It
has always been clear that if Moscow were to firm up its support of North
Vietnamese policy objectives in Indochina, Hanoi would tend to moderate the
degree of its open support for Peiping in the Sino-Soviet dispute, and once again
attempt to play its assumed role of 'honest broker' seeking to bring at least an
operative unity between Peiping and Moscow." Moscow, however, wished to

maintain the existing détente with the United States and feared the possibility of an enlarged war in Vietnam. Evidently alarmed at the mounting signs of American escalation, the Soviets were regarded by U.S. intelligence as desiring to defuse a crisis that threatened to leave them on the horns of a dilemma: refusal to continue economic assistance and military supplies to Hanoi would leave them vulnerable to a predictable charge by Peking of abandoning a fraternal communist state; sustaining this support risked undermining détente with Washington. "The Soviets," the CIA reported, "almost certainly hope that North Vietnam avoids actions which might provoke US reprisals and produce further escalation. Kosygin will almost certainly urge this point of view in Hanoi. . . ."[34]

Thus, at the time of Kosygin's visit to Hanoi, Moscow was probably anxious to bring about a negotiated settlement of the Vietnam War. Following the January 31 announcement that he would head the delegation, *The New York Times* noted that there was "speculation in the Administration and among informed diplomats that Mr. Kosygin's trip might be the opening move in a broad Soviet attempt to mediate between the United States and the Hanoi regime for a settlement of the Vietnamese war," and that Washington expected that after his visit Moscow "would start a campaign to reconvene the Geneva Conference on Vietnam." There were differences within the administration as to Kosygin's purposes, but some State Department officials, especially in its offices of Asian Communist Affairs and Intelligence and Research, believed that "the USSR might well find it in its interests to act as an agent of moderation and compromise, providing the U.S. with an avenue of graceful retreat from a seemingly irretrievable situation." It is clear, however, that this was not what most senior administration officials desired. They still remained opposed to a negotiated solution until such time as the position of the U.S. and that of its Saigon client were strong enough so they could impose a settlement that would maintain a separate anticommunist South Vietnamese state.[35]

Though it might have seemed plausible to assume that nothing would be more likely to kill a Kosygin negotiating initiative than to bomb North Vietnam while he was there, that was not the consequence. The premier did not drop the proposal, and, to Washington's discomfiture, the Soviet government indicated its support of U Thant's February 12 appeal for a negotiated settlement. On February 16, following his return to Moscow, Kosygin proposed a new international conference on Indochina, and on February 23 Moscow announced its support of de Gaulle's call for a negotiated peace and a reconvening of the 1954 Geneva Conference.[36]

More predictable, perhaps, with respect to the bombing attack, which Kosygin regarded as "a personal insult," was Moscow's warning the next day that as a consequence it was now necessary "to take further measures to safeguard the security and strengthen the defense capability" of the Hanoi government, and Kosygin's announcement two weeks later that a military-aid agreement concluded while he was in Hanoi was already being implemented. (In now urging further escalation of U.S. air strikes against the North, the Joint Chiefs anticipated that the probable Soviet response would consist "both of a vigorous diplomatic and propaganda effort to bring the US to [the] conference table and provision of military support to North Vietnam" and that this "almost certainly would include anti-aircraft artillery and radars" with about an even chance that this would include SA-2 surface-to-air missiles.)[37]

For its part, the Peking government had by mid-February responded to the U.S. expansion of the war in the North with what the State Department saw as a "more truculent public posture." It noted that while avoiding "commitment to any specific course of action under specific circumstances," China's repeated promises of assistance strongly implied a "direct involvement of their own forces" to an extent that "committed their prestige to a more vigorous response to any future escalation." It saw official editorials as implying that Peking was "ready to assist Hanoi [to] exercise its 'right' to hit back across the demarcation line" (seventeenth parallel), with China having the "right to employ 'every possible means' to assist North Vietnam since the United States had provided the GVN with 'troops' and materiel."[38]

The Joint Chiefs believed that Peking would be reluctant to become directly involved in the fighting, but concluded that, as the number and severity of U.S. attacks against North Vietnam increased, the Chinese would "probably feel an increased compulsion to take some dramatic action to counter [the] impact of U.S. pressures," with a "fair chance" that they would introduce "limited numbers of Chinese ground forces as 'volunteers' [the designation used in Korea] in North Vietnam, and/or northern Laos. . . ."[39]

The Pleiku "streetcar" not only precipitated the almost immediate launching of the first Phase I bombing of North Vietnam, but was well timed for strengthening the efforts of those who argued that it be promptly succeeded by Phase II. Bundy and Taylor had agreed, before the former had left Washington, to include the topic "Extension of the War Beyond SVN" on the agenda for their talks in Saigon. There, the day before the attack on Pleiku, they and Alexis Johnson, McNaughton, and Westmoreland had reached agreement on the draft of a variant of Phase II replete with "analysis, rationale, and illustrative scenario."[40]

During his first day in Saigon, Bundy focused on the president's request for an assessment of the local political situation. Via CIA channels, he promptly informed him:

> We have pressed throughout the day to see whether any member of the country team believes that we can prevent continued deterioration in the absence of a "reasonably effective and stable government." The country team appears to share the President's judgement that such a government is necessary on all counts. Getting it is something else again. . . . A day of inquiry reveals no present prospect of a government acceptable to us that would be acceptable to leaders of the Buddhist institute. The current situa-

tion among non-Communist forces gives all the appearances of a civil war within a civil war. In this situation, the construction of a Government of national unity may well require sharp confrontation with Buddhists before, during, or after the construction job.[41]

Discussions the next day shifted to the agenda item of "Extension of War Beyond SVN." Bundy and Taylor concentrated on Phase II, the sustained bombing project, with Phase I apparently being taken for granted. As McNaughton cabled McNamara from Saigon, in these sessions the Bundy group and the Saigon mission discussed at length a "graduated reprisal program"—an objective clearly supported by both. In encapsulating the consensus arrived at, McNaughton reported that "through a measured, controlled sequence of actions against the DRV," sufficient pressure would be brought to bear "to persuade it to stop its intervention in the south." The judgment, he said, had been reached that with "the fabric of SVN . . . pulling apart" and a widespread belief among the South Vietnamese that "the U.S. is on the verge of bugging out," such a program would probably "dampen VC activities in due course" and inspire the South Vietnamese to more effective efforts. This cabled summation conformed to the much more detailed delineation of the graduated reprisal program that Bundy's group and senior mission members had drawn up the day before Pleiku. Acknowledgment that Lyndon Johnson was not yet behind their plans was indicated by the first item in their program's suggested sequence of events: "Presidential approval and preparations of supporting rationale." And it was evident from McNaughton's cable that the Bundy-Taylor group was unclear even as to whether the president would regard the Pleiku reprisal as "a single-shot affair like Gulf of Tonkin" or as the start of a sustained "reprisal-oriented squeeze."[42]

Before the psychological climate induced by the Pleiku attack and bombing reprisal could dissipate, McGeorge Bundy moved to persuade the president to commit the United States to a Phase II escalation. The arguments Bundy put forward strongly influenced the president in his decision to cross this Rubicon only some three weeks after having finally authorized the retaliatory bombing triggered by Pleiku.[43]

Bundy's opening paragraphs struck a note of crisis, invoked American prestige as the central factor, and moved to denigrate negotiations as a possible course. Since his first two paragraphs set the tone and provided the assumptions upon which the remainder of his memorandum rested, they should be read in their entirety:

The situation in Vietnam is deteriorating, and without new U.S. action defeat appears inevitable—probably not in a matter of weeks or perhaps even months, but within the next year or so. There is still time to turn it around, but not much.

The stakes in Vietnam are extremely high. The American investment is very large, the American responsibility is a fact of life which is palpable in

the atmosphere of Asia, and even elsewhere. The international prestige of
the United States, and a substantial part of our influence, are directly at risk
in Vietnam. There is no way of unloading the burden on the Vietnamese
themselves, and there is no way of negotiating ourselves out of Vietnam
which offers any serious promise at present. It is possible that at some future
time a neutral non-Communist force may emerge, perhaps under Buddhist
leadership, but no such force currently exists, and any negotiated U.S.
withdrawal today would mean surrender on the installment plan.[44]

This assessment of indigenous possibilities for a negotiated settlement was
in fact grossly misleading. Contrary to what he assured the president, a "neutral
non-Communist force" had indeed already emerged, and it was "under Buddhist
leadership." If, nevertheless, Johnson might possibly be attracted to this route or
be seriously enough concerned about international pressures at least to explore
it, the end of Bundy's memorandum was likely to dissuade him. It read:

> . . . we should *not* now accept the idea of negotiations of any sort except
> on the basis of a stand down of Viet Cong violence [a condition that he and
> some other presidential advisers hoped would later be achieved through the
> inducement brought about by a sufficiently punishing weight of bombing].
> A program of sustained reprisal, with its direct link to Hanoi's continuing
> aggressive actions in the South will not involve us in nearly the level of
> international recrimination which would be precipitated by a go-North
> program which was not so connected. For this reason the international
> pressures for negotiation should be quite manageable.

"The best available way of increasing our chances of success in Vietnam," Bundy
argued, was what he referred to as a policy of "sustained reprisal," continuing
air and naval action against the North—in effect, Phase II. This was to be
"justified by and related to the whole Viet Cong campaign of violence and terror
in the South" and not simply to particular Viet Cong attacks, such as at Pleiku.
"We are convinced," he stated, "that the political values of reprisal require a
continuous operation. Episodic responses geared on a one-for-one basis to 'spectacular' outrages would lack the persuasive force of sustained pressure."

In his rationale for escalating to this level of sustained air and naval bombardment of the North, Bundy directly confronted the conviction of the president
and Rusk that political and military improvement of the Saigon regime was a
necessary precondition for carrying the war to the North. Assuring the president
that the members of his group had made it their "particular business" to examine
"whether and to what degree a stable government" was necessary, he contended
that this was an unrealistic prerequisite, and that governmental authority in
Saigon "need be no stronger than it is today with General Khanh as the focus
of raw power while a weak caretaker government goes through the motions. Such
a government can execute military decisions and it can give formal political

support to joint US/GVN policy." And that, he acknowledged, "is about all it can do."

Though Khanh would be adequate for launching the bombing of the North, once that was under way beneficial political and psychological consequences in the South would make possible the establishment of a better government there. "We emphasize," he said, "that our primary target in advocating a reprisal policy is the improvement of the situation in *South* Vietnam." "The immediate and critical targets are in the South—in the minds of the South Vietnamese and in the minds of the Viet Cong Cadres." As a consequence of the reprisal bombing, he assured the president, "it seems very clear that . . . there will be a sharp immediate increase in optimism in the South among nearly all articulate groups. . . . This favorable reaction should offer opportunity for increased American influence in pressing for a more effective government—at least in the short run." The United States could also expect to secure better control over the Saigon military establishment, he argued. "Joint reprisals [that is, carried out along with the South Vietnamese air force and navy] would imply military planning in which the American role would necessarily be controlling, and this new relation should add to our bargaining power in other military efforts. . . . We have the whip hand in reprisals as we do not in other fields." Continuing in this euphoric vein, he concluded, "The Vietnamese increase in hope could well increase the readiness of Vietnamese factions themselves to join together in forming a more effective government."

The United States, Bundy continued, would also benefit from the likely "substantial depressing effect" that sustained reprisals, "even in a low key," would have upon the morale of Viet Cong cadres in South Vietnam. Employing language well suited to engaging the president's pride, he said that this judgment was based, among other things, "upon the solid general assessment that the determination of Hanoi and the apparent timidity of the mighty United States are both major items in Viet Cong confidence." Finally, Bundy turned to relate this policy to the domestic and global reputation and prestige of the administration and the United States. Though acknowledging that the policy of sustained reprisal bombing might not succeed, he asserted:

> What we can say is that even if it fails, the policy will be worth it. At a minimum it will damp down the charge that we did not do all that we could have done, and this charge will be important in many countries, including our own. Beyond that, a reprisal policy—to the extent that it demonstrates U.S. willingness to employ this new norm in counter-insurgency—will set a higher price for the future upon all adventures of guerrilla warfare, and it should therefore somewhat increase our ability to deter such adventures. We must recognize, however, that that ability will be gravely weakened if there is a failure for any reason in Vietnam.

Thus Bundy argued that, even if the policy did fail, it was worth undertaking. Despite his admission at the very beginning of his brief that it would mean "significant U.S. air losses" and that "U.S. casualties would be higher—and more visible to American feelings—than those sustained in the struggle in South Vietnam,"* he concluded that "even if it fails to turn the tide—as it may—the value of the effort seems to us to exceed its cost."

Immediately after his return to Washington late in the evening of February 7, Bundy presented the full text of his memorandum to the president, with copies distributed to McNamara and Rusk. The next morning, after further discussions with Bundy and with some of his other senior advisers, the president called a meeting of the National Security Council, at which all of his Washington-based senior advisers (except Rusk, who was ill) were present, along with four leading Democratic and Republican congressmen—all of whom, Johnson writes, had read the Bundy report or knew its main elements.[46]

At the meeting Bundy summarized his report, and Johnson later wrote that among those present there was unanimous support for its "principal recommendation: a program of sustained reprisal against the North." Some reservations were, however, voiced by Ball and Vice President Humphrey, who a week later wrote a long dissenting memorandum, arguing primarily in terms of domestic political considerations. A subsequent memorandum by Rusk indicated that he too now supported a sustained bombing campaign.[47]

According to the NSC's summary notes of the meeting, the president referred to his early-December approval in principle of "further pressure against North Vietnam," and stated, "We are now ready to return to our program of pushing forward in an effort to defeat North Vietnamese aggression *without escalating the war*" (emphasis added). He went on to explain that Taylor's efforts since December had not produced a better government in Saigon, but "it is our hope that current U.S. action may pull together the various forces in Saigon and thus make possible the establishment of a stable government."[48]

Johnson's endorsement of Bundy's recommendations was in fact somewhat oblique and couched in language sufficiently ambiguous to leave him some latitude regarding actual implementation. The confusion created by this ambiguity was reflected in the questions seeking clarification from Representative Gerald Ford, and in some of Johnson's responses.[49] (Indeed, the president's position was vague enough to prompt Bundy to plead for elucidation and greater precision a week later.)

Some of the same caution and ambiguity persisted in Johnson's cable that evening to Taylor:

> I am now prepared to go forward with the best government we can get, and accordingly I have today decided that we will carry out our December plan for continuing action against North Vietnam with modifications up and

*Casualties already sustained by the U.S. military in Vietnam resulting from hostile action had not been insignificant, totaling 346 killed and 1,524 wounded by the end of 1964. This figure did not include casualties from noncombat accidents or inadvertent "friendly fire."[45]

down in tempo and scale in the light of your recommendations as Bundy reports them, and our own continuing review of the situation. . . . I am impressed by argument that the building of a minimum government will benefit by some private assurances from us to the highest levels that we do now intend to take continuing actions. Therefore you are authorized to convey this in general terms to key leaders and political figures as you see fit. At the same time, you should say we want to work with a unified and ongoing government, and that the sooner they can work out such a government the better we can plan and execute the continuing actions we have in mind.[50]

This last phrase must have encouraged Taylor in his own conviction that escalation required a different government from the existing Saigon regime.

Whether or not those attending the meeting of February 8 had reason to be uncertain as to the strength of the president's own support for the sustained bombing program recommended by Bundy, acceptance was one thing and implementation was another. It was five days before Johnson formally endorsed the proposal, twenty days before he publicly announced his decision to embark upon the program, and two more days until, on March 2, it could be implemented. During this period events in and outside Vietnam affected that progression.[51]

XI

The Decision
for Sustained Bombing

Lyndon Johnson clearly demonstrated his reluctance to authorize reprisal bombing in his response to the Viet Cong attack launched against a U.S. army billet in Qui Nhon on February 10, in which twenty-three Americans were killed and twenty-one wounded. He turned down an immediate JCS recommendation for eight weeks of sustained bombing and the deployment of a marine brigade to Danang, and was willing to order no more than a one-shot Pleiku-type reprisal, carried out the next day by some 130 U.S. planes.[1]

Johnson, however, was being subjected to additional pressures from outside, as well as within his administration. Ten days before Pleiku, former Vice President Nixon had attacked the administration for losing the war, warning that the United States would be thrown out of Vietnam if it did not change its strategy. Just after the retaliation for the Qui Nhon assault, Nixon declared that single strikes were not enough and insisted that the United States must now attack North Vietnam hard and consistently "day by day" and "night by night." He said that even though the average American probably favored disengagement this was "no time for consensus government. . . . It's a time for leadership. The average citizen doesn't know what the stakes are in Vietnam."[2]

When he heard of the Qui Nhon attack, Wesley Fishel, chairman of the now-resurgent American Friends of Vietnam, phoned the State Department to inform it and the White House staff that the lobby's executive committee urged a strong stand, with retaliation against North Vietnam, including the introduction of American troops to seal off infiltration trails. If such advice was not acted upon, his group, "all of whom he described as experts and prolific writers on South Vietnamese affairs, would proceed to publish highly critical articles on U.S. policy in South Vietnam," and within a week or two would run a full-page advertisement in *The New York Times*. Soon afterward, in a public policy statement, the organization called for "stronger American action and involvement" in Vietnam, including "perhaps as many as two brigades" of U.S. troops to serve as a general reserve in South Vietnam, which would engage Viet Cong troops in fixed positions, and a "North Vietnam Liberation Movement," which would sponsor psychological programs, including paramilitary action.[3]

The much more influential China lobby was also still affecting the public atmosphere in which Washington made its decisions on Vietnam. Among the adherents of Chiang Kai-shek's well-funded cause, it was especially the Committee of One Million Against the Admission of Communist China to the United Nations that helped nourish the widespread belief among members of the Congress and the American public that Hanoi and the NLF were acting as agents of Peking. This committee was able to secure the endorsement of more than half the Congress to a policy of opposition, not only to China's admission to the United Nations and to American diplomatic and trade relations, but also to "any policy of accommodation which might be interpreted as U.S. acquiescence in, or approval of Communist China's aggression, direct or indirect, against her neighbors." It was presumably in the context of this last plank in its platform that the Committee of One Million extended its mandate to Vietnam, where, it warned the public, "Red Chinese-supported troops are killing young Americans."[4]

The tendency of the public to see communist China as the *éminence grise* manipulating America's enemy in Vietnam was reflected in a confidential poll Louis Harris conducted for the administration just after the February 10 reprisal bombing. When asked, "Who do you think is behind the attacks by the Viet Cong?," 53 percent blamed the Chinese communists and 26 percent North Vietnam (only 7 percent said "Civil War"; and 14 percent said "Not Sure"). Of those polled, 58 percent believed that a continuation of the bombing would cause China to send in planes and troops (22 percent did not and 20 percent were unsure); 43 percent felt that, even if this happened, "a longer war could be avoided" (42 percent said it could not); and 36 percent as against 40 percent favored "bombing China if that is the only way to save South Vietnam" (24 percent were unsure). In summing up the poll (which included numerous other questions), Harris concluded, "The American people feel that China is testing our will. The majority favor the action the President has taken. They do not believe we can walk away from South Vietnam. . . ."[5]

This survey was undertaken as a check against a well-publicized Gallup poll a few days previously which had found that the president's overall rating had gone from 66 percent positive on February 1 to 69 percent just after the two reprisal bombings, with approval of his "handling the situation in Vietnam" rising from 41 percent to 60 percent during that interval. Released on February 15, the Gallup poll found that out of 91 percent of Americans who had heard or read about the reprisal bombings of North Vietnam during the previous week, 67 percent approved, and only 15 percent disapproved. Sixty-four percent favored the United States continuing its efforts in Vietnam, as against 18 percent wanting a "pull out." When this 64 percent was asked, "Should the U.S. continue its present efforts in South Vietnam at risk of nuclear war?," about half (31 percent) were in favor, with 21 opposed and 12 claiming no opinion.[6]

Clearly, then, the president had reason to believe that a substantial majority of Americans supported the retaliatory bombing program on which he had just embarked and that a sizable number would favor more hawkish policies than he had yet approved. Nevertheless, to the apparent disappointment of Bundy and McNamara, as well as the JCS, he continued to balk at actually authorizing Phase II's implementation. Possibly this reluctance stemmed from indications that the reprisal bombings had not reduced Viet Cong military morale,* and, probably of greater importance, also from the fact that these attacks against the North were not bringing about in the South either political coherence or a greater dedication to prosecuting the war. Indeed, the bombings provided a major impetus to the peace movement in Vietnam, gave it a sharper anti-American edge, and placed the Buddhist monks even more effectively at its head. Thus, on February 9, Ambassador Taylor cabled:

> Increasing indications that Buddhist Institute orchestrating strong anti-American campaign with neutralist overtones, evidently to picture U.S. presence and interference as main obstacle to peace in Vietnam and present selves as only independent group capable of leading Vietnamese people to settlement of conflict without heavy intensification of war effort. Institute leadership apparently playing on what they feel is widespread popular desire for peace, as well as on latent nationalism of younger generation in particular.[7]

Outside Vietnam, pressures were converging for an end to the fighting through a negotiated settlement, and the two reprisal bombings lent a sense of greater urgency to French, Indian, and Soviet efforts to achieve this. On February 12, responding to the now rising concern within the United Nations, U Thant publicly called on all parties to move "from the field of battle to the conference table," either inside or outside the U.N., and to revive the 1954 Geneva Conference. Though this appeal enlisted Hanoi's support and soon secured French and Soviet backing for reconvening the Geneva Conference, the U.S. administration's response was sharp and negative. The same was true for U Thant's follow-up plea of February 24 for a negotiation that would enable the United States to "withdraw its troops with dignity."[8]

But among the president's senior advisers there was little desire to move away from military escalation toward even reconnoitering possibilities that negotiations might uncover. As James C. Thomson, Jr., complained to McGeorge Bundy on February 19, "we have failed to do any significant exploration of Hanoi's actual private terms for a settlement," and, with respect to "the specifics of a realistic U.S. negotiating position, the Administration has made no concerted effort to staff this out with any of the care and vigor given to target selection and

---

*The CIA reported that during the first two weeks of February the ARVN lost 1,312 weapons compared with only 279 captured from the Viet Cong—a ratio almost twice as high as during January. It also observed that "Viet Cong main forces in the northern provinces are the best organized and strongest in South Vietnam and, as yet, have not been committed to their full military potential." It reckoned total Viet Cong main-force personnel at 34,900.

the like." Presumably Thomson would have foreseen the futility of such an appeal
if he had been aware—as he was not—of Bundy's private memorandum to the
president that same day. Strongly opposing any move toward negotiations, Bundy
advised Johnson how to handle an important newspaper editor. "The pressure for
negotiations is coming mostly from people who simply do not understand what
that word means in Asian ears right now. If the U.S. proposes negotiations, or
even indicates a desire for them, the word in Saigon will be that we are getting
out, and the consequences of that rumor would be very severe for our whole
position." As Max Frankel, a *New York Times* Washington correspondent, wrote
at this time, "Even a vague commitment to negotiations is feared here because
officials suspect that it would destroy the morale of South Vietnam's army and
further undermine the coalition, already shaken, of military, civilian and religious
leaders."[9]

The administration would not consider negotiations until after its Vietnamese adversaries had in effect thrown in the towel and agreed in advance to
its central demand that Vietnam remain divided into two "nations," with the
southern half maintained as a separate political entity controlled by an anticommunist regime. That position had been publicly reiterated just the day before the
Pleiku attack by William Bundy:

> Negotiation will in the end certainly be an answer if it produces an indepen-
> dent and secure South Viet-Nam. But, on the other hand, there's no sign
> that Hanoi would really go for that at the present time. Any negotiation
> that admitted communism to South Viet-Nam or legalized it, that didn't
> get Hanoi and the North Vietnamese out, or that set up some structure
> under nebulous, not very clear guarantees, simply would not provide the
> independent and secure South Viet-Nam that nation is entitled to and that
> we're after.[10]

Secretary Rusk drove this message home on February 25, at a press conference at which he was said to be "determined to deflect pressures for unconditional
negotiations and to maintain the pressure on North Vietnam begun by the air
raids." There could be no negotiations, he emphasized, until Hanoi first agreed
to respect the security and independence of South Vietnam. "The heart of the
problem," he said, "is an assault upon the safety and the territorial integrity and
independence of South Vietnam. If that is relieved and removed, then things can
begin to move." In elaborating on this theme a few months later, he added that
no political settlement was possible so long as the Viet Cong kept its arms. If
elections in the South were necessary in order to arrive at one, then a precondition
for that would have to be the disarming of the armed forces of the NLF while
the Saigon government kept its arms.[11]

In view of the increasing international pressures for negotiations, and support for them by *The New York Times* and several liberal journalists including
the influential Walter Lippmann, and the fact that a private Harris poll had

disclosed that 75 percent of the American public favored the United States' asking for negotiations "to settle the war in Vietnam," the administration regarded it as all the more important to establish as convincingly as possible that the fighting in the South was the consequence of Hanoi's aggression. The fruit of this project in public relations, first known as the Jorden Report (named after William Jorden, author of an earlier version), ultimately emerged on February 27 as a White Paper, entitled *Aggression from the North: The Record of North Viet-Nam's Campaign to Conquer South Viet-Nam.* Set in train over two months before under the direction of McGeorge Bundy's aide Chester Cooper, this report was to focus on infiltration of military personnel and supplies from North to South and provide "a reconciliation, or at least an explanation of past low estimates of infiltration given in Congressional testimony and to the press," possible questions and suggested answers for use with the press or the Congress, and documentary evidence and graphic materials to aid in public presentations. On February 9 a cable was sent to General Westmoreland which began, "Sec def [Secretary of Defense] needs to know ASAP what recently-captured physical evidence you have that can be brought to Washington for public presentation. Purpose is to serve as part of hard-hitting and convincing demonstration establishing history of DRV involvement and direction of V.C., with emphasis on recent period." A measure of disingenuousness attended Cooper's efforts, as was reflected in his February 9 memorandum for Bundy: "Re the White Paper, we will have a catalogue of sins and Hanoi's culpability by the end of the week, if possible. Meanwhile D.O.D. [Department of Defense] is preparing a justification for further early strikes in the event there are no additional spectaculars in the next few days."[12]

If the retrospective account of Philip Liechty, a former CIA officer, is reliable, it would appear that the agency also did its share in preparing the case. After concluding a fifteen-year career there, Liechty charged that the agency had fabricated "evidence" in mid-February 1965 to help prove that large quantities of Chinese and Czechoslovak arms were being sent from North Vietnam to the Viet Cong. He stated that from its warehouses the CIA filled a boat with more than a hundred tons of weapons manufactured in communist countries and sank this in shallow water just off the shore of South Vietnam's Phu Yen province. After staging a "phony firefight," it invited foreign correspondents to inspect this evidence. An account of such a North Vietnamese ship and its cargo of arms was in fact incorporated as a centerpiece of the State Department's White Paper, where it was introduced as "dramatic new proof . . . exposed just as this report was being completed." Whatever the reality, the discovery of the sunken ship and weapons cache was beautifully timed, with Taylor cabling Washington on February 20, "Journalists and I.C.C. [International Control Commission] team have been taken to site and background briefings for journalists and ICC team in Saigon arranged. We are continuing major effort exploit this impressive evidence DRV interference in SVN." Max Frankel of the *Times* was clearly persuaded by this feature of the White Paper, referring to it as "conclusive proof" of "an increased southward flow of more sophisticated weapons." Absent from the

White Paper was any mention of what Charles Mohr had reported in the *Times* only three weeks before: "American military advisers in Vietnam have long conceded that the majority of Vietcong weapons are American-made ones captured in battle from South Vietnamese forces." Undoubtedly this story of the sunken boat gave greater credibility to the White Paper's final assertion that "The record is conclusive. It establishes beyond question that North Viet-Nam is carrying out a carefully conceived plan of aggression against the South."[13]

In its timing, as another *New York Times* correspondent aptly reported from Washington, the White Paper appeared to have a twofold objective: "To provide a justification for continuing American air strikes against targets in North Vietnam" and "to reinforce the Administration's position that any negotiations on the Vietnamese crisis are impossible until North Vietnam indicates that it will cease its aggression."[14]

On February 13 the president formally authorized a sustained bombing program and instructed Taylor to seek the immediate agreement of the Saigon government. "We will execute a program of measured and limited air action jointly with GVN against selected targets in DRV remaining south of 19th parallel until further notice. FYI [For Taylor's information, and presumably not to be relayed to GVN] Our current expectation is that these attacks might come about once or twice a week and involve two or three targets on each day of operation." There was as yet no authorization for implementation. This program was for "immediate future actions," and the president would not announce it until directly after the "next authorized air action," but said, "We believe this action should take place as early as possible next week." As Herbert Schandler has observed, "Details of these air actions . . . were sketchy, indicating that the President still wished to preserve as much flexibility as possible concerning the scope and character of this action."[15]

It is evident that Johnson's position still fell short of a full and clear-cut adoption of a sustained bombing plan, leaving Bundy, and apparently McNamara, dissatisfied. A meeting of the two advisers with the president on February 15 did not resolve these differences, and, in an effort to get him more fully aboard and bring him to a firmer and less ambiguous position, Bundy sent him a memorandum the next day. It seemed essential to him and McNamara, he said, "that there be an absolutely firm and clear internal decision of the U.S. government and that this decision be known and understood by enough people to permit its orderly execution." McNamara "simply has to know what the policy is so that he can make his military plans and give his military orders. This certainly is equally essential if we are to get the necessary political efforts in Saigon."[16]

Beyond this, the burden of Bundy's memorandum was, in effect, that the president was waffling between a variant of reprisal bombing and the sustained program recommended to him the week before. "If we limit ourselves to reprisals

for spectaculars like Pleiku and Qui Nhon, we leave the initiative in the hands
of the Communists, and we can expect no good result." This pattern had to be
clearly distinguished from the sustained bombing:

> Rightly or wrongly, those of us who favor continuing military action
> against the North do see it as a major watershed decision. However much
> it is based on continuing aggression in the South (as it should be), it amounts
> to a U.S. decision to mount continuing pressure against Hanoi by use of our
> air and naval superiority. This is not the same, in operational terms, as we
> did last August [Tonkin Gulf]. And it is not the same as a policy of episodic
> retaliation for particular attacks against large numbers of Americans. It is
> very different indeed, and the difference is just what we are counting on as
> the one means of turning around a desperate situation which has been
> heading towards a disastrous U.S. defeat.

Johnson's response was sufficiently encouraging for Bundy to draft a new set
of instructions to Taylor that more fully accorded with his own interpretation of
sustained bombing. The president, however, insisted on making a number of
amendments to the draft, which effectively retained his freedom to maneuver. He
substituted "our current thinking" for Bundy's phrase "current policy," and,
most important of all, changed the key sentence from "We have recommended,
and the President has concurred in, continuing air and naval action against North
Vietnam whenever and wherever necessary" to "We have recommended, and we
think the President will concur in . . ." The next sentence left considerable
flexibility of interpretation and action: "Our thinking has been and continues to
be that any such action shall be limited and fitting and adequate as a response
to the continuous aggression in South Vietnam directed in Hanoi."[17]

Though he had moved close to the Bundy-McNamara-Taylor position on
sustained air strikes, the president had clearly not yet fully endorsed it. On the
16th Bundy had assured Johnson that Henry Cabot Lodge and the editor of the
Washington *Post,* J. Russell Wiggins, both supported that program. Now heavier
artillery was resorted to when General Eisenhower was brought to the White
House on the morning of the 17th for a long session with Johnson. His position
was closer to Bundy's than to that of McNamara and Taylor. Not only did he
endorse the bombing campaign and counsel against negotiating from a position
of weakness, but he also suggested that if it were necessary the United States
should be prepared to send in six to eight divisions of ground forces.[18]

At a meeting of the National Security Council late in the afternoon of
February 18, Johnson still gave no indication when he might order implementation of Phase II, or "Rolling Thunder," as it was now generally called.[19]
McNamara reported that General Khanh had agreed to bombing targets in the
southern part of North Vietnam. But some of the president's advisers, especially
Taylor, did not interpret Khanh's acquiescence as a sufficiently legitimate basis
for launching Rolling Thunder, hard as the ambassador had been pressing for this

policy. Taylor believed that Khanh was too unreliable and unpredictable to justify resting a major new U.S. military investment on a Saigon political base still dominated by him. But McGeorge Bundy, backed by McNamara and apparently also by some in the State Department and the CIA, read Khanh differently and believed that, despite his deficiencies, he provided a sufficient political base from which to project the escalated U.S. military power that they all advocated.

Behind Bundy's and Taylor's sharply differing assessments of Khanh lay the more fundamental question of what constituted a sufficient semblance of indigenous government in Saigon. If possible, this should be a regime that would lend credibility to the proposition that the United States was launching a sustained aerial bombardment of the North in response to the request of a legitimate representative of the people of the South. Bundy held to the position taken in his memorandum to the President that such a government "need be no stronger than it is today with General Khanh as the focus of raw power while a weak caretaker government goes through the motions," for that general, despite all his faults, was "by long odds the outstanding military man currently in sight—and the most impressive personality generally." Consequently he continued to oppose Taylor's demand for Khanh's removal from the scene. McNamara apparently held a view similar to Bundy's; his deputy John McNaughton reported to him from Saigon on February 7, "Not much of a government is required for the GVN to play its role [in support of a sustained bombing campaign against the North]. The present government, for example, ineffectual as it is, is enough to participate in such a program," even though "it is not good enough" to carry out the struggle against the Viet Cong. Taylor, however, continued to reject this position and also Bundy's view that the Buddhists could be incorporated into a government compatible with U.S. aims. Although no one was a more enthusiastic advocate of sustained bombing than Taylor, he insisted that the Saigon regime needed more substance than Bundy felt was required. Taylor referred to the difficulties he faced in obtaining "authentic Government of Vietnam concurrence" for the bombing, given the existing condition of "virtual non-government" in Saigon, and argued that something better had to be found to provide a base. "We need the first team," he cabled, "and we need it fast."[20]

Taylor had been prepared to accept as sufficient Vietnamese endorsement for the retaliatory bombings General Khanh's acquiescence, as reported by General Westmoreland, and the specific permission he himself had secured from Nguyen Xuan Oanh, now the "lame duck acting prime minister" who had served as third deputy prime minister in the recently ousted Huong Cabinet. Because of his previous employment by the U.S. government and long residence in the United States, Oanh was widely regarded by Vietnamese as standing so close to American officials—who referred to him as "Jack Owen"—and so reliably "pro-American" as to be virtually an expatriate. Indeed, Taylor himself had slight regard for him. Only five months before, when Oanh was briefly substituting for Khanh, the ambassador had advised Washington that "Jack Owen is the personification and incarnation of this vacuum; he has no strength to back him up. . . . His occupancy of Khanh's office . . . and the motions through which he is going pretending to act as Prime Minister cannot be taken seriously."[21]

But the ambassador did not believe that this sort of backing was reliable enough for launching Phase II, or likely to be regarded as "authentic Government of Vietnam concurrence." In order to give the long-term program a firmer Vietnamese political foundation, he hoped to install a more dependable and cooperative government than General Khanh's, and one that was served by a prime minister of greater political stature and stronger nationalist credentials than Oanh. For the administration was anxious to be perceived by Americans and an international audience as acting in the interests of the Vietnamese, and at this time, because of U Thant's peace campaign, these audiences were unusually attentive.

In view of the limitations imposed by American objectives in Vietnam, it is difficult to visualize what in Taylor's view might constitute a "first team." But one thing was certain: he did not intend it to include Khanh or the Buddhists. Though agreeing that "we should not encourage the formation of a government which is unnecessarily provocative to the Buddhist Institute"* (the organization led by Tri Quang, Tam Chau, and other politically oriented monks), he argued for one in which the military would have dominant power, and cautioned, "Our efforts should be discreet and invisible to the naked eye since no VN [Vietnamese] official will thrive long who can be accused of being a U.S. puppet."[22]

General Khanh's reliance on the Buddhists was now clear. Knowing that Taylor was doggedly out to unseat him, and with his support among the divided Saigon military now shakier than ever—while the ambassador's efforts continued to erode what remained—Khanh appreciated that his political future depended critically on his retaining the backing he had won from the Buddhists by ousting Prime Minister Huong. And this, it soon became evident, would require aligning himself with their objectives of a negotiated settlement with the NLF and a neutralized South Vietnam. The Buddhist leaders, it must be noted, were confident that they shared sufficient common ground with the NLF to make a compromise solution possible.[23]

Khanh's marriage of necessity with the Buddhists, and the consequent realignment with their aims, gave him a powerful reason for taking a covert step beyond what even his few remaining supporters in Washington could tolerate. For this former hawk, whom the United States had backed just a year before in ousting a suspected proneutralist government, now decided to follow that road himself.[24]

Certainly Khanh's "re-coup" of January 27 and the embassy's appreciation

---

*"Buddhist Institute" was the shorthand designation of U.S. officials for the Vien Hoa Dao, the Institute for the Propagation of the Faith, which was the most active and politically significant component of the United Buddhist Association of Vietnam.

of his growing dependence on Buddhist support began to crystallize fears among U.S. officials that he might be tempted to move toward a neutralist position. Even the day before this coup, Deputy Ambassador Alexis Johnson cabled State that Khanh was "at least as well aware as we are of the increasing number of statements by [Buddhist] Institute leaders with respect to a negotiated solution." "This," he observed, "gives ground for some suspicion that Khanh may see his future as being the Sihanouk [the strongly neutralist chief of state of Cambodia] of South Vietnam." Similar warnings soon followed from Taylor and the CIA, which reported on February 3 that some generals were convinced that "Khanh is plotting, either through his own contacts or with full Buddhist collusion, to make himself the 'Prince Sihanouk' of Vietnam by negotiating a deal with the Viet Cong's National Liberation Front to neutralize South Vietnam."[25]

Not only have a number of senior South Vietnamese officers charged that Khanh was in fact attempting to arrive at an understanding with the NLF, but he himself has subsequently acknowledged this. Lieutenant General Tran Van Don's account of what occurred closely parallels that of Khanh.

> Knowing that the Americans were losing confidence in him, Khanh sought to open clandestine negotiations with and to gain support from the NLF. This proved to be his ultimate downfall because when the Americans became aware of it they undoubtedly felt that he was about to lead both Vietnam and the United States into a type of negotiated settlement possibly favorable to the Communists. At just this time, of course, the United States administration was preparing itself for military intervention; so Khanh had to go.[26]

Khanh's first contacts with the NLF appear to have been initiated in late December, soon after his acrimonious exchanges with Taylor, and after he was convinced that the ambassador was maneuvering to oust him. In addition to putting out some indirect feelers through the Vietnamese community in France, Khanh moved to establish direct contact with the NLF in South Vietnam. His adversary and critic Tran Van Don charges, and Khanh acknowledges, that he took the initiative in contacting Huynh Tan Phat (then secretary of the Central Committee of the NLF) and paved the way for discussions by releasing Phat's wife from jail.[27]

An initial exchange of letters with Phat was followed by a second, including the NLF leader's reply of January 28, which both Khanh and Don believe was itself, at least in its substance, soon afterward known to U.S. intelligence. In this Phat wrote:

> Replying to a number of your ideas, I previously had occasion to write you a long letter in which I clearly set forth our point of view, and also informed you that we were prepared to offer you our friendly cooperation and join with all who manifested these same desires and aspirations.

I heartily approve of your determined declaration against American intervention and I congratulate you for having made it. You stated quite clearly in fact that "the USA must let South Vietnam settle the problems of South Vietnam." In your recent press-conference your attitude was equally clear. . . . The road you have taken will be a difficult one. . . . As. you pursue this goal, you may rest assured that you also have our support, as we stated in our last letter.

We are convinced, given our common determination to serve our people and our country, valiantly to fight for national sovereignty and independence, and against foreign intervention, that whatever our differences of political opinion, we can join together and coordinate our efforts to accomplish our supreme mission, which is to save our homeland.[28]

Certainly this letter would have confirmed the U.S. embassy's maturing suspicions, and given Taylor reason to accelerate his efforts to oust Khanh.

Apparently, a little after the middle of February, information on Khanh's approaches to the NLF was firm enough to overcome the remaining resistance in Washington to Taylor's plans. Once it had become clear that the ambassador's shrewd adversary was indeed moving toward an accommodation with the NLF, it was evident not only that the political character of the Saigon regime was at stake, but also that the possibility of launching a retaliatory bombing campaign was in jeopardy. Consequently, McGeorge Bundy and McNamara had no reason to defend him further.

Over the previous weeks, despite lack of support from these two, Taylor and his staff had been cultivating opposition to Khanh and trying to encourage senior South Vietnamese military officers to organize a coup against him.[29] But this task was not easy. Not only had Taylor's own barracks-room diplomacy in late December outraged a number of important officers and temporarily pushed them closer to Khanh, but as a group the ARVN leadership was less integrated and more variegated than the two other principal political forces in the Saigon-controlled arena—the U.S. mission and the Buddhists. The political orientation of some of the ARVN's most powerful officers was often shifting and unpredictable. Generals Nguyen Khanh and Nguyen Chanh Thi had come to align themselves increasingly with the Buddhists, while Nguyen Van Thieu, Lam Van Phat, and Tran Thien Khiem had close ties with Catholic elements. But that apart, opportunism and personal ambition dominated their actions, and these men and most other senior officers had made no clear commitments by which their moves could be anticipated. There was, however, one consistently operative factor: all were keenly sensitive to the fact that not only the Saigon military establishment in general, but also their own enhanced professional positions, economic status, and political power, remained absolutely dependent upon the United States, just as earlier in their careers they had been on France.

The critical nature of U.S. financial support gave Taylor a basis for hoping that Khanh's resort to anti-American rhetoric might be used to drive a wedge between him and the Young Turks and make it easier to replace him with some more cooperative leader—assuming a reasonably effective one could be found. In some of his anti-Taylor tirades, Khanh had touched on this sensitive nerve by suggesting that, if necessary, he and his fellow officers could get along without U.S. aid. For most senior members of the officer corps that was a chilling and heretical proposition. Taylor and his supporters in the State Department saw an opening, which they persistently endeavored to exploit. The ambassador and his staff ensured that the issue did not die, even though Khanh did his best to back away from it, and their efforts to use it to undermine his position vis-à-vis other powerful officers undoubtedly eroded his support. The anxiety provoked by Khanh and nourished by Taylor and other members of the U.S. mission was so great that even Nguyen Chanh Thi, the Young Turk general most openly critical of American policy, regarded it as of central importance in his decision to work for Khanh's ouster. As Thi later put it, "It was necessary to move against him because our army was dependent on the Americans, and we could not get along without them." And in Khanh's final removal on February 21, Taylor assessed this fear of a loss of U.S. support as the crucial factor "which raised the courage level of the other generals to the point of sacking him."[30]

Stimulated by Taylor's courting of Khanh's military rivals, fresh coup planning had begun during the second half of January, particularly by Catholic Dai Viet officers. But the embassy, although lending them encouragement, still could not assure them of Washington's blessing. Before his ouster the beleaguered Prime Minister Huong had backed what was at first probably the most promising of the plots, which was aimed at preempting the anticipated moves against him by Khanh and the Buddhists. This plot would have ousted Khanh as commander-in-chief in favor of General Khiem—still exiled as ambassador to Washington. Although by January 23 this plot had reportedly enlisted the support of two powerful generals—Nguyen Van Thieu and Nguyen Huu Co—Alexis Johnson had regarded it as poorly planned and potentially embarrassing to the United States, since it required U.S. transport of a key plotter from Saigon to Washington and his return to South Vietnam with General Khiem. Alexis Johnson had therefore been unwilling to give Huong any support other than the promise of sanctuary should he be endangered by the plotting.[31]

On February 3, only hours before McGeorge Bundy was to leave Washington for Saigon, Taylor mounted a renewed and major effort to oust Khanh, apparently hoping that Bundy would be faced by a *fait accompli* on his arrival. He hinted at this in a cable that reached Bundy just before he left. The ambassador's follow-up message to Bundy provided the immediate rationale for the coup he was hoping to set in motion. He stated that, because senior ARVN officers were now convinced that "once in control of the govt Khanh would follow the neutralist route attempting to become Sihanouk of SVN in alliance with the Buddhist Institute," and because of Khanh's projected reassignment and neutralization of "the key military figures who have taken firm position in attempting to control Buddhist Institute agitation . . . we are contacting selected members of

the 'watch dog group' on the Armed Forces Council today to probe the depth
of their feelings in what they propose to do, if anything, to oppose Khanh."[32]

Taylor did his best to convince Ky and other top generals that they now had
a green light to move against Khanh. Two hours after his last cable to Bundy,
he informed his own sympathizers in the State Department that he had made
clear to General Nguyen Cao Ky, and through him "his colleagues," that the
United States was "in no way propping up General Khanh or backing him in any
fashion." The next day Taylor cabled that his message to Ky "had fallen on fertile
ground" and that he had authorized a "similar message to be conveyed discreetly
to seven other key generals." The embassy, he said, saw "three leading candidates" to replace Khanh—General Nguyen Huu Co (commander of II Corps),
General Nguyen Van Thieu (deputy prime minister), and Admiral Chung Tang
Cang (head of the navy)—but General Tran Thien Khiem was not ruled out,
despite his absence from the scene to serve in Washington. Of these four, all but
Co were Catholics or regarded as politically aligned with them. Observing that
Khanh might try to stay in power behind a screen of civilian officeholders, Taylor
concluded, "I can well visualize necessity at some time of using full U.S. leverage
. . . to induce our Vietnamese friends to get Khanh out of position of commander-
in-chief (from which he pulls the strings) and to install their very best governmental line-up." The ambassador acknowledged the strong likelihood that Khanh was
aware of his plotting, but assured the State Department, "I am not particularly
concerned now over an excessively conspicuous showing of [the] US hand."[33]

Taylor's additional encouragement to the potential coup-makers proved
insufficient for the time being. Despite mounting allegations regarding Khanh's
neutralist plans, these charges had not yet been made to stick, and during his
four-day stay in South Vietnam and for at least a week thereafter, Bundy refused
to withdraw his support from the durable Vietnamese commander. But Taylor's
encouragement of Khanh's opponents had an enduring effect.

In the meantime, the ambassador persevered in his efforts to shape a Cabinet
led by a prime minister as reliably pro-American as the recently ousted Huong.
Unable to enlist sufficient support for his own candidate (Dr. Nguyen Luu Vien,
who had been first deputy prime minister under Huong), Taylor and the ARVN
officers through whom he was working felt obliged to accept Dr. Phan Huy Quat,
a compromise candidate minimally acceptable to the Buddhists, whom the astute
Khanh prevailed on the Military Council to appoint on February 14. The new
prime minister was a Buddhist, though without strong ties to the Buddhist
political leadership. He was acceptable to them and to most of the senior Vietnamese military—possibly because, as the CIA speculated, both thought he could
be controlled. Khanh, of course, expected that as commander in chief of the
armed forces he himself would actually control his appointee. Although the
Catholic community was opposed to a Buddhist prime minister, the situation was
not completely polarized, for one of the most influential Catholic officers, General
Nguyen Van Thieu, was appointed minister of defense as well as one of the three
deputy prime ministers. (The other two were Tran Van Do, a Buddhist who had

once been Bao Dai's foreign minister, and Tran Van Tuyen, who, like Quat, had been jailed by Diem in 1960.) On the same day, the Armed Forces Council reappointed to the largely ceremonial post of chief of state, Pham Khac Suu, a man acceptable to both Buddhists and Catholics.[34]

It was presumably very soon after Quat's Cabinet was installed that American intelligence confirmed reports of Khanh's covert contact with the NLF. No one in the Johnson administration now opposed Khanh's ouster, and his aspiring successors in Saigon no longer hesitated for fear they lacked Washington's blessing. And thus, despite Khanh's brief success in outmaneuvering Taylor and once more installing a government subject to his own domination, he had no time to consolidate his position.

Taylor's efforts to promote Khanh's ouster now suddenly precipitated action, but not exactly what he had bargained for. Except for General Khiem, the men backing the coup were not among those Taylor preferred to work with. The Young Turks, upon whom he had been counting, were not yet sufficiently organized to act and had been bypassed by another group spurred on by that inveterate coup promoter, Colonel Pham Ngoc Thao. With good reason to believe the colonel was plotting against him from his post as press attaché in South Vietnam's Washington embassy, Khanh had recalled him to Saigon. Fearing arrest, Thao had immediately gone underground after his return in early January. Soon he was in touch with U.S. officials, with whom, the CIA reported, he "left little doubt that he was coup planning against Khanh." A well-informed Vietnamese source holds that Thao consciously pre-empted a move by other anti-Khanh generals: "Thao acted first, out of fear that if he did not, the other generals would overthrow Khanh and get rid of him as well. He knew that if the others overthrew Khanh his fate would be worse than Khanh's." Thao's nominee for replacing Khanh was Tran Thien Khiem, the ambassador to Washington, whom Taylor also regarded as a suitable replacement. The U.S. embassy's other preferred candidates, Generals Nguyen Huu Co, and Nguyen Van Thieu and Admiral Chung Tang Cang, appeared content to wait in the wings to see how the balance of forces developed before committing themselves.[35]

U.S. intelligence was close to the mark in describing the coup effort as "primarily a move by die-hard neo-Diemists and Catholic military militants disturbed at the rise of Buddhist influence, opposed to Gen. Khanh and—in a vague, ill-thought-out way—desirous of turning back the clock and undoing some of the results of the November 1963 ouster of Diem." Led by Catholic officers mostly with Dai Viet connections, the coup had the support of influential Catholic civilian militants such as Father Hoan Quynh and Mai Ngoc Khuc, as well as the militant Catholic organization, the National Defense Force. Led by Nguyen Bao Kiem, a professor at the U.S.-supported National Institute for Administration, this semiclandestine organization was partly an outgrowth of Diem's old Can Lao, and was reported by the CIA as numbering among its members or close associates several important military officers, including Nguyen Van Thieu, Nguyen Huu Co, and Nguyen Bao Tri.[36]

Since December, Ambassador Khiem had helped develop the coup's ratio-
nale by charging that Khanh and the Buddhists were working for a "neutralist
solution" and that "Khanh was leading the nation into negotiating with the
Communists." Whether the coup's principal planner was Khiem, Pham Ngoc
Thao, Nguyen Bao Kiem, General Tran Van Don, or General Lam Van Phat,
the top commander of the coup troops (and leader of the aborted effort of
September 13, 1964), *The New York Times* was not alone in concluding that
Khiem's embassy in Washington had been deeply involved in the coup's plan-
ning.[37]

In the early afternoon of February 19, General Lam Van Phat and Colonel
Pham Ngoc Thao led troops into Saigon. Spearheaded by the armored units of
Colonel Duong Huu Nghia, the coup forces quickly seized the radio station and
various other strategic points, including the airfield and general staff headquar-
ters, capturing several high-ranking officers who were members of the Armed
Forces Council. They barely missed catching Khanh as well. Convinced that
Taylor and Westmoreland were in collusion with the coup leaders to set him up
for arrest, Khanh recalls Taylor's insistence that, as commander in chief of the
South Vietnamese armed forces, he, Khanh, had to be on hand on the afternoon
of the 19th, when Quat held his first Cabinet meeting as the new prime minister.
Both Taylor and Westmoreland attended, and Khanh, as agreed, was also present. He says that in the middle of the discussions he sensed that it would be wise
to leave and go "on tour." Outside he found the coup troops already beginning
to assemble around the building, and he only narrowly escaped to Tonsonhut air
base at the edge of the city. There he found Air Marshal Ky, whom the rebels
were apparently also bent on capturing. (Ky had supported him against the
September 13 coup attempt and was initially disposed to side with him again.) The
two left the airport in Ky's plane just as the tanks were approaching it. Khanh
was flown to the main marine base at Cape Saint Jacques to rally support, and
he ordered Ky to go to the air force's second major base at Bien Hoa to do the
same. Ky arrived there and got his fighter bombers off the ground before General
Phat's tanks arrived. Although, with Taylor's knowledge and encouragement, Ky
had been laying plans during the previous two weeks to oust Khanh, he was
anything but a friend of the present coup leaders. And, in fact, he was about to
bomb General Phat's troops at Tonsonhut, when he was dissuaded from doing
so by the energetic intercession of General Westmoreland, who pointed out that
this would put at hazard over six thousand Americans who were stationed there.[38]

Broadcasts over Saigon Radio by a few of the coup leaders seriously undercut
the anticipated support from other army units. Nguyen Bao Kiem not only
repeated Pham Ngoc Thao's earlier announcement that the pro-Catholic General
Khiem was about to return from Washington to replace Khanh, but also went
on to assert that ousting Diem had been wrong; following this, a Catholic major
broadcast a long eulogy of Ngo Dinh Diem. To many, all this appeared to presage
Catholic rule, a return to power of Diemist officers, and possible retribution
against those who had staged the 1963 coup.[39]

These announcements also precipitated a strong Buddhist reaction. Over the Nhatrang radio station the influential Buddhist leader, Thich Tam Chau, called for all Buddhists to back the Armed Forces Council. The pro-Diem broadcasts also alarmed Nguyen Chanh Thi, Nguyen Huu Co, and other Buddhist officers. All this made it more likely that Khanh, having now escaped, might well be able to rally sufficient troops both to crush the coup forces and to stay in power. And, indeed, a number of units loyal to him were beginning to converge on Saigon.[40]

Whatever the extent of Taylor's and Westmoreland's earlier backing of General Khiem, the political polarization his adherents were inducing, their political gaucherie, and the opportunities they were inadvertently giving Khanh to return to power could only diminish American support. U.S. officials—civilian and military—viewed with alarm the dangerously increased tensions between Buddhists and Catholics and the immediate prospect of heavy internecine fighting, which could end in renewed credentials for a victorious Khanh and were certain to open up wide opportunities to the Viet Cong. Moreover, the coup leaders' willingness to abandon even the pretense of political continuity by their apparent determination to oust Quat and his Cabinet as well as Khanh further alienated American officials.[41]

It was thus clear that, if U.S. objectives were not to be put further at hazard, Taylor and Westmoreland would have to get off the sidelines and quickly enter much more directly into the power struggle; and this they did. The coup leaders in Saigon had counted on a U.S. plane's bringing General Khiem in from Washington to lead their movement. But, following an appeal from the marine brigade commander, General Le Nguyen Khang, to the U.S. embassy that Washington not permit Khiem to leave, Taylor cabled the State Department on the 19th: "Regardless what ultimate outcome may be we feel Khiem's arrival here . . . would only add tinder to what this evening appears to be very explosive situation with possibilities of internecine strife between armed forces units . . . Urge he not try return [to] Saigon until situation more clarified."

With the coup attempt now perceived to be running contrary to U.S. interests, Taylor and Westmoreland moved to freeze it in mid-passage while trying to ensure that its major objective—the removal of Khanh—was still realized. They now called for a standstill in troop movements. They also instructed U.S. military advisers in dealing with their Vietnamese counterparts to maintain this, refuse to accompany any unit that was marching on Saigon, and "deny that the U.S. was informed concerning the coup attempt but otherwise maintain a neutral position insofar as the contending factions are concerned."[42]

In attempting to deny power to Khiem and his supporters while sustaining the momentum of their floundering effort to dislodge Khanh, Taylor and Westmoreland relied heavily on Air Marshal Ky, whom Khanh erroneously assumed was still supporting him, and on General Nguyen Chanh Thi, commander of I Corps, who was known to be strongly opposed to both Khanh and the coup leaders. Ky was prevailed upon to withdraw his support of Khanh and instead cooperate with the U.S. mission for the twin objectives of ousting him and keeping

Phat and Khiem from taking power—the latter being a prospect that Ky had found distasteful from the outset. As a retrospective CIA assessment concluded, "Ky's command of the air force made him instrumental" in rescuing Khanh from the coup forces "until Ky changed his mind." Liaison was easy, for Westmoreland could work directly through Ky's U.S. air-force adviser, Brigadier General Robert R. Rowland, and the major U.S. and South Vietnamese air bases were cheek by jowl at Tonsonhut. Westmoreland and Taylor now endowed Ky with the mandate of "moderator," with the clear backing of the United States. His marching orders were that the forces of Khanh and his opponents were to be held in place and to avoid conflict while Ky made arrangements for a meeting of the Armed Forces Council. Illustrative of the use Westmoreland made of Ky was the American general's instruction to Colonel Gruenther, the U.S. adviser to General Nguyen Bao Tri, the Seventh Division commander. While Tri met with General Khanh at Phu Lam, just south of Saigon, preparatory to entering the city to help oust the coup group, Gruenther "recommended" to Tri that he "call General Ky about the situation prior to moving his troops." Soon afterward it was reported that General Tri had halted his troops' advance on the capital.[43]

U.S. officials worked concurrently with Generals Thi and Cao Van Vien, commander of III Corps, to organize a Capital Liberation Force made up of military units prepared to oppose both the rebels and Khanh. An American plane flew General Thi to Saigon from his headquarters in Danang so that he could take command of this force and attend a critical meeting of the Armed Forces Council. As the Capital Liberation Force was being marshaled, but before Khanh's supporter, General Tri, had halted his troops or it was clear whether they would be joined by the marine brigade in an assault against the rebels, General Rowland took General Phat and Colonel Thao to the Bien Hoa air base to confer with Ky. Very early on the morning of the 20th, an agreement was reached that the coup leaders would undertake to release the members of the Armed Forces Council they held and withdraw their forces from Saigon, on condition that Khanh be removed. It was arranged that Phat and Thao were immediately to visit the chief of state, Pham Khac Suu, and direct him to sign a decree relieving Khanh of the post of commander in chief and also to call a meeting that day between the Armed Forces Council and Quat's Cabinet. A series of reports from Westmoreland to Washington described how the first contingent of anticoup forces then entered Saigon at 6:40 a.m. and gave Phat's armor thirty minutes to get out of the city, and how Phat and Pham Ngoc Thao took leave of their troops. Pham Ngoc Thao broadcast a final message over Saigon Radio stating that the purposes of his group had been accomplished because General Khanh was being replaced, and then he and General Phat went into hiding.[44]

Immediately after this, a meeting of fifteen of the twenty members of the Armed Forces Council was convoked at Bien Hoa, with Prime Minister Quat and his Cabinet attending, and the United States providing the necessary transport. Urged on by Generals Thi and Ky, a majority of the council voted to remove Khanh from his position of commander in chief while affirming support for Quat and his Cabinet. Phat and Thao were merely to be stripped of their rank, and no action would be taken against Khiem, who was to remain ambassador to Washington. Quat and Pham Khac Suu immediately endorsed the decree of the rump Armed Forces Council, and its secretary, General Huynh Van Cao, was delegated to telephone Khanh at his base in Vung Tau to apprise him officially. Khanh exploded, insisting—with some justification—that only a meeting of the full Armed Forces Council could remove him, and warned that he intended to fight all efforts to do so. Believing Khanh "was determined to go for broke," General Cao states, "I panicked and went to see General Westmoreland." It was then arranged for General Rowland, Ky's U.S. adviser, to meet with a second rump session of the Armed Forces Council (now with only eight out of fifteen members attending) to work out a strategy to prevent Khanh's return to power.[45]

Unable himself to persuade Khanh to yield, Westmoreland ordered Colonel Jasper Wilson, who a year before had been Khanh's U.S. adviser, to fly to the headquarters of the marines at Vung Tau, where Khanh was now based. Westmoreland cabled Washington that he expected Wilson to "capitalize" on his "close personal relationship with Khanh to persuade him to accept the decision of the Armed Forces Council." From Vung Tau the CIA officer accompanying Wilson reported that Khanh accused the United States of sponsoring the coup against him and declared that his ouster would simply confirm its deep involvement. However, after several hours of discussion he was persuaded that his position was hopeless, and was promised a dignified, face-saving way out. The American colonel who had worked so closely with Khanh in his coup against General Duong Van Minh thirteen months before was able to report to Westmoreland that Khanh had now capitulated. Secretary Rusk cabled Taylor that the State Department thought it prudent not to comment on this achievement, stipulating, "Naturally we would also wish leave settlement Khanh issue to appear as much as possible the doing of Vietnamese themselves."[46]

On February 24, Khanh brought joy to Taylor and Westmoreland: with Washington's warmest blessing, he left South Vietnam as Saigon's "roving ambassador." Fearing Khanh's ability to "re-coup," Taylor waited until his plane had actually taken off before he felt it safe to advise Washington of the removal of this major impediment to carrying out "Rolling Thunder," the program of sustained bombing against the North. But the delay he and Westmoreland had both advocated while the coup attempt was in progress was not quite over. Khanh and the political risks involved in working with him had been eliminated, but the "authentic Saigon concurrence" Taylor had postulated as a prerequisite to the bombing campaign was still far from achieved. As Carl T. Rowan, the apparently bewildered head of the United States Information Agency, then put the matter to President Johnson: "The continuing turmoil . . . leaves us uncertain as to whom to work with and the Vietnamese people confused as to who constitutes the government we are asking them to rally round."[47]

True, the new military leadership that American efforts had helped put in place, led by the triumvirate of Ky, Thi, and Thieu, could be relied upon to give strong support to "Rolling Thunder." But what of the incumbent prime minister, Pham Huy Quat, whom Khanh had established in office only a month before at the expense of the United States' first preference, Tran Van Huong? Quat had been willing—some thought reluctantly—to endorse the two reprisal bombings, following the Viet Cong attacks against Pleiku and Qui Nhon; but could he be relied upon to back the sustained bombing campaign that President Johnson publicly announced on February 28? In terms of real power Quat was clearly overshadowed by the new military leadership, but to audiences in the United States and elsewhere abroad he was important as a symbol of political continuity and a legitimizing civilian cloak of governance that many American officials still thought important to maintain. "Authentic Saigon concurrence" would seem much less credible without the support of this civilian face of the government. But against the background of a clearly dramatic upsurge in antiwar sentiment precipitated by the retaliatory air strikes of February 6 and 10, it was not clear what position Quat would take on the major escalation represented by "Rolling Thunder."

The rising neutralist tide raised fears among American officials that despite the full backing of the U.S. and the Armed Forces Council, Quat might be unable to head off negotiations and neutralization. On the heels of Khanh's departure the CIA Office of Current Intelligence reported Tri Quang and his cohorts as "moving towards an openly espoused neutralism." On February 27, Taylor cabled that the Buddhist Institute had been "articulating with increasing intensity what it feels is popular sentiment for peace," with Thich Tam Chau appearing "to have gone further than any Buddhist leader so far in calling publicly for peace," and Thich Tri Quang giving a "strong hint of Buddhist initiatives in [the] direction of [an] open and unequivocal call for negotiations."[48]

Although the Buddhist's provided the main channel for peace sentiment, it was now being articulated by secular groups as well, the most effective of which was the Peace Movement Committee led by a former Cabinet member and Commissioner for Refugees, Dr. Pham Van Huyen. After circulation of its February resolution calling for a cease-fire and negotiations between the Saigon government and the NLF, the organization's membership expanded rapidly, especially among civil servants, with more than four thousand signing the resolution despite the risk this entailed.[49]

Under concurrent pressures from the U.S., the Armed Forces Council, and this burgeoning peace movement, Quat seemed to waver. At the end of February he and his Cabinet closeted themselves for two days of intensive discussions to work out a policy for coping with the upsurge of antiwar sentiment and the stance to be taken on bombing. As *The New York Times* staff correspondent in Saigon reported: "A guarantee by the Quat Government that the war would continue was considered here to be a necessity for a United States decision to proceed with further air strikes against the North."

The outcome of this meeting was a decisive victory for the element led by Deputy Prime Minister General Nguyen Van Thieu which advocated expanding the war and opposed a negotiated peace. Though still fearful of confronting the Buddhists, Quat did fire three hundred civil servants who were members of the Peace Movement Committee and arrested nearly a hundred of them, including Pham Van Huyen. The next day, March 1, Quat made the public announcement the American officials had been waiting for. He declared that the war in South Vietnam was "obviously a case of self-defense" and that there could be no peace until "the Communists end the war they have provoked and stop infiltration." Just in case members of Quat's Cabinet might be having any second thoughts on this issue, Air Marshall Ky, now spokesman for the Armed Forces Council— where the real power lay and upon which the Cabinet depended for its survival —declared that the council would replace any government that in its judgment "threatened to betray the country."[50]

The day after Quat's announcement, American planes launched their first attack in the sustained bombing of the North.

XII

The Call for
U.S. Ground Forces

It was soon evident that bombing the North was ineffective. There were none of the positive consequences in the South—either political or military—that Lyndon Johnson's advisers had confidently predicted. However inclined he may have been to take some wry satisfaction in having correctly resisted for so long their pressures to escalate, the president could not, of course afford to do so; for he, not they, was the lightning rod of responsibility for the policies he had endorsed. As the political and military fabric of the southern regime continued to unravel even more rapidly than before, almost all of his advisers pressed for a second dimension of escalation—the introduction of U.S. ground combat forces. Only if this level of U.S. military intervention was added, they now contended, would the bombing sorties against the North yield successful results in the South. At first, only relatively modest numbers of troops were seen as necessary, with their mission limited to protecting the U.S. air bases in the South from which sorties were now being flown against both the North and the Viet Cong. But within five months it was being argued that massive forces were in fact essential—not simply to protect American bases, but to take over from a rapidly collapsing ARVN the central role in fighting the Viet Cong. This argument became stronger with the increasing evidence that Hanoi was unleashing its own ground combat units in response to the additional U.S. military intervention.

To understand how this happened and why the United States so rapidly reached this ultimate level of military intervention requires a closer look at the developments in Vietnam that precipitated the escalatory steps, as well as at Washington's new decisions and the rationales accompanying them.

There is little doubt that the launching of a sustained bombing campaign against the North, together with the progressive introduction of U.S. troops, removed the constraints that had previously kept Hanoi from sending its own ground combat units into the South. Probably the bombing alone would have precipitated this; but aerial attack coupled with the arrival of troops made such a response almost inevitable. During the previous four years, although military, technical, and supply cadres—mostly southern in origin—had been infiltrated into the South from North Vietnam, Hanoi had always held back from dispatching combat units, for fear of provoking further U.S. military intervention. Now that the bombing had in fact been launched, however, it had little to lose. The DRV leaders must have concluded they had even less to lose once the first American combat units went ashore at Danang on March 6. Whether or not the North Vietnamese army (PAVN—People's Army of Vietnam) was already poised to move once the bombing started, they of course needed time to trek into the South—usually via the mountainous and forested back door of eastern Laos.[1]

Beginning with Diem, Saigon regimes had repeatedly reported PAVN units fighting in the South, but U.S. officials had regularly discounted these allegations, regarding them as ploys to obtain greater support. In fact, the available record indicates that it was not earlier than April 21, 1965, that U.S. intelligence first confirmed that a North Vietnamese combat unit was operating in South Vietnam. At the time this was reported as a regiment, but on May 13, General Westmoreland informed Johnson that it was only a single battalion.[2]

On May 5 MACV had still not confirmed that more than one North Vietnamese battalion had yet crossed into South Vietnam. Then, on May 27, Maxwell Taylor cabled, "While evidence exists that one battalion of 325 Div. is presently in Kontum province and one battalion of 305 Div. is known to have been in central panhandle of Laos in March, 1965, MACV has no firm intelligence suggesting massive PAVN buildup on RVN/Laos Border."[3]

On June 11, the chairman of the Joint Chiefs of Staff reported, "Elements of the 101st Regiment of the 325th North Vietnamese Army (PAVN) Division are in the northern zone of II Corps area, and it is possible that elements of two other regiments of the division are now deployed within the provinces of Kontum-Pleiku and Phu Bon or in nearby Laos. Elements of the 304th PAVN Division are suspected to be in Southern Laos, capable of early movement into RVN." A month later Taylor cabled that Westmoreland's headquarters had been able to confirm the presence of only one PAVN regiment, the 101st, in the South, but that the presence of a second, the Eighteenth, would probably be reported soon.[4]

It should be observed, then, that on April 21, the day American intelligence confirmed the existence of what later emerged as a single battalion of PAVN troops in the South, many times more American combat units were already there. Indeed, at that time even the number of South Korean soldiers in South Vietnam (2,000) was greater than this North Vietnamese unit. The total of approximately 56,000 U.S. military personnel then in South Vietnam (23,000 military advisers plus some 33,000 combat troops including four marine battalion landing teams) significantly exceeded MACV's estimated total of 39,517 infiltrators* who had come down from North Vietnam between 1959 and April 1965, *plus* the approximately 1,000-man battalion which constituted the only PAVN military unit yet

---

*Individuals or small groups of cadre with military training, most of whom at this stage were still southerners who had regrouped north of the seventeenth parallel in 1954, after the Geneva Conference.

known to have entered the South.* Though the PAVN build-up was slow, with its total troop strength in the South lagging far behind that of the United States throughout the Johnson administration, this new feature of the war worried U.S. officials: once the dike had been breached by a battalion, who could tell whether and when further increments of the remaining 300,000 or more PAVN soldiers might follow? In reality, however, the increase in North Vietnamese forces was slow. In March 1966, General Wheeler reported that there were only 13,100 of them in the South, along with 225,000 Viet Cong, and that facing them were 216,400 U.S., 690,000 South Vietnamese, and 23,000 third-country (mostly Korean) troops.[5] Because several accounts have taken liberties with the relevant chronology, it should be emphasized that the available evidence indicates that Hanoi's initial units arrived in the South after the first American combat forces were introduced there and after the U.S. had begun bombing the North.

Even after Johnson had endorsed the sustained bombing campaign against the North, Westmoreland remained pessimistic about military prospects in the South. In essential agreement with the CIA's analysis of the same day, on February 25 he "foresaw in six months a Saigon government holding only islands of strength around provincial and district capitals that were clogged with refugees and beset with 'end the war' groups asking for a negotiated settlement, and six months after that a Viet Cong takeover except for major towns and bases held with U.S. help." Two weeks after the sustained bombing campaign had begun, he predicted that no tangible results would follow from this until June at the earliest, and that in the meantime the ARVN needed American reinforcements to hold the line against growing Viet Cong strength.[6]

Nor did the bombing induce any improvement in Saigon's morale and in the political situation in South Vietnam. The Saigon government, led by Khanh's appointee, Pham Huy Quat, remained weak and under siege by antineutralist Catholics as well as by a peace movement that appeared to draw considerable additional strength from the reaction to the bombing. American officials, however, were initially disposed to keep Quat in place. They apparently assumed that, without Khanh's power behind him and without Khanh to coach him, Quat could be easily influenced to cooperate with pro-American ARVN officers—especially Ky, Thi, and Thieu—whose power had increased with Khanh's removal. Moreover, from Washington's perspective (as previously noted), Quat served as a useful symbol of continuity for audiences outside Vietnam—much more so than

---

*On July 11, 1965, when Westmoreland confirmed that a full PAVN regiment was operating in the South, a JCS study group reported that this brought the total strength of enemy combat units up to approximately 48,500, organized into 10 regimental headquarters, 65 battalions, and 188 companies. (Thus, approximately 97 percent of these enemy combat forces were Viet Cong.) There were an additional 17,600 Viet Cong personnel considered to be engaged in "combat support type operations." As of June 30, 1965, there was a total of 59,980 U.S. military personnel in Vietnam, of which 27,300 were army, 18,100 marine corps, 10,780 air force, and 3,800 navy.

the inconspicuous chief of state, Phan Khac Suu. Thus, despite ongoing Catholic opposition, Quat continued to enjoy sufficient American backing to retain his position for a further three and a half months—until Thieu and Ky, with U.S. acquiescence, ousted him.

Despite repeated Catholic allegations that Quat was secretly in contact with the NLF, and though one of his three deputy prime ministers, Tran Van Tuyen, may have been, there is no evidence that Quat himself had such contacts. In fact, his agreement to the U.S. air war against the North and to the introduction of U.S. marines to protect air bases argues strongly against this. Nor did Quat's efforts—ultimately unsuccessful—to increase his authority over the Saigon generals, through establishing a joint military command in which they would be brought under "the steadying influence of General Westmoreland," square with such a posture.[7]

Despite the mass arrests of the secular proponents of negotiations and an end to the war, and the Military Council's standing orders to arrest anyone who advocated such a course, the Buddhists were not deterred. They forged ahead with what Taylor reported as "an upsurge in 'peace' talk" in which "several Buddhist Institute leaders, including Tri Quang and Tam Chau as well as secondary leaders Ho Giac and Quang Lien, have been publicly quoted in vague and fuzzy statements as favoring an end to the war and the withdrawal of foreign forces." Chester Cooper advised McGeorge Bundy that the pressure for negotiations in South Vietnam had reached a "critical" stage.[8]

The popular backing enjoyed by the Buddhist and secular peace movements was sufficient to affect the outlook of at least one of the four army regional commanders. On March 11, the CIA reported that General Nguyen Huu Co, commander of II Corps, planned to drop offensive military operations in his command because, even though he himself did not favor neutralism, he expected the government eventually to enter into negotiations, possibly in 1965. His strategy, he felt, would "put the government in a better bargaining position should truce talks materialize."[9]

Pressed by both the Armed Forces Council and the U.S. embassy to act against the growing peace movement, Quat's government in mid-March arrested some twenty-seven members of the Cao Dai religious sect who had been calling for a neutral, unified Vietnam, and then took the dramatic step of expelling Pham Van Huyen and two other prominent members of his movement, pushing them across the seventeenth parallel into North Vietnam. The prime minister was still reluctant, however, to take such action against members of the powerful Buddhist Institute, drawing a somewhat spurious distinction between their viewpoint and that of the weaker peace groups. Finally, however, in mid-April, under American pressure and the mounting threat of a coup by Catholic officers, he felt obliged to move against an important second-echelon Buddhist, Thich Quang Lien, who had gone beyond the generally more ambiguous stance of the top Buddhist leaders in his call for the withdrawal of all U.S. troops. Quang Lien was forced to leave the country for "medical treatment abroad."[10]

With these examples before them, and fearful that, should Quat be removed, he might be replaced by a pro-Catholic prime minister more strongly opposed to their own goals, the Buddhist leadership stopped short of any greater confrontation and adapted to what they perceived as the realities of the power balance.[11]

Taylor and Westmoreland were not alone in their alarm. That the military and political deterioration of the Saigon regime was accelerating was now, in fact, becoming a broadly based perception within the administration, and was eloquently reflected in a White House memorandum prepared for Chester Cooper on March 22.[12] This memorandum shows a striking preoccupation with the absence of indigenous political foundations for the U.S. military effort. Two of the "three major problem areas" it regarded as of "overriding importance in the precariousness" of the U.S. position related to this deficiency. "The lack of a political base for the GVN [Saigon government] of sufficient strength to counter Viet Cong political and psychologic superiorities" was perceived as being so great that, to compensate, an American effort was needed "of the scope undertaken by the U.S. in support of the Diem government in 1954–55." Coupled to this "political action effort," "psychological operations" would have to be mounted for "motivating the government administration, military forces and populace in support of the government."

There was, the memorandum continued, a "growing lack of confidence among the GVN leadership—political and military—and the populace in the ultimate success of the counterinsurgency." This was "a direct result of the apparent superiority of the Viet Cong in the military, political, and psychological fields." Neither "U.S. punitive expeditions against North Vietnam" nor "the limited deployment of U.S. ground forces to provide security for rear installations" had induced "the morale boost necessary to offset this lack of confidence." In view of all this, together with the Saigon forces' ineffectiveness in countering the threat posed by the Viet Cong main-force battalions and regiments, substantial reinforcements were needed. Otherwise there was likely to be "continued deterioration—possibly at an accelerating rate." Since the ARVN was already "too thinly spread," only by "abandoning wide areas," with a consequent "serious adverse impact on morale," could its forces be regrouped for a more effective confrontation of the Viet Cong. It was argued that the only alternative was "introducing additional forces from outside Vietnam." "If done on a sufficiently large scale [this] would have a substantial favorable impact on the military situation and on morale in South Vietnam, would adversely affect morale of the Viet Cong, and would clearly demonstrate to Hanoi and Peking the extent of U.S. determination and will to end Communist aggression in South Vietnam." About three divisions—the amount then being proposed by the JCS—were needed "to have the necessary impact on the military situation," and they "should be employed essentially in offensive and counteroffensive operations against major Viet Cong troop concentrations rather than in security or pacification missions."[13]

John McNaughton's draft memorandum for McNamara written during the period March 10–24 reveals the administration's state of mind as to military and political prospects in the South. It also makes more understandable why West-moreland and the JCS succeeded in their now insistent campaign for introducing substantial U.S. ground combat forces.[14] Concerning the "deteriorating situation," McNaughton reported that "militarily, SVN has been cut in two with GVN [Saigon's] control in [the] north [of South Vietnam] reduced to enclaves" and "politically, 50% chance of coup within 3 weeks." In terms of basic U.S. objectives in Vietnam, his "Prognosis" forecast a progressive political and military deterioration leading to unmitigated disaster:

(a) GVN officials will adjust their behavior to an eventual VC takeover.
(b) Defections of significant military forces will take place.
(c) Whole integrated regions of the country will be totally denied to GVN.
(d) Neutral and/or left wing elements will enter the government.
(e) A popular-front regime will emerge which will invite the U.S. out.
(f) Fundamental concessions will be made to the VC.
(g) Accommodations to the DRV will put SVN behind the Curtain.

McNaughton's scenario depicted the perceived course of events if the existing level of U.S. power were not increased. He posited three possible alternative courses of action: "progressively squeeze North Vietnam; or add massive U.S. ground effort in South Vietnam; or downgrade the apparent stakes." The increasing bombing pressure and covert actions to implement the first course were already well under way, with the tonnage of bombing and scope of targets soon to grow. The ground effort envisaged in the second alternative was very soon to be approved and set in motion. But the third option, that of downgrading the stakes in Vietnam, was not given a serious hearing. Yet had this been followed in 1965, the United States might well have achieved at least as many of its objectives as it secured ten years later, and without the enormous losses of life that this delay entailed. The terms of this option should be noted.

If and when it is estimated that even the best US/GVN efforts mean failure (undesirable escalation or defeat), it will be important to act to minimize the damage to the U.S. effectiveness and image thereafter by such steps as these:

(a) Deliver ultimatum to coup-prone generals to "shape up or ship out," and when they patently fail to shape up, we ship out.

(b) Publicize uniqueness and congenital impossibility of SVN case (e.g., Vietminh held much of SVN in 1954, long uncontrollable borders, unfavorable terrain, absence of national tradition or administrators, mess left by French, competing factions, Communist LOC [line of communications] advantage, late U.S. start, etc.).

(c) Create diversionary "offensives" elsewhere in the world (e.g. to shore up Thailand, Philippines, Malaysia, India, Australia); launch an "anti-poverty program" for underdeveloped areas.

(d) Enter multi-nation negotiations calculated to shift opinions and values.

(e) Shift to Saigon focus of decision and discussion.

In his initial draft McNaughton did not append to this third option any mention of the risks it might entail. However, two weeks later, presumably after feedback from McNamara and others, the new version did contain such a caveat, which in its entirety reads, "Risks. With the physical situation and the trends as they are the fear is overwhelming that an exit negotiated now would result in humiliation for the US."[15]

This fear of national humiliation, and the attendant damage to their own prestige, remained at the forefront of the minds of the president's advisers and of the president himself, and the same was to be true of Nixon's administration. Moreover, most of the president's associates were apparently still confident that through the injection of U.S. power they could engineer the survival of a separate state in the southern half of Vietnam, regardless of the continuing lack of any significant indigenous foundation. With reservoirs of U.S. military might still available, they were not interested in any serious exploration of a disengagement —whether negotiated or otherwise—at least until they could assess the consequences of applying this additional power. They clearly hoped that the results would vindicate them and the advice they had already given the president, while saving him, the country—and themselves—from the humiliation that they believed would ensue from switching to a negotiations track at a time when their South Vietnamese ward was so weak. Perhaps later, if the balance of internal forces had been favorably affected by an injection of sufficient additional American power, they would be willing to risk taking that route, but not now.

In Robert McNamara's policy memorandum of mid-March 1964 the central U.S. objective had been "an independent non-communist South Vietnam," which had to be maintained both to keep the rest of Southeast Asia from falling under communist dominance and to demonstrate to the rest of the world through this "test case" the capacity of the United States "to help a nation meet a Communist 'war of liberation.' "[16]

In the internal rationale of a year later, however, these considerations were much less prominent; indeed, the fate of the South Vietnamese themselves seems to have become a minor consideration. Partly because the administration had publicly endowed the struggle in Vietnam with enormous importance—through its apocalyptic rhetoric as well as its actions—the American involvement had become the focus of such a glaringly intense spotlight of worldwide attention that Johnson's advisers now placed much greater emphasis on how the United States looked in its efforts to manage events in this increasingly prominent part of the world. And both the president and his advisers often seemed to have difficulty in distinguishing between their personal prestige and that of the United States.[17] These advisers clearly believed that further American military escalation might work. In any case it was consistent with the primarily military approach with which they and their careers had already become so closely identified, and consistency is usually a prerequisite for protecting a public career.

Perhaps the most succinct articulation of the internal rationale that had now emerged was incorporated in the above-mentioned memorandum of McNaughton, an official upon whose judgment McNamara relied heavily. This weighted United States objectives in Vietnam as: "70% To avoid a humiliating U.S. defeat (to our reputation as a guarantor), 20% To keep SVN [South Vietnam] (and the adjacent) territory from Chinese hands, 10% To permit the people of SVN to enjoy a better, freer way of life." This preoccupation with the reputation of the United States, and of the administration in office and its top officials, was to influence American policy heavily during the next decade. Equally revealing of the paramount importance now attached to U.S. prestige was one of the concluding paragraphs in McNaughton's memorandum, captioned "Evaluation."

> It is essential—however badly SEA [Southeast Asia] may go over the next 1–3 years—that U.S. emerge as a "good doctor." We must have kept promises, been tough, taken risks, gotten bloodied and hurt the enemy very badly. We must avoid harmful appearances which will affect judgments by, and provide pretexts to, other nations regarding how the U.S. will behave in future cases of particular interest to those nations—regarding U.S. policy, power, resolve and competence to deal with their problems. In this connection, the relevant audiences are the Communists (who must feel strong pressures), the South Vietnamese (whose morale must be buoyed), our allies (who must trust us as "underwriters") and the U.S. public (which must support our risk-taking with U.S. lives and prestige).

McNaughton's category of "humiliating defeat" was, of course, relevant not only to audiences outside the United States, but also to the domestic political considerations so ingrained in the minds of the president and his advisers as to be taken for granted and require no explicit articulation in a strictly internal memorandum. This was the political calculation that failure to keep South Vietnam free of communist control would leave the Democratic Party open to a Vietnamese analogue of the damaging "loss of China" charge. That consideration had been pertinent even in Truman's approach to Vietnam, and for Johnson as well as Kennedy it remained an abiding obsession that any administration that could be charged with responsibility for "losing" more Asian territory to communist control would stand vulnerable to serious domestic political attack.

The rationales the administration presented for its Vietnam policy internally and publicly diverged widely. For the public the relative importance of McNaughton's three objectives was reversed (and, of course, the "loss of China" syndrome was not referred to). Thus, conspicuous in Lyndon Johnson's major speech of April 7 was self-determination—albeit highly qualified and built on the premise of there being an "independent nation of South Vietnam." The American objective was that the Vietnamese "be allowed to guide their own country in their own way," and "free from outside interference." (However bizarre such an objective must have seemed to the South Vietnamese people in view of the heavy American political presence among them, this proposition had appeal for an American citizenry that had only recently begun to focus on Vietnam and was still largely ignorant of the political dimension of the U.S. involvement there.) "The first reality," the president asserted, was aggression against "the independent nation of South Vietnam." And containment of the power of communist China remained a central concern, for Peking was accused not only of urging on Hanoi against South Vietnam, but also of "helping the forces of violence in almost every continent," its role in Vietnam merely "part of a wider pattern of aggressive purposes." Eisenhower's domino theory and the lesson of Munich were still very much alive: if the United States retreated from Vietnam, "the battle would be renewed in one country and then another," for "the appetite of aggression is never satisfied." As it had done in Europe, the United States had to draw a line in Southeast Asia against the spread of communist power. And then, more akin to his administration's internal rationale, the president affirmed that over many years America had made a commitment, "a national pledge to help South Vietnam defend its independence." To leave that nation to its fate would shake the confidence of people "around the globe, from Berlin to Thailand," in the value of a commitment by the United States that they could count on if attacked; there would be "increased unrest and instability, and even wider war."

The JCS and McGeorge Bundy had long urged the introduction of U.S. ground combat forces. McNamara had recently joined them, and Rusk, who almost until the end had stood by the president in his reluctance to initiate a sustained bombing program, now provided no such brake. Once it had been decided that jet air power would be used against the Viet Cong in the South and against North Vietnam, the foundation had been established for the final great escalation. Much of this aerial offensive needed to be launched from fields in South Vietnam, which would naturally become targets for the Viet Cong and later Hanoi.* It was almost immediately evident that U.S. air power alone could not protect these fields, nor was it often very accurate in operations against the Viet Cong. A laconic report from Cooper to McGeorge Bundy on March 1 vividly illustrated this: "Much activity by U.S. bombers against VC concentrations. Damage (i.e. V.C. casualties) may well be considerable, but reliable readout lacking. The only thing we *know* has happened is that we knocked out an ARVN regimental command post. . . . Largest chopper operation of the war (about 170) netted nothing."[18]

---

*U.S. planes were also based on carriers of the Seventh Fleet and in Thailand. The B-52s employed against both the North and the Viet Cong in the South flew from Guam until 1967, when airfields able to accommodate them were built in Thailand. The Manila government would not permit B-52s to be based in the Philippines.

Airfields and other major U.S. installations, it was clear, could only be secured by ground troops, but it was equally evident that Saigon's disintegrating forces themselves could not effectively protect them. In addition to the concern that many ARVN units were unwilling to court confrontation with Viet Cong forces by carrying out the patrolling necessary to protect American installations, there were now doubts over what at the end of February was termed the lack of "integrity" of some ARVN units. Several of them had participated in demonstrations that were against the United States as well as the Saigon government.[19]

A month before the attack at Pleiku, Westmoreland had advised the president that, if U.S. soldiers alone were to provide "maximum security" to all U.S. personnel and facilities in Vietnam, a total of thirty-four battalions or approximately seventy-five thousand U.S. troops would be required. He pointed out that there were a total of "16 important airfields, 9 communications facilities, one large POL [petroleum, oil, lubricants] storage area, and 289 separate installations where U.S. personnel work or live," and that "any one of these is conceivably vulnerable to VC attack in the form of mortar fire or sabotage." It was from three airfields—Tonsonhut (Saigon), Bien Hoa (near Saigon), and Danang—that most U.S. bombing and napalm attacks against the Viet Cong emanated, and it was natural that these fields would be priority targets. The one at Danang was regarded as by far the most vulnerable.[20]

Thus, even those who opposed the introduction of U.S. ground forces, such as Ambassador Taylor, reluctantly agreed that American soldiers had to augment ARVN units in protecting Danang. Taylor acknowledged this in a cable following a visit to that base just before the sustained bombing campaign got under way:

Am deeply impressed with the magnitude of the security problem as are General Westmoreland and his principal military colleagues. Except for chronic shortage of GVN forces in I Corps area, we would be inclined to urge GVN to allocate several additional battalions to the Danang area. But we know that such forces could not be made available except at prohibitive cost to the security of other areas of SVN. For these reasons we are driven to consider a solution which we have always rejected in the past, the introduction of US ground combat forces to reinforce the defense of Danang until GVN forces become available for the purpose.

With Taylor's agreement, then, two U.S. marine-corps battalion landing teams (totaling thirty-five hundred men) were brought ashore on March 6, raising the number of U.S. military personnel in the Danang area up to around seventy-three hundred.[21]

To be effective, the marines who were assigned to help protect the Danang air base had to patrol out beyond it, at least up to four thousand yards—the range of the U.S. 81-mm. mortars that the Viet Cong had captured from the ARVN. Thus, Westmoreland had pointed out that "to keep enemy mortar fire off any one given point one must secure an area roughly 16 square miles." The sort of active patrolling required, of course, increased the incidence of combat, leading in turn to a sharp rise in U.S. casualties. Whole units of American soldiers were now operating in hostile territory—exposed, with their lives hostage to enemy reactions to their presence. Ultimately this armed the proponents of sustained and increased military intervention with a more effective weapon than they had ever possessed for advancing their cause within the U.S. domestic political arena: "defense of the lives of our boys in Vietnam." As James Thomson later put it, "Once we had all those men out there to protect, the stakes were no longer primarily that of sustaining the Saigon government, but rather, our boys out there —a change that gave our military a much greater say in policy."[22]

As a result of his experience in Vietnam, Taylor possessed a more realistic basis for assessing the quality of Saigon's armed forces than General Wheeler in Washington, and he foresaw serious long-term dangers for the United States if large numbers of American combat forces were introduced. Accordingly, at the beginning of March he reported to the president that, though he accepted the justification for the "important departure from former policy" in the decision to use U.S. jet aircraft in the South against the Viet Cong and to introduce marine combat units for the defense of the Danang airfield, he was concerned that the United States "not rush in and take over the conduct of the war from the Vietnamese," arguing that "it would be a political and psychological mistake to change our past position that this is a Vietnamese war in which we are helping in areas where the Vietnamese cannot help themselves." Taylor's views soon came to be shared in spades by the CIA's Office of National Estimates. It presciently observed, "There will be constant danger that the war weary people of South Vietnam will let the U.S. assume an even greater share of the fighting," with the "danger that U.S. troop commitment will lead more South Vietnamese to accept the Communist line that U.S. colonialism is replacing French," and "turn increasing numbers of Vietnamese toward support of the Viet Cong effort to oust the U.S."[23]

Digging in his heels against additional U.S. ground forces, Taylor urged instead that the tempo of bombing the North be increased, "to convince Hanoi authorities they face prospect of progressively severe punishment." He commented, "I fear to date Rolling Thunder in their eyes has been merely a few isolated thunder claps."[24]

Once the Rubicon had been crossed, however, there were swiftly increasing pressures from the JCS and their civilian allies for the dispatch of additional combat elements. After a week in South Vietnam, the army chief of staff, General Harold K. Johnson, recommended to McNamara on March 14 the deployment of a full U.S. division, either to defend the Bien Hoa and Tonsonhut airfields plus some coastal enclaves or to take on the Viet Cong in the highland provinces of Kontum, Pleiku, and Darlac. (Both he and McNamara opted for the latter.) General Johnson also urged the introduction of a four-division force comprised of U.S. and allied SEATO forces to form a counter-infiltration cordon running approximately along the seventeenth parallel, near the demilitarized zone, from the South China Sea to Laos and on to the Mekong River. Taylor promptly parried this recommendation, arguing successfully that judgment on it be reserved.[25]

On March 29, the day Taylor left Saigon for Washington, the Viet Cong exploded a 250-pound bomb outside the Saigon embassy, which killed twenty-two people (two of them American) and injured 186 others (including fifty-two Americans) while providing additional dramatic testimony of the ARVN's inability to protect American installations.[26]

In Washington, Taylor found the JCS pressing for the introduction of two divisions for operations against the Viet Cong, with Westmoreland supporting this and possibly more if bombing the North still proved unsuccessful. The JCS was also proposing the dispatch of one South Korean division for use against the Viet Cong. In discussions with the president on April 1–2, Taylor argued that there was no military necessity for such measures, and that the South Vietnamese might resent being inundated by so many Americans, a concern shared by Prime Minister Quat. Taylor had already found Quat to be sensitive about the proposed introduction of just two marine battalions limited to one small enclave.[27] Three foreign divisions, some with "search and destroy" missions, and supporting logistical elements would total around 100,000 and give the war an entirely different character.

McNamara, who had been inclined to favor the three-division proposal, and Rusk then recommended postponing a decision on this until the situation could be reviewed sixty days later. For the present they suggested—and in this compromise Taylor concurred—the United States should send in two additional marine battalions, plus one air squadron and eighteen to twenty thousand U.S. support troops ("to fill out existing units and provide needed logistic personnel"). McGeorge Bundy proposed that U.S. troops in Vietnam be allowed the freedom to engage in combat rather than be confined to static defense. The CIA's John McCone was strongly opposed to Bundy's suggestion and argued against an American ground combat role in the South unless it was accompanied by a much greater weight of air strikes against the North, but his memorandum did not reach the president until well after these crucial discussions—too late to support Taylor or affect the president's decision to approve the McNamara/Rusk and Bundy proposals and what was termed "the present slowly ascending tempo" of Rolling Thunder operations. Indeed, McCone's memorandum was apparently withheld from the president, and the CIA chief was obliged to hand-deliver a copy to him as his last official act before resigning.[28]

The decisions arrived at in these discussions were embodied in an NSC Action Memorandum of April 6, drafted by McGeorge Bundy. He enjoined that the president desired that all these actions he had approved "be taken as rapidly as practicable, but in ways that should minimize any appearance of sudden changes in policy. . . . The President's desire is that these movements and changes should be understood as being gradual and wholly consistent with existing policy."[29]

. . .

Having successfully fended off the three-division proposal, Taylor had gone along with the McNamara/Rusk compromise. But McCone was on his way out and on April 28 was replaced by Admiral William F. Raborn, a CIA director more in tune with Bundy and McNamara, and Ambassador Taylor soon found himself more isolated than before from the center of policymaking. Outflanked by both Westmoreland and the JCS, he stood fast a scant three weeks against the advocates of a major deployment of U.S. ground combat forces, now spearheaded by an aggressive Robert McNamara and quietly backed by both McGeorge Bundy and Rusk.

Taylor had left Washington with the understanding—embodied in a National Security Council decision of April 2—that the administration would "experiment with the Marines in a counterinsurgency role before bringing in other U.S. contingents." Apparently, however, Westmoreland and the JCS were able to convince the president that the ARVN was deteriorating too fast to test this. On April 11, Westmoreland urgently revived his request for the dispatch of the 173rd Airborne Brigade. This was promptly supported by CINCPAC and the JCS, recommended by McNamara on April 13, and apparently endorsed by the president that same day.[30]

It is unclear whether Johnson was aware his ambassador had been completely bypassed in this decision. But Taylor certainly knew it, as he informed Rusk the next day, and was clearly resentful. McGeorge Bundy therefore advised the president later on the 14th to restrain McNamara from sending Taylor implementing orders, explaining that this would be "very explosive right now because he will not agree with many of them and he will feel he has not been consulted." Informing the president of a cable in which Taylor "gravely questions the usefulness of immediate additional ground deployments," Bundy reassured Johnson, "I am sure we can turn him around if we give him just a little time to come aboard."[31]

Taylor was also bypassed in the concurrent decision to escalate along another axis—which he referred to in a follow-up cable on April 17 as "what I take to be a new policy of third-country participation in ground combat." In the April 1–2 meetings, it had been agreed that the "possibility" of deploying third-country troops in combat roles (South Korea, Australia, and New Zealand being specifically mentioned) was to be the object of "urgent exploration." That exploration was now proceeding apace, even before Taylor had had a chance to discuss the matter with Quat. Some three months before, Prime Minister Huong and Khanh had agreed to the introduction of two thousand South Korean troops—a battalion of engineers and supporting elements. But five days before the April 1 meeting, Taylor had informed Washington that both Quat and his deputy and minister of defense, General Thieu, believed there was "no present requirement to consider the introduction of third country ground combat forces."[32]

When Taylor received instructions from Rusk on April 15 to secure a request from Quat as soon as possible for the introduction of a South Korean regimental combat team, and was asked by the Pentagon the next day to discuss "several possible uses of U.S. forces beyond the NSC decisions of April 2," the ambassador rebelled. He replied that he could not present these matters to Quat until he himself was given "clarification of our purposes and objectives" with regard to the introduction of third-country and U.S. combat forces. "Before I can present our case to [the] GVN, I have to know what the case is and why. It is not going to be easy to get concurrence for the large-scale introduction of foreign troops unless the need is clear and explicit." And even so, he warned, Washington's request might initiate "a sharp debate within the GVN."[33]

On April 18, informed of Taylor's views, Johnson directed that all these actions be suspended until after McNamara's scheduled meeting with Westmoreland in Honolulu two days later. Thereafter, the president would review the situation and consult with Taylor. But the reprieve was brief. When Taylor joined McNamara and Westmoreland at Honolulu, he found himself faced by four additional strong advocates of an increased U.S. ground combat role—William Bundy, John McNaughton, Admiral Ulysses G. Sharp (CINCPAC), and General Earle Wheeler (chairman of the JCS). Confronted by this Macedonian phalanx, Taylor capitulated and, as McGeorge Bundy had predicted, now climbed aboard. The unanimous recommendation that McNamara gave to the president on April 21 called for a major escalation. Thirteen U.S. combat battalions, numbering 82,000 men, were to be added to the 33,500 U.S. troops already in Vietnam (this including the four marine battalions stationed at Danang and Chu Lai) along with three South Korean (ROK) and one Australian battalion (totaling 7,250 men).[34]

This was not presented to the president as a prescription for winning the war, but, rather, simply for denying victory to the Viet Cong. The "victory" envisaged for the United States, McNamara explained, was "to break the will of the DRV/VC by depriving them of victory," or, as Taylor had put it, "a demonstration of Communist impotence, which will lead to a political solution." It was agreed that a settlement would come "as much or more from VC failure in the South as from DRV pain in the North," and that it would take "more than six months, perhaps a year or two, to demonstrate VC failure." The participants were also in accord that the existing tempo of air strikes against the North was about right, that this bombing program should continue "at least six months, perhaps a year or more," and that in any case it was "very important that strikes against the North be continued during any talks." The Hanoi–Haiphong–Phuc Yen* areas were to be avoided, for all those present appeared to share Taylor's view that it was "important not to 'kill the hostage' by destroying the North Vietnamese assets inside the 'Hanoi do-nut.' " By this Taylor and the others at Honolulu meant that if too much of North Vietnam were destroyed, its leaders, with little left to lose, could not be expected to be influenced by changes in either the bounds or intensity of the bombing. They believed that by sparing the capital

---

*Phuc Yen was the most important MiG air base in the DRV and was located eighteen miles northwest of Hanoi.

and Haiphong (the only major port) the United States could still exert leverage on Hanoi's leaders by threatening to increase the weight and geographic extent of its bombing. If these assets were destroyed, there would be no feasible way of pressuring the DRV's leaders either to limit the flow of arms to the Viet Cong or to induce the Viet Cong to end or at least reduce the level of their insurgency. For most of the president's advisers, it was still an article of faith that Hanoi had this capacity.

It is not clear to what extent Lyndon Johnson had been won over to this view, but he had another reason, more immediate and compelling, for limiting the tempo and geographical extent of the bombing. This was his abiding fear that too rapid an escalation of the bombardment, or one that extended to Hanoi, Haiphong, or the China border areas, might provoke a massive Chinese military response and possibly greater Soviet involvement as well. Though the president's advisers differed as to the point at which they believed the Chinese would intervene, nearly all were convinced that Peking would not passively stand by and see her southern neighbor completely destroyed by American bombing. Some later critics have faulted Johnson for not having "gone for the jugular" and sent American combat troops into the North, but there was scarcely any doubt among his advisers—military or civilian—that, Vietnamese resistance and U.S. casualties aside, such a move might well have led to the introduction of Chinese ground combat forces. Few believed that bombing China would deter such action, and no one wished to risk provoking in Vietnam a repetition of the Chinese role in the Korean War.[35]

Though none of the participants in the April 20 Honolulu meeting expected their measures to lead to any dramatic or immediate improvement in the South, they did believe that the deployment of these additional troops would "bolster the GVN forces while they are building up." What McNamara and his supporters were proposing to Lyndon Johnson, then, was in effect a holding action—a recommendation for a sufficient increment of combat soldiers at least to hold the Viet Cong at bay. That was the minimum, but there was also the hope that with additional external support the Saigon regime might in time become strong enough, and the Viet Cong sufficiently stymied, for the United States to risk negotiations that would preserve the South as a separate, noncommunist state.

For a president whose major preoccupation was a domestic program embodying the revolutionary changes envisaged for his "Great Society," even that minimum objective was sufficient. To secure that, and obviate the loss of prestige and enormous American domestic political backlash he expected would follow a Saigon collapse, Lyndon Johnson evidently did not regard the investment in men and treasure advocated by McNamara and other advisers as excessive. Part of their recommendation he approved on April 21 and the balance on May 15.[36]

The slow pace at which Johnson escalated—still significantly slower than that advocated by the JCS, Westmoreland, and most of his civilian advisers—must in considerable part have reflected his mounting concern that a sharp, clear-cut escalatory move in Vietnam might so rock the boat as to threaten passage of many as-yet-unrealized pieces of Great Society legislation. That program was his highest priority, and with some of the most important bills (including the Voting Rights Act and Medicare) under consideration or soon to be presented, he apparently did not want to risk losing needed support by alarming and antagonizing members of Congress over his actions in Vietnam. He did buy a little time by obfuscating the degree of escalation inherent in implementing McNamara's April 21 recommendations, having the secretary not announce these troop increases publicly until June 16. But by holding back the release of this information, the president laid the foundations for what came to be known as the "credibility gap."

For some Americans Johnson's credibility was further strained when, on April 29, he launched his misinformed intervention in the Dominican Republic, sending in some twenty thousand marines in a clumsy effort to preempt what he believed to be a possible communist takeover and Castroism. By this alarmist reaction to what George Ball later termed "the questionable threat posed by a small number of alleged Communists dubiously reported to be in the Dominican Republic," he lost what William Bundy referred to as "a hunk of liberal sentiment" that became "deeply antagonized." At the time, neither Ball nor the president's other advisers criticized the intervention, and in extenuation Ball observed that "Johnson's use of excessive power and effort in the Dominican Republic reflected a wider preoccupation. We were just on the verge of committing large numbers of American combat forces to Vietnam and the President feared that a disaster close to home might lead more Americans to challenge our adventure ten thousand miles away." From this Dominican intervention, however, William Bundy realized that there was a significant fallout inimical to public support for the administration's escalation in Vietnam. "I think there was a very unfortunate degree of link-up that weakened public support in a critical 'liberal,' 'intellectual'—but somewhat broader than either area."[37]

This intervention did appear to harden the opposition of what was becoming an increasingly articulate, though still small, minority of senators opposed to military escalation in Vietnam. In addition to Ernest Gruening and Wayne Morse, this group now included Frank Church, George McGovern, Mike Mansfield, Gaylord Nelson, and William Fulbright, chairman of the Senate Foreign Relations Committee. The president, however, tidily outmaneuvered even these critics and in the process achieved greater legitimacy for his policies. On May 4, at a time when the full scope of his April 21 decision was not yet known to Congress, he couched a request for an additional $700 million in support of his Vietnam policies in terms that made it extremely difficult to refuse without appearing to oppose the effort to halt communist aggression and—most inhibiting of all—becoming vulnerable to the charge of denying support to those American soldiers already in the field. Though this garnered him no little resentment from congressional Vietnam critics who consequently felt obliged to go along, it produced favorable votes in the House and Senate of 408-7 and 88-3 respectively, providing a basis for claiming congressional backing for his policies in addition

to the Tonkin Gulf Resolution and SEATO. Some of his phraseology deserves
attention:

> This is not a routine appropriation. For each member of Congress who
> supports this request is also voting to persist in our effort to halt Communist
> aggression in South Vietnam. Each is saying that the Congress and the
> President stand united before the world in joint determination that the
> independence of South Vietnam shall be preserved and Communist attack
> not succeed. . . . The additional funds I am requesting are needed to
> continue to provide our forces with the best and most modern supplies and
> equipment. . . . They are needed to build facilities to house and protect our
> men and supplies. . . . To deny and delay this means to deny and delay the
> fullest support of the American people and the American Congress to those
> brave men who are risking their lives for freedom in Vietnam.[38]

Though the president temporarily outmaneuvered the congressional opposition to his Vietnam policies, it was evident that criticism among a minority of the
public and from a few influential newspapers and columnists was becoming
increasingly vocal (notable among the dissenters were *The New York Times* and
columnists Walter Lippmann and Drew Pearson). The strongest and most
focused surge of protest came from some of the major universities, and became
particularly articulate with the launching of campus "teach-ins," which were
generally critical of the administration's Vietnam policies. Pioneered at the University of Michigan, these discussion sessions sought to provide students with as
much factual information as possible about Vietnam and the American intervention. The movement reached full flower with the National Teach-In held in
Washington, D.C., on May 17–18. Organized primarily by a faculty group from
Michigan, it rapidly enlisted support from faculty and students at several hundred
colleges and universities across the country and in Canada. These institutions sent
delegations to the Washington teach-in and in most of them classes were dismissed so that students could watch on television or listen over the radio to the
debates held in the capital. From that time on, the campus Vietnam teach-in was
an ongoing phenomenon at an increasing number of American academic institutions, and it became a source of growing concern to the administration.[39] It was,
however, to be another twelve to eighteen months before a majority of students
appeared to be definitely against the war.

By the spring of 1965, Lyndon Johnson had been conditioned by his advisers to
assume that pursuit of a negotiated solution was not yet in the national interest.
George Ball apart, they continued as vehemently as ever to admonish that such
a course was unthinkable until Saigon could bargain politically and militarily
from a position of greater strength—sufficient to ensure its survival as a separate,
noncommunist state. And for the Johnson administration—like Eisenhower's and

Kennedy's—*that* condition remained fundamental and nonnegotiable. Yet for the NLF and Hanoi, the obverse of this remained equally nonnegotiable. For them no solution was conceivable that left their country torn in two as a consequence of the interjection of Western power, with the southern half controlled by a government dependent upon and subserviently aligned with the United States. Negotiations, of course, require compromise arrived at through mutual concessions, but given the incompatibility of fundamental objectives between Saigon and Washington on the one hand, and Hanoi and the NLF on the other, there was little basis for compromise. As Paul Warnke, who was John McNaughton's successor as assistant secretary of defense, later put it, "The intractable fact was that neither Hanoi nor Washington could compromise its position without in effect admitting defeat. . . ." For Hanoi to "compromise," as Washington defined that term, "would be to capitulate and accept the defeat of an idea that had motivated its leadership since World War II. For the United States to 'compromise' and permit the indigenous forces in Vietnam to work their own way would be to condone the demise of the anti-Communist regime we had supported in Saigon for twenty years."[40] The separate southern state that three administrations had been trying to build during the previous decade was still essentially an appendage of the United States. The fragile edifice still lacked a sufficient indigenous foundation to support it. Without massive American economic and military buttresses, the walls would collapse, and U.S. officials knew it. They could not, therefore, envisage a settlement that did not register the heavy impact of American power, and that sort of outcome neither Hanoi nor the NLF would accept.

The basic incongruity of the American position lay, of course, in the effort to keep a nation divided in two—a nation whose nationalist ferment was as strong as that of any country in the twentieth century. The president and his advisers evidenced precious little empathy for Vietnamese nationalism and never seemed to appreciate its strength and breadth. But their own sense of nationalism—usually defined in terms of American prestige and invincibility—loomed very large in their calculations.

Given the nature and power of Vietnamese nationalism, Dean Rusk's repeated assertions that the American intervention would cease when Hanoi "left its neighbors alone" appears all the more incongruous; for as Warnke observes, "Hanoi regarded the South Vietnamese not as neighbors, but as part of the same family." If there were to have been any progress toward a negotiated solution, the process would have had to provide a significant role for the United States' main adversary, the NLF—whatever its relationship to Hanoi. At this time—before the saturation bombing of American B-52s, U.S. ground and naval artillery, and Phoenix-type assassination teams had destroyed or chewed up a major part of the NLF's infrastructure and combat units—the front-line American adversary in Vietnam was the NLF. The first PAVN units had just arrived in the South and for more than a year were to remain no more than a small fraction of NLF combat strength. Indeed, until at least the end of 1965 the total manpower of PAVN units in the South was less than that of the United States' Korean auxiliaries there, and much less than that deployed by the United States. This must be understood to appreciate Hanoi's approach to negotiations, its leaders insisting that their soldiers had a considerably greater right to be in the southern half of Vietnam than those from two foreign countries. As Warnke observes, "At no point was North Vietnam ever willing to accept the description of its forces as foreign in any part of Vietnam, or to equate its withdrawal with ours."[41]

No political solution could escape providing a place for the NLF. To insist, as did the president's advisers, that to participate politically its adherents would first have to surrender their weapons and submit to the mercy of the well-armed Saigon military was to take up residence with Alice in Wonderland. Yet this was precisely the advice Lyndon Johnson was getting.

Maxwell Taylor later observed: "From 1965 to the end of 1967, there was nothing in the power relationship between the two sides which offered hope of successful negotiations, even if we got them started." Certainly a negotiated settlement that registered the relative political and military power of the contestants would have fallen far short of minimum U.S. objectives. It could not have left all of the South in the hands of those opposed to the NLF, nor barred that area's ultimate reunification with the North. With South Vietnamese leaders acknowledging privately to American officials that their regime could not risk political competition with the NLF, those officials could only hope that in time —after the introduction of sufficient additional U.S. military power—the NLF could be sufficiently weakened to permit this.[42] When this additional American power had weighted the scales sufficiently, then it would be safe to conduct bona-fide negotiations leading to a political settlement. In the meantime, however, Washington would avoid negotiations while hoping to make sufficient gestures in support of them to blunt the efforts of their proponents both in the United States and among allies abroad. And during this period the administration would continue to insist—implicitly or explicitly—upon the same precondition for negotiations that was in fact the nub of its controversy with the NLF and Hanoi— preservation of a separate, anticommunist state in the South. It was some two and a half years later, after the introduction of half a million American troops had shown the unattainability of this objective, before the administration would begin to modify its conditions and its approach to negotiations.

In the spring of 1965, Lyndon Johnson had to reckon with the fact that the same opinion polls which assured him of his having the support of a large majority of Congress and the American public for his military escalations of February-March also indicated that an even larger majority looked favorably on a negotiated solution of the Vietnam conflict. In response to this sentiment, he now seemed to be moving toward negotiations, but his statements were so hedged with preconditions that they undercut the possibility. Thus, Chester Cooper later assessed Johnson's much-cited March 25 announcement as "merely rhetoric, a public relations holding-action. . . ." Although "its tone and content were soothing to an anxious American and foreign public," it was in fact "heavily insured against any immediate negotiation initiatives on the part of Hanoi."[43]

A careful reading of Johnson's address discloses the conditionality of his approach: "The United States will never be second in seeking a settlement in Vietnam that is based on an end of Communist aggression," i.e., the NLF would have to stop fighting and Hanoi would have to stop supporting it; "I am ready to go anywhere at any time, and meet with anyone whenever there is promise of progress towards an honorable peace," i.e., one reflecting U.S. terms. And two weeks later, in his Johns Hopkins speech, he spoke of his readiness to engage in "unconditional discussions," i.e., not negotiations, with the "governments concerned," thereby ruling out the NLF.[44] The reason the United States was in South Vietnam was to help "defend its independence" (as an anticommunist state separate from the North).

This speech also contained the president's offer to ask the U.S. Congress for "a billion dollar investment" in the economic development of all the countries of Southeast Asia, North Vietnam included. Eugene Black, former president of the World Bank, was asked to head a team to inaugurate U.S. "participation in these programs"—including a Mekong River equivalent of the TVA. The reluctant Black found a bewildered Washington bureaucracy unprepared to provide the immediate planning required by the president and in desperation approached Cornell University's even less prepared Southeast Asia Program for ideas.[45]

The NLF had issued a five-point manifesto on March 22 expressing its refusal to enter into negotiations until after U.S. troops had been withdrawn. In rebroadcasting and publishing this statement, Hanoi effected several minor moderating changes, the most important of which could be read as implying that a U.S. withdrawal need not precede negotiations so long as it was pledged beforehand. Peking's translation of the NLF's five points was in accord with Hanoi's version.[46]

It is, of course, understandable that those living in the part of Vietnam where U.S. forces were actually operating should be more insistent than those living above the seventeenth parallel on getting these foreign troops out as soon as possible. But U.S. intelligence was uncertain how to interpret differences on what the CIA saw as "key issues" in the statements. The Saigon embassy cautioned against regarding these divergences "as necessarily a reflection of differences in basic position" and believed they were "more apt to reflect different tactics, local situations, and at times lack of immediate coordination." Its analysis of "recent variances between the Front and Hanoi" indicated these were "differences of tone rather than substance—the Front's tone being somewhat sharper," and it concluded, "It appears doubtful, at present, that any split exists between the Front and Hanoi."[47]

The CIA's Directorate of Intelligence, however, noted that during the past year the DRV government had resurrected its principal mass organization, the Fatherland Front, "to serve as a focal point for expressing Hanoi's support and cooperation with the Liberation Front in South Vietnam" and had called a meeting of its Central Committee on April 7, where one of the two main themes had been "the unity of purpose" between the Vietnamese in North and South Vietnam in the struggle against the U.S. aggressors. An additional effort to emphasize this unity, the CIA suggested, might have been the appointment on the same day of a former southern resistance leader, Nguyen Duy Trinh, as the DRV's new minister of foreign affairs.[48]

Whatever the validity of this speculation, publication of Hanoi's own "four points" confirmed that its approach to negotiations was somewhat more moderate than the NLF's. Since these four points provided the basis for Hanoi's negotiating position for some three years, the full text should be noted:

> The unswerving policy of the DRV Government is to respect strictly the 1954 Geneva agreements on Vietnam and to implement correctly their basic provisions as embodied in the following points:
>
> 1—Recognition of the basic national rights of the Vietnamese people— peace, independence, sovereignty, unity, and territorial integrity. According to the Geneva agreements, the U.S. Government must withdraw from South Vietnam U.S. troops, military personnel, and weapons of all kinds, dismantle all U.S. military bases there, and cancel its military alliance with South Vietnam. It must end its policy of intervention and aggression in South Vietnam. According to the Geneva agreements, the U.S. Government must stop its acts of war against North Vietnam and completely cease all encroachments on the territory and sovereignty of the DRV.
>
> 2—Pending the peaceful reunification of Vietnam, while Vietnam is still temporarily divided into two zones the military provisions of the 1954 Geneva agreements on Vietnam must be strictly respected. The two zones must refrain from entering into any military alliance with foreign countries and there must be no foreign military bases, troops, or military personnel in their respective territory.
>
> 3—The internal affairs of South Vietnam must be settled by the South Vietnamese people themselves in accordance with the program of the NFLSV [NLF] without any foreign interference.
>
> 4—The peaceful reunification of Vietnam is to be settled by the Vietnamese people in both zones, without any foreign interference.[49]

In presenting these four points, Pham Van Dong opened a way to negotiations. He explained that they were to be regarded as a "basis for the soundest political settlement." Recognition of this "basis," he said, "would create favorable conditions for the peaceful settlement of the Vietnam problem, and it will be possible to consider the reconvening of an international conference along the pattern of the 1954 Geneva conference on Vietnam." The four points were sufficiently broad and undetailed to provide ample scope for negotiation—if the United States had wished to pursue them; nor would acceptance of them as a basis for discussion have pledged it in advance to an outcome it could not support. As a staff assessment prepared for McGeorge Bundy concluded, "If we choose to make them so, Pham Van Dong's proposals could provide the basis for a negotiating dialogue." And McGeorge Bundy, while characterizing Hanoi's terms of settlement as "quite unacceptable to us," acknowledged that the Hanoi government regarded them "as a basis for discussion" and that he; Llewellyn Thompson, former ambassador to Moscow; and Ray Cline, acting head of the CIA, all agreed that there was "at least a hint of real interest from Hanoi in eventual discussions."[50]

With this opening, Ball went straight to Johnson the next morning to revive and promote some of the arguments for a negotiated settlement he had made the previous October. The president's reaction was sufficiently encouraging for Ball to prepare a long memorandum for him that afternoon. Although he made copies for the president's senior advisers, this time he sent the memorandum directly to Johnson.[51]

Ball's point of departure in this April 21 memorandum was that, if the Vietnam situation was to be settled without a major war, the United States would have to prepare itself for a settlement that fell short of its publicly stated goals. Hanoi's four points and the NLF's program he saw as providing a basis for negotiations. "Hanoi obviously does not expect us to accept its four points as a pre-condition for negotiations" and had set them forth "for the purpose of staking out a bargaining position." He saw much in them that the United States could accept. "I think it is possible that these four points were deliberately drawn to test the possibility of beginning a dialogue—and we would do well to examine them in that light."

The United States, Ball argued, should "try to find some common ground that would save face for Hanoi and permit it to pull back even though that action were only tactical and Hanoi hoped to prevail at some later date. In my view such a tactical withdrawal is probably the most we can realistically try to achieve short of totally destroying North-Vietnam." Such a tactical withdrawal, even if temporary, could, of course, also save American face.

Negotiation of a political solution "in accordance with the program" of the NLF, Ball later explained to me, he saw as constituting an opportunity rather than an obstacle. Its call for the establishment of a coalition government followed by an election in which he believed, with good reason, it would support monitoring by an international commission, could yield a government that, in his opinion, would be reasonably representative, even though pro-American elements might not come out on top.

With this in mind, Ball suggested to the president the broad outlines of a possible settlement incorporating the following elements:

1. All hostilities would be terminated. Hanoi would stop infiltrating men and equipment and the Viet Cong would stop their guerrilla activities. The United States would halt its bombing and both the South Vietnamese and the United States would stop attacking the Viet Cong.
2. The Saigon Government would declare a general amnesty—subject to the faithful carrying out of paragraph 1 by Hanoi and the Viet Cong. As part of the amnesty all Viet Cong wishing to return to the North would be

permitted to do so. Transportation would be provided and a regrouping encouraged—but not required—along the lines of that arranged in 1954.

3. An International Commission would undertake to police the cease-fire by the appropriate deployment of adequate inspection teams at key points throughout the country.

4. An agreed future date would be set for elections. The Liberation Front would be recognized as a political party and would be permitted to present candidates and conduct an election campaign by peaceable means.

5. An International Force would supervise the elections. Once the new Government was installed the United States would withdraw. However, the new Government would have the right to request assistance from the United States or any other country in the event that its independence were again threatened.

6. Reunification would be permitted at a specified future date if desired by the people of South Viet-Nam and their Government.

Although the president's advisers attacked Ball's plan as unrealistic, it is now evident that his proposal, whatever its defects, could have achieved at least as much of the administration's aims as the heavy escalation in U.S. military intervention which the advisers advocated, and without the enormous physical destruction of the society and land of Vietnam and the great loss of American and Vietnamese lives which it caused. Bundy, McNamara, and Rusk doggedly continued to oppose negotiations—at least until Saigon and the United States were in a position to bargain from much greater strength. In the meantime they argued that a known American disposition to negotiate would take the starch out of the ARVN and whatever government sat in Saigon. Thus McGeorge Bundy informed the president that "We have not yet had serious discussions with the Republic of Vietnam" regarding any prospect of negotiations. With respect to the problems involved, he observed, "it is very hard for us to look these questions in the eye with Quat and Company lest each of us begin to suspect the determination of the other."[52]

But apparently Johnson's mind was not yet completely closed to arguments in favor of negotiations. Two days later Richard Goodwin, a member of the White House staff, pointed out to him that Pham Van Dong "did not specifically say we would have to accept these four points before there could be negotiations. The point seems to be ambiguous." He went on to explain:

Some of the brightest experts in State Intelligence feel there is a real possibility that (a) these were not set forth as conditions, (b) they were meant as a statement of ultimate objectives, just as we say any final settlement has to provide for an independent South Vietnam, tied to no alliance, etc. . . . (c) they said this in order to reassure the Liberation Front that they would not sell them out at a Conference, just as we say things to reassure Saigon.

Goodwin then suggested that Pham Van Dong might have meant his statement to be an overture, and that Hanoi might have regarded the president's recent statements as rejections of negotiations. "Thus, they may feel the ball is in our court." It was because of this, Goodwin said, that he had earlier proposed to the president a statement designed to say, "Of course, we can't accept your four points as the basis for a final settlement, but we are willing to discuss them, just as you will discuss our position." This, he added, "does not mean we accept them as conditions or that we have changed our mind about the essentials of final settlement." Johnson's interest in this memorandum is indicated by the scrawl in his handwriting at the bottom: "Bill [presumably Moyers], you and Dick see me re this. Talk it out also with Mac."[53]

It was the third of Hanoi's points that was seized upon by the president's advisers as the most plausible basis for refusing to engage in such negotiations. With very few exceptions, U.S. officials insisted on reading it as meaning an NLF takeover of the Saigon government. But that was not what the NLF's program stipulated. Moreover, at an April 15 meeting of the front's top leadership, its own position on point 3 had been clarified in what the CIA's Directorate of Intelligence regarded as a "relatively cautious formulation" that, it concluded, "may have been intended to leave some room for maneuver on the exact role and status of the Front in any future move towards a settlement in Vietnam." Certainly the phrase in the clarification on which the CIA based this conclusion could not easily be interpreted as meaning the exclusion of everyone but the NLF from the envisaged Saigon government; it stated that any solution for South Vietnam would be "unrealistic and impractical" if it "disregards the participation and decisive position of the NLFSV."[54] Whatever the case, any American official who gave more than lip service to the idea of self-determination, and who had actually read the extensive ten-point program put forth by the NLF when it was established, would have found it difficult to fault its current proposals.

As may be recalled from chapter IV, the NLF program envisaged replacement of the Saigon regime by a national assembly elected on the basis of universal suffrage, with provision for a broad coalition administration pledged to a wide range of social and economic measures. Chester Cooper recalls that he and several other Washington staff members argued that the enemy's views should be probed and that, if the NLF's idea of free elections provided scope for their monitoring by "an international policing mechanism (a strengthened International Control Commission or some other body)," the United States could accept point 3.[55]

There was scope, then, for interpreting the NLF program referred to in point 3 as a political process providing for genuine self-determination—assuming the United States wanted this. Only through negotiations, however, could the point be further clarified. The views of Cooper and Goodwin and their supportive second-echelon colleagues were, however, not acceptable to the president's senior advisers, except Ball. An exercise in self-determination was not something the United States could risk in South Vietnam—at least as long as its central objective was to maintain as much of that area as possible free of NLF control. It would be a long time before the administration made any serious effort to probe the enemy's views on a political settlement, and a long time too before it felt it could even discuss such prospects with the Saigon regime.

If there were any doubts left as to the administration's intention to avoid serious negotiations until the results of applying more military power had been tested, such doubts were removed after the U.S. briefly halted the air raids on North Vietnam—the well-publicized "bombing pause" of May 12–17. The pause resulted neither in a reduction in Viet Cong military activity nor in any move toward negotiations. It was, however, useful in temporarily blunting charges that the administration was not receptive to negotiations; *The New York Times* noted "strong indications" that one "motivation for the pause was the Administration's desire to convince its critics at home and abroad that North Vietnam and China were preventing negotiations, not the United States."[56] The non-public face of the exercise, however, could serve only to convince the NLF and Hanoi that Washington was presenting an ultimatum rather than seeking negotiations. In a scholarly account of the relation between coercion and diplomacy in the Vietnam War, Wallace J. Thies has observed: "Faced with the prospect of having to expand the war, a pause offered the President a convenient tool for defusing the criticism that would inevitably accompany any escalation, since if a pause were held and the North Vietnamese failed to respond, the President would be free to claim that it was they who were blocking the path to peace and that he had no choice but to step up pressure."[57]

William Bundy later recalled that he and his brother were largely responsible for drafting the message informing Hanoi of the pause. He says that it was approved by Rusk (over whose signature it was sent), and "Of course it was reviewed by the President; but it was reviewed as the considered opinion of his advisers." Bundy acknowledges that this message had been "well and truly criticized to me privately since. . . . And I think it's a great pity that we didn't have the extra reflection and somebody to draw back from it. . . . It was a crisp, kind of lawyer's document. . . . And I don't think it was . . . well handled."[58]

One has only to read that message to understand why it should have convinced Hanoi that the United States was bent on applying military leverage and was uninterested in negotiations; and also why the administration, concerned about possible domestic criticism, refused to release it to the American public. Not until Hanoi Radio broadcast Rusk's message on December 10, 1965, did a few American newspapers publish it and the American public learn what the Hanoi government had known for the previous seven months.[59]

> The highest authority in this Government has asked me to inform Hanoi that there will be no air attacks on North Vietnam for a period beginning at noon, Washington time, Wednesday the 12th of May, and running into next week.
>
> In this decision, the United States Government has taken account of repeated suggestions from various quarters, including public statements by

Hanoi representatives, that there can be no progress toward peace while there are air attacks on North Vietnam.

The United States Government remains convinced that the underlying cause of trouble in Southeast Asia is armed action against the people and Government of South Vietnam by forces whose action can be decisively affected from North Vietnam. The United States will be very watchful to see whether in this period of pause there are significant reductions in such armed actions by such forces.

The United States must emphasize that the road toward the end of armed attacks against the people and Government of [South] Vietnam is the only road which will permit the Government of [South] Vietnam and the Government of the United States to bring a permanent end to their air attacks on North Vietnam.

In taking this action, the United States is well aware of the risk that a temporary suspension of these air attacks may be understood as an indication of weakness, and it is therefore necessary for me to point out that if this pause should be misunderstood in this fashion by any party, it would be necessary to demonstrate more clearly than ever, after the pause has ended, that the United States is determined not to accept aggression without reply in Vietnam.

Moreover, the United States must point out that the decision to end air attacks for this limited trial period is one which it must be free to reverse, if at any time in coming days, there should be actions by the other side in Vietnam which required immediate reply.

But my Government is very hopeful that there will be no such misunderstanding and that this first pause in air attacks may meet with a response which will permit further and more extended suspension of this form of military action in expectation of equal constructive actions by the other side in the future.

It will be noted that this statement ignored Hanoi's four points and made no reference at all to negotiations or even discussions. To this ultimatum there was no positive response from Hanoi—direct or indirect. "The foreign minister of Hanoi," George Ball observes, "denounced the pause as a 'deceitful maneuver to pave the way for American escalation'—which I thought a perceptive appraisal."[60] When the bombing resumed on May 18, Hanoi continued in its stance of refusing to participate in negotiations or discussions as long as American planes were bombing its territory.

And so, because of the political and military weakness of its client Saigon regime, the administration hung back from any serious exploration of a negotiated settlement. Before risking that course, it planned to wait until after greater increments of U.S. military power had weighted the political scales more heavily in Saigon's behalf.

XIII

Constraints on U.S. Policy

Despite the troop increases ordered on April 21, Johnson soon realized that such American forces alone could not even sustain a holding action in South Vietnam. So Washington now made a major effort to secure help from its allies. Attempts to gain their support had already been under way for almost a year, but thus far the results of this "Third Country Support," or "Many Flags Program" as it was often referred to, had been keenly disappointing. Now that U.S. ground combat forces had been committed, however, the president thought it much more urgent to get such support and called for an all-out effort for rapid acceleration of the program.

The Many Flags Program was attractive to the administration for two reasons. It had the potential of significantly reducing the U.S. military burden, and it also had the political advantage—in dealing with American as well as global audiences—of providing visible proof that the increased military intervention was sanctioned by, and enjoyed the tangible support of, some of Washington's allies.

Nine months earlier, when on American initiative Khanh's government had appealed worldwide for assistance, nine countries other than the United States were already providing modest amounts of economic, educational, and technical (mostly medical) assistance to South Vietnam, but, except for the Chinese Nationalist government on Taiwan, none had sent troops. In July 1964 the "several hundred military and paramilitary" personnel from Taiwan constituted by far the largest third-country contingent in Vietnam, and its government was prepared to make additional personnel "available as required."[1]

The presence of Chinese nationalists ("Chinats"), however, was potentially dangerous, for it might provoke military intervention by the Chinese communist government, an action that, in the opinion of U.S. officials, Chiang Kai-shek was hoping for in order to bring Washington into conflict with Peking. In addition, there was strong anti-Chinese sentiment among Vietnamese. Consequently, the Chinat airplane pilots and technicians, as well as other ethnic-Chinese elements that were brought in to fight in the South, or carry out sabotage in the North, were frequently represented as Nungs—a mountain minority that straddled the frontier between North Vietnam and China.[2]

Probably the largest single Chinat contingent was a component of the Sea Swallows, a special military unit originally based near the extreme southern tip of Vietnam, which was directly supported by the United States and led by a Catholic, Father Nguyen Loc Hoa. With the residue of an original nucleus that had fled with Father Hoa from China in 1951, this group enrolled ethnic-Chinese recruits from Vietnam and a considerable number of soldiers seconded from Chiang Kai-shek's army on Taiwan. It is not clear whether the Sea Swallows were being supported by the Eisenhower administration in 1959, when Diem invited Father Hoa to settle in South Vietnam following a seven-year sojourn in Cambodia. From the beginning of the Kennedy administration, however, Hoa did receive U.S. support and a major public-relations boost from Kennedy himself —without, of course, any acknowledgment of the Chinat connection. With General Khanh's approval, the dispatch of an additional 112 soldiers from Taiwan was authorized in September 1964. But there was always a danger that the identity of Hoa's non-Vietnamese force might be revealed, and fear of this was a constraint against any large increases in it. (Thus, Maxwell Taylor was understandably nervous about the indiscretion of an aide of the Taiwan general in charge of sending these soldiers to Vietnam, who informed the U.S. embassy in Saigon that their arrival there was the "first step en route to [the Chinese] mainland.") In April 1965 the Sea Swallows mustered six companies of combat infantry, but their numbers apparently were not appreciably increased thereafter.[3]

Although Washington made a great effort to enlist assistance from its European allies, they were willing to provide no more than small amounts of economic and technical aid to Saigon. None would send soldiers. The United States publicly excused Britain, whose backing it had been especially keen to secure, from sending troops because her hands were full in beating off Indonesian probes into Malaysia. But the real reason London was reluctant to supply even the small token force that Washington hoped for was the unpopularity of America's Vietnam role among the British public, despite the considerable support it received from the British press.[4]

Thus, up to the end of May 1965, the Many Flags Program had attracted troops from just three allies—Australia, South Korea, and New Zealand—and within another year and a half only the Philippines and Thailand had joined them. But, except for Australia (whose first complement of an infantry battalion and support troops was sent in June 1965 and whose total contribution rose to 7,500 by 1967) and New Zealand (with an artillery battery of 517 men integrated with the Australian infantry), these countries were not responding as genuine allies— that is, without remuneration. Seoul, Manila, and Bangkok all demanded very heavy prices—payment so high that these governments, if not their troops, might fairly have been regarded as mercenary.[5]

An infantry engineering task force of 2,200 South Koreans plus ten karate instructors had arrived in South Vietnam in early 1965, and by October they had been augmented by an infantry division and a combat brigade. A second infantry division and a regimental combat team arrived in 1966, with about 3,000 additional troops, for a total of approximately 50,000 men. Negotiations to send in a Philippine combat engineer battalion with a supporting "security group of infantry, armor and artillery detachments" consisting of 2,200 men began in December 1964, but the first units did not actually leave for Vietnam until August 16, 1966. Arrangements for bringing in Thai troops, which finally totaled about 11,000, were not concluded until late in 1966, with the first contingent arriving in Saigon on July 15, 1967.[6]

The delays in obtaining these contingents from Manila and Bangkok were largely caused by financial bargaining. When negotiations with the Philippine government commenced in December 1964, it was insisting on what U.S. officials regarded as "an outrageous pay and allowances bill ($8 per diem for a Filipino GI)." By May 1965 Manila had raised the ante to what these Americans referred to as "exorbitant financial demands" of $15 per day. When the troops were finally dispatched on August 16, 1966, and President Ferdinand Marcos announced, "There is no price too high to pay for freedom," he was clearly thinking of the American, not the Philippine, treasury. Chester Cooper calculated that the $39 million ultimately paid the Philippine government for the period 1967–69 worked out to $26,000 per man. In addition to supplying the amounts that increased pay and allowances of Philippine troops in Vietnam by about 80 percent, the United States gave them access to American post exchanges there—an enormously lucrative operation whereby purchases averaged $1,000 per man, and, as Senator Stuart Symington observed, were "a good deal more than their salary." The State Department's representative was unable to account for this discrepancy, but possibly the answer lay in the fact that Filipinos in Vietnam were paid in U.S. dollars, which could be exchanged on the black market at far above the official rate.[7]

Marcos exacted considerably more—for use in the Philippines, not Vietnam: two patrol boats, rifles, and machine guns for a battalion combat team, and accelerated funding to equip three engineering construction battalions. In September 1966, just after Philippine troops were finally dispatched to Vietnam, Marcos paid a state visit to the United States, where he addressed Congress and was promised a substantial increase in economic assistance. Beyond that, the Philippines benefited considerably from remittances home of nearly five thousand Filipino civilians working for the U.S. government in Vietnam, who from 1966 to 1969 earned $118.5 million. In view of all this, it is understandable why, when a U.S. Senate hearing in 1969 was about to divulge this information, the State Department was said to fear that publication "might create the impression that Filipino troops went to South Vietnam not as a willing contribution of an ally, but as mercenary troops paid by the United States."[8]

The Thai government was also successful in its bargaining. The annual cost to the United States of the Thai troops was approximately $50 million a year. The overseas allowance paid by the United States amounted to an additional 150 percent for privates and corporals and over 200 percent additional for lieutenants and captains. (It should be noted that the Thai government was also supporting

U.S. objectives in Southeast Asia by contributing twenty-five battalions to the CIA's "Secret Army" [Armée Clandestine] in Laos. There the United States paid Thai privates an allowance of 300 percent over and above their regular pay, with a total cost to the United States by 1971 of about $100 million per year.) The Thai government also directly benefited. U.S. economic and military assistance increased markedly, approximately doubling between 1965 and 1968. It is, however, difficult to distinguish to what extent this was a *quid pro quo* for the deployment of Thai troops, or for the rights Bangkok granted Washington to establish a network of air bases for use by bombers and other planes operating over South and North Vietnam. From 1965 to 1968 at least 75 percent of all U.S. bombing of North Vietnam emanated from Thai bases.[9]

Of the three Asian contingents, the U.S. military regarded the South Koreans (ROK) as most valuable for their training and fighting ability. But the price the United States paid for these fifty thousand troops was astronomical. Officers and enlisted men who served in Vietnam were given much greater remuneration (eighteen times higher for sergeants and twenty times for enlisted men) than they received in Korea. The troops also had access to the goods in U.S. post-exchange facilities.[10]

As a further *quid pro quo,* the U.S. gave South Korean firms a disproportionate number of civilian contracts in Vietnam. Some of this was pure featherbedding, such as a Korean firm's being hired to remove garbage in Saigon. (In 1966 I observed its crews manning huge Manhattan-style trucks that mechanically ingested the refuse, when there were thousands of destitutes in the city who desperately needed work and could have removed the garbage more cheaply and without the government's having to import such costly equipment.) By 1969 Koreans numbered over sixteen thousand out of a total of twenty-six thousand foreign civilian employees of the U.S. government in South Vietnam. The dollar remittances sent home by Korean soldiers and civilian employees in Vietnam, together with other foreign-exchange earnings garnered by Korea from the Vietnam War, was $135 million in 1967, $165.5 million in 1968, and nearly $200 million by 1969, or 20 percent of Seoul's annual foreign-currency revenue.[11]

The United States also provided substantial direct inducements to the South Korean government itself. Besides meeting all costs of sending, maintaining, equipping, and remunerating Korean forces sent to Vietnam, Washington undertook to

> provide substantial items for modernizing ROK forces in Korea . . . equip, train, and finance replacement forces for those going to Vietnam; improve the ROK anti-infiltration capability; improve the ROK arsenal for ammunition production; improve the living quarters for ROK forces in Korea; . . . continue to procure commercial consumables in Korea for the military assistance program . . . make special efforts to procure goods and services in Korea in support of the Vietnam war; and provide more economic assistance loans to Korea.[12]

The total costs of all U.S. Vietnam-related payments and benefits to Korea for the five fiscal years 1966–70 alone amounted to $927 million. About one-quarter of the Korean soldiers were withdrawn in 1971, but most of the remainder stayed until early 1973, at which time they were more numerous than U.S. ground troops.[13] Thus, the costs to the United States must be increased significantly if the last two years of the Vietnam service by Koreans is to be included.

Because these highly secret arrangements were concealed from public view, the administration was able to refer to Korea, Thailand, and the Philippines as "staunch allies" who were "volunteering to fight for the Free World." Had the true relationship been known, an adverse public reaction could certainly have been expected with regard to South Korea, where the number of U.S. troops guarding its northern frontier—approximately fifty thousand—was virtually the same as the contingent of Korean troops ultimately sent to Vietnam. A similar reaction could have been expected with regard to the Philippines, which in addition to its Pacific-wide Mutual Defense Treaty with the United States had a commitment under SEATO. As Tom Wicker later observed in *The New York Times,* since the Philippines "agreed publicly with the United States that the war in Vietnam was being fought in accordance with the SEATO treaty, it should have obligated them to participate in the war." This was particularly true in that the Philippines had been receiving Military Assistance Program funds from the United States for a combat battalion designated for "use as a SEATO commitment."[14] Another reason for not making public the extent to which these Asian troops and their home governments were rewarded was the disparities in remuneration—the Koreans and Filipinos reportedly receiving considerably more per soldier than did the Thais.

By June 1965, with no more than five thousand third-country forces in Vietnam, it was clear that even the considerable increase scheduled for the next few months could not come close to providing the needed reinforcement of U.S. forces. The ARVN was now disintegrating ever more rapidly and had suffered a further series of defeats even though most of the Viet Cong main-force regiments and battalions had not yet been committed. Moreover, though by mid-May no more than one battalion of North Vietnamese (PAVN) forces had yet been confirmed in South Vietnam, Hanoi clearly had the capacity to send many more units south to reinforce the Viet Cong.[15]

Though the bombing of the North had removed Hanoi's constraints against sending PAVN units south, overall it had apparently not reduced the fighting capacity of the NLF itself. Not only was the NLF able to rely on its own primitive arsenals and on U.S. weapons captured from the ARVN to offset whatever loss in weapons was being caused by the American bombing of supply routes from the North, it was also able to recruit and train additional troops at a rate significantly in excess of its casualties. All this was awkward for proponents of escalation, for the situation was still roughly the same as a year before when

William Bundy, in an internal memorandum, referred to "the fact that the Viet Cong *do* have a lot of appeal in South Vietnam and *do* rely heavily on captured U.S. weapons."[16]

Nor, apparently, had bombing and napalming the northern targets adversely affected morale there or reduced its government's and people's disposition to support the southern insurgency. A major study by the State Department's Division of Intelligence and Research sent to Rusk on June 29 concluded:

> Rather limited but quite uniform and convincing evidence indicates that the U.S. strikes against North Vietnam have had no significantly harmful effects on popular morale. In fact, the regime has apparently been able to increase its control on the populace and perhaps even to break through the political apathy and indifference which have characterized the outlook of the average North Vietnamese in recent years.[17]

This study noted there was "no sign of dissidence." And it took issue with one of the U.S. military's rationales for bombing—namely, that the consequent "intense mobilization of North Vietnamese society for defense" represented an economic "cost" inflicted by the attacks—because of the "disruption caused by the evacuation of urban dependents, the excessive air raid and militia organization and drill, the expansion of military mobilization, and the reforming of [economic] enterprise organizations along military lines." According to the State Department study, that argument "mistakes the regime's use of patriotism as a lever of social control for a 'cost.'" On the contrary, it concluded, "It seems clear that as a result of these actions the North Vietnamese population has become considerably more regimented, mobile, and responsive to the regime's demands, resulting in economic gains outweighing the economic 'costs.'"

As a consequence of the bombing, the study noted, the DRV's previously lagging program of transferring nonessential activities—educational, administrative, and industrial—and dependent population from urban to rural areas had now moved forward much more effectively, with even the population of Hanoi (which had not been bombed) reduced by as much as a third. And the flagging program of settling a million peasants from the overcrowded Red River Delta in mountain areas had now been accelerated, with quotas nearly met. Noting that "the rationale and design of the air attacks has been to interfere with the military support given to the Viet Cong in South Vietnam through destroying military facilities south of the 20th parallel," the study concluded that, though the attacks made the support more difficult and costly, few expected that Hanoi would sharply reduce this support. With current overland military traffic from North to South estimated to be only about a hundred tons per day, the attacks "could hardly present any major problem or costs."[18]

JCS pressures to extend the bombing to Haiphong and the smaller ports were resisted not simply because it was feared this might precipitate retaliation by communist China, but also because a detailed Pentagon study had demonstrated the strategy's marginal effectiveness. The forty-five thousand tons per month (65 percent of total DRV imports) that were funneled through Haiphong could be shifted to southern Chinese ports and then transported via rail and road across the northern DRV border. (Thirty percent of import tonnage was already entering by rail, and 5 percent by highway.) Although this heavier overland traffic would still be subjected to U.S. bombing, it was evident that alternative land routes could soon largely compensate for the destruction or blockading of North Vietnam's ports, and the flow of imports would only temporarily be disrupted. (It is worth noting that the ineffectiveness of bombing and mining North Vietnam's ports was conclusively demonstrated during the Nixon administration, when Hanoi compensated by utilizing an already prepared spider web of auxiliary truck roads reaching down from the Chinese border and a gasoline pipeline.) The Pentagon study also pointed out the dangers Haiphong's bombing would bring to international shipping. Apart from the fact that sinking a Soviet ship might produce a major confrontation with Moscow, only a third of Haiphong's shipping came from communist countries, with another third carried by British ships and the remainder from other noncommunist countries, mostly American allies— primarily Japan, Norway, and Greece.[19]

One course of action that was opposed by nearly all of the president's advisers (a notable exception being Walt W. Rostow) was a U.S. ground-force invasion of North Vietnam. Estimates differed as to the resistance Hanoi's forces could mount against such an assault, and there was a widely shared belief that such a move would bring in Chinese troops. There was much less fear of Soviet intervention. In a section of his July 20 memorandum captioned "Communist reaction to the expanded program," McNamara opined, "The Soviets can be expected to continue material assistance to North Vietnam and to lodge verbal complaints, but not to intervene otherwise." Still in pursuit of détente with the United States, Moscow in fact hewed pretty closely to this scenario, though providing more and better antiaircraft equipment (SAMs) than the Pentagon had apparently expected. Though American officials soon concluded that the Soviets were sending technicians to North Vietnam, including military personnel to train the PAVN to use this equipment, there was apparently little fear of their ever sending in military units. The possibility of a major Chinese intervention was, however, taken very seriously. This was evident in the same McNamara report: "At least as long as we do not invade North Vietnam, do not sink a Chinese ship and, most important, do not strike China—[the Chinese] will probably not send regular ground forces or aircraft into the war."[20]

In recent years the Johnson administration's unwillingness to go all out and invade North Vietnam has been criticized in some quarters. These observers have tended to brush aside the likelihood that the United States would then have confronted large numbers of Chinese combat forces, as well as the certainty that it would have faced some three hundred thousand well-trained North Vietnamese. The record shows not only that the administration was deeply concerned about so provoking Peking, but that in fact it had very good reason to be. During June and July 1965 quite palpable evidence emerged indicating that an American invasion of North Vietnam would be seen as such a threat to China's security as to precipitate the dispatch of Chinese combat troops across the border. Such a probability was accepted by U.S. intelligence, and clearly conditioned and constrained the Johnson administration's conduct of the war

With respect to the use of American air power too there was a widely shared belief in State, the CIA, and much of the Pentagon that an all-out bombing offensive against the North, particularly if extended to Hanoi and Haiphong, seriously risked China's intervention in the war. The certainty of this was not so great as in the case of an American invasion of the North, whether by land or by sea, but as the record now shows, this concern was also well founded.

Chinese actions as well as statements during 1965 should by themselves have constituted a sufficient warning. But because of still-vivid memories of China's unanticipated entry into the Korean War, they were paid even greater heed. To the hawkish minority who discounted any serious Chinese reaction, Johnson retorted, "That's what MacArthur thought." Undoubtedly it was because of the Korean experience that the warnings of Allen Whiting, who from 1962 to 1966 headed the Far East division of the State Department's Office of Intelligence and Research, were listened to with special attention. His book on China's entry into the Korean War *(China Crosses the Yalu)* was widely respected by many in the administration, including Dean Rusk, who during the first two years of that war had served as assistant secretary of state for Far Eastern affairs.

Chinese statements alone were enough to give Washington some pause. One example appeared in the *People's Daily* of June 1, 1965: "The United States, all the way from the other side of the ocean, has sent troops to China's neighboring country, threatening China's security daily. Why should socialist China not give all-out support to socialist, fraternal Vietnam?" More threatening was the reproduction in the July 23 *Peking Review* of the statement by the head of a visiting DRV delegation that "large numbers of the Chinese People's Liberation Army and Chinese youth have volunteered to go to Vietnam and take part in the fighting there."[21]

Much more persuasive, however, were the clearly visible actions of the Chinese. A retrospective intelligence summary from the CIA's Office of Current Intelligence concluded, "The Chinese Communists in June 1965 began deploying a limited number of military support units into North Vietnam (DRV). This marked the first time that Chinese troop units had been stationed outside China since 1958, when Peking withdrew the last of its troops from North Korea." The first such unit detected had appeared in the northeast coastal areas of the DRV in mid-June, "probably a special division-size organization which has a border defense/coastal security mission." Other Chinese forces being introduced were logistic support and antiaircraft units. Though, according to this report, there was no evidence that these included combat forces, the confirmed deployment of logistic support troops and available intelligence suggested that "the Chinese are taking some of the necessary steps to move more units rapidly into Vietnam should the war escalate."[22] These actions, as Whiting points out in his study, *The Chinese Calculus of Deterrence,* were meant not only to help the DRV, but also to send a clear message to the United States.

The build-up of the Chinese forces in North Vietnam was rapid, with some thirty-five thousand crossing the border by December and reaching nearly fifty thousand by the early spring of 1966. They remained in North Vietnam until the cessation of massive American bombing of the North above the twentieth parallel in March 1968, following which they began gradually to go back to China. (They did not, however, return to Vietnam when Nixon resumed heavy bombing in the spring of 1972.) Whiting's assessment is especially instructive. He notes that, though Peking could easily have done so, it made no effort to conceal the presence of these troops from American intelligence. They wore regular uniforms and there was no pretense of their being civilians or, as in the Korean War, "volunteers." The logical conclusion was that their presence "was deliberately made known in a manner so as to be credible without appearing provocative by publicly confronting the United States." Except for the previously mentioned coastal-defense unit, they were all antiaircraft, road and railroad engineering, and supply formations; none were ground combat units. Nevertheless, Whiting observes, they "did not remain in passive reserve but engaged in combat, inflicted losses, and suffered casualties. The anti-aircraft division fired on American planes and was bombed in return. Engineer and railroad construction battalions, the bulk of the deployment, worked to keep communications open despite repeated [air] attack." They provided Washington "with a highly credible token" of the Chinese army's determination to keep open transport lines from China (a railroad and a network of truck roads), "regardless of the attendant risks in escalation."[23]

If all this did not deter some American officials from toying with the idea of a U.S. invasion of North Vietnam, another feature of the Chinese presence there was well calculated to do so. This was their construction at Yen Bai, in the DRV's northwest, of a major base complex, readily visible to American planes. Incorporating a large runway and growing to nearly two hundred buildings, it was protected by antiaircraft guns mounted on rails and revetted into caves "that permitted a prompt response against American aircraft reported from radar stations to the south." Whiting writes, "The purpose of Yen Bai was ambiguous, perhaps intentionally so. It could become a DRV redoubt in the event of an invasion. . . . However, the Korean precedent raised the possibility of Yen Bai serving a massive Chinese intervention should this become necessary." He concludes:

> In sum, Peking's posture in the fall and winter of 1965 signaled a willingness to increase the risk of war with the United States by open statements, by unpublicized war preparation in south China [known to U.S. intelligence] and by the covert deployment of troops to the DRV for construction and

combat against American bombings. The signals were consistent and credible and, insofar as they addressed a willingness to help in the event of an American invasion, they communicated a feasible Chinese response, underlined by repeated allusions to a "Korea-type war." In addition, their implications of possible intervention to protect border communications and vital targets in Hanoi-Haiphong further cautioned against expanding United States raids beyond existing limits.[24]

The Johnson administration revealed very little about the Chinese presence in North Vietnam and its implications to either Congress or the U.S. public. Whiting states that "American officials couched their revelations in such a manner as to minimize attention and reaction in congressional and press circles where concern about a possible Sino-American war was acute." This "unobtrusive release of information," he declares, "avoided alarm while alerting Peking" that the administration "was aware of Chinese activity in the DRV and intended to abide by its implications."[25]

This more militant Chinese posture in North Vietnam, it should be emphasized, had already been noted in U.S. intelligence reports as early as mid-June 1965. Undoubtedly this tangible earnest of Chinese intent, then, was a factor in deterring U.S. officials who felt that the North Vietnamese armies alone could not have inflicted unacceptable casualties on American forces if they ventured to invade North Vietnam. The China factor conditioned and constrained American Vietnam policy throughout the remainder of the Johnson administration. It was clearly evident in McNamara's July 20 policy prescription and presumably influenced all those advisers with whom the president conferred in the weeks leading up to his decision at the end of July.

Prime Minister Quat's government was not well suited to recieve the large increases in U.S. ground combat forces for which the JCS and Westmoreland were now pressing. Whether or not Quat himself was opposed to this expansion, his political foundations were too insecure to permit him to accept it rapidly or unquestioningly. Besides his dependence on the United States, he was reliant on two incompatible elements—the Buddhists and the armed forces. And from the very outset he was under siege from most of the Catholic community, which regarded him as too close to the Buddhists and—quite unjustifiably, from the available evidence—likely to negotiate with the NLF. Catholic opposition was increased by the severe sentences his courts meted out on May 7 to many of those who had backed Pham Ngoc Thao and Lam Van Phat in their aborted February coup.[26]

As Khanh's appointee, Quat was in a weak position vis-à-vis much of the South Vietnamese military establishment; yet without at least the grudging support of its top officers, his position was untenable. At the same time, however, it was essential that he not alienate the Buddhist monks, whose backing had never been enthusiastic. Like Khanh in his days of ebbing power, Quat had to walk a narrow path between these political forces. If he himself was now prepared to accept the large influx of foreign troops that the U.S. military was urging, it was clear that the Buddhists were not, and that, if he became identified with this American policy, he would forfeit their support.[27]

Thus, although Quat had agreed to the U.S. bombing campaign, American officials found him reluctant to acquiesce in the introduction of large numbers of U.S. and South Korean ground combat forces. As early as March 24, Assistant Secretary of Defense John McNaughton had observed to McNamara that Quat was "queasy" about U.S. troop deployments, and Ambassador Taylor clearly sensed Quat's opposition when he counseled Washington that the United States could not count upon the prime minister's automatic acceptance of such plans. On May 19 Taylor warned the administration that the troops added under the president's April 21 decision had strained the limits of South Vietnam's absorptive capacity, and he urged a halt until there was a clear and undisputable necessity for an increase. By June 7, however, Taylor was persuaded of that necessity and supported Westmoreland's urgent request for more troops; but the absorptive capacity of South Vietnamese society had not changed, and any government that overlooked this invited a nationalistic backlash.[28]

Taylor's hopes that American troops could be concentrated in enclaves to minimize their visibility and contact with Vietnamese civilians did not square with Westmoreland's need for active patrolling in depth, and his later desire for "search and destroy" operations. The rapid Americanization of the war was a phenomenon that could not be disguised. One of Quat's deputy prime ministers, Tran Van Tuyen, found him preoccupied by the fear that, if more U.S. forces arrived, his government would appear to be "a lackey of the Americans." Taylor reported that "there is no doubt" that Quat and his ministers were "very sensitive to recurring charges that Americans are in control and that Washington is calling the shots."[29]

Quat had been a suitable partner in an American escalation restricted to an air war against the North and an enclave deployment of limited U.S. ground forces, but he was clearly not the man to head a government tied to a massive U.S. military presence and a visible Americanization of the war. During the early spring, it became increasingly evident that his own views and political require-ments were not sufficiently compatible to satisfy Westmoreland and the JCS, or, ultimately, Taylor. As early as April 12 the report of Army Chief of Staff Harold K. Johnson clearly took a very dim view of Quat's government. Although the U.S. mission gave no credence to Catholic accusations that Quat was seeking a neutral-ist solution, it was concerned about the weakness of his government and strongly faulted his unwillingness to take measures that risked alienating the Buddhist political leadership. In a meeting with Quat arranged by the embassy at the end of April, Henry Cabot Lodge (who in two months was scheduled to resume his post and replace Taylor) took Quat to task, advising him to "show more determi-nation and strength in taking all measures necessary to prosecute the war successfully" and to see to it that his government did not "waste its efforts looking ahead to ceasefire and negotiations." He criticized Quat for not arresting the Buddhist monk Quang Lien and breaking up his peace movement as decisively as he had done with those not led by Buddhists. "By not dealing forcefully with this and other issues," Lodge admonished, Quat had given the impression of "weakness and indecision."[30]

In his efforts to retain Buddhist support Quat worked through, and helped improve the position in Saigon of, General Nguyen Chanh Thi, the powerful commander of I Corps. He appointed Thi's candidate, Colonel Pham Van Lieu, as the new head of the national police, and Lieu quickly replaced over half of the precinct chiefs in Saigon—a move that enhanced Thi's power base and antagonized some other military leaders. Though a strong anticommunist, Thi had never been keen on accepting American advice and was himself too reliant on the Buddhist organization in the northern provinces of South Vietnam to suit U.S. military or civilian officials.[31] Quat's ties with Thi, then, clearly helped crystallize their initial misgivings about the prime minister's usefulness in promoting U.S. objectives.

Quat's position was further undermined by a series of reverses during April and May, which included: a mutiny in the navy; his potentially adroit but ultimately unsuccessful maneuvering to tighten his hold on the armed forces; persistent efforts of Catholic elements to discredit him on unproved charges of planning a deal with the NLF; and an aborted incipient coup effort against him on May 20 by an assortment of disgruntled Catholic and other elements led by Colonel Pham Ngoc Thao. Although there were accusations from some of Quat's Cabinet that U.S. officials encouraged this poorly organized coup effort, the available evidence is meager, with some of the key U.S. documents bearing on the coup attempt still classified or too heavily sanitized to permit a judgment. Thao's arrangements—however far advanced—were cut down by preclusive police actions. Some forty military and civilian leaders were arrested, but Thao escaped and again went into hiding. Finally tracked down by the police and shot on July 15, he died in custody the next day.[32]

Quat and the military leaders who supported him were, according to the CIA, "apparently using the [coup] incident to purge some elements considered anathema to the Buddhist hierarchy." These arrests further antagonized much of the Catholic community, which on May 27 presented a resolution to the chief of state, Phan Khac Suu, accusing Quat of collusion with neutralists and calling for his replacement. Following Pham Ngoc Thao's coup attempt, both Quat's position and his U.S. backing became noticeably weaker.[33]

The Saigon mission—with the concurrence of Taylor, Alexis Johnson, and Westmoreland—cabled Washington on June 5 that Quat's continuing inability to work out an accommodation among the competing political and military interests "had not been reassuring." If this persisted or the military situation continued to deteriorate, they stated, "we will have to assess the situation . . . and consider various alternatives, of which a more active military involve-

ment in the political situation may be best from both political and military
points of view." As *New York Times* correspondent Jack Langguth reported
from Saigon, the United States mission's efforts began "to shift from maintaining Dr. Quat in power to paving the way for an orderly transfer of the Premiership to someone else"—namely, the Saigon generals. Westmoreland was already
bypassing the prime minister, making clear that in committing American troops
he would not respond to Quat's requests, but only those coming from the Vietnamese military themselves. Three days after that move, on June 8, President
Johnson met Westmoreland's request and authorized him to commit U.S.
ground troops to combat if their assistance was requested by the South Vietnamese army.[34]

The ostensible factor precipitating Quat's ouster was his inability to secure
the military's backing in his dispute with the normally passive chief of state, Phan
Khac Suu, over the replacement of several Cabinet ministers. Quat was sufficiently innocent of the military's plans that on June 9 he put his fate in their
hands, requesting the Armed Forces Council's mediation. To his surprise it not
only refused to back him, but told him he would have to step down. Nor could
he find support from the U.S. mission. Any residue of confidence in Quat there
had undoubtedly been dissipated when he indicated that if he wasn't asked to stay
on he would turn over the office to General Thi. With the U.S. mission, most of
the military, and the Catholics ranged against Quat, and the Buddhists having
no strong reason for giving him the sort of wholehearted backing he needed to
stand any chance of contesting this alignment, he was out.[35]

The Saigon military were now firmly in the saddle—exercising power out in
front as well as behind the scenes. And there they would remain until the regime
collapsed ten years later. Their only potential challengers within the area controlled by Saigon were the Buddhists, but it was to be another year before the
monks had sufficient power to mount a major confrontation. And when they did,
the greatly augmented American presence stood firmly behind the South Vietnamese military leadership.

The new military government was headed by a council of ten senior officers
—the National Leadership Committee—led initially by a triumvirate of Generals
Nguyen Chanh Thi, Nguyen Van Thieu, and Nguyen Cao Ky. Of the three, Thi
was the most powerful, enjoying backing from the Buddhists as well as a considerable number of officers, and the committee voted that he serve as prime minister.
This was a prospect thoroughly alarming and repugnant to the U.S. mission. For
whatever reasons—or inducements—Colonel Pham Van Lieu, Thi's top adviser,
now persuaded him to turn down the offer and wait for a few months until
conditions were more propitious. To the great relief of the mission, Thi accepted
this advice; to his own bitter disappointment, he was never given a second chance.
The mission's first choice had been Thieu, but some U.S. officials, as well as a
number of senior ARVN officers felt, with justification, that if a Catholic were
to assume this office the Buddhists would be provoked into a reaction of equal,
or greater, force than the one that had ejected Prime Minister Huong five months

before. Not for two years, until the Buddhists' political power had been crushed, would it be possible for Thieu to become prime minister.

Of the three men who had sufficient support among senior officers to assume the office, Nguyen Cao Ky, a nominal Buddhist, was judged the safest bet, and, despite reservations (especially Taylor's) concerning his personal character and political abilities, the mission settled for him. With its blessing, Phan Khac Suu was ousted as chief of state, and Thieu took over this largely ceremonial position. But that general's real authority—now considerably augmented—was more accurately reflected by his position as chairman of the powerful military junta, the National Leadership Committee.[36]

Thieu, Ky, and Defense Minister Nguyen Huu Co were all regarded as "pro-American," and all supported a full-blown Americanization of the war.[37] The proponents of escalation now had in place the appropriate instrument through which to work toward the final phase of U.S. military intervention, in which the American military presence would soon heavily outweigh and overshadow the armed forces of the Saigon regime.

When the new military government officially took office on June 14, General Thieu, acting as its spokesman, made the sort of statement the Johnson administration had been waiting for. He promised a war government dedicated to unity, discipline, and victory over the Viet Cong. And the newly installed prime minister, Nguyen Cao Ky, announced a program for which American officials had long pressed—a full-scale mobilization of all able-bodied men into military service—and at the same time stated that he was doubling army pay. (The United States, of course, was paying the bill.) Emphasizing his opposition to any manifestation of neutralist sentiment, he went even further than the embassy wished when, a few days after his inauguration, he severed diplomatic relations with France. Nor was the embassy happy about his statement that the country needed a leadership like Adolf Hitler's, an assertion the Americans tried hard, if not altogether successfully, to get him to explain away. But no one could have been more cooperative with respect to the introduction of large U.S. combat forces. Ky repeatedly urged that additional troops be sent to Vietnam, soon requesting even more than were available.[38]

Regardless of its public stance, within the administration there was no longer any pretense that the United States was supporting a genuine political entity in South Vietnam. As Senator Mike Mansfield put it to the president at the time Quat was being displaced, "We are no longer dealing with anyone who represents anybody in a political sense. We are simply acting to prevent a collapse of the Vietnamese military forces which we pay for and supply. . . ." Ky and Thieu themselves acknowledged their lack of popular support, privately informing U.S. officials that under conditions of peace they would not be able to compete successfully with the NLF politically.[39]

The new heads of the Saigon establishment were equally aware of their military weakness vis-à-vis the NLF. On July 16 they urged that the total U.S. expeditionary force be brought up to two hundred thousand men, and Thieu assured McNamara that "If U.S. troops were to relieve ARVN to work actively on a pacification program," his regime "could demonstrate to the people" it was "capable and qualified to govern." Ky declared that their government "desired more U.S. troops not because the Vietnamese were unwilling to fight but that it would relieve ARVN for important pacification tasks," and since Saigon "did not like to lose terrain to the VC," that "US/allied forces [should] help hold terrain" while his government "reorganized the rear."[40] That was a fair description of the relationship that now developed between Washington and Saigon.

XIV

The Decision on Major
U.S. Ground Forces: Phase I

Lyndon Johnson was now faced with the fact that bombing the North, applying greater air power in the South, introducing third-country forces, and the installation of more amenable agents in Saigon were not sufficiently augmenting the ability of the current level of U.S. troops to effect even a holding operation against the tide of Viet Cong victories. Equally evident was that existing American political objectives in Vietnam could not be secured by negotiations. This left the administration with just two alternatives: it could lower its sights and settle for more modest political goals via negotiations; or, if it insisted on striving for its original objectives, it could send in a much larger number of U.S. ground combat units. The JCS, Taylor, Westmoreland, Ambassador-designate Lodge, and all of the president's top-level Washington advisers except George Ball and his unofficial adviser, Clark Clifford, supported the second course.[1]

Westmoreland's alarming dispatches undoubtedly encouraged proponents of a military solution to urge the introduction of additional U.S. combat forces. On June 7, 1965, he reported that over the previous weeks the balance of forces had shifted further to the NLF's favor. Even with only two out of its nine regiments and a similar proportion of separate battalions heavily engaged, its troops were inflicting heavy defeats on the ARVN. A week later he cabled that during the previous three weeks, these Viet Cong had mauled five ARVN battalions so badly they were "inoperative." ARVN desertion rates had become "inordinately high" and the fighting strength of many of its battalions "unacceptably low." The Viet Cong were "destroying battalions faster than they can be reconstituted and faster than they were planned to be organized under the buildup program."[2] And apart from the adverse trend in Viet Cong–ARVN force ratios, some PAVN troops had entered South Vietnam and were available to reinforce the Viet Cong. Elements of the PAVN's 325th Division, though not yet in combat, were now reportedly deployed in the Second Corps area, and some of the 304th Division were in the panhandle of Laos with a " 'doorstep' capability to reinforce the VC with sizeable forces."

In order to cope with this situation, Westmoreland cabled, "I see no course of action open to us except to reinforce our efforts in SVN with additional U.S. or third country forces as rapidly as practical during the critical weeks ahead." Additionally, he warned, plans should be developed "to deploy even greater forces, if and when required, to attain our objectives or counter enemy initiatives." But for the present he was asking for just two more marine-battalion landing teams (8,000 men), an air mobile division (21,000 men), a corps headquarters (1,500 men), an ROK regimental combat team, and the balance of an ROK army division (18,500 men), with supporting U.S. logistic personnel (1,500 men). These forces would not be expected to defeat the Viet Cong; their "basic purpose" would be simply "to convince the VC that they cannot win." In other words, Westmoreland was telling Johnson that to continue even a successful holding action urgently required 32,000 more U.S. ground troops and 18,500 more South Koreans, and might soon require more.

By highlighting the appalling weakness of America's Saigon ward, the fall of Quat's government and the roughly concurrent series of ARVN military disasters enhanced the credibility of Westmoreland's request for troops. An initially skeptical Ambassador Taylor soon confirmed the general's estimate of the seriousness of the situation and closed ranks with the JCS and McNamara in supporting that call. The president, however, held off. At an NSC meeting on June 11, he concluded, "We must delay and deter the North Vietnamese and Viet Cong as much as we can, and as simply as we can, without going all out. When we grant General Westmoreland's request, it means that we get in deeper and it is harder to get out. They think they are winning and we think they are. We must determine which course gives us the maximum protection at the least cost."[3]

On June 19 Johnson approved preparatory steps for the troops Westmoreland had requested, without, however, deciding to approve the request itself. On June 22, the JCS upped the ante by adding ten more battalions, and queried Westmoreland as to whether, with such an expansion of his original request (which would now total forty-four additional combat battalions and an overall number of about 180,000), he would be able to convince the enemy it could not win. Westmoreland replied that, though there was no evidence the Viet Cong and Hanoi would alter their plans regardless of U.S. actions over the next six months, such an increase should be enough to establish a favorable balance of power in that time. If the United States were to seize the initiative from the enemy, however, further increments would be required into 1966 and beyond.[4] So, just to prolong the holding action until the end of the year would now require more than double the 82,000 the president had authorized on April 21.

Johnson was clearly reluctant to approve this recommendation. Only after more than five weeks of vigorous and extended debate, during which almost all of his senior advisers came to support this increase, did he agree to authorize it. How was a clearly reluctant president prevailed upon to take this major step— one that set the course of U.S. Vietnam policy until almost the end of his administration and locked it into a major ground war, the war that the just-retired military leadership had argued so adamantly against? The recently disclosed record of this critical five weeks provides us with a relatively clear picture of the advice he received and his own reaction to it. It should destroy some stereotypes and significantly alter perceptions that have become embedded in the conventional wisdom.

There were two important phases in the process of shaping a decision concerning the JCS/Westmoreland recommendations. The first ran from June 7 to July 20, when Robert McNamara offered his final recommendation and laid much of the groundwork for the second and more critical phase, which involved the most intense discussions and lasted for a full additional week.

During the first phase, Maxwell Taylor's influence rapidly faded. His tour of duty as ambassador in Vietnam was scheduled to end in July. By early June it was known he would not be invited to serve a second year, and would soon be replaced by his predecessor, Henry Cabot Lodge. Because of his lame-duck status and failure to keep Saigon on an even political keel, Taylor's voice in Vietnam policy had become significantly weaker than that of the JCS, Westmoreland, McNamara, or McGeorge Bundy. Taylor had previously been regarded as more hawkish than these last two civilian advisers, but he now found them more ardent advocates than he of an increase of U.S. ground forces—with Rusk soon joining them—and also less restrained than he in their recommendations for using air power against the North. By June 5 Bundy was advocating "an occasional limited attack inside the Hanoi perimeter—probably in the Haiphong port area"—and was finally, a month later, joined in this view by an initially reluctant McNamara.[5]

McNamara had apparently given considerable support to Westmoreland's June 7 request but was at first unwilling to back the larger figure urged by the JCS four days later.[6] During this first phase of decision shaping, Rusk rather unobtrusively kept moving toward McNamara's slightly moderated support of the JCS/Westmoreland position; its two leading opponents were Senator Mike Mansfield and George Ball. McGeorge Bundy, from his position of proximity in the White House, appears to have interacted most frequently with the president and clearly spent considerable time in undercutting the arguments of Ball and Mansfield. Though initially critical of the size of McNamara's proposed escalation in ground forces, Bundy was evidently no less convinced that a greater military effort on the ground was the only feasible route.

Perceiving that the United States was no longer supporting even the semblance of a government in South Vietnam, but merely the Saigon military, Mansfield raised with the president fundamental questions as to the American purpose in Vietnam.[7] He declared that the administration had not made this clear. "What do we mean when we say we are going to stay in South Vietnam and for what specific United States or Vietnamese ends are we going to stay there? . . . And it is the crucial question because the answer to it should control the extent and nature of our military involvement in Vietnam." If the administration was planning to stay in Vietnam "until we or our Vietnamese military allies prevail everywhere south of the 17th parallel down to the smallest hamlet," then "we are talking in terms of years or decades, and upwards of a million American soldiers on the ground in South Vietnam, assuming that the Chinese do not become involved with men." If, instead, the administration had lowered its sights to "holding the military situation about where it is now," he contended that the estimate of three hundred thousand ascribed to McNamara was too low. Assuming the North Vietnamese army did not "move in full and open force across the 17th parallel," something "in the range of 500,000 might do it."

Or, Mansfield asked, was the administration planning to stay on in order "to hold a bargaining position for negotiations which might be expected to permit some reasonable choice—self-determination—on the part of the South Vietnamese people as to their political future" and provide "some protection for Vietnamese who have been on our side" with "some prospect of a bonafide peace based on eventual withdrawal of all foreign forces." In this case, he declared, American forces and the ARVN should be withdrawn from exposed positions in the interior to central bases and Saigon, and the United States should itself conduct a "powerful diplomatic peace offensive" and get to the conference table rather than waiting for signals from the other side. "Unless the situation is already totally hopeless," Mansfield estimated that such a course might be feasible, "at least for a year or so with something on the order of 100,000 or less United States combat forces on the ground backed by powerful naval and air units."

"The absence of a decision as to which of the above approaches really serves our national interests," Mansfield declared, "seems to me to be the crux of the difficulty. . . . But as things are now going, it is apparent that you are being advised to continue to take at least the second course." He was correct in that assumption and prescient in warning that "A course once set in motion . . . often develops its own momentum and rationale whatever the initial intentions."

It was presumably because of his concern about the questions raised by this senator for whom he had great respect that Lyndon Johnson now gave more scope and appeared to be unusually attentive to George Ball, his adviser with views closest to Mansfield's. Ball submitted to the president on June 18 a memorandum headed "Keeping the Power of Decision in the Vietnam Crisis." He sent it directly, through presidential assistant Bill Moyers, rather than routing it via Rusk, McGeorge Bundy, or McNamara. Moyers called him three days later to tell him Johnson had read it over the weekend and agreed in substance "with most of the memorandum—[with] one or two slight changes possibly."[8]

Ball recalled that he had been "sensitive to President Johnson's almost obsessive determination never to lose command" when he gave his memorandum its title and began it with the famous words of Ralph Waldo Emerson: "Things are in the saddle and ride mankind." It was not difficult to surmise that the "things" he saw in the saddle were the pressures for escalation. His central argument was that "the best formula for maintaining freedom of decision is (a) to limit our commitments in time and magnitude and (b) to establish specific time schedules for selection of optimal courses of action on the basis of preestablished criteria."

In raising its commitment from fifty to a hundred thousand or more men and deploying most of the increment in combat roles, the administration, he warned, was beginning a "new war—the United States *directly* against the Viet Cong." Even five hundred thousand American soldiers would not necessarily secure existing objectives: "Before we commit an endless flow of forces to South Vietnam we must have more evidence than we now have that our troops will not bog down in the jungles and the rice paddies—while we slowly blow the country to pieces."

Ball's doubts on this score hinged heavily on the record of France's unsuccessful efforts in Vietnam. "To be sure, the French were fighting a colonial war while we are fighting to stop aggression. But when we put enough Americans on the ground in South Vietnam to give the appearance of a white man's war, the distinction as to our ultimate purpose will have less and less practical effect. . . . Today no one can say for certain how many Vietnamese are for us or against us. . . . And our popularity will diminish even further as we are forced to indulge in more and more bombing, crop burning, etc."

Ever since 1961, Ball continued, "we have tended to underestimate the strength and staying power of the enemy. We have tended to overestimate the effectiveness of our sophisticated weapons under jungle conditions. . . . We have been unable to bring about the creation of a stable political base in Saigon. . . . The French had much the same experience." This did not mean that Americans could not succeed where the French had failed, for the United States had things going for it that the French did not have, "but we cannot yet be sure." Moreover, there was still insufficient evidence "that the South Vietnamese will stand up under the heightening pressure—or, in fact, that the Vietnamese people really have a strong will to fight after twenty years of struggle." And the more forces the United States deployed in South Vietnam, "the harder we shall find it to extricate without unacceptable costs if the war goes badly. With large forces committed, the failure to turn the tide will generate pressures to escalate. There will be domestic demands that we expand our air attacks on the North so as to destroy Hanoi and Haiphong. Yet if our air attacks threaten this total destruction of the North Vietnamese economy, Red China can hardly help but react. And our best Soviet experts do not believe that the Soviet Union could stand down in the event we became involved directly with China."

For all these reasons Ball urged the president to hold back from a major escalation and first test the results of "a *controlled commitment* for a *trial period* of three months" with "an aggregate level of 100,000 U.S. troops—but no more. . . . On the basis of our experiences during that trial period we will then appraise the costs and possibilities of waging a successful land war in South Vietnam and chart a course of action accordingly."

Then, "contingent upon a minimum level of stability in Saigon," if the president was "satisfied that United States military power *can* stop and throw back the Viet Cong without unacceptable United States losses, you are then in a position to decide on a longer-term aggressive strategy. . . ." But, "if the evidence accumulated during the test period *provides no reasonable assurance* that the United States can conduct a successful land war in South Vietnam without a vast protracted effort, you should seek means of limiting the American commitment and finding a political solution at a level below the total achievement of our declared objectives."

Ball concluded with the suggestion that the United States needed at least to plan for this second contingency.

> During the past weeks we have concentrated on seeking a political solution that would fully meet our stated objectives in South Vietnam. Such a solution will not be feasible so long as the Viet Cong are winning or believe they are winning. Since we cannot be sure that we will be able to beat the Viet Cong without unacceptable costs, we would be prudent to undertake an additional study of the political means to achieve less than a satisfactory solution—or, in other words, a solution involving concessions on our side as well as the Viet Cong.

Moyers's notes on the president's reaction to Ball's memorandum suggest that he agreed with its substance. Johnson commented:

> I don't think I should go over one hundred thousand but I think I should go to that number and explain it. I want George to work for the next ninety days—to work up what is going to happen after the monsoon season. I am not worried about running off in the wrong direction. I agreed that it might build up bit by bit. I told McNamara that I would not make a decision on this and not to assume that I am willing to go overboard on this. I ain't. If there's no alternative, the fellow who has the best program is the way it will probably go.[9]

So Ball was being invited to compete with McNamara, and he followed up over the next two weeks with complementary memoranda for the president.[10] It was soon evident, however, that he had to compete with McGeorge Bundy as well.

The impact of Ball's arguments, especially those developed in the memorandum described above, was sufficient to inspire Bundy to prepare a nine-page memorandum that he presented to the president on June 30, captioned "France in Vietnam, 1954, and the U.S. in Vietnam, 1965—A Useful Analogy?" The thrust of Bundy's brief was that there was no fundamental analogue and that the president should not be discouraged by Ball's argument from continuing to use U.S. military power to achieve the administration's objectives. In referring to the regime then led by Ky and Thieu, which American soldiers were called upon to save, Bundy credited it with attributes these two Vietnamese would have found astonishing. Their regime, he explained to the president, was involved in a process of "social and political revolution." (Johnson was not informed that, as later recounted by some of Bundy's own assistants, in the drafting of the program for Ky's "New Society" that durable operative Edward Lansdale "did some of the ghost writing.")[11]

Bundy then reassured the president as to the public's backing of his current Vietnam policies, declaring that, whereas the French had lacked the will in 1954 to continue their fight in Vietnam, there was general support among Americans for the present U.S. course. Despite considerable concern about various aspects of the war in some quarters, he told him, "in general, the public appears unenthusiastic but reconciled to our role in this conflict." The latest Harris poll, he pointed out, had shown that 62 percent of the public expressed "overall approval of the President's handling of the Vietnam crisis" and of those having an opinion "almost 80 percent approve of the bombing and over 60% believe we should send more troops." He concluded, "At home we remain politically strong and, in general, politically united. Options, both military and political, remain to us that were no longer available to the French."

On July 1 the president received four memoranda for discussion at a meeting the following day. These were described in Bundy's covering memorandum as: "Dean Rusk's four-page statement of the basic issues"; "George Ball's paper on a compromise solution"; "Bob McNamara's recommendation for expanded military action"; and "my brother Bill's program offering a middle course for the next two months."[12] The meeting, Bundy advised, would not actually make decisions —which he said should be made in about ten days—but would be for "sharpening the issues you want studied." He added, "My hunch is that you will want to listen hard to George Ball and then reject his proposal. Discussion could then move to the narrower choice between my brother's course and McNamara's."

Evidently pushing for his brother's proposal, Bundy observed, "The second-level men in both State and Defense are not optimistic about future prospects in Vietnam and are therefore very reluctant to see us move to a 44 battalion force with a call-up of reserves. So they would like to cluster around the middle course suggested by my brother. They would like to see what happens this summer before getting much deeper in."

Rusk, in his July 1 memorandum, had avoided identifying himself with any particular military proposal, contenting himself with warning against attacking targets in the Hanoi-Haiphong area "for the present," and, as McGeorge Bundy had said, discussing the issues involved—and in familiar terms. The secretary's assessment of prospects was closer to utopian than that of any other senior adviser. That American pacification efforts were falling behind did not mean that the Viet Cong were winning. They had "the power to disrupt, but they are not capable of occupying and organizing the country or any major part of it. The Viet Cong can be denied a victory, even if complete pacification will be a long and tortuous prospect." Even further from reality was Rusk's belief that the United States had the capacity to improve the performance of the Saigon government. "We must use the leverage of the U.S. presence and assistance to insist that the

South Vietnamese leaders declare a moratorium on their bickering and knuckle down to the increased effort needed to defeat the Viet Cong. They must be told bluntly that they cannot take us for granted but must earn our help by their performance."

Ball's memorandum did have real import for a president called upon to react to the proponents of escalation. He urged that U.S. force levels be held at the existing presidential authorization of fifteen combat battalions and a total of seventy-two thousand men, with their mission restricted to base security and as a reserve to support the ARVN in situations where Westmoreland regarded this as necessary.

> No one can assure you that we can beat the Viet Cong or even force them to the conference table on our terms no matter how many thousand *white foreign* (US) troops we deploy. . . . Once we suffer large casualties we will have started a well-nigh irreversible process. Our involvement will be so great that we cannot—without national humiliation—stop short of achiev-ing our complete objectives. *Of the two possibilities, I think humiliation would be more likely than the achievement of our objectives—even after we had paid terrible costs.* [13]

McNamara's memorandum was the clear precursor of the one he would submit three weeks later, following another visit to South Vietnam.[14] The central U.S. political objective was unchanged—maintenance of a separate, noncommu-nist southern state. But this was to be achieved by a less ambitious military objective than before. Creation of the military conditions for attaining this politi-cal settlement would no longer require the enemy's defeat, but merely the demon-stration that "the odds are against their winning." However, under existing conditions, he pointed out, "the chances of achieving this are small—and the VC are winning now—largely because the ratio of guerrilla to anti-guerrilla forces is unfavorable to the government." In facing this situation there were just three options open to the United States: "(1) Cut our losses and withdraw under the best conditions that can be arranged; (2) continue at about the present level, with US forces limited to, say, 75,000, holding on and playing for the breaks while recognizing that our position will probably grow weaker; or (3) expand substan-tially the US military pressure against the Viet Cong in the South and the North Vietnamese in the North and at the same time launch a vigorous effort on the political side to get negotiations started."

Opting for the third alternative, McNamara then proceeded to urge an increase of U.S. and ARVN military strength to the level required "to counter current and likely VC ground strength" and prove to the Viet Cong that it could not win. Assuming that ARVN strength held its own, U.S./third-country combat strength should be brought to forty-four battalions within the next few months. In addition, he endorsed Westmoreland's request for thirteen more U.S. helicop-ter companies, five U.S. Chinook (helicopter) platoons, and an unspecified number of "additional US artillery batteries and engineers to reinforce ARVN divisions and corps." To supply these U.S. forces it would be necessary to "call up selected [U.S.] reserve forces (approximately 100,000 men)" and "extend tours of duty in all Services."

Over and above this, the air war was to be sharply stepped up both in the South and the North, with much heavier reliance on B-52s (whose carpet-bombing technique, it should be noted, precluded anything approaching "precision bombing"). These were to carry out eight hundred sorties per month "in strikes against VC havens" in the South and were to be heavily employed against the North, where the object was to "destroy the war-making supplies and facilities . . . wherever they may be located," including the railroad yards of Hanoi. Of sixty-four new targets to be struck in the North, about half, including the two railroad yards in the city of Hanoi, were regarded as "suitable for B-52 attack." (One wonders what statistics McNamara was relying on when he gave the assurance that only in five of the sixty-four new targets would the bombing be "likely to lead to more than 100 civilian casualties.") And in addition to destroying all rail and highway bridges leading from China to Hanoi, the United States was to undertake the highly controversial action of mining harbors in the North.

It was Westmoreland's belief, McNamara advised, that these measures together, if all taken on schedule, "should reestablish the military balance by the end of December," but would "not per se cause the enemy to back off."

While these military moves were being taken, McNamara called for the United States to carry out what he termed "expanded political moves." The cast to his arguments suggests that he may have been as much concerned with the manipulation of public opinion in the United States and among its allies as in any search for a negotiated settlement. The series of "political initiatives" that Washington was to take would be "in order (a) to open a dialogue with Hanoi, Peking and the VC looking toward a settlement in Vietnam, (b) to keep the Soviet Union from deepening its military involvement and support of North Vietnam until the time when settlement can be reached, and (c) to cement the support for US policy by the US public, allies and friends, and to keep international opposition at a manageable level. While our approaches may be rebuffed until the tide begins to turn they nevertheless should be made."

Prominent among the political initiatives were: (1) a high-level representative in contact with Moscow to discuss U.S. intentions and "desire to find common ground to work with them rather than come into conflict" and "press the Soviets to avoid any deeper involvement"; (2) "after consultation with the GVN [we] should initiate contacts with the Liberation Front and North Vietnam, making clear a readiness to discuss ways and means of achieving a settlement in Vietnam"; (3) "contact with the Chinese to set forth the US position including our limited objective and the dangers to China of continuation of the war" and to "press the Chinese to bring the aggression against the South to an end"; (4) United Nations: "As a prelude to expansion of our military effort, we should consider once more putting before the UN the Vietnam question for discussion with Chicoms and North Vietnamese present. They will almost surely refuse to attend and will provide us with a better position for expanding military action; but if they accept we will have the prospect of negotiations without having stopped our bombing." These political initiatives, he held, "are likely to be successful in the early stages only to demonstrate US good faith: they will pay off toward an actual settlement only after the tide begins to turn (unless we lower our sights substantially)."

McNamara acknowledged there were some risks involved in the military course he, Westmoreland, and the JCS were now advocating. "Increased US bombing of Vietnam, including targets in Hanoi and Haiphong, SAM sites and airfields, and mining of North Vietnamese harbors, might oblige the Soviet Union to enter the contest more actively with volunteers and aircraft. This might result in minor encounters between US and Soviet personnel." As for China, "So long as no US or GVN troops invade North Vietnam and so long as no US or GVN aircraft attack Chinese territory, the Chinese probably will not send regular ground forces or aircraft into the war. However, the possibility of a more active Soviet involvement in North Vietnam might precipitate a Chinese introduction of land forces probably dubbed volunteers [as in Korea] to preclude the Soviets' taking a pre-eminent position in North Vietnam."

North Vietnam, McNamara predicted, would "not move towards the nego-tiating table until the tide begins to turn in the south," but when that happened "they may seek to counter it by sending large numbers of men into South Vietnam." He was even less confident about what the NLF might do. They might continue to fight "almost indefinitely," and "a key question on the political side is whether any arrangement acceptable to us would be acceptable to the VC."

"The test of endurance may be as much in the United States as in Vietnam," McNamara admonished, but he nevertheless assured that "Even though casual-ties will increase and the war will continue for some time, the United States public will support this course of action because it is a combined military-political program designed and likely to bring about a favorable solution to the Vietnam problem."

What lay behind McNamara's bellicose brief? And how did he arrive at a set of conclusions that seemed so to lack inner logic? The file made available to the staff he later selected to assemble and edit the *Pentagon Papers* is singularly bare of documents relating to this,[15] and very little pertinent material has subsequently been released. To gain some further insight into these questions we are obliged, therefore, to rely heavily on the views of John McNaughton, the person on whom McNamara depended most in developing his approach to Vietnam during this period.

The draft McNaughton prepared for McNamara on July 13 (with an eyes-only copy to McGeorge Bundy) is remarkably consistent with the secretary's July 1 proposals and a clear precursor to his more formal July 20 memorandum for the president—with the basic ideas similar and the actual wording of some important passages precisely the same.[16] The significance of the McNaughton draft lies in the fascinating candor with which it describes some of the thinking that lay behind these proposals.

McNaughton's statistical approach to Vietnam was very much in harmony with McNamara's; and his definition of U.S. aims remained very close to what he had posited four months before:

70% – To preserve our national honor as a guarantor (and the reciprocal: to avoid a show-case success for Communist 'wars of liberation'?)

20% – To keep SVN (and their adjacent) territory from hostile expansive [sic] hands

10% – To "answer the call of a friend," to help him enjoy a better life.

Also – To emerge from crisis without unacceptable taint from the methods used.

Using almost exactly the same words as emerged in McNamara's July 20 memorandum, McNaughton described the situation obtaining in Vietnam, then went on to liken a "win" outcome there to what had occurred in counterinsurgency efforts in Malaya and the Philippines; a "compromise" outcome to the settlements arrived at in Vietnam in 1954 and Laos in 1962 (a coalition government, including the communists); and U.S. capitulation to what had happened to France in Algeria. He assessed the likelihood of these various outcomes in terms of five options involving varying inputs of U.S. forces.

All these options open to the United States, in McNaughton's view, assumed "maximum ingenuity on the all-important political side"—a tall order in itself. In presenting his probabilities he arranged outcomes by percentage in three columns: the first "success," the second "inconclusiveness," and the third "collapse."

Outcome/Effort Combinations	Probabilities of Success/Inconclusiveness/Collapse		
	By 1966	By 1967	By 1968
"win" with 200–400,000+ U.S.	20/70/70	40/45/15	50/30/20
"win" with 75,000 U.S.	10/70/20	20/50/30	30/30/40
"compromise" with 200–400,000 U.S.	40/50/10	60/25/15	70/10/20
"compromise" with 75,000 U.S.	20/60/20	30/40/30	40/20/40
"capitulate & withdraw"	0/0/100	0/0/100	0/0/100

"A collapse at a 75,000 level," he concluded, would probably be worse than "an inconclusive situation at a 200,000–400,000+ level."

On the basis of these expectations, McNaughton called for expanding the U.S. military presence to the forty-four battalions that the JCS had requested and recommended a call-up of selected reserves and an extension of the duty tour of those already in the armed forces. He ended with a prognosis that was the same as in McNamara's memorandum of a week later, though with a little more detail. With respect to the odds he had provided, he concluded that "even if 'success' [were achieved], it is not obvious how we will be able to disengage our forces from South Vietnam. It is unlikely that a formal agreement good enough for the purpose could possibly be negotiated—because the arrangement can reflect little more than the power situation. Most likely in the case of 'success' is a settling down into a 'compromise'-like situation . . . with a large number—perhaps 2 divisions—of US forces required to stay for a period of years. During that period of time, any number of things can change the picture beyond prediction."

There is no indication as to whether McNaughton's assessment of probabilities was ever communicated to Lyndon Johnson. If it had been, it would probably have given him greater pause and stronger reservations as to the course of action McNamara was recommending to him.

The day before McNamara had submitted his July 1 recommendations, McGeorge Bundy had sent him a memorandum strongly protesting the extent and rapidity of his proposed escalation and voicing particular concern over the mining of North Vietnamese ports.[17] Presumably after discussing it with McNamara, Bundy told the president in his own July 1 memorandum that, though the JCS wanted to go after even more targets in the Hanoi area than McNamara, he believed McNamara "would readily accept advice to tone down those of his recommendations which move rapidly against Hanoi by bombing and blockade." Dean Rusk, he said, "leans toward the McNamara program, adjusted downward in this same way." Reflecting McNamara's pressure for the prompt deployment of a U.S. air mobile division, where a decision was being pressed for in about ten days, Bundy told the president that a decision should be made between the course advocated by William Bundy and McNamara's slightly moderated JCS proposal (incorporating the recommendation for the urgently requested air mobile division).

In the meantime, McGeorge Bundy advised the president, "I think you may want to have pretty tight and hard analyses of some disputed questions like the following":

　　1. What are the chances of our getting into a white man's war with all the brown men against us or apathetic?
　　2. How much of the McNamara planning would be on a contingency basis with no decision until August or September?

3. What would a really full political and public relations campaign look like in both the Bundy option and the McNamara option?

4. What is the upper limit of our liability if we now go to 44 battalions?

5. Can we frame this program in such a way as to keep very clear our own determination to keep the war limited? (This is another way of stating question 4.)

6. Can we get a cold, hard look at the question whether the current economic and military situation in Vietnam is so very bad that it may come apart even before this program gets into action? (I don't believe that it is that bad, but no one seems to be really sure of the facts today.)

Though nothing in the available record indicates that these questions received the thoughtful attention they merited—beyond that contained in the memoranda Ball and Mansfield had sent the president—William Bundy's memorandum "A 'Middle' Course of Action in South Vietnam" was attuned to some of the concerns they raised. And it was this option that his brother was now recommending to the president. It was a "middle" way largely with respect to McNamara's recommendations, meeting it about halfway, but it was 100 percent opposed to Ball's call for negotiating a compromise settlement.

In effect, William Bundy's memorandum called for a two-month deferment of a decision on both increases in ground-force deployment in the South and an expansion of the air war against the North, while planning for this course was readied so that it could then be followed if the president so elected. "In essence," he stated, "this is a program to *hold on* for the next two months, and *to test* the military effectiveness of US combat forces and the reaction of the Vietnamese army and people to the increasing US role."

American combat strength during this period would be limited to eighteen battalions and an overall U.S. strength of about eighty-five thousand. The administration would "prepare to meet the possible military need for 44 combat battalions by the end of the year, but defer any decision on deploying these troops and on calling up major reserve units." As for the air mobile division to which the JCS had assigned such a high priority, it was to be alerted so that it "*could* be sent to South Vietnam three weeks after decision at any time, but *not* decide now that it will in fact be sent." Domestic political reaction was also a concern. "While military effectiveness is the basic reason for holding at about 85,000, we must also reckon the Congressional and public opinion problems of embarking *now* on what might appear *clearly* to be an open-ended ground commitment."

There should be "maximum air action in the South, including B-52's," but existing limitations on air strikes against the North were to be maintained. A decision on "mining North Vietnamese harbors and/or cutting the rail and railroad lines from China to North Vietnam" should be deferred "for the mining would tend to throw North Vietnam into the arms of Communist China and diminish Soviet influence," while the attempt to cut the roads and railroads was "useful added pressure" that should be held in reserve. Bombing of the urban areas of Hanoi and Haiphong was to be avoided, because hitting them "would not *now* lead Hanoi to give in but might on the contrary toughen it" and "would almost certainly lose us the support of such key governments as the UK and Japan. Above all, it would probably intensify the Soviet commitment and probably remove the chance of the Soviets exerting restraint in the fall." But "negotiating concessions in any form" were to be rejected. The program provided for "the possibility of discreet contacts with Hanoi, and cut-out contacts (*not* identified with the US) with the Liberation Front." These, however, "would not be with any serious negotiations expectations, but to open channels and soften both up by playing on Hanoi's fear of Peking and the possible Liberation Front fear of being totally under Hanoi's domination."

Worried by the considerable range of conflicting advice from his regular advisers, Johnson now turned to fresh counsel—men of national stature seasoned by positions of earlier stewardship in the conduct of American foreign policy. This distinguished group of about fifteen discussed several foreign-policy issues of which Vietnam was the foremost. They were divided into three panels, each of which received a briefing on July 7, met separately the next day in the three panels during the morning and lunch, and then assembled together for a joint afternoon discussion at the end of which they presented their conclusions to the president. The Vietnam panel included General Omar Bradley, former chairman of the JCS; Roswell Gilpatric, former deputy secretary of defense; Dr. George Kistiakowsky, former presidential science adviser; Arthur Larson, former director of the U.S. Information Agency; and John J. McCloy, former high commissioner to Germany and assistant secretary of war during World War II. After reading what William Bundy refers to as "papers covering the situation and the key questions on which their advice was sought," they met with him, McNamara, Rusk, and Ambassador to the Soviet Union Llewellyn Thompson.[18] Stating the "government position" was a paper drafted by William Bundy that he describes as "pretty close to the consensus viewpoint [among the president's advisers], George Ball excepted." (Ball was engaged as the administration's principal spokesman before a separate panel dealing with Europe, and was able to make only a brief oral statement on Vietnam to the full group when the three panels assembled together during the final hours.)

The Vietnam panel was asked three questions:

A. If it is accepted that a Communist takeover in South Vietnam would lead fairly rapidly at least to the accommodation of the rest of Southeast Asia to the Chinese Communists, and possibly to outright Communist Chinese and North Vietnamese control of mainland countries, how serious would this basically be for US security?

B. To what extent would a Communist takeover in South Vietnam, in the face of the US commitment, affect US credibility and standing in holding to the key areas such as Northeast Asia, the Philippines, India, and even Europe?

C. To what extent would a "compromise" settlement that preserved South Vietnam for a time but that involved risks of eventual Communist takeover by political means, have the same consequences?

Bundy states that the panel's reaction was "clear and unmistakeable," and that "with the exception of Arthur Larson, the members felt that the stakes were very high indeed . . ., they thought that not only would Thailand fall under Chinese sway, but that the effects in Japan, India, and even Europe could be most serious. In Europe, deGaulle would then find many takers for his argument that the US could not now be counted on to defend Europe. . . . The Panel accepted both the argument that Vietnam was a test case of 'wars of national liberation' and the argument that a US defeat would lead to widespread questioning whether US commitments could be relied on." "What was important," he recalls, was that "the Panel thought that standing firm in Vietnam was of very great importance to American interests and to the independence of many nations and areas" and "felt that there should be no question of making whatever combat force increases were required."

Bundy observes that this meeting had not been envisaged as any rubber-stamp exercise, and that although the president "probably expected that *most* of the Panel would be *generally* in favor of a firm policy," he found that "*almost all* were *solidly* of this view, and this must have had a distinct impact on his personal and private deliberations. There can be no doubt that a large strand in the President's make-up [was] that he should not fall short of the standards set by those who had played leading parts in World War II and throughout the period of American successes in the Cold War. Now a fair sample of these men, or the American 'Genro' if you will, had advised him to see this one through."

With this additional advice before him, Lyndon Johnson still held back from any final decision on major new ground-force deployments. On July 10 he agreed to the dispatch of 10,400 logistic and support troops (due to arrive August 15) "to support current force levels and to receive the airmobile division, *if deployed*" [emphasis added].[19] But he would not go further before he had sent McNamara back to Vietnam to confer with Taylor and Westmoreland and make another assessment of the condition of the Saigon government and U.S. military requirements, and until he then had an opportunity for extensive discussion of these findings with his other senior advisers.

McNamara and an entourage that included General Wheeler and Ambassador-designate Lodge spent July 16 with Taylor and Westmoreland in extensive discussions with General Thieu and Ky. Thieu affirmed that "at least half the manpower" in South Vietnam was controlled by the Viet Cong and requested that, over and above the contemplated forty-four battalions, an additional U.S. infantry division be sent there to bring U.S. forces up to approximately two hundred thousand. And it was then that he declared that with these U.S. troops relieving the ARVN his government "could demonstrate to the people that it is capable and qualified to govern," and Ky added that U.S. forces should "help hold terrain while the GVN 'reorganized the rear.' "[20]

No further accounts of McNamara's discussions in Saigon are available. It is clear, however, that when the secretary left Washington on July 15, the president had not yet made a decision with regard to his July 1 recommendations, and did not do so until five or six days after McNamara returned on July 20 with his revised proposals.[21]

This is evident from the very explicit consecutive paragraphs in McGeorge Bundy's memorandum to the president of the evening of July 24:

> . . . on June 11, after discussions with MACV and Ambassador Taylor, the Joint Chiefs recommended additional deployments to a total of 116,000. The most important element in this recommendation was the airmobile division. On June 19 you gave approval to the necessary preparatory steps for these deployments, without deciding on deployment itself.
>
> On July 2, the Joint Chiefs produced a further recommendation for a total troop strength of 179,000, again in coordination with MACV and Ambassador Taylor. Before approving this recommendation, you sent McNamara to Vietnam. With marginal modifications, it is this recommendation which is now before you for decision.[22]

In his July 20 memorandum to the president, McNamara painted a stark but accurate picture of Saigon's political and military deterioration—a picture well suited to win support for the dispatch of additional U.S. ground forces to Vietnam. "The situation in South Vietnam is worse than a year ago (when it was worse than a year before that)," he reported. Since June 1, the GVN had been forced to abandon six district capitals, with only one having been retaken; the government was able to provide security to "fewer and fewer people in less and less territory"; cities and towns were being isolated, and "a hard VC push was on" to dismember the nation and maul the army."[23]

The overall ratio of Saigon to Viet Cong military forces, McNamara continued, had dropped to "only a little better than 3-to-1, and in combat battalions little better than 1.5-to-1. Some ARVN units have been mauled; many are under-strength [in fact averaging less than 54 percent of strength in infantry and Ranger battalions][24] and therefore 'conservative.' Desertions are at a high rate, and the force build-up has slipped badly." Despite having also sustained high casualties, the Viet Cong "seem to be able to replace their losses" and they now controlled "a manpower pool of 500,000 to 1 million fighting-age men." In the face of this, Saigon's forces were "not capable of successfully resisting the VC initiatives without more active assistance from more US/third country ground forces than those thus far committed. . . . Early commitment of additional US/third country forces in sufficient quantity . . . should stave off GVN defeat."

As for the air war against the North, he reported, "There are no signs that we have throttled the inflow of supplies for the VC or can throttle the flow while their material needs are as low as they are. . . . Nor have our air attacks in North Vietnam produced tangible evidence of willingness on the part of Hanoi to come to the conference table in a reasonable mood."

McNamara offered the president the same three limited options of three weeks before, once again couched in language that could lead to only one conclusion. But to the first—"Cut our losses and withdraw under best conditions that can be arranged"—he now added, "almost certainly conditions humiliating the United States and very damaging to our future effectiveness on the world scene." The wording of the second option—continuing at the present level—was exactly the same as on July 1; the third option—for "substantially" expanding the U.S. military input, and again the one he was recommending—stood unchanged except that McNamara now stipulated it was something to be undertaken "promptly" and added the sentence "This alternative would stave off defeat in the short run and offer a good chance of producing a favorable settlement in the longer run; at the same time it would imply a commitment to see a fighting war clear through at considerable cost in casualties and material and would make any later decision to withdraw even more difficult and even more costly than would be the case today."

This third alternative, McNamara stated, was his recommendation "as the course of action involving the best odds of the best outcome with the most acceptable cost to the U.S." He held to his proposal for a concurrent political effort "to lay the groundwork for a favorable outcome by clarifying our objectives and establishing channels of communication," but acknowledged that the U.S. embassy did not support this. "Ambassador Lodge states 'any further initiative by us now (before we are strong) would simply harden the Communist resolve not to stop fighting.' Ambassadors Taylor and [Alexis] Johnson would maintain discreet contacts with the Soviets, but otherwise agree with Ambassador Lodge."

The expanded American forces provided under McNamara's recommended option were to be used aggressively "to take the offensive—to take and hold the initiative . . . keeping the enemy at a disadvantage, maintaining a tempo such as to deny them time to recuperate or regain their balance, and pressing the fight against VC/DRV main force units in South Vietnam to run them to ground and destroy them." There would be "increased use of air in-country, including B-52s night and day to harass VC in their havens." Air strikes against North Vietnam would gradually be increased from the existing level of twenty-five hundred sorties per month to four thousand or more. McNamara acknowledged that by the end of the year this program might result in a rise in the level of U.S. soldiers killed in action to "the vicinity of 500 a month," but assured the president that the U.S. public could be counted on to support it.

The third option was designed to lead to a "favorable outcome" that would encompass a sequence of what McNamara termed "nine fundamental elements":

a) VC stop attacks and drastically reduce incidents of terror and sabotage;

b) DRV reduces infiltration to a trickle, with some reasonably reliable
method of our obtaining confirmation of this fact;

c) US/GVN stop bombing North Vietnam;

d) GVN stays independent (hopefully pro-US but possibly neutral)

e) GVN exercises governmental functions over substantially all of South
Vietnam;

f) Communists quiescent in Laos and Thailand;

g) DRV withdraws PAVN forces and other North Vietnamese infiltrators (not regroupees) from South Vietnam;

h) VC/NLF transform from a military to a purely political organization;

i) US combat forces (not advisors or AID) withdraw.

These nine fundamentals, McNamara explained, could evolve with or without an express agreement and, except for a cease-fire, were more likely to evolve
without than with one.[25] "We do not need now to address the question whether
ultimately we would settle for less than the nine fundamentals; because deployment of the forces recommended . . . is prerequisite to the achievement of *any*
acceptable settlement, and a decision can be made later, when bargaining becomes
a reality, whether to compromise in any particular."

Thus, no settlement acceptable to the United States could be negotiated until
after the United States had applied the additional military force McNamara was
proposing. The package he now recommended to the president was endorsed by
Taylor, Lodge, Alexis Johnson, Admiral Sharp, General Wheeler, and General
Westmoreland. It provided for an increase of thirty-four combat battalions by
October—or forty-three of them if the South Koreans were unable promptly to
provide an expected nine (the Australians had already supplied one battalion).
These, plus increases in helicopter lift, air squadrons, advisory personnel, etc.,
would bring total U.S. personnel in Vietnam to 175,000, or 200,000 if the South
Koreans did not send the nine additional battalions. He warned, however, that
additional troops might soon be required. "It should be understood that the
deployment of more men (perhaps 100,000) may be necessary in early 1966, and
that the deployment of additional forces thereafter is possible but will depend on
developments."

To carry out this program, McNamara recommended the call-up of approximately 235,000 men in the U.S. Reserve and National Guard and an increase in
the regular armed forces by approximately 375,000. The latter would necessitate
expanding the draft and extending tours of duty of men already in the service.
By mid-1966 these measures would together yield "approximately 600,000 additional men (approximately 63 additional maneuver [combat] battalions) as protection against contingencies."

McNamara's conclusion demonstrated his recognition that all this might not
in the long run end up as more than an extended holding action: "It should be

recognized also that, even in 'success' it is not obvious how we will be able to disengage our forces in Vietnam. It is unlikely that a formal agreement good enough for the purpose could possibly be negotiated—because the arrangements can reflect little more than the power situation. A fairly large number of US (or perhaps 'international') forces may be required to stay in Vietnam."

It is remarkable that in his next and concluding sentence McNamara was able to give this soothing assurance: "The overall evaluation is that the course of action recommended in this memorandum—if the military and political moves are properly integrated and executed with continuing vigor and visible determination—stands a good chance of achieving an acceptable outcome within a reasonable time in Vietnam."

With that advice before him, the president embarked upon a week of the most intensive discussions with his advisers he had ever conducted.

XV

The Decision on Major
U.S. Ground Forces: Phase II

Intense discussions between Lyndon Johnson and his advisers during the last week of July 1965 resulted in the administration's second major escalatory step —the decision to commit large numbers of U.S. ground combat forces to South Vietnam. Once taken, this action led quickly to the war's Americanization, which, as George Ball had predicted, took on a momentum of its own, involving ever-increasing numbers of men, until the president finally called a halt at more than half a million American troops.

The critical nature of the decision calls for a close scrutiny of the process by which it was reached. As Neil Sheehan has noted, the *Pentagon Papers* analyst who dealt with it "apparently did not have access to White House memoranda, so he is able to give only a sketchy account of Mr. Johnson's role." Fortunately, however, during the last few years, declassification of pertinent documents has substantially compensated for the scanty account available in the *Papers.*[1]

The record now available for this crucial week challenges the view that during this shaping of Vietnam policy Johnson decisively dominated a group of intimidated, acquiescent advisers. It also casts some doubt on the allegation that, before he participated in these discussions, the president had already made up his mind in favor of a substantial increase in U.S. ground forces. Like George Ball, both McGeorge Bundy and William Bundy believe that by July 21 Johnson was inclining toward McNamara's recommendation but had not yet made up his mind. In later reconstructing the discussions of that day, William Bundy observes that this was "no charade" and that as late as July 24 the president "was still framing his decision and retaining the option to reverse" the gathering consensus for McNamara's position. Ball thought that Johnson was becoming "a prisoner of the momentum generated by a monolithic body of senior advisers," but saw him as still very much open to consideration of alternative courses and deeply desirous of exploring them.[2] Chester Cooper, who himself believes that Johnson had made up his mind by July 21, has nicely summed up the lack of agreement still surrounding this question:

Many government officials close to the developments of that week are convinced that the image of a soul-searching and agonizing examination of alternatives, including the option of cutting our losses and pulling out, was an accurate reflection of what actually occurred. They believe if one or two senior participants had joined George Ball in opposing new troop deployments, the President might have been induced to think through the issue of whether more troops should be sent, rather than simply worrying about how many. There are others who feel the President almost certainly knew by the end of the first day's discussion, and perhaps even before the meeting started, what he planned to do, but it suited his purpose and his style to give the impression that he was engaging in a lengthy and thorough appraisal in which all points of view were advanced and weighed. To back up their position they maintain the decision had been reached earlier by McNamara when he conferred with senior military officers in Honolulu on his way home from Vietnam.[3]

Because of these conflicting views, it is best to let the now considerably enlarged record speak for itself.

The first and apparently most crucial of the week's meetings occurred on July 21. There are three records of this: an unsigned account from the NSC files rendered in abbreviated, semiverbatim style; the slightly less comprehensive but apparently verbatim record of the president's aide Jack Valenti; and the extensive and more inclusive summary by Cooper—the most recently declassified of the three.[4] For the most part these records are remarkably congruent, but sometimes they differ significantly. Though the coverage Valenti provides checks with that of the other two records, in certain areas they, especially Cooper's, go beyond Valenti's, providing important parts of the discussions that he has omitted. Thus the three accounts are here woven together, relying as much as possible on Valenti's generally more detailed version, but closing its gaps with appropriate passages from the other two.

Attending these meetings in the Cabinet Room of the White House on July 21 were: McGeorge Bundy, Horace Busby, Cooper, and Valenti from the White House; Rusk, Ball, William Bundy, Ambassador Lodge, and Ambassador to Thailand Leonard Unger from State; McNamara, Cyrus Vance, and John McNaughton from Defense; General Wheeler, chairman of the JCS; Admiral Raborn and Richard Helms of the CIA; Carl Rowan and Leonard Marks of the U.S. Information Agency; and, for just the final session of the day, Johnson's friend and unofficial adviser, Clark Clifford, chairman of the Foreign Intelligence Advisory Board.

McNamara, who had returned from Saigon earlier that morning and presumably had already talked briefly to Johnson and given him a copy of his memorandum, now distributed copies to all in the room. (Probably all present would have seen McNamara's precursor drafts on June 26 and July 1, and most would presumably have seen at least some relevant reporting from him during

his four-day stay in Saigon.) McNamara noted that his "specific recommendations" had been concurred in by Lodge, Sharp (CINCPAC), Taylor, Alexis Johnson, and Westmoreland, but that with respect to the rest of the paper he had not
sought or received their agreement.

McNamara then stated, according to Cooper's account, that though no
attempt had been made to "coordinate" the remainder of the paper, the comments of other members of the group had been solicited. No attempt had been
made to resolve certain shades of difference, but Ambassador Lodge's concerns
about early political moves to obtain a negotiated settlement (paragraphs 4c and
9) were recorded in footnotes.

[Valenti account follows]

LODGE: If I thought a diplomatic move would be successful, I would be for it.
Now, it would harden the enemy. This is not the time to do it. Clarifying
objectives is good for the world public, but not necessary for governments.
They understand it.

McNAMARA: It seems to me that our call-up and the increase in budget is
evidence that we are not taking over North Vietnam, nor do we want to.

McG. BUNDY: Our public utterances will make it clear that we are not trying
to take over North Vietnam.

McNAMARA: Our public actions must do this. We must show that we are not
in accord with Ky's objective to invade North Vietnam. We are building such
a force that the North might think that is what we are going to do.

LODGE: Remember that this "on to North Vietnam" movement is part of a
propaganda move and nothing more.

[NSC account follows]

McG.B.: Isn't it true that most of the diplomatic moves come from other
nations rather than from the U.S.

McNAMARA: That is exactly what I'm talking about.

LODGE: The President has done a remarkable job of forming public opinion.
Very skillful.

[Valenti account resumes]

BUNDY: Are there divergences between the GVN and the U.S. in troop use?

McNAMARA: GVN wants us to use [U.S.] troops in the highlands. This is
unacceptable to us. While GVN originally recommended this, they are now
in agreement with us.

[Cooper account]

> In response to a series of questions from Secretary Rusk, Secretary McNamara doubted that the GVN could raise the necessary forces to counter increasing VC capabilities (the country team was more optimistic, but we should be prudent to take a pessimistic and skeptical view of the abilities of the GVN—"a non-government"—to push forward with any major program); morale of U.S. forces was excellent (General Wheeler heartily agreed); the monsoon offensive was under way and "there was more to come"; the VC lacked the capability to seize any of the major US bases, or Saigon.

[Valenti account resumed]

WHEELER: Our advisors are pleased with the Vietnamese. They speak very highly of the Vietnamese foot soldier. The officer corps, however, is very different. Some officers are not of the highest quality. But this is not total. The big weakness in the GVN forces are lack of adequate officer material, in their training and their attitude. But they are getting better.

RUSK: Any summary of enemy troubles?

McNAMARA: Nothing more than we already know. They are suffering heavy losses. They are well supplied with ammunition. I suspect much of the inflow of supplies is water-borne. The only part of our action that is unsatisfactory is our patrol of the seashore. But even if we did have tight control, it would make little difference in the next six to nine months.

RUSK: What is the timing on how we should proceed?

McNAMARA: There ought to be a statement to the American people no later than a week, once the president's decision is reached.

BUNDY: It is quite possible the message to the Congress, once the president has determined our position, would be a message to the public.

[NSC account]

RUSK: We ought to get civilians in the Congressional testimony to [dis?]abuse the feeling that the military is making the decisions.

[McG] BUNDY: Perhaps Rusk should follow up the President's speech with statement of total unanimity.

BALL: It is one thing to ready the country for this decision and another to face the realities of the decision. We can't allow the country to wake up one morning and find heavy casualties. We need to be damn serious with the American public.

MCNAMARA: We discussed the command arrangements; they are to be left as they are—parallel commands.

[Cooper account]

> Secretary McNamara felt that we should make it clear to the public that American troops were already in combat.

At 11:30 the president joined the meeting, and, according to the Cooper account, McGeorge Bundy "suggested the following agenda for the discussion to follow":

> 1. The Action Recommendations (para 5 of the McNamara report)
> 2. The political situation and prospects in Vietnam.
> 3. The basic diplomatic position.
> 4. A scenario for action.

The President stressed the need for utmost care to avoid any leaks or speculation on the subjects under discussion.
Secretary McNamara summarized his recommendations.

[Valenti account]

> PRESIDENT: What I would like to know is what has happened in recent months that requires this kind of decision on my part. What are the alternatives? I want this discussed in full detail, from everyone around this table. Have we wrung every single soldier out of every country that we can? Who else can help us here? Are we the sole defenders in the world? Have we done all we can in this direction? What are the compelling reasons for this call-up? What results can we expect? Again, I ask you what are the alternatives? I don't want us to make snap judgments. I want us to consider all our options. We know we can tell the South Vietnamese we are coming home. Is that the option we should take? What would flow from that? The negotiations, the pause, all the other approaches we have explored, are these enough? Should we try others?

[NSC account]

> PRESIDENT: Let's look at all our options so that every man at this table understands fully the total picture.

[Cooper account]

> McNamara discussed the situation: the VC has greatly expanded its control of the country, populous areas are now isolated, both the VC and ARVN have been suffering heavy casualties. Unless the US steps in with additional forces, the VC will push the GVN into small enclaves and [it will] become increasingly ineffective. The VC now controls about 25 percent of the

population. (CIA Director Raborn estimated that the VC controlled about 25 percent of the population during the day and about 50 percent at night.) A year ago the VC controlled less than 20 percent.

The President felt that our mission should be as limited as we dare make it. General Wheeler agreed, but felt that we should engage in offensive operations to seek out and fight the VC main force units. Although this is difficult because of lack of tactical intelligence, we know where these base areas are.

Director Raborn reported the CIA's estimate that the VC will avoid major confrontations with US forces and concentrate on destroying our LOCs [lines of communication] and on guerrilla war generally. General Wheeler felt that the VC will have to "come out and fight" and that this will probably take place in the highlands where they will probably attempt to establish a government seat.

[Valenti account]

BALL: Isn't it possible that the VC will do what they did against the French —stay away from confrontation and not accommodate us?

WHEELER: Yes, that is possible, but by constantly harassing them, they will have to fight somewhere.

McNAMARA: If the VC doesn't fight in large units, it will give the ARVN a chance to resecure hostile areas. We don't know what VC tactics will be when the VC is confronted by 175,000 Americans.

RABORN: We agree. By 1965's end, we expect NVN (North Vietnam) to increase its forces. It will attempt to gain a substantial victory before our buildup is complete.

PRESIDENT: Is anyone here of the opinion we should not do what the memorandum says? If so, I want to hear from them now, in detail.

BALL: Mr. President, I can foresee a perilous voyage, very dangerous. I have great and grave apprehensions that we can win under these conditions. But let me be clear. If the decision is to go ahead, I am committed.

PRESIDENT: But, George, is there another course in the national interest, some course that is better than the one McNamara proposes? We know it is dangerous and perilous, but the big question is, can it be avoided?

BALL: There is no course that will allow us to cut our losses. If we get bogged down, our cost might be substantially greater. The pressures to create a larger war would be irresistible. The qualifications I have are not due to the fact that I think we are in a bad moral position.

PRESIDENT: Tell me then, what other road can I go?

BALL: Take what precautions we can, Mr. President. Take our losses, let

their government fall apart, negotiate, discuss, knowing full well there
will be a probable take-over by the Communists. This is disagreeable, I
know.

PRESIDENT: I can take disagreeable decisions. But I want to know can we make
a case for your thoughts? Can you discuss it fully?

BALL: We have discussed it. I have had my day in court.

PRESIDENT: I don't think we have made any full commitment, George. You
have pointed out the danger, but you haven't really proposed an alternative
course. We haven't always been right. We have no mortgage on victory.
Right now, I am concerned that we have very little alternative to what we
are doing. I want another meeting, more meetings, before we take any
definitive action. We must look at all other courses of possibility carefully.
Right now I feel it would be more dangerous to lose this now, than endanger
a greater number of troops. But I want this fully discussed.

RUSK: What we have done since 1954 to 1961 has not been good enough. We
should have probably committed ourselves heavier in 1961.

ROWAN: What bothers me most is the weakness of the Ky government. Unless we put the screws on the Ky government, 175,000 men will do us no
good.

LODGE: There is not a tradition of a national government in Saigon. There are
no roots in the country. Not until there is tranquility can you have any
stability. I don't think we ought to take this government seriously. There is
simply no one who can do anything. We have to do what we think we ought
to do regardless of what the Saigon government does. As we move ahead on
a new phase, we have the right and the duty to do certain things with or
without the government's approval.

PRESIDENT: George, do you think we have another course?

BALL: I would not recommend that you follow McNamara's course.

PRESIDENT: Are you able to outline your doubts? Can you offer another course
of action? I think it's desirable to hear you out, truly hear you out, then I
can determine if your suggestions are sound and ready to be followed, which
I am prepared to do if I am convinced.

BALL: Yes, Mr. President. I think I can present to you the least bad of two
courses. What I would present is a course that is costly, but can be limited
to short-term costs.

PRESIDENT: Alright, let's meet again at 2:30 this afternoon to discuss George's
proposals. Meanwhile, let Bob tell us why we need to risk all these Americans' lives. I don't choose to do that casually.

[Cooper account]

McNamara proceeded to develop his option. In essence the VC now had the capability to push ARVN out of positions they now control with a consequent inevitable takeover of the Government. He would not recommend that we hold our forces at the present level. We should increase our forces or get out.

General Wheeler pointed out that the ARVN strength had sharply declined because of casualties and desertions. With increased US forces we will have proportionately less casualties. He could not assure the President, however, that an additional 100,000 men would be sufficient.

[Valenti account]

McNamara and Wheeler proceeded to outline the reasons for more troops. Essentially, they said, 75,000 men are just enough to protect the bases. It would let us lose slowly instead of rapidly. The extra men, they insisted, would stabilize the situation, and then improve it. It also would give the ARVN a breathing space, they said. We would limit the incursion of more troops to 100,000 because it might not be possible to absorb more in South Vietnam at this time. Both McNamara and Wheeler declared there was no major risk of a catastrophe. . . .[5]

PRESIDENT: It seems to me that you will lose a greater number of men. I don't like that.

WHEELER: Not precisely true, Mr. President. The more men we have there the greater the likelihood of smaller losses [according to Cooper's account, "proportionately less losses"].

PRESIDENT: Tell me this. What will happen if we put in 100,000 more men and then two, three years later you tell me you need 500,000 more? How would you expect me to respond to that? And what makes you think if we put in 100,000 men, Ho Chi Minh won't put in another 100,000, and match us every bit of the way?

WHEELER: This means greater bodies of men from North Vietnam, which will allow us to cream them.

PRESIDENT: But what are the chances of more North Vietnamese soldiers coming in?

WHEELER: About a fifty-fifty chance. The North would be foolhardy to put one-quarter of their forces in SVN. It would expose them too greatly in the North.

[Cooper account]

Admiral Raborn stated that CIA's estimate was that Hanoi would send 20–25,000 PAVN troops into South Vietnam by the end of the year.

[Valenti account]

PRESIDENT: Do you have people in North Vietnam?

RABORN: Not enough, Mr. President. But what we have we think are reliable.

PRESIDENT: Why can't we improve our intelligence in North Vietnam?

RABORN: We have a task force working on this, Mr. President.

[Cooper account]

The President urged the DCI [Raborn] to increase CIA's capabilities for intelligence collection in the North. Anything that was needed to accomplish this would be made available. Mr. McNamara stressed the need to increase combat intelligence as well (CIA and MACV-J-2 were working on this problem.)

The President indicated his deep concern about press stories from Saigon that US forces were bombing innocent civilians. There followed a general discussion on the overall press situation with the President urging State Department officials to work on the matter.

The President closed this session with a request to Messrs. Ball and McGeorge Bundy constantly to explore alternatives to proposed policies. (Adjournment from 1.00 to 2.30 p.m.)

[Valenti account—opening of July 21 afternoon session]

PRESIDENT: Alright, George.

BALL: We cannot win, Mr. President. This war will be long and protracted. The most we can hope for is a messy conclusion. There remains a great danger of intrusion by the Chinese. But the biggest problem is the problem of the long war.

The Korean experience was a galling one. The correlation between Korean casualties and public opinion showed support stabilized at 50 percent. As casualties increase, the pressure to strike at the very jugular of North Vietnam will become very great.

I am concerned about world opinion. If we could win in a year's time, and win decisively, world opinion would be alright. However, if the war is long and protracted, as I believe it will be, then we will suffer because the world's greatest power cannot defeat guerrillas.

Then there is the problem of national politics. Every great captain in history was not afraid to make a tactical withdrawal if conditions were unfavorable to him. The enemy cannot even be seen in Vietnam. He is indigenous to the country. I truly have serious doubt that an army of westerners can successfully fight orientals in an Asian jungle.

PRESIDENT: This is important. Can westerners, in the absence of accurate intelligence, successfully fight Asians in jungle rice paddies? I want McNamara and General Wheeler to seriously ponder this question.

BALL: I think we all have underestimated the seriousness of this situation. It is like giving cobalt treatment to a terminal cancer case. I think a long, protracted war will disclose our weakness, not our strength.

The least harmful way to cut losses in SVN is to let the government decide it doesn't want us to stay there. Therefore, we should put such proposals to the GVN that they can't accept. Then, it would move to a neutralist position. I have no illusions that after we were asked to leave South Vietnam, that country would soon come under Hanoi control.

What about Thailand? It would be our main problem. Thailand has proven a good ally so far, though history shows it has never been a staunch ally. If we wanted to make a stand in Thailand, we might be able to make it.

Another problem would be South Korea. We have two divisions there now. There would be a problem with Taiwan, but as long as the Generalissimo is there, they have no place to go. Indonesia is a problem, as is Malaysia. Japan thinks we are propping up a lifeless government and are on a sticky wicket. Between a long war and cutting our losses, the Japanese would go for the latter. My information on Japan comes from Reischauer [the American ambassador to Japan].

PRESIDENT: But George, wouldn't all these countries say that Uncle Sam was a paper tiger, wouldn't we lose credibility breaking the word of three presidents, if we did as you have proposed? It would seem to be an irreparable blow. But I gather you don't think so.

BALL: No, sir. The worse blow would be that the mightiest power on earth is unable to defeat a handful of guerrillas.

PRESIDENT: Then you are not basically troubled by what the world would say about our pulling out?

BALL: If we were actively helping a country with a stable viable government, it would be a vastly different story. Western Europeans look upon us as if we got ourselves into an imprudent situation.

PRESIDENT: But I believe that these Vietnamese are trying to fight. They're like Republicans who try to stay in power, but don't stay there long. Excuse me, Cabot.

BALL: Thieu spoke the other day and said the Communists would win the election.

PRESIDENT: I don't believe that. Does anyone believe that? (His hand circled the table. McNamara, Lodge, Bill Bundy, Leonard Unger all expressed views contrary to Ball's.) [Several Saigon government leaders had, in fact, told McNamara, Lodge, and Unger, in meetings with them in Saigon a few days before, that in a political competition the NLF would win.][6]

MCNAMARA: Ky will fall soon. He is weak. We can't have elections there until there is physical security, and even then there will be no elections because as Cabot said, there is no democratic tradition. (Wheeler suggested that McNamara was right about Ky, but said: "I am very much impressed with Thieu.")

PRESIDENT: There are two basic troublings within me. First, that westerners can ever win a war in Asia. Second, I don't see how you can fight a war under direction of other people whose government changes every month. Now, go ahead, George and make your other points.

BALL: The costs, as well as our western European allies, are not relevant to their (European) situation. What they are concerned about is their own security, that is, troops in Berlin have real meaning, troops in Vietnam have none.

PRESIDENT: Are you saying that pulling out of Korea would be akin to pulling out of Vietnam?

MCGEORGE BUNDY: It is not analogous. We had a status quo in Korea. It would not be that way in Vietnam.

BALL: We will pay a higher cost in Vietnam. This is a decision one makes against an alternative. On one hand, a long, protracted war, costly, very costly, with North Vietnam digging in for the long-term. This is their life and driving force. The Chinese are taking the long term view by ordering blood plasma from Japan. On the other hand, there are short-term losses if we pull out. On balance, we come out ahead of the McNamara plan. Of course, it is distasteful either way. [As Ball later observed to me, "The problem was that I couldn't make it look like a victory."]

[Cooper account][7]

Mr. Bundy [McGeorge] agreed with the McNamara proposals. He felt that no government which could hold power is likely to be one that is likely to invite us out. The basic lesson of Mr. Ball's view is that: 1) The post-monsoon season will not see us in the clear. 2) No single speech will be sufficient to reassure the American people. We will have to face up to the serious ominous implications of our new policy. This is not a continuation of our present approach. "We are asking Americans to bet more to achieve less." We will have to engage in a much more massive political and economic effort. New organizational changes may be necessary in our mission in Saigon and in our governmental structure in Washington. There are no early victories in store, although casualties are likely to be heavy.

Mr. Bundy did not believe that Mr. Ball's "cancer analogy" was a good one. Immaturity and weakness, yes. A non-Communist society is struggling to be born. Before we take our decision to the American people, Ambassador Taylor should go back to the GVN and get greater, more positive assurances. There will be time to decide our policy won't work after we have given it a good try. (Mr. Ball disagreed here, feeling that the larger our commitment, the more difficult would be the decision to get out. "We won't get out; we'll double our bet and get lost in the rice paddies.")

Mr. Bundy felt that the kind of shift in US policy suggested by Mr. Ball would be "disastrous." He would rather maintain our present commitment and "waffle through" than withdraw. The country is in the mood to accept grim news.

Secretary Rusk emphasized that the nature and integrity of the US commitment was fundamental. It makes the US stance with the USSR creditable. It would be dangerous if the Communist leadership became convinced that we will not see this through. It is more important to convince the Communist leadership of this than to worry about the opinion of non-Communist countries. He is more optimistic about the outcome of the war than some. The effects of our force increment will be to force the VC into guerrilla activity, to remove the capability of the other side to use major forces against the GVN. The VC must now be faced with difficult decisions. An increased US commitment does not change the nature of the war—we have already gone a long way in the air and on the ground without escalating. Consequently he wondered whether we should be too dramatic about the increase in US forces. (Mr. Bundy pointed out here that calling up the reserves will require a certain amount of "drama.")

[Valenti account]

RUSK: If the Communist world finds out we will not pursue our commitments to the end, I don't know where they will stay their hand. I have to say I am more optimistic than some of my colleagues. I don't believe the VC have made large advances among the Vietnamese people. It is difficult to worry about massive casualties when we say we can't find the enemy. I feel strongly that one dead man is a massive casualty, but in the sense that we are talking, I don't see large casualties unless the Chinese come in.

[Cooper account]

McNamara felt that Mr. Ball understated the cost of cutting our losses. He agreed with Mr. Rusk on the international effect of such an action at this time. Mr. Ball also overstates the cost of his (McNamara's) proposal. He [McNamara] agreed that it would take at least two years to pacify the country and we must be prepared to increase our forces by another 100,000.

General Wheeler said that it was unreasonable to expect to "win" in a year regardless of the number of US troops involved. We might start to reverse the unfavorable trend in a year and make definite progress in three years.

The President wondered whether we could win without using nuclear weapons if China entered the war.

General Wheeler felt we could in "Southeast Asia." He believes US forces can operate in the terrain of Southeast Asia. This is the first "war of National Liberation"; if we walk out of this one, we will just have to face others.

The President asked why, when we've been undertaking military efforts for 20 months, this new effort will be successful.

General Wheeler felt that our additional forces will stave off a deteriorating situation.

[Valenti account]

LODGE: I feel there is a greater threat to start World War III if we don't go in. Can't we see the similarity to our own indolence at Munich? I simply can't be as pessimistic as Ball. We have great seaports in Vietnam. We don't need to fight on roads. We have the sea. Let us visualize meeting the VC on our own terms. We don't have to spend all our time in the jungles. If we can secure our bases, the Vietnamese can secure, in time, a political movement to, one, apprehend the terrorist, and two, give intelligence to the government. The procedures for this are known. I agree the Japanese agitators don't like what we are doing, but Sato is totally in agreement with our actions. The Vietnamese have been dealt more casualties than, per capita, we suffered in the Civil War. The Vietnamese soldier is an uncomplaining soldier. He has ideas he will die for.

LEONARD UNGER: I agree this is what we have to do. We have spotted some things we want to pay attention to.

PRESIDENT: How can we get everybody to compete with McNamara in the press? We are trying to do many other things with our economic and health projects. Can't we constantly remind the people that we are doing something besides bombing?

UNGER: We have taken this question up with Barry Zorthian and the press people.

[Cooper account]

The President stressed his desire to get more third country troops into South Vietnam. He also raised the possibility of a Vietnam Task Force which would meet daily.

The meeting adjourned at 5:30.

At noon the next day, July 22, the president met with the country's military leadership and a few of his civilian aides. Present in addition to McGeorge Bundy,

Clifford, McNamara, Vance, and Valenti were: General Wheeler; General Harold K. Johnson, army chief of staff; General John P. McConnell, air force chief of staff; Admiral David L. McDonald, chief of naval operations; General Wallace M. Greene, Jr., commandant of the marine corps; Harold Brown, secretary of the air force; Paul Nitze, secretary of the navy; Stanley Resor, secretary of the army; and Eugene M. Zuckert, assistant secretary of the air force. The fullest account of this meeting is from the Cabinet Room Meeting Notes File, and it follows (with abbreviations spelled out):*

THE PRESIDENT: I asked Secretary McNamara to invite you here to counsel with you on these problems and the ways to meet them. Hear from the chiefs the alternatives open to you and then recommendations on those alternatives from a military point (of view). Options open to us: one, leave the country —the "bugging out" approach; two, maintain present force and lose slowly; three, add 100,000 men—recognizing that may not be enough—and adding more next year. Disadvantages of number three—risk of escalation, casualties will be high, and may be a long war without victory. I would like you to start out by stating our present position and where we can go.

ADMIRAL McDONALD: Sending Marines has improved situation. I agree with McNamara that we are committed to extent that we can't move out. If we continue the way we are, it will be a slow, sure victory for the other side. By putting more men in it will turn the tide and let us know what further we need to do. I wish we had done this long before.

PRESIDENT: But you don't know if 100,000 will be enough. What makes you conclude that if you don't know where we are going—and what will happen —we shouldn't pause and find this out?

McDONALD: Sooner or later we will force them to the conference table. . . .

PRESIDENT: But if we put in 100,000 men won't they put in an equal number?

McDONALD: No, if we step up our bombing . . .

PRESIDENT: Is this a chance we want to take?

McDONALD: Yes, when I view the alternatives. Get out now or pour in more men.

PRESIDENT: Is that all?

McDONALD: I think our allies will lose faith in us.

PRESIDENT: We have few allies really helping us now.

*In a few cases where this record is garbled or unclear, the wording of the somewhat more attenuated Valenti account is drawn on, being inserted within parentheses.

MCDONALD: Thailand for example. If we walk out of Vietnam, the whole world will question our word. We don't have much choice.

PRESIDENT: Paul, what is your view?

PAUL NITZE: In that area not occupied by US forces, it is worse, as I observed on my trip out there. We have two alternatives—support Vietnam all over the country or (stick to the) secure positions we do have. Make it clear to populace that we are on their side. Gradually turn the tide of losses by aiding Vietnam at certain points. If we just maintained what we have—more the Pres. problem than ours—to acknowledge that we couldn't beat the VC, the shape of the world will change.

PRESIDENT: What are our chances of success?

NITZE: If we want to turn the tide, by putting in more men, it would be about sixty-forty.

PRESIDENT: If we gave Westmoreland all he asked for, what are our chances? I don't agree that North Vietnam and China won't come in.

NITZE: Expand the area we could maintain. In the Philippines and Greece it was shown that guerrillas (can lose).

PRESIDENT: Would you send in more forces than Westmoreland requests?

NITZE: Yes. Depends on how quickly they . . .

PRESIDENT: How many? Two hundred thousand instead of 100,000?

NITZE: We would need another 100,000 in January.

PRESIDENT: Can you do that?

NITZE: Yes.

MCNAMARA: The current plan is to introduce 100,000—with the possibility of a second 100,000 by first of the year.

PRESIDENT: What reaction is this going to produce?

GENERAL WHEELER: Since we are not proposing an invasion of North Vietnam, the Soviets will step up materiel and propaganda—same with the Chicoms. North Vietnam (might) introduce more regular troops.

PRESIDENT: Why wouldn't North Vietnam pour in more men? Also, call on volunteers from China and Russia?

WHEELER: First, they may decide they can't win by putting in forces they can't afford. At most they would put in two more divisions. Beyond that, they strip their country and invite a countermove on our part. Second, on volunteers —the one thing all North Vietnam fears is the Chinese. For them to invite

Chinese volunteers is to invite China taking over North Vietnam. Weight of judgment is that North Vietnam may reinforce their forces, but they can't match us on a buildup. From military view, we can handle, if we are determined to do so, China and North Vietnam.

PRESIDENT: (Don't you) anticipate retaliation by the Soviets in the Berlin area?

WHEELER: You may have some flare-up but lines are so tightly drawn in Berlin, that it raises the risk of escalation too quickly. Lemnitzer thinks there will be no flare-up in Berlin. [General Lyman L. Lemnitzer, a former chairman of the JCS, was then commander of Allied forces in Europe.] In Korea, if Soviets undertook operations it would be dangerous.

PRESIDENT: Admiral, would you summarize what you think we ought to do?

McDONALD: First, supply the forces Westmoreland has asked for. Second, prepare to furnish more men—100,000—in 1966. Third, commensurate building in air and naval forces, step up air attacks on North Vietnam. Fourth, bring in needed reserves and draft calls.

PRESIDENT: Any ideas on what cost of this would be?

McNAMARA: Yes. $12 billion dollars in 1966.

PRESIDENT: Any idea what effect this will have on our economy?

McNAMARA: It would not require wage and price controls in my judgment. The price index ought not go up more than one point or two.

GENERAL McCONNELL: If you put in these requested forces and increase air and sea effort, we can at least turn the tide to where we are not losing anymore. We need to be sure we get the best we can out of South Vietnam. We need to bomb all military targets available to us in North Vietnam. As to whether we can come to a satisfactory solution with these forces, I don't know. With these forces properly employed, and cutting off their (VC) supplies, we can do better than we are doing.

PRESIDENT: Have results of bombing actions been as fruitful and productive as we anticipated?

McCONNELL: No, sir, they haven't been. (They have been) productive in South Vietnam, but not as productive in North Vietnam because we are not striking the targets that hurt them.

PRESIDENT: Are you seriously concerned when we change targets we escalate the war? They might send more fighters down. (Can you be certain it won't) escalate efforts on the ground? Would it hurt our chances at a conference if we killed civilians in this bombing?

McCONNELL: We need to minimize killings.

PRESIDENT: Would you go beyond Westmoreland's recommendations?

McCONNELL: No, sir.

PRESIDENT: How many planes lost?

McCONNELL: 106 of all types—small percentage of (our) total.

PRESIDENT: How many (do we have) out there?

McCONNELL: One hundred and forty-six combat. We have lost 54 combat.

PRESIDENT: How many Navy planes?

McDONALD: It's in the thirties—[of] about 125 (Navy) combat.

EUGENE ZUCKERT: It's worth taking a major step to avoid long-run consequences of walking away from it.

PRESIDENT: Doesn't it really mean if we follow Westmoreland's requests we are in a new war? (Isn't) this going off the diving board?

McNAMARA: This is a major change in U.S. policy. We have relied on South Vietnam to carry the brunt. Now we would be responsible for satisfactory military outcome.

PRESIDENT: Are we in agreement we would rather be out of there and make our stand somewhere else?

GENERAL JOHNSON: The least desirable alternative is getting out. The second least is doing what we are doing. Best is to get in and get the job done.

PRESIDENT: But I don't know how we are going to get that job done. There are millions of Chinese. I think they are going to put their stack in. Is this the best place to do this? We don't have the allies we had in Korea. Can we get our allies to cut off supplying North Vietnamese?

McNAMARA: No, we can't prevent Japan, Britain, (and the others) to charter ships to Haiphong.

PRESIDENT: Have we done anything to get them to stop?

McNAMARA: We haven't put the pressure on them as we did in Cuba, but even if we did, it wouldn't stop the shipping.

BROWN: It seems that all of our alternatives are dark. I find myself in agreement with the others.

PRESIDENT: Is there anything to the argument that this South Vietnamese government is likely to fail, and we will be asked to leave. If we try to match the enemy we will be bogged down in protracted war and have the government ask us to leave?

BROWN: Our lines of communication are long.

PRESIDENT: How long?

BROWN: 7,000 miles from the West Coast, but not too much greater than China's. Biggest weakness of political base is lack of security they can offer their people.

PRESIDENT: Are we starting something that in two to three years we simply can't finish?

BROWN: It is costly to us to strangle slowly, but chances of losing are less if we move in.

PRESIDENT: Suppose we told Ky of requirements we need—he turns them down—and we have to get out and make our stand in Thailand.

BROWN: The Thais will go with the winner.

PRESIDENT: If we didn't stop in Thailand where would we stop?

MCNAMARA: Laos, Cambodia, Thailand, Burma, surely affect Malaysia. In 2–3 years communist domination would stop there, but ripple effect would be great (in) Japan, India. We would have to give up some bases. Ayub [Khan, head of Pakistan government] would move closer to China. Greece, Turkey would move to neutralist positions. Communist agitation would increase in Africa.

GENERAL GREENE: Situation is as tough as when it started. But not as bad as it could be. Marines in the First Corps area is example of benefits. (Here are the stakes as I see them.) One, national security stake; (it is a) matter of time before we (would have to) go in some place else. Two, pledge we made. Three, prestige before the rest of the world. If you accept these stakes, there are two courses of action. One, get out. Two, stay in and win. How to win (in the North and in the South)? The enclave concept will work. I would like to introduce enough Marines to do this. Two Marine divisions and one air wing. Extend. 28,000 there—(we need an) additional 72,000.

MCNAMARA: Greene suggests these men over and above the Westmoreland request.

PRESIDENT: Then you will need 80,000 more Marines to carry this out?

GREENE: Yes. I am convinced we are making progress with the South Vietnamese, in food and construction. We are getting evidence of intelligence from the South Vietnamese. In the North, we haven't been hitting the right targets. We should hit pol (petroleum) storage—essential to their transportation. Also, (we must destroy their) airfields, MGs and IL28s. As soon as SAM installations are operable.

PRESIDENT: What would they do?

GREENE: Nothing. We can test it by attacking pol storage. Then we should attack industrial complex in North Vietnam. Also, they can be told by pamphlet drop why we are doing this. Then we ought to blockade Cambodia —and stop supplies from coming down. How long will it take? Five years, plus 500,000 troops. I think the (American) people will back you.

PRESIDENT: How would you tell the American people what the stakes are?

GREENE: The place where they will stick by you is the national security stake.

GENERAL JOHNSON: We are in a face-down. The solution, unfortunately, is long-term. Once the military (problem) is solved, the problem of political solution will be more difficult.

PRESIDENT: If we come in with hundreds of thousands of men and billions of dollars, won't this cause China and Russia to come in?

GENERAL JOHNSON: No. I don't think they will.

PRESIDENT: MacArthur didn't think they would come in either.

GENERAL JOHNSON: Yes, but this is not comparable to Korea. . . . [garbled]

PRESIDENT: But China has plenty of divisions to move in, don't they?

GENERAL JOHNSON: Yes, they do.

PRESIDENT: Then what would we do?

GENERAL JOHNSON [after a long silence]: If so, we have another ball game.

PRESIDENT: But I have to take into account they will.

GENERAL JOHNSON: I would increase the build-up near North Vietnam, and increase action in Korea.

PRESIDENT: If they move in thirty-one divisions, what does it take on our part?

McNAMARA: Under favorable conditions they could sustain thirty-one divisions and assuming the Thais contributed forces, it would take 300,000 plus what we need to combat the VC.

STANLEY RESOR: I'm a newcomer— [interrupted by President]

PRESIDENT: But remember they're going to write stories about this like they did the Bay of Pigs—and about my advisors. That's why I want you to think very carefully about alternatives and plans. Looking back on the Dominican Republic would you have done any differently, General?

GENERAL JOHNSON: I would have cleaned out part of the city and gone in— and with same numbers.

PRESIDENT: Are you concerned about Chinese forces moving into North Vietnam?

GENERAL JOHNSON: There is no evidence of forces—only teams involved in logistics. (They) could be investigating areas which they could control later.

PRESIDENT: What is your reaction to Ho's statement he is ready to fight for twenty years?

GENERAL JOHNSON: I believe it.

PRESIDENT: What are Ho's problems?

GENERAL JOHNSON: His biggest problem is doubt about what our next move will be. He's walking a tightrope between the Reds and the Chicoms. Also, he is worrying about the loss of caches of arms in South Vietnam.

PRESIDENT: Are we killing civilians along with VC?

WHEELER: Certain civilians accompanying the VC are being killed. It can't be helped.

PRESIDENT: The VC dead is running at a rate of 25,000 a year. At least 15,000 have been killed by air—half of these are not a part of what we call VC. Since 1961 a total of 89,000 have been killed. South Vietnamese are being killed at a rate of 12,000 per year.

STANLEY RESOR: Of the three courses the one we should follow is the McNamara plan. We can't go back on our commitment. Our allies are watching carefully.

PRESIDENT: Do all of you think the Congress and the people will go along with 600,000 people and billions of dollars (being spent) 10,000 miles away?

RESOR: Gallup poll shows people are basically behind our commitment.

PRESIDENT: But if you make a commitment to jump off a building and you find out how high it is, you may withdraw the commitment. I judge though that the big problem is one of national security. Is that right? [murmured assent] What about our intelligence. How do they (the VC) know what we are doing before we do it? What about the B-52 raid—weren't they gone before we got there?

McNAMARA: They get it from infiltration in the South Vietnamese forces.

PRESIDENT: Are we getting good intelligence out of North Vietnam?

McNAMARA: Only reconnaissance and technical soundings. None from combat intelligence.

[Valenti in his account recalls that before the meeting Johnson had instructed McGeorge Bundy to prepare a paper on how the U.S. had gotten to where it was in Vietnam and to pose the tough questions that needed to be asked.]

PRESIDENT: Some Congressmen and Senators think we are going to be the most discredited people in the world. What Bundy will now tell you is not his opinion nor mine—I haven't taken a position yet—but what we hear.

BUNDY (reading from his paper): The argument we will face: For ten years every step we have taken has been based on a previous failure. All we have done has failed and caused us to take another step which failed. As we get further into the bag, we get deeply bruised. Also, we have made excessive claims we haven't been able to realize.

Also after twenty years of warnings about war in Asia, we are now doing what MacArthur and others have warned against. We are about to fight a war we can't fight and win, as the country we are trying to help is quitting.

(There is) the failure on our own to fully realize what guerrilla war is like. We are sending conventional troops to do an unconventional job.

How long—how much. Can we take casualties over five years—aren't we talking about a military solution when the solution is political. Why can't we interdict better. Why are our bombings so fruitless? Why can't we block-ade the coast? Why can't we improve our intelligence? Why can't we find the VC?

PRESIDENT: Gerald Ford has demanded the President testify before the Congress and tell why we are compelled to up the reserves. Indications are that he will oppose calling up the reserves.

MCNAMARA: I think we can answer most of the questions posed.

CLIFFORD: If the military plan is carried out what is the ultimate result if we are successful?"

WHEELER: Political objective is to maintain SVN as free and independent. If we follow the course of action, we can carry out this objective. Probably after success, we would withdraw most of our forces; [though some,] international or otherwise, would have to stay on. If we can secure the military situation, it seems likely that we can get some kind of stable government."

On the afternoon of the same day, July 22, Johnson met with his regular senior aides and several prominent *ad hoc* civilian advisers—Clark Clifford, John McCloy, and Arthur Dean—to report to them on his morning meeting with the military. Here the president invited Clifford, whose opposition to escalation had been known to him for more than two months, to present his views. No full record of this meeting is available, but Ball records his delight at Clifford's strong argument against the commitment of U.S. combat forces and his assessment of the probable domestic consequences. In this discussion, Ball recalls, "Clifford emerged as a formidable comrade on my side of the barricades."[8]

Immediately afterward Ball caucused with his new ally and gave him copies of the memoranda he had previously submitted to the president. The next day, he says, Clifford informed him that he had spent until 2:00 A.M. studying them and found them "impressive and persuasive." Clifford advised him that, though he hoped their combined exertions might help block the advocates of escalation, he was not sanguine. Evidently referring to some of the president's other advisers, he observed, "individuals sometimes become so bound up in a certain course it is difficult to know where objectivity stops and personal involvement begins."[9]

On this point Clifford later observed that "even more important" than Johnson's inheritance of Kennedy's stated position on Vietnam—"We are in Vietnam, and let me assure you we intend to stay"—was his inheritance of his predecessor's senior advisers. "He encountered a practically unanimous sentiment" among them that the United States was headed correctly in Vietnam, and that "the domino theory is unquestionably so," and he "proceeded at that time on the basis of a solid phalanx of advice from the main advisers" on Vietnam that it was the United States' mission to help the South Vietnamese defend themselves against "Communist aggression."[10]

After the July 22 meetings Johnson repaired to Camp David "to reflect." In pondering over McNamara's July 20 recommendations and the advice proffered by his advisers, he of course had more than Vietnam on his mind. For, however cogent the arguments for these proposals may have appeared to him in terms of U.S. objectives in Vietnam, they clearly involved a potentially heavy domestic price, disruptive of the political harmony required if he was to shepherd his Great Society program through Congress. Especially was this so with respect to those features of the McNamara/JCS plan requiring a call-up of the Reserve and National Guard, extension of tours of duty, and an increase in the draft.

On the day after Johnson went to Camp David, McGeorge Bundy presumably assuaged some of his anxiety regarding the possible incompatibility of increased military spending with his Great Society programs, when he sent him memoranda arguing against the necessity of a large fiscal appropriation to meet the costs of McNamara's package. (McNamara had estimated the proposed escalation would require $2 billion through the end of 1965, and Vance that it would run to about $8 billion in 1966.) An appropriation for such an amount, Bundy contended, would be "a belligerent challenge to the Soviets" and would "stir talk about controls over the economy and inflation—at a time when controls are not needed and inflation is not that kind of a problem." It was not necessary, he said, "because there are other ways of financing our full effort in Vietnam for the present."[11]

Though Bundy's plans for financing are not clear, what he had in mind by "our full effort in Vietnam" was evident the next evening (July 24) in his memorandum to the president recommending his approval of the JCS proposal with its "marginal modifications" by McNamara for a total troop strength of 179,000 men. These should be sent to Vietnam through November, but any decision on further major deployments reserved.[12] Bundy was thereby advocating a little over double the deployment recommended in his brother's "Middle Course" and backing the central component of the 1965 phase of the McNamara/JCS proposal. No longer was he standing as a buffer between the president and the military chiefs, but now, as with McNamara, was more of a conduit.

With McGeorge Bundy now backing the McNamara/JCS/Westmoreland recommendation, the president appears to have agreed to approve some measure of ground-combat-force increase, but had not yet decided on how much or how he would raise these troops. That he had now decided on some increase was implicit in orders he gave Bundy on the 24th, apparently after receiving his endorsement of the recommendation.[13] But how far he would go was still up in the air.

For a meeting on the afternoon of July 25—probably the last and one of the most critical in making his decision—the president invited to Camp David just three people: Clark Clifford, Arthur Goldberg (ambassador to the U.N.), and McNamara. During the discussions the only others present were Johnson's two aides Horace Busby and Jack Valenti. (Goldberg, then U.S. representative to the United Nations, was there primarily because some advisers were pressing for a U.N. resolution that would demonstrate the administration's peaceful intent and desire to negotiate a Vietnam solution.) The record of these discussions is limited, with no available direct account of what McNamara said.

It is not clear whether at this point Johnson had been provided with all the relevant information needed to make a sound judgment of the McNamara/JCS proposal. McNamara's July 20 report had not incorporated Westmoreland's "Concept of Operations," presented orally to him in Saigon a few days before, and, according to a knowledgeable high-level U.S. official, it does not appear that this was given to Johnson until well after the Camp David meeting: in late August it was finally dispatched from Saigon in writing. Westmoreland's concept envisaged three phases of military operations. Phase I (requiring that U.S. ground combat strength be brought up to a total of forty-four battalions, or about 175,000 men) was directed toward halting the losing trend in the war by the end of 1965. Phase II (requiring a further twenty-four combat battalions, fourteen artillery battalions, three air defense—Hawk—battalions, eight engineer battalions, twelve helicopter companies, "and additional support units," for an overall 1966 increase of about a hundred thousand) was designed for "the resumption of offensive operations" during the first half of that year "in high priority areas necessary to destroy enemy forces, and [for the] reinstitution of rural reconstruction activities." Phase III was the vaguest and most open-ended. It would, "if the enemy persisted," run for another year to a year and a half (mid-1968) and would require an unspecified number of additional forces—whatever was "necessary to extend and expand clearing and security operations throughout the entire populated area of the country and those forces necessary to destroy VC forces and their base areas."[14] It would seem appropriate to ask whether Johnson, if he had had this more detailed projection before him, might not have questioned the McNamara/JCS proposal more critically than he did.

From the NSC files, there is an abbreviated official record of Clifford's remarks at Camp David, along with the president's follow-up reading of a letter, and there is an almost verbatim amplification of Clifford's statement as taken down by Valenti (substantially similar to the NSC version). Clifford's views were consistent with those in his May 17 letter to the president but more emphatic, and now also addressed the pending question of a U.N. resolution. Goldberg strongly supported such a resolution, but found both Clifford and McNamara opposed.[15]

[Clifford's views, as recorded in Valenti's notes]*

I do not think it advisable to go to UN with resolution. You don't need to re-inforce your peaceful intentions this way. It is inconsistent with your going in with more troops.

Stop talking about Vietnam. Rusk, Harriman, the President, everyone ought to take this out of the public consciousness—particularly continually saying why we are there. The enemy will not be forced to a conference table by any UN proposal. Underplay Vietnam until January and then reassess.

Both the above statements are based on this reason: I don't believe we can win in South Vietnam. If we send in 100,000 troops, the North Vietnamese will match us. And when they run out of troops, the Chinese will send in "volunteers." Russia and China don't intend for us to win this war. If we lose 50,000 men there, it will be catastrophic in this country. Five years, billions of dollars, hundreds of thousands of men—this is not for us. At the end of the monsoon season, let us QUIETLY probe and search out with other countries—even if we have to moderate our position—a way for us to get out. I cannot see anything but catastrophe for our nation in this area. A resolution in the UN with all the dramatic debate it would produce is bad for us.

Following this, the President read from a letter which incorporated views largely consistent with those just stated by Clifford and whose content suggests it was probably from [Mike] Mansfield.[16]

---

*Clifford has informed me (letter of June 24, 1985) that to the best of his recollection Valenti's account of his position is correct.

[NSC record]

> Vietnam is not of intrinsic value. If [deletion] There is no high principle involved. Basic issue is not to get thrown out under fire.
> Political questions are what we make them.
> 1. Instruct officials to stop saying all human kind is at stake.
> 2. Stop saying we are going to pacify the country.
> 3. [undecipherable] patience—pressure—quietly working areas we can hold. Hold there for years if need be. Make a safe haven.
> 4. Vietcong cannot attack those places frontally.
> 5. Gradually stop bombing north and south. Maximum attention to it which is wrong.
> 6. Keep negotiations open.

These views, Clifford's, and Goldberg's diverged sharply from McNamara's, and one presumes the president then asked McNamara for his comments. Unfortunately, no record of such presumptive comments has been released.

Goldberg joined Clifford in opposing McNamara's recommendation that the president call up the reserves. He recalls feeling so strongly on this point that "I advised the President that if he accepted this recommendation I would withdraw my resignation from the Supreme Court because calling up the Reserves would be tantamount to a full scale war with widespread complications involving possibly the Soviet Union."[17]

Johnson turned down the call for reserves. Apparently, however, McNamara had anticipated the possibility of having to retreat on this issue, and according to William Bundy had come to Camp David prepared to advise Johnson that an overall expansion of American armed forces by six hundred thousand men* could be managed without calling up the reserves, "and that his senior military advisers thought that the drawbacks of the draft method—confusion, slower rate of build-up, less experienced men—were acceptable."[18]

On July 26, the day after his Camp David discussions, the president had final meetings on Vietnam with McNamara and his other top advisers (with Clifford and Goldberg also present), but much of the record of these proceedings has still not been declassified.[19] It was presumably here that he either arrived at or announced his decision on the McNamara/JCS recommendation. Later it became clear that with respect to troop deployment, the president had now decided to meet their recommendation about halfway—an immediate increase of 50,000 U.S. troops to total 125,000 rather than the proposed 104,000 increase to total 179,000—

---

*This overall figure was predicated on the assumption that roughly one and a half additional men were required in the total force in order to maintain one additional man in Vietnam after allowances had been made for training time, travel, and the expected short terms of duty there. This figure was at the same time regarded as sufficient to maintain the U.S. global strategic reserve at previous levels.

but with the expectation that the latter figure might be required by the end of the year and that more men would be needed in 1966. He had refused to call up the reserves while agreeing to a substantial increase in the draft and an extension of tours of duty. By not calling for the reserves, he avoided the necessity of requesting a new mandate from Congress and the almost inevitable heavy debate this would have precipitated. The escalation now being set in motion would look less abrupt and more consistent with previous policy than was actually the case.

Informed of this decision soon afterward, Senator Mansfield worked hard to alert Johnson to the dangers involved. After talking with the president on the morning of the 27th, he met at 3:30 that afternoon with five of the Senate's most influential leaders—two Republicans, (George Aiken and John Sherman Cooper) and three Democrats (J. William Fulbright, Richard Russell, and John Sparkman) —and told them of Johnson's decision. Their discussion resulted in a nineteen-point memorandum that Mansfield sent to the president that same day, but which probably did not reach him until after he had given a formal cachet to his decision at a meeting of the National Security Council which began at 5:30 P.M. In any case, Mansfield had presented the president with his views that morning, and the semi-consensus ("very substantial agreement") of the six senators was considerably more moderate than the position he had himself conveyed beforehand.

The memorandum from this group of senators was prefaced by their "general sense of reassurance that your objective was not to get in deeply and that you intended to do only what was essential in the military line until January, while Rusk and Goldberg were concentrating on attempting to get us out. A general desire to support you in this course was expressed." But the senators' nineteen points raised many important cautions. One of them may have been particularly unsettling, for it closely paralleled Clifford's warning in the president's meeting with the Pentagon representatives just five days earlier. "The main perplexity in the Vietnam situation," they pointed out, "is that even if you win, totally, you still do not come out well. What have you achieved? It is by no means a 'vital' area of U.S. concern. . . ." Their final point expressed dissatisfaction with McNamara's role: he had been "a disappointment in his handling of this situation, probably because he is being used in a way which he ought not to be used."[20]

Later that afternoon (July 27), in his meeting with the National Security Council, it is even more certain that a decision had already been reached, for the president announced at its outset that before "formalizing" decisions on the deployment of additional U.S. forces to Vietnam he wished to review the present situation. The discussion that then developed, as recorded in the NSC summary, is, nevertheless, useful to an understanding of the administration's internal rationale for the decision just made.[21]

SECRETARY RUSK:

    a. The Chinese Communists are most adamant against any negotiations between the North Vietnamese and the U.S./South Vietnamese. The clash between the Chinese Communists and the Russians continues.

b. [sanitized] We have asked many times what the North Vietnamese would do if we stopped the bombing. We have heard nothing to date in reply.

c. There appear to be elements of caution on the other side—in Hanoi as well as in Moscow. Our purpose is to keep our contacts open with the other side in the event that they have a new position to give us.

d. The U.S. actions we are taking should be presented publicly in a low key but in such a way as to convey accurately that we are determined to prevent South Vietnam from being taken over by Hanoi. At the same time, we seek to avoid a confrontation with either the Chinese Communists or the Soviet Union.

SECRETARY McNAMARA: Summarized the military situation in Vietnam:

a. The number of Viet Cong forces has increased and the percentage of these forces committed to battle has increased.

b. The geographic area of South Vietnam controlled by the Viet Cong has increased.

c. The Viet Cong have isolated the cities and disrupted the economy of South Vietnam. The cities are separated from the countryside.

d. Increased desertions from the South Vietnamese Army have prevented an increase in the total number of South Vietnamese troops available for combat.

e. About half of all U.S. Army helicopters are now in South Vietnam in addition to over 500 U.S. planes.

The military requirements are:

a. More combat battalions from the U.S. are necessary. A total of 13 additional battalions need to be sent now. On June 15, we announced a total of 75,000 men, or 15 battalions.

b. A total of 28 battalions is now necessary.

c. Over the next 15 months, 350,000 men would be added to regular U.S. forces [overall U.S. strength—not all earmarked for Vietnam].

d. In January, we would go to Congress for a supplementary appropriation to pay the costs of the Vietnam war. We would ask now for a billion, in addition to the existing 1966 budget.

The attack on the SAM sites in North Vietnam was necessary to protect our planes. Attacks on other priority targets in North Vietnam are required.

AMBASSADOR LODGE: Asked whether the ratio of government to guerrilla ground forces had to be 10:1. During his testimony before the Senate Foreign Relations Committee, he had been asked this question. Comment had been made about the astronomical size of U.S. forces required if this traditional 10:1 ratio was valid.

GENERAL WHEELER: The mobility and fire power of U.S. and South Vietnamese forces has put an imponderable element into the traditional ratio of 10:1. Perhaps 4:1 is the right ratio.

With the additional forces to be sent to South Vietnam, General Westmoreland believes we can hold our present position and possibly move back
into areas now contested. The one exception would be in the Fourth Corps.

Secretary Rusk and Secretary McNamara expressed differences of view
concerning a map brought to the meeting by Secretary McNamara which
purported to show the amount of territory in South Vietnam controlled by
the Viet Cong. Secretary Rusk thought the map overstated the size of Viet
Cong controlled areas. Secretary McNamara said it understated the area
they control. At least 26% of the population of South Vietnam is controlled
by Viet Cong, according to Secretary McNamara's figures.

THE PRESIDENT: The situation in Vietnam is deteriorating. Even though we
now have 80 to 90,000 men there, the situation is not very safe. We have these
choices:

a. Use our massive power, including SAC [Strategic Air Command] to
bring the enemy to his knees. Less than 10% of our people urge this course
of action. [Presumably implicit in this course of action would be a willingness to resort to nuclear warfare.]

b. We could get out, on the grounds that we don't belong there. Not very
many people feel this way about Vietnam. Most feel that our national honor
is at stake and that we must keep our commitments there.

c. We could keep our forces at the present level, approximately 80,000
men, but suffer the consequences of losing additional territory and of accepting increased casualties. We could "hunker up." No one is recommending this course.

d. We could ask for everything we might desire from Congress—money,
authority to call up the reserves, acceptance of the deployment of more
combat battalions. This dramatic course of action would involve declaring
a state of emergency and a request for several billion dollars. Many favor
this course. However, if we do go all out in this fashion, Hanoi would be
able to ask the Chinese Communists and the Soviets to increase aid and add
to their existing commitments.

e. We have chosen to do what is necessary to meet the present situation,
but not to be unnecessarily provocative to either the Russians or the Communist Chinese. We will give the commanders the men they say they need
and, out of existing materiel in the U.S., we will give them the materiel they
say they need. We will get the necessary money in the new budget and will
use our transfer authority until January. We will neither brag about what
we are doing [nor] thunder at the Chinese Communists and the Russians.

This course of action will keep us there during the critical monsoon
season and possibly result in some gains. Meanwhile, we will push on the
diplomatic side. This means that we will use up our manpower reserves. We
will not deplete them, but there will be a substantial reduction. Quietly, we

will push up the level of our reserve force. We will [not?] let Congress push us but, if necessary, we will call the legislators back.

We will hold until January. The alternatives are to put in our big stacks now or hold back until Ambassadors Lodge and Goldberg and the diplomats can work.

TREASURY SECRETARY HENRY FOWLER: Do we ask for standby authority now to call the reserves but not actually call them?

THE PRESIDENT: Under the approved plan, we would not ask for such authority now.

When this NSC record was first declassified, in July 1980, its final sentence was deleted. That sentence was restored following a subsequent declassification request, and reads "There was no response when the President asked whether anyone in the room opposed the course of action decided upon."[22] Ball and Clifford opposed this escalation, while Wheeler, representing the Joint Chiefs, and McNamara had been pressing for much more, and the president knew this. But with his decision presumably having been reached (or at least announced) in their presence the previous day, it was not to be expected that any of them would now argue against it before this wider audience. It is equally clear that none of those now acquainted with the decision for the first time took this opportunity to register dissent.

In the final paragraph of his own record of this NSC meeting, which he reconstructed on November 2, 1968, on the basis of his 1965 notes, McGeorge Bundy states, "The notes also record my own feeling that while the President was placing his preference for alternative five [e] as against four [d], on international grounds, his unspoken objective was to protect his legislative program [i.e., his Great Society program] or at least this had appeared to be his object in his informal talk as late as Thursday and Friday of the preceding week—July 22 and July 23." Bundy is here undoubtedly singling out one of the president's paramount considerations. But to focus so heavily on this is to present a somewhat unbalanced picture of what we know of Lyndon Johnson's approach to Vietnam. He was in fact also deeply concerned about the international implications of the all-out fourth alternative—especially the danger that this courted military intervention by the Chinese communists and increased Soviet aid to Hanoi. Perhaps if Bundy had been with the president on the 24th and 25th at Camp David, particularly when Clark Clifford so forcefully pointed out the dangers of an escalation provoking such reactions by the two major communist powers, he might have given greater weight to this factor.

Fifteen minutes after meeting with the National Security Council, the president, with all senior advisers except Ball, sat down with some of the top congressional leaders to brief them on the decision.[23]

PRESIDENT: (Quoted Elisha Cook about the responsibilities of the leader) (Reviewed the five courses open to us)

So the fifth alternative is the one that makes the most sense. We don't know if this will be 2 years or 4 years or what. We didn't know World War I was going to be one year or five years.

RUSK: The attitude of the Communist world is the key question.

[SENATOR GEORGE] SMATHERS: We are denying the VC the victory, aren't we? Is not our purpose not to be driven out—and avoid WW III by not bringing in China and Russia. Is this a change of policy?

PRESIDENT: As aid to the VC increases, our need to increase our forces goes up. There is no change in policy.

[REPRESENTATIVE HALE] BOGGS: Any substantial surrender of government forces to VC—or officers? How about government?

MCNAMARA: No. Indicates willingness to fight—even though suffering heavy casualties.

PRESIDENT: I couldn't call you down until I had all the information.

WHEELER: (Described guerrilla operation)

[SENATOR RUSSELL] LONG: If we back out, they'd move somewhere else. Ready to concede all Asia to Communists? Not ready to turn tail. If a nation with 14 million can make Uncle Sam run, what will China think?

SPEAKER MCCORMACK: I can't think we have any alternatives. Our military men tell us we need more and we should give it to them. The lesson of Hitler and Mussolini is clear. I can see five years from now a chain of events far more dangerous to our country.

[REPRESENTATIVE GERALD] FORD: I fully understand why we can't do 1, 2 or 3 but I need an explanation of 4 and 5. In either case, Westmoreland would be supplied with what he wants. The question is how? Under 4, money would follow a request by you for additional funds from the Congress. Under 5, you use what you have and come back in January for more money.

PRESIDENT: We will ask Congress for money on either side. We would ask for reasonable request now and see what happens. If you call up reserves now, their year starts ticking immediately. If we wait until January, we can bring in reserves and put them to work immediately. We'll have firm plans then.

Under #5, we ask for no legislation, call up no reserves, don't scare the Russians, and send troops in as we need them.

FORD: You will increase draft calls and extend enlistments?

PRESIDENT: Yes. I want to use this period to show them they can't run us out.

FORD: Double draft calls—how much a strain on training command?

MCNAMARA: About the same as #4. If we call up reserves, it will be for a limited period (one year). Congress is not likely to increase this. It means that we have a perishable asset and seek to replace it by doubling the draft call.

FORD: What does it do to the ceiling on armed forces?

MCNAMARA: We lift the ceiling. We have authority to do that now.

FORD: It is not entirely clear. Appropriations bill is in Senate. Under 4 you would . . .

PRESIDENT: Would call up reserves now and make out estimates in new bill.

MCNAMARA: The rate of activity is difficult to forecast. Considering increasing chopper and plane activity. Don't know what the total is. Under #4 we ask Congress for blank check. Under #5 we can be more specific—come back to Congress in January with clear understanding.
Under #5 we would ask for $1.5 billion.

FORD: How much is the difference?

[REPRESENTATIVE CARL] ALBERT: In both cases Westmoreland gets what he wants—with less fanfare.

[REPRESENTATIVE LES] ARENDS: How many men?

MCNAMARA: We don't know—we will meet requirements. Right now 50,000 additional. We will ship NOW—as soon as the decision is made.

RUSK: During monsoon season, there has not been a sharp increase in conventional fighting. Increase is in their tactics.

PRESIDENT: I've asked you to come here not as Democrats or Republicans but as Americans. I don't want any of you to talk about what is going on. The press is going to be all over you. Let me appeal to you as Americans to show your patriotism by not talking to the press. I'm going to do everything I can, with honor, to keep Russia and China out.

[SENATOR EVERETT] DIRKSEN: I quite agree with your premise. The first business is to peel off dramatics. Tell the country we are engaged in very serious business. People are apathetic. Afraid we are stripping Europe components.

MCNAMARA: Baloney on stripping. We are *not* stripping. It is not necessary.

DIRKSEN: We don't need to withhold information.

PRESIDENT: We won't withhold. We want to announce as soon as troops arrive.

In the morning I will consult Ike and tell him what we hope to do and get his views.

I will see the Chairmen of Foreign Relations, Appropriations and Armed Forces.

Then announce decision in press conference.

DIRKSEN: Five months is a long time. I don't think you can wait. If you need the money, you ought to ask for it.

PRESIDENT: We have the money, 50 Billion plus 800 million. When you come back in January you'll have a bill of several billion dollars.

MANSFIELD: I agree with Dirksen on apathy in the country.

I would not be true to myself if I didn't speak. This position has certain inevitability. Whatever pledge we had was to *assist* SVN in its own defense. Since then there has been no government of legitimacy. We ought to make that decision every day. We owe this government nothing—no pledge of any kind.

We are going deeper into war. Even total victory would be vastly costly. Best hope for salvation is quick stalemate and negotiations.

We cannot expect our people to support a war for 3–5 years. What we are about is an anti-Communist crusade, on . . .

Escalation begets escalation.

From this group of congressmen, then, the only one who registered opposition to the president's announced course at the time was Senator Mike Mansfield, and his assessment was to prove remarkably prescient. Other members of Congress—Aiken, Church, McGovern, Morse, Nelson, and Pell notable among them—strongly opposed increasing U.S. military involvement in Vietnam, but at this point they remained a small minority of that body. When Johnson informed the public of his decision on July 28, it is clear that most of the Congress stood behind it. But, as Mansfield had warned in his memorandum of that same day, the country was backing him on Vietnam primarily because he was president, "not necessarily out of any understanding or sympathy with [your] policies on Vietnam; beneath the support, there is deep concern and a great deal of confusion which could explode at any time. . . ."

The president communicated his decision to the country at a televised news conference on July 28. His address and responses to questions were couched in language emphasizing that continuity with past policy and objectives was being maintained. He announced that there would be an almost immediate increase of U.S. fighting strength in Vietnam from an existing 75,000 to 125,000, but additional forces would be required later and would be sent "as requested": General

Westmoreland would be provided with the troops he needed. "Over a period of time" the monthly draft of Americans into the armed forces would be doubled, from 17,000 to 35,000, but it was not now necessary to call up the reserves. The United States stood ready, if possible via the United Nations, to enter into discussions with Hanoi (once again, the word "negotiations" was eschewed) or with any other "government" (again excluding the NLF). The United States, he explained, was in Vietnam to "fulfill one of the most solemn pledges of the American nation," one shared by Eisenhower and Kennedy, "to help defend this small and valiant nation. . . . And we just cannot now dishonor our word, or abandon our commitment, or leave those who believed us and who trusted us to the terror and repression and murder that would follow."

Most members of Congress, *The New York Times* reported the next day, were relieved by the course Johnson had announced, heartened especially by the fact he was not calling up the reserves and by his apparent willingness to look to negotiations. At an ongoing conference of forty-five of the nation's governors, all but Mark Hatfield of Oregon and George Romney of Michigan endorsed the president's stand, and the first poll, taken hours after his speech, showed a substantial margin of approval among that majority of those interviewed who registered an opinion.[24]

Johnson had kept to his holding action—authorizing the deployment of what he believed would be enough additional U.S. military strength to (a) keep the American position in Vietnam from eroding to a point where domestic opponents could level the politically crippling attack that a Vietnamese analogue of the "loss of China" charge would provoke (such a debate, he believed, would be "even more destructive of our national life than the argument over China had been"[25]); (b) skirt the greater danger of a major conflict with China and the attendant possibility of nuclear war that would be risked by an all-out increase in military input; (c) maintain what he construed to be U.S. global prestige. If these concurrent objectives could be achieved, there should be time and scope for attainment of the domestic legislation embodied in his Great Society program.

Johnson had stressed continuity of policy, that nothing fundamental had changed. In the words of Doris Kearns, who later had unusual access to his thinking:

> By pretending there was no major conflict, by minimizing the level of spending, and by refusing to call up the reserves or ask Congress for an acknowledgment or acceptance of the war, Johnson believed he could keep the levers of control in his hands. He had worked hard to reach the position where he could not only propose but pass his Great Society legislation. . . . "I was determined to keep the war from shattering that dream," Johnson later said, "which meant I simply had no choice but to keep my foreign policy in the wings. I knew the Congress as well as I know Lady Bird, and I knew that the day it exploded into a major debate on the war, that day would be the beginning of the end of the Great Society."[26]

And by minimizing the extent of the war, he argued, he also took less chance of provoking Chinese and Russian intervention. These tactics did secure the president a reprieve from the gathering storm of opposition in the Congress—sufficient time to push through most of his cherished domestic legislation. But the consequent increase in his credibility gap on the war made it all the more difficult to handle the much greater domestic opposition to it that later developed.

Lyndon Johnson had been advised that even the increment of 104,000 troops (above the existing 75,000 he had authorized three months before) requested by the JCS, Westmoreland, and McNamara could be counted on to hold the line no longer than the end of 1965. In his own mind the president was evidently prepared to move up to that number later in the year when it became necessary, rather than sticking to the immediate increase of 50,000 stipulated in his July 28 public address. Indeed, in that television appearance he had stated forthrightly that to meet Westmoreland's requirements it would later be necessary to exceed 50,000—with no upper ceiling being indicated. It is doubtful, however, that either he or McNamara expected that once that door was opened, Westmoreland's demands would escalate to the extent that they did. Within eight and a half months of the president's late-July decision, mounting pressures from Westmoreland and the JCS had brought him to schedule build-ups to 383,500 men by the end of 1966. Their continuing demands brought him to authorize 425,000 to be reached by June 30, 1967, with these military chiefs actually having asked (as early as August 5, 1966) for a deployment of 542,588 men by the end of 1967. By mid-March 1967, Westmoreland was requesting even more—which would bring the total to 671,616. With McNamara himself acknowledging, as early as mid-October 1966, the ineffectiveness of any increase beyond 470,000 the president yielded only a little more to these unending troop requests, and when he left office at the end of 1968 was holding the line at 536,100.[27] With these successive large additional deployments, the war had now indeed been Americanized, the ARVN becoming no more than a heavily dependent adjunct of a massive U.S. expeditionary force.

Two major factors combined to bring Westmoreland and the JCS to insist on increasing the size of U.S. military forces in Vietnam so rapidly. The first was the continuing high rate of desertions from the ARVN, and the growing propensity of most of its commanders to retire behind the shield of American combat power that was being put in place. Thus protected, Saigon's army tended to concentrate on less hazardous mopping-up operations in the rear and garrison duty, often relaxing in the face of the rapidly mounting Americanization of the fight against the Viet Cong. The second was the courage and stamina of both the NLF and Hanoi in the face of what in the annals of human warfare was an unprecedented tonnage of bombs and napalm. What Maxwell Taylor retrospectively concluded about Hanoi also fit the NLF:

In 1965 we knew very little about the Hanoi leaders other than Ho Chi Minh
and General Giap and virtually nothing about their individual or collective
intentions. We were inclined to assume, however, that they would behave
about like the North Koreans and Red Chinese a decade before; that is, they
would seek an accommodation with us when the cost of pursuing a losing
course became excessive. Instead, the North Vietnamese proved to be in-
credibly tough in accepting losses which, by Western calculation, greatly
exceeded the value of the stake involved.[28]

Johnson was never willing to risk the heavy casualties—and uncertain outcome—that Walt Rostow's proposed invasion of North Vietnam would have
entailed. Quite apart from the fact that to raise enough American troops for such
a campaign would have so drained them from the South as to open it up to a Viet
Cong takeover, it was by no means clear how they would fare against North
Vietnamese combat forces that were larger and better equipped than the total of
Viet Cong and Hanoi combat forces then deployed in the South. And the knowledge that such an invasion would be highly likely to trigger the intervention of
large numbers of Chinese combat troops on Hanoi's side remained a further
constraint against any such adventure.

The same expectation governed the president's reluctance to wage an all-out
bombing campaign extending to Hanoi and Haiphong, in accordance with the
maxim of the air force's chief, General Curtis LeMay, of bombing the country
"back into the stone age." That too would have been very likely to bring in
substantial Chinese combat forces. With U.S. intelligence establishing that the
level of bombing reached in July 1965 had already provoked the Chinese to
introduce antiaircraft, coastal defense, and engineering units into North Vietnam,
this prospect seemed all the more probable.[29] And since the U.S. military's plans
for dealing with such a contingency called for escalating to the level of nuclear
warfare, it is understandable that any responsible American president would
refuse to risk either Rostow's or LeMay's prescriptions.

In the face of these limitations, the options open to Johnson were very
restricted. He could negotiate a settlement or continue along the same strategic
track he had been pursuing with whatever increase in U.S. military forces was
necessary to keep the Saigon government from being overwhelmed. Serious
negotiations were out, in part because almost all the president's top advisers had
steered him away from that course, generally denigrating it and insisting it could
not be risked until greater infusions of U.S. military might would have so worn
down the Viet Cong as to permit Saigon to deal with the NLF from a position
of superior strength. In addition, the advisers had done virtually nothing to
explore and develop formulae for him that might have stood some chance of
bridging his concern for U.S. prestige and the reality of the political forces
indigenous to South Vietnam, whose weight would have to register heavily in any
exercise in self-determination. Most fundamentally, any negotiated settlement
would have required a degree of compromise by the United States that could not

possibly have been reconciled with its ongoing objectives of maintaining a separate, anticommunist state in the southern half of Vietnam.

Refusing to accept such a compromise, and the adverse domestic political reaction that it feared this would entail, the Johnson administration concluded that, short of the unacceptable choices of saturation bombing of the North or its invasion by U.S. ground forces, there was no other course open for keeping its Saigon ward from being overrun than to increase substantially America's military input in accordance with existing strategy. Once having made this decision, the United States would remain locked on course for more than seven years—until the bankruptcy and hopelessness of the policy had become so widely understood by the American Congress and public as to force Johnson's successor finally to yield to reality and call a halt.

The Johnson administration's July decision led to an enormous increase in the fire power being projected by air and artillery into Vietnam—most of it in the South. The impact of this soon not only devastated the physical landscape of Vietnam but also produced a strong indigenous political reaction, resulting in the last major noncommunist challenge to the United States and to the pursuit of its objectives in Vietnam.

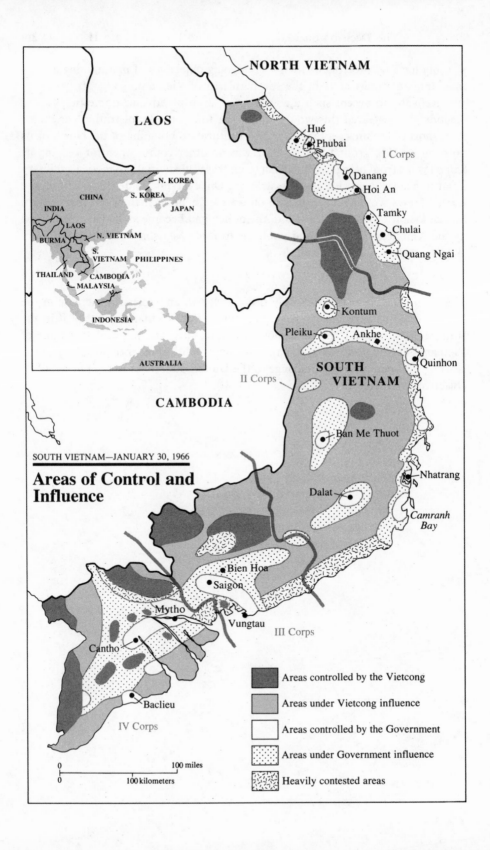

NORTH VIETNAM

LAOS

I Corps

Hué
Phubai
Danang
Hoi An
Tamky
Chulai
Quang Ngai

Kontum
Pleiku
Ankhe
Quinhon

SOUTH
VIETNAM

II Corps

CAMBODIA

Ban Me Thuot

Nhatrang

SOUTH VIETNAM—JANUARY 30, 1966

**Areas of Control and
Influence**

Dalat

Camranh
Bay

Bien Hoa
Saigon

Mytho

Vungtau

III Corps

Cantho

Baclieu

IV Corps

N. KOREA
CHINA   S. KOREA
INDIA   JAPAN
LAOS
N. VIETNAM
BURMA
S.
VIETNAM PHILIPPINES
THAILAND CAMBODIA
MALAYSIA

INDONESIA

AUSTRALIA

Areas controlled by the Vietcong

Areas under Vietcong influence

Areas controlled by the Government

Areas under Government influence

Heavily contested areas

0   100 miles
0   100 kilometers

XVI

The Final Polarization

The major ground-force escalation unleashed by the Johnson administration beginning in the fall of 1965 had an enormous impact on South Vietnam, and not only physically. The weight of search-and-destroy missions and the fire power projected by American planes and artillery into rural Vietnam altered the relationship between man and land, progressively tearing asunder its social fabric; and this had inescapable political consequences. Against the background of a much-broadened and more visible U.S. role in the fighting, popular revulsion in South Vietnam against the widening bloodshed tended to have an increasingly anti-American cast. And the public's erstwhile grudging acceptance of a Ky/Thieu government, now unquestionably regarded as a subservient agent of the United States, was further undermined.

In this situation, the political position of the Buddhist monks in South Vietnamese society was inevitably strengthened by their continued championing of the widespread and increasingly desperate desire for peace and for Vietnamese self-determination. These attitudes became even more broadly based and more salient among the population as the impingement of vastly augmented American fire power brought what U.S. officials acknowledged was "considerable public apprehension over growing civilian casualties."[1] The Buddhists understood how deeply the rural inhabitants, who bore the brunt of the war in the South, longed for the fighting to end. And they appreciated what some American officials knew but rarely publicly mentioned—how little air power and artillery could discriminate between the Viet Cong soldier and the unarmed civilian.

Following a trip to Vietnam in February 1966, Representative Clement Zablocki reported to the House Foreign Affairs Committee that an average of two civilians were killed for every Viet Cong, and that in some recent search-and-destroy missions against the VC the ratio had been six civilians to one enemy soldier.[2] The credibility of his estimate was enhanced because he was known as one of the most prominent hawks in Congress.

Ambassador Lodge's top-secret internal administration commentary—approved by Westmoreland—on Zablocki's report made very clear why so many rural inhabitants were streaming into the cities to find safety. Lodge pointed out that the "superiority of Allied forces . . . lies largely in almost unlimited quantities of sophisticated equipment of war. We have weapons of tremendous power, ranging from B-52's, 175 [mm.] guns, and 8 inch naval guns, down to rapid firing M-16 rifles. . . . Some of these powerful weapons are long-range, and although extreme caution is used when they are employed it is inevitable that they will produce civilian casualties, most of which we will never learn about." Any restrictions on the use of these weapons, he warned, would have to be "balanced against military requirements or they could become so tight as to inhibit our military activities to [a] point where our superiority in weapons is completely negated." He observed that the number of civilians actually killed could not be established, since the peasants and Viet Cong often wore the same black clothing, and that the "black-clad corpses" of civilians were "inevitably counted as VC." Moreover, Lodge asked, "How do you learn whether anyone was inside structures and sampans destroyed by the hundreds every day by air strikes, artillery fire, and naval gunfire? Even if you find casualties in them, how do you know whether they were innocent civilians or VC?" He concluded by urging that the administration not get involved in a "statistical numbers game" and urged that it "continue to impress on public and Congress that reason for civilian casualties is essentially cruel yet totally deliberate VC tactic of using civilians innocent or otherwise, and that casualties caused by VC, being deliberate, are much more cruel and morally reprehensible than those inadvertently caused by Allied forces."[3]

The inability of many U.S. weapons to discriminate between enemy soldiers and the civilian population was in fact much greater than Lodge indicated. This was certainly true of napalm, which both incinerated houses and adhered to and burned deep into flesh. According to Michael Krepon of the staff of the Arms Control and Disarmament Agency, it "became a staple part of U.S. military tactics in Indochina, despite misgivings by some political officials." (It constituted "approximately 8–9% of the yearly bomb tonnage" dropped in Indochina from 1965 on, with a total of over 338,000 tons dropped in the course of the war.)[4]

The question of civilian napalm casualties was a sensitive subject, and it was officially denied that there were significant numbers of them. Vietnamese medical interns at several hospitals informed me that it was government policy to disperse napalm patients as widely as possible, so that visitors would not realize how numerous they were. Officially, "absolutely no napalm cases" were being treated at Saigon's central hospital. Only by visiting on Christmas Day 1966, when most of its senior staff were at home, was I able to inspect the wards at that hospital where such cases were lodged. Nurses and interns then guided me to wards where thirty-five severe cases were being treated, about half of them children. On the same day I saw additional napalm victims at the Saigon Children's Hospital. (Hospital staff told me that many victims of napalm attacks died on the spot, and others before they could be brought to hospitals.)

Probably the most extensive cause of civilian casualties were such antipersonnel weapons as "Lazy Dog," a delayed-action bomb, and the CBU (Cluster Bomb Unit), both of which were authorized for use in South Vietnam on September 26, 1964 (initially in "Yankee Team" flights of planes jointly manned by South Vietnamese and American pilots).[5]

According to Krepon, the CBU was regarded as "the most indiscriminate and lethal area weapon developed for the Vietnam War." Though undoubtedly effective against enemy guns or personnel, it was not a weapon of precision. When one considers that these fragmentation bombs, which were detonated at an altitude of six hundred feet, dispersed fragments that could kill or wound people in an area approximately nine hundred by three thousand feet, it can be appreciated how large an area could be covered by an F-4 Phantom, each of which could normally carry eight bombs and up to twenty with special racks. Dropped extensively in the South as well as in North Vietnam, these bombs were not just used against gun emplacements but, in Krepon's words, "became *the* weapon for area denial." In his comprehensive study he observes that "no formal rules of engagement were placed on where, when, and how CBUs were to be used," and concludes, "CBUs must have caused extensive civilian casualties, and in a high ratio to the military damage unquestionably inflicted on their intended targets."[6]

The original American strategy for the use of ground combat forces in Vietnam had been predicated on the assumption that the search-and-destroy operations mounted by U.S. and South Korean troops would be followed up by complementary actions of the South Vietnamese army, designed to hold and pacify the territory into which these allies had penetrated. This strategy failed in large part because of the incapacity (or unwillingness) of the South Vietnamese troops to carry out their part of the operation. Thus, although U.S. forces were equipped with such overwhelming fire power that they could cut into and through any of the extensive areas of South Vietnam controlled by the NLF—albeit sometimes suffering heavy casualties—the results of these actions were almost always transitory, with no effective follow-up with respect to either military or political control. This was so even after the major build-up of U.S. ground forces had been completed, for General Westmoreland was still rarely able to spare enough of his own men to nail down control over the areas they had penetrated. Thus, military operations yielded little in terms of any lasting territorial control. Moreover, the political consequences were frequently negative, for these actions could not help antagonizing the civilian population, which was frequently mauled in the process.

As it became evident that the United States lacked the military and political resources to consolidate control over disputed territories, Westmoreland began to concentrate on a new strategy of simply denying as much territory and population as possible to the enemy, while at the same time employing other fire power to grind down their military units in what he termed a policy of "attrition." Gradually, beginning on a small scale early in the second half of 1965, this strategy of "territorial denial" increasingly came to supplant reliance on search-and-destroy missions. More and more rural territory that U.S. and South Vietnamese forces were unable to control was turned into largely uninhabitable "harassment and interdiction [H and I] areas" or "free fire zones" (later officially referred to as "specified strike zones").

The close air support given to U.S., South Korean, and South Vietnamese troops accounted for fewer than 10 percent of all air strikes in South Vietnam. The remainder fell into the "wide and diffuse" category of "interdiction." Originally defined as "preventing or hindering enemy use of an area or route, or as a selective-campaign against the enemy's total logistic organization," this category soon came to embrace these "H and I" areas or "free fire zones." "By virtue of residence," anyone who elected to remain in these territories after warning of attack (often a very short interval) was regarded as enemy. As the emphasis moved in this direction, interdiction took on the character of strategic warfare, with the objective of denial to the enemy of territory, manpower, and food.[7]

A former U.S. marine intelligence officer who served in Vietnam has described this development: "An integral part of this strategy was the forced depopulation of vast areas of South Vietnam. . . . Early American designation of large 'free fire zones,' followed by B-52 raids, F-4 Phantom attacks on vague 'targets of opportunity,' long-range artillery and naval 'harassment and interdiction' fire, and movement of villagers at gunpoint during 'search and destroy' missions, had already made many South Vietnamese refugees, but now U.S. commanders proceeded to co-ordinate every weapon in their arsenal to separate the remaining Vietnamese rural population" from the NLF. Noting Mao Tse-tung's remark that revolutionaries were to the people as fish to the sea, he concluded, "Having failed to annihilate the fish or even locate them properly, U.S. strategists proposed to drain the water from the fish and leave the latter floundering, finally vulnerable to identification and destruction."[8]

Beginning in late June 1965 with the first air strike by a flight of twenty-seven B-52s, these planes from the Strategic Air Command became the principal instrument of the strategy, delivering approximately half the tonnage of aerial munitions dropped on South Vietnam from 1965 to 1970. Originally designed to drop atomic bombs, each of them could carry thirty tons of conventional explosives. A typical mission of six planes could saturate an area of at least one square mile. Flying at thirty thousand feet, their pilots could normally not see what they were hitting and had to be instructed from the ground or by forward air controllers (FACs) in spotter planes. Because the planes were too high to be seen or heard, their bombs often fell before people on the ground could even look for cover. Sometimes they were employed in close air support missions for ground troops, but most B-52s were used for territorial denial. In a study heavily reliant on official U.S. military records, Guenter Lewy ascertained that during 1966 "some 65 percent of the total tonnage of bombs and artillery rounds used in Vietnam involved such unobserved [H and I] fire," and that by the first half of 1967, 41 percent of this was being dropped by B-52s.[9]

Area denial was sought not simply through air power and the U.S. navy's big guns, with their capacity to reach over twelve miles inland. The sustained fire of land-based U.S., ARVN, and ROK artillery also rendered many populated areas uninhabitable to adherents of the NLF or anyone else. Sometimes this fire was intended to deprive the enemy of a potential staging area, but often its objective was to clear out peasants from territory over which it was too difficult to exercise authority and push them into refugee camps, where they could be more easily controlled. An account in the official U.S. Marine Corps history is illustrative of such an action. Describing the marines' "first measurable success in the struggle for the people," the authors refer to an action carried out by a Lieutenant Colonel Clements in mid-June 1965. Having found that the population of two neighboring hamlets located five and a half miles from his base refused to move, Clements "decided to convince the villagers that they were in a combat zone and that they would be safer to accept refugee status and relocate near Le My," his base. In this battalion commander's words: "I directed that H & I fires be brought close to the hamlet, night after night. The attitude of the people about relocation 'improved' in time and the relocation operation was scheduled. . . ." Then on June 18 Clements's battalion moved through the hamlets with ARVN forces and "brought out" more than 350 villagers, who were then moved into his base area. In the colonel's words, "I suppose given a free choice, the people would not have left their hamlet. I influenced their decision by honesty, sincerity, and a hell of a lot of H and I fires." Immediately following that quote, the Marine Corps chroniclers observe: "By this time Le My had become a show case for pacification," and they quote Colonel Clements's conclusion that this "permitted a great deal of person-to-person confidence to develop, and along with it, a personal commitment to the government cause."[10]

Such views were certainly not confined to members of the U.S. military. Jonathan Schell has described his interview with James A. May, a civilian who was senior adviser for the U.S. pacification program in Quang Ngai province. In response to Schell's questions about the villages destroyed by U.S. forces, May said:

> "This is a necessary side effect if you're going to fight hard. We've invited people to come on out of the V.C. village to secure areas where it's safe. The V.C. use villages as protection, the way a gangster uses a hostage. . . . You just can't get at the enemy unless you get at them where they're at. There isn't any way to get them but level the villages they are located in. . . . Gradually, we're depriving the V.C. of his labor force and food. Now we've got about fifty thousand people in camps [in Quang Nam province] and about seventy-five thousand [resettled people] who have built their own houses or are living with friends."

May then responded to Schell's question about "the official policy toward the people who continued to live in the zones of harassment-and-interdiction artillery fire."

"These people have had a choice. They still think Charlie's [the VC] going to win. We've plastered the place with Chieu Hoi [*Open Arms*] leaflets [a promise of clemency and rehabilitation]. And when we bring them into secured areas we try to get them to stay, but the pull of the land is very strong. . . . Still we've been encouraged by the number of people who have come to live along the highway, and also by the number who have started living on the beaches. We know they're not dangerous out there, because they haven't any cover and they can't dig underground as well there." When asked if he thought it was a good idea "to hold all the villagers responsible when the Vietcong chose to fire at our troops from the village," May replied: "If you let him in your village, you're an accomplice, aren't you?"

When Schell asked about conditions in the camps, May answered:

"There's always plenty to eat and a roof over their head. . . . Some people want to know, 'Aren't we going to create a nation of refugees living on the dole?' This has been proven totally without foundation. The refugees have a better standard of living than they did in the villages. Look at the tin on their roofs. It's better than the old thatched roofs—it doesn't leak. And the refugee camps bring the people in closer to the urban centers, where they can have modern experiences and learn modern practices. It's a modernizing experience."[11]

It is not suggested that the official marine-corps chroniclers' apparent approval of Colonel Clements's approach was representative of the opinions of all those officers who served in General Westmoreland's command,[12] or that all U.S. civilian advisers in the pacification program held the same views as James May. Certainly many were more sensitive to the political consequences of Westmoreland's policies, though never strong enough to challenge them effectively. I recall vividly the frustration and anguish expressed by one marine battalion commander over the civilian casualties being inflicted in his sector. "I have to operate blind," he complained, explaining that he didn't have a single man in his outfit who could really understand Vietnamese and that he was obliged to use Vietnamese interpreters who had their own axes to grind and whom he didn't trust.

One of the best-qualified critics of Westmoreland's strategy was John Paul Vann. After serving in Vietnam as a U.S. lieutenant colonel and an adviser to the Vietnamese Seventh Division, he resigned from the army in mid-1963 in order to criticize these policies. He was regarded as so knowledgeable, however, that in early 1965 he was appointed coordinator of field operations for the U.S. Operations Mission in Vietnam, ultimately being given a civilian rank equivalent to lieutenant general. His reputation as a soldier and the respect in which he was held for his understanding of the political context and consequence of military actions kept him in close contact and rapport with a good many U.S. officers in both Vietnam and the Pentagon—if not with General Westmoreland's headquarters. When, after seven more years of service in Vietnam, he died in a helicopter crash, *Newsweek* referred to him as "the third most influential American in Vietnam (outstripped only by the American Ambassador and commanding general)," and Robert Komer, former director of the U.S. pacification program in Vietnam, reckoned his death as the equivalent of losing two divisions.[13]

Vann's internally circulated memorandum of September 10, 1965 (recirculated largely unchanged on April 1, 1967), incorporated a scathing criticism of General Westmoreland's population-removal strategy and its political consequences:

> Recently, when advocating the establishment of a large, new free bombing zone in a populated area, a US officer stated: "If these people want to stay there and support the Communists, then they can expect to be bombed."
> Completely ignored or unknown in this type of thinking are the considerations that:
>
> 1. These people have lived there all their life.
> 2. They are ancestral worshippers who feel it necessary to daily pray at the graves of their ancestors.
> 3. They have no place to go where they can continue to earn a living.
> 4. Most of them have never heard of Communism, and sincerely believe that their husbands, sons or brothers, if involved in the conflict, are doing so to fight oppression.
> 5. It is primarily the GVN absence, as opposed to the NLF presence, that has involved a majority of them in the conflict.
> The question arises as to the wisdom of a policy that, despite its objective, results in the exodus from a contested area of those elements of the population who do not support the NLF. This is surrendering an area and its resources to the enemy, and, even worse, removing those who might later provide the base of resistance to the enemy. The subsequent free bombing and unrestricted artillery firing that results may well provide an opportunity to polish conventional military techniques, but is worse than useless in accomplishing the ultimate objective of winning the population.[14]

The escalation in fire power had a mounting geopolitical impact. Because of this and the destruction of their crops by bomb craters or the increasing application of aerial-delivered herbicides, a large part of the peasantry fled their villages to the safe sanctuary of the cities and their satellite refugee camps. Extensive areas of South Vietnam were no longer being farmed, with the reduction of the land under cultivation in the First Corps area (the one where the exodus from the countryside was greatest), reaching 50 percent in 1967. The old ratio between urban and rural inhabitants shifted dramatically. Overwhelmingly rural when Diem's state had been established, South Vietnam's population had now become

more urban than rural, and the imbalance continued to grow. A U.S. Senate
report estimated that by the end of 1974 "some 65% of South Vietnam's population lives in an urbanized setting—mostly in a false urban situation, without a
sustained economic base." As early as the end of 1966, Saigon's inhabitants had
increased to about four times their earlier number, now totaling more than 2.5
million, and, proportionately, Danang had grown even more, to about one million. By conservative estimate (the amount officially acknowledged by the Saigon
government), the refugees numbered 1,616,633 by the end of November 1966—this
not including an estimated 150–200,000 new refugees in the Saigon area, and some
100,000 in Danang. McGeorge Bundy's aides reported to him that a total of
745,800 refugees had been processed by the Saigon government just between July
and December 31, 1965.[15]

The swollen urban population and the satellite refugee camps became even
more dependent than before on deliveries of food from the United States. In 1940
the South, even after supplying the deficit of the North, had exported approximately a million tons of rice. In 1965, despite the heavier use of fertilizers and the
introduction of higher-yielding strains, the net export of rice had ceased and
imports had risen to 130,000 tons, reaching 750,000 tons in 1967.[16]

Not only was there a large expansion of the festering slum areas in the urban
centers, but increasingly the uprooted rural populations were herded into concentrations on the outskirts of the cities and towns, where they lived at "little more
than a subsistence level of existence." These refugee camps were usually fenced
with barbed wire, and their inhabitants controlled by informers, a system of
passes, and the periodic distribution of rations. Though the United States did
provide food and medicine, the inhabitants often received considerably less than
their allocation, because a portion of the funds or supplies was siphoned off by
South Vietnamese officials.[17]

Refugees from rural Vietnam who were of age were frequently forced to
enter military service, but most of the others were unemployed. U.S. economic
programs were not geared to incorporating uprooted peasants into the economic
life of South Vietnam's expanding urban areas, and political considerations, plus
the widespread corruption within the Saigon military and civilian bureaucracy,
led to the channeling of American resources primarily to the expanding urban
middle class. Corruption sometimes exceeded what the embassy could countenance, as was the case with pilferage by Vietnamese officials in charge of Saigon's
major port area, which became so great during 1966 that the U.S. government felt
obliged to use its own military units to work the docks.

The heavy increase in American and other foreign troops and the burgeoning
number of U.S., South Korean, and Filipino civilian contractors and employees
also had an adverse psychological impact on much of the urban population. As
at least some U.S. officials were aware, the greater the number of these often
highly visible aliens, the greater the affront to nationalist sensitivities, and the
more the regime of Ky and Thieu appeared subservient to outside power. Moreover, the enormous growth of the urban economy, resulting from the expanded

American intervention and the personal expenditures by the influx of Americans and other aliens, led to socioeconomic distortions.

Many times larger than the small Vietnamese bourgeoisie existing during the last years of French colonial rule, the now largely artificial urban middle class incorporated elements that were affected differently by the increased inflationary pressures caused by the U.S. military effort. American officials believed it vital to dampen the continuing inflationary pressures, but could find no really effective way of doing so.[18] The rise in purchasing power that was spread so unevenly usually meant that the richest South Vietnamese and/or those with the closest political ties to the government grew richer, while many other members of the middle class, along with the enormously expanded number of white-collar workers, soon began to suffer from the inflation—often with a consequent increase in their resentment against the government, the war, and the United States.

John Paul Vann clearly understood the political implications of the American economic-assistance program. In his September 1965 memorandum, he observed that the Saigon regime had "demonstrated that it cannot establish stability, even with dictatorial powers, let alone achieve a popular base among the people." He continued: "Assistance from the United States, both military and economic, is used to perpetuate a regime that, despite lip service to the contrary, has not demonstrated a sincere interest in bettering the lot of the rural population." Its leaders had demonstrated that they were "incapable of surmounting a system of which they are a product, and a participant and have vested interest in perpetuating." He noted that "the only apparent condition imposed or required by our assistance programs has been that the GVN be anti-Communist," and that "those Vietnamese who are most ardently anti-Communist are the affluent members of the urban areas who stand to lose most if the Communists take over." And "being politically articulate and influential," these were "the same people who inherited and are propagating a government which is intrinsically opposed to the social revolution in progress." Then, in a statement which was especially heretical coming from a high USOM official, he concluded: "Realistically . . . a viable non-Communist government" in South Vietnam may be more easily attained "through socialist-inclined leaders who are more in tune with the aspirations of the rural population." He regarded "the existing government" as "oriented towards the exploitation of the rural and lower class urban population," and saw no prospect of the emergence of "a more representative type of government" until "a political base among the population" had developed, "a matter of years and decades."

Vann held that "It has been the default of the GVN more than the appeal of Communism" that forced nationalists who objected to fence straddling to "throw in their lot with the National Liberation Front," and found it to be "a scathing indictment of our political awareness that we have sat idly by while many patriotic and non-Communist Vietnamese were literally forced to ally themselves with a Communist dominated movement in the belief that it was their only chance to secure a better government." He saw "hopes of a military victory now denied to the NLF by the US presence,"[19] but felt there was no prospect of the Saigon government's securing a rural political base. Observing that "the Government of South Vietnam has failed to appeal to its rural population since its formation in 1955," Vann stated that the peasantry's dissatisfaction had "become increasingly evidenced each year since the late fifties" and "today is largely expressed through alliance with the NLF." But the character of the Saigon government to which the United States was tied, he decided, was incompatible with any policy that could compete politically with the NLF.

Vann was bitter over the fact that in villages that had recently been wrested, with considerable difficulty, from Viet Cong control by U.S. forces, nearly all the land given the peasantry by the NLF had been reclaimed by absentee landlords who sat safely in Saigon or behind a screen of U.S. artillery and air power in the provincial capital. Like Colonel Sam Wilson, the politically sensitive officer in charge of local U.S. forces who accompanied us on a trip we took together, he was intensely frustrated over their helplessness in getting the district and provincial officials—almost all military officers—to carry out the U.S.-supported agrarian reform program, which still existed largely on paper. Both complained that because these officials themselves had a vested interest in continuation of the existing exploitative pattern of agrarian relationships, it was impossible to secure their cooperation in implementing the regulations.[20]

Protected by an expanding shield of American fire power and a now overshadowing U.S. military presence, the military junta headed by Nguyen Cao Ky and Nguyen Van Thieu, which had been in office since mid-1965, readily abandoned more and more of the battlefield to the United States. And it entered 1966 no more willing to risk transferring the contest with the NLF to the political level than it had been six months before—a reluctance it would maintain until Saigon fell a decade later. Thus, on January 7, 1966, two of McGeorge Bundy's aides reported to him, "To date Ky's government has been notably unsuccessful in developing significant popular enthusiasm or positive political support. . . . Currently Saigon's ruling generals continue to express opposition to . . . any settlement in which the South Vietnamese [i.e., their regime] would be forced to compete politically with the Viet Cong."[21]

Later that year General Pham Xuan Chieu, chief political adviser to Ky and Thieu and secretary of their Military Directorate (the new name of the National Leadership Council), spelled out their position:

> To defeat the Communists we must win against them both politically and militarily. First militarily.
> But we are very weak politically and without the strong political support of the population which the NLF have. Thus now even if we defeat them militarily, they can come to power because of their greater political strength.

After defeating them militarily, we will have to be able to destroy their political organization and political infrastructure among the people.

Thus we now only have—with the support of our Allies (the U.S., Korea, etc.)—a strong military instrument, but we are without a political instrument that can compete with the communists in the South. Such a political instrument we must now begin to create, a process that will take a generation or at least 10 years. . . .

It is unrealistic to speak of a cease-fire until after we have built up our political strength to a point where we can compete with the Communists successfully. . . .

Thus, President Johnson's statement at Manila [February 1966] that the U.S. troops would begin withdrawal within 6 months of a settlement makes no sense. We must have military victory plus political superiority first.[22]

The Ky/Thieu government, Chieu asserted, was convinced that to secure military victory it would ultimately be necessary to carry the war into North Vietnam. He acknowledged that this might take a million American troops, could drive the North Vietnamese across the border into Chinese sanctuaries, and would probably bring China into the war. If larger U.S. and Korean forces were insufficient to defeat the Viet Cong and Hanoi, contingents from Chiang Kai-shek's armies should be used.[23] Should this cause Peking's combat units to join the war, and should the United States not then attack mainland China itself, Chiang's forces could be so employed. In any case, it might be necessary to move on to World War III in order to remove the menace of communism from Vietnam.

Although these views were well known to some U.S. civilian and military officials and consistent with highly classified memoranda, they were rather different from the heroic stance the Johnson and Nixon administrations publicly attributed to the Saigon leadership. Chieu's elucidation does, however, provide insights helpful to understanding the limitations under which the United States operated during the decade when Ky and Thieu served as its political instruments. For although the new junta that Washington treated as the government of South Vietnam proved even more eager than U.S. officials had hoped to endorse American military escalation, it constituted a weaker military ally than its predecessor. On most of the increasingly rare occasions when they were willing to stand firm, ARVN units were badly mauled by the Viet Cong, and Saigon's military desertion rate mounted almost as fast as the expanded draft which Ky and Thieu instituted in accordance with their promise to the United States. The South Vietnamese military leaders, then, saw the increased infusions of U.S. and third-country (largely Korean) ground forces as an opportunity for further reducing their own combat roles and retiring behind the battlements of external military power.

.   .   .

In the face of this situation, Vietnam's politically engaged Buddhists, with their Vien Hoa Dao (or Buddhist Institute) providing most of the leadership, had been working steadily at strengthening their organization. Their ultimate objective remained an end to the fighting and a negotiated political settlement with the NLF. But to avoid a confrontation with American power, their leaders recognized that they could not openly declare this. They emphasized instead the intermediate aim of elections, a step awkward for the U.S. mission to oppose, which, if reasonably honest, would ensure Ky and Thieu's replacement by a Saigon regime in tune with these Buddhist aims. When he was prime minister, Phan Huy Quat had announced plans for the election of a legislative assembly to be held in August 1965. U.S. officials, however, had then disapproved, fearing unpredictable and probably adverse consequences, and when Ky and Thieu assumed power the plans had been shelved. But once out of the bottle, this genie could not be put back, for the idea had widespread appeal.[24]

At the end of March 1966, Robert Komer, the interim successor to McGeorge Bundy (prior to the appointment of Walt Rostow), discerned that "an essential missing element in the present GVN structure [was] a vehicle for popular participation." Some U.S. officials also recognized this and realized that this absence was "in part responsible for the political crises with the Buddhists." Nevertheless, Lodge, with the backing of most top officials in the Johnson administration, remained determined to avoid elections until after the war had been won, or at least until after the Saigon military were solidly and unchallengeably in control. Ky, however, believed the popular demand to be so strong that it would be wise to give lip service to the idea, and he made several vague pledges that elections would eventually take place. As Takashi Oka wrote, the government led by Ky and Thieu "had not a single concrete achievement to point to in the field of progress towards democratic civilian rule. All it could cite were promises, and promises alone, after nine months in office, simply were not good enough." Yet even though the South Vietnamese public remained skeptical that meaningful elections would ever be held under the junta, the Buddhists seized on the hope that had been stirred by Ky's many unimplemented promises and commenced energetically to build on it.[25]

Not long after, I had a series of talks with some Buddhist leaders concerning the views that governed their actions during this period. (These were not, it should be emphasized, the views that they felt it prudent to express to U.S. officials.) Thich Thien Hoa and Thich Phap Tri, after mid-1966 respectively president and vice-president of the Vien Hoa Dao, prefaced their discussion with the observation: "It is the popular opposition to the American invader, whom the people generally see as they did the French, that gives the communists so much popular support. Remove the American military presence and you remove the main cause for the communists' popular support. Peace can only come with the departure of the United States." Through their network of social-service organizations, as well as their religious ties, the Buddhist leaders had developed a rapport with and an understanding of the rural population that the Saigon military and their U.S. mentors could never hope to attain. They understood clearly what one of their number, Thich Nhat Hanh, put so poignantly: "The Vietnamese peasant doesn't know what anticommunism is except the bomb." Moreover, they saw the Americans and their Vietnamese protégés as enhancing the reputation of communism through the same gaucherie as the French—the tendency to label critics of whatever actual political persuasion as "communist" or "procommunist." With Lodge and Ky now both describing the politically active Buddhists in these terms, the blunder pioneered by the French was surpassed.

The Buddhist leadership saw the NLF as a predominantly nationalist organization, with the overwhelming mass of its adherents made up of noncommunists who had joined it because they saw it as fighting for national independence against an intruding Western power and its venal Vietnamese agents. They regarded its procommunist leadership as strongly nationalist, and were convinced they could deal with them and arrive at a mutually beneficial agreement. And they held that, even if the NLF leaders did not want a cease-fire and the compromise political settlement necessary to sustain it, they would have to take that course once it was offered by a Saigon government free of U.S. control. Otherwise, they believed—and on this point their conviction was unqualified—the NLF would lose nearly all of its supporters. Many U.S. officials contemptuously denounced such a view as naïve. But the Buddhists were in an infinitely better position to assess Vietnamese political attitudes and dynamics than were Americans, whose perceptions were informed so heavily by their own prejudices and by their often sycophantic Vietnamese retainers.

The steps that the Buddhist leadership hoped to take through 1966 and thereafter were clearly spelled out by Thich Thien Minh, their chief organizer. The United States, Thien Minh emphasized, was the principal political power in the Saigon regime, and, having installed the Ky/Thieu government and maintained it in office, the Americans would have to remove that government if there was to be any progress toward an end to the fighting and a political compromise. "We can't negotiate peace through the present government . . . for it is weak and without popular support and not recognized by either the NLF or Hanoi as representing the people here, which is true. We do not want to negotiate from weakness. This government must be changed—not with Buddhist leaders in government positions—but changed so as to be representative." He went on to spell out the position held by the Buddhist leadership from early 1966, that, if there were ever to be peace and a negotiated settlement, the United States would have to remove the political obstacles that it had interposed. It would have not only to end its bombing of the North but also to permit a sufficient change in the Saigon leadership "so that there is a government whom the people will trust to carry out reasonably honest elections. . . . The new elected leaders would form a government sufficiently representative to undertake negotiations with the NLF." Coincident with these negotiations, or as soon as possible after they were under way, there should be a cease-fire—an action that in itself would enhance the newly elected government's appeal. "An impartial international presence should be brought in if possible to supervise execution of the cease-fire and armistice." One of the major objectives of the negotiations would be "to prepare for subsequent countrywide elections in the South wherein the elected Saigon government and the NLF would yield place to a government more representative than either."[26]

The immediate goal for which these Buddhists fought during the first half of 1966 was a freely elected constituent assembly that would have legislative as well as constitution-drafting powers, with the military leadership stepping down as soon as the assembly was established. They calculated that it would be possible to carry out the elections and effect this transfer of power within a period of six months. Pending election of the constituent assembly, they called for the immediate convening of an interim body composed of delegates elected by provincial councilors from their own numbers. These councilors, themselves elected during the last days of Quat's government, had thus far been powerless, exercising only an advisory role to the appointed province chiefs, nearly all of whom were army officers. The Buddhists envisaged, however, that representatives from this group elected by their provincial colleagues would serve in an interim national assembly and be vested with interim legislative authority—and during this transitional period Ky and his Cabinet would exercise executive powers alone.[27]

Since the crisis of early 1965, U.S. civilian and military officials in Saigon had become increasingly distrustful of the Buddhist political leaders. Quite correctly, they regarded the Buddhists as more than just opponents of military rule. Henry Cabot Lodge had been wrong in describing Thich Tri Quang and other militant Buddhist leaders as equivalent to "card-carrying Communists"; but he was right in thinking that they opposed a military solution of their country's problems, wished to end U.S. political dominance, and wanted the Vietnamese free to settle their affairs on their own; and he was also correct in believing that for the Buddhists, free elections were an essential step toward those goals. American officials were not long in appreciating that a freely elected government would by its very nature move to end the fighting and negotiate a political settlement with the communists. As "a most authoritative spokesman for U.S. policy in Saigon" (presumably Lodge) put it to Newsweek's Emmet John Hughes, "If any elected assembly sits in Saigon, it will be on the phone negotiating with Hanoi within one week." A genuinely representative government would, in the terminology of U.S. officials, be "neutralist," and as such could be expected not only to seek an accommodation with the NLF and Hanoi, but also to put the United States in the humiliating position of being asked to leave.[28]

Lodge's assessment soon came to be shared in Washington, where William Bundy and other officials were reported to fear that Tri Quang "might yet attempt to work for a coalition government with the Vietcong or to find other compromise with the Communists."[29] Consequently—with Lodge and Westmoreland taking the critical initiatives—from the time that Ky and Thieu came to office, American power was ranged against the Buddhists and in full support of the two military leaders, working to ensure that elections be deferred until their positions had been strengthened and a political system established that would assure their continuing dominance.

During their first seven months in power, Ky and Thieu had felt too weak to assert any significant degree of authority over the ARVN's four corps commanders, who ran their areas very much as "personal satrapies,"[30] continuing to assert considerable regional independence as their price for acquiescing to the new Saigon leadership's political paramountcy—such as it was. In the fall and early winter of 1965–66 this became a matter of growing concern for U.S. officials. They were especially worried about General Nguyen Chanh Thi, the Buddhist commander of I Corps, an area embracing South Vietnam's five northernmost provinces and its second- and third-largest cities, Danang and Hué. Recognized by the U.S. military as an effective combat officer, Thi governed with an even greater degree of independence from Saigon than the other three corps commanders. He was locally popular—at least in and around the cities—and feared by Ky and Thieu as a threat.

Because he depended on the support of politically active Buddhists in his area, Thi understandably refrained from active opposition to their peace program and political strategy. This led Lodge to worry that the general might find it expedient to back the same program. Thus, by early April the ambassador assessed as "consistent with General Thi's character" reports that "he cherished some resentment against the Americans in respect of what he considers political and military interference and infringement of sovereignty," and that he was "considering the possibility of establishing a government in the south which would be of such a character that the bulk of the population including the Vietcong would support it—and presumably neutralization of the country and possibly federation with the North would be possible. . . ."[31]

In early February of 1966 the Johnson administration took a step that it hoped would strengthen Ky and Thieu, but which inadvertently helped precipitate the confrontation with the Buddhists that most U.S. officials wished to avoid. At a conference in Honolulu to which Johnson summoned the two leaders, the president physically embraced Ky—an action that, together with what was viewed as a peremptory summons, symbolized for the Vietnamese a dependency that further diminished Ky's standing. For Ky himself, however, the meeting demonstrated a public U.S. commitment to him personally that would assure American backing for whatever moves he might take against his rivals.[32]

Knowing that Lodge and Westmoreland were critical of Thi, Ky was now emboldened to move against him. Lodge, however, was mindful of Thi's power, and urged Ky not to fire him unless he was certain of success. The other generals of the Military Directorate felt better able to cope with Ky than with this powerful rival of his, and on March 10 they voted to oust Thi from his command. In a meeting with Johnson just afterward, McNamara strongly endorsed this move, with Taylor chiming in, "He's a bad character and good riddance." Lodge

and Westmoreland then urged Thi to leave gracefully, offering him the pretext
of a face-saving physical examination in the United States, and promising him a
good living there and an education for all of his children. With the support of
the Buddhists, however, Thi resisted American pressures to depart for nearly
three months. His ability to hold on was also a consequence of the tacit support
of General Lewis Walt, commander of the U.S. marines in the First Corps area,
with whom he had gotten along well and who evaluated him much more positively than did Westmoreland.[33]

The news of Thi's dismissal sparked widespread protest throughout the First
Corps area, and even in Saigon, where paratroopers (whom he had once commanded) marched in his support. Buddhist leaders quickly capitalized on this
unpopular decision in order to give a sharper edge to their already well developed
political demands on Ky and Thieu. In Danang and Hué they moved to assert
control over the protest, "seeking to turn it from one simply demanding Thi's
reinstatement into one calling for national elections to replace the military junta
with a civilian government." From Danang and Hué on March 15, large mass
meetings called for Ky to rescind the order for Thi's removal and for the Saigon
junta to retire to the battlefield and make way for a democratically elected civilian
government. The next day in Saigon, Thich Ho Giac, the Buddhist Institute's
most effective orator, picked up the demands for an elected civilian government
and the exclusion of the military from political roles, and to a crowd of at least
ten thousand pledged an all-out effort to secure these goals.[34]

Because of the public cynicism and frustration at Ky's repeated but still-
unfulfilled promises for elections—or even the first steps toward preparing for
them—these moves were well timed. Public support for Tri Quang, Tam Chau,
Thien Minh, and other Buddhist leaders of what was now known as "the Struggle
Movement" became broader and bolder throughout most of the five provinces of
the First Corps area—the movement's main bastion—as well as in Saigon. Most
alarming for Ky and Thieu and their American backers was the sympathy many
of the troops in I Corps showed toward the movement. Throughout most of that
area not under NLF control, the movement now began to exert authority. And
it called publicly not only for the prompt establishment of an interim legislative
assembly and a clear-cut schedule for elections to a constituent assembly, but also
for the end of the military's political leadership in Saigon.

After assessing the strength of the Struggle Movement, Major General
Nguyen Van Chuan, whom the Saigon junta had appointed as Thi's successor,
refused to employ military force to restore control and urged a political settlement. The U.S. embassy and the junta regarded the situation as so dangerous that
they suspended their plans to exile Thi, and, in what Lodge termed "a calculated
risk," sent him back to the First Corps area in the hope that he would try to quiet
the situation. Arriving in Danang on March 16, Thi made a series of ambiguous
public addresses while privately giving much more explicit assurances of his
sympathy for local grievances against the Saigon regime. He refused to return to
Saigon and, despite the circumspection of his public addresses, undoubtedly

helped encourage the Struggle Movement. Whatever Thi's own immediate ambitions, events soon passed him by, and Thich Tri Quang and other influential Buddhists, supported by the student leaders of Hué University, retained the political initiative.[35] Popular backing for the movement continued to mount throughout most of the five northern provinces, with officers and men of the army's First Division soon beginning to join it openly.

The Johnson administration was alarmed at these developments, and Dean Rusk authorized Lodge to convey to Tri Quang and other Buddhist leaders "the President's considered view that, if they persist in their present irresponsible and destructive course, not only will they lose the U.S. public and official sympathy that they have heretofore had, but they may well bring about a situation of chaos and anarchy in which U.S. Government support to Vietnam could no longer be effective."[36]

To stem the antigovernment tide now rising in Saigon and other cities, as well as in the northern provinces, Ky concluded after consultation with Lodge that, as an immediate tactical move "to steal the political initiative from the Buddhists," it was necessary to announce that elections for a "constituent assembly" would be held during the current year, followed by a presidential election in 1967. Accordingly, on March 17, while Lodge had a long talk with Tri Quang, Ky and Thieu consulted with Tam Chau, to acquaint him with their new proposal. The promises made by the two military leaders were ambiguous, but their general message was that there would be a return to civilian government and the speeding up of both constituent-assembly elections and a subsequent presidential vote. Tri Quang returned to the embassy to inform Lodge that the political crisis would end if the government kept its promise.[37]

Having gained this reprieve, Ky and Lodge met on March 22 for a long discussion of tactics on plans for the elections and a constituent assembly. Calculated ambiguity remained the hallmark of Lodge's approach. He counseled Ky that his statements should not "exclude the possibility of elections later on for a constitutional convention" but his words "should be deliberately fuzzed and left open by implication." He admonished the prime minister to drop the "pernicious" term "constituent assembly" in favor of "constitutional convention," pointing out that the latter body would simply meet to adopt a constitution and then disband, whereas a constituent assembly, to which the junta and the Buddhists had already agreed, "stays around and makes trouble for an indefinite period." Accepting only reluctantly the idea of an elected government in the future—well after a constitution had been drafted—Lodge considered "preservation of the junta as an interim government vital." There was support for these views in Washington, where, as Max Frankel reported, the administration wanted the military to remain in power "while a constitution is written and ratified and an acceptable coalition of non-communist civilians is organized—a period of at least another year or so."[38]

Having defused the situation with his promises and bought a week of tranquillity, Ky then, on advice from Lodge, reneged on some of his most important

pledges to the Buddhists. The junta would manage "democratization" through
a process whereby, it was clear, they themselves would continue to hold a tight
rein on governmental power. There was to be no possibility for an elected constituent assembly to exercise governmental powers during the period it was
writing a constitution. Indeed, there would be no constituent assembly at all, but,
rather, a "Constitutional Preparatory Commission," whose members would be
selected by the junta, to draft the constitution while the military remained in
power. Thus, Ky and Thieu would be free to apply pressure on the body drafting
the constitution and the election law; and the elections—when ultimately held—
would be carried out under their aegis. Moreover, instead of sticking to the date
of early 1967 for the elections, as he and Thieu had promised, Ky now questioned
whether they would ever be held, declaring that the date would depend on
progress against the Viet Cong and would have to be deferred until Saigon
controlled 75–80 percent of South Vietnam's population. Since the junta's own
secretary general, General Pham Xuan Chieu, had just acknowledged to provincial leaders that no more than 50 percent was then under the government's
control,[39] it was clear that elections, if they were ever to take place, were a long
time off. And Ky warned that he would if necessary take "very, very strong
measures" should the Buddhists and their supporters now return to the antigovernment demonstrations that they had called off pending the elucidation of his
intentions.

Lodge was unwilling to explore possibilities for compromise with the Buddhists and their supporters. He dismissed a suggestion, apparently emanating
from Rusk, that he call a conference of the contending parties, asserting that this
would not be able to work out a solution unless Ky's government were prepared
to implement the compromises it had previously negotiated. And against that
course he remained adamantly opposed. An effort to split the Struggle Movement
"by trying to make minimum concessions on the political timetable for a constitution and election" was unsuccessful, though Lodge and some other U.S. officials
persevered in their efforts to achieve this objective.[40]

The Buddhist leaders were not prepared to accept what they saw as an
outright betrayal. For them the gauntlet had been deliberately flung down, and
the predictable reaction was prompt. Popular support further solidified behind
the Struggle Movement. Anti-Ky demonstrations broke out in Hué to demand
the overthrow of his government. In Saigon as well, Buddhists mounted large
antigovernment demonstrations, and, to the surprise of the American embassy,
even the leaders of the South Vietnamese Catholic community joined the demand
for an end to military rule. Lodge's role behind Ky's belligerent stance was widely
perceived, and statements and broadcasts from Hué Radio took on a clearly
anti-American tone. The major themes, as the Saigon mission reported to President Johnson, were that Ky's "corrupt" government was "merely a puppet, with
national sovereignty held by others"; that the people and soldiers had been
betrayed by Thieu and Ky, who "would not dare stand up to the people if they
were not backed by a foreign country"; that the "rascals in Saigon are receiving

orders from the White House and American Embassy in Saigon"; and that "the U.S. wants to conquer our country under the guise of helping to fight communists."[41]

On April 2 Johnson was advised that in Hué and Danang "the police, civil servants, and large elements of the local 1st Division are in total sympathy with the 'struggle' group" and that "anti-American themes have been increasing." He was told that the Cao Dai had joined the Buddhists in labeling Ky's government illegal, and he was warned that the Struggle Movement "seems to be imbued with ideas of 'neutralization' and reducing the U.S. role," although it was not asking the United States to get out "as of now." Never had any South Vietnamese government stood more naked of indigenous backing. In the words of a retrospective U.S. intelligence assessment, there was an "almost total absence of *any* organized popular *support,* or even sympathy for the American-backed regime."[42]

After impatient urging from Lodge, and in accordance with plans worked out with him and Westmoreland, the junta struck to crush the opposition. Inside the enclave within the U.S. Danang air base assigned to his own air force, Ky set up a "black operation" clandestine radio station, which purported to be a "Voice of the Struggle Movement," and beamed broadcasts to Saigon that made the Buddhists appear to have embraced communism. On April 3, he declared that communists had taken over control of the Struggle Movement in Danang and that he was sending troops there to liberate the city. (A direct assault on Hué was regarded as too difficult, and possible only after first taking Danang.)[43]

With twenty thousand of the forty thousand U.S. marines in the First Corps area stationed in Danang itself, Ky's allegations that the town was in communist hands must have seemed a bit absurd to General Wallace B. Greene, Jr., marine corps commandant, who happened to be visiting the city. In a public broadcast the next day he stated, "I don't consider that we have an insurrection in process," adding that "the situation was calm." Greene was clearly reflecting the views of his commander on the spot, General Lewis Walt, who, along with the new commander of the First Corps area, General Nguyen Van Chuan, believed that a political resolution of the issues between Saigon and the Struggle Movement was the only sensible course. Moreover, Walt feared that, if Saigon were to employ military force, his own troops might be caught in the crossfire. He apparently played no role in the planning that Westmoreland (with whom he was then believed to have strained relations) and Lodge had carried out with Ky and Thieu, and he seems to have had little advance warning of the provocative move that they launched. The orders from Walt's superiors, however, along with his own concern for the safety of the American troops under his command, dictated that he play a role that on balance weighed heavily in favor of the junta in Saigon.[44]

The tendentious nature of Lodge's reporting to Washington at this time may explain why neither Rusk nor Johnson was willing to challenge his insistence on forceful measures against the Buddhists. Shortly before American transports began shuttling the junta's troops to Danang, the ambassador sent Rusk one of his more vivid cables. Describing a meeting of the previous day, he reported that

Ky turned to him "with a very serious expression on his face and, looking somewhat shaken, said: 'We have waited too long. Now we must be very firm. . . . All these different groups and minorities and sects make an infernal combination.' " He said that Ky believed Tri Quang to be a communist and had warned Lodge that "we face a great communist conspiracy to take over the government, ask the Americans to leave, and turn the country over to Hanoi." Declaring that "he had had too much faith in the value of making concessions to the Buddhists," Ky told Lodge that he wanted to move three battalions to Danang and bring up one division from IV Corps for security in Saigon. He asked for U.S. aircraft to reinforce Danang, and said that he knew Westmoreland was ready but needed an order from Lodge. The ambassador promptly agreed to the request (which presumably he and Westmoreland had been expecting) and ordered the American commander to provide the planes. Lodge concluded his cable by quoting Ky— "History will judge whether I have done well or not, but I am ready to make the supreme sacrifice"—and ended with the remark "He was deeply moved and so was I."[45]

The president and his aides in Washington took Lodge's bizarre account of a heroic Ky with a good measure of salt, but they were now clearly worried and appeared initially unclear as to what course to take. A still heavily censored account of their meeting on the evening of April 4 gives some flavor of their thinking:

> President thinks it important to keep our troops and equipment out of riot area. We don't want to become involved. President approved telegram (first one) on what posture [American mission] Vietnam people should take— *hands off.* President wonders about (second telegram) on political situation. Says appeasement never wins. Worried about a constitutional assembly— rather have someone we can control rather than a Communist takeover of the Assembly. . . . President gave approval for a second telegram to go out. (Now he looked at this telegram on alternative governments.)

[Several sentences sanitized]

RUSK: Alternatives are less desirable than what we have.

PRESIDENT: [Sentence sanitized] Time has come when the alternative is to get out—or do what we need to do to get the government shored up—move in with power and stay there.

[Full paragraph sanitized]. . . .

PRESIDENT: The way I see it, Ky is gone, the last gasp. Doubt he can pull it off. When he goes there'll be hell in this country [sanitized]

PRESIDENT: What do we tell the world[?]

GENERAL TAYLOR: We can minimize our losses if Ky goes and the Directory [the rest of the military junta] stays. We have to take sides this time.

PRESIDENT: Thought Ky made bad judgment in saying Mayor of Danang ought to be shot. Any other bad judgment we know about?

TAYLOR: The Hitler statement—but I thought he had matured.[46]

On that discouraging note the meeting ended, but if the president and at least most of his advisers in Washington were reluctant to give Ky all-out backing, Lodge and Westmoreland were not. Despite Rusk's admonition to the embassy of a week before that in dealing with the opposition the United States "should avoid as far as possible providing Ky with clearly identifiable U.S. facilities not presently at GVN disposal," Lodge and Westmoreland, with the prompt support of CINCPAC, did just that. On the morning of April 5, ten huge C-130 transports, piloted by Americans and specially flown in from bases outside Vietnam for the operation, began shuttle flights carrying nineteen hundred elite South Vietnamese troops, with ten M-41 tanks, sixty armored personnel carriers, and other equipment from Saigon to Danang airport. Designed to effect a rapid and overwhelming build-up of forces loyal to Ky and Thieu, this operation, in which U.S. and South Vietnamese planes together funneled in some four thousand troops, was protected by the United States at both ends. U.S. marines ringed the adjacent South Vietnamese and U.S. air bases at Danang, blocking any access to the area by the military forces that had rallied to the Struggle Movement. Ky had thus been provided a privileged sanctuary far north of his own power base and in the very heart of the dissidents' stronghold.[47]

Once the build-up at the air base had been completed, Ky himself flew in to take charge. But instead of overawing the supposedly wavering dissident elements in the First Corps area, the actions he and his American mentors had taken further outraged its inhabitants and crystallized the hostility of the local military toward his government. Deploying the soldiers under his command in Danang so that they blocked all routes from the air base, General Nguyen Van Chuan told Ky that his forces would not be permitted out, and warned that there would be bloodshed if they tried. Chuan announced that the problem was political and had to be solved by political means and not by force. Within hours of the airlift, General Phan Xuan Nhuan, commander of the ARVN's First Division, headquartered in Hué, with his men backing him declared for the Struggle Movement and threatened to fight Ky's troops if they came to that city. The odds were no longer decisively in Ky's favor, who now, lacking the military superiority he had counted upon, was reluctant to move into Danang even against the smaller number of lightly armed soldiers manning the city barricades.[48] But this was a deficiency that Ky and Westmoreland would not forget when they launched a second such effort five weeks later.

Their little blitzkrieg of April 5 quickly collapsed, and Ky, ignominiously obliged to apologize publicly to the citizens of Danang for having called them communists, announced he would withdraw to Saigon the forces he had inserted into the air base. To head off the public pressure building against it, the junta in Saigon the next day ratified Ky's decision to seek an accommodation with the Buddhists and yielded to the demand that he withdraw his troops from Danang —a promise that in fact remained unkept. Thus, Lodge, in a cable to the State Department, referred to "pseudo-retiring troops" and stated, "There is no intention of removing any of them."[49] But because Ky's troops remained well inside the American-held perimeter of the air base, it was impossible for the Struggle Movement to know that they were actually not aboard planes flying to Saigon.

Soon after the April 5 operation began, Westmoreland had informed Washington that it had "an excellent prospect of success," and the Pentagon's initial reaction to the resulting fiasco was confused and uncertain. McNamara informed the president that the "Struggle movement may be too strong to throw off. We don't know much about their objectives. They obviously have strength we didn't know about, and I don't want to go to war against them." It was apparently at this point that the challenge mounted by the movement precipitated within the administration what William Bundy refers to as an "abortive re-look at policy." The review was ultimately aborted because before it could get well under way Lodge and Westmoreland had helped Ky mount a second military campaign against the movement massive enough to crush it without fail. And in the end, viewing the political dominance of the Vietnamese military as crucial to the U.S. interest, the administration supported the initiatives of its assertive proconsuls in Saigon and did indeed go to war against the Struggle Movement.[50]

In the weeks following the April 5 fiasco, a series of meetings was held between Ball, William Bundy, George Carver (the CIA's Vietnam specialist), McNaughton, and Leonard Unger to work out a set of new options that addressed the clearly altered political balance within South Vietnam and the fact that the Buddhists constituted the major organized political force there apart from the NLF. McNaughton and Unger produced memoranda which in varying degrees recognized the need to bring the Saigon government into some sort of negotiated compromise settlement with the NLF. Ball, while still supporting such a compromise, pressed for "cutting our losses" and disengaging unless the Saigon government shaped up. William Bundy appeared to reserve his position. At this point it seems that McNamara now favored pressing for a deal between Saigon and the NLF. But Maxwell Taylor and Walt W. Rostow, who had just replaced McGeorge Bundy as National Security Adviser, gave the President very different advice, both of them urging that a tough line be taken against the Buddhists and in support of Ky. Rostow went furthest, arguing a position consistent with that of Lodge and Westmoreland: U.S. "counterforce and counter-politics" had to be brought to bear. "Right now, with the latest Buddhists communique," Rostow advised Johnson, "we are faced with a classic revolutionary situation—like Paris in 1789 and St. Petersburg in 1917." Tri Quang "is going for the jugular," and "assuming he is not a VC himself, the VC obviously regard him as a potential

Kerensky. . . . we have to bring into play the factor in the equation that was not present in Russia in 1917: the presence of U.S. force. . . . In the face of defeat in the field and Kerensky's weakness, Lenin took over in November. This is about what would happen in Saigon if we were not there; but we are there. And right now we have to find the ways to make that count."[51]

With its policy apparently being made as much in Saigon as in Washington, the administration now followed a two-pronged strategy. On the one hand, in accordance with Rostow's recommendations, sufficient concessions were to be granted—particularly a promise to hold elections within four to six months—to win the temporary support of both Buddhist and non-Buddhist proponents of civilian government. But at the same time there would be efforts to divide the Buddhist leadership, strong measures taken against further Buddhist and student demonstrations in Saigon, and plans readied for a second military expedition against Danang. As Neil Sheehan reported from Saigon, senior American officials there recognized that these forceful measures would probably cause bloodshed, but they argued that though they "must be used judiciously, [they] should not be shrunk from."[52]

The military junta remained under such sustained pressure from the Buddhists and their allies that it felt obliged to promise political concessions beyond what American officials thought necessary. Responding to the public mood in Saigon, the National Political Congress, appointed by the military leadership in the hope of bypassing and outmaneuvering the Buddhists, came out in mid-April with a set of demands that, to the junta's dismay, were virtually identical to those of the Buddhists. In the face of this, General Thieu, as chief of state, read a decree on behalf of the junta on April 14 promising that elections for a constituent assembly would be held within three to five months, and he and Ky agreed to abide by all the decisions that the Buddhists and the National Political Congress had arrived at. These called for their military government to resign as soon as the elections for the assembly had been held, to promise that it would use political rather than military means in reaching solutions in the First Corps area, with no reprisals against those who had agitated against the government, and to grant the assembly legislative powers while it was drafting a constitution. Prime Minister Ky agreed in writing not to punish or retaliate against anyone who had taken part in the demonstrations.[53]

On the basis of these promises, which they understood Lodge had concurred in, Tri Quang and Thich Don Hau—probably the most respected and influential monk in Hué—and other Buddhist leaders undertook to call off antigovernment agitation and restore order in the five northern provinces. They had held back from insisting that Ky and Thieu step down before the elections because they appreciated this was not politically realistic: it would risk a major confrontation with American power. Tri Quang went to Hué and appealed to its residents to "stop all activities causing disturbances" and, over considerable opposition, prevailed in his argument that "the present government may remain in power until a constitutional assembly is set up."[54]

Tri Quang's willingness to put his own prestige and future on the line in calling for this compromise can only be appreciated in terms of the assurances he believed he had received from Lodge. He was not alone in this understanding: one of the largest and most respected Catholic newspapers in Saigon later stated that Lodge had "pledged on his honor to the Venerable Tri Quang that the U.S. would never allow a suppression of the Buddhists in central Vietnam to take place, if the Buddhists agreed to put an end to their struggle after 14 April, 1966," the day on which Thieu issued the decree promising establishment of a constituent assembly. Tri Quang, this Catholic source observed, "had agreed and had carried out this agreement; the struggle was stopped and the situation in South Vietnam was stabilized; but the Americans did not keep their promises with the Buddhists, and the generals also broke their promises." It concluded, "These facts showed the Buddhists had fallen into the trap of the Johnson administration."[55]

In the meantime, Lieutenant General Ton That Dinh, the officer assigned by the junta to replace the only recently appointed General Chuan as I Corps commander, had, like his predecessor, quickly sensed the strength of the Struggle Movement's local backing. He assured soldiers and civilians there that he had come to restore harmony, not to compel submission, and that there would be no reprisals; he found that General Walt shared his conclusion that what was called for was political compromise rather than military confrontation. On the basis of Ky and Thieu's mid-April promises, Dinh worked with support from Thich Tri Quang and Thich Don Hau to defuse possibilities for violence further by inducing some eighteen hundred students throughout the area to turn in the small arms that they had been issued by Thi and Chuan. Though not trusting Ky and Thieu, Dinh, like the two monks, understood that the United States had guaranteed their promises.[56]

The resulting calm lasted only a few weeks, for the junta's concessions had been made merely as a tactic to gain time until conditions conducive to mounting a second and more heavily armed military effort had been secured. The junta's intentions were foreshadowed at the end of April when it abruptly cashiered the head of the national police, Colonel Pham Van Lieu, replacing him with Colonel Nguyen Ngoc Loan, a confidant of Ky's known for his ruthlessness and strong-arm methods.[57] But Dinh, the Buddhist leaders, and apparently Rusk and Walt were nevertheless quite unprepared for Ky's sudden return to a policy of brute force. It is evident, on the other hand, that Lodge and Westmoreland were not surprised.

Suddenly, on May 4 and 7, Ky made a series of announcements reneging on most of his government's promises. The constitutional assembly would be given no legislative powers, and Ky and his government would not resign after constituent-assembly elections were held, but would, rather, remain in power "at least for another year." Not until a second election—for a legislative assembly—had been held at an unstipulated time after the constitutional assembly had completed its work would a civilian government be formed.[58]

This about-face caused an immediate rise in the level of tension that became a source of sharp anxiety for the National Security Council, which saw it as likely to increase anti-American sentiment. A staff memorandum for the council's May 9 meeting observed that, although this increase might be transitory in nature, "the large-scale American presence, increased frustration with a seemingly endless war, and continued unattained political objectives on the part of the Buddhist militants could combine to produce more deep-seated anti-U.S. feelings with serious implications for our objectives in Vietnam." Although it is evident that the NSC staff, Secretary Rusk, and some others in the State Department, along with General Walt, wanted to avoid a further confrontation and hoped for a reconciliation between the Military Directorate and the Buddhists, other American officials—certainly including Lodge and Westmoreland—had very different views and continued to encourage Ky and Thieu to take decisive action against the Buddhists.[59]

Lodge and Westmoreland had approved the decision to replace General Chuan with General Dinh, but they were no more happy with Dinh's efforts at peaceful compromise than they had been with his predecessor's. At Dinh's subsequent trial, Ky described Westmoreland as telling him that Dinh's "actions and words were very dangerous and causing serious disturbances" and as asking what he, Ky, was doing to remove him. Lodge, Ky stated, expressed the same view. General Walt, on the other hand, as Neil Sheehan reported, felt that Dinh "had been making considerable progress toward reconciling Danang and Hué to government authority" and deplored the new attack on Danang that Lodge and Westmoreland were encouraging Ky to mount.[60]

Planned without Dinh's knowledge, a major military expedition against Danang was launched without warning early on the morning of May 15. This time the preparations were much more thorough, and were calculated to ensure not only a substantial superiority in troops, but a preponderance in heavy weapons as well. Ky's air force along with commandeered commercial planes flew a steady stream of elite units into his enclave inside the American-protected Danang air base, augmenting the substantial number remaining from the previous airlift to the equivalent of two-thirds of a division. In the meantime, U.S. military advisers had induced Dinh to send most of his local forces to southern Quang Nam and northern Quang Ngai provinces to fight Viet Cong forces, and his remaining troops in the Danang area were heavily outnumbered.[61]

Dinh states that on the evening before the attack, forty U.S. heavy tanks of a kind never previously used in the First Corps area were offloaded from ships in the U.S.-run port of Danang and early the next morning joined Ky's forces. *The New York Times* reported that other ships transported armored personnel carriers that were also employed against the Struggle Movement and its military supporters. In addition, according to Dinh, helicopters ferried about two thousand small arms made available from U.S. Special Forces stocks to Phong Dien and Quang Dien districts where they were turned over to anti-Buddhist members of the local Dai Viet and VNQDD parties for use against the Struggle Movement in these outlying areas. And air power was brought to bear from Ky's U.S.-

protected Danang sanctuary in a way that General Walt—apparently overruled by his superiors—had previously refused to countenance. But it was the heavy tanks with their 90-mm. cannon that made the crucial difference.[62]

Early in the morning of May 15, as some of the newly arrived tanks were being deployed to surround General Dinh's house, he escaped to Walt's headquarters, where he was given asylum, and later a helicopter took him to Hué. He states that Walt was surprised by the course of events, saying he had not expected Westmoreland to permit Ky to act in this way, and that he himself was about to put a call through to McNamara. Dinh accepted Walt's invitation to talk with the secretary, and was shaken by what he was told. He says that McNamara, while assuring him that the assault was not aimed at him personally, referred to it as a "pacification operation," the same term used for actions against the Viet Cong. Following his protests, Dinh claims, the secretary promised to discuss the matter with Johnson and Lodge, who had returned to Washington, and said he would send Philip Habib (chief of the political section of the American embassy) to Danang to contact him as soon as possible. Credited with having worked effectively with the military government in Korea, Habib had been brought to Saigon just after Ky and Thieu had assumed power. In view of his known hostility toward the Buddhist leadership, he was a surprising choice for a mission of reconciliation.[63]

Habib did arrive that afternoon, Dinh relates, and was considerably blunter than McNamara. Dinh says he was informed that the move against Danang had been undertaken with President Johnson's approval, and that the United States was resolved to support the junta in this operation. There might be a settlement with the Buddhists "under certain conditions, so long as U.S. policy in South Vietnam could be carried out," but only if the situation in Danang improved would Hué be spared a similar "pacification program." Habib, he says, then tried unsuccessfully to persuade him to go to Saigon so that another general could take his place, assuring him that the U.S. government guaranteed he would not be arrested and that he would be given a diplomatic post abroad.[64]

Ky and Thieu then relieved Dinh of his command of I Corps and replaced him with a Catholic officer, General Huynh Van Cao. Cao at first refused to authorize an attack against the Struggle Movement's armed pagoda strongholds in Danang and, according to Westmoreland, finally agreed to this only after one of the officers accompanying Ky's aide, Colonel Nguyen Ngoc Loan, held a pistol to his head. At this point, Westmoreland writes, Cao's life was saved by the timely arrival of Colonel Arch Hamblen, Walt's deputy senior adviser. Thereafter Cao was given sanctuary in U.S. military headquarters at Danang.[65]

Despite the odds against them, the local troops, which still backed the Struggle Movement in Danang, might have been successful if expected reinforcements had arrived. But the troops immediately available to the Struggle Movement, led by Colonel Dam Quang Yeu, from the garrison at Hoi An, some twenty miles to the south, were unable to relieve Danang. The only bridge providing access to Danang across the Tourane River had been seized by U.S.

marines, who refused to permit them to pass. Without support from Yeu's larger force, the anti-Ky troops in Danang were soon outnumbered at least five to one. The Saigon forces within the U.S.-protected base were able to sally forth and retire as battlefield expediency dictated, while their planes rocketed and strafed positions held by the local troops. Ky's pilots were so inaccurate that they managed to inflict casualties on nine U.S. marines as well as Vietnamese civilians. When the Danang defenders prepared to shell Ky's military units and his air-force installations within the base area, American marines threatened to turn U.S. fire power against them because of the danger to adjacent U.S. installations.[66]

After six days of troop build-up, Ky sent forth his heavy tanks and elite troops (airborne and marines) against the city. As Neil Sheehan reported, "The tanks led the way, hurling shells from 90 mm. cannon and raking foxholes, concrete block and sandbag machine-gun positions and the houses along both sides of the streets with a hail of bullets from machine guns." There were two days of bitter fighting, at the end of which Ky's forces had captured the Struggle Movement's strongholds, including one pagoda compound described by Sheehan as looking like "a charnel house." The seven hundred local troops who backed the Struggle Movement surrendered, along with the monks, Buddhist boy scouts, students, and other civilians aligned with them. On May 24, in the final act of this episode, American marines ousted Colonel Yeu's troops from a large ammunition dump south of Danang's southern river border, which he had threatened to blow up if Ky's forces crossed the bridge (the same one the marines had previously blocked against Yeu when he sought to reinforce his comrades in Danang). At this point, as Westmoreland observes, "It was an advantage having a fearful General Cao hiding out in the American headquarters while still nominally in command of I Corps, for it enabled Arch Hamblen virtually to command the I Corps." After resistance in the Danang pagodas had collapsed, "Hamblen and [Samuel] Thomsen [a political adviser from the embassy] then went from one dissident ARVN unit to another with written appeals that Cao willingly signed urging their units to desist. One by one they gave in."[67]

With the odds now so heavily adverse, and U.S. support of Ky so palpable, General Thi apparently concluded it would be prudent to mend his fences, and under U.S. auspices he met with Ky at the U.S. air base at Chu Lai to work out an accommodation. Thi now agreed to Westmoreland's terms for his departure from Vietnam. His family and he would be looked after in the United States, and his face partly saved by his acceptance of Westmoreland's still-outstanding offer of March 11, to come to the United States for "a complete physical examination and check-up" with the promise of "administration of whatever treatment is found necessary." In the event, the "treatment" called for Thi's remaining indefinitely in the United States, at the expense of the American government, and being forbidden to return to Vietnam. (He was ensconced in a handsome apartment on Connecticut Avenue in Washington, D.C., across from the Hilton Hotel, but after about seven years the U.S. government suddenly cut off his substantial allowance.) General Dinh was less fortunate: after declining the offer of an ambassador-ship, he was jailed.[68]

Emboldened by his success in Danang, Ky moved quickly against the Buddhists in Saigon, his troops using fixed bayonets and tear gas to drive some two thousand monks, nuns, and others into a pagoda compound, and arrested twenty leaders at the Buddhist Youth headquarters along with several labor leaders. Apparently to offset further his mid-April humiliation, he once again publicly denounced Tri Quang as a "Communist." As for his oft-promised elections, he announced on May 24 that they could not be held until after his government had created "security and order," with Thieu adding that another precondition would be the achievement of "social discipline."[69]

In reaction to what they regarded as an American betrayal in Danang, student supporters of the Struggle Movement in Hué, as an "act of retribution," burned the U.S. consulate and USIS library there. But there were now few troops left to defend this old imperial capital when Ky's forces moved against it from Danang, fifty-five miles to the south. Again the United States tipped the scales in his favor. As the *New York Times* correspondent R. W. Apple, Jr., reported from Hué, "Almost the entire First Division was moved out of the city, lured to Quangtri Province by American advisers, who hoped that Air Vice Marshal Ky would send paratroopers here as he sent them to Danang." Although some of its units returned before Ky could take full advantage of the situation, he was still favored by the absence of much of the division. In a rapid build-up of troops inside the protective ring of U.S. marines guarding the nearby Phu Bai air base, Ky sent in two airborne and two marine battalions, part of the Seventh Armored Cavalry Regiment, and four hundred combat police, all under the direct command of Colonel Nguyen Ngoc Loan. At least two of these battalions were transported from Saigon in U.S. air-force planes, and American police advisers accompanied Colonel Loan.[70]

Ky's battalions quickly overwhelmed the outnumbered and outgunned local forces. By June 19 his troops were in control of all Hué, and soon arrested Tri Quang and several hundred other Buddhist monks and university and high-school students. Tri Quang was released soon after being flown to Saigon, but many of the others were still in prison nine years later when the Saigon government fell. Many of the Hué University students who evaded arrest felt that they had no option but to take to the mountains and join the NLF.[71]

Having succeeded in Danang and Hué, Ky and the junta felt strong enough to clamp down on what remained of Buddhist power in Saigon. One of the top three Buddhist leaders, Thich Thien Minh, was seriously wounded on June 1 by a grenade attack generally believed to have been carried out by operatives of Ky's deputy, Colonel Loan. On June 19, police and troops blockaded the compound of the pagoda housing the Vien Hoa Dao in Saigon, and five days later they stormed the building and ousted its occupants.[72]

On the same day that Hué fell and the Vien Hoa Dao was blockaded, the military junta rejected the election law drawn up two weeks before by the electoral-law commission Ky himself had appointed. Overruling it, and abrogating the promises earlier made to the National Political Congress as well as those made to the Buddhists, the military leadership now issued a revised electoral law and stripped the envisaged constituent assembly of all legislative powers. Ky and Thieu stipulated, moreover, that even after the six months needed to draft a constitution, their junta would remain in power for an additional period until—under their aegis—subsequent elections had been held for a president and legislature. (When those finally took place, in August 1967, Ky and Thieu had no trouble organizing and managing the process so as to ensure that the presidency remained in their hands.) During this period, then, it would be the junta itself that would arrange for the various governmental institutions provided by the constitution. Thus, Ky and Thieu were to remain in power throughout the constitution's drafting and during the subsequent round of voting that was in theory to produce a government to replace them. Lodge and the dominant voices in the Johnson administration had gotten what they wanted, and on June 25 the ambassador publicly praised Ky's regime for its stand in putting down the Struggle Movement, referring to this as "a solid political victory."[73]

Stunned and embittered by this American intervention, the Buddhist leaders believed that Lodge had calculatedly betrayed them. "The most obvious reality in our country today," wrote Tri Quang to one of his close associates, Thich Nhat Hanh, "is that the Americans behave as colonialists." Many Buddhists found it difficult to understand why U.S. behavior contrasted so sharply with American support of them three years before against Diem. But certainly two of the top leaders—Tri Quang and Thien Minh—understood very clearly.[74]

The principal reason the United States had thrown its weight against the Saigon government in 1963 had not been that that regime had suppressed the Buddhists, but that Diem and Nhu had been insufficiently cooperative and effective as instruments for securing American objectives. Following the events of 1966, both Tri Quang and Thien Minh more keenly appreciated this and had come to conclude that the Kennedy administration's concern about the Diem regime's repressive actions against Buddhists, which the American press had then so fully covered, had occurred primarily because the administration understood their adverse effect on the U.S. public's support of the war. The year 1966 saw a Saigon government in power that was equally opposed to Buddhist aims, but one that the mission and Washington judged to be fully supportive of U.S. objectives and sufficiently amenable to American direction. For Washington policymakers, these qualities substantially outweighed whatever criticism the American public might register of the use of U.S. power to crush the politically active Buddhists and their supporters. And this time there was little such criticism, for with few exceptions, the American media paid relatively little attention to the event.[75]

In 1963 American officials did not believe that the Buddhist leaders favored negotiating a compromise political settlement with the NLF or were opposed to a continuation of military action against it. But by 1966 they had come to regard the Buddhist-led Struggle Movement as ultimately committed to these "neutralist" goals and to ending America's military and political roles in Vietnam. In the spring of 1966 the Struggle Movement marshaled so much popular backing that unless U.S. military power had supported Ky and Thieu against it, the Buddhists' immediate political demands would have had to be met. Otherwise these two military leaders would probably have been ousted or faced with the likely secession of most of the South's five northern provinces, including its second largest city, Danang, and the traditional capital of all Vietnam, Hué. The Johnson administration could countenance none of these alternatives, and it quickly moved to apply the force necessary to forestall them.

The challenge mounted by the militant Buddhists and their supporters in the spring of 1966 was the last that Ky and Thieu had to face (apart, of course, from the NLF and Hanoi). From then on, Vietnamese who lived in the Saigon-controlled areas remained convinced that the dominance of these two generals could not be contested so long as the United States stood solidly behind them; and that was precisely what both the Johnson and Nixon administrations did. The middle ground that the Buddhists had been building up between the Saigon military and the NLF was cut away and prospects destroyed for anything resembling a viable "third force." The even more rigid polarization now imposed upon the people of South Vietnam continued to deny them the option of political compromise, permitting only two active choices—supporting the NLF or a Saigon regime shaped by and dependent upon the United States.

American objectives in Vietnam remained incompatible with any assertion of the actual balance of indigenous political forces. Quite apart from the U.S. role in the broader campaign against the NLF and Hanoi, it was continuously necessary to inject American power into the areas of South Vietnam under Saigon's administration so that local levers of control remained in the hands of Vietnamese prepared to act in conformity with U.S. interests. For nine more years the decisive weight of this American intervention would continue to register heavily on the political scales, offsetting the pulls of indigenous political gravity sufficiently to maintain in power a leadership devoid of significant popular support—and guaranteeing that one of the U.S. government's main public rationales for its Vietnam involvement would continue to ring hollow:

> "We seek only to insure that the South Vietnamese have the right and opportunity to control their own destiny. . . ."[76]

Notes

I. The Beginnings of American Intervention

1. See especially Walter LaFeber, "Roosevelt, Churchill and Indochina," *American Historical Review,* December 1975, pp. 1277–95; George C. Herring, "The Truman Administration and the Restoration of French Sovereignty in Indochina," *Diplomatic History,* Spring 1977, pp. 97–117.

2. For extensive documentation concerning the incompatibility of trusteeship for Indochina and these other U.S. goals, see Herring, "Truman Administration," p. 99, n. 4; see also LaFeber, "Roosevelt, Churchill and Indochina," p. 1289. For the series of Vichy French agreements with Japan, see David G. Marr, "World War II and the Vietnamese Revolution," in *Southeast Asia Under Japanese Occupation,* ed. Alfred McCoy (Yale University Southeast Asia Studies, 1980), pp. 133, 153.

3. LaFeber, "Roosevelt, Churchill and Indochina," pp. 1289–92; Herring, "Truman Administration," p. 100.

4. Herring notes that on Truman's first full day in office a top-level administration foreign-policy coordination body asked the State Department for clarification of the American position on Indochina. (Herring, "Truman Administration," p. 100.)

5. Some of the more discerning American officials were quite aware of this tactic. See Abbot Low Moffat's Congressional Testimony in U.S. Congress, Senate, Committee on Foreign Relations, *Hearings on Causes, Origins, and Lessons of the Vietnam War,* 92nd Cong., 2nd sess., May 9–11, 1972, p. 169.

6. De Gaulle, speaking to Jefferson Caffery, the U.S. ambassador to Paris, quoted in Caffery to Stettinius, March 13, 1945, in *Foreign Relations of the United States* (U.S. Government Printing Office, 1969–) [hereafter cited as *FRUS*], *1945,* 6:300.

7. *The Pentagon Papers: The Defense Department History of United States Decisionmaking on Vietnam: The Senator Gravel Edition,* 4 vols. (Beacon Press, 1971) (hereafter *PP* [Gravel]), 1:15. There are two other published versions of the Pentagon Papers: *United States–Vietnam Relations, 1945–1947; Study Prepared by the Department of Defense,* 12 vols., printed for the use of the House Committee on Armed Services (U.S. Government Printing Office, 1971), sometimes known as the "Hebert Edition," which will be referred to in this study as *PP* (GPO); and *The Pentagon Papers as Published by "The New York Times,"* by Neil Sheehan, Hedrick Smith, E. W. Kenworthy, and Fox Butterfield (Bantam Books, 1971), referred to in this study as *PP* (NYT). For a discussion of the strengths and weaknesses of the three sets, see George McT. Kahin, "The Pentagon Papers: A Critical Evaluation," *American Political Science Review,* 64, no. 2 (June 1975): 675–84.

The American position on Indochina

was conveyed to the U.S. ambassador in Paris the next day, May 9, but was not sent to Ambassador Patrick Hurley in Chungking until June 2. (Allan W. Cameron, *Viet-Nam Crisis: A Documentary History*, vol. 1, *1940–1956* [Cornell University Press, 1971], p. 36.)

8. For Moffat's views and his discerning assessment of the weaknesses in the majority position, see his testimony and written statement in Senate, *Causes, Origins, and Lessons*, pp. 161–79. Theoretically the Southeast Asia Division, originally established in the spring of 1944 under the name of Division of Southwest Pacific Affairs, had primary jurisdiction over Thailand, no jurisdiction over the Philippines (still the preserve of the War and Interior Departments), and "concurrent" jurisdiction with the European desks on matters relating to the European colonies in Southeast Asia. See *ibid.*, pp. 161–62.

This assessment of the European desk officers was made by the several members of the Southeast Asia Division with whom I discussed this matter in the immediate postwar years. Dominance of the European desks in shaping U.S. policy toward Vietnam was then equally apparent in the U.S.-approach to the Dutch-Indonesian dispute. See George McT. Kahin, *Nationalism and Revolution in Indonesia* (Cornell University Press, 1952).

9. Prepared at the request of Secretary of War Henry L. Stimson, the paper was described by Acting Secretary of State Joseph Grew as "representing the considered views of the Department of State as a whole." (Cameron, *Viet-Nam Crisis*, 1:39 ff.)

10. Cable to Max Bishop in New Delhi, as repeated on October 5 to Walter Robertson in China, in *FRUS, 1945*, 6:313. Acheson added that it was not American policy "to assist the French to reestablish their control over Indochina by force," and that "the willingness of the U.S. to see French control reestablished assumes that French claim to have the support of the population of Indochina is borne out by future events," an assumption that in fact remained no more than a persistently repeated hope.

11. Cameron, *Viet-Nam Crisis*, 1:39–43.

12. On OSS and military views on Vietnamese nationalists, see U.S. Congress, Senate, Committee on Foreign Relations, *The United States and Vietnam: 1944–1947*, Staff Study, April 3, 1972 (U.S. Government Printing Office, 1972), p. 4; Huynh Kim Khanh, *Vietnamese Communism: 1925–1945* (Cornell University Press, 1982), pp. 316–18; Ellen Hammer, *The Struggle for Indochina* (Stanford: Stanford University Press, 1954), p. 130; Chester L. Cooper, *The Lost Crusade: America in Vietnam* (Dodd, Mead, 1970), p. 40. By far the most comprehensive account of the role and perceptions of American OSS and military personnel in Vietnam during the last year of the war and the months immediately thereafter is found in Archimedes Patti, *Why Vietnam?* (University of California Press, 1980); see also R. Harris Smith, *O.S.S.: The Secret History of America's First Central Intelligence Agency* (University of California Press, 1972).

On Ho, see Bernard Fall, *Ho Chi Minh on Revolution: Selected Writings, 1920–1966* (Praeger, 1967), especially p. ix; Jean Lacouture, *Ho Chi Minh: A Political Biography* (Random House, 1968); Patti, *Why Vietnam?* Khanh prefers "patriotism" to "nationalism" in this context. (*Vietnamese Communism*, pp. 60–62.) For the fullest accounts of Ho's intellectual and political development, see Khanh, *Vietnamese Communism*, and David Marr's superb analysis of modern Vietnamese nationalist thought, *Vietnamese Tradition on Trial, 1920–1945* (University of California Press, 1981). For Moffat's statement, see Senate, *Causes, Origins, and Lessons*, p. 169.

13. The statement on neutrality prepared by John Carter Vincent was carried in the *Department of State Bulletin*, October 21, 1945, p. 646. See also Acheson's cable to Walter Robertson of October 5, 1945, in *FRUS, 1945*, 6:313. See also *PP* (GPO), 1 (IV.A.a):1, 20. With respect to the Lend-Lease equipment, see U.S. Joint Chiefs of Staff, *History of the Indochina Incident, 1940–1954* (Historical Division, Joint Secretariat, Joint Chiefs of Staff, 1971), declassified

1981, and hereafter cited as *JCS History*. This refers with apparent approval (on p. 115) to a New York *Herald Tribune* dispatch of March 10, 1947, which stated that the equipment the British provided the French was valued at over $77,040,000. It is difficult to know what portion of this was of U.S. origin, some presumably being Japanese. But among the items the British turned over to the French were some eight hundred U.S. Lend-Lease jeeps and trucks, an action approved by President Truman. (*PP* [GPO], 1 [A-24].) With respect to the continued use of U.S. insignia, see Robert Shaplen's report in *Newsweek*, August 19, 1946, p. 42; Harold Isaacs, *No Peace for Asia* (Macmillan, 1947), p. 161.

14. The fullest account I have encountered of the use of American ships in the transport of French troops to Vietnam in the fall of 1945 is Michael Gillen's "Sailing into War: The American Troopship Movement to Vietnam in 1945," paper read at the Mid-South Sociological Association Convention, Birmingham, Ala., October 28, 1983. In this carefully researched essay, Gillen has positively identified seven (of what may have been as many as twelve) U.S. ships that sailed for Saigon during October 1945 alone, and estimates that these seven carried more than thirteen thousand French troops. Archimedes Patti cites a report from U.S. Ambassador to France Jefferson Caffery wherein a representative of the French Foreign Office on September 22, 1945, expressed "deep appreciation for shipping the United States has offered to make available in the Pacific." (*Why Vietnam?*, p. 380.) See also Noel Clinton Eggleston, "The Roots of Commitment: United States Policy Toward Vietnam, 1945–50," Ph.D. dissertation, University of Georgia, 1977, p. 55, citing "Memorandum Relating to Shipping Claims," May 28, 1946, U.S. Department of State, *Treaties and Other International Agreements of the United States of America, 1776–1949*, comp. Charles Bevans, 12 vols. (U.S. Government Printing Office, 1968–1974), 7:1146.

For the official U.S. position, see Department of State Circular to certain diplomatic and consular officers, January 23, 1946, cited in *PP* (GPO), 1 (IV,A.2):1, 20. For the September 27 statement, see *FRUS, 1948*, 6:45.

For Robert Blum's statement, see Council on Foreign Relations Study Group on Indo-China, meeting of February 6, 1957, "Digest of Discussion," p. 28. Though most of the military equipment provided the French in Indochina was made available indirectly through France, considerable nonlethal items were transferred more directly; thus, in late 1946, Washington extended Paris a credit of $160 million for the purchase of "vehicles and miscellaneous industrial equipment in Indochina." (*PP* [Gravel], 1:51.) See also Smith, *O.S.S.*, p. 347; he refers to this as "war equipment for use against the Viet Minh in Cochin China."

15. See Department of State report prepared for NSC, "U.S. Policy Toward Southeast Asia," NSC 51, July 1, 1949, para. 58; Comptroller General of the United States, *Audit Report to the Congress of the United States: Economic and Technical Assistance Program for Vietnam, International Cooperation Administration, Department of State, Fiscal Years 1955–1957*, p. 18. As Robert Blum put it, "There was, technically, no aid being supplied to Indo-China. But the United States was aware that the balance of payments presented by the French in their accounting of the use of American aid funds, included the deficit represented by expenditures in Indo-China." (Council on Foreign Relations Study Group on Indo-China, "Digest of Discussion," February 6, 1957, p. 26.) See also *PP* (GPO), 1 (IV, A.2):1.

On the basis of a substantial body of pertinent documentation, Noel C. Eggleston observes, "The Truman Administration was aware of the fact that it was, in essence, providing substantial indirect aid to the French side in the Vietnam war. In fact appropriations evidently took into account French needs in Indochina." As for the Marshall (European Recovery) Plan, he concludes that it "may have contained no direct financing for French Indochina, but the indirect aid provided by the plan was indeed substantial. . . . The French Government was able to divert surreptitiously to Vietnam Marshall Plan aid intended for France." ("Roots of Commitment," p. 87.) At least a few members of Congress suspected this. In talks with Senators Owen Brewster (Republican of Maine) and Frank Graham (Democrat of North Carolina) in 1949, I learned that they believed, but could not get the State Department to acknowledge, that the military operations of both the Dutch in Indonesia and the French in Vietnam were being supported by funds diverted from Marshall Plan aid that Congress understood to be destined for the economic reconstruction of the Netherlands and France.

16. See George McT. Kahin, "The United States and the Anticolonial Revolutions in Southeast Asia," in *The Origins of the Cold War in Asia*, ed. Yonosuke Nagai and Akira Iriye (University of Tokyo and Columbia University Press, 1977, 1978), pp. 338–61. For U.S. policy toward Indonesia and the Netherlands, see Robert J. McMahon, *Colonialism and Cold War: The United States and the Struggle for Indonesian Independence, 1945–49* (Cornell University Press, 1981); and Kahin, *Nationalism and Revolution*. For the CIA assessment, see CIA, *Review of the World Situation As It Relates to the United States, November 14, 1947*, para. 15, Southeast Asia (National Archives, Washington, D.C.). On the basis of my own research in Indonesia during 1948–49, I can testify to the accuracy of this assessment for that country.

17. It should be noted that the political leverage of this bank stemmed from a much broader base than Indochina: since 1945 it had invested no new funds in the Far East and had concentrated its expansion in the Middle East and Africa. (*FRUS, 1952–1954*, 13:50.)

18. For other analogies employed by French leaders comparable to the "ten-pin theory" see Stein Tønneson's excellent dissertation, "The Outbreak of the War in Indochina, 1946," University of Oslo, 1982, especially pp. 279–82.

There were apparently no American journalists in Madagascar during this rebellion, and scarcely any mention of it was made in the American press. For several decades Madagascar had been used by the French as the principal place of exile for Vietnamese nationalists, and it is understandable why contacts should have been developed and sustained between nationalists of the two countries. Some Vietnamese communists who had been exiled to Madagascar were taken by the British (who had taken the island from the Vichy French) in early 1945 and parachuted into areas of northern Vietnam controlled by the Vietminh. See Smith, *O.S.S.*, p. 330; Joseph Buttinger, *Vietnam: A Dragon Embattled*, 2 vols. (Praeger, 1967), 1:294. According to Buttinger, these Vietnamese were sent in by the British "under the assumption, shared increasingly also by the French, that this would help the Vietminh to multiply the problems their guerrillas were allegedly causing the Japanese." (*Ibid.*, 2:1017, n. 27.)

19. The timing of this precipitate and premature uprising against the French was occasioned by the fact that several units of the Vietnamese colonial militia sympathetic to the communists were about to be sent to fight against a Thai military force (which the Japanese had invited in to annex part of Cambodia) and would have been lost to the movement after their departure. See Marr, "World War II," p. 141. Khanh quote is from *Vietnamese Communism*, p. 256; see also pp. 180, 185–86, 253, and 255–7. Khanh observes that throughout the 1930s Ho Chi Minh held "no known official post in either the Comintern or the ICP [Indochinese Communist Party]," and that he spent much of his time teaching illiterate Vietnamese in Moscow to read their own language and composing lessons in Vietnamese history and geography for them. (*Ibid.*, pp. 180–81.)

20. For the fullest discussion of Ho's experience in China in the early 1940s, see King Chen, *Vietnam and China, 1938–1954* (Princeton University Press, 1969). Khanh states that not one of the party leaders who attended the May 1941 meeting could be

identified with what he terms "the internationalist faction," and that all Central Committee members present were either from northern or central Vietnam. (*Vietnamese Communism,* pp. 257–59.)

21. Further details can be found in William J. Duiker, *The Communist Road to Power in Vietnam* (Westview Press, 1981); Khanh, *Vietnamese Communism;* Marr, "World War II," and "Vietnam: Harnessing the Whirlwind," in *Asia—The Winning of Independence,* ed. Robin Jeffrey (St. Martin's Press, 1981); Alexander B. Woodside, *Community and Revolution in Modern Vietnam* (Houghton Mifflin, 1976), as well as the doctoral dissertations of David Elliott, "Revolutionary Re-Integration: A Comparison of the Foundation of Post-Liberation Political Systems in North Vietnam and China," Cornell University, 1976; Edwin Moise, "Land Reform in China and North Vietnam," University of Michigan, 1977; and Christine Katherine Pelzer White, "Agrarian Reform and National Liberation in the Vietnam Revolution: 1920–1957," Cornell University, 1981.

22. A valuable coverage of the Japanese occupation, including the roles of Cuong De, Diem, and the establishment of the Bao Dai–Tran Trong Kim government, is provided in the unpublished, strongly documented monograph (drawing on extensive Vietnamese and Japanese sources) of Masaya Shiraishi, "The Japanese and the Vietnamese 'Nationalists' During World War II," Seminar on the International Relations of Southeast Asia, Cornell University, Ithaca, N.Y., 1979. His account is based on extensive interviews with many of the Japanese military and civilian officials who served in the occupation, as well as on Japanese and Vietnamese records. The fullest published account is in Marr, "World War II." Also valuable is ch. 4 of Philippe Devillers's classic study, *Histoire du Viet-Nam de 1940 à 1952* (Editions du Seuil, 1952). See also Buttinger, *Dragon Embattled,* 1:289–90. Marr points out that the Tran Trong Kim Cabinet in fact achieved more than generally credited. "It was able to moderate Japanese

rice confiscations, reduce taxes, introduce the Vietnamese language to the civil bureaucracy, loosen censorship, eliminate many symbols of French rule, expand paramilitary training and encourage youth groups to assume quasi-police roles." (Marr, "World War II," p. 145.)

23. Charles Fenn, *Ho Chi Minh: A Biographical Introduction* (Scribner's, 1973), pp. 72–75 (Fenn was an OSS agent in Kunming who dealt with Ho); Chen, *Vietnam and China,* pp. 93–94.

24. For the area of Vietminh control, see Smith, *O.S.S.,* p. 330. The fullest account of Ho's relations with the Kuomintang generals is in Chen, *Vietnam and China;* Patti's *Why Vietnam?* provides additional pertinent data. On U.S. assistance to the Vietminh, see Senate, *Causes, Origins, and Lessons,* p. 3. Chu Van Tan, the Vietminh commander assigned to protect the American OSS teams, told me that the quantity of arms actually delivered was not extensive—largely carbines, and only enough of them to equip one company. (Interview, Viet Bac, September 1972.) He and General Vo Nguyen Giap were the principal architects of the Vietminh's army, and he became the Democratic Government of Vietnam's first minister of defense. Probably the major acquisition of arms came soon after the Japanese coup of March 6, 1945, when the Vietminh recruited some three thousand of the Vietnamese members of the disbanded French colonial army, some of whom apparently still had their arms. See Khanh, *Vietnamese Communism,* p. 310.

25. On Vietminh control of ten provinces, see Woodside, *Community and Revolution,* pp. 229, 233. On the famine, see Marr, "Harnessing the Whirlwind," pp. 192–93, and "World War II," pp. 135–36; Ngo Vinh Long, *Before the Revolution: The Vietnamese Peasants Under the French* (M.I.T. Press, 1973), pp. 130–33. Duiker quote is from *Communist Road to Power,* p. 103. White quote is from "Agrarian Reform," p. 107. For the period in general, see Duiker, *Communist Road to Power;* Elliott, "Revolutionary Re-Integration"; Khanh,

Vietnamese Communism; Moise, "Land Reform"; White, "Agrarian Reform"; Woodside, *Community and Revolution.*

26. See Marr, "World War II," pp. 146–47.

27. Quoted in Robert Shaplen, *The Lost Revolution* (Harper and Row, 1965), p. 30, and cited by Marr in "World War II," p. 147.

28. Marr, "World War II," p. 146.

29. Marr states that the Tran Trong Kim Cabinet had resigned just prior to the Japanese surrender, in the hope of reconstituting itself with broader support. (*Ibid.,* p. 158, n. 99.) See below concerning these Chinese-supported parties. Truong Buu Lam estimates that by September 1940 the Phuc Quoc, with their major base at Langson (across the border from a part of China occupied by the Japanese), had five thousand rifles at their disposal. ("Japan and the Disruption of the Vietnamese Nationalist Movement," in *Aspects of Vietnamese History,* ed. Walter F. Vella [University of Hawaii Press, 1973], p. 245.)

30. Moffat's written statement is in Senate, *Causes, Origins, and Lessons,* p. 177.

31. On the day of Ho's declaration, see Smith, *O.S.S.,* p. 354. At the Friendship Association's inaugural meeting on October 17, General Gallagher presented a friendly, even fraternal attitude, singing songs (according to one account, the Vietnamese national anthem) and endorsing the Vietnamese proposal for an exchange of students with the United States—an idea that Ho Chi Minh tried fruitlessly to follow up in a letter to the U.S. secretary of state that was never acknowledged. (*Ibid.,* p. 357; Senate, *United States and Vietnam: 1944–1947,* pp. 4–6.)

32. On "The Star-Spangled Banner," see Smith, *O.S.S.,* p. 355; Patti, *Why Vietnam?,* pp. 368–69. Excerpts from the independence proclamation can be found in George McT. Kahin and John W. Lewis, *The United States in Vietnam,* 2nd ed. rev. & enl. (Delta, 1969), pp. 419–21.

33. See Marr, "Harnessing the Whirlwind," p. 195. The Bao Dai–Tran Trong Kim regime was not permitted to administer Hanoi, Haiphong, and Danang until July.

34. Useful descriptions of all these groups can be found in Devillers, *Histoire du Viet-Nam;* Patti, *Why Vietnam?;* Gareth D. Porter, "Imperialism and Social Structure in Twentieth Century Vietnam," Ph.D. dissertation, Cornell University, 1976. Porter provides the most extensive available account of the several interrelated but sometimes competing Dai Viet parties. The fullest account of the background of Prince Cuong De, whom the Phuc Quoc hoped to establish in power, can be found in David G. Marr, *Vietnamese Anticolonialism* (University of California Press, 1971).

35. See Patti, *Why Vietnam?,* pp. 499–500; Edward G. Lansdale, *In the Midst of Wars* (Harper and Row, 1972), p. 153.

36. The fullest treatments of the Cao Dai are Jayne Werner's "The Cao Dai: The Politics of a Vietnamese Syncretic Religious Movement," Ph.D. dissertation, Cornell University, 1976, and her more recent *Peasant Politics and Religious Sectarianism: Peasant and Priest in the Cao Dai in Vietnam* (Yale Southeast Asia Studies, 1981). There is also a succinct and informative account in Patti, *Why Vietnam?,* pp. 500–03. Werner states that at the end of 1944, the Japanese permitted formation of three unarmed Cao Dai military corps, the largest of which numbered 3,240 men. The most substantial treatment of the Hoa Hao is the 1981 Harvard Ph.D. dissertation by Hue Tam Ho Tai, "Dreams of Peace and Plenty: Vietnamese Millenarianism and Its Modern Fate." Porter, "Imperialism and Social Structure," also contains important material on the Hoa Hao, based on his own interviews as well as Vietnamese and French publications. See also Marr, "World War II," p. 140; Bernard Fall, "The Political-Religious Sects of Vietnam," *Pacific Affairs,* 28, no. 3 (September 1955): 235–53.

37. Quote on the Hoa Hao is from Hue Tam Ho Tai, "Dreams of Peace and Plenty," p. 192. On differences between the sects and the Vietminh, see Werner, "Cao Dai," pp. 291–92n., citing her interview with Major A. M. Savani, a former head of French military intelligence, and pp. 303–5.

38. As far as I have been able to discover, there exists no balanced, comprehensive account of the Vietminh's relations with these two religious sects and with the Trotskyists. According to David Marr, Tran Van Giau, leader of the party in the South in the second half of 1945, stated that it was divided into two groups and that there had been no contact with the Central Committee from 1941 until early 1945. (Personal communication to the author from David Marr, who interviewed Tran Van Giau in Hanoi in 1980.)

39. For Mountbatten's admonition, see "Extract from the Report to the Combined Chiefs of Staff by the Supreme Allied Commander, Southeast Asia, 30 June, 1947," *Documents Relating to British Involvement in the Indo-China Conflict,* Command 2834 (Her Majesty's Stationery Office, 1965), p. 47. Gracey acknowledged the political character of his intervention, reporting on September 22 to Mountbatten, "I would stress that though it may appear that I have interfered in politics of the country, I have done so only in interest of maintenance of law and order and after close consultation with Senior French representatives." This is incorporated in Mountbatten's cable to the U.S. Chiefs of Staff [SEACOS 488], September 23, 1945. For further details of the British occupation and its consequences, see George Rosie, *The British in Vietnam: How the Twenty-five-Year War Began* (Panther, 1970); Daniel Bart Valentine, "The British Facilitation of the French Re-entry into Vietnam," Ph.D. dissertation, University of California at Los Angeles, 1974. See also Isaacs, *No Peace for Asia,* pp. 152–54.

40. With respect to Gracey's *faits accomplis,* see Vice-Admiral The Earl Mountbatten of Burma, *Report to the Combined Chiefs of Staff: Section E, Post Surrender Tasks* (Her Majesty's Stationery Office, 1969), pp. 286, 288, 293. On September 28, Mountbatten summoned Gracey to Singapore to confer with the British secretary of state for war, who confirmed Mountbatten's view that British policy was not to interfere in Vietnam's internal affairs. Three days later, however, Mountbatten received new orders from the British Chiefs of Staff instructing him "to use British/Indian troops to give assistance to the French throughout the interior of southern F.I.C. [French Indochina] so long as this did not prejudice my primary responsibility for Saigon." In relaying these instructions to Gracey, he stated that his troops were to be used only in a preventive role and not in offense. (*Ibid.,* p. 288.) Additional confusion as to Gracey's mandate arose from the fact that his immediate superior was General Sir William Slim, commander of Allied land forces in Southeast Asia. On September 28, Mountbatten had reported to the British Chiefs of Staff that Gracey had stated there need be no fear that the French would call on British forces for assistance outside of the Saigon-Cholon area. (United Kingdom, Public Records Office, WO [War Office] 203/42, 43.) The evidence available suggests that whereas the Secretary of State for War backed Mountbatten in his relatively moderate position, General Slim and the Chiefs of Staff supported Gracey. For further elucidation of this complex problem, Valentine's above-cited dissertation, which makes extensive use of British documents (though not those most recently released), should be consulted.

41. On Gracey's use of the Japanese, see *JCS History,* pp. 80–86; "Extract from the Report of the Combined Chiefs of Staff, 1947." On casualties for this period, see United Kingdom, Public Records Office, FO [Foreign Office] 371, Far Eastern 1946, General File No. 8, pp. 1394–2112. The total British breakdown was:

	Killed	Wounded
British	3	6
Gurkhas	38	104
French	85	314
Japanese	129	167

On Gracey's acknowledgment, see Isaacs, *No Peace for Asia,* p. 159. As an on-the-spot *Newsweek* correspondent, Isaacs provides graphic details of the use of Japanese troops in offensive as well as defensive operations. It was not until November 30, 1945, that Gracey's political adviser reported, "We are now seriously getting down to our task of disarming the Japanese. . . ." (FO 372, Far Eastern 1946, General File No. 8, p. 1393.)

42. On French civil administration as "sole authority," see cable from Ambassador in France (Caffery) to Secretary of State, October 12, 1945, in *FRUS, 1945,* 6:314. Mountbatten's announcement came in a telegram to British Chiefs of Staff, March 17, 1946, FO 371, 53961/044172, pp. 3, 5. As of March 17, Mountbatten reported that, apart from French naval and air units, a total of 68,688 French army troops were in the southern half of Indochina, "exclusive of 2,-450 enrolled partisans," and that 3,887 vehicles and 324 armored cars had been turned over to the French along with 2,590 tons of ordnance (including weapons) and 2,710 tons of ammunition. "Honorary Citizen of Saigon" was in Despatch #20, Interservices Mission to FO, February 1, 1946, FO 371, General File No. 8. The French also wished to present military decorations to Gracey and his officers, but their offer was declined because of the political inferences that might have been drawn.

43. The most comprehensive accounts of the Chinese occupation are to be found in Chen, *Vietnam and China,* ch. 3; Devillers, *Histoire du Viet-Nam;* John T. McAlister, Jr., *Vietnam: The Origins of the Revolution* (Alfred A. Knopf, 1969); Hammer, *Struggle for Indochina,* ch. 6. One of the most searching analyses of the Chinese occupation I have encountered is the unpublished research monograph of Harold E. Meinheit, "The Chinese Intervention in Vietnam: 1945–1946," Seminar on Political Problems of Southeast Asia, Cornell University, Ithaca, N.Y., December 1976. The 152,500 figure is King Chen's in *Vietnam and China,* p. 120. The total given in the *J.C.S. History* is 180,000. For an account of the complexities of politics among the Chinese generals and between them and Chiang Kai-shek, see

Chen, *Vietnam and China,* ch. 3; Devillers, *Histoire du Viet-Nam,* ch. 11. See also Donald Lancaster, *The Emancipation of French Indo-China* (Oxford University Press, 1961), p. 126.

44. For Indochinese Communist Party's declaration, see Khanh, *Vietnamese Communism,* p. 328. Duiker quote is from *Communist Road to Power,* p. 117. On Hsiao Wen, see *JCS History,* p. 99. Because of his own apparent procommunist sympathies (as well as previous contact with Ho Chi Minh in Kuomintang China), Hsiao Wen was presumably already predisposed in favor of the Vietminh. On his political leanings, see Chen, *Vietnam and China,* pp. 65, 83. According to Devillers, Hsiao Wen rallied to the Chinese communists in 1950 and was then used by them to contact the Vietminh. (*Histoire du Viet-Nam,* p. 456.) On Ho's Cabinet, see Hammer, *Struggle for Indochina,* p. 144.

45. On Gallagher's efforts to influence Lu Han, see Edward R. Drachman, *United States Policy Toward Vietnam, 1940–1945*: (Fairleigh Dickinson University Press, 1970), pp. 135–37; this well-documented study draws upon Gallagher's papers. In the treaty with Chiang Kai-shek's government France gave up all her extraterritorial rights in China, her territorial concessions in Canton, Hankow, Kwangchowan, Shanghai, and Tientsin; relinquished that part of the Yunnan-Haiphong Railroad that was in China; exempted Chinese goods transported over the railway's Vietnam section from customs and transit duties; and improved the economic rights and legal position of Chinese resident in Vietnam. See Chen, *Vietnam and China,* pp. 141–42. The text of the military agreement can be found in Memorandum for the Combined Chiefs of Staff from the French Military Attaché in Washington, March 8, 1946, FO 371/53961; 044172. For the date of actual signing, see Memorandum by Lt. Com. (R.N.V.R.) P. T. Simpson-Jones, "Sino-French Negotiations," March 15, 1946, FO 371/53963; 044208. (Simpson-Jones was British liaison officer with the Chinese occupation forces.) By refusing to

wait for the actual signing of this military agreement, the French exposed their naval vessels to heavy fire from Chinese shore batteries at Haiphong on March 5, the British having noted the day before that, in ordering this movement, General Leclerc had "jumped the gun." (H. M. Eyers, British Embassy, Chungking, telegram to Far Eastern Department, Foreign Office, March 4, 1946, FO 371/53961; 044172.)

46. On the simultaneity of the final stages of the two sets of negotiations, see n. 45 and telegram from SACSEA to Cabinet Offices, FO 371, 1946, General File No. 8, pp. 2190–3465. For Leclerc's statement, see Tønneson, "Outbreak of War," p. 73. On duress from the Chinese, Jean Sainteny, the French negotiator, writes, "I had found an unexpected ally in the person of a Chinese officer, General Chao, who . . . had taken the initiative of persuading Ho Chi Minh to reach an agreement with France." (Jean Sainteny, Ho Chi Minh and His Vietnam: A Personal Memoir [Cowles, 1972], p. 63.) The British also clearly appreciated that the Sino-French alignment forced Ho "to come to terms with the French." (Telegram from Saigon to Foreign Office, February 22, 1946. See also Meiklereid [British consul in Saigon] to Foreign Office of the same date; C. M. Anderson's report to the Foreign Office, March 17, 1946, F 4178/8/61, FO 371, Far Eastern 1946, General File No. 8.) General Giap observed, "Chiang would force our people to accept the terms he had signed with the French," and that on the eve of the March 6 agreement Chinese representatives came to see Ho, asking why the Vietminh had not signed an agreement with the French and "counselled us not to be too uncompromising." The next morning, after the unexpected localized outbreak of fighting between Chinese land batteries and French naval forces of Haiphong, Giap reports that the Chinese "were demanding precisely that we settle with the French." (Vo Nguyen Giap, Unforgettable Months and Years, trans. Mai Van Elliott [Cornell University Southeast Asia Program, 1975], pp. 90, 99, 101.) On this point see also Chen,

Vietnam and China, p. 144. The 1970 official history of the Lao Dong [Workers Party] also referred to the danger of having to confront both the Chinese and the French concurrently if the Vietminh did not arrive at an agreement with the French. (Historical Research Committee of the Lao Dong Party Central Committee, 40 Years of Party Activity [Hanoi, 1970]; translated in [U.S.] Joint Publications Research Service [hereafter JPRS] 49867, February 27, 1970, p. 24.) Writing in 1975, Nguyen Khac Vien stated, "In order not to have to fight both French and Chinese troops, the Vietnamese government preferred seeking a compromise with the former to end the occupation of the country by Chiang Kai-shek men." (The Long Resistance [1858–1975] [Hanoi: Foreign Languages Publishing House, 1975], p. 118.)

47. On the departure of the Chinese, see FRUS, 1946, 8:48. The Chinese informed American officials on May 22, 1946, that they had transferred all garrison duties to the French, with four of their divisions still remaining but scheduled to leave by June 16. (Ibid., p. 45.) Chen quote is from Vietnam and China, p. 145. Giap, in his public address, argued that the agreement was "a necessary step to preserve the revolution." (Duiker, Communist Road to Power, p. 120; see also Chen, Vietnam and China, pp. 147–48.)

48. For terms of this agreement, see Chen, Vietnam and China, p. 145; for its implementation, see Meiklereid telegram to Bevin, April 11, 1946, p. 2. FO 371/53963; 04428. Lancaster states that the Chinese gave permission for the first French troops to enter Hanoi on March 16. (Emancipation of French Indo-China, p. 149.)

49. For the full text of the agreement and its annex, see Allan B. Cole, ed., Conflict in Indo-China and International Repercussions: A Documentary History, 1945–1955 (Cornell University Press, 1956), pp. 40–42. As late as May 1950, a senior American official could write, "No one knows what the French Union means." (PP [Gravel], 1:368.)

50. When the Union was finally defined,

membership was made compulsory, and under Article 62, members had "to pool all the means at their disposal to guarantee the protection of the whole Union." This same article, as David Schoenbrun has pointed out, in effect gave the president of the French Republic "a constitutional right to raise troops, levy taxes, requisition crops, in fact take over any member country at will." (David Schoenbrun, *As France Goes* [Atheneum, 1968], p. 218.)

51. Quote is from Donald Zagoria, *Vietnam Triangle: Moscow/Peking/Hanoi* (Pegasus, 1967), p. 36. See also Charles McLane, *Soviet Strategies in Southeast Asia* (Princeton University Press, 1966), p. 432; Ruth T. McVey, *The Calcutta Conference and the Southeast Asian Uprisings* (Cornell Modern Indonesia Project, 1958). McLane also notes that, in his much-cited authoritative article in *Pravda* of August 7, 1947, E. Zhukov, who was to emerge as the principal Soviet spokesman on colonial affairs after the war, was restrained, did not exhort the colonial peoples to turn to violence in defense of their rights, and provided no assurance that Moscow would support their cause "except in words." (McLane, *Soviet Strategies*, p. 257.)

52. McLane, *Soviet Strategies*, p. 432.

53. Zagoria, *Vietnam Triangle*, pp. 36–37.

54. On the party's fears of losing votes, see Zagoria, *Vietnam Triangle*, p. 37; *PP* (GPO), I (A-32). On Thorez's promise to de Gaulle, see *New York Times*, November 27, 1946. Thorez quote is in Sainteny, *Ho Chi Minh and His Vietnam*, pp. 70–71. On the shift in communist policy, see McLane, *Soviet Strategies*, pp. 273, 440; Bernard Fall, *Viet-Nam Witness, 1953–1956* (Praeger, 1966), pp. 22–29; Hammer, *Struggle for Indochina*, pp. 297–98.

55. A prominent member of the Socialist Party, Louis Caput, who was an old acquaintance of Ho's, served as one of his chief advisers in his negotiations with French government representatives leading to the agreement of March 6, 1946. (Stephen Richard Lyne, "The French Socialist Party and the Indochina War," Ph.D. dissertation,

Stanford University, 1965, pp. 94, 110.) On December 10, six days before he formed a new government, Léon Blum, head of the Socialist Party, had stated in its journal *Le Populaire* that "independence" was the only solution for Vietnam. (Hammer, *Struggle for Indochina*, p. 186.) Moffat quote is from his Memorandum to John Carter Vincent, in *FRUS, 1946*, 8:52–54. The text is also available in Gareth Porter, *Vietnam: A History in Documents* (New American Library, 1981), pp. 46–47. On the "Republic of Cochin China," see Hammer, *Struggle for Indochina*, pp. 168–69, 180–81.

56. On the French cruiser incident, see Schoenbrun, *As France Goes*, p. 236, n. 3; Hammer, *Struggle for Indochina*, p. 183, n. 9. Hammer notes that this estimate may have been conservative. The text of Morlière's ultimatum of November 28 and the subsequent exchange of notes between him and General Giap, who proposed a joint commission to discuss the demand, can be found in Porter, *Vietnam: A History in Documents*, pp. 52–53. This excellent, well-annotated selection of important documents, like Porter's larger, two-volume compilation, provides a valuable research and teaching aid to anyone studying the Vietnam War, often significantly supplementing documents in the *Pentagon Papers*.

57. On Ho's cable to Blum, see Devillers, *Histoire du Viet-Nam*, pp. 351–52; Tønnesson, "Outbreak of War," pp. 198–200; Hammer, *Struggle for Indochina*, p. 186; *PP* (GPO), I (A-32). The text of Giap's order is in Porter, *Vietnam: A History in Documents*, pp. 58–59. Blum became premier of a short-lived, transitional, all-socialist Cabinet on December 15 (Hanoi time). The estimate of troop strength comes from *JCS History*, p. 115.

58. Leclerc January 1947 quote is in Devillers, *Histoire du Viet-Nam*, p. 367; see also *PP* (GPO), I (A-34). Leclerc's quote on "xenophobic nationalism" is in Schoenbrun, *As France Goes*, pp. 237–38, n. 4.

59. S. M. Bao Dai, *Le Dragon d'Annam* (Plon, 1980), pp. 152–61. Bao Dai asserts, rather lamely, that he did not return to

Hanoi and his position in its government, because just as he was about to go he received a note from Ho Chi Minh discouraging him from doing so. This seems highly implausible, for Bao Dai's presence in the government was useful to Ho and the Vietminh. For brief, puzzled references to Bao Dai's departure from Hanoi, see Bernard Fall, *The Two Vietnams: A Political and Military Analysis* (Praeger, 1964), p. 208; Chester Cooper, *Lost Crusade*, p. 56.

60. Quoted in Fall, *Two Vietnams*, p. 208.

61. For a full text of the Elysée Agreement, see Cole, *Conflict in Indochina*, 1:72–79. A detailed account of the establishment of Bao Dai's regime can be found in Buttinger, *Dragon Embattled*, 2:667–734. See also Devillers, *Histoire du Viet-Nam*, pp. 394–424. Marr quote is from a personal communication with the author.

62. Quote is from a communiqué from Léon Pignon to Admiral D'Argenlieu, January 4, 1947, quoted in Devillers, *Histoire du Viet-Nam*, p. 364.

63. State Department cable is in *PP* (GPO), 1 (A-46): 49–50. "Capturing control" quote is from Department of State Policy Statement on Indochina, September 27, 1948, in *FRUS, 1948*, 6:44. On the lack of evidence for Vietnam, see Senate, *United States and Vietnam: 1944–1947*, especially pp. 20–22.

64. Both quotes are from Department of State Policy Statement on Indochina, September 27, 1948, in *FRUS, 1948*, 6:48.

65. *Ibid.*, pp. 48–49.

66. Quoted in Gary Hess, "The First American Commitment in Indochina: The Acceptance of the 'Bao Dai Solution,' 1950," *Diplomatic History*, Fall 1978, p. 339.

67. Quote is from Department of State report prepared for NSC, "U.S. Policy Toward Southeast Asia," July 1, 1949, NSC 51, para. 59. This report referred to "the false issue of French imperialism, which cements communists and non-communists in unity." (*Ibid.*, para. 60.)

68. Statement of George C. Marshall, "Transcript of Proceedings, Meeting on

U.S.-China Problems, October 8, 1949," mimeo, U.S. Department of State, Division of Central Services, 1949, p. 405.

69. National Security Council Report of the Executive Secretary, "United States Objectives and Courses in Southeast Asia," June 25, 1952, pp. 10–12.

70. National Security Council quotes are in *PP* (Gravel), 1:82, 83, 361–62.

71. As Richard M. Freeland observes, with respect to the announcement of the Truman Doctrine in March 1947, "The President adopted the position taken by Forrestal and Byrnes early in 1946 that popular support for extensive foreign aid could be achieved only in the framework of an exposition of the expansionist nature of Soviet policy and the announcement of a policy of resistance to it." (*The Truman Doctrine and the Origins of McCarthyism* [Alfred A. Knopf, 1972], p. 87.) For further discussion of this factor see Walter LaFeber, *America, Russia and the Cold War* (John Wiley, 1976), pp. 54–59. Baruch quote is in Freeland, *Truman Doctrine*, p. 89; see also p. 101. George Kennan observed with reference to the Truman Doctrine that "It placed our aid to Greece in the framework of a universal policy rather than that of a specific decision addressed to a specific set of circumstances. . . ." (Quoted in Freeland, *Truman Doctrine*, pp. 100–101.)

72. See *PP* (GPO), 1 (A-42), Evelyn Colbert, *Southeast Asia in International Politics* (Cornell University Press, 1977), p. 89; Martin J. Murray, *The Development of Capitalism in Colonial Indochina (1870–1940)* (University of California Press, 1980), p. 167. This last is by far the most comprehensive analysis of the French colonial economy in Indochina.

73. The Truman administration's thinking on the relation of Southeast Asia and Japan was set forth with particular clarity in an NSC Staff Study of February 13, 1952, "United States Objectives and Courses of Action with Respect to Communist Aggression in Southeast Asia." This stated, among other things, that "Exclusion of Japan from trade with Southeast Asia would

seriously affect the Japanese economy, and increase Japan's dependence on United States aid. In the long run the loss of Southeast Asia, especially Malaya and Indonesia, could result in such economic and political pressures in Japan as to make it extremely difficult to prevent Japan's eventual accommodation to the Soviet Bloc." (*PP* [Gravel], 1:375.) This position was foreshadowed two days before in Memorandum from Assistant Secretary of State for Far Eastern Affairs (Allison) to Secretary of State, February 11, 1952, in *FRUS, 1952–54,* 13:28–30. For the fullest account of the argument that Japan required compensatory trade with Southeast Asia, see Michael Schaller, "Securing the Great Crescent: Occupied Japan and the Origins of Containment in Southeast Asia," *Journal of American History,* 69, no. 2 (September 1982): 393–414.

74. British investment and trade were still dominant in Thailand and, though under assault from Rangoon's socialist government, in Burma as well. The equating of Burma with Indochina as a barrier to the advance of Chinese communist power is clear in the above-cited Allison memorandum of February 11, 1952, p. 30. Burma's importance in this context is illustrated by the major covert U.S. campaign, especially strong in the early 1950s, to support a substantial body of Chiang Kai-shek's troops there, despite strong opposition from the Burmese government. For details, see Robert Taylor, *Foreign and Domestic Consequences of the KMT Intervention in Burma* (Cornell Southeast Asia Program, 1973).

75. On the diversion of French officers from NATO, see *FRUS, 1952–54,* 13:76, 159; see also the statement of George C. Marshall, in U.S. Dept. of State, "Meeting: U.S.-China Problems, October 8, 1949," p. 405. The French reported that "the equivalent of the whole current American contribution to French defense is being absorbed in Indochina." (*FRUS, 1952–54,* 13:75.) On France's military expenditures, see p. 39 and n. 17 to ch. II of this book.

76. See Draft Memorandum Prepared by Department of Defense, "A Cold War

Program to Save Southeast Asia for the Free World," April 3, 1952, *FRUS, 1952–54,* 13:-120. The British ambassador to Washington reported in mid-December 1949 that Acheson thought the communists' seizure of power in China would likely be followed by their expansion south- and eastward, beyond the borders of China. (Sir Oliver Franks to Bevin, December 17, 1949, in the personal papers of Ernest Bevin, PRO 800/462, document FE/49/40; I am indebted to Walter LaFeber for this document.)

77. For substantial documentation on France's hints about pulling out, see Eggleston, "Roots of Commitment," pp. 210–11, n. 26. Gary Hess has noted that the threat of withdrawal had been resorted to as early as May 1948, "when the State Department discussed with the French embassy the implications of Congressional criticism of the extent to which the Indochina war was draining French resources and Marshall Plan assistance." (Hess, "First American Commitment," p. 338.)

78. Gary Hess has put the administration's position succinctly: "The only feasible remedy for the acknowledged shortcomings of the 'Bao Dai solution' was American recognition and support, not a liberal French colonial policy." ("First American Commitment," p. 339.)

79. Dean Acheson, *Present at the Creation* (W. W. Norton, 1969), p. 673.

80. *Ibid.,* p. 674.

II. To the Brink of War in Support of France

1. Quote is from *New York Times,* January 25, 1949.

2. Cable: State to Saigon, May 10, 1949, in *PP* (Gravel), 1:63. (Bracketed words are per Gravel edition.)

3. *Department of State Bulletin,* July 18, 1949, p. 75.

4. On Washington and London's laying the groundwork, see Dean Acheson, *Present at the Creation* (W. W. Norton, 1969), p. 672; see also Washington's cables to U.S.

embassies in Manila, Jakarta, and Bangkok, January 7, 11, 12, in *FRUS, 1950,* 6:691–94, which are reproduced in Gareth Porter, *Vietnam: A History in Documents* (New American Library, 1981), pp. 220, 221. For the text of the DRV appeal, the Chinese and Soviet responses, and Acheson's reply, see Allan W. Cameron, *Viet-Nam Crisis: A Documentary History,* vol. 1, *1940–1956* (Cornell University Press, 1971), pp. 141–45.

5. It will be remembered that many Americans came to identify the Korean War with China, and that the conventional wisdom held that Peking, as much as Pyongyang or Moscow, was responsible for its outbreak. The Dulles quote is from *New York Times,* September 3, 1953.

6. David Schoenbrun, *Vietnam: How We Got In, How to Get Out* (Atheneum, 1968), p. 35.

7. Kennedy quote is in *The War in Indochina* (U.S. Government Printing Office, 1954), p. 7. A decade and a half later, when writing about this period, Acheson apparently still clung to the analogue: "We recognized in a communiqué that the struggle in Indochina was part of the world-wide resistance to 'Communist attempts at conquest and subversion,' that France had a 'primary role in Indochina,' such as we had assumed in Korea, and stated that within the authority given by Congress we would increase our aid to building the national armies [of the Indochina states]." (Acheson, *Present at the Creation,* p. 676.)

8. Thus, with reference to the July 1952 U.S. agreement to support the French fiscal-year-1953 budget to the extent of $525 million, the JCS historians observe, "It is not clear, however, what part of this sum was used for Indochina and what part for French requirements in Europe." (*JCS History,* p. 262.) A Dulles telephone memorandum indicates that almost half of this U.S. contribution to the French budget was made up of ECA counterpart funds released "for French military budget purposes for use in Indochina." (Memorandum of Telephone Conversation, John F. Dulles to Mr. Nolting, May 11, 1954.)

9. On "lending" the first aircraft carriers, see Memorandum for the Secretary of Defense, "U.S. Aid to Indochina," JCS, WGL, January 26, 1951. On C-47s, etc., see *JCS History,* pp. 267, 268. With C-47s in short supply in the United States, and crucial for dropping three parachute battalions in a series of French operations in Indochina, it was necessary to augment the twenty-one lent by the U.S. air force with planes diverted from U.S. MDAP (Mutual Defense Assistance Program) deliveries to NATO (including twenty destined for Belgium). See also *FRUS 1952–1954,* 13:387.

10. *JCS History,* pp. 262, 486.

11. *Ibid.,* p. 261. For figures as of May 28, 1952, see *FRUS, 1952–1954,* 13:156–57.

12. For the 1952 assessment, see U.S. Joint Intelligence Committee, "Current Situation in Southeast Asia," January 2, 1952.

13. All quotes are from *JCS History,* pp. 206–7.

14. Melvin Gurtov, *The First Vietnam Crisis: Chinese Communist Strategy and United States Involvement, 1953–1954* (Columbia University Press, 1967), pp. 28–29 and nn. 174–75, citing *New York Times* and Department of State Press Release No. 160, March 28, 1953.

15. See Bernard Fall's letter to *New York Times,* March 11, 1966.

16. Vietminh and Indochina Command totals are from Report of the U.S. Special Mission to Indochina, prepared by General J. W. O'Daniel, February 5, 1954. Breakdown of Indochina Command is from *FRUS, 1952–1954,* 13:159. For the French government quote, see Embassy of France (Washington), Service d'Information et de Presse, October 1952, p. 9; two divisions were based in North Africa and one in various other French colonies. For Marshall's statement, see Department of State, Division of Central Services, Transcript of Proceedings, Meeting, "U.S.-China Problems," October 8, 1949, p. 405.

17. France's military expenditures are in *FRUS, 1952–1954,* 13:158. NSC quote is from Memorandum from State Department to National Security Council, "Further United

States Support for France and the Associated States of Indochina," August 5, 1953, p. 1.

18. On 148,000 casualties, see *ibid.* On comparison with Saint-Cyr graduates, see Embassy of France (Washington), Service d'Information, p. 16. Quote is from "Further United States Support," p. 4; see also *PP* (Gravel), 1:407; *JCS History*, p. 301.

19. Laniel's statement is quoted in Hammer, *Struggle for Indochina*, p. 312. Ho's response is in Philippe Devillers and Jean Lacouture, *End of a War: Indochina, 1954* (Praeger, 1969), pp. 44–47.

20. Quotes on Laniel government and domino theory are from "Further United States Support," p. 4; see also *PP* (Gravel), 1:407. NSC quotes are from NSC, Planning Board, Special Annex to Report to NSC, No. 177, "United States Objectives and Courses of Action with Respect to Southeast Asia," December 31, 1953, pp. 4, 7, 8. Even including two divisions scheduled for redeployment from Korea in March 1954, the United States would have had only five readily available divisions.

21. Secretary Dulles's opinion is in Acting Secretary of State and Acting Secretary of Defense, Progress Report to the NSC, No. 124/2, "United States Objectives and Courses of Action with Respect to Southeast Asia," August 5, 1953, p. 8. French fear of spread of U.N. debate is in cable from Bedell Smith (Geneva) to Dulles, May 5, 1954, DDE Library; see also *JCS History*, p. 302. The French were unable to elicit an assurance of American support even if the Chinese intervention were limited to air power: Dulles indicated that the U.S. response would depend on circumstances. (*Ibid.*, p. 371.) On the other hand, "Paris was so fearful of provoking the Chinese" that as late as March 24 its chief of staff, General Ely, "would not hazard a guess whether his government would ask American help to save Dienbienphu." (*Ibid.*, p. 373.)

22. On the plans that were developed, see NSC, Planning Board Report to NSC, December 31, 1953, No. 177, pp. 1–9. Dulles's phraseology was used as early as his speech

in St. Louis, in *Department of State Bulletin,* September 14, 1953, pp. 341–42.

23. Eisenhower's realization is in *Hagerty Diary,* February 7, 1954. (Photostat copy in Dwight D. Eisenhower Library, Abilene, Kansas. James C. Hagerty was Eisenhower's press secretary.) Paris quote is from *JCS History,* pp. 420–21.

24. Quote on dropping South Korean troop idea is from NSC, Record of Actions at its 185th Meeting, February 17, 1954, pp. 2–3, and 187th Meeting, March 4, 1954, p. 2. Dulles quote is from his cable to Amconsul, Geneva, June 9 [1954]; see also *JCS History,* pp. 420–21; *FRUS, 1952–1954,* 13:1053–54, 1716. As late as the NSC meeting on July 22, 1954, this Korean option was to be "kept under review in the light of future developments." (NSC Action #1178, Record of Actions, 207th Meeting, July 22, 1954.)

25. See cable from Dillon to Secretary of State, May 14, 1954.

26. Plans for boosting aid are in *PP* (Gravel), 1:408, 77. Apparently there was another augmentation of the U.S. outlay amounting to $124 million in March 1954. (*FRUS, 1952–1954,* 13:1111.) It is difficult to establish the total value of the U.S. contribution for fiscal 1954 with any precision, for official sources vary significantly. The compilers of the JCS study observe, "The figures given by various sources reveal serious conflict." (*JCS History,* p. 486 n.) See *New York Times,* April 7, 1954, for the proportion of global U.S. aid. *JCS History,* pp. 487–88, gives the following breakdown:

Military Assistance	$1,308,000,000
Financial Support of French Budget	1,285,000,000
Military Support Program	75,000,000
Defense Support Program	95,000,000
Total	$2,763,000,000

27. NSC quote is from Operations Coordinating Board, Progress Report on NSC 5405 (Southeast Asia), August 5, 1954, p. 9. MDAP figures are from *JCS History,* pp. 306, 370, 488–89. Both carriers, the USS *Belleau Wood* and the *Lafayette* (formerly

USS *Langley*), had been transferred by September 5, 1953. The British had also loaned the French a carrier, the *Arromanches* (formerly the HMS *Colossus*). See also *FRUS, 1952–1954,* 13:1170. On the involvement of U.S. personnel, see *FRUS, 1952–1954,* 13:-938, 944, 984, 1016, 1170; *JCS History,* p. 489.

28. On the ten more battalions, see J. F. Dulles, January 7, 1954, before Senate Foreign Relations Committee, in U.S. Congress, Senate, Committee on Foreign Relations, *Executive Sessions,* 83rd Cong., 2nd Sess. vol. 6 (1954), p. 6. One of these ten battalions had been withdrawn from Korea.

29. According to an NSC report "The light Vietnamese battalions would remain in these areas [southern and central] to guarantee territorial security while the regular units (French Union and Vietnamese) would be moved to Tonkin to increase the forces available there for operations against the bulk of the enemy's forces." (NSC, Progress Report, "U.S. Objectives and Courses of Action with Respect to Southeast Asia," August 5, 1953, NSC 124/2, p. 14.) On the increase in weapons after the Korean War, see Gurtov, *First Vietnam Crisis,* pp. 14–15. Dulles's estimate is in cable from American Embassy, Paris, to Department of State, April 21, 1954, in "Minutes of Conversation Held in Paris by the Secretary of State and Foreign Minister Bidault with Relation to 'Unified Action' in Southeast Asia," April 14, 1954, p. 4.

30. Quote is in cable from Dulles (Paris) to Secretary of State [paraphrasing Bidault], April 24, 1954, in DDE Library. The classic account of the Battle of Dienbienphu, its background and context is Bernard Fall's *Hell in a Very Small Place: The Siege of Dienbienphu* (Lippincott, 1966). On Eisenhower's support, see Memorandum (Personal and Confidential) from C. D. Jackson for Mr. Luce, July 27, 1954, DDE Library. Jackson, who was in close contact with Eisenhower during this period, states, "The President kept viewing the Indo-Chinese military situation like an American General with American troops under his command. When Dienbienphu started shaping up and Allen Dulles gave him the order of battle

showing that the Vietminh outnumbered the garrison by three or four to one, he made some comment that this was a rather good situation to chew up the enemy; that in a siege operation you could easily hold against four and five times your number."

31. The estimate of the days of labor is from *Nhan Dan,* September 5, 1955, trans. Christine White. On the Vietminh attack, see Bernard Fall, *Street Without Joy* (Stackpole, 1961), p. 290. Fall notes, "In order to strafe those emplacements, the Air Force's fighter-bombers had to fly directly into the axis of the guns and of their attending antiaircraft guns and machine guns. . . . Wet foliage proved almost impervious to napalm. . . ." See also Fall's account of the battle in *Hell in a Very Small Place.*

32. For the carrier-based bomb option, see Brig. General Sidney F. Griffin, Study Group on Indochina, Council on Foreign Relations, May 6, 1957, pp. 4, 6; see Memorandum from C. D. Jackson to Henry Luce, "U.S.-Indochina Mess," July 27, 1954, C. D. Jackson Papers, DDE Library. According to Jackson, Radford suggested that flights of carrier-based planes could have their U.S. markings obliterated and "no one would know where they came from, or who they were." The allegation that Secretary Dulles on two occasions actually offered Foreign Minister Bidault American atomic bombs for use by French forces in Indochina has not been conclusively verified. Bidault so stated to two American reporters, Drummond and Coblenz, and earlier in August 1954 a senior French official (Roland de Margorie) had asserted that this was the case. In an exchange of cables with Ambassador Dillon, Dulles categorically denied the charge. (Roscoe Drummond and Gaston Coblenz, *Duel at the Brink* [Doubleday, 1960], pp. 121–22; *PP* [GPO], 10: 705–8. See also Fall, *Hell in a Very Small Place,* esp. p. 307; Richard K. Betts, *Soldiers, Statesmen, and Cold War Crises* [Harvard University Press, 1977], p. 106.)

33. Gavin quote is from his *Crisis Now* (Random House, 1968), p. 48. As early as March 24, Radford had advised Eisenhower

that to avoid a French failure in Vietnam, which he said could "well lead to the loss of all S.E. Asia to Communist domination," the U.S. "must be prepared to act promptly and in force possibly to a frantic and belated request by the French for U.S. intervention." (Memorandum for the President from Arthur Radford, "Discussions with General Ely Relative to the Situation in Indo-China," March 24, 1954.) For Ridgway's position, see *JCS History*, p. 388; see also Memorandum from Joint Chiefs of Staff for Secretary of Defense, "Studies with Respect to Possible U.S. Action Regarding Indochina," May 26, 1954; NSC, "Summary of Studies with Respect to Possible U.S. Action Regarding Indochina," NSC 5421, June 10, 1954, p. 4; Matthew Ridgway, *Soldier* (Harper and Brothers, 1956), pp. 275–78. For NSC and ICS estimates as to the likelihood of Chinese intervention, see NSC 5421, June 10, 1954, p. 2; JCS Memorandum, "Studies," May 26, 1954; and Gavin, *Crisis Now*, p. 47.

34. Nixon later stated that Secretary Dulles shared the view expressed in his April 16 statement but insisted that the speech had not been made at his suggestion: "It was not an administration trial balloon. It was mine, absolutely, and the sole responsibility was mine." (Nixon interview, February 24, 1966, Dulles Oral History File, Princeton University Library.) On Eisenhower's decision to side with Ridgway, see Ridgway, *Soldier*, p. 277. "With reference to the Far East" quote is from JCS Memorandum, "Studies," May 26, 1954; see also *JCS History*, p. 389.

35. "When the day comes" quote is from Ridgway, *Soldier*, p. 278.

36. In an "eyes only" cable to Eisenhower and Bedell Smith on April 29, Secretary Dulles, then at Geneva, reported, "The attitude here of Molotov and Chou En-lai's statement yesterday lead me to rate more high than heretofore the probability that any open U.S. intervention would be answered by open Chinese intervention with consequence of general war in Asia." (Cable from Dulles [Dulte] 21, April 29, 1954.)

37. For indications of greater administration support, see *Hagerty Diary*, April 24 and July 26, 1954; *JCS History*, p. 388. For several references to accounts stating that atomic bombs were to be used, see Betts, *Soldiers, Statesmen and Cold War Crises*, pp. 106, 253. Radford quote is in *JCS History*, p. 373a.

38. For Radford's acknowledgment, see his Memorandum for the Secretary's [Dulles] File, April 5, 1954. In a meeting with Dulles and key congressional leaders on April 3, Radford stated that only if U.S. air power had been committed at least three weeks earlier did he feel "reasonably certain" that the Vietminh would have been defeated.

39. Quote is in *JCS History*, p. 380; see also p. 379; *Hagerty Diary*, April 20, June 11, 1954. The decision to approve the use of U.S. C-119 transport for dropping napalm, "provided no U.S. crews were involved," was apparently made at Radford's initiative. (Memorandum for the President from Arthur Radford, March 24, 1954.)

40. Quote is from Dulles's draft of April 2, 1954, following revisions made during his visit to the White House that day. As far as I have been able to determine, this was the final draft. On the April 3 meeting, see Memorandum from Dulles for the Secretary's File, April 5, 1954. The congressmen present were Senators Knowland, Milliken, Lyndon Johnson, Russell, and Clements, and Representatives Martin (Speaker of the House), McCormack, and Priest. The French were especially eager for American bombing runs aimed at the Vietminh's supply depot, which was dispersed over an eight-square-mile area near Dienbienphu. (Anthony Eden, *The Memoirs of Anthony Eden: Full Circle* [Houghton Mifflin, 1960], p. 112.)

41. Dulles quotes are from Dulles's Memorandum, April 5, 1954. Possibly Dulles did not then regard the condition of an earnest of genuine independence as of major importance, for he did not mention it in either a call he made to Eisenhower that day or in his personal memorandum. How-

ever, it does appear in other accounts of this meeting, and in his later discussions with the French he frequently emphasized it.

42. The second plea is relayed in cable from Dulles (Paris) to Secretary of State, April 23, 1954. Georges Bidault's request is in Memorandum by Dulles, "French Requests Involving Possible United States Belligerence in Indochina," undated, p. 4. It was on the occasion of this request that Dulles was alleged to have offered Bidault two atomic bombs for use in Vietnam. Eden quote is from his *Full Circle,* pp. 113–19.

43. Dulles quote is from his cable to Secretary of State, April 25, 1954. For Dulles's April 24 message to Laniel, see his cable to Secretary of State, April 24, 1954, and letter to Bidault, April 24, 1954. For Eisenhower's statement to these congressmen, see *Hagerty Diary,* April 26, 1954. The group included Senators Knowland, Milliken, Saltonstall, Ferguson, and Bridges, together with Representatives Martin, Halleck, Arends, Allen, and Leonard Hall, as well as Vice President Nixon, Deputy Secretary of Defense Anderson, and the Budget Director Hughes.

44. Dulles had begun to explore the idea of United Action with the House Foreign Affairs Committee as early as March 23. (Memorandum [Personal and Private] by J. F. Dulles, "French Requests Involving Possible United States Belligerency in Indochina," p. 6. This undated retrospective memorandum was apparently prepared by Dulles shortly after the conclusion of the Geneva Conference.) For Churchill and Eden's views, see Eden, *Full Circle,* pp. 117–19. Dulles quotes are from Secretary's Briefing for Members of Congress, May 5, 1954, p. 7; see also Dulte 21, cable from Dulles (Geneva) to Eisenhower and Bedell Smith, April 29, 1954. For Eisenhower's suggestions for a letter to Churchill, see Memorandum of Conversation with the President by J. F. Dulles, May 19, 1954.

45. On Eisenhower and Dulles's hope, see n. 54 below. On Eisenhower's view by mid-May, see Memorandum of Telephone Conversation from J. F. Dulles to Admiral Radford, May 10, 1954, DDE Library; cable from Dillon (Paris) to Secretary of State, May 14, 1954; see also *FRUS, 1952–1954,* 13: 1583.

46. Quotes on the French communication are in Dulles's Memorandum, "French Requests," p. 13. Laniel's warning is in cable from Dillon (Paris) to Secretary of State, May 10, 1954. For Radford's proposal, see Memorandum of Conversation, Secretary's residence, May 9, 1954 (participants: Radford, Anderson [deputy secretary of defense]; Captain George Anderson, and Mr. Douglas MacArthur II). For Dulles's May 11 response to the French, see Dulles's Memorandum, "French Requests," pp. 14–15.

47. At the beginning of the Geneva negotiations, the Joint Chiefs appeared to have reached a consensus, and their position was that "the allocation of more than token" U.S. forces to Indochina "would be a serious diversion of limited U.S. capabilities," an observation that coincided with their "central philosophy that the real solution to Far Eastern difficulties lay in the neutralization of Communist China." (*JCS History,* p. 429.) Efforts to obtain specific commitments from the French for sending reinforcements from France and North Africa to Indochina had been unsuccessful, though they talked vaguely of increasing their forces by three divisions. (Cables from Dillon to Secretary of State, May 27, May 30, 1954.) Dulles quotes are from his Memorandum of Conversation with the President, May 19, 1954. This resolution (drafted by Dulles on May 17) was approximately the same as that of April 2, except that it was broader, referring to "Asia," rather than "Southeast Asia." For the text of the May 17 version, see *FRUS, 1952–1954,* 13: 1585.

48. That Eisenhower and Dulles were still hoping for a congressional mandate is evident in Dulles's cable to Paris embassy on May 26, 1954, in *FRUS, 1952–1954,* 13:1618–19. For a blistering and knowledgeable critique of this third draft presidential message to Congress and the assumptions upon which it rested, see Memorandum by Charlton Ogburn, May 26, in *ibid.,* p. 1620.

Quotes are from Special National Intelligence Estimate (SNIE), June 15, 1954, in *ibid.,* p. 1585. The U.S. position was spelled out in Dulles's cable to American embassy in Paris of that date, in *ibid.,* pp. 1689–90. See also *JCS History,* pp. 383, 389, 390, 446; *Hagerty Diary,* April 19, 1954.

49. Figures are from *FRUS, 1952–1954,* 13:1699–1700.

50. All quotes are from *JCS History,* pp. 422–27.

51. June 2 decision is in *FRUS, 1952–1954,* 13: 1657–58. See also, Memorandum from Robert Cutler, Special Assistant to the President, for Secretary John Foster Dulles, June 2, 1954, concerning the conference that morning in the president's office where he made this decision.

52. Cables from Dulles (Geneva) to Secretary of State, May 15, 1954; from Dillon (Paris) to Secretary of State, May 30, 1954.

53. The Pentagon chronicler observes that no French authority doubted the Vietminh's "capability to eliminate the French from Tonkin with one major offensive, and to drive on for further gains in the South against a weakened, demoralized Franco-Vietnamese army." (*PP* [GPO], 1 [D.9].) On Smith's informing Congress, see Memorandum for the Record by Bryce Harlow, June 23, 1954, of meeting between President Eisenhower, Secretary Dulles, and Smith with congressional leaders. Smith stated that "Ho Chi-minh is in command of 75% of the country, that elections tomorrow would give him 80% of the vote; that the Bao Dai regime is corrupt and the French are still colonialists." British Chiefs of Staff quote is in Memorandum of Conversation, Eden, Dulles, *et al.,* Geneva, April 25, 1954, p. 3.

54. Dulles's hope is in *JCS History,* p. 446. "Essential" and "so as to have" quotes are from cable from Dulles to Acting Secretary of State, April 22, 1954, as quoted in *JCS History,* p. 390. Eden's course is in Memorandum of Conversation, Eden, Shuckburgh, and Caccia with Dulles and McArthur [Jr.], April 25, 1954. Smith quote is from Statement of Walter Bedell Smith, February 16, 1954, Senate Foreign Relations

Committee, *Executive Sessions* (1954), p. III. As for the possibility of U.S. intervention, even the conference's most peripheral member, Bao Dai's "foreign minister," Tran Van Do, clearly appreciated this prospect. (Discussion with the author, Saigon, January 14, 1970.)

55. "7 Points" discussed in cable from Dulles to Amembassy, Paris, July 3, 1954, in *PP* (GPO), 9:603. Four days later Dulles explained that the term "respect" did not mean that the United States would actually "guarantee" a Geneva settlement that conformed to the seven points, or that it would "necessarily support it publicly," but that the U.S. "would not seek directly or indirectly to upset [such a] settlement by force." (*Ibid.,* p. 617.)

56. Eden, *Full Circle,* p. 149.

57. Cable from Dulles to Amembassy, Paris, July 10, 1954, in *PP* (GPO), 9:627.

58. In addition to heavy French financial dependence on the United States, Washington exercised significant leverage through its ability to withdraw its support from the precarious French position in Algeria and Tunisia. (*PP* [Gravel], 1:117.) On the possibility of Parliament's supporting the EDC, see cable from Dillon to Secretary of State, May 8, 1954, in *JCS History,* p. 397; see also *PP* (Gravel), 1: 115. Premier Mendès-France argued to Dulles on July 13, 1954, that there never had been a majority for EDC in the French Parliament and that he did not believe there was then a majority. (Memorandum of Discussion, Ambassador Dillon's Residence, Paris, July 13, 1954, pp. 6–7.)

59. For Parliament's turning the EDC down, see Donald Lancaster, *The Emancipation of French Indochina* (London: Oxford University Press, 1961), pp. 336–37; Daniel Lerner and Raymond Aron, eds., *France Defeats the E.D.C.* (Praeger, 1957), pp. 16–17. After the defeat of the EDC, Dulles agreed with Congressman Walter Judd that "the price of the truce [in Vietnam] was the defeat of E.D.C." (Memorandum of Telephone Conversation, September 14, 1954.) On the Russian understanding, see *PP* (GPO), 1 (III, C. 1):19.

60. See *PP* (GPO), 1 (III, C.1)18–19. As noted above, this fear of the Indochina conflict escalating into World War III was shared by the British.

61. Evelyn Colbert, *Southeast Asia in International Politics, 1941–1956* (Cornell University Press, 1977), p. 283.

62. On Washington's original expectations, see *PP* (GPO), 1 (III, C.1): 21; cable from Smith to Secretary of State, May 23, 1954, sec. 3, p. 3.

63. On China's desire to confine the French-Vietnamese conflict and her fear of an eventual American intervention there, see especially the excellent study of François Joyaux, *La Chine et le règlement du premier conflit d'Indochine (Geneva 1954)* (Paris: Publications de la Sorbonne, 1979), p. 200. Eden quotes are from Anthony Eden, *Toward Peace in Indochina* (Houghton Mifflin, 1966), p. 2. On Peking's security interests, see *PP* (GPO), 1 (III, C.1): 20.

64. For "peaceful co-existence," see *PP* (GPO), 1 (III, C.1): 20–21; Joyaux, *La Chine,* p. 89. Eden and Molotov also served as co-chairmen of the sessions devoted to Korea.

65. Dulles quote is from Report by the Secretary of State, July 16, 1954, Senate Foreign Relations Committee, *Executive Sessions* (1954), p. 657. Quotes on Chauvel are from cable from Johnson [U.S. Ambassador to Geneva] to Secretary of State, July 9, 1954, in *PP* (Gravel), 1:549.

66. White quotes are from "Agrarian Reform," pp. 196–97. March 1954 editorial is in Gareth Porter, ed., *Vietnam: The Definitive Documentation of Human Decisions,* 2 vols. (Earl Coleman Enterprises, Inc., Publishers, 1979), 1:506–7. Ho Chi Minh quote is in White, "Agrarian Reform," p. 234, citing Ho's speech at the Sixth Plenum of the Central Committee (July 15–18, 1954) as reproduced in *Ho Chi Minh's Selected Writings (1920–1969)* (Hanoi: Foreign Languages Publishing House, 1973), pp. 178, 180.

67. *PP* (GPO), 1 (III, C.1): C5–8. (The account of the DRV's position presented in the Gravel edition is attenuated.)

68. The opening French position is outlined in Bedell Smith's cable to Dulles of May 5, 1954. François Joyaux, in his comprehensive analysis of the Chinese role at the Geneva Conference, marshals convincing evidence for his conclusion that "the Chinese delegation took an attitude towards the Viet-Minh that was more constraining than that of the Soviet delegation." (*La Chine,* especially p. 286.)

69. *PP* (GPO), 1 (III, C.8–11); Joyaux, *La Chine,* pp. 240, 227–28, 231–32.

70. For Chou En-lai's concessions, see cable from Smith to Secretary of State, June 19, 1954, sec. one, p. 2; see also cable from Dillon to Secretary of State, June 24, 1954; Joyaux, *La Chine,* p. 231. Colbert quote is from her *Southeast Asia,* p. 281; for a fuller discussion, see Joyaux, *La Chine.* "A major breakthrough" quote is in *PP* (GPO), 1 (III, C.24–25); see also Joyaux, *La Chine,* pp. 227–29. Within a week of Chou En-lai's informing Eden, on June 17, that it "would not be difficult" to get the Vietminh to agree to withdraw their "volunteers" from Laos and Cambodia, Hanoi agreed to do so. On Smith's expectations, see *Hagerty Diary,* June 23, 1954; Outline of General Smith's Remarks to the President and Bipartisan Congressional Group, June 23, 1954, p. 2. Smith foresaw communist control of no territory in Cambodia. Moreover, as Joyaux points out, Chou's position, implicitly at least, acknowledged that the two royal governments were free to receive arms from outside to be used against the Pathet Lao and Khmer Isarak forces. (Joyaux, *La Chine,* pp. 228–29.)

71. Molotov is quoted in cable from Smith to Secretary of State, June 19, 1954, sec. one, p. 3, and sec. two, p. 2. Chou specifically requested that the Pathet Lao's regroupment zone front on China as well as Vietnam. (Joyaux, *La Chine,* p. 231.) On French vs. Vietminh influence, see *PP* (GPO), 1 (III, C.13).

72. On French abandonment of "leopard spot" formula, see cable from Smith to Secretary of State, June 18, 1954. Quote is in *PP* (GPO), 1 (III, C.11).

73. Joyaux, *La Chine,* p. 282.

74. *PP* (GPO), 1 (III, D.8–9). Pierre

Mendès-France's statement is in *Journal Officiel de la République Française, Débats Parlementaires, Assemblée Nationale,* July 23, 1954, p. 3580.

75. On the meeting, see *PP* (GPO), 1 (III, C.23). Ambassador Johnson reported shortly afterward that China's vice minister of foreign affairs, Chang Wen-tien, had informed the French that Chou En-lai had had a "very good meeting" with Ho Chi Minh and that the results "would be very helpful to [the] French." (Cable from Johnson [Geneva] to Secretary of State, July 9, 1954.) On the highway and on Chinese pressure on the Vietminh to yield on this question, see Joyaux, *La Chine,* pp. 283–84.

76. Outline of General Smith's Remarks to the President and Bipartisan Congressional Group, June 23, 1954, p. 3.

77. Chou En-lai position is from cable from Dillon (Paris) to Secretary of State, June 24, 1954. "Still little more" quote is from *PP* (GPO), 1 (III, D.13); see also Joyaux, *La Chine,* p. 279.

78. For the full text of all three of the signed armistice agreements, see Robert F. Randle, *Geneva 1954: The Settlement of the Indochinese War* (Princeton University Press, 1969), pp. 572–607. The World Court held in 1933 that an oral agreement between authorized representatives of countries is legally binding. (Case of Denmark and Norway with regard to Eastern Greenland, Permanent Court of International Justice, A/b No. 53 [1933], p. 71.) See also Herbert Briggs, *The Law of Nations,* 2nd ed. (Appleton-Century-Crofts, 1952), p. 838. The full text of the Final Declaration, with a record of the orally stated positions of the participants, as well as the Franco-Vietnamese armistice agreement, can be found in Randle, *Geneva 1954;* Cameron, *Viet-Nam Crisis;* George McT. Kahin and John W. Lewis, *The United States in Vietnam,* 2nd ed. rev. & enl. (Delta, 1969); Porter, *Definitive Documentation.* For the U.S. position, see Cameron, *Viet-Nam Crisis,* pp. 314–15; Kahin and Lewis, *United States in Vietnam,* pp. 446–47; Porter, *Definitive Documentation,* pp. 655–66. For the objections of Bao Dai's rep-

resentative, see Cameron, *Viet-Nam Crisis,* pp. 284–85, 309–10. For the positions of the Royal Lao and Royal Cambodian governments, see Cameron, *Viet-Nam Crisis,* pp. 312–13; Kahin and Lewis, *United States in Vietnam,* pp. 445–46. In declaring his support, the Cambodian representative insisted —unsuccessfully—that note be taken of his country's claim to certain southern-Vietnamese border areas.

79. Eden, then Lord Avon, made the point absolutely clear in discussions with me and others at Cornell, March 11–12, 1969. Tran Van Do expressed his endorsement of Eden's view to me in Saigon, January 14, 1970.

80. Quote is from Article 14(a) of the armistice agreement. On French fears of "spontaneous rebellions," see French General Assembly Debates, Christian Pineau [head of the French Parliamentary Mission to Vietnam], December 17, 1954, pp. 6512–13.

81. With respect to France's obligation for observance and enforcement, see, for example, the statements of French Cabinet ministers in Roger Pinto, "La France et les états d'Indochine devant les accords de Genève," *Revue Française de Science Politique,* 5, no. 1 (January-March, 1955). Regarding the obligation of a successor Vietnamese regime's assumption of France's responsibilities, see article 27 of the armistice agreement. In the treaty of June 4, 1954 (unsigned, but initialed and operative), wherein the French undertook to transfer authority to Bao Dai's government, it was made clear that this would entail its assumption of all obligations "resulting from international treaties or conventions contracted by France in the name of the State of Vietnam." (Secretariat of State for Foreign Affairs of the Republic of Vietnam, Bureau of Archives, "Treaties on Vietnamese Independence and Franco-Vietnamese Association," quoted in Ngo Ton Dat, "The Geneva Partition of Vietnam and the Question of Reunification during the First Two Years [August 1954 to July 1956]," Ph.D. dissertation, Cornell University, 1963, pp. 452–53. The writer of this dissertation served at the

Geneva Conference as aide to Prince Buu Loc, who was Bao Dai's prime minister prior to Ngo Dinh Diem. For the text, see also Porter, *Vietnam: A History in Documents,* pp. 150–51.)

82. Quote on precedent for North Africa is from cable from Bedell Smith to Secretary of State, May 5, 1954. Eisenhower's threat is from Memo for Record, Secretary Dulles's telephone call to Ambassador Lodge (in New York), June 24, 1954. In instructing Lodge, Dulles stated that Eisenhower wanted to avoid making this representation "in the form of a threat," but that there should be "a clear understanding that if they don't take into account our needs and considerations in this matter, it will be a two-way street, and they must accept it." For more on this controversy see *Hagerty Diary,* June 24, 1954.

83. The Department of State understood this. See the analysis of its Division of Research for Far East, Intelligence Report No. 7045, "Probable Developments in South Vietnam Through July 1956," September 15, 1955, p. 61.

84. Stipulation is from Final Declaration, para. 6. Eden's statement came in discussions with me and others in Ithaca, N.Y., March 11–12, 1969. In his public lecture at Cornell on March 11, he took the same position (that the seventeenth parallel was not expected to become a lasting political boundary), though acknowledging (with obvious reference to the American delegation at Geneva), "I wouldn't say it was absolutely excluded out of anybody's mind."

85. Articles 16–19 of the armistice agreement. When war materiel was worn out or damaged, however, it could be replaced on a piece-for-piece basis, and the French were permitted to rotate military personnel on a limited man-for-man basis, in units no larger than a battalion.

86. Articles 41–43 of the armistice agreement.

87. U.S. officials' private thoughts are from telephone conversations, Bedell Smith and Dulles, July 20, 21, 1954. In reporting on the conference's outcome to the NSC on

July 22, Dulles stated that "Communist demands had turned out to be relatively moderate in terms of their actual capabilities." (*FRUS, 1952–1954,* 13:1869.) For Eisenhower's view, see *Hagerty Diary,* July 8, 1954. According to Anthony Eden, Dulles chose to disassociate himself from the agreements because "American public opinion would never tolerate 'the guaranteeing of the subjection of millions of Vietnamese to Communist rule.' " (Eden, *Full Circle,* p. 156.) Remaining quotes are from telephone conversations, Dulles and Ambassador Bonnet, July 20, 1954; Dulles and Senator Smith, July 20, 1954.

III. The Establishment of a Separate Southern State

1. For this NSC directive, see National Security Council, "U.S. Policy in Mainland Southeast Asia," April 2, 1958, NSC 5809, p. 12, para. 55, and *PP* (Gravel), 1:267.

2. On November 20, 1954, Dulles informed Eisenhower that he was "in the midst of a terrible crisis with Mendès [-France]. He wants to drag us into the North African situation up to our necks. . . . He wants us to commit ourselves." (Memorandum of Telephone Call from Dulles to the President, November 20, 1954.)

3. Thus, Dulles observed to Secretary of Defense Anderson, "So far we have been able to say that the losses in that area [Vietnam] have been French failures." (Memorandum of Telephone Call from Dulles to Secretary Anderson, November 19, 1954.)

4. This assessment of Dulles's views is based primarily on a long discussion I had with him in mid-1950 that was focused largely on the Southeast Asian national revolutions. The conversation took place shortly after he had been appointed as special adviser to the State Department and charged with responsibility for working out the terms of a peace treaty with Japan. As late as mid-1954, Dulles informed an Executive Session of the Senate Foreign Relations Committee that independence had been

given the Indonesians prematurely. ("Report of the Secretary of State," January 7, 1954, U.S. Congress, Senate, Committee on Foreign Relations, *Executive Sessions*, 83rd Cong., 2nd sess. vol. 6 [1954], pp. 23–24.)

5. Quotes in this and the following paragraph are from the personal notes made by Ambassador Hugh S. Cumming immediately after his briefing by Eisenhower and Dulles in late 1953. The views expressed to Cumming are rendered with greater precision and detail but are consistent with those Dulles conveyed to me some three years before. I am grateful to Cumming for permission to quote from his notes and for his generosity in discussing this matter at length with me in 1970. He became one of Dulles's closest confidants. Following his posting to Indonesia (1953–56), he was appointed director of the State Department's Bureau of Intelligence and Research. This had previously been a position lacking much influence, but under Cumming—thanks to the reliance that Dulles placed on him—it became much more important, and soon he was briefing the secretary every morning on incoming cables, having the authority to select those meriting his attention.

6. See n.5. In 1957–58 Dulles took the lead in organizing covert operations to encourage and support a coup designed to unseat Indonesia's President Sukarno (because of a mistaken view that he was then leading the country toward communism) or, failing that, to bring about the secession of the oil-rich island of Sumatra and Celebes (Sulawesi) from the rest of Indonesia. He was on the verge of extending *de facto* diplomatic recognition to these areas as a separate state when the rebels, despite a lavish supply of American arms and CIA instructors, succumbed to the Indonesian army's actually strongly anticommunist central command. See the accounts of the two U.S. ambassadors who served in Indonesia during this period: John Allison, *Ambassador from the Prairie* (Houghton Mifflin, 1973), and Howard P. Jones, *Indonesia: The Possible Dream* (Harcourt Brace Jovanovich, 1971).

7. Ambassador Cumming saw their reading of "the lesson from China" as having an applicability that extended well beyond Indonesia.

8. For a relevant account of the U.S. intervention in Greece, see Richard J. Barnet, *Intervention and Revolution* (World Publishing, 1968), pp. 97–131. Following his experience in Greece, William Bundy served as a member of the CIA's Office of National Estimates, and from 1952 to 1956 was CIA alternate on the NSC Planning Board. He was deputy assistant secretary of international security affairs in the Defense Department under Kennedy, who authorized his promotion to assistant secretary shortly before Kennedy died. Johnson endorsed that decision and in March 1964 appointed Bundy to succeed Roger Hilsman as assistant secretary for Far Eastern affairs. William Bundy expressed his "Greek solution" view in meetings with the State Department's East Asia Advisory Council and in discussions with me. See also Ernest R. May, *Lessons of the Past* (Oxford University Press, 1973), pp. 110–11; Richard J. Barnet, *Roots of War* (Penguin Books, 1971), p. 105.

9. An able American ambassador, Myron Cowan, also deserved much of the credit in the Philippines, but since he was less inclined than Lansdale to claim it, his contribution was not so widely recognized. Lansdale was in a favorable position to conduct the covert side of the effort, having operated in the Philippines before with assignments including the reorganization of Philippine intelligence. In 1954 he knew much less about Vietnam, his first assignment there having been in the previous year, when he was involved in covert activities that he later described as relating to certain "unconventional warfare annexes of the Navarre Plan"; during this time he made contact with some of the Cao Dai leaders.

10. Covered by the treaty was "the general area of Southeast Asia, including also the entire territories of the Asian Parties, and the general area of the Southwest Pacific not including the Pacific area north of 21 degrees 30 minutes north latitude" (article VIII). With respect to Cambodia's rejection

of SEATO and the status of Laos, see U.S. Congress, Senate, *Hearing Before the Committee on Foreign Relations,* 93rd Cong., 2nd sess., March 6, 1974, "U.S. Commitment to SEATO," pp. 71, 72, 79.

11. *Ibid.,* p. 77.

12. The analysis provided in this and the following paragraph, given by the writer when testifying before the 1974 Senate Foreign Relations Committee hearings on SEATO (*ibid.,* p. 36), was fully endorsed by Senator William Fulbright, the committee chairman, and Senator Frank Church, the committee member who requested the hearing. As to the State Department's unambiguous interpretation that a recommendation for measures under para. 2 required unanimity, see William Bundy's unpublished 1972 manuscript (hereafter cited as "W. Bundy manuscript"), ch. 3, pp. 23–24.

13. U.S. Congress, Senate, *The Southeast Asia Collective Defense Treaty,* 83rd Cong., 2d sess. (U.S. Government Printing Office, 1954), pp. 1, 3, 13, 21–22, 25, 28, 33. For further discussion of this treaty, see Senate, "U.S. Commitment to SEATO" (including the appended study by the Congressional Research Service of the Library of Congress); George McT. Kahin and John W. Lewis, *The United States in Vietnam,* 2nd ed. rev. & enl. (Delta, 1969), pp. 300–301.

14. All quotes are from National Security Council, "Review of U.S. Policy in the Far East," August 20, 1954, NSC 5492/2, *PP* (GPO), 10:736–37.

15. "Report of the Secretary of State," Senate Foreign Relations Committee, *Executive Sessions* (1954), pp. 642–43.

16. Figures are from B. S. N. Murti, *Vietnam Divided* (Asia Publishing House, 1964), pp. 223–24. Murti, a London University Ph.D. in history, served in Vietnam from 1954 to 1957, where he was deputy secretary general of the International Control Commission that had been set up to oversee implementation of the Geneva Agreements. He states that 130,000 Vietminh moved north, consisting of 87,000 soldiers and 43,000 administrative cadres, liberated POWs,

and their families. The number arrived at by the compilers of the *Pentagon Papers* as the "best current estimate" was 134,269; they also concluded that 5,000 armed Vietminh and 3,000 cadres were left behind. (*P.P.* [GPO], 2 [IV, A.5, Tab 1]: 17.) R. B. Stebbins and the Research Staff of the Council on Foreign Relations calculated that approximately 150,000 Vietminh troops were transported north on Polish and Russian vessels, and that many were accompanied by their families. (*The United States in World Affairs, 1954* [Harper and Bros., 1956], p. 285.)

By August 1, 1955, the strength of French forces in the North had declined to 60,000 and was to dip to 35,000 by October. (Cable from Chief MAAG [Saigon] to CINCPAC, August 9, 1955.) The message noted the "French need for ground forces elsewhere, primarily North Africa," and observed that they "can see no future in sacrificing French lives in a country that is outside the French empire." By June 30, 1956, all French combat troops had been withdrawn from Vietnam. (Operations Coordinating Board [OCB], NSC, Progress Report, "U.S. Objectives and Courses of Action in Southeast Asia," July 11, 1956, NSC 5405, p. 6.) For the U.S. funding of 150,000 Vietnamese troops, see CIA National Intelligence Estimate, "Probable Developments in Vietnam to July 1956," October 11, 1955, No. 63.1-3-55, p. 7.

17. Paul Ely statement is from cable from Ambassador Heath (Saigon) to Department of State, July 23, 1954, in *FRUS, 1952–1954,* 13:1872. There is considerable disagreement as to the numbers and percentage of Catholics. The Operations Coordinating Board of the NSC estimated the total of civilians who had been evacuated by May 19, 1955, to be 620,000, with an additional 150,000 moving south by December 23. (OCB, *Memorandum* for James S. Lay, Jr., Executive Secretary, Progress Report [Southeast Asia], December 23, 1955, NSC 5405.) The ICC, "citing chiefly the Saigon government as its source," came up with a total of 892,876 civilians, but this included a figure of

70,000 "arrivals not registered" provided by Diem's government. (*PP* [GPO], 2 [IV, A.5, Tab I]:9.) For a discussion of various estimates, see Joseph Buttinger, *Vietnam: A Dragon Embattled,* 2 vols. (Praeger, 1967), 2:900, 1116–17. Estimate of civil servants, etc., is from *PP* (GPO), 2 (IV, A.5, Tab I):11. Robert Scigliano notes that in 1960 Catholic authorities estimated "the Catholic population of North and South Vietnam at 1,807,-784, with 793,000 members of the faith still living above the 17th parallel." (Scigliano, *South Vietnam,* p. 53.)

18. "Not spontaneous" quote is from Chester L. Cooper, *The Lost Crusade: America in Vietnam* (Dodd, Mead, 1970), p. 130. See also Murti, *Vietnam Divided,* pp. 85–86; Philippe Devillers and Jean Lacouture, *End of a War: Indochina, 1954* (Praeger, 1969), pp. 334–35; Tran Tam Tinh, *Dieu et César* (Quebec: Sudestasie, 1975, 1978), pp. 93–95; Bernard Fall, *The Two Vietnams: A Political and Military Analysis* (Praeger, 1964), pp. 153–54. The French informed Dulles they were attempting to support a formula that "would be the best proof" that life south of the seventeenth parallel was preferable to life in the North. (*FRUS, 1952–1954,* 13:-2010.)

19. With respect to the black propaganda, see *PP* (NYT), pp. 16–17; *PP* (Gravel), 1:579. For a detailed account of CIA psychological warfare and clandestine paramilitary operations in the North in the year following the Geneva Conference, see "Lansdale Team's Report on Covert Saigon Mission in 1954 and 1955" in *PP* (Gravel), 1:573–83; see also Tran Tam Tinh, *Dieu et César,* pp. 94–95. Devillers quote is from Devillers and Lacouture, *End of a War,* p. 335. Murti quote is from *Vietnam Divided,* p. 83; also in *PP* (GPO), 2 (IV,A.5, Tab. I): 11.

20. Seventh Fleet figures are *PP* (GPO), 2 (IV,A.5, Tab I): 15. The fullest coverage of the refugee program is in the *First* and *Second Interim Reports of the International Commission for Supervision and Control in Vietnam,* Vietnam No. 1 (1955), Command 9461, and the *Third Interim Report of the*

International Commission for Supervision and Control in Vietnam, Vietnam No. 2 (1955), Command 9499 (both published by Her Majesty's Stationery Office, London, in May and June 1955 respectively). For the December 1954 allocation, see Interview, Leland Barrows, Director, U.S. Operations Mission in Vietnam, with John D. Montgomery, Saigon, May 27, 1958, John D. Montgomery Papers, Hoover Institution on War Revolution and Peace, Stanford University, Box 6. See also *PP* (Gravel), 1:248.

21. The bitterness of some non-Catholic nationalists toward these Catholics was, in the words of one CIA evaluation, "epitomized by the tradition saying that 'Vietnamese Catholics are the claws by which the French crab has been able to crawl across and devour our land.' " (Central Intelligence Agency, Memorandum, September 19, 1964, OCI No. 2230/64, p. 2.)

22. To the French National Assembly, the minister of state for relations with the associated (Indochina) states, Guy La Chambre, explained the choice of Ngo Dinh Diem: "We did not choose Mr. Ngo Dinh Diem. He was already designated when our government came into the act." (*Journal Officiel de la République Française, Débats Parlementaires, Assemblée Nationale,* December 17, 1954, 2nd sess.) See also cable from Dillon to Department of State, May 26, 1954, in *FRUS, 1952–1954,* Indochina, 2:1615. See also S. M. Bao Dai, *Le Dragon d'Annam* (Plon, 1980), p. 328, who acknowledges conversing with Dulles just before appointing Diem, and Cooper, *Lost Crusade,* pp. 127–28, who states that Dulles met with Bao Dai in Paris in the spring of 1954 "in an effort to persuade him to join Diem in Vietnam and help Diem defend the South," but that the emperor declined to go back to a partitioned country. Dulles and Bao Dai agreed, he said, that Bao Dai should "remain in France and return to Vietnam after Diem had won over the country." On the training of South Vietnamese armed forces, see Cable: Dillon to Department of State, May 26, 1954, *FRUS, 1952–1954,* 13:1615.

23. "On balance" quote is from cable

from Dillon to Department of State, May 24, 1954, in *FRUS, 1952–1954,* Indochina, 2:1609. "Diem is a messiah" quote is from McClintock to Department of State, July 4, 1954, in *ibid.,* pp. 1783–84.

24. Buttinger quote is from *Dragon Embattled,* 2:846. For further details of Diem's background, see Fall, *Two Vietnams,* p. 239; Robert Shaplen, *The Lost Revolution* (Harper and Row, 1965), pp. 107–8.

25. On Diem and the Japanese, see Masaya Shiraishi, "The Japanese and the Vietnamese 'Nationalists' During World War II," Seminar on the International Relations of Southeast Asia, Cornell University, Ithaca, N.Y., 1979, pp. 19, 20, 23, 27, 30, 36; Ralph B. Smith, "The Japanese Period in Indochina and the Coup of March 9, 1945," *Journal of Southeast Asian Studies,* 9, no. 2 (September 1978): 274, 286, 388. Prince Cuong De had been in exile in Japan since 1906, and Diem clearly held him in higher esteem than Bao Dai. For Diem's relations with the Japanese, see also Buttinger, *Dragon Embattled,* 1:289–90, 602–3.

26. A Maryknoll priest with service in Vietnam, Thomas O'Melia, attempted unsuccessfully, through Senator James Duff of Pennsylvania, to arrange a meeting for Diem in a letter to Dulles of June 6, 1953. (John Foster Dulles Papers, Princeton University Library, IIa correspondence 1953 [I–K].) Diem acknowledged Ho Chi Minh's stature as a nationalist and expressed the conviction that he could provide an effective alternative to Ho in February 1953, when he visited Cornell University and spent an afternoon discussing his ideas about Vietnam and its future with my seminar. I also had an opportunity to talk with him extensively in private meetings. For accounts of the American Friends of Vietnam, see especially Buttinger, *Dragon Embattled,* 2:927 ff.; Robert Scheer, *How the United States Got Involved in Vietnam* (Center for the Study of Democratic Institutions, 1965), pp. 31–33. Bedell Smith quote is from sess. of February 16, 1954, Senate Foreign Relations Committee, *Executive Sessions,* p. 143.

27. On the organization's dependence

on the U.S. government, see Memoranda from Chester Cooper for Mr. Valenti, "The American Friends of Vietnam Program," May 5, June 7, 1965. This editorial venture, which sought respectability by attempting to enlist several academic Southeast Asian specialists, ultimately aborted, presumably because the academics approached refused to join despite the offer of a handsome monetary retainer. I have in my possession copies of documents explicitly describing the arrangement between Colonel Dupuy and Wesley Fishel, a key member of the American Friends of Vietnam who was to serve as editor of the journal. See also Cooper's Memorandum, "American Friends," May 5, 1965.

28. Delivered by Ambassador Donald R. Heath on October 23.

29. The quote concerning the Central Intelligence Agency is from Cooper, *Lost Crusade,* p. 129. Cooper was to have long experience, in various capacities, in helping shape U.S.-Vietnam policy. See also Edward G. Lansdale, *In the Midst of Wars* (Harper and Row, 1972), ch. 10. Dulles's instructions to Lansdale are from a statement by Lansdale in Michael Charlton and Anthony Moncrief, *Many Reasons Why: The American Involvement in Vietnam* (Hill and Wang, 1978), p. 42. Lansdale's "how to be a Prime Minister" quote is from Charlton and Moncrief, *Many Reasons Why,* p. 55. On helping Diem dominate the military forces, see *PP* (Gravel), 1:580. According to Lansdale, the Binh Xuyen, founded in 1940 as a social club of day laborers and charcoal-makers, had been organized, trained, and armed by the Japanese Kempeitei, who had used them in the 1945 coup against the Vichy French colonial establishment. The French had used them as a militia, assisting their own forces in guarding Saigon and its environs. Lansdale characterized their leader, Bay Vien, as having "developed rapidly into the combination role of the city's Boss Tweed and Al Capone." (*In the Midst of Wars,* p. 153.)

30. In explaining the U.S. leverage to the French Chamber of Deputies, Guy La

Chambre made clear that because of dependency on American funds it was "necessary to determine a policy in common," and that "To find ourselves alone in Indochina meant to cover, with the help of our funds only, the entirety of the expenses of the expeditionary corps and the national armies. We didn't have the means for it yesterday, and we don't have them today." (*Journal Officiel de la République Française, Débats Parlementaires, Assemblée Nationale,* December 17, 1954, 2nd sess.)

On the French need for U.S. support in North Africa, see Memorandum for the Record, Telephone Call from Secretary Dulles to Ambassador Lodge, June 24, 1954; Devillers and Lacouture, *End of a War,* p. 358. French vulnerability vis-à-vis the United States had already been registered by Prime Minister Mendès-France in his September 5 instructions to the French delegation at the Manila Conference: "It is essential that our policy towards South Vietnam must be worked out in conjunction with the United States. We have a number of points at issue with them in other areas. There must be no additional reasons for a clash over Vietnam." (Devillers and Lacouture, *End of a War,* p. 324; see also *PP* [Gravel], 1:223.)

31. On Buu Hoi, see Buttinger, *Dragon Embattled,* 2:719, 1024, 1099–1100; Cooper, *Lost Crusade,* p. 126; especially Devillers and Lacouture, *End of a War,* pp. 32, 337, 347, 358, 363. Buu Hoi, grandson of the Emperor Minh Mang and Bao Dai's cousin, was a respected cancer specialist with his own laboratory in France. He had earlier been with the Vietminh, and his father had elected to live in the North after the Geneva partition. Ely's report is in Devillers and Lacouture, *End of a War,* p. 363. For Washington's position on Buu Hoi, see *ibid.,* pp. 364–65, n. 5; George Chaffard, *Les Deux Guerres du Vietnam: De Valluy à Westmoreland* (La Table Ronde, 1969), p. 167. See also *PP* (Gravel), 1:221.

32. Probably the fullest account of the struggle between Diem and Hinh can be found in the account of Tran Van Don, then a colonel on Hinh's staff, serialized in late 1970 and early 1971 in the Saigon newspaper *Dien Tin.* (I am indebted to James Nach for a translation of this.) Don was obviously an admirer of Hinh, and the account is partial to the general's position. For Hinh's statement, see George McT. Kahin and John W. Lewis, *The United States in Vietnam,* 2nd ed. rev. & enl. (Delta, 1969), p. 69. Bao Dai states that Hinh was informed by General Ely that if he mounted a putsch against Diem, the United States would end all financial aid and military supplies. (*Dragon d'Annam,* p. 335.) Diem replaced Hinh with the much more tractable General Le Van Ty.

33. In sec. two of his cable to Dulles of April 7, 1955, Collins stated that he had been obliged to conclude that "Diem does not have the capacity to achieve the necessary unity of purpose and action from his people which is essential to prevent this country from falling under Communist control." Concerning Dulles's reluctance to remove Diem, as late as April 11 he and his brother Allen, who headed the CIA, agreed that they wanted to hold on to Diem a bit longer. (Memorandum of Telephone Call from J. F. Dulles to Allen Dulles, April 11, 1955.) For Diem's alienation of the Cao Dai and Hoa Hao, see Kahin and Lewis, *United States in Vietnam,* p. 70; NSC, Progress Report (Southeast Asia), NSC 5405 (supplement). Collins had assumed Diem would take over these payments to the sects from funds provided him by the United States, and that the figure would total approximately $5 million. (Cable from Collins to Secretary of State, January 20, 1955.) CIA, "Probable Developments to July 1956," October 11, 1955, No. 63, 1-3-55, states, "The national police and security forces were commanded by Bay Vien, the leader of the Binh Xuyen gang who had bought them from Bao Dai in April 1954." The U.S. ambassador to Saigon estimated that Bao Dai was receiving an annual "gratification" equivalent to more than $1 million U.S. dollars from the Binh Xuyen for its gambling concession alone. (*FRUS, 1952–1954,* 13:228.) According to Lansdale, "The Binh Xuyen were participating in one of the world's major arteries of the dope traffic,

helping move the prized opium crops out of Laos and South China. The profits were so huge that Bao Dai's tiny cut was ample to keep him in yachts, villas, and other comforts in France." (Memorandum to Ambassador Bunker and Members, U.S. Mission Council, Saigon, "On the Cao Dai," May 1968, p. 17.)

34. CIA, "Probable Developments to July 1956," is explicit in using the term "bribery" (pp. 3, 5). It does not say that the bribes were dispensed by American agents or emanated from American coffers, but Diem, of course, was almost totally reliant on U.S. financing and could not have met these costs from his own meager resources. Fall's estimates are from *Two Vietnams,* p. 246. For additional sources concerning these bribes, see Buttinger, *Dragon Embattled,* 2:-1101. Tran Van Don, then a colonel in the Vietnamese army's Joint General Staff, states that the salaries of soldiers of several of the sects' military units that were induced to rally to Diem, including Trinh Minh Thé's Cao Dai army, received subsidies that amounted to a "rather considerable figure," but that he did not know where they were coming from. ("Tran Van Don Remembers," extracts from his memoirs printed in *Dien Tin* [Saigon], March 1971, as translated by James Nach.) Lansdale himself does not mention the bribery, but states that the Cao Dai were integrated "with American help" and that he himself "negotiated the integration" of the regiments of the Hoa Hao regiments of General Ngo. He says that he was also in contact with the Binh Xuyen chief of staff, who attempted to bring "battalions loyal to him" over to Diem but was killed by his superiors before this could be accomplished. (Lansdale, "On the Cao Dai," pp. 9, 16, 17.) With respect to Lansdale's payment of funds to Trinh Minh Thé, see *PP* (NYT), p. 20. Cable from CINCPAC to DEPTAR, August 11, 1955, states that by that date twenty-three thousand Cao Dai had been integrated. Ultimately, Lansdale states, a total of twenty-seven thousand Cao Dai were integrated. (Lansdale, "On the Cao Dai," p. 14.) The CIA credited only fifteen of the

thirty thousand as constituting the Cao Dai's "trained army." (CIA, National Intelligence Estimate, October 11, 1955, p. 4.) According to the CIA's assessment, three thousand Hoa Hao were then cooperating with Diem; twenty-five hundred, "though ostensibly rallied" to Diem, were neutral; and two other groups, totaling about twenty-five hundred, were still resisting. "By bribery, persuasion, and finally force," as this CIA report put it, "Diem virtually eliminated the Binh Xuyen and the most important elements of the Hoa Hao as threats to his authority." (CIA, "Probable Developments to July 1956," p. 3.)

35. Fox Butterfield in the *New York Times* edition of the *Pentagon Papers* states, "With permission from the embassy, the Saigon Military Mission [the local CIA] then [fall of 1954] began secretly paying funds to a Cao Dai leader, Gen. Trinh Minh Thé, who offered his services to Premier Diem." In the unpublished footnotes to the GPO edition of the *Pentagon Papers* it is stated, "Lansdale was accused of having bribed Thé to win his support but vigorously denies this. However, the SMM did secretly reimburse Thé's Lien Minh forces who moved into Saigon and acted as Diem's palace guard in October." ([IV,A.1]: 49, n. 131.) Lansdale was bitter at Graham Greene's description of Trinh Minh Thé in *The Quiet American,* and even more put out by Greene's characterization of Lansdale himself in the character Alden Pyle. According to Lansdale, Trinh Minh Thé had "a platform of political aims compatible with American aims for Vietnam," and was "kin in spirit and political ideas to our forefathers who once stood against the Redcoats on Lexington Green and at Concord Bridge." ("On the Cao Dai," pp. 2, 11, 13.) Lansdale's own, rather flamboyant description can be found in his book, *In the Midst of Wars.* Tran Van Don's more temperate account of these events and much of their context can be found in his memoirs as serialized in the Saigon newspaper, *Dien Tin,* during March 1971.

36. Memorandum of Telephone Call from Dulles to Assistant Secretary Hoover,

8:38 A.M., April 28, 1955. On April 11, Dulles
had yielded to Collins's urging that Diem be
replaced and authorized him to look for a
suitable successor. (Cable [Eyes Only] from
Dulles to Collins, April 11, 1955.)

37. *PP* (Gravel), 2:248.

38. By the end of the Eisenhower administration, South Vietnam had become
the fifth-largest recipient of U.S. aid in the
world, and by 1958 its U.S. economic aid
mission was the largest anywhere. (*PP*
(Gravel), 1:268.) *Newsweek,* some seven
years after the American economic assistance program had been under way, expressed the relation between U.S. aid and
the new bourgeoisie thus: "The government
has used American aid to build up a new
dominant economic class that staunchly
supports the regime. . . ." (November 6, 1961,
p. 46.)

39. See Comptroller General of the
United States, *Audit Report to the Congress
of the United States: Economic and Technical Assistance Program for Vietnam, International Cooperation Administration, Department of State, Fiscal Years 1955–1957,* p.
27.

40. Aid figures are from John D. Montgomery, *The Politics of Foreign Aid* (Praeger, 1962), p. 284. He notes that CIP
amounted to roughly 80 percent of all U.S.
aid in 1958 and 1959. The figure of 87 percent
is extrapolated from the breakdown for 1955
provided in the J. D. Montgomery Papers.
There was an additional $95.6 million in ec-
onomic loans during this seven-year period.
(Box 6, "American Aid to Vietnam,"
Hoover Library.) The CIP had reached a
high of $398 million in 1966, and stood at
$233 in 1973. In these later years it was aug-
mented in its piaster-generating capacity for
Saigon's budget by programs for selling surplus U.S. agricultural products (FFF, Title
I, and PL 480, Title I) that amounted to $81
million in 1966 and $150 million in 1973.
(ADCCA/CIP/FOB, "The AID Commercial
Import Program for Viet-Nam," mimeo,
1969; "Enclosure A," letter from John R.
Mossler, Minister-Director, U.S. Aid Mission to Vietnam, to Luu Van Tinh, Director

General for Budget and Foreign Aid, February 23, 1973.)

41. According to Leland Barrows, head
of the U.S. Economic Aid Mission to Vietnam, during the period 1955–59 the South
Vietnamese government provided only 10
percent of its total military expenditures
from its own resources. (Cited in D. Gareth
Porter, "Imperialism and Social Structure,"
p. 249.) A CIA estimate calculated that only
about 30 percent of the total 1955 budget of
the government of South Vietnam estimated
at $521 million would be raised from local
resources. (CIA, "Probable Developments
to July 1956," p. 9.) On military grants, see
Montgomery, *Politics of Foreign Aid,* p. 284.
For the dollar reserves, see Milton C. Taylor, "South Vietnam: Lavish Aid, Limited
Progress," *Pacific Affairs,* 34, no. 3 (Fall
1961): 248. Of income tax assessed in 1955 for
the previous year on 19,749 individuals, only
4 percent was collected. (J. D. Montgomery
Papers, "From Notes of the M.S.U. Summer
Seminar," Hoover Library.) Gareth Porter
observes that in 1959 direct taxes constituted
only 5 percent of government revenues, and
that the figure had declined to 4 percent in
1963. ("Imperialism and Social Structure in
Twentieth Century Vietnam," Ph.D. dissertation, Cornell University, 1976, p. 264.)

42. Thus, Diem stated to Professor
Lloyd Musolf, head of the Michigan State
Public Administration Advisory Team, "We
have created a middle class in business and
industry by controlling import and export."
(I am indebted to Professor Musolf for permission to quote from his December 4, 1960,
interview notes.)

43. On sale of dollars for piasters and
original number of importers, see Comptroller General, *Economic and Technical Assistance Program for Vietnam, 1955–1957.*
Quotes are from Montgomery, *Politics of
Foreign Aid,* pp. 91–92.

44. "Served the political value" quote is
from John D. Montgomery Papers, Box 5,
Hoover Library; also cited in Porter, "Impe-
rialism and Social Structure," p. 262.
Gareth Porter has established that Leland
Barrows said this in an interview with Mont-

gomery on June 4, 1958. In the Hoover Library collection, the name of the interviewee has been deleted. "Extravagant standard" and "hard-won" quotes are from Lawrence Morrison, "Industrial Development Efforts," in *Viet-Nam, The First Five Years, an Inter-Symposium,* ed. Richard Lindholm (Michigan State University Press, 1959), p. 215, cited in Porter, "Imperialism and Social Structure," p. 260. "A standard" and "a significant" quotes are from "Prospects for North and South Vietnam," *PP* (GPO), 10:-1194. This is apparently a CIA National Intelligence Estimate and probably dates from mid-1959. Interview of Dr. Dan by the author, Saigon, January 12, 1967.

45. All quotes are from Memorandum from Office of the Deputy Assistant Secretary of Defense (Stephen Enke) to W. W. Rostow, Special Assistant to the President, "Vietnam Anti-Inflation Measures," April 6, 1966.

46. Taylor, "South Vietnam: Lavish Aid," p. 256.

47. "Binding commitment" quote is from Division of Research for Far East, Department of State, "Probable Developments in South Vietnam Through July, 1956," September 15, 1955, Intelligence Report No. 7045, p. 64. Concerning the fear of destroying the military armistice, French officials expected there would probably be "spontaneous rebellions in the whole country" if elections were not held. (*Journal Officiel de la République Française, Débats Parlementaires, Assemblée Nationale,* December 17, 1954, pp. 6512–13. See also NSC, "Progress Report [Southeast Asia]," July 11, 1956, NSC 5405, p. 6.) NSC quote is from National Security Council, "U.S. Policy on All-Vietnam Elections," May 17, 1955, pp. 7, 10. On SEATO meeting, see Brian Crozier, "The Diem Regime in Southern Vietnam," *Far Eastern Survey,* 24, no. 4 (April 1955): 56.

48. Department of State, September 15, 1955, Intelligence Report No. 7045, pp. 64, 69–70, 76. See also CIA, "Probable Developments to July 1956," pp. 2, 5, 6.

49. Quote is from cable from Rusk to

American Embassy, November 11, 1961 (drafted by State Department legal counsel A. Shayes and approved by U. Alexis Johnson).

50. American intelligence sources on Diem's election prospects are CIA, "Post Geneva Outlook in Indochina," August 3, 1954, National Intelligence Estimate 63-5-54; Department of State, "Probable Developments Through July 1956," p. 66; Department of State, Division of Research for Far East, "Considerations Bearing on the Problems of the 1956 Elections in Vietnam," February 1, 1955, Intelligence Report No. 6818, pp. ii, 9, 16. As early as March 17, 1954, a memorandum prepared for the Special Committee of the NSC had acknowledged that the holding of a "truly representative plebiscite" was not feasible since it would "lead to the loss . . . [of Vietnam] to Communist control." (*PP* [Gravel], 1:453.) Quotes are from Department of State, "Considerations Bearing on the 1956 Elections," February 1, 1955, Intelligence Report No. 6818, pp. ii, 9, 16.

51. Department of State, "Probable Developments Through July 1956," p. 65.

52. Planning Board quote is from National Security Council, Draft Statement, "U.S. Policy on All-Vietnam Elections," May 17, 1955, NSC 5519, pp. 1, 3. U.S. contingency plans are in Memorandum from Executive Office of the President for National Security Council, "U.S. Policy in the Event of a Renewal of Aggression in Vietnam," September 16, 1955. (Incorporating a study prepared by the Joint Chiefs of Staff, dated September 9, 1955.) It was estimated that "to repulse and punish overt Vietminh aggression" would require two to four U.S. divisions and that "to destroy Vietminh forces and take control of the North" would require "up to eight U.S. divisions." The report warned that in either case "the effects upon other U.S. military commitments . . . would be significant." It pointed out that the JCS believed that "the major threat to South Vietnam continues to be that of subversion."

53. This argument, in effect, turned ar-

ticle 7 of the multinational Geneva Final Declaration on its head. See ch. II.

54. On U.S. wanting Diem to attend preliminary consultations, see Department of State, "Probable Developments Through July 1956," p. 65. NSC conclusions are in NSC, "U.S. Policy on All-Vietnam Elections," p. 7.

55. On the French troop withdrawals, see NSC, "Progress Report (Southeast Asia)," July 11, 1956, p. 6. McNamara quote is from Memorandum for the President from the Secretary of Defense, March 13, 1964. Exactly the same wording appears in William Bundy's March 1, 1964, draft of this memorandum (p. 10), which was circulated the next day to William Sullivan, John McNaughton, and Adam Yarmolinsky.

56. For the most comprehensive coverage of the record of Hanoi's requests and appeals for consultations, see Franklin Weinstein, *Vietnam's Unheld Elections* (Cornell Southeast Asia Program, 1966). According to Paul Kattenburg, who during this period served as head of the State Department's Vietnam Task Force, in the two years following the Geneva Conference Hanoi sent "more than 200" messages to Diem and the Geneva co-chairmen regarding elections during this period. (Interview, Washington, D.C., September 26, 1970.) See also *PP* (Gravel), 1:247. Britain's interest in the Geneva settlement appears to have waned after April 1955, when Eden moved from foreign secretary to prime minister and was preoccupied with a broader range of problems. Moreover, his government's serious tension with Washington over the Suez in mid-1956 presumably reduced any disposition to challenge American policies in Vietnam.

On lack of interest of these three countries in carrying out Geneva provisions, see Department of State, "Probable Developments Through Mid-1957," Intelligence Report No. 7256, pp. v, 2, 88, 94; CIA, Probable Developments to July 1956," p. 8; Memorandum of Telephone Call from Dulles to Ambassador Lodge, June 24, 1954; cable from Chief MAAG (Saigon) to CINCPAC, August 9, 1955.

57. Department of State, "Probable Developments Through Mid-1957," pp. 88–90, 104.

58. Statement on Gromyko is in *ibid.,* p. 87. On Khrushchev's proposal, see *PP* (Gravel), 1:247, 262, 288.

For Peking's position, see the commentary by "Observer" in the official PRC newspaper, *Jenmin Jihpao,* January 27, 1957. "Observer" wrote: "As a measure of transition before the unification of Korea and Vietnam, this [Soviet] proposal is just and reasonable, because it can enable the Korean people and the Vietnamese people to get the representation they deserve in the United Nations. [Both Hanoi and the ex-Vietminh in the South must have found it astonishing that Diem's regime was regarded as the representation that southerners deserved.] Besides it can promote contacts and consultation between the north and south of Korea and of Vietnam, so as to achieve peaceful unification there." Elsewhere in the same issue, *Jenmin Jihpao* reported Hanoi's position in the form of a telegram sent by its prime minister to the U.N. stating that only a unified Vietnam could join the U.N. and that Saigon's application for South Vietnam's membership was not in accord with the principles agreed upon at the Geneva Conference. (Translation made for me by a Chinese scholar fluent in English.) On Ho's "evident surprise," see *PP* (Gravel), 1:262.

59. See Department of State, "Probable Developments Through Mid-1957," pp. v, 2.

60. *New York Times,* May 9, 1957.

IV. Diem and the Rise of the NLF

1. NSC, Progress Report (Southeast Asia) (NSC 5405) and Portions of NSC 5429/5, December 21, 1955, pp. 5, 6.

2. Diem's understanding of U.S. anticommunist issues was noted by the author in discussions with him at Cornell, February 20, 21, 1953. See also *PP* (Gravel), 1:253.

3. On the U.S. Information Service, see Robert Scigliano, *South Vietnam: Nation*

Under Stress (Houghton Mifflin, 1963) p.
207. Quotes are from NSC, Progress Report
(Southeast Asia) (N.S.C. 5405 and Portions
of NSC 5429/5), July 11, 1956, p. 7.

4. On defying and deposing Bao Dai,
see Scigliano, *South Vietnam,* p. 207. On the
election procedure, see Donald Lancaster,
The Emancipation of French Indo-China
(Oxford University Press, 1961), p. 398. Referendum choices are in S. M. Bao Dai, *Le
Dragon d'Annam* (Plon, 1980), p. 343. Por-
trayal of Bao Dai and Diem from Edward G.
Lansdale, *In the Midst of Wars* (Harper and
Row, 1972), pp. 333–34. On election fraud,
see Bernard Fall, *The Two Vietnams: A Political and Military Analysis* (Praeger, 1964),
p. 257; Lancaster, *Emancipation of French
Indo-China,* p. 399n.

5. Scigliano quote is from *South Vietnam,* pp. 44–45; this still remains the most
scholarly study of the period.

6. For the characterization of Ngo
Dinh Can, see Paul M. Kattenburg, *The
Vietnam Trauma in American Foreign Policy, 1956–1975* (Transaction Books, 1980), p.
55; *PP* (Gravel), 1:299. The full name for the
Can Lao was Can Lao Nhan Vi Cach Mang
Dang (Personalist Labor Revolutionary
Party). On this party and its subordinate
mass organization, the National Revolutionary Movement, see Scigliano, *South Vietnam,* p. 75. For the most comprehensive account of Personalism, the philosophy which
was supposed to underlie both organizations, see John D. Donnell's "Personalism in
Vietnam," in *Problems of Freedom: South
Vietnam Since Independence,* ed. Wesley R.
Fishel (Free Press, 1961), pp. 29–67. State
Department intelligence quotes are from Division of Research for Far East, Department
of State, "Probable Developments in Vietnam Through Mid-1957," May 23, 1956, Intelligence Report No. 7256, p. 101. Quotes on
the Can Lao are from Memorandum from
Brig. Gen. Lansdale, OSO/OSD, for Secretary of Defense/Deputy Secretary of Defense, "Vietnam," January 17, 1961, in *PP*
(GPO), 11:9. Carlyle Thayer reports that
Geoffrey Warner, then a faculty member at
the Australian National University, was

told by Lansdale in 1973 that the "American Foreign Service professional" who
created the Can Lao was G. Frederick
Reinhardt, the U.S. ambassador to Saigon
who succeeded General Lawton Collins in
1955. (Carlyle Thayer, "The Origins of the
National Front for Liberation of South Vietnam" [Ph.D dissertation, The Australian
National University, 1977] pt. 2, p. 428, n.
130.)

7. For percentages of Vietminh, see Scigliano, *South Vietnam,* p. 134; see also Joseph Alsop, "A Reporter at Large," *New
Yorker,* June 25, 1955, p. 48.

8. "Thoroughly terrified" quote is from
PP (Gravel), 1:255. On the acknowledged
numbers jailed, see John Osborne, "The
Tough Miracle Man of Vietnam," *Life,* May
13, 1957; Georges Chaffard, *Indochine: Dix
Ans d'indépendance* (Calman-Lévy, 1964),
pp. 168, 169; see also *PP* (Gravel), 1:253. An
Xuyen figures are from United States Opera-
tions Mission, *Saigon Daily News Round-up,*
February 28, 1959, as quoted in Scigliano,
South Vietnam, p. 169. The report by the
governor is in *Time,* April 21, 1961, cited in
Fall, *Two Vietnams,* p. 272.

In the face of the obstacles put in its
path by Diem, the International Control
Commission declared in September 1956,
"While the Commission has experienced
difficulties in North Vietnam, the major part
of its difficulties has arisen in South Vietnam." (*Sixth Interim Report of the International Commission for Supervision and Control in Vietnam,* Vietnam No. 6 [1957],
Command 31 [Her Majesty's Stationery
Office, 1957], p. 30.)

9. Osborne, "Tough Miracle Man."

10. For Devillers quote, see his "The
Struggle for the Unification of Vietnam,"
China Quarterly, 9 (January-March 1962):
12. For Henderson quote, see his "South
Vietnam Finds Itself," *Foreign Affairs,* 35,
no. 2 (January 1957): 285, 288. For Buttinger's quote, see his *Vietnam: The Unforgettable Tragedy* (Horizon Press, 1977), p.
48.

11. For a fuller text and relevant documentation on Law 10/59, see George McT.

Kahin and John W. Lewis, *The United States in Vietnam,* 2nd ed. rev. & enl. (Delta, 1969), pp. 101–2, 121–22; see also *PP* (Gravel), 1:252.

12. On village councils, see *PP* (Gravel), 1:255; Robert Shaplen, *The Lost Revolution* (Harper and Row, 1965), p. 133; Scigliano, *South Vietnam,* p. 32.

13. "Having no roots" and "strangers" quotes are from John D. Montgomery, *The Politics of Foreign Aid* (Praeger, 1962), p. 71. Scigliano quote is from *South Vietnam,* p. 54.

14. On the land-tenure and rent issues, see Montgomery, *Politics of Foreign Aid,* pp. 124, 126; Shaplen, *Lost Revolution,* p. 144; Scigliano, *South Vietnam,* p. 123.

15. On the "agrarian reform" program, see Scigliano, *South Vietnam,* pp. 122–23.

16. Most Montagnard tribal groups spoke variants of either the Malayan-Polynesian or Mon-Khmer language groups. The ancestors of many of them had been pushed inland when the Vietnamese had forced their way south three to four centuries before. The fullest account of the interaction between Diem's governance and the Montagnards can be found in Gerald Hickey, *Free in the Forest: Ethnohistory of the Vietnamese Central Highlands, 1954–1976* (Yale University Press, 1982). By 1961 half of the Montagnard population of Kontum province had been forcibly regrouped. (*PP* [Gravel], 1:312.) Some six thousand of the Rhade tribe had elected to go north in 1954–55. According to an official DRV account, the first of the large tribes to be involved in armed uprisings against the Diem regime were the Bahnar and Raglay [Roglai]. (Ta Xuan Linh, "How Armed Struggle Began in South Vietnam," *Vietnam Courier* [Hanoi], March 1974, p. 22.) Quotes are from *PP* (Gravel), 1:255.

17. Quote is from Scigliano, *South Vietnam,* pp. 179–80.

18. See Joseph Buttinger, *Vietnam: A Dragon Embattled,* 2 vols. (Praeger, 1967), 2:483. Denis Warner, in *The Last Confucian* (Macmillan, 1963), p. 89, observes, "Summary Viet Cong justice for a village chief guilty of corruption or brutality did not offend the peasants. On the contrary, it tended to endow the Viet Cong with some of the characteristics of Robin Hood and his band of merry men."

19. On Can Lao and Catholics, see CIA Memorandum, September 19, 1964, OCI No. 2230/64, p. 3. On Personalism, see *ibid.;* Scigliano, *South Vietnam,* p. 55. Quote is from CIA Memorandum, September 19, 1964, p. 3.

20. "For many Vietnamese peasants" and "opprobrium" quotes are from *PP* (Gravel), 1: 252. Scigliano quote is from *South Vietnam,* p. 158.

21. On the numbers of dissidents, see Thayer, "Origins of the National Liberation Front," pt. 2, p. 485; Ta Xuan Linh, "How Armed Struggle Began," p. 21. U.S. intelligence reports estimated "as many as 1500" armed noncommunist dissidents as late as April 1958. (*PP* [GPO], 2 (IV,A.5.Tab 4):18.

22. On southern dissidents with relatives in the North, see B. S. N. Murti, *Vietnam Divided* (Asia Publishing House, 1964), p. 224.

23. Most scholars who have researched this matter acknowledge the existence of the differences between the South and the North. See especially the subsequent references to Race and Thayer. Three other Vietnam specialists—David Elliott, David Marr, and Gareth Porter—concur. (Discussions with the author.) See also Patric McGarvey, *Visions of Victory* (Hoover Institution, 1969), which discusses later years. Elliott, on the basis of several years of interviewing Viet Cong prisoners for the Rand Corporation as well as a careful scrutiny of documents, concludes, "We know from analysis of the available written record that [within party channels] there was constant argumentation between the leaders in the South (including those sent down from the North) and Hanoi over questions of strategy." (Letter to the author, June 7, 1983.)

My own understanding of this period and of the National Liberation Front's origins and character owes a substantial debt to David Elliott, David Marr, and Gareth Porter, who all read earlier drafts of this chapter and from whose criticisms and suggestions I have greatly benefited. I have also benefited considerably from the studies of William J. Duiker, *The Communist Road to Power in Vietnam* (Westview Press, 1981); Douglas Pike, *Vietcong: The Organization and Techniques of the National Liberation Front of South Vietnam* (The MIT Press, 1966); Jeffrey Race, *War Comes to Long An* (University of California Press, 1972); Thayer, "Origins of the National Liberation Front," and "Southern Vietnamese Revolutionary Organizations and the Vietnam Workers' Party: Continuity and Change, 1954–1974," in Joseph J. Zasloff and MacAlister Brown, eds., *Communism in Indochina* (Lexington Books, 1975), pp. 27–56. Likewise, I have profited from Mai Elliott's translation of Nguyen Thi Dinh's *No Other Road to Take* (Cornell Southeast Asia Program, 1976) and Joseph J. Zasloff, *Political Motivation of the Viet Cong: The Vietminh Regroupees* (The Rand Corporation, 1968). In addition, I have had useful discussions with several senior NLF officials, including two former secretaries general—Nguyen Van Hieu and Tran Buu Kiem—and its foreign minister, Nguyen Thi Binh. I also had many good talks with non-NLF Vietnamese in close touch with that organization, including Trinh Dinh Thao, who soon afterward, in April 1968, emerged as chairman of the NLF-sponsored Alliance of National Democratic and Peace Forces.

24. For details of Soviet and Chinese relations with Hanoi in the immediate post-Geneva years, see Thayer, "Origins of the National Front," pp. 565–89. During this precarious period, Chinese and Soviet aid was indeed of enormous importance in rehabilitating the northern economy, which, it must be emphasized, had suffered much greater damage in the struggle with France than had that of the South. An analyst in the *Pentagon Papers* concluded that during the period 1955–60 Chinese and Soviet economic assistance to the North totaled at least \$578.5 million. (*PP* [GPO], 2[IV,A.5. Tab. 3]:29.) Roy Jumper and Marjorie Weiner

Normand arrive at a roughly similar figure for this period—\$563.5 million. Their breakdown is \$300 million (of which \$200 million was as grant aid and \$100 million on a credit basis) from China, and \$237 million (of which \$100 million was as grant aid and \$137 million as credits) from the Soviet Union, plus \$26 million in credits from Eastern European countries. ("Vietnam," in *Governments and Politics of Southeast Asia,* 2nd ed., George McT. Kahin, ed [Cornell University Press, 1964], p. 107.) Bernard Fall concludes that total foreign aid accounted for between 38.6 percent and 65.3 percent of the DRV's budget in 1955 and had declined to between 17.7 percent and 21 percent in 1960. (*Two Vietnams,* p. 177.) A Pentagon analyst notes that Moscow "had virtually cut off aid during the 1962–1964 period." (*PP* [Gravel], 4:116.) Following the U.S. escalation in February 1965, however, Soviet aid increased sharply.

25. For a comprehensive and knowledgeable account of these developments and the agrarian situation in the North generally, see Christine Katherine Pelzer White, "Agrarian Reform and National Liberation in the Vietnam Revolution: 1950–1957," Ph.D. dissertation, Cornell University, 1981. For a careful, well-documented assessment of the character and scope of the excesses attending the reform program, see Gareth Porter, *The Myth of the Bloodbath: North Vietnam's Land Reform Reconsidered,* International Relations of East Asia Project (Cornell University, 1972). Porter estimates in this study that a maximum of twenty-five hundred landowners were executed during the campaign. In the course of his research he found that Hoang Van Chi, the principal source Western writers have relied on for estimates of these executions, had heavily doctored and seriously distorted Giap's above-mentioned speech. He also discovered that Chi's book, *From Colonialism to Communism* (Praeger, 1964) had been subsidized by the U.S. Information Agency. (For this see also *New York Times,* September 28, 1966.) Porter states that Hoang Van Chi informed him that he had worked for Diem's

Ministry of Information for some eight months in 1955–56, and also as a translator for the U.S. Information Agency, and that Chi's *The New Class in Vietnam,* published in Saigon in 1958 (where he first discussed North Vietnam's land reform), was partly subsidized by Diem's Ministry of Information. (Porter, *Myth of the Bloodbath,* p. 6.) Porter writes that when he interviewed Hoang Van Chi in 1972 in Washington, where the Vietnamese was then lecturing at the USAID Training Center, he defended his translations by saying, "I tried to convey the real meaning more than the literal translations." (*Ibid.,* p. 45, n. 18.) Porter notes that *Time* magazine (July 1, 1957, p. 27) estimated the number killed during the campaign at 15,000, and that in 1963 Bernard Fall gave a figure of "probably close to 50,-000" (*Two Vietnams,* p. 156). The next year Hoang Van Chi escalated the figure to "about 5% of the total population," which, Porter observes, would have amounted to a total of 675,000. He concludes that the ultimate level of official U.S. escalation came with President Nixon, who, after first using Fall's figure of 50,000 in 1969, asserted on April 16, 1971, that "a half million by conservative estimates . . . were murdered or otherwise exterminated." (*Myth of the Bloodbath,* pp. 53–54.)

26. Race quote is from *War Comes to Long An,* p. 75. See also "CRIMP Document" (forty-two-page English translation), p. 2. So named because it was captured by U.S. forces in "Operation CRIMP" north of Saigon in early 1966, this document is generally regarded as legitimate; it is believed to be the notebook of a high-level political cadre probably written around early 1963. The fullest published rendition of "The Path of the Revolution in the South" is the translation by Gareth Porter in his *Vietnam: The Definitive Documentation,* 2:24–30. The original is document No. 1002 in Jeffrey Race's Collection of Communist Documents, deposited with the Center for Research Libraries in Chicago. Thayer quote is from "Origins of the National Front," p. 362. "A new long-range strategy" quote is

from Race, *War Comes to Long An,* p. 75. Race, in the introduction to his own translation of "The Path of the Revolution in the South" (typescript), states, "The policy of peaceful political struggle remained in force until superseded by the decision of the 15th Conference of the Central Committee"— that is, until January 1959. Thayer regards this document as serving as the party's "basic document until at least the last quarter of 1958." (Thayer, "Origins of the National Front," p. 366.)

27. Race quotes are from *War Comes to Long An,* pp. 77, 80. Quotes from "The Path" are in Porter, *Vietnam: Definitive Documentation,* 2:25.

28. On the military weakness, of the party and its adherents in the South see Race, *War Comes to Long An,* p. 80. Quotes from "The Path" are in Porter, *Vietnam: Definitive Documentation,* 2:25. Jeffrey Race, in his study of the pivotal province of Long An (abutting on Saigon to the southwest), cites informants who told him that in party discussions at the provincial level and above during this period, "it was taken for granted that armed uprising would be employed in the future, but this was not communicated to lower levels for fear of causing 'confusion.' " (Race, *War Comes to Long An,* p. 81.)

29. Duiker states that "The Path of the Revolution in the South" "was apparently presented as a proposal to the Eleventh Plenum [of the Lao Dong's Central Committee] held in December." (*Communist Road,* p. 178.) Quotes from "The Path" are in Porter, *Vietnam: Definitive Documentation,* 2:27–29. An implicit recognition of the unpopularity of this line and the ongoing tensions generated between southern cadres and the party's Central Committee is suggested by the fact that in the semiofficial retrospective account of 1974 by Ta Xuan Linh ("How Armed Struggle Began," p. 22) it is asserted that part of "the gist" of the directive in "The Path of the Revolution in the South" was "Political struggle must be supported by military activities," a prescription that in fact appears nowhere in the doc-

ument. This sort of revisionism—suggesting that the party leadership had urged a more militant line than it actually had—was to become even more pronounced after the collapse of the Saigon regime in 1975.

30. On arming propaganda teams, see "CRIMP Document" (English translation), p. 12. On assassinating local officials, see Race, *War Comes to Long An,* p. 82. For varying estimates and Saigon's breakdown of figures, see Thayer, "Origins of the National Front," pp. 507, 511–13.

31. Quotes are from "CRIMP Document," p. 10.

32. Quotes are from Ta Xuan Linh, "How Armed Struggle Began," pp. 20–23. With respect to this fusion with residual Cao Dai, Hoa Hao, and Binh Xuyen military units, see also War Experiences Recapitulation Committee of the High-Level Military Institute, *The Anti-U.S. Resistance War for National Salvation 1954–1975: Military Events (Cuoc Khang Chien Chong My Cuu Nuoc 1954–1975: Nhung Su Quan Su)* (Hanoi, 1980 [Translated by U.S. Joint Publication Research Services, 1982]), p. 11. Hereafter referred to as *Anti-U.S. War.* According to Douglas Pike, when the National Liberation Front was finally formed in 1960, "the bulk" of its early support came from ten of the eleven Cao Dai sects, with the Hoa Hao also serving as "an early and major participant." (Pike, *Vietcong,* pp. 68–69.)

33. See Thayer, "Origins of the National Front," pp. 493–97; Ta Xuan Linh, "How Armed Struggle Began," p. 23; *Anti-U.S. War,* pp. 22–25.

34. Thayer quotes are from "Origins of the National Front," pp. 533–38. He cites Ta Xuan Linh's semiofficial retrospective account, "Armed Uprisings by Ethnic Minorities Along the Truong Son," pt. II, *Vietnam Courier,* October 1975, p. 19. See also Thayer's "Southern Vietnamese Revolutionary Organizations," pp. 41–42; Duiker, *Communist Road,* pp. 185–86. For the small-scale attacks south of the Montagnard areas, see "CRIMP Document," p. 10; Ta Xuan Linh, "How Armed Struggle Began," p. 23. The latter states that these included an at-

tack on October 10, 1958, in which "resistance units" routed a battalion of Diem's troops and put the headquarters of a military subsector out of action. Both accounts describe an attack of October 25, 1958, on U.S. MAAG Headquarters at Bien Hoa in which American military advisers were killed. This appears to be unreported in U.S. and Saigon sources, which do, however, refer to a similar attack on July 8, 1959. See *Vietnam Press* (Saigon), January 3, 1960, pp. 12–13, and *Vietnam—Presse Bulletin d'Informations Confidentielles,* January 11, 1960, pp. 6–7. (This limited and restricted edition of *Vietnam Presse,* largely devoted to monitoring Hanoi broadcasts, was circulated to only a few top officials of Diem's government.)

35. Apparently the first Western scholar to note and appreciate the significance of the "Voice of the South Vietnam Liberation Front" broadcasts was Christine White, in a research seminar paper at Cornell in 1965. Carlyle Thayer has, so far as I know, done the most extensive and searching analysis of these broadcasts and Hanoi Radio's "Commentary." He concurs as to the likelihood that this radio was "a 'black' RVN [Saigon government] operation from its inception." According to his investigation, "the former head of the RVN's Psychological Warfare Directorate (1956–1962) stated that his government ran a clandestine radio service which pretended to be 'Liberation Radio,' " and "a senior official in the Central Intelligence Agency [George Carver], who originally used transcripts" of this radio's broadcasts in an article written for *Foreign Affairs,* "has now admitted that they were 'black propaganda.' " Thayer also notes that in April 1958 the U.S. National Security Council listed among American objectives in Vietnam "Assist the [Saigon] Government of Vietnam to undertake programs of political, economic, and psychological warfare against Viet Minh Communists." (These quotes, plus the one in the text, are from Thayer, "Origins of the National Front," pp. 517–28.) For Hanoi's reaction, see the statement of Le Duan, reported

in *Vietnam Presse Bulletin d'Informations Confidentielles,* July 21, 1958; "Voice of the South Vietnam Liberation Front," September 2, 1958, and Hanoi Radio "Commentary," July 10, 1958. For further discussion of these broadcasts, including a point-by-point denunciation of American intervention broadcast by the NLF radio August 4, 1958, see Kahin and Lewis, *United States in Vietnam,* pp. 111–12, 123–24.

36. General Tran Van Tra, *Ket Thuc Cuoc Chieu Tranh 30 Nam (History of the Bulwark B2 Theatre),* vol. 5 (Van Nghe Publishing House, 1982), p.53. After a limited printing, the book was apparently banned soon after it appeared. This volume, the only one in the 5-vol. series translated by the JPRS, appears as its Southeast Asia Report No. 1247, JPRS 82873, February 2, 1983.

37. Race, *War Comes to Long An,* pp. 110–11.

38. *Anti-U.S. War,* p. 25.

39. Carlyle Thayer points out that there has been confusion over the dating of the Fifteenth Plenum, a number of accounts indicating it was in May 1959—when the plenum's communiqué was actually published —rather than in January. (Thayer, "Origins of the National Front," p. 670, n. 7; see also "CRIMP Document," p. 10.) Quote from the new directive is from *Anti-U.S. War,* p. 30. Race quote is from *War Comes to Long An,* pp. 105–6. Though parts of his assessment refer to the important province of Long An alone, they appear to be valid for the situation throughout the South.

40. Some post-1975 official accounts of the new directive have been colored by a certain amount of revisionism to suggest that the party's stance was more militant than this directive actually was. See, for instance, the 1976 edition of *An Outline History of the Viet Nam Workers' Party (1930–1975)* (Foreign Languages Publishing House, 1976), p. 105. For the date when the new directive reached the South, see *Anti-U.S. War,* p. 34. It did not reach provincial cadres in Ben Tre province, according to Nguyen Thi Dinh, until the end of December 1959. (*No Other Road,* pp. 17, 62–64.) See also Thayer, "Origins of the National Front," pp. 672–73; "South Vietnamese Revolutionary Organization," pp. 43–44. Duiker, referring to the 1959 decision, notes that the "CRIMP Document" refers to "an initial hesitation" in the party, which caused "a short period of time to be lost." (*Communist Road,* p. 195.) On the directive's application in the Central Highlands, see *Anti-U.S. War,* pp. 28–29.

41. Race quote is from *War Comes to Long An,* p. 113. On the June and October rebellions, see Ta Xuan Linh, "How Armed Struggle Began," p. 23. July 8 report is in *PP (GPO),* 2 (IV,A.4): 1:338. DRV sources quoted in Duiker, *Communist Road,* p. 192; see also Ta Xuan Linh, "Armed Uprisings by Ethnic Minorities," p. 20; *Anti-U.S. War,* p. 34. On September 26 ambush, see *PP (Gravel),* 1:338; see also David Halberstam, *The Making of a Quagmire* (Random House, 1965) pp. 63–64. The term "Viet Cong," sometimes rendered "Vietcong," was a contraction of "Viet-Nam Cong San," meaning "Vietnamese communists." It was introduced by Diem's regime in or before 1959, and widely used thereafter, often indiscriminately, by Diem's officials and Americans serving in Vietnam.

42. Race quote is from *War Comes to Long An,* p. 120. Mai Elliott quote is from Nguyen Thi Dinh, *No Other Road,* p. 18. For other accounts of the incident, see Duiker, *Communist Road,* pp. 191–92; Ta Xuan Linh, "Ben Tre, Land of Concerted Uprisings," *Vietnam Courier,* no. 27, August 1974, p. 6. See also An Bao Minh, "Uprising in Ben Tre," in *South Vietnam: Realities and Prospects,* ed. Nguyen Khac Vien (Hanoi: Vietnamese Studies 18/19, 1968), pp. 130–50; *Anti-U.S. War,* p. 38.

43. On the uprising's accomplishments, see Dinh, *No Other Road,* pp. 63–64. Its "exemplary nature" is noted in *Anti-U.S. War,* p. 38. On the January 25 attack, see *PP (Gravel),* 1:338; Race, *War Comes to Long An,* pp. 106–7; Ta Xuan Linh, "How Armed Struggle Began," p. 24 (describing this attack in considerable detail but dates it

February 25, 1960); *Vietnam Press* (Saigon), February 7, 14, 1960; *Anti-U.S. War*, p. 39.

44. On bypassing the party line in Long An province, Race observes: "In carrying out the new policy, according to the Regional Committee, many local organizations had been overenthusiastic and premature in their actions, believing that the time for the overthrow of the Diem regime had already arrived." (*War Comes to Long An*, p. 118.) Substantial excerpts from the March 1960 declaration can be found in Kahin and Lewis, *United States in Vietnam*, pp. 458–61. I have a copy of the document that accords with one in Jeffrey Race's collection, and am indebted to Mai Elliott for its translation. Race states that "according to defectors' statements" this declaration "was simply the product of a meeting called in accord with Central Committee policy." (*War Comes to Long An*, p. 107. n. 5.) Such an interpretation, however, is clearly incompatible with the directive of the Regional Committee for the South of March 28, 1960, or with the April 20 address of the secretary general of the Lao Dong, both cited below. David Elliott observes that this March 1960 initiative by the former fighters is omitted in all postwar official accounts and that "this episode has now become a non-event—possibly because it was too open a rebuke to the Party's hesitancy at a critical juncture." (Letter to the author, June 7, 1983.) Philippe Devillers appears to have been the first Western scholar to have noted the importance of this declaration. See his "The Struggle for the Unification of Vietnam," in *North Vietnam Today*, ed. P. J. Honey (Praeger, 1962), pp. 15–16.

45. Porter, *Vietnam: Definitive Documentation*, 2:59–68. This document, generously made available to scholars by Jeffrey Race from his own valuable collection, was translated by Mai Elliott.

46. On Le Duan's speech, see Donald Zagoria, *Vietnam Triangle: Moscow/Peking/Hanoi* (Pegasus, 1967), p. 105; Porter's Commentary in his *Vietnam: Definitive Documentation*, 2:68. Zagoria regards the speech as including a "frank plea for 're-

stricting' the Southern resistance movement so that it would not interfere with world peace—a clear warning of the danger of a larger war with the Americans if the Southerners pushed too hard," and Porter sees the "new element" in the speech as being "the clarity and emphasis with which Le Duan indicated that the North wished to avoid at all costs a war in the South which could engulf the North." A substantial extract of Le Duan's speech can be found in Porter, *Vietnam: Definitive Documentation*, 2:68–70. Zagoria's observation is from *Vietnam Triangle*, p. 106.

47. All quotes are from "Resolution of the Third National Congress of the Viet Nam Workers' Party on the Tasks and Line of the Party in the New State," in *Third National Congress of the Viet Nam Workers' Party: Documents* (Foreign Languages Publishing House, Hanoi, n.d.), 1:221–22, 224–26.

48. All quotes are from *Anti-U.S. War*, pp. 45–46.

49. December 20, 1960, is the date given in official DRV accounts. On the location of the meeting, see Ta Xuan Linh, "How Armed Struggle Began," p. 19. Hanoi's announcement was on Hanoi Radio, January 29, 1961. Phnom Penh announcement came in "La Dépêche du Cambodge," January 25, 1961; Saigon's was in the newspaper *Ngon Luan*, January 20, 1961, and Saigon Radio, January 22, 1961.

50. For substantial excerpts of the text of the ten-point program, see Kahin and Lewis, *United States in Vietnam*, pp. 464–69; the full text in English translation can be found in *Political Program of the South Viet Nam National Front for Liberation* (Giai Phong Editions, 1968), pp. 14–33.

51. On Nguyen Huu Tho, see *Anti-U.S. War*, p. 46; Ta Xuan Linh, "How Armed Struggle Began," pp. 19, 24; *An Outline History of the Vietnam Workers' Party (1930–1975)* (Foreign Languages Publishing House, 1976), p. 108.

52. Thayer quote is from "Origins of the National Front," p. 680. Pike quotes are from *Vietcong*, p. 83. He estimates that NLF

membership had grown to three hundred thousand by early 1962 and that until the overthrow of Diem in November 1963 the Cao Dai and Hoa Hao were the most numerous components. (*Ibid.,* pp. 115, 68, 69.) Race states that this movement of ex-southerners back into the South began during 1960. (*War Comes to Long An,* p. 113.) It may have commenced during the latter months of 1959, but it would seem doubtful that the Laotian route could have been viable before sometime in 1960. On the authorization of this trail, see *Anti-U.S. War,* pp. 30–31.

53. Elliott bases his conclusion on several years of extensive interviewing of captured Viet Cong/NLF cadres for the Rand Corporation. (Discussion with the author, July 1983.) Jeffrey Race points out that the acronym "COSVN" derived from a translation of "Office Central de la Région Sud," which was itself a mistranslation of the actual Vietnamese term. (Race, *War Comes to Long An,* p. 288.)

54. All quotes are from *Declaration of the First Congress of the South Vietnam Front for Liberation* (Foreign Languages Publishing House, 1962), pp. 20–21, 23–24, 30–31.

55. July 20 declaration quotes are in Tran Van Giau and Le Van Chat, *The South Viet Nam Liberation National Front* (Foreign Languages Publishing House, 1962), p. 38. For more of the text of this statement, see *New York Times,* July 2, 1962; Pike, *Vietcong,* pp. 350–51. (There are some slight but unimportant differences among these translations.) As to attitudes in the North, Le Van Chat and Tran Van Giau, both prominent Hanoi officials of southern origin, one of whom (Tran Van Giau) had been a top Vietminh leader in the South in 1945–46, wrote that, as citizens of the DRV and natives of the South, "we admit that at first reading, the program of the NLF is not likely to get our full approval. The neutrality of the South means for Viet Nam a divergence of political character each side of the 17th parallel, while our country has always constituted a 'single entity.'" They acknowledged, however, that neutrality was "acceptable to all patriots and would constitute an important step forward compared with the present disguised colonial regime. To speak of the necessity of uniting all national and democratic forces, is to recognize their necessity to make concessions to one another, each group drawing nearer to its allies to actively contribute to the defense of national interests." (*South Viet Nam Liberation National Front,* p. 31.) The transitional coalition was to be made up of representatives of "all political parties, sects and groups belonging to all political tendencies, social strata, classes, religions and nationalities existing in South Vietnam." (From the NLF's 1962 program.)

56. For the main text of the NLF's November 8, 1963, statement, see Kahin and Lewis, *United States in Vietnam,* pp. 473–76. For the December 20, 1964, statement, see Pike, *Vietcong,* p. 357. For the main text of the May 8, 1969, statement, see Kahin and Lewis, *United States in Vietnam,* pp. 512–16. The importance the NLF still attached to these features was underlined by the former secretaries general with whom I spoke: Nguyen Van Hieu, in a discussion in Phnom Penh on August 11, 1967, and Tran Buu Kiem, then head of the NLF (PRG) delegation to the Paris peace talks, in a long discussion with me in Paris in May 1969 which focused primarily on an elucidation of the May 8, 1969, statement. (The PRG, or Provisional Revolutionary Government, was the final manifestation of the NLF, its emergence in June 1969 as a separate government rather than just a revolutionary movement.) For biographical data on the two former secretaries general, see Pike, *Vietcong,* pp. 429, 432. The first secretary general of the NLF was Dr. Phung Van Cung.

57. At the time of my talk with Nguyen Van Hieu, he was nominally NLF ambassador to Cambodia, but was regarded as the top NLF official in charge of its foreign affairs. (Pike has considerable data on his role in this.)

58. On Hanoi's view of the PRP, see Devillers, "Struggle for Unification," p. 23; Jean Lacouture, *Vietnam Between Two*

Truces (Random House, 1966), pp. 57–58. See also Pike, *Vietcong,* p. 217. On the PRP's establishment, see *Hoc Tap* no. 1 [Hanoi] 1966; Pike, *Vietcong,* pp. 136 ff. My discussion with Manac'h took place in Paris on September 9, 1968. He stipulated that this interview remain off the record for a decade.

59. For recurring indications of differences, see Pike, *Vietcong,* pp. 107, 363, 369. The principal difference in negotiating stances following the introduction of U.S. combat troops was the NLF's initial insistence that there could be no negotiations until the United States had removed the troops from Vietnam, whereas Hanoi indicated its willingness to begin negotiations following an agreement in principle that the United States would later withdraw. For a fuller discussion of this and less important differences at this time, see Kahin and Lewis, *United States in Vietnam,* pp. 208–9; Marcus G. Raskin and Bernard B. Fall, *The Viet-Nam Reader* (Vintage Books, 1965), pp. 233–52. NLF leaders with whom I talked include Nguyen Van Hieu (1967), Tran Buu Kiem (1969), and Nguyen Thi Binh (1970 and 1972). I also had discussions with DRV officials in Paris or Hanoi in 1968, 1969, 1971, and 1972. A striking difference between the NLF and Hanoi was evident to me in October 1972, when the NLF (PRG) foreign minister, Nguyen Thi Binh, appeared to be stunned and deeply worried by Hanoi's willingness to attach less importance to the release of political prisoners vis-à-vis other objectives in the negotiations.

60. David Elliott's observation came in a private communication; he is one of the most knowledgeable scholars in this matter. For Pike's views, see *Vietcong,* pp. 107, 369.

61. Noting the party's revision of history, David Elliott observes that those ex–NLF members who have defected since reunification have also had an incentive to magnify the extent of party control (letter to the author, June 7, 1983). For an example of Hanoi's revisionism on this point, see *Outline History of the Vietnam Workers' Party,* p. 105. For a bitter account of the demotion or displacement of NLF (PRG) leaders after

1975, see the account of Truong Nhu Tang (formerly minister of Justice in the PRG [NLF] Cabinet), "The Myth of Liberation," in the *New York Review of Books,* October 21, 1982, pp. 31–36.

62. Although many American officials were aware of the fragility of the "aggression from the North" rationale, successive administrations found it useful in dealing with American and world audiences. Thus, early in the Kennedy administration, Walt W. Rostow, initially that president's top Vietnam adviser, explained to Secretary of State Dean Rusk: "As I see it, the purpose of raising the Viet-Nam issue as a case of aggression is either to induce effective international action or to free our hands and our consciences for what we have to do. . . . At the minimum we put ourselves in a political position to salvage South Laos and save Viet-Nam with a more rational military plan than we have now." (Memorandum from W. W. Rostow for the Secretary of State, July 13, 1961.)

Efforts to shape American public opinion to ensure acceptance of the thesis that the southern insurgency was in fact a case of northern aggression increased during Kennedy's administration and reached their zenith in 1965–66 under Lyndon Johnson. A few examples of this are in order if the durability of the myth is to be understood. The Kennedy administration, in its widely disseminated fall 1961 "White Paper" on Vietnam, entitled *A Threat to the Peace: North Viet-Nam's Effort to Conquer South Viet-Nam,* spoke of the "fiction" that armed uprising in the South had been an internal matter and asserted that the NLF was a Hanoi creation which was "neither independent nor southern." (U.S. Department of State [U.S. Government Printing Office, 1961], pp. 14–23.) The same claim was made with greater elaboration in the Johnson administration's 1965 White Paper, *Aggression from the North: The Record of North Vietnam's Campaign to Conquer South Viet-Nam,* prepared for wide public dissemination on the eve of, and to help justify, the enormous escalation of U.S. military intervention about to be unleashed. (U.S. Department of State [U.S. Government Printing Office, 1965]; see especially pp. 19, 22.) Even more misleading was Rusk's statement that the NLF's struggle with Saigon "could end literally in 24 hours . . . if these people in Hanoi should come to the conclusion that they are not going to seize Vietnam and Laos by force." U.S. Congress, Senate, *Supplemental Foreign Assistance Fiscal Year 1966 —Vietnam,* 89th Cong., 2nd sess. (U.S. Government Printing Office, 1966), p. 15. In a public address on May 13, 1965, before the Dallas World Affairs Council, the assistant secretary of state for Far Eastern affairs, Wiliam Bundy, went even further. Positing two separate countries in Vietnam with nationalist feelings that "differ to a significant degree," he spoke of "the myth that the Viet Cong movement has any significant relationship to the political opposition to Diem. . . . There should be no doubt of the true nature of the Viet Cong and its National Liberation Front. They are a completely different movement from the political opposition to Diem." (Though there was a significant body of opposition to Diem apart from the NLF, it was certainly not the only opposition, or as strongly and broadly based as the NLF.) As for Diem's repression, it was "never drastic by the standards we should apply to governments in new nations." Hanoi's call for honoring the elections stipulated at Geneva was only "propaganda," whereas "the Eisenhower Administration had fully supported the principle of free elections under international supervision." Bundy's speech was republished in the *State Department Bulletin* and, in revised form, in a much more widely distributed department publication entitled—appropriately enough—"South Vietnam: Reality and Myth." With this sort of information, it is understandable why the American public and much of Congress were so easily misled.

One of the more sophisticated examples of deception was undertaken by the CIA with the cooperation of the influential journal *Foreign Affairs.* George Carver, one of the agency's top Vietnam specialists, wrote the two lead articles on Vietnam in its April 1965 and April 1966 issues, both of which were commended to the public by administration officials. In each case he was disingenuously identified for readers as simply "student of political theory and Asian affairs with degrees from Yale and Oxford; former officer in the U.S. aid mission in Saigon; author of 'Aesthetics and the Problem of Meaning.' " The chairman of the Senate Foreign Relations Committee, Senator William Fulbright, was outraged when he later learned of this subterfuge, and asked the CIA to look at the propriety of its analysts' presenting official statements and conclusions to American readers in the guise of independent scholarship. But probably few of *Foreign Affairs'* readers were aware of this deception. (Fulbright's criticism was expressed to me; on his request to the CIA, see *New York Times,* April 30, 1966.) Particularly in the second of Carver's articles, "The Faceless Viet Cong," which characterized the NLF as "a contrived political mechanism with no indigenous roots," there was indeed "a problem of meaning" (pp. 360–61, 372). Compounding this chicanery, in support of his thesis Carver used the spurious statements in the above-mentioned "black operation" radio broadcasts that purported to be the voice of "the Liberation Front." And among the few sources he cited, and which he recommended as meriting "the careful attention of anyone interested in Vietnamese affairs," was a book, Hoang Van Chi's *From Colonialism to Communism* (Praeger, 1964), whose publication was reported by the *New York Times,* on September 28, 1966, as having been subsidized by the U.S. Information Agency.

63. The skeptical officials included George Ball, Chester Bowles, Averell Harriman, and James Thomson. Even the hawkish Henry Cabot Lodge acknowledged in an internal report regarding what he termed "the true nature of the Viet Cong" (NLF) that it was composed of "indigenous communists" of whom many derived from cadres developed in southern Vietnam in the struggle against France who had remained in the South after Geneva, could not now be

expected to withdraw to the North, and would "disappear only through their physical liquidation or by winning them away from communism." (Cable from Lodge to Secretary of State, March 9, 1964.) William Bundy also clearly harbored reservations, as indicated by a section of his March 2, 1964, Memorandum for Messrs. Sullivan, McNaughton, Yarmolinsky, wherein he observed that "the fact that the Viet Cong *do* have a lot of appeal in South Vietnam and *do* rely heavily on captured U.S. weapons has left the impression even in some U.S. circles that the North Vietnam role is actually marginal at best and that the conflict is 'just a civil war.' "

V. The Decline of Diem's Regime

1. In Laos an ineffective right-wing military government, created and nourished by the United States, was rapidly losing ground to both neutralist and communist forces. For the fullest, most scholarly account of the Eisenhower administration's Laotian intervention, see Charles A. Stevenson, *The End of Nowhere: American Policy Toward Laos Since 1954* (Beacon Press, 1972). On March 26, 1960, the U.S. army's chief of staff called for urgent measures to improve the South Vietnamese army's counterguerrilla activities, and on March 30, the JCS agreed that "anti-guerrilla capability should be developed within [the] organization of the regular armed forces by changing emphasis in training [of] selected elements [of the] ARVN and other forces from conventional to anti-guerrilla warfare." (*PP* [GPO], 2 (IV,A.5, Tab. 4):83.

2. For Durbrow's March 7 dispatch, see *PP* (GPO), 10:1256. For the full text of the manifesto, see Bernard Fall, *The Two Vietnams: A Political and Military Analysis* (Praeger, 1964), pp. 442–48.

3. Quotes are from Department of State, Intelligence Report, "Restive Political Situation in South Vietnam" (8 pp.), August 29, 1960.

4. See cables from Durbrow to Herter, September 16 and October 15, 1960, Memorandum from Durbrow to Diem, October 14, 1960, in *PP* (GPO), 10:1311–24.

5. Among the most prominent civilians was Dr. Phan Quang Dan, who, during the first day of the coup, made a strong radio broadcast in favor of the rebels and was identified as a "political commissioner of their Revolutionary Committee."

6. The quote is from Department of State, "Restive Political Situation in South Vietnam," August 29, 1960, p. 8. At least some of the rebels wished the prime minister in the new government to be General Le Van Kim, then commandant of the National Military Academy at Dalat, who, according to his brother-in-law, General Tran Van Don (in discussions with me), was willing to assume the position once the coup was successful, but was unwilling to commit himself openly in advance.

7. Apparently Thi was not privy to the planning of the coup and was brought into it just as it got under way, presumably because of his suspected lingering loyalty to Diem (though decidedly not to Nhu). According to ex-Generals Nguyen Khanh, Ton That Dinh, and Tran Van Don, in separate discussions with the writer, Thi was forced at pistol point to accompany Colonel Dong into the company of the paratroopers who were surrounding the palace and, having been so compromised, had to remain with the rebels. The parachutist regiment he commanded had, according to ex-Colonel Pham Van Lieu, been maneuvered into position without his knowledge after the rebels had killed Major Ngo Xuan Soan, his subordinate, an action of which he was presumably ignorant until after the coup attempt had collapsed. Quotes are from Saigon Radio (in Vietnamese) as monitored November 11, 1960, by the U.S. Foreign Broadcast Intelligence Service (FBIS) GGG1, and reported November 14, 1960.

8. Diem had appointed Le Van Ty to chief of staff some five years before to replace General Nguyen Van Hinh. Although not a power within the armed forces, he was not regarded as aligned with any particular faction and was therefore well suited to serve as

intermediary. Ty's announcement and the rebels' broadcast are in FBIS, November 14, 1960, GGG2.

9. Diem indicated his suspicion of the coup's American backing to a number of people—including me, when I talked with him two months after the event. Several senior army officers then stationed in Saigon, one of them a top coup leader, have in subsequent discussions with me, been explicit in charging American encouragement of the rebels. Also former General Tran Van Don, then in Saigon, states that during the first day of the coup a CIA agent accompanied the coup leaders. See his *Our Endless War Inside Vietnam* (Presidio Press, 1978), p. 79. Robert Shaplen writes, "The Americans had known in advance that the coup was coming and while they did not assist it, they did nothing to stop it. . . ." (*The Lost Revolution,* [Harper and Row, 1965], pp. 141–42.) Stanley Karnow in his account of the coup observed that "Most Americans in Saigon were sympathetic to the rebels. But neither the general [head of MAAG] nor Ambassador Elbridge Durbrow could risk involvement in the revolt." He reports Nhu as emphasizing to him that "the principal culprits in the revolt were the 'western embassies' and individual Americans in particular," and that "American military advisers were helping the paratroopers during the revolt." ("Diem Defeats His Own Best Troops," *Reporter,* January 19, 1961, pp. 28–29.)

10. Cable from Lansdale to Deputy Secretary Douglas, November 15, 1960, in *PP* (GPO), 10:1330–31. On alleged American perfidy, see cables from Durbrow to Secretary of State, December 4, 1960, in *PP* (GPO), 10:1335, 1338. See also Karnow, "Diem Defeats His Own Best Troops," p. 28. Diem sent one of his confidants, Gene Gregory, to Ambassador Durbrow with what he stated was explicit evidence of "American support of and complicity in the coup." (Discussions of the author with Gene Gregory.)

11. Regarding Lansdale's heavy backchannel criticism of Durbrow to Washington, see his cables to the Department of Defense just after the coup attempt, in *PP* (GPO), 10:1329–31. For this and his thinly veiled request for Durbrow's job, see also *PP* (GPO), 2 (IV, A.5): 68, 69.

12. In Southeast Asia, this difference in attitude was clearly apparent with respect to Burma and Indonesia.

13. In the holdings of the John F. Kennedy Library are numerous private polls he ordered during 1961 to determine how he looked in comparison with Eisenhower. Pelz quote is from "John F. Kennedy's 1961 Vietnam War Decisions," *Journal of Strategic Studies,* 4, no. 4 (December 1981): 363, 365.

14. Quotes are from Memorandum for the Record of Assistant to the President [Eisenhower], General Wilton R. Persons, January 19, 1961. This partly sanitized nine-page account is the fullest available. Secretary of State Christian A. Herter's Memorandum for the Record of this meeting runs a scant four pages and also has deletions. The heavy emphasis Eisenhower placed at this meeting on support of the existing right-wing Laotian government, and on control of Laos as the key to all Southeast Asia, was also observed by Clark Clifford, then a confidant of Kennedy, who also attended the meeting. (For Clifford's record see *PP* [Gravel], 2: 635–37.)

15. "Without taking troops" quote is from Roger Hilsman, *To Move a Nation* (Doubleday, 1967), p. 128; see also Stevenson, *End of Nowhere,* p. 143. "Stunned silence" is from Stevenson, *End of Nowhere,* p. 135.

16. On Kennedy to his aides, see Arthur M. Schlesinger, Jr., *A Thousand Days* (Houghton Mifflin, 1965), p. 339; John Kenneth Galbraith in NBC, White Paper, "Vietnam Hindsight, Part I: How It Began" (full transcript of December 21, 1971, broadcast), sec. III, pp. 11–12. Galbraith states Kennedy told him, "There are just so many concessions that one can make to the communists in one year and survive politically. . . . We just can't have another defeat this year in Vietnam."

17. By early November 1961, McGeorge Bundy and apparently other advisers were

urging Kennedy to replace Bowles with George Ball. (Memorandum from McG. B., "Week End Reading for the President," November 4, 1961; see also Chester Bowles, *Promises to Keep: My Years in Public Life, 1941–1969* [Harper and Row, 1971], p. 363.) As for Southeast Asia, Pelz cites a memorandum of March 29, 1961, from Bowles to Kennedy urging a neutralization of that region, with India and Japan as guarantors. ("Kennedy's 1961 Decisions," pp. 364, 382; see also Bowles, *Promises to Keep*, p. 409.) Rusk strongly opposed Bowles's idea for neutralizing Vietnam.

18. Strictly speaking, 685 was about double the number that a rigorous interpretation would permit; but, as a consequence of Dulles's heavy lobbying of Nehru, the Indian chairman of the ICC agreed, with Canadian support, to an interpretation permitting that total. It appears that subsequently, in early 1960, New Delhi was apprised that if "conditions in Southeast Asia should deteriorate seriously," the United States reserved the right to increase the number of its advisers to 888, which was apparently the maximum that the most generous interpretation of the Geneva limitations would permit. See cable from Durbrow to Secretary of State, February 7, 1961. In the same cable the ambassador argued that, since the combined number of U.S. and French training and advisory military personnel in Vietnam at the conclusion of the Geneva Agreements was 1,847, this would "permit us to argue that we could increase MAAG strength by 1,162."

19. On the meeting, see Memorandum from W.W.R. [Rostow] for Mr. Bundy [McGeorge], "Meeting Saturday Morning, January 28, in the President's Office, on Viet-Nam," January 30, 1961, p. 4. This bore the notation: "This memorandum is designed for Mr. Bundy only. It aims to give more detail than should go into a memorandum for the record." Included in the meeting were Secretary of Defense McNamara, Secretary of State Rusk, Allen Dulles (still head of the CIA), Graham Parsons (still assistant secretary for the Far East), Lansdale,

Rostow, and probably McGeorge Bundy as well. Lansdale's report was Memorandum for Secretary of Defense/Deputy Secretary of Defense, in *PP* (GPO), 2 (IV, A.5): 66–77.

20. In the course of the January 28, meeting, there was obvious agreement that Durbrow would have to be replaced and discussion as to whether Lansdale or Kenneth Young should get the post. Young was made ambassador to Thailand and Lansdale remained in Washington, where he continued to have the ear of Walt Rostow and Deputy Secretary of Defense Roswell Gilpatric.

21. All quotes in this and following paragraph are from Rostow's January 30 memorandum on the January 28 meeting. For Kennedy's approval see: Memorandum from JFK to Secretaries of State and Defense, January 30, 1961.

22. The new measures were approved by the president at the NSC meeting of April 29, 1961. (*PP* [NYT], pp. 120–24.) That the Green Berets were described as being sent for training purposes did not in fact differentiate them from other U.S. military personnel serving in Vietnam. The arrival of these men placed Ambassador Nolting in an awkward position vis-à-vis his British, French, and other diplomatic colleagues in Saigon, who asked him whether this represented an increase in MAAG. (Cable from Nolting to Secretary of State, May 24, 1961.)

23. Memorandum to the President from WWR[ostow], March 29, 1961.

24. The lack of understanding was strikingly clear to me among officers in counterinsurgency training at Maxwell Field, where I was invited to lecture in 1961. Kattenburg quotes are from *The Vietnam Trauma, in American Foreign Policy, 1956–1975* (Transaction Books, 1980), pp. 111–12.

25. For quote and Nixon's comment, see Pelz, "Kennedy's 1961 Decisions," pp. 365–66. On the June summit meeting, see Paul M. Kattenburg, *Vietnam Trauma,* p. 114.

26. Quote is from "A Program of Action to Prevent Communist Domination of South Vietnam," April 26, 1961, p. 2. On

Kennedy's following Lansdale, see Pelz, "Kennedy's 1961 Decisions," pp. 368–69. Kennedy also insisted that the expansion of counterinsurgency activities not be dependent upon Diem's agreement to accept a joint integrated plan.

27. JCS May 10 report is in *PP* (Gravel), 2:49. The previous day the JCS had recommended the dispatch of U.S. forces to Thailand.

28. *Ibid.*, p. 54. Kennedy announced Johnson's trip on May 5, just after an NSC meeting devoted to discussing steps to reassure both the Thai and Vietnamese leaderships.

29. Nolting quotes are from cables from Nolting to Department of State, received May 18, 1961, and May 26, as corrected May 29, 1961. Four months later, following mounting NLF successes, Diem indicated his desire for a bilateral security treaty, but by that time the United States had concluded it would not be desirable.

CIA quote is from Information Report, "Views of Dr. Tran Kim Tuyen [director of Diem's Presidential Security Service] on Vietnamese Reactions to U.S. Military Aid," November 22, 1961. Pentagon analyst quote is in *PP* (Gravel), 2:69. For Johnson's recommendations, see *ibid.*, pp. 57–59; Schlesinger, *Thousand Days,* p. 543.

30. On the insurgency attacks overrunning the Mekong Delta, see David Halberstam, *The Making of a Quagmire* (Random House, 1965), p. 65. For CIA findings, see CIA, SNIE 53-2-61, "Bloc Support of the Communist Effort Against the Government of Vietnam," October 5, 1961, pp. 3–6, 70–71. Another reason for Diem's reconsideration was his anxiety over the situation in Laos and American policy there. See cable from Nolting to State, October 1, 1961.

31. Quotes are from Memorandum to the President from WWR[ostow], "Southeast Asia," October 5, 1961, pp. 2–3.

32. *PP* (Gravel), 2:74.

33. Rostow proposal quote is from Memorandum to the President, October 5, 1961. Kennedy quotes are in *PP* (Gravel), 2:79–80.

34. Quote is in *PP* (Gravel), 2:84. Arguments against such a treaty were forcibly made by Sterling Cottrell of the State Department in the appendixes to Taylor's report; he held that it would shift responsibility to the United States or engage a full U.S. commitment to defend Vietnam. (*PP* [GPO], 2 (IV, B.1): 18.)

35. On proposals of McGarr, Lansdale, and JCS, see *PP* (Gravel), 2:65–66, 85, 101, 103–4. On Taylor's meeting with Diem, see *ibid.*, pp. 84–87. In the course of Vice-President Johnson's talk with Diem, McGarr, who was present, had pressed Diem for an acknowledgment of his willingness to accept an increase in U.S. training personnel that would permit introduction of combat units; but Nolting, also present, reported that he wasn't sure Diem understood what McGarr was driving at. (Cable from Nolting to State Department, May 18, 1961.) Taylor assured Washington that "Diem's reaction on all points was favorable," but the memorandum he is referring to touched very lightly on any combat role for the task force. (*PP* [Gravel], 2:86–87.) All that he was able to report on that score was that Diem was favorably inclined to the proposition that such a task force might contain some combat troops to protect the engineer, medical, signal, and transportation elements, and that the force as a whole "would constitute [a] military reserve in case of heightened military crisis." A week after Taylor returned to Washington, Diem, in meeting with General McGarr, made very clear that he still wanted American-piloted planes and helicopters, but "did not mention the flood task force, or anything else that might imply a request for ground troops." (*Ibid.*, p. 101.)

36. All quotes are in *PP* (Gravel), 2:90–92.

37. *Ibid.*, p. 89.

38. *Ibid.*, pp. 93–94, Quotes regarding Rostow are on pp. 98–99.

39. Apropos of advisers who agreed with Taylor and Rostow, McGeorge Bundy, in conveying memoranda from Rostow to Kennedy on October 7, had warned the

president, "This is genuinely coming to a head, and I myself am now persuaded that we must promptly find a way of acting much more vigorously in South Vietnam." (Kennedy's Weekend Paper), "Papers to Newport," October 7, 1961.) For the views of William P. Bundy (then acting assistant secretary of defense for international security affairs), see *PP* (Gravel), 2:79. For McNamara's original reaction as described in his memorandum for the president of November 8 (sent on behalf of himself, the JCS, and Gilpatric), see *PP* (Gravel), 2:108–10. Rusk's views are in *ibid.*, p. 105.

For Ball's views, see George W. Ball, *The Past Has Another Pattern* (W. W. Norton, 1982), p. 366. Bowles's views are in his *Promises to Keep,* p. 409; see also Hilsman, *To Move a Nation,* p. 423; George Herring, *America's Longest War: The United States in Vietnam 1950–1975* (John Wiley, 1979), pp. 81–82; Pelz, "Kennedy's 1961 Decisions," pp. 377–78; Schlesinger, *Thousand Days,* pp. 545–58. For more on Galbraith's views, see *PP* (Gravel), 2:121–25.

Harriman quotes are from his Memorandum for the President, November 11, 1961. In a handwritten covering note marked "Personal," Harriman wrote, "I have given a copy of this Draft Memorandum to Dean Rusk. He asked me to tell you his comment. 'It is a matter of timing,' bearing in mind 'other communications' on the same subject." That Kennedy had read Harriman's memorandum was evident in references to him and some of these ideas in the president's memorandum of November 14. (See n. 41.)

40. This account of the genesis of the November 11 memorandum is the interpretation of a number of knowledgeable scholars who have written about this matter and seems to me to be the most plausible explanation. See *PP* (Gravel), 2:110, 113; see also Ball, *Past Has Another Pattern,* p. 368. In the November 11 memorandum McNamara retreated from the position he had taken in his memorandum of November 8, which had recommended commitment of the United States to the "clear objective of preventing

the fall of South Vietnam to Communism" through "the necessary military actions" and support of Taylor's plans "as the first steps towards its fulfillment." For the full text see *PP* (Gravel), 2:108–9. On the excluded point, see *PP* (Gravel), 2:117. The full NSC Action Memorandum of November 22 can be found in Porter, *Vietnam: The Definitive Documentation,* 2:146–48.

41. All quotes are from Kennedy's Memorandum for Secretary of State [and] Secretary of Defense, November 14, 1961. Rostow's critique is in his Memorandum for the President, "Negotiations about Vietnam," November 14, 1961. The whole of section B of the president's memorandum (a full page) is taken verbatim from Rostow's.

42. The analyst in the *Pentagon Papers* is clearly incorrect in stating that the president's instructions to Nolting were sent on the 14th. (*PP* [Gravel], 2:117.) A subsequently declassified document of these instructions bears the date November 15, and later references to the instructions explicitly refer to that date. (Task Force Vietnam, Department of State, "Status Report on the Instructions to Ambassador Nolting," November 20, November 28, 1961.) Quotes are from *PP* (Gravel), 2:111.

43. "A crucial element" quote is in *ibid.,* p. 119. Diem's arguments are in Task Force Vietnam, "Status Report on Instructions to Ambassador Nolting," November 28, 1961; interview of the author with Diem, Saigon, January 26, 1961.

44. On the White Paper, see ch. IV. Kennedy's perception of its use is suggested in his August 7 memorandum to Rostow and Taylor: "By what means can we bring to world public opinion the action of the North Vietnam [*sic*] in Laos and South Vietnam? I agree with you that groundwork has to be laid or otherwise any military action we take against Northern Vietnam will seem like aggression on our part." (Staff Memos, Evelyn Lincoln's Notebook.) Halberstam quote is from *Making of a Quagmire,* p. 68. On Nolting and Harkins, see Schlesinger, *Thousand Days,* p. 548. For the administration's June

instructions to its Saigon mission, see Homer Bigart, *New York Times*, June 3, 1962.

45. Figures through April 1962 are from *PP* (Gravel), 2:454. Presumably the figures for MAAG did not include U.S. Special Forces. Totals by the end of 1962 are from "Statistics on US Army Operations in Vietnam," Talking Paper, OPS OD Fe/72796, January 21, 1963. (Prepared for the Secretary of the Army General Staff.)

46. On the ICC mission's meeting, see *PP* (Gravel), 2:126–27. Quote is from International Commission for Supervision and Control in Vietnam, *Special Report to the Co-Chairmen of the Geneva Conference on Indo-China,* Command Paper 1755 (Her Majesty's Stationery Office, 1962), p. 7; see also p. 10.

47. A third helicopter company was shipped to Vietnam on December 15, 1961. (Task Force Viet-Nam, "Status Report on Instructions to Ambassador Nolting," November 20, 1961.) Quotes are from message from CINCPAC to JCS (Nr. 110740Z), March [21], 1962. On the combat roles of the helicopters, see also *New York Times*, October 16 and 18, 1962; Halberstam, *Making of a Quagmire*, p. 81. An NSC decision of November 11, 1961, authorized that "Aircraft, personnel and chemical defoliants" be sent to Vietnam "to kill Viet Cong food crops and defoliate selected border and jungle areas to assist in uncovering enemy hideout and transit areas." On November 27, it was reported that "spraying equipment had been installed on Vietnamese H-34 helicopters, and is ready for use against food crops." (It is not clear how soon after this the order was given to implement the program.) (Operations Directorate, J.3, Joint Chiefs of Staff, "Status Report of the Military Actions Resulting from NSC Meeting, 11 November, 1961," November 27, 1961, p. 10.)

48. All quotes are from Hilsman, *To Move a Nation,* pp. 444, 442.

49. Counterinsurgency enthusiasts' quotes are in *PP* (Gravel), 2:455. Among the differences between Malaya and Vietnam

was that in Malaya the insurgents, being predominantly Chinese, could look for no support from the Malay majority. In their relocation program, then, the British were dealing with a largely foreign-born ethnic minority—the Chinese (and actually only part of that minority)—in a country where the majority component—the Malays—worked closely in support of the British effort. The rural Chinese squatter population that was moved consisted for the most part of unrooted recent arrivals, and probably totaled less than one-fifth of the number of the rural Malay population. For an extensive analysis of the strategic hamlet program and comparison of it and the British experience in Malaya, see Milton Osborne, *Strategic Hamlets in South Vietnam* (Cornell Southeast Asia Program, 1965). McNamara quotes are in *PP* (Gravel), 2:148.

50. On use of the program to control the peasantry see *PP* (Gravel), 2:152.

51. "Indicating" quote is from *ibid.,* p. 149; see also p. 151. Halberstam quote is from *Making of a Quagmire*, p. 188.

52. September 1962 figures are from *PP* (Gravel), 2:151. June 1963 figures are from Scigliano, *South Vietnam,* p. 181.

53. Mecklin quotes are from *Mission in Torment* (Doubleday, 1965), pp. 99–100. On François Sully, see David Halberstam, *The Best and the Brightest* (Random House, 1972), p. 252. Pentagon office's assurances are in Letters from Arthur Sylvester, Assistant Secretary of Defense, to Kennedy, April 7, 1962; to McGeorge Bundy, April 7, 1962.

54. For a comprehensive and vivid account of the battle of Ap Bac, see Halberstam, *Making of a Quagmire*, pp. 147–58; see also Hilsman, *To Move a Nation,* pp. 447–49; and Chester L. Cooper, *The Lost Crusade: America in Vietnam* (Dodd, Mead, 1970), pp. 199–202, who estimates ARVN manpower superiority in the battle at ten to one. For Harkins quote, see Halberstam, p. 158, and Hilsman, p. 449. Kennedy's and McNamara's appraisals are in Cooper, pp. 199–201. For claims as to success of

the military campaign and Strategic Hamlet Program, and plans for withdrawal of U.S. troops, see *PP* (Gravel), 2:179–81; force level projections are in *ibid.*, p. 183.

55. Rusk's March 8 quote is in *Department of State Bulletin*, March 25, 1963, pp. 435–36. April 22 speech is in *ibid.*, May 11, 1963, pp. 729–30.

56. "Privileged" quote is from General Tran Van Don, in discussion with the author. " 'Arrogance of power' " quote is from William Corson, *The Betrayal* (W. W. Norton, 1968), p. 96.

57. Quotes are from CIA, Information Report, "Indications of Government of Vietnam Plan to Request Reduction of American Personnel in Vietnam [as of mid-April 1963]," April 22, 1963.

58. Diem's call for a reduction in U.S. forces was already prominent on the agenda of the NSC meeting of April 10. (National Security Council Agenda for the Meeting of April 10, 1963, 511th Meeting.) Quotes are from Department of State, Incoming Telegram from Nolting, received April 6, 1963. In signing the report, Nolting indicated that he had the concurrence of Harkins and Brent, the Embassy's chief economic affairs officer (as director of USOM).

59. As early as May 1961, Walt Rostow had advised Kennedy: "Although we have no alternative except to support Diem now, he may be overthrown. . . . If so, we should be prepared to move fast with the younger army types who may then emerge." (Memorandum to the President from WWR[ostow], "Vietnam NSC Paper," May 10, 1961.) In a report of December 3, 1962, to the secretary of state, Hilsman acknowledged the possibility of a coup, mounted most likely by military leaders, but did not advocate this course. If the military were not polarized into pro- and anticoup groups, he saw a coup by this element as having "a better than even chance of succeeding," with the prospect that the new leadership "would probably maintain South Vietnam's pro US orientation." (*PP* [Gravel], 2:716.)

VI. The Overthrow of Diem

1. For the Mansfield report, see *New York Times*, February 25, 1963, p. 1; U.S. Congress, Senate, Committee on Foreign Relations, *Vietnam and Southeast Asia, Report of Senator Mike Mansfield, Senator J. Caleb Boggs, Senator Claiborne Pell, and Senator Benjamin Smith*, 88th Cong., 1st sess. (U.S. Government Printing Office, 1963), especially pp. iii, iv, 8–9.

2. Kenneth P. O'Donnell and David F. Powers with Joe McCarthy, *"Johnny, We Hardly Knew Ye": Memories of John Fitzgerald Kennedy* (Little, Brown, 1972), p. 16. Much more than Kennedy's appointments secretary, O'Donnell is described by Pierre Salinger as the member of the White House staff with "the greatest responsibility, influence, and accessibility to the president."

3. Probably around three-quarters to four-fifths of the population in the South could be regarded as at least nominally Buddhist. See "The Situation in Vietnam," SNIE 53-2-63, July 10, 1963, in *PP* (Gravel), 2:730. On conversion to Catholicism, see CIA Memorandum, September 19, 1964. On arousing of a new political consciousness, see Memorandum from Thomas L. Hughes, Director of the State Department's Bureau of Intelligence and Research, to Acting Secretary "Diem Versus the Buddhists: The Issue Joined," August 21, 1963, p. 2; see also Chester L. Cooper, *The Lost Crusade: America in Vietnam* (Dodd, Mead, 1970), p. 210. Quote is from Memorandum from Thomas L. Hughes to Secretary, "The Problem of Nhu," September 15, 1963, p. 1.

4. For the May 8 incident and culpability of Diem's troops, see *PP* (Gravel), 2:226.

5. On exacerbation of tensions between U.S. Embassy and Diem, and increasing U.S. domestic political price, see *PP* (Gravel), 2:229–31.

6. For the demonstrations, government reaction, Duc's self-immolation, and the June 16 agreement, see Hughes, "Diem Versus the Buddhists," p. 3; *PP* (Gravel), 2:-226–27.

7. For American intelligence's contrary conclusion, see SNIE, July 10, 1963, in *PP* (Gravel), 2:731. Quotes are from Hughes, "Diem Versus the Buddhists," pp. 3–4.

8. July 4 and 10 quotes are in *PP* (Gravel), 2:728, 733. The July 10 SNIE noted "accumulating evidence of serious disaffection and coup plotting in high military and civilian circles." (*Ibid.*, p. 731.)

9. For Harkins's and others' assurances, see *PP* (Gravel), 2:230–31. On the choice of Lodge, see Cooper, *Lost Crusade*, p. 211n. According to Kenneth O'Donnell, it was Rusk who suggested appointing him, and for Kennedy "the idea of getting Lodge mixed up in such a hopeless mess as the one in Vietnam was irresistible." (O'Donnell and Powers, *"Johnny, We Hardly Knew Ye,"* p. 16.)

10. On Lodge's preparations for assuming the post of ambassador, see *PP* (Gravel), 2:728. "Entrusted him" quote is from Geoffrey Warner, "The United States and the Fall of Diem: I. The Coup That Never Was," *Australian Outlook*, December 1974, p. 247. In his interviews, Warner found that Nolting was "inclined to believe that Lodge was entrusted with such a mission" but that Taylor believed he left for Saigon with an open mind. McCone quote is from his briefing to a new Saigon station chief, as recorded in Peer da Silva, *Sub Rosa: The C.I.A. and the Uses of Intelligence* (Times Books, 1978), p. 208. Apparently Lodge's last meeting with the president before leaving for Saigon was on August 14, and was regarded by McGeorge Bundy as "a good chance to give the Ambassador guidance he will need." Before this meeting the president was to read the report of Nolting's final visit and "tough talk" with Diem. (Reading for the President from McG. B[undy], August 13, 1963.

11. "Uneasiness" quote is from SNIE 53-2-63, July 10, 1963, "The Situation in South Vietnam," partially reproduced in *PP* (Gravel), 2:730. Remaining quotes are in *ibid.*, p. 732.

12. On July 17 news conference, see *PP* (Gravel), 2:824;

13. Account of raids and quote is from Hughes, "Diem Versus the Buddhists," p. 5.

14. It is difficult to assess the extent of the encouragement given, or the level and standing of the Americans who gave it, because so few of the pertinent U.S. documents covering this period have been declassified.

15. On the June plot, see *PP* (Gravel), 2:237; Robert Shaplen, *The Lost Revolution* (Harper and Row, 1965), p. 205; Major Pham Van Tuy, "The Coup D'Etat of November 1, 1963," *Lap Truong*, June 4–July 31, 1971, especially pp. 15–23. *Lap Truong* was a Saigon newspaper that supported Nguyen Cao Ky and ceased publication in August 1971. Major Pham Van Tuy, not actually identified as the writer of this long serialized article, had been aide to Lieutenant General Tran Van Don, and was assisted in writing some of the sections by another of Don's aides, Dong Hong Duyet. Understandably, they present General Don's version of the coup and its background. Although suffering from a somewhat biased (pro-Don) interpretation of events, this is by far the most detailed account available. I am much indebted to James Nach for his translation, running 132 pages in its English version, which has been deposited in Cornell University's Olin Library.

A retrospective CIA report credited Thao by late June 1963 with "leading one of three groups which had [later] united to overthrow Diem," having extensive contacts with middle-level troop commanders, and apparently having done "considerable spadework among them for the November 1963 coup." The agency found "no firm evidence he has not completely severed his ties with the Communists" and concluded that some of the allegations that he retained them "may be due to jealousy over Thao's aggressiveness and public renown." It reported him to be a Catholic, with close ties to Diem's brother Archbishop Ngo Dinh Thuc. He had rallied to Diem's government in 1956, joined the Can Lao, and become its organizer in the southwestern provinces. (CIA, Office of Current Intelligence, Intelligence Memorandum, "Colonel Pham Ngoc Thao," February 20, 1965, pp. 1–6.)

16. The ten generals were Huynh Van

Cao, Ton That Dinh, Tran Van Don, Nguyen Khanh, Tran Thien Khiem, Le Van Kim, Nguyen Ngoc Le, Duong Van Minh, Do Cao Tri, and Mai Huu Xuan. General Don informed the CIA's Colonel Lucien Conein that the martial-law decree was envisaged as the first phase of a larger plot. (CIA Information Report, "Major General Tran Van Don Details the Present Situation in South Vietnam: The Plan to Establish Martial Law; and His Views on South Vietnam's Future" [as stated August 23, 1963], August 24, 1963, p. 14.) It is evident that not all the officers who joined in the request for martial law perceived its implications for widening the coup possibilities.

17. See *PP* (Gravel), 2:233.

18. His "brazenness" culminated in an interview with Joseph Alsop, then one of the most influential American columnists. (New York *Herald Tribune,* September 18, 1963.)

19. "Speculation" quote is from CIA, Office of Current Intelligence, "South Vietnamese Government Contacts with the Viet Cong and Liberation Front," November 26, 1965, p. 3. For Conein's statement, see NBC News White Paper, "Vietnam Hindsight, Part II: The Death of Diem," transcript of broadcast, December 22, 1971, VIII, p. 5.

20. Interview of Nguyen Ngoc Tho with the chief political officer of a major embassy in Saigon friendly to the U.S., December 25, 1969. Nguyen Ngoc Tho responded similarly to me when I asked him the same questions in Saigon on January 15, 1970.

21. Discussions of the author with Gene Gregory, Washington, D.C., September 28, 1970, and Paul Kattenburg, Ithaca, N.Y., March 18, 1981. Kattenburg believes Diem was too strongly anticommunist to have ever actually gone through with such an arrangement. Tran Van Don quote is from discussions with the author in Washington and Ithaca, 1978, 1979, 1981; see also Don's book, *Our Endless War Inside Vietnam* (Presidio Press, 1978), p. 53.

22. Warner, whose research included interviews with Roger Lalouette, states, "There is little doubt that the RVN government was negotiating with the Commu-

nists." (Warner, "Coup That Never Was," p. 248; see also p. 249.) See Georges Chaffard's *Les Deux Guerres du Vietnam: De Valluy à Westmoreland* (La Table Ronde, 1969), pp. 307, 310, 322. See also Arthur Dommen's account, in the Los Angeles *Times* of December 15, 1968, of Chaffard's article covering this ground in the French weekly *L'Express.* For the most detailed and comprehensive account see Mieczyslaw Maneli, *War of the Vanquished* (Harper and Row, 1971).

23. Chaffard, *Deux Guerres du Vietnam,* p. 312; see also Los Angeles *Times,* December 15, 1968. For further data on Hanoi's response to Nhu's initiative, see Warner, "Coup That Never Was," p. 248.

24. Lodge had already argued against further efforts to persuade Diem to get rid of Nhu because he was sure Diem would refuse, and such a move risked exposing the generals to the danger of the brothers' retribution. Hilsman quotes are from *To Move a Nation* (Doubleday, 1967), p. 493. Rusk quote is from Cable (Eyes Only) from Rusk to Lodge, August 29, 1963.

25. CIA, "Contacts with Vietnamese Generals, 23 August Through 23 October, 1963."

26. CIA, Information Report, "Major General Tran Van Don Details the Present Situation in South Vietnam; the Plans to Establish Martial Law; and His Views on South Vietnam's Future, 23 August and As Stated," distributed August 24, 1963. (Sanitized copy; sanitization limited to removal of name of Don's CIA interlocutor, who from other sources is known to have been Lucien Conein.)

27. Nothing in Don's long account supports Hilsman's statement that he believed Nhu was plotting the generals' execution or that "Nhu might attempt to make a deal with Hanoi and sell out the whole country." (Hilsman, *To Move a Nation,* pp. 484–85.)

28. Letter from Rufus Phillips to the author, May 28, 1985. See also PP [Gravel], 2:234.

29. *Ibid.,* p. 234.

30. They would have reached him early on August 25, Saigon time. Drafted by Hils-

man, Undersecretary of State George Ball, Averell Harriman, and Michael Forrestal, with some additional input by Rusk, the cable was approved by the president without consultation with McNamara, McCone, or Taylor but with at least tacit concurrence of their senior subordinates. Regarding Rusk's input, see Cooper, *Lost Crusade,* p. 212. For the text of the cable, see *PP* (Gravel), 2:-734–35. For an account of the subordinates' concurrence, see George Ball, *The Past Has Another Pattern* (W. W. Norton, 1982), pp. 371–72.

31. For the quotes and full text, see *PP* (Gravel), 2:734.

32. Lodge quote is in cable to Rusk and Hilsman, August 25, 1963, in *ibid.,* p. 735.

33. For "Volunteered" and the divisions within Washington, see *PP* (Gravel), 2:238; Oral Histories of John A. McCone (pp. 15–16) and Maxwell Taylor (pp. 21–22), LBJ Library. On the generals' distrust of Harkins, see CIA cable (Eyes Only) to the Director, November 16, 1963, p. 3. (Sanitized.)

34. On the limited support for the coup, see Pham Van Tuy, "Coup d'Etat of November 1," p. 33. Quotes are from Cable from Taylor to Department of State, September 2, 1964 (this retrospective account was prompted by an assessment of Pham Ngoc Thao and Do Mau's prospects in another coup attempt, a year later, against General Khanh's government). On August 30, see *PP* (Gravel), 2:239–40; Pham Van Tuy, "Coup d'Etat of November 1," pp. 33–34.

35. On Khanh and American agent on August 25, see CIA, "Contacts with Vietnamese Generals," p. 1. Quote is in *ibid.*

Tran Van Don, who subsequently had good reason to hate Khiem, as well as Khanh (see ch. VII), rather grudgingly acknowledges Khiem's role. See Pham Van Tuy, "Coup d'Etat of November 1," pp. 23–24, who alleges Khiem's group was really not assembled until early September.

36. CIA, "Contacts with Vietnamese Generals," p. 2, and *PP* (Gravel), 2:237–38.

37. CIA, "Contacts with Vietnamese Generals." See also *PP* (Gravel), 2:237.

38. Khanh's being assigned a CIA liaison officer emerged in discussions with the author, Ithaca, N.Y., December 6, 7, 1974. It is impossible to corroborate Khanh's claim to have been in touch with Michael Forrestal of the White House staff sometime in August, but he clearly was in close contact with CIA agents. Regarding Nhu's being informed, Khanh says Don recounted how Nhu had called him in and said, "Don't be an idiot and attempt a coup; we know everything."

As for Harkins and Richardson as informers, General Ton That Dinh came to the same conclusion. Because Richardson's cables to Washington at this time were so strongly supportive of a coup, it would seem unlikely that he was the one who warned Nhu.

39. The reference to an aid cut stemmed from the practice on the "Voice" of reporting what was in the American press where there had been speculation as to such a move. For a plausible explanation of this mix-up, see Hilsman, *To Move a Nation,* p. 489. Memorandum for the President, "Voice of America Goof," from M. V. Forrestal, August 26, 1963. Noting that "the problem in Vietnam is rapidly becoming an operational one," Forrestal stated that "it is of the utmost importance that the execution of your decisions be lodged in one person, in one office," and that McGeorge Bundy agreed Hilsman was "the logical person for this for the time being." Hilsman quote is from *To Move a Nation,* p. 490.

40. On McNamara, Taylor, and McCone, see Hilsman, *To Move a Nation,* p. 490; *PP* (Gravel), 2:238. Rusk, though cautious, evidently stood closer to Hilsman, Harriman, Ball, Forrestal, and other supporters of a coup than to these three other senior officials. Observing to Lodge in late August that "the only point on which you and General Harkins have different views is whether an attempt should be made with Diem to eliminate the Nhus," Rusk urged the ambassador "to explore further question of possible attempt to separate Diem and the Nhus," but acknowledged that "perhaps it is inconceivable that the Nhus could be

removed without taking Diem with them or without Diem's abandoning his post." Citing Paul Kattenburg's recent conversations with Diem, he thought it unlikely that Diem would take seriously anything less than "a real sanction, such as a threatened withdrawal of our support." As noted above, however, he worried about the possibility that this might provoke the regime to move against the generals or even bring it to call for North Vietnam's assistance in expelling the Americans. Thus, he urged that such a sanction "await the time when others were ready to move immediately to constitute a new government." (Cable [Eyes Only] from Rusk to Lodge, August 29, 1963.) On generals' hesitation and knowledge that Nhu was aware of plans, see *PP* (Gravel), 2:240.

41. The record of this meeting is incorporated in a seven-page report by Bromley Smith, Memorandum of Conference with the President, August 27, 1963—6 P.M., "Subject: Vietnam." (A total of a little more than two pages is deleted.) Attending the meeting were Rusk, Ball, McNamara, Roswell Gilpatric, Robert Kennedy, Taylor, General Marshall S. Carter (acting director of CIA), Edward Murrow, Nolting, General Victor Krulak, Hilsman, Richard Helms, William Colby, McGeorge Bundy, Michael Forrestal, and Bromley Smith.

42. Rufus Phillips's confirmation and Lodge's authorization are in CIA, "Contacts with Vietnamese Generals," pp. 2, 3; *PP* (Gravel), 2:239. "Sensitive information" quote is in *PP* (NYT), p. 171, quoting a CIA cable October 5, Lodge's appeal is in PP (Gravel), 2:738–39.

43. Kennedy met Lodge's request in Cable (Eyes Only) from Rusk to Lodge and Harkins, August 29, 1963. The message was sent 5:00 P.M. Washington time, and its file copy bears the notation that Kennedy had read it. Quotes from Kennedy's private message to Lodge are in *PP* (NYT), pp. 162, 173. This important message is not found in either of the other two editions of the *Pentagon Papers*. A somewhat longer version of the president's cable, incorporating most but not all of the *New York Times* account, can be found in U.S. Congress, Senate, Select

Committee to Study Governmental Operations, *Alleged Assassination Plots Involving Foreign Leaders: Interim Report,* November 20, 1975 (U.S. Government Printing Office, 1975), p. 219.

44. Roger Hilsman, Memorandum for Secretary of State, "Possible Diem-Nhu Moves and U.S. Responses," August 30, 1963. This important document was declassified by authority of President Johnson on February 14, 1968, but was subsequently reclassified and, except for its first page, has not been available under the Freedom of Information Act. Much of it was, however, cited in John Roche, "The Jigsaw Puzzle of History," *New York Times Magazine,* January 24, 1971, pp. 39, 42; and in David Wise, *The Politics of Lying* (Random House, 1973), pp. 172–73, 177–78. The full text appeared in the Chicago *Sun-Times* of June 23, 1971.

45. The president's concern about the danger to Americans is suggested by the fact that the only materials McGeorge Bundy prepared for him as "Week-End Reading" for August 31 dealt with Vietnam, the first of these being three papers entitled "Availability of U.S. Forces for Deployment," which had been prepared the previous day by Admiral Riley. Rusk's "Eyes Only" cable of August 29 to Lodge and Harkins stated: "On movement of U.S. forces, we do not expect to make any announcement or leak at present and believe that any later decision to publicize such movements should be closely connected to developing events on your side. We cannot of course prevent unauthorized disclosures or speculation, but we will in any event knock down any reports of evacuation."

46. Among others whom Minh suspected of betraying coup plans to Nhu was General Khiem, who he subsequently (October 5) told Conein might have played "a double role" in August. (*PP* [Gravel], 2:768.) Assessment of Dinh is in Hilsman, *To Move a Nation*, p. 493.

47. On Tri Quang, see Cable from Lodge to Secretary of State, September 1, 1963. Lodge was so favorably impressed by Tri Quang that he seriously considered recommending his inclusion in a successor

government. (*PP* [GPO], 12:591.) In a September 7 cable, the State Department authorized Lodge to inform Diem "that before release of bonzes can be considered U.S. must be satisfied that GVN [South Vietnamese Government] is taking positive and demonstrable steps to insure religious tolerance and redress specific Buddhist grievances. . . ." A cable from the CIA's Saigon station to Washington, August 31, 1963, stated, "This particular coup is finished. . . . There is little doubt that GVN aware US role and have considerable detail." (reproduced in U.S. Senate, *Select Committee Interim Report,* November 20, 1975 [U.S. Government Printing Office, 1975], p. 220.) Lodge's August 31 cable is in *PP* (Gravel), 2:240.

48. A record of the meeting prepared by General Krulak can be found in *PP* (Gravel), 2:741–43.

49. For the Krulak and Mendenhall reports and Kennedy's reaction, see Hilsman, *To Move a Nation,* p. 501; *PP* (Gravel) 2: 243–45.

50. NSC, Memorandum of Conference with the President, prepared by Bromley Smith, "Subject: Vietnam," September 10, 1963, 10.30 am. [10 lines sanitized.]

51. Cable ("Eyes Only") from Lodge to Secretary of State, September 11, 1963, passed to the White House the same day.

52. Memorandum from Thomas L. Hughes to Secretary, "The Problem of Nhu," September 15, 1963.

53. Memorandum from Roger Hilsman for Secretary, "Viet-Nam," September 16, 1963. (Declassified by President Johnson on February 14, 1968.)

54. All quotes are from Memorandum from Chester Cooper for Director, "Possible Rapprochement Between North and South Vietnam," September 19, 1963.

55. "South Vietnam: An Action Plan," September 16, 1963, pp. 6–8. This particular section of the document has not been sanitized in declassification. Documents that might reveal Kennedy's reaction to these suggestions have not been released.

56. Arthur M. Schlesinger, Jr., *A Thou-*

sand Days (Houghton Mifflin; 1965), pp. 995–96.

57. *PP* (GPO), 12 (V,B.4): 554–73.

58. "United States Objectives in South Vietnam," September 11, 1963. Probably prepared for an NSC meeting, this memorandum indicates no author or designee, but comes from the NSC files, "Meetings on Vietnam," 9/11/63–9/12/63. An AID tabulation of the status of CIP apparently prepared in early September indicated that, of $80 to $100 million of CIP funds scheduled for 1964, $70 to $75 million worth of CIP commodities were already in the pipeline. *(Current AID and PL 480 Programs for Vietnam—FY 1964.)* (AID, mimeo, 1963.)

59. Khiem's September 26 report is in CIA, "Contacts with Vietnamese Generals," pp. 3–4.

60. For Minh's suspicion of Khiem, "cold feet" and "specific plan" quotes, see *ibid.,* p. 4. For Minh's insistence on clarification of U.S. position, his three plans and check on Camp Longthanh, see *PP* (NYT), pp. 213–15; see also Shaplen, *Lost Revolution,* p. 203.

61. Richardson's cable, partly sanitized, is in Porter, *Vietnam: Definitive Documentation,* 2:206. For McCone's response, see Senate, *Alleged Assassination Plots,* p. 221.

62. On October 6, a new acting station chief had taken over Richardson's functions. See the reference to this in McCone's cable to Lodge of that day. (Porter, *Vietnam: Definitive Documentation,* 2:206.) McCone's statement is in his Oral History, p. 16. As early as August 28, in a cable to McCone, Richardson had indicated a willingness to see both Diem and Nhu removed from office and predicted disaster for South Vietnam and U.S. objectives there if they remained. *(PP* [Gravel], 2:736.) Hilsman quote is from *To Move a Nation,* p. 515. Perhaps Hilsman was unaware that Richardson had changed his position, for he states that Richardson "argued persistently" that the United States should continue to support Nhu as well as Diem. *(Ibid.,* pp. 498–99.) Hilsman's account makes understandable why Richard-

son had the reputation of being pro-Nhu. (*Ibid.,* pp. 499–500.) Richardson may have altered his stand without some U.S. officials' having become aware, but in any case, his successor, Peer da Silva, writes that his long pro-Diem stance had put him "on the wrong side of Lodge." (*Sub Rosa,* pp. 208–9.) For perhaps the clearest insight into the matter, see Cooper, *Lost Crusade,* p. 218.

63. Conein's message to Minh is in *PP* (Gravel), 2:217, 257–58; see also Shaplen, *Lost Revolution,* p. 203. The wording in quotation marks is from Washington's cable of October 6, authorizing this policy, in *PP* (Gravel), 2:769. On freezing CIP subventions, see *PP* (NYT), p. 178. On cutting off Special Forces funding, see *PP* (Gravel), 2:-217–18, 253.

64. On Conein's efforts, see Pham Van Tuy, "Coup d'Etat of November 1," pp. 31, 33–34. The writer's reference is to "one with hairy hands, the most able adviser to Colonel Le Quang Tung." "Hairy hands" was the colloquial term for an American, and Conein was U.S. military adviser to Tung. See also Shaplen, *Lost Revolution,* p. 205.

65. According to Dinh, Don told him Washington supported the coup "100 percent." I discussed the coup and its background extensively with both Dinh and Don separately on several occasions in Washington and Ithaca in 1978, 1979, and 1981.

66. Dinh spoke of being criticized as military governor in a seminar at Cornell University on November 17, 1979, and in subsequent discussions with me. This accords with Tran Van Don's account to me. Dinh's account of his interaction with Diem at this time is confirmed by Don's account to me and consistent with a previously published description, approved by Don, in Pham Van Tuy, "Coup d'Etat of November 1," p. 29. See also *PP* (Gravel), 2:265. According to Shaplen, "Don had egged Dinh on to ask Diem and Nhu to make him Minister of Interior," with Diem reacting furiously and telling Dinh that he had grown

too big for his breeches, "just what Don and the other generals had expected." (Shaplen, *Lost Revolution,* p. 202.) Quote on General Don is from Pham Van Tuy, "Coup d'Etat of November 1." "The plotting generals" quote is in *PP* (Gravel), 2:265. Don's aide, Pham Van Tuy, gives him full credit for bringing Dinh aboard, and states that Don promised Dinh he would become minister of the interior in the government that succeeded Diem's.

67. On persuading Diem to transfer the Seventh Division, see Pham Van Tuy, "Coup d'Etat of November 1," pp. 40, 41. Dinh states that although he actually sent Co south to take control of General Cao's Seventh Division, he informed Nhu that he'd just shot Co for being a traitor. For detailed accounts of the plotting and maneuvers generally consistent with briefer mentions in *PP* (Gravel), 2:265–66, see Halberstam, *Making of a Quagmire,* pp. 284–85; Shaplen, *Lost Revolution,* pp. 203–4; see also Pham Van Tuy, "Coup d'Etat of November 1," pp. 41, 47–49.

68. Up to this point the accounts of Shaplen, *Lost Revolution,* pp. 204–7; *PP* (Gravel), 2:266; and those given me in discussions with Dinh and Don are largely congruent.

69. On Nhu wanting the Special Forces out of Saigon, see Halberstam, *Making of a Quagmire,* pp. 286–87; Shaplen, *Lost Revolution,* pp. 204–5. The *Pentagon Papers'* narrative is evidently based largely on these two sources. Ton That Dinh's account is fully corroborative. Pham Van Tuy's account states that units of the Special Forces, "the best and most loyal to the regime, had been brought together at Camp Le Van Duyet (III Corps Headquarters) early in the morning [of November 1] and had then received instructions from General Dinh to move out of the city, disperse and carry out operations at three separate locations." ("Coup d'Etat of November 1," p. 47.)

70. The CIA reported, "Harkins was telling Don that it was not time to run a coup. . . ." (Cable to the Director, November 16, 1963.) According to Don, Harkins ad-

vised him that "he was strongly against any coup we might be planning; that he certainly did not support it." (Tran Van Don, *Our Endless War*, p. 98.) This is consistent with what Don told me. For Harkins's version, see *PP* (Gravel), 2:258.

71. For Conein's assurances to Don, see CIA, "Contacts with Vietnamese Generals," p. 5. Hedrick Smith's observations are in *PP* (NYT), p. 181.

72. *PP* (GPO), 12:591.

73. CAS [CIA] message (Eyes Only), to Ambassador Lodge and General Harkins, October 15, 1963. This message, minus the deleted sentence is in *PP* (Gravel), 2:782.

74. Meeting and cables are in *PP* (Gravel), 2:255, 784–89. Quotes are on pp. 784–85.

75. "Still have" quote is in cable of October 30 in *ibid.*, p. 782. White House instructions to Lodge are from cable from Bundy to Lodge, October 30, 1963, in *PP* (GPO), 12:593–94. For October 30 cables to Lodge and Felt, see *PP* (GPO), 12:593–94; *PP* (Gravel), 2:783; White House, "Check List for 4 PM Meeting," October 29, 1963, John F. Kennedy Library, NSF, NSC Exec. Comm. folder, "Meetings on Vietnam 10/1/63–11/22/63," Box 316.

76. On Felt's known stance against the Nhus, see *PP* (Gravel), 2:234.

77. "He wanted to talk" quote is in *ibid.*, p. 267; see also Hilsman, *To Move a Nation*, p. 518. Pham Van Tuy quote is in "Coup d'Etat of November 1," pp. 46–47. General Don testified to me that the account by this former top aide is "fully reliable," except that he (Don) actually "choked" rather than "cried" upon being informed of Diem's death. For different speculation concerning Felt's visit with Diem, see Mecklin, *Mission in Torment*, p. 251.

78. Pham Van Tuy, "Coup d'Etat of November 1," pp. 50–52, 58–59.

79. Don told me Harkins had been bypassed in discussions in Washington and Ithaca, 1978, 1979, and 1981. Hilsman confirms Don's call to Stilwell and states he was awakened by the State Department's duty officers shortly after 2:00 A.M. (Washington time) with news of the coup. (Hils-

man, *To Move a Nation*, p. 519.)

80. Lodge's request is in *PP* (Gravel), 2:791. Later, in testifying before the Senate, Conein stated that he had brought these funds along at Don's request so that he could "procure food for his troops and . . . pay death benefits" for those killed in the coup, and that this amounted only to the equivalent of about $42,000. Senate, *Alleged Assassination Plots*, p. 222.

81. Quotes are in *PP* (Gravel), 2:268.

82. On Khanh's phone call, see Pham Van Tuy, "Coup d'Etat of November 1," p. 70. In discussions with the writer, Don and Dinh, both of whom are strongly prejudiced against Khanh (because of his later coup against them), have independently maintained that he remained on the sidelines until prospects for the November coup looked favorable, and had been prepared to play a role in Nhu's countercoup, having agreed to prepare an alternative haven for the brothers (in case use of that at Cape Saint Jacques were not feasible) at the Cateka Rubber Plantation, to which they alleged he had ordered the commander of his Twenty-third Division.

83. For Minh's orders to pick up the brothers, see *PP* (Gravel), 2:269. The analyst in the *Pentagon Papers* states that most accounts place blame for the murders on General Mai Huu Xuan (*ibid.*, p. 269). For other assessments, see Le Tu Hung, *Bon Tuong Da-lat* [*The Four Dalat Generals*] (Saigon: Dong Nai, 1971), pp. 74–76, 89; Pham Van Tuy, "Coup d'Etat of November 1," pp. 100–113 (this of course follows Don's version); Colonel Duong Hieu Nghia's interview with the Saigon newspaper, *Hoa Binh*, July 27, 1971; NBC's Alvin Davis in "Death of Diem." Regarding a possible comeback, Tran Van Don observes that if the brothers had lived, perhaps after three months the Americans would have replaced him and the other generals by bringing Diem and Nhu back to power. (Discussion with me in Ithaca, N.Y., March 24, 1981.) See also Halberstam, *Making of a Quagmire*, p. 297.

84. Da Silva quote is from *Sub Rosa*, p. 215.

85. Cable (Eyes Only) for Ambassador

Lodge from the President (via Department of State), November 6, 1963. (Not declassified until March 25, 1983.)

86. See *PP* (Gravel), 2:222, 271.

VII. "The Pentagon's Coup"

1. The other five council members were Major Generals Tran Van Minh, Pham Xuan Chieu, Tran Thien Khiem, Mai Huu Xuan, Le Van Nghiem.

2. "Actually" quote is from William P. Bundy, MIT Group Meeting, January 21, 1970, Adam Yarmolinsky Papers, John F. Kennedy Library. (The meeting was to discuss a draft of Bundy's projected book on the United States and Vietnam—a book never published.)

3. As noted in ch. IV, Douglas Pike, a U.S. foreign-service officer regarded as a specialist on the NLF's organization, acknowledges that the Cao Dai constituted "the bulk of the early NLF support" and that the Hoa Hao was also "an early and major participant in the NLF." *Vietcong: The Organization and Techniques of the National Liberation Front of South Vietnam* (The MIT Press, 1966), pp. 68–69, 369.

4. Mahayana Buddhists dominated social and political functions of the organization, but Theravada leaders were well represented, even though one of them, Mai Tho Truyen, soon broke away—because (I inferred in a discussion with him) he was not given a position as high as he believed he deserved. The two most powerful leaders of the association, both Mahayana, were Thich Tri Quang, secretary general of its High Council, and Thich Tam Chau, director of that body's executive arm, the Institute for the Propagation of the Faith (Vien Hoa Dao). Within the Vien Hoa Dao were six functionally differentiated commissions: Personnel; Rites; Finance and Construction; Lay Affairs; Propagation of the Faith; and Youth. The last two were the most important in social and political matters, with Thich Thien Minh, head of the Youth Commission and a close ally of Tri Quang, soon emerging as the third-most-powerful leader.

Initially Tam Chau was the most influential, but by 1966 was overshadowed by Tri Quang, who remained closely allied to Thien Minh. It was to their leadership that the well-known poet Thich Nhat Hanh was most closely linked.

5. Tam Chau's address and the embassy comment are incorporated in a cable from Marvin L. Manfull, Counsellor of Embassy for Political Affairs, American Embassy, Saigon, to Department of State, "Recent Buddhist Developments," March 26, 1964.

6. The importance of this generally unappreciated development has been emphasized to me by both Paul Kattenburg, then head of the administration's Vietnam task force, and David Marr, at that time in Vietnam as a lieutenant in the U.S. Marine Corps Intelligence; it accords fully with my own discussions with senior Buddhist leaders.

7. The views of Tho and Minh were consistent with what both of them stated in confidence to a senior political officer of an embassy of a major government (not France) friendly to the United States and to two senior correspondents (Henry Kamm of *The New York Times* and Jean Claude Pomonti of *Le Monde*). My own discussions with Tho were in Saigon in 1970, with Minh in Saigon in 1970 and 1971, and with Don in Saigon, Washington, D.C., and Ithaca, N.Y., in 1970, 1973, 1978, and 1979–80. On contacts with the NLF, see CIA, Office of Current Intelligence, Intelligence Memorandum, "South Vietnamese Government Contacts with the Viet Cong and Liberation Front," November 26, 1965, p. 3. For a fuller text of the NLF appeal, see George McT. Kahin and John W. Lewis, *The United States in Vietnam,* 2nd ed. rev. & enl. (Delta, 1969), pp. 473–76; also pp. 134–37. The CIA report is Memorandum from John A. McCone, "Highlights of Discussions in Saigon 18–20 December, 1963," December 21, 1963. (Probably prepared for the president.)

8. Regarding the shake-up, by December 20 about 70 percent of the province chiefs had been replaced. (McCone, "Highlights of Discussions.")

9. See Oral Histories of Taylor and McCone, LBJ Library.

10. On strategic hamlets in Long An, see Memorandum for the President from M. V. Forrestal, December 11, 1963. On Hoa Hao and Cao Dai rallying to Saigon, see McCone, "Highlights of Discussions"; Hedrick Smith, *New York Times,* December 28, 1963.

11. Generals Minh, Don, and Dinh, and Prime Minister Tho all regarded their opposition to the U.S. military's bombing plans as the major reason for the coup that was mounted against them. "Aerial bombardment" quote is from Memorandum from JCS for Secretary of Defense, January 22, 1964, in *PP* (Gravel), 3:498–99; see also p. 35. Among other things, the JCS recommended that the U.S. "commit additional U.S. forces as necessary, in support of the combat action in South Vietnam" and "in direct action against North Vietnam." In response to a directive apparently from the JCS, General Harkins and the Saigon CIA's Covert Action Branch on December 19, 1963, forwarded a plan, supported by CINCPAC, providing for a "spectrum of capabilities for the RVNAF [South Vietnamese air force] to execute against North Vietnam." (*PP* [Gravel], 3:117.) Roger Hilsman quote is from *To Move a Nation* (Doubleday, 1967), p. 534. Hilsman also claims that McNamara had not yet joined those who advocated bombing the North (not the impression received by the South Vietnamese leaders who met with him) and that President Johnson was in complete sympathy with his general approach.

12. Chuan quote is from an interview with *Hoa Binh* (a moderate Catholic newspaper in Saigon), July 20, 1971. His account of this meeting is corroborated by Tran Van Don, one of those attending it.

13. McNamara's report is referred to in a cable from the President to Ambassador Lodge, May 14, 1964, NSF, Vietnam, vol. 9, Cables.

14. *PP* (Gravel), 2:307.

15. Both quotes are in *ibid.,* 2:307–8.

16. Minh's complaint is in *ibid.,* p. 307.

Mai Huu Xuan's statement was corroborated by General Ton That Dinh, then minister of security in the Minh government, and General Tran Van Don, its minister of defense. The CIA's Saigon station criticized Xuan's handling of police affairs, reporting to Washington that he continued "to pack the Directorate-General and police with old cronies, some of whom are of questionable repute and to pursue with perhaps greater than necessary zeal the roundup for questioning of officials connected with the Diem regime." (CIA, "Situation Appraisal as of 30 November, 1963," distributed December 2, 1963.)

17. Minh was not the only junta member whom Lodge wished to transform into a politician: see *PP* (Gravel), 2:307. In retrospect, both Ton That Dinh and Tran Van Don conclude that Minh's rebuff to Lodge was unwise, and that if he had indulged him in these requests the ambassador might have been more supportive against Harkins's efforts to undermine the junta's standing in Washington.

18. For de Gaulle's August 29 offer, see *New York Times,* August 30, 1963. NLF's endorsement of Sihanouk proposals came on NLF Radio, December 13, 1963. The culminating external event in building up an atmosphere conducive to belief in the possibility of a neutralist solution came on January 25, with France's recognition of the People's Republic of China and the attendant speculation that the West's opposition to a China regarded as supportive of Hanoi was diminishing. Mansfield's opinions in his Memorandum to President Johnson, "Southeast Asia and Vietnam," December 7, 1963. (This refers to a conversation the two men had held on the previous Thursday.)

19. Cable from Lodge to Secretary of State, December 4, 1963.

20. Memorandum to the President from McG.B[undy], "Senator Mansfield's Views on South Vietnam," January 6, 1964.

21. Memorandum from W. W. Rostow to Secretary [of State], "Southeast Asia and China," January 10, 1964.

22. CIA Weekly Report, "The Situation in South Vietnam 28 February 1964," p. 4.

23. Hedrick Smith quote is from *New York Times,* December 10, 1963. State Department's response to Dinh is in cable from Ball to American Embassy, Saigon, December 16, 1963.

24. Tran Van Don quote is from *Our Endless War Inside Vietnam* (Presidio Press, 1978), p. 133.

25. McNamara quotes are from Memorandum for the President from Secretary of Defense, December 21, 1963.

26. Letter to the President from John A. McCone, Director of Central Intelligence, December 23, 1963, with McCone's attached memorandum; "Highlights of Discussion in Saigon 18–20 December 1963," dated December 21, 1963.

27. For American disillusionment, see, for instance, Hedrick Smith, *New York Times,* February 2, 1964.

28. For the new regime's view of Harkins, see CIA ("Eyes Only") cable to Director [from Saigon], November 16, 1963. On the weakening of Harkins's position vis-à-vis Lodge's, see the reports of David Halberstam and Jack Raymond, *New York Times,* November 13, 15, 1963, January 29, 1964. For Harkins's awareness that Lodge wanted to replace him, see cable to Director [partly sanitized, and presumably from the CIA Saigon station chief], November 16, 1963.

29. On the military men's worry about transfers, see CIA, "Situation Appraisal as of December 14, 1963," distributed December 16, 1963, p. 6. Quote is from CIA, "Situation Appraisal as of 7 December 1963," p. 4.

30. Quote is from "Background on Coup in SVN, 30 January 1964," a report prepared by U.S.-marine intelligence shortly after the coup. Information on Duong Ngoc Lam is from private communication with General Tran Van Don; see also Robert Shaplen, *The Lost Revolution* (Harper and Row, 1965), pp. 231–32.

31. Khiem resented the fact that some of his authority as chief of staff had been taken over by General Don as defense minister.

32. "U.S. pressure" quote is from *PP* (Gravel), 2:303. The account states that other coup-protection units stayed near Saigon for this purpose. If that was so, when the crisis arose they were apparently too far from the center of action to play a role. As early as November 29, General Harkins had cabled General Taylor, chairman of the JCS, and Admiral Felt, CINCPAC, "General Dinh is still reluctant to give up command of III Corps. I'm still working on this. . . ." (Cable [naval message], November 29, 1963.) The major and apparently final U.S. effort to secure Dinh's removal was conveyed by Lodge on behalf of President Johnson, as part of the third of eleven points of advice presented orally to Minh at the beginning of January (probably January 1), 1964. (White House Memorandum from McGeorge Bundy to General Clifton at LBJ Ranch in Texas for the President, December 30, 1963.) Dinh informed me that he had been under sustained heavy pressure by the U.S. military to give up his command. Don observations are from discussions with the author.

33. For the argument that Khiem was initially most important in the planning, see Le Tu Hung, *Bon Tuong Da-lat* [*The Four Dalat Generals*] (Saigon: Dong Nai, 1971), p. 14. Quote is in *ibid.,* pp. 11–12. Although nominally a Buddhist, Khiem was, according to a CIA report, "generally identified with the Catholic group," and was regarded as having been very close to Diem. (CIA Report [undated], NSF, Vietnam, vol. 23.) In so identifying Khiem, this report states that "some Buddhist elements have considered him to be a holdover from the Ngo Dinh Diem period," and that "he commanded the forces which relieved the siege of Diem's Palace in the 1960 coup attempt, but went along with the other generals in the successful 1963 coup." For the U.S. military's and CIA's estimates of Khanh, see CIA, *Biographic Register,* January 29, 1965; naval message (Personal) from Harkins to Admiral Felt and General Taylor, November 29, 1963; CIA Memorandum, March 20, 1964, p. vi.

34. The CIA's own apparent confusion

as to where Khanh had stood in November 1963 is suggested by its retrospective appraisal in the Office of Central Reference's *Biographic Register* of January 29, 1965, which observed: "During the suspected coup planning of August and September 1963, Khanh gave no indication of being involved in an anti-government coup plan. He reportedly regarded Ngo Dinh Nhu as the most intelligent and astute individual in Vietnam and as one who could provide the leadership that Vietnam needed. However, Khanh's name was linked with a coup group reportedly directed by Nhu [designed to preempt and compromise the leaders of the actual coup] and with one led by Tran Kim Tuyen. . . . Khanh's participation in the November 1963 coup that deposed Ngo Dinh Diem is not clear." For Khanh's awareness Minh did not trust him, see CIA, Current Intelligence Memorandum, Annex, March 20, 1964, p. iv. On Khanh's motive, see CIA, *Biographic Register,* January 29, 1965.

35. Although Tho had served as Diem's vice president, members of the new government regarded him as having acted as a moderating force against repression of the Buddhists, and Minh in particular felt he was indispensable to the effective administration of the successor government because of his knowledge of administrative and economic matters. This assessment of his stand regarding the Buddhists was consistent with that of the CIA in its "Situation Appraisal as of 14 December 1963," distributed December 16. Johnson's instructions to Lodge are from "Instruction for Oral Presentation," attached to Memorandum from McGeorge Bundy to General Clifton at LBJ Ranch in Texas for the President, December 30, 1963.

36. That the coup would not have taken place without U.S. support emerged in the author's discussions with Khanh, Don, and Dinh, and in their presentations in seminars at Cornell University as well. Regarding pertinent U.S. government documents, the Freedom of Information Act has made it possible to get some important material through the now increasingly tight mesh of constraints, even though successive administrations have refused to declassify many documents relating to Minh's ouster that were precisely identified in requests made for declassification.

37. Regarding Harkins's encouragement, Robert Shaplen, who noted that "a number of meetings between Khanh and American officers in the North [where Khanh was area commander] took place in the first two weeks of January," is undoubtedly correct in surmising that "it is very likely that they dealt partly with the new coup." (*Lost Revolution,* pp. 232–33.) Khiem, though not a member of the Dai Viet, enjoyed cordial relations with them. So important was the role of Dai Viet officers in the coup that subsequently they tended to refer to it as "their" coup. (See cable from Saigon Embassy to Department of State, June 3, 1964.) Vis-à-vis Nghiem's role, a U.S. marine-corps intelligence report noted that he had traveled to Hué on January 13 and obtained General Khanh's backing for moves against two of Minh's principal lieutenants—Tran Van Don and Ton That Dinh —as well as Tho, and then returned to Saigon, where he was in contact with Khiem and Nguyen Van Thieu, who, it notes, were "both essential to the success of the coup." ("Background on the Coup in SVN, January 30, 1964" [undated, but apparently February 1964]). On the role of Do Mau, see Shaplen, *Lost Revolution,* pp. 230–33.

38. See joint CAS [CIA] MACV message to McGeorge Bundy, January 29, 1964.

39. Lodge's January 30 cable is in *PP* (Gravel), 3:37–39.

40. Khanh's report is in joint cable CAS/MACV to White House, McGeorge Bundy, January 29, 1964. On rumors about Minh and the NLF, see Jean Lacouture, *Vietnam: Between Two Truces* (Random House, 1966), p. 132.

41. Khanh's description came in discussions with the author, and at the Cornell seminar.

42. Quotes are from cable from Harkins to Taylor, January 30, 1964. Permission for declassification of his dispatches during this crucial field trip has been denied.

43. Quotes are from Central Intelligence Agency, Intelligence Information Cable, "Subject: Background of Coup Staged by General Nguyen Khanh," Saigon, January 30, 1964. This report went on to state that on January 30 Nghia supported the coup led by Khanh, and that Lieutenant Colonel Ly Tong Ba, commander of the Sixth Armored Squadron, joined Brigadier General Lam Van Phat, commander of the Seventh Division—like Thieu's Fifth Division part of General Khiem's III Corps—in doing so.

44. Harkins's report was in cable from Harkins to Taylor, January 30, 1964.

45. Nhung was seized and promptly taken to jail, where he was found hanged—having allegedly taken his own life for fear of torture. See Tran Van Don, *Our Endless War,* pp. 112–13; Le Tu Hong, *Bon Tuong Da-lat,* p. 9.

46. Chuan's account is a translation from the Vietnamese by Mai Elliott from the moderate Catholic daily *Hoa Binh* [Saigon], July 14, 16, 1971.

47. *Ibid.,* July 20, 1971. General Chuan's conclusion regarding the centrality of the American role in these events is consistent with the accounts given me by Generals Minh, Don, and Dinh and Prime Minister Tho.

48. Khanh quote is from interview with the author, Ithaca, N. Y., June 6, 1973. For the official U.S. position, see, for instance, James Reston and Jack Raymond, *New York Times,* January 30, 31, 1964. Final quote is from *PP* (Gravel), 2:37. The other, somewhat more forthright account provided in the *Papers* states that "there is no record of an official U.S. reply" to Khanh's request of January 28 for U.S. support in staging a coup (*ibid.,* pp. 308–9), but obviously no U.S. reply could be "official," for room had to be left for "plausible denial" in case the coup effort failed to oust a government that Washington formally recognized.

There is an incongruous disparity between the *Pentagon Papers'* accounts of the coups against Diem and against Minh. In view of the issues involved, the ousting of Minh was in fact as much a watershed in the relations between Washington and Vietnam as the removal of Diem. Yet though the extent of U.S. involvement in the earlier coup is spelled out with great detail, there appears to be a deliberate effort to obscure the American role in the second. It is natural to ask whether the chroniclers in the Pentagon-commissioned study may not have been willing to have the U.S. role in the removal of Diem rather extensively described because of the Pentagon's opposition to it, whereas the clear involvement of the U.S. military mission in the overthrow of Minh made them reluctant to disclose details of this part of the record.

49. That as late as January 25 Lodge had no inkling of plans for the coup is suggested by his cable of that date to President Johnson, asking that he send Minh "a message of congratulations" on "the progress achieved so far." (Department of State cable from Lodge to Harriman, January 25, 1964.) A knowledgeable French source states that it is the generally accepted thesis that Lodge was presented with a *"fait accompli."* (Chaffard, *Les Deux Guerres du Vietnam: De Valluy à Westmoreland* [La Table Ronde, 1969], p. 351, n. 2.) Lodge himself, in a cable to Washington a few days after the coup, stated, "General Khanh's coup was extremely disconcerting at first blush." (*PP* [Gravel], 3:38.) Very soon after the event, the ambassador of a major U.S.-aligned power found the usually well informed Lodge to be surprisingly ignorant about the character and views of General Khanh. According to Harkins, Lodge did not inform Washington that the coup was to be executed until about forty-five minutes beforehand. (Cable from Harkins to Taylor, January 30, 1964.)

50. Outgoing telegram, Department of State, 7:47 P.M., January 29, 1964. (With Saigon twelve hours ahead of Washington time, this presumably reached the embassy around 8:00 A.M. on the 30th.)

51. In the scant coverage of the coup provided by the Department of Defense in the *Pentagon Papers,* there appears to be an

effort to shift any suspicions of U.S. involvement from Harkins to Lodge. The ambassador is portrayed as the American most privy to the coup plotters' plans and as the person who conveys news of the coup from Wilson to Harkins, even though Wilson in fact reported directly to the general, who, after all, was his immediate superior.

52. Situation report is in CIA cable from Saigon prepared at 0725 A.M., January 30, NSF, Vietnam, vol. 3. Harkins quote is from his Cable to Taylor, January 30, 1964.

VIII. The Rise and Decline of General Khanh

1. Cable from Lodge to Secretary of State, January 31, 1964, NSF, Vietnam, vol. 3.

2. Khanh's statements on the United States are in cables from Lodge to Secretary of State, January 31, February 4, 1964. Rusk cable was to Amembassy Saigon, February 1, 1964. Johnson's note is in White House Central Files, CO 312.

3. For a list of new MRC members, see *Vietnam Press,* February 5, 1964. The Dai Viet was split into southern, central, and northern factions, which rarely cooperated. A contemporary CIA assessment aptly observed that it was "not now an organized political party, and never has been more than a factional coalition of individual politicians holding vaguely similar political goals and banded together for mutual advantage. At least since 1955, in fact, there has been no centralized party structure. A number of quarreling factions headed by individual aspirants for political power have claimed the party label, but otherwise have had little in common beyond opposition to the Ngo Dinh Diem regime." (Annex, CIA Memorandum, "The Situation in South Vietnam," February 28, 1964.) Hoan, who had actually been promised the premiership, a position Khanh himself took, was furious at his demotion, and as early as February 25 was reported to be intriguing against Khanh. See

CIA Intelligence Information Cable, from Saigon, February 29, 1964.

4. "Young Turks" is in CIA Intelligence Memorandum, October 8, 1964; see also Le Tu Hung, *Bon Tuong Da-lat* [*The Four Dalat Generals*] (Saigon: Dong Nai, 1971), p. 26; *New York Times,* February 14, 1964. Khanh's description of Minh is in Cable from Lodge to Secretary of State, February 7, 1964.

5. Cable from Lodge to Secretary of State, February 27, 1964.

6. Memorandum for the President from Secretary of Defense, March 16, 1964.

7. On Khanh's cooperation with the U.S. military, see cables from Westmoreland to JCS, June 25, 1964; Taylor to State, July 27, 1964. Peter Grose quote is in *New York Times,* September 4, 1964, p. 8. On Khanh's reaction to Lodge's replacement, see *PP* (Gravel), 2:327. At approximately the same time, Westmoreland replaced General Harkins, for whom he had been serving as deputy.

8. "Designed to result" quote is in *PP* (Gravel), 3:150. Low success and high casualty rates are discussed in Memorandum for the President from McG. B.[undy], "Air Drops on North Vietnam," July 24, 1964. On the mobilization decrees, see cable from Rusk to Amembassy Saigon, April 4, 1964. Khanh later, however, dragged his feet, and never actually implemented the decrees. (*PP* [Gravel], 2:316.) Johnson's request is in *ibid.,* p. 317. "We Vietnamese" quote and Lodge's response are in cables from Lodge to President, April 30, May 1, 1964.

9. "In our effort" quote is from cable from Department of State to American Embassy, Saigon, April 28, 1964. Increased figures are in *PP* (Gravel), 3:72; cable from State to American Embassy Saigon, July 21, 1964; figure for aid is in Peter Grose, "Crisis in Vietnam: How it Developed," *New York Times,* September 4, 1964.

10. On U.S. efforts to discourage coup planning, see, for instance, the instructions in the cable from Rusk to Amembassy Saigon of March 18, 1964. "Neutralist flavor" quote is from Department of Defense (ISA)

Draft Memorandum for the President, March 5, 1964. The first indication (or rumor) of a coup came on February 7, when the CIA suboffice in Hué reported alleged plans for a neutralist coup in the First Corps area on February 10. U.S. officials promptly informed Khanh, who then was reported to be taking "appropriate action." (Cable from CIA Saigon to CIA Washington, February 7, 1964.) Whether or not such a coup was actually planned at this time, this report was used by General Khanh to replace Colonel Phong as commander of the First Division by Colonel Nguyen Chanh Thi. (Cable from Heble [U.S. consul in Hué] to Dept. of State, February 8, 1964.)

11. Lodge's advice to Khanh is in cable from Lodge to Department of State, March 26, 1964. Lodge's advice to the USIA is in Memorandum for the President from Carl T. Rowan, United States Information Agency, June 4, 1964. Rowan quotes are in *ibid*.

12. All quotes are from Memorandum for the President from Secretary of Defense, March 16, 1964. (See also the March 13 draft for some additional data.) Almost all of the points in these memoranda noted above can be found in *PP* (Gravel), 2:311–14.

13. McCone's suggestions are to be found in a page-long footnote to the March 13 draft of McNamara's March 16 Memorandum. "Several hundred" and "third largest" quotes are from cable from CIA Taipei to Department of State, July 7, 1964.

14. Quotes are from *PP* (Gravel), 3:78.

15. Cablegram from Johnson to Lodge, March 20, 1964, in *PP (NYT)*, p. 285.

16. Lodge, who had pressed for action against North Vietnam since at least October 30, 1963, again urged this course in a cable to the president on February 20, 1964. Shortly before submitting his March 16 report, McNamara had attended a meeting with the JCS in which these military leaders had pressed with "vehemence" for "strong overt U.S. actions against the North." (Memorandum from Michael Forrestal to McGeorge Bundy, March 18, 1964.)
In the JCS recommendation made on

May 11, 1961, these military chiefs stated that, if Southeast Asia was to be held "outside the Communist sphere," it would be necessary to deploy U.S. forces "immediately" to South Vietnam. (Cable from JCS to CINCPAC, May 11, 1961.) This view was brought into greater focus on January 22, 1964, with a JCS memorandum calling for "aerial bombing of key North Viet-Nam targets, using U.S. resources under Vietnamese cover," and for the commitment of "U.S. forces as necessary" both "in direct actions against North Viet-Nam" and "in support of the combat action within South Vietnam." (Memorandum from JCS for Secretary of Defense, "Re: Vietnam and Southeast Asia," January 22, 1964, in *PP* [Gravel], 3:-498. Later clarification of Khanh's views disclosed that what he had had in mind after achieving rear-area security was "reprisal tit-for-tat bombing" rather than a massive sustained bombing campaign or the use of land forces against the North. (Cable from Taylor to Department of State, July 27, 1964.)

17. On the NSC meeting, see National Security Action Memorandum No. 288, March 17, 1964. Johnson quote is from his cablegram to Lodge, March 20, 1964, in *PP* (Gravel), 2:314. The full text of this cable can be found in Gareth Porter, *Vietnam: The Definitive Documentation of Human Decisions,* 2 vols. (Coleman Enterprises, 1979), 2:261.

18. Quotes are from cable from William P. Bundy to Ambassador Lodge, April 4, 1964, p. 5. This important cable, for which I originally requested declassification in 1976, was only released, after a long appeal procedure, in 1983. Bundy had been deputy assistant secretary of defense at the beginning of the Kennedy administration and had been nominated assistant secretary by Kennedy shortly before the president died, a promotion Johnson approved.

19. McNamara's talks with Lodge and Harkins are discussed in *ibid.,* p. 1; see also William P. Bundy, Oral History, tape I, p. 16, LBJ Library.

20. Wheeler and Khanh's meeting is re-

ported in *PP* (Gravel), 3:64. "War footing" is in Memorandum for Secretary [of State], apparently from Michael Forrestal, May 4, 1964. Comparison to Lincoln is in *PP* (Gravel), 3:66; *PP (NYT)*, p. 246. Lodge quote is from cable to Secretary of State, May 4, 1964.

21. Quotes on McNamara's position are from Talking Paper for the Secretary of Defense, from Benjamin Read for McGeorge Bundy ("For Information") (Nodis), May 7, 1964, pp. 2, 4, 6. NSC quote is from Summary Record of National Security Council Meeting, No. 532, May 15, 1964, p. 5.

22. Rusk's advice to Lodge is from cable, May 5, 1964. The final quote is from cable from Rusk to Lodge, May 21, 1964.

23. Bundy quote is in *PP* (Gravel), 2:-319.

24. For Khanh on attacking the North, see *ibid.*, 3:72. All quotes are in *ibid.*, 2:-321–22.

25. For Honolulu meeting, see *ibid.*, 3:-172–73. For quote from Pentagon analyst, see *PP* (GPO), 3 (IV, C.1):83, and *PP* (Gravel), 3:77.

26. On preparing American public opinion, see *PP* (Gravel), 2:325, 291. Regarding Lodge's militancy, Michael Forrestal, a White House aide, observed on April 28 that "almost any of the actions suggested by Lodge . . . could start a chain of escalation for which we are not yet prepared." (Memorandum for Mr. Bundy, "Vietnam," April 28, 1964.) Lodge was opposed to keeping Khanh in the dark about plans for introducing a congressional resolution, and urged he be informed, stating that this would "give him a shot in the arm." (Cable from Lodge to State, June 13, 1964.) Quotes are from cable from Lodge to State, June 12, 1964.

27. Quotes are from Wallace J. Thies, *When Governments Collide: Coercion and Diplomacy in the Vietnam Conflict, 1964–1968* (University of California Press, 1980), pp. 36–37, 40.

28. *Ibid.*, pp. 37–38.

29. For JCS and Pentagon innuendos, see Memorandum from Michael Forrestal for Mr. Bundy, "Vietnam," March 18, 1964;

see also Forrestal's memorandum for him, "Vietnam Planning," April 16, 1964. For some of Goldwater's statements on Vietnam, see Theodore H. White, *The Making of the President 1964* (Atheneum, 1965), pp. 106, 325.

30. Bundy's list of possible candidates to succeed Lodge included Sargent Shriver, Roswell Gilpatric, Robert McNamara, Robert F. Kennedy, and William Gaud. Except for Gaud (strongly supported but characterized as being "at the next level down in the Administration"), he evaluated the other candidates in terms unlikely to enhance their prospects. He reported McNamara as having "gone a little stale" and having "rather mechanized the problem [Vietnam] so that he misses some of its real political flavor." (Memorandum for the President from McGeorge Bundy, "Subject: Possible Successor to Lodge," June 6, 1964.) Bundy has informed me that he didn't really want the position, but felt it his duty to offer himself. Johnson's preoccupation with keeping the JCS aboard was stressed in discussions with me by James Thomson, a White House aide who devoted much of his time to Vietnam in this period, and was emphasized by Anthony Eden in a talk with me immediately after he had visited Lyndon Johnson in 1968. (Eden, feeling that in the democratic system the military should be depended upon to follow policies set by the civilian leadership, remarked, "Winston and I would have never let the military interfere in policy the way President Johnson has.")

31. On Khanh's concurrence with Ky's statement, see CIA Intelligence Information Cable, "Prime Minister Nguyen Khanh's Plan to Involve the United States in North Vietnam," July 24, 1964. The sabotage missions had recently been increased, eight covert teams having been parachuted in since April. In a Memorandum to the President, July 24, 1964, McGeorge Bundy described these as having been "only moderately successful" and with high casualty rates. Ky is quoted by Peter Grose in *New York Times*, July 20, 23, 1964.

32. Taylor's protest is in *PP* (Gravel),

2:328; he had presented his diplomatic credentials on July 8. Khanh's response is quoted by Peter Grose in *New York Times,* July 24, 26, 1964.

33. Taylor's plea and the quote about him are in *PP* (Gravel), 2:328.

34. For U Thant's proposal and the international response, see *New York Times,* July 9, 1964; "President de Gaulle Holds Tenth Press Conference," Ambassade de France, Service de Presse et d'Information (New York), No. 208, July 23, 1964, p. 11; Hanoi Radio, July 24, 28, 29, 1964; Moscow Radio, July 26, 1964, as quoted in *Documents Relating to British Involvement in the Indo-China Conflict 1945–1965,* Command 2834 (Her Majesty's Stationery Office, 1965), p. 239; Peking Radio, August 2, 1964. See also *Peking Review,* VII, No. 32 (August 7, 1964): 22.

35. Johnson's and Khanh's statements are in *New York Times,* July 25, 1964. Military mission figures are in *ibid.,* July 28, 1964.

36. As early as February 29, 1964, a CIA cable from Saigon had reported that "Dai Viet leaders are planning to increase their power within the government with the ultimate objective of replacing Major General Khanh." "The full enlistment" quote is from Memorandum by Dean Rusk, "Summary of Additional Steps in South Vietnam," April 20, 1964.

37. Rusk quote is from outgoing telegram, Department of State, July 25, 1964.

38. Rusk quotes are from cable to Taylor, July 25, 1964.

39. State Department quote is from one of the authors of the *Pentagon Papers* and may not be verbatim. (*PP* [Gravel], 2:329.) "State of emergency" is from cable from Taylor to Department of State, July 27, 1964.

40. See Memorandum for Discussion [Draft], June 10, 1964, "Alternative Public Positions for U.S. on Southeast Asia for the Period July 1–November 15." See also Agenda for 5:30 Meeting, June 10 [1964], The White House, NSF, Country File, Vietnam, vol. 11, Memos. For memo prepared at June 10 meeting, see *PP* (GPO), 3 (IV, C.1):82–84.

41. Quotes are from *PP* (GPO), 3 (IV, C.1): 84.

42. Forrestal quote is from his Memorandum to Bundy, June 15, 1964. William Bundy quote is in Porter, *Vietnam: Definitive Documentation,* 2:285–87.

43. Instructions for June 15 meeting are in *PP* (Gravel), 3:181; Chester L. Cooper, *The Lost Crusade: America in Vietnam* (Dodd, Mead, 1970), p. 235.

44. Rusk quotes are from Memorandum for the President, "Legal Basis for Sending American Forces to Vietnam," June 29, 1964. (This bore the notation "This memorandum has been reviewed in the Department of Justice and approved by Mr. Schlei, Assistant Attorney General in charge of the Office of Legal Counsel.")

45. Particularly revealing is a cable from Department of State for Ambassador Taylor, September 12, 1964, in response to his request for a record of his testimony in executive session before the Senate Foreign Relations Committee, which was finally released in September 1979. See also Rusk's August 3, 1964, cable to Taylor acknowledging that he believed the North Vietnamese attack of the day before was "directly related to their effort to resist" these OPLAN 34-A activities. This cable is available in Porter, *Vietnam: Definitive Documentation,* 2:301–2. On the air strikes, see NMCC Operational Survey: Corigendum, August 6, 1964. Two U.S. planes were lost in the operation. According to William Bundy, the drafters of the Tonkin Gulf Resolution had available "the text [of the draft resolution] that had been fiddled with in May and June." (William P. Bundy, Oral History, May 26, 1969, tape 1, p. 28.)

46. In the opinion of the general counsel of the Department of Defense, the debate in the Senate preceding passage of the resolution revealed "quite clearly the understanding of both proponents and opponents" that the resolution granted the president "advance authority to take whatever action he may deem necessary regarding the [*sic*] South Vietnam and its defense." (Memoran-

dum from L. Niederlehner for Honorable Cyrus Vance, June 10, 1965.)

47. For the most comprehensive accounts of the Tonkin Gulf episode and the controversy surrounding it, see Anthony Austin, *The President's War* (Lippincott, 1971); Joseph C. Goulden, *Truth Is the First Casualty* (Rand McNally, 1969); and Eugene Windchy, *Tonkin Gulf* (Doubleday, 1971). Subsequent to the publication of these books, a considerable body of relevant, previously classified documents have been made available through the LBJ Library, but as of 1985 many of the most important still have not. An excellent recent reconstruction, drawing on most of the most pertinent documents that have been released, appeared in the July 23, 1984, issue of *U.S. News and World Report,* pp. 56–67, under the title "The Phantom Battle That Led to War."

48. U.S. Congress, Senate, Committee on Foreign Relations, "The Gulf of Tonkin, the 1964 Incidents," Hearings, 90th Cong., 2nd Sess., February 20, 1968 (U.S. Government Printing Office). Unless otherwise indicated, the account of the hearings is drawn from this. With respect to the hearings' mention of the psychiatric-ward episode, Goulden (p. 204), cited in n. 47, establishes that the commander remained there about four weeks.

49. The fullest coverage of these intercepts is in "Phantom Battle."

50. Stockdale amplifies this Washington *Post* account in his subsequently published book co-authored with his wife, Sybil Stockdale, *In Love and War* (Harper and Row, 1984), pp. 3–36.

51. Summary Notes of 538th NSC Meeting, August 4, 1964, by Bromley Smith. Material in brackets is drawn from Senate, "Gulf of Tonkin, the 1964 Incidents."

52. Quote is from *New York Times,* August 5, 1964.

53. Eric F. Goldman, *The Tragedy of Lyndon Johnson* (Alfred A. Knopf, 1969), pp. 235–37.

54. For Taylor's views on Khanh's position, see cable from Taylor to State, September 2, 1964.

55. "All but absolute power" is from CIA, Weekly Report, "The Situation in South Vietnam," August 13, 1964; a CIA assessment of August 20, 1964, qualified this conclusion: "Under a semblance of democratic framework, Khanh has broad powers as president, but his power is not absolute. His actions may still be vetoed by the MRC, which at present stands behind him." (CIA, Weekly Report, "The Situation in South Vietnam," August 20, 1964.) Peter Grose report is from *New York Times,* August 28, 1964. Taylor cabled the State Department that it had been Khanh's "purpose to use the galvanizing force" of the Tonkin incident "to narrow the base of his government, give him more flexibility and make his political/military efforts more effective," but that he had "succeeded only in the partial elimination of General Minh, the dissolution of the MRC and the disaffection of the Dai Viets." (Cable from Taylor to State, September 1, 1964.) On Khanh's new post, see cable from Taylor to State, August 12, 1964; *New York Times,* August 17, 1964. On August 20, President Johnson, on the suggestion of his advisers, cabled Khanh his "congratulations and warm best wishes" on his "assumption of office as President." (Cable from Rusk to Amembassy, Saigon, August 20, 1964.) On U.S. recommendations for Khanh, see cables from Rusk to Amembassy Saigon, August 11, 1964; from Taylor to Secretary of State, August 12, 1964.

56. On the protests, see *New York Times,* August 20, 22, 24, 1964. One Vietnamese account characterized these demonstrations as the biggest since the coup against Diem. (Le Tu Hung, *Bon Tuong Dalat,* p. 33.)

57. On Dai Viet officers involved in the early stages of this coup plotting, see CIA Weekly Report, "The Situation in South Vietnam," August 5, 1964, p. 2. For the Buddhist demands and Khanh's consultations with Taylor and Johnson and quote see *PP* (Gravel), 3:86; see also 2:334.

58. CIA Intelligence Information Cable, Saigon, August 25, 1964 [sanitized]; *PP* (Gravel), 3:86; 2:334.

59. The Buddhists' demands were that

Khanh's ill-starred August 16 constitution be rescinded; that he relinquish his briefly occupied position of president; that the MRC dissolve itself, but before doing so appoint a temporary chief of state, who at the end of a year was to step down in favor of a successor chosen by popular election. Westmoreland quotes are from "Résumé of Questions and Answers Telecon with General Westmoreland," August 25, 1964, p. 2; plus addendum. CIA quotes are from CIA, Weekly Reports, "The Situation in South Vietnam," August 20, 27, 1964; and CIA, Office of Current Intelligence, "The Situation in South Vietnam," August 25, 1964.

60. Taylor and Westmoreland's recommendations are in incoming message from COMUSMACV (Westmoreland) for JCS August 25, 1964. On Westmoreland's reassurance of Khanh, see PP (Gravel), 3:86; 2:335. Taylor quote is from cable to Secretary of State ("Pass Exclusively to McGeorge Bundy"), February 3, 1965.

61. CIA, Weekly Report, "The Situation in Vietnam," August 13, 1964, p. 3.

62. On MRC's indecision, see ibid. Though it was stated publicly that the three members of the "troika" were to share power equally, Taylor made it clear to them that the United States strongly favored Khanh's remaining as head of government. (Cable from Rusk to Lodge, August 26, 1964.) On continuing splits in the military, see PP (Gravel), 2:334–35; 3:86–87. "More window dressing" quote is from cable from Taylor to State, September 2, 1964, sec. 2. For Taylor's cautions to Khanh, see PP (Gravel), 2:335. Taylor-to-Washington quote is from cable from Taylor to State, September 2, 1964, sec. 2.

63. Cable from Taylor to State, September 2, 1964, sec. 2.

64. CIA, Intelligence and Reporting Subcommittee of the Interagency Vietnam Coordinating Committee, Weekly Report, "The Situation in Vietnam," August 27, 1964.

65. Pham Ngoc Thao was one of the very few former Vietminh officers to join Diem. As a Catholic and a man of considerable intelligence, he gained Diem's confidence and was appointed head of Kien Hoa Province where he became famous because of his success in pacifying most of the province— or at least appearing to do so (some alleged that he simply arrived at a "live-and-let-live" arrangement with the local NLF). He joined Tran Kim Tuyen in plotting a coup against Diem in September 1963 and, when Tuyen was fired, joined the coup group led by Minh and Don. They promoted him to colonel following Diem's overthrow. Despite his close relationship with some Catholic officers, others in the military suspected him of being a Viet Cong agent. He was close to Khiem and, when Khanh exiled that general to Washington, followed him there as press attaché. After a second and more successful coup against Khanh in February 1965, he went into hiding and was later discovered and shot on July 16, 1965. (Further biographical data can be found in Le Tu Hung, Nhung cai chet trong cach mang 1-11-63 [The Deaths in the November 1, 1963, Revolution] [Saigon: Dinh Minh Ngoc, 1971], pp. 125–31, 142–43, 160–64; CIA, Office of Current Intelligence, Intelligence Memorandum, February 20, 1965, "Colonel Pham Ngoc Thao." According to the latter report, Thao's close acquaintance with Diem's brother Archbishop Ngo Dinh Thuc had made him acceptable to Diem, even though one of his own brothers was a high official in Hanoi.) On the headed-off Dai Viet coup, see cable from Taylor to State, September 2, 1964; PP (Gravel), 3:87. The immediate background to this plot is described in a CIA report of September 1, 1964, "The Loyalties of the Armed Forces Commanders and the Possibility of Success If a Coup d'Etat Is Attempted: Situation Appraisal as of 31 August 1964." This report saw Colonel Pham Ngoc Thao as masterminding the planning. On rehabilitating the Dalat generals, see Le Tu Hung, Bon Tuong Da-lat, pp. 108–10. The author states that Nguyen Chanh Thi "was determined to overthrow Khanh if he brought the four generals back to Saigon," and that both Ky and Thi wanted to keep them in Dalat indefinitely. On Khanh's announcement, see CIA, Infor-

mation Cable, September 9, 1964, "Appointments to the Interim Government and Scheduled Departure from South Vietnam of Several Generals"; cable from Taylor to State, September 6, 1964; Memo from Thomas L. Hughes, Director of Intelligence and Research, Dept. of State, to Secretary, "Prospects for an Imminent Coup in Saigon," September 4, 1964; cable from Alexis Johnson to State, September 8, 1964. See also Le Tu Hung, *Bon Tuong Da-lat,* p. 70.

66. On the September 13 coup, see CIA, SNIE 53–64, "Chances for a Stable Government in South Vietnam," September 8, 1964. One Vietnamese school of thought, to which, for example, General Tran Van Don subscribes, holds that Khanh himself provoked and indirectly encouraged the coup so as to expose his chief enemies, especially Khiem, and thus have an excuse to oust them and also to rally American support for himself. In any event, Khanh was soon afterward able to win U.S. support for exiling General Khiem to the post of Saigon's Ambassador to Washington. An early embassy report on the ongoing coup attempt stated, "Generals Khiem, Thieu, and Lam seem so passive that they appear to have been either tacitly supporting or associated with this move by Duc and Phat." (Cable from Deputy Ambassador Alexis Johnson, September 13, 1964.) In an interview with the moderate Catholic newspaper *Hoa Binh* (January 29, 1972), General Huynh Van Cao later recounted that Khiem had invited him to join the coup effort, and he had refused, chiding Khiem, "You're part of the 'Troika' now; if you want to carry out a coup d'état, won't you be overthrowing yourself?," and then pointed out that the United States, being in the midst of a presidential election, would not want to have the boat rocked. On Saigon Radio announcement, see CIA report from Saigon, "The Situation in South Vietnam," September 10–16, 1964; cable from Westmoreland to JCS, September 13, 1964.

67. "Counter plan" is in Cable from COMUSMACV (Westmoreland) to Department of Defense, September 13, 1964. "In position" quote is from cable from JCS to MACV, September 13, 1964. Khanh states that he was initially unsure as to whether he still had full U.S. backing and asked for the "Voice of America" broadcast both to test this and to undercut support that some officers might otherwise have given to the coup attempt. (Interviews with the author, Ithaca, N.Y., December 6–7, 1973.) A running account of the efforts of the U.S. military advisers is provided in a series of cables from Westmoreland to the Department of Defense on September 13. Westmoreland quote is from incoming message to Department of Defense, September 13, 1964. Regarding the coup leaders' underestimation of U.S. support for Khanh, General Phat later maintained at his trial that he and General Duc had met with Alexis Johnson ten hours after the start of the coup attempt and had been given what they understood was his tacit approval. (*New York Times,* October 16, 1964.) If at that stage they did receive such an impression, it was clearly mistaken.

68. A CIA post-mortem on the coup noted that both Khiem and Thieu "issued expressions of firm support for Khanh somewhat belatedly, as did the commanders of II and III Corps," and concluded, "Potential fence-sitters among the military rallied to Khanh's support when it became clear that Ky was prepared to resist the coup militarily and that the U.S. would not sanction Khanh's overthrow." (CIA, "The Situation in South Vietnam," September 10–16, 1964.) On Ky and Thi, see cable from Alexis Johnson in response to queries from Rusk *et al.,* September 13, 1964, pp. 8, 13. According to Professor Cao Huy Thuan, himself an influential Buddhist leader, Ky and Thi discussed their plans for supporting the coup in his presence in Danang a few days before it took place. (Interview with the author, Ithaca, N.Y., October 29, 1974.) The speculation concerning Ky and Thi is one of the possibilities Robert Shaplen perceived in his *The Lost Revolution* (Harper and Row, 1965), p. 289. There he also observes, "It was later learned that a number of Americans had been aware that the coup was in the works the day before it took place and had

played an odd catalytic role, cancelling each other out."

69. On Khiem's appointment as ambassador, see *PP* (Gravel), 2:339. For conclusion that Minh had to go, see *PP* (Gravel), 2:340–41.

70. On the Young Turks' enhanced status, see CIA, Intelligence Memorandum, "The Young Generals' Group in South Vietnam," October 8, 1964. Khanh had announced his intention to restore the Dalat generals to office shortly before the September 13 coup attempt, and the Young Turks had remained opposed.

71. General Minh, on behalf of the transitional "troika" administration, had actually appointed most of this council shortly before the September 13 coup.

72. Quotes are from CIA cable to White House and Defense Intelligence Agency, August 25, 1964. A CIA Intelligence Memorandum of the same date concluded, "The confused situation is extremely vulnerable to exploitation by the Communists and by proponents of a negotiated settlement." (CIA, Office of Current Intelligence Memorandum, "The Situation in South Vietnam," August 25, 1964.)

73. Quotes are from CIA, SNIE 53-64, "Chances for a Stable Government in Vietnam," September 8, 1964. The next day's report is CIA, Information Cable, September 9, 1964, "Appointments to the Interim Government and Scheduled Departure from South Vietnam of Several Generals."

74. The U.S. concern with Khanh's reliance on the Buddhists was spelled out as early as August 25 by Westmoreland in Department of Defense, "Additional Question and Answer Telecon with General Westmoreland." Quotes are from CIA Memorandum, "Tri Quang and the Buddhist-Catholic Discord in South Vietnam," September 19, 1964. That this conclusion as to the Buddhists' ultimate intentions was correct was substantiated in my talks with Tri Quang and his top lieutenant, Thich Thien Minh, in Saigon several years later.

75. Cable from COMUSMACV (Westmoreland) to RUHL HQ/CINCPAC,

November 26, 1964; see also *PP* (Gravel), 2:342.

IX. Escalation and Political Viability

1. For Joint Chiefs' recommendations and criticism of Taylor, see cable from Taylor to State, August 18, 1964, in *PP* (Gravel), 3:545–48, 550–52. Taylor, who was still chairman of the JCS on June 2, had not endorsed the position taken by the other members of that body.

2. Memorandum for the President from McGeorge Bundy, August 31, 1964.

3. Quotes are in *PP* (Gravel), 2:335–36.

4. *Ibid.*, p. 336.

5. Memorandum for the Record by McGeorge Bundy, "Meeting on South Vietnam, 9 September, 1964, 11:00 A.M., Cabinet Room," September 14, 1964.

6. Johnson's caution conformed to the consensus arrived at by Taylor, Rusk, McNamara, and Wheeler in a Memorandum to the President of September 8, where they recommended, "We should be *prepared* to respond on a tit-for-tat basis against the DRV in the event of any attack on U.S. units or any *special* DRV/VC action against South Vietnam." (*PP* [Gravel], 3:562.) Quotes are from National Security Action Memorandum, No. 314, September 10, 1964, in *PP* (Gravel), 3:565–66. (Emphasis added.)

7. On the JCS push for reprisal strikes, see *PP* (Gravel), 3:194–95. For Johnson's reaction to the alleged September 18 Gulf of Tonkin attack, see Memorandum for the Record by McGeorge Bundy, "The Gulf of Tonkin Incident, September 18," September 20, 1964. As is often the case when Bundy prepared such memoranda, it is difficult to ascertain where he himself stood on the question. On the Bien Hoa attack, see cable from COMUSMACV to Rusk, November 1, 1964. Four U.S. military were killed and approximately twenty others wounded in the attack against the Bien Hoa air base. Ten planes were destroyed and eight damaged.

8. James C. Thomson, Jr., "How Could Vietnam Happen?," *Atlantic Monthly,* April 1968, pp. 52–53.

9. As William Bundy observed, "There are plenty of papers in the '64 period that say 'We have got to be in a stronger position before we can have any realistic hope of negotiations.' " (Oral History, tape 2, May 29, 1969, p. 23, LBJ Library.) Paul Warnke quote is from "The Search for Peace," in *The Vietnam Legacy,* ed. Anthony Lake (New York University Press, 1976), p. 319.

10. Ball's opinions emerged in discussion with the author, Princeton, N.J., January 16, 1985.

11. The full text of Ball's 1964 memorandum and an account of the circumstances surrounding it can be found in "A Light That Failed," *Atlantic Monthly,* July 1972, pp. 33–49.

12. On U Thant's August 6 meeting see Memorandum of Conversation Between Adlai E. Stevenson and U Thant, February 16, 1965; Wallace J. Thies, *When Governments Collide: Coercion and Diplomacy in the Vietnam Conflict, 1964–1968* (University of California Press, 1980), p. 48; William Bundy, unpublished Vietnam study, 1972, ch. 22, p. 17. See also n. 14 below.

13. On Moscow and Hanoi's response and Johnson's not being informed, see Philip L. Geyelin, *Lyndon B. Johnson and the World* (Praeger, 1966), p. 204; Mario Rossi, "U Thant and Vietnam: The Untold Story," *New York Review of Books,* November 17, 1966, p. 8; David Kraslow and Stuart H. Loory, *The Secret Search for Peace in Vietnam* (Random House, 1968), pp. 103, 106–8; John Bartlow Martin, *Adlai Stevenson and the World: The Life of Adlai Stevenson* (Doubleday, 1977), p. 830. For Thomson and Bundy, see William Bundy, M.I.T. Study Group, Adam Yarmolinsky Papers, John F. Kennedy Library; Bundy, Oral History, tape 1, p. 40.

14. This account is based primarily on a draft report prepared by the State Department in early November 1965 at President Johnson's request, "to reconstruct events [some of which Johnson appeared to have just been informed about] re. [the Secretary General's] 1964 suggestion that US and DRV meet in Rangoon to discuss peace in Vietnam," embodied in an urgent cable of November 10 sent by Ball to Rusk (then in Rio de Janeiro) requesting his "comments or modifications" on a three-and-a-half-page chronology running from August 1964 to March 10, 1965; and two other documents: Memorandum of Conversation Between Adlai Stevenson and U Thant, February 16, 1965, and Memorandum from Harlan Cleveland to Dean Rusk, Secy. of State, and George Ball, Under Secy., February 17, 1965. William Bundy's substantial account in his unpublished Vietnam manuscript is largely consistent with these documents, as is Eric Sevareid's less comprehensive "The Final Troubled Hours of Adlai Stevenson," *Look Magazine,* November 30, 1965. For further corroborative evidence of various aspects of these accounts, see Geyelin, *Lyndon B. Johnson,* p. 208; Kraslow and Loory, *Secret Search for Peace,* pp. 101, 108; Rossi, "U Thant and Vietnam," p. 8; Richard Walton, *The Remnants of Power: The Tragic Last Years of Adlai Stevenson* (Coward-McCann, 1968), pp. 141–42; U.S. Senate, Committee on Foreign Relations, *A Conversation with U Thant, Secretary General of the United Nations,* March 22, 1967 (U.S. Government Printing Office, 1972), p. 3; Norman Cousins, "How U.S. Spurned Three Chances for Peace in Vietnam," *Look Magazine,* July 29, 1969, p. 46; Martin, *Adlai Stevenson,* p. 830; *The Papers of Adlai E. Stevenson,* vol. VIII, *Ambassador to the United Nations, 1961–1965,* ed. Walter Johnson et al. (Little, Brown, 1979), pp. 664, 666.

15. On U Thant's proposal, see *New York Times,* February 25 and 26, 1965.

16. United Nations Press Service, n. 3075, February 24, 1965.

17. Officials' public denials are in *New York Times,* February 25, 26, 1975. For Stevenson's private communication with U Thant, see Memorandum of Conversation, February 27, 1965.

18. Editorial is from *New York Times,* November 17, 1965.

19. Robert Gallucci quote is from *Neither Peace nor Honor: The Politics of American Military Policy in Viet Nam* (Johns Hopkins Press, 1975), p. 44.

20. Thomson, "How Could Vietnam Happen," p. 52. See *PP* (Gravel), 3:111; see also *PP (NYT)*, p. 324; Gallucci, *Neither Peace nor Honor*, p. 42.

21. On the fear of China's involvement, see Bundy, Oral History, tape 5, May 29, 1964, pp. 9–11, 21–22. As Bundy here notes, there was also concern that this would induce an adverse Soviet reaction. U.S. military assessments credited Hanoi with the capability of sending two infantry divisions to attack across the Demilitarized Zone (at the seventeenth parallel) within just forty-eight hours after initiation of a U.S. air strike against the North, while concurrently moving into southern Laos with "two infantry divisions and two infantry brigades, supported by one tank regiment and eight artillery regiments." (William P. Bundy, Draft, "Likely Developments and Problems If the Communist Side Engaged in Major Retaliation at Some Point," November 13, 1963, p. 4.) Taylor quotes are in Memorandum for the President from Robert S. McNamara, April 21, 1965.

22. The first meeting of this NSC Working Group was on November 3. It included William Bundy, John McNaughton, and representatives from the JCS and CIA. On the role of the JCS representative and his differences with the other members, and for the Bundy/McNaughton view on the sources of Communist strength in the South, see *PP* (Gravel), 3:113–14, 656. For Taylor quotes, see Memorandum for the President from McGeorge Bundy, August 31, 1964. For the views on ground forces, see *PP* (Gravel), 3:239.

23. Following a negative reaction from the majority of Johnson's senior advisers when they discussed this draft on November 24, the quote "probably . . . Vietnam" was excised from the draft of November 26, which was presented to Taylor and then the president.

24. Quotes are from Revised Draft 11/

21/64, as amended 11/26/64, W. P. Bundy/J. McNaughton, "Courses of Action in Southeast Asia," in *PP* (Gravel), 3:656–66.

25. *Ibid.,* pp. 114–15, 661; see also p. 664.

26. See Memorandum for Secretary Rusk, Secretary McNamara, Mr. McCone, General Wheeler, Mr. Ball, Mr. McGeorge Bundy, "Issues Raised by Papers on Southeast Asia," November 24, 1964, from William Bundy. Bundy's caption is from Memorandum of Executive Meeting, November 24, 1964, November 25, 1964. It should be noted that the *Pentagon Papers'* treatment of this important memorandum is not fully accurate. See especially *PP* (Gravel), 3:237, 239.

27. The full text of Taylor's November 27 briefing is in *PP* (Gravel), 3:666–73.

28. The memorandum issuing from this meeting can be found in *PP* (Gravel), 3:-674–76. The group included the same participants as on November 24–25, with the addition of Michael Forrestal and John McNaughton.

29. Memorandum for the President from McGeorge Bundy, "Courses of Action in Southeast Asia," November 28, 1964.

30. On the conditions for negotiation, see *PP (NYT)*, p. 324; Gallucci, *Neither Peace Nor Honor*, p. 42. Thomson quote is from "How Could Vietnam Happen?," p. 52; see also *PP* (Gravel), 3:111–12. Johnson quote is from Oral History, p. 22.

31. McNaughton's handwritten notes for this meeting indicate that he, the president, the vice president, Rusk, McGeorge Bundy, William Bundy, McNamara, McCone, Taylor, and Wheeler participated.

32. On chroniclers' awareness of their lack of documents, see *PP* (Gravel), 3:248. Quotes are from *ibid.,* p. 251. See "Position Paper on Southeast Asia, December 2, 1964" (White House Letterhead), National Security Files; and Instructions from the President to Ambassador Taylor as Approved by the President, December 3, 1964. December 7 quote is from Memorandum from the President to Secretary of State, Secretary of Defense, Director of Central Intelligence, December 7, 1964.

33. Instructions from the President to Ambassador Taylor, December 3, 1964.

34. *Ibid.*

35. Johnson quotes are in *ibid.* Intensification of covert actions in Laos was begun on December 14. (*PP* [GPO], 3[IV, C.1.]: 102.) The provision in Taylor's instructions for intensification of MAROPS (marine operations) aimed at "harassing the enemy" is not included in the December 2 position paper. Paragraph D of the position paper provided that the initial thirty-day period could "be continued without change," or be followed by "a transitional phase" (short of Phase II) wherein "additional military measures may be taken, including deployment of a large number of U.S. aircraft to the area, low-level reconnaissance of infiltration targets in the DRV near the borders, and the possible initiation of strikes a short distance across the border against the infiltration routes from the DRV." "If the GVN" quote is from "Position Paper on Southeast Asia," December 2, 1964, p. 2. Its paragraph relating to a conditional Phase II program went on to state: "Such a program would consist principally of progressively more serious air strikes, of a weight and tempo adjusted to the situation as it develops (possibly running from two to six months) and of appropriate US deployments to handle any contingency. Targets in the DRV would start with infiltration targets south of the 19th parallel and work up to targets north of that point. This could eventually lead to such measures as air strikes on all major military-related targets, aerial mining of DRV ports, and a US naval blockade of the DRV. The whole sequence of military actions would be designed to give the impression of a steady, deliberate approach, and to give the US the option at any time (subject to enemy reaction) to proceed or not, and to quicken the pace or not. Concurrently, the US would be alert to any sign of yielding by Hanoi, and would be prepared to explore negotiated solutions that attain US objectives in an acceptable manner." In the president's instructions to Taylor, "subsequent to Phase I" and "after the GVN has shown itself firmly in control," the U.S. would be "prepared to consider" a Phase II program against the DRV.

36. Quotes are from "Instructions from the President to Ambassador Taylor," December 3, 1964. On December 7 and 9 Taylor met with Khanh and Prime Minister Huong and, according to the *PP (NYT)*, "exacted the desired promises in exchange for the bombing" (p. 335).

37. It was widely, and soon publicly, understood that the dispensing of the substantial funds involved was to be dependent upon political performance. See Seymour Topping, *New York Times,* January 16, 1965.

38. See Memorandum for the President from Chester L. Cooper and McGeorge Bundy, December 14, 1964.

39. "The problem of immediate priority" is from outgoing telegram, Department of State, from Ball to Amembassy, Saigon, December 12, 1964. Taylor quotes are from his cable for Acting Secretary, December 16, 1964. Bundy and Cooper quote is from their Memorandum for the President, "Political Developments in South Vietnam," December 14, 1964. Johnson scrawled on Memorandum for the President, from Chester L. Cooper and McGeorge Bundy, "Political Development in South Vietnam," December 18, 1964. "To educate" quote is from cable from Taylor for Acting Secretary, December 16, 1964.

40. On internecine warfare among the officer corps, see cable from Taylor to Department of State, December 16, 1964, p. 3; CIA, Weekly Report, "The Situation in South Vietnam," December 16, 1964, pp. 3–4. On the refusal of the High National Council and the embassy's position, see CIA report of December 23, 1964, NSF, Vietnam, vol. 24 [provenance not indicated]. On the abolition of the High National Council, see cable from Taylor for McNamara, McG. Bundy, McCone, Wheeler, Rusk, and Sharp, December 21, 1964; cable from MACV to Department of Defense (National Military Command Center), December 20, 1964. On the Armed Forces Council, see cable from Taylor for Rusk, McNamara, [McGeorge] Bundy, McCone, and Wheeler,

December 20, 1964; see also *PP* (Gravel), 2:346.

41. Quotes are from cables from Taylor to State, December 22, 1964; Taylor to White House, December 22, 1964; Taylor to Rusk *et al.,* December 20, 1964.

42. Quotes are in cable from Robert H. Miller, First Secretary of Embassy, Saigon, to Department of State, "Summary of Conversation, Sunday, December 20," December 24, 1964.

43. Taylor acknowledged that his dressing down of the generals had helped drive them closer to Khanh. (*PP* [Gravel], 2:349.)

44. On these events, see cables from Taylor to State, December 22, 1964; message to the President and McNamara from Bundy, December 22, 1964; CIA Cable, December 23, 1964. The foregoing account, based on American sources, is consistent with the version given me by General Khanh in Ithaca, N.Y., in 1973. Taylor's rather lame explanation that Khanh "asked" him if he should resign fits only Taylor's cables to Washington during this period (see, for instance, Taylor to Department of State, December 21, 1964) and not other declassified U.S. documents bearing on these events (such as CIA cable of December 23, 1964). That Taylor was taken in by Khanh's strategy was made clear in the ambassador's cable to the Department of State on the morning of December 22: "Khanh has just telephoned me indicating that he is prepared to step down as Commander-in-Chief and asks whether I can provide funds to allow him to travel in U.S. and elsewhere. He further asked would I give similar assistance to other generals who may wish to travel. I asked him to provide me a list of the latter and to call me back this afternoon. Unless otherwise directed, I intend to agree to support Khanh's travel on a reasonable basis and take a hard look at any others of the military who may want to leave the country. We do not want a mass exodus from the battlefield." Rusk, it should be noted, was taken in as well and urged Taylor to accept Khanh's offer to leave, but to "carefully scrutinize any other names in

order to prevent any serious impairment of the military leadership for [the] war effort." (Cable from Rusk to American Embassy, Saigon, December 22, 1964.) Nguyen Chanh Thi's threats are in CIA, Information Cable, "Remarks by General Nguyen Thi Reflecting His Unhappiness with the United States," December 22, 1964.

45. For speculations on Thieu and Ky, see cables from Rusk to AmEmbassy, Saigon, December 21 and 24, 1964. On Westmoreland's contacts with Ky, see cables from Rusk to AmEmbassy, Saigon, December 24, 1964; Westmoreland to RUHL HQ/CINCPAC, November 26, 1964. On Huong's resisting Taylor, see Memorandum for the President from Chester Cooper and McGeorge Bundy, "Political Developments in South Vietnam," December 21, 1964.

46. On Khanh's order of the day, see articles by John Finney and Peter Grose, *New York Times,* December 23, 1964. For the full text of the letter about Taylor and its signatures, see cable from Taylor to Department of State, December 26, 1964. The officers' threat is in CIA cable (240442Z-ZFF-1) [probably December 23, 1964], NF-CF, Vietnam, vol. 24. U.S. response is in cable from Rusk to Ambassador or Deputy Ambassador, December 24, 1964.

47. Charges from Taylor's background briefing are in his cable to Department of State, December 24, 1964. Westmoreland quote is from cable from COMUSMACV to RUHPA/CINCPAC, December 24, 1964; also in orders to Commander of 7th Fleet, December 25, 1964.

48. "Very heart" quote is from cable from Taylor to Department of State, December 30, 1964. "In view of" quote is from cable from Johnson to Taylor, December 30, 1964. (In this the president used the term "the Front" rather than "Viet Cong.") See also cables from State and Rusk to American Embassy, Saigon, December 24, 25, 1964. A message from MACV to Washington on the 26th established that the U.S. military mission itself acknowledged that "political problems in Saigon raise [the] question if bombing could have been perpe-

trated by others than VC," but concluded, "It is becoming clear that this is most unlikely." See also *PP* (Gravel), 2:350, 3:262–63.

X. Bombing the North Will Save the South

1. Quote is from cable from the President of the United States to Taylor only, December 30, 1964.

2. Discussions with McGeorge and William Bundy, New York and Princeton, December 1984 and January 1985.

3. Cable from Taylor (General Westmoreland and Alexis Johnson concurring) to Secretary of State, December 31, 1964, with exclusive distribution to McNamara, McGeorge Bundy, McCone, and Sharp (CINCPAC).

4. On desertion in the army, see Jack Langguth, *New York Times,* January 10, 1965. On Binh Gia, see *ibid.,* January 3, 1965. Casualty figures are in Memorandum from Earle G. Wheeler for Mr. McGeorge Bundy, "Binh Gia Engagements, 28 December–4 January," January 5, 1965; also "Binh Gia—An Appraisal," Annex to the CIA's Weekly Report of January 6, 1965, "Situation in South Vietnam." Referring to this and other recent engagements, Wheeler concluded: "This series of battles could reflect a growing Viet Cong confidence in their military capabilities. Despite the relative RVN superiority in numerical strength, fire power and mobility, the Viet Cong may now feel that they are strong enough to compete in a war of movement by negating the RVN superiority through better intelligence, more intimate knowledge of the terrain, control over the local populace and their inherent ability to revert rapidly to guerrilla tactics."

5. Taylor quotes are from his cable ("For the President") to Secstate, January 6, 1965. Bundy quotes are in *PP* (Gravel), 3:684–85.

6. In two earlier drafts of this cable, the president indicated "someone" might be McGeorge Bundy. Presumably prepared by the White House staff under Bundy's supervision, the cable's initial drafts contain several other points that did not appear in the version finally approved by the president, and it is possible that their deletion provides some further insight into his thinking at this stage. Notable among these omissions were "We concur in your judgement that large new American forces are not now desirable for security or for combat roles"; "We concur in your view that any action against the North should be designed for political and psychological results"; and "Reprisal planning should be aimed explicitly at political and psychological effect."

7. Draft cable from the President to the Ambassador, bearing the written notation "This draft discussed in Sec State's Office Jan 13."

8. Cable from Taylor to Secretary of State, January 22, 1965.

9. CIA, SNIE 10-3-65, "Communist Reactions to Possible US Actions," February 11, 1965, pp. 9–10.

10. Khanh informed me that Taylor was by then working to remove him. His conclusion is supported by his critic Lieutenant General Tran Van Don, with whom I have also discussed this matter. Don has written in the same vein in *Our Endless War Inside Vietnam* (Presidio Press, 1978), p. 139. On the Young Turks' attitude toward Khanh, see the handwritten note from Chester Cooper to McGeorge Bundy, "Quick Roundup on F[ar] E[ast] in Event President Wants Latest from You," January 2, 1965. This also noted that "Khanh might be cooking up scheme for virtual military take-over of government." The views of Taylor quoted are referred to in the cable sent under Rusk's name to the American Embassy, Saigon, January 11, 1965.

11. Rusk's advice is in his cables to AmEmbassy, December 23, 24, 1964. Westmoreland quotes are from cable from COMUSMACV to RUHLHQ/CINCPAC, December 24, 1964.

12. Cable from Rusk to AmEmbassy, Saigon, January 11, 1965.

13. On the compromise, see Memoran-

dum for the President from Chester L. Cooper and McGeorge Bundy, January 13, 1965; *PP* (Gravel), 2:352, 3:261; *New York Times,* January 16, 1965. Taylor quotes are from his cable to Department of State, January 16, 1964. On the Cabinet shuffle, see *New York Times,* January 19, 1965. On increasing the armed forces, see *ibid.,* January 16, 1965.

14. On Thi's attitude toward protests, see cable from Alexis Johnson to State, January 26, 1965. On Buddhist charges and the actions against the USIS buildings, see cable from Taylor to Department of State, January 25, 1965; *New York Times,* January 23–26, 1965.

15. On the January 22 "treaty," see cables from Taylor to Department of State, January 12, 13, 20, 24, 1965. Alexis Johnson quotes are from his cable to State, January 26, 1965.

16. For Bundy's remarks to Johnson see his handwritten note on Memorandum for the President by Bundy and Chester Cooper, "Subject: Political Developments in South Vietnam," January 13, 1965; on "consulting with psychiatrists" see Memorandum from Chester Cooper and James C. Thomson, Jr., for Mr. [McGeorge] Bundy, "The Week That Was" January 15, 1965.

17. On Westmoreland's close relations with Ky, see cable from Rusk to AmEmbassy, Saigon, December 24, 1964; Alexis Johnson quote is from his cable to State, January 26, 1965.

18. *PP* (Gravel), 2:353; *New York Times,* January 27, 1965.

19. Quotes are from cables from McGeorge Bundy to Taylor, January 30, February 1, 1965.

20. Quotes are from CIA, Memorandum for the National Intelligence Board, SNIE 53-65, "Short Term Prospects in South Vietnam," February 2, 1965.

21. Quotes are from cables from Taylor to State, January 29, 31, 1965, and Ball to Taylor, January 30, 1965.

22. See Bundy memorandum in *PP* (Gravel), 3:684–85; cable from Taylor to Secstate, January 6, 1965; CIA, SNIE 53-65, "Short Term Prospects in South Vietnam,"

February 2, 1965; *New York Times,* January 31, 1965.

23. On Westmoreland's proposal and concurrences, see cable from Westmoreland to RUHPA/CINCPAC, January 26, 1965; JCS to CINCPAC, January 27, 1965; *PP* (Gravel), 3:687. On the B-52s, see *PP* (Gravel), 2:353; Admiral U. S. G. Sharp and General W. C. Westmoreland, *Report on the War in Vietnam (as of June 30, 1968)* (U.S. Government Printing Office, 1969), p. 98.

24. Regarding the fear of a neutralist government, see n. 23; *PP (NYT),* pp. 339, 341, 392. As early as November 6, 1964, the man upon whom McNamara leaned most heavily for advice on Vietnam, John McNaughton, predicted that the collapse of the regime might happen in as little as six months unless the United States took new actions. See *ibid.,* p. 365. But during December and January, estimates of the time within which a debacle might occur had been reduced considerably.

25. Humphrey quote is from MIT Meeting on William Bundy's Vietnam ms., Cambridge, April 16, 1970. The same point is made by James Thomson in his article "How Could Vietnam Happen?," *Atlantic Monthly,* April 1968, p. 51, where the remark is attributed to "one of the very highest figures in the Administration."

26. McGeorge Bundy promised to develop a paper in his Memorandum for the President, January 26, 1965. On McNamara, see *PP (NYT),* p. 342. Quotes are from Memorandum for the President from McG.B[undy], January 27, 1965. This memorandum remained closely held and, according to McGeorge Bundy (in discussion with the author, December 1984), was shown to neither of his two Vietnam assistants, Chester Cooper or James Thomson. Thomson did not learn of it until the document was declassified some ten years later, and Cooper makes no mention of it in his book, *The Lost Crusade: America in Vietnam* (Dodd, Mead, 1970).

27. February 2 report is in the National Security File. The president's standards, Taylor acknowledged, had been meant to

include "the ability to provide leadership to the people, to maintain law and order in urban centers, to make operational plans and effect their execution by loyal military and police forces, to keep the in-country base secure from any VC/DRV reaction to Phase II and, following air strikes against the DRV, to exploit their success in carrying out a national pacification plan." (This last point was frequently emphasized at this time, since it was clear that air strikes against the DRV would not in themselves eliminate the problem posed by the Viet Cong in the South.)

28. George W. Ball, *The Past Has Another Pattern* (W. W. Norton, 1982), p. 389.

29. Thomson quote is from a discussion with the author, November 1979, and MIT Meeting on William Bundy's Vietnam ms., Cambridge, April 6, 1970, Adam Yarmolinsky papers, JFK Library. "The Administration" and "The President" quotes are from Cooper, *Lost Crusade*, p. 256. "The option" quote is from Cooper, Oral History, interview of January 1969 (released June 7, 1974), p. 14, LBJ Library.

30. The president's intent to dispatch someone was clear from a draft of the cable he sent Taylor on January 7, which in its final form designated no particular person (see above). "The shape" quote is from Memorandum for the President from McG.B., "Subject: Draft Message for Taylor," January 27, 1965; see also Summary Notes of 544th NSC Meeting, February 1, 1965. Taylor quote is from his cable for Bundy, February 3, 1965.

31. *PP* (Gravel), 2:319; Memorandum for the President from McG.B., August 31, 1964. The first quote gives the interpretation of the Pentagon chronicler, while the second and third are from Bundy's memorandum.

32. For the Pleiku casualties and the other nine attacks, see CIA, Office of Current Intelligence, "Viet Cong Military Activity in South Vietnam," February 10, 1965. Taylor and the Joint Chiefs of Staff had already argued that a much smaller incident in Saigon on January 16, involving a pool-side explosive charge, constituted a sufficient

provocation to justify evacuation of all U.S. dependents and a retaliatory bombing. See Memorandum for the President prepared by James C. Thomson, Jr., "Report on Saigon Cable Traffic," January 19, 1965. For the President's meeting with his advisers, see Summary Notes ("For the President Only") by Bromley Smith of 545th NSC Meeting, February 6, 1965. Illness prevented Rusk from attending. Ball states that, "faced with a unanimous view, I saw no option but to go along." (Ball, *Past Has Another Pattern*, p. 390.) Hubert Humphrey reports an earlier "ad hoc meeting" with the president the night before, in which he, Ball, and Adlai Stevenson opposed the bombing but were outvoted by the majority. (Hubert H. Humphrey, *The Education of a Public Man* [Doubleday, 1976], p. 319.) Because of bad weather, only forty-nine of the navy jets were able to deliver their bombs and rockets. A flight of twenty-four planes from South Vietnam's air force was to have participated in this attack, but because of weather conditions did not fly against the North until the following day. *PP* (Gravel), 3:286.

33. "Streetcar" quote is in Townsend Hoopes, *The Limits of Intervention* (David McKay, 1969), p. 30. "Actually" quote is from Allen S. Whiting, *The Chinese Calculus of Deterrence* (University of Michigan Press, 1978), p. 178 and n. 23. In a letter to the author of April 17, 1982, Whiting states that the above interpretation of his remarks is "wholly correct," and that he predicted such an attack even before he knew that Soviet Prime Minister Kosygin would be visiting Hanoi. Bundy's statement that he could not recall having been informed of an impending attack on a U.S. installation was made to the author in December 1984. Mohr's question is in *New York Times*, February 8, 1965. The commander of U.S. naval forces in the Pacific, Admiral U. S. G. Sharp, states that three attack carriers were indeed in the Tonkin Gulf at this time, but that, "in order to avoid any incident that might worsen United States–Soviet relations," two of them were ordered eastward to Subic Bay after it was learned Kosygin

would be in Hanoi, yet that "within hours" of the Pleiku attack they were ordered to steam back to the Tonkin Gulf. (Sharp and Westmoreland, *Report on the War in Vietnam*, p. 14.) Mohr, a former correspondent in Vietnam whose candor in reporting had led to his resignation from *Time*, also noted that the heaviest weapons used by the Viet Cong in the attack were captured U.S. 81-mm mortars. Whiting's observation is from his letter to the author, April 17, 1982.

34. Soviet 1965 aid program is discussed in CIA, Office of Current Intelligence, Intelligence Memorandum, "The Kosygin Visit to Vietnam," February 1, 1965. This report noted that the Soviet Union had extended to North Vietnam about $370 million worth of economic aid since 1955, "mainly in the form of factories and machine shops, power plants and coal mine equipment," with the last major credit having been extended in 1960. "It has always" quote is from *ibid.* "The Soviets" quote is from CIA, Memorandum for the United States Intelligence Board, SNIE 10–65, "Communist Military Capabilities and Near Term Interventions in Laos and South Vietnam," February 1, 1965, p. 8. See also *New York Times*, February 1, 1965 (three articles); *PP* (Gravel), 3:301; William B. Bollis, "Relations Between the U.S.S.R. and Vietnam," in *Vietnam and the Sino-Soviet Dispute*, ed. Robert A. Rupen and Robert E. Farrell (Frederick A. Praeger, 1967), p. 53; Donald Zagoria, *Vietnam Triangle: Moscow/Peking/Hanoi* (Pegasus, 1967), p. 47.

35. "Speculation" quote is from *New York Times*, February 2, 1965; see also *ibid.*, January 31, and February 1, 1965. "The USSR" quote is in *PP* (Gravel), 3:301; see also Zagoria, *Vietnam Triangle*, pp. 47–48; Max Frankel, *New York Times*, February 18, 1965; Bernard Fall, "The Year of the Hawks," *New York Times Magazine*, December 12, 1965.

36. On Kosygin's proposal, see Director of Intelligence and Research, INR, Thomas Hughes, to Secretary of State, "Kosygin's Speech Contains Some New Elements but Reiterates Basic Soviet Position,"

February 26, 1965, p. 1. See also *New York Times*, February 24, 1965.

37. "A personal insult" is from Cooper, *Lost Crusade*, p. 261. Moscow's warning is in *New York Times*, February 9, 1965. On the military-aid agreement, see State Department, INR report, February 24, 1965, p. 2. Joint Chiefs quotes are from their cable to CINCPAC, February 17, 1965.

38. Quotes are from Thomas L. Hughes memorandum to the Secretary, "Tough Chinese Communist Posture on Vietnam," February 19, 1965.

39. Quotes are from cable from JCS to CINCPAC, February 17, 1965.

40. "Extension of the War Beyond SVN" is listed as the third of eight topics in Taylor's cable to Bundy, February 1, 1965. "Analysis" quote is from cable from McNaughton to McNamara and Vance, via Taylor and Department of State, February 7, 1965.

41. Memorandum for the President from Bromley Smith, February 4, 1965 (incorporating Bundy's reply as forwarded via John McCone).

42. McNaughton quotes are from his cable to McNamara and Vance, February 7, 1965. Presumably to ensure that McNamara and Vance alone were properly clued in for the NSC meeting that was scheduled to take place before Bundy's plane could arrive from Saigon, McNaughton's cable was prefaced "Assure personal delivery prior to 0800 NSC Meeting, No distribution, Eyes Only." "Presidential approval" and "a single-shot" quotes are from "A Graduated Reprisal Program to Stop DRV Intervention in SVN: A Suggested Scenario" (M. L. Manfull, Counsellor, Political Affairs, US Embassy, Saigon, Rapporteur), February 6, 1965. This suggested an approach toward Phase II whereby after an initial act of specific retaliatory reprisal the pattern would shift into what was described in their agenda for discussion as a "transitional phase" toward Phase II in which the United States would "continue reprisal actions against DRV targets at times and places of our own choosing linking them only in general terms

to the level of VC outrages." Among other measures to be taken, they prescribed stationing a U.S. Hawk antiaircraft battalion off Danang, and alerting the 173rd Airborne.

43. On the president's decision, see Johnson, *Vantage Point,* p. 128.

44. The analysis here provided is from the full text of the Bundy report. For the introductory "Summary Conclusions" of the Bundy report, see *PP* (Gravel), 3:309. Extracts of his assessment of the relation between Saigon politics and escalation can be found in *ibid.,* pp. 310–11. His accompanying memorandum, "A Policy for Sustained Reprisal," can be found in *ibid.,* pp. 312–15, and in *PP* (NYT), pp. 423–27.

45. For U.S. casualties through 1964, see FER/ISA, "U.S. Costs and Casualties in South Vietnam," February 10, 1965.

46. The four congressional leaders included two Republicans, Representative Gerald Ford and Senator Everett Dirkson, and two Democrats, Senator Mike Mansfield and Speaker of the House John McCormack.

47. Johnson quote is from *Vantage Point,* p. 126; see also p. 127. For Humphrey's views, see Humphrey, *Education of a Public Man,* pp. 310–24. Rusk's are in Memorandum from National Security Files [sanitized] of February 23, 1965, attributed to Rusk, NSF, Vietnam, vol. 29. In this Rusk also stated that he favored "the immediate stationing in Danang of a Marine battalion combat team, to be reinforced promptly to a brigade if the security situation calls for it."

48. Summary Notes of 547th NSC Meeting, February 8, 1965.

49. The NSC minutes state that in response to Ford's question whether Bundy was now recommending the program proposed in December, "The President responded by saying that Mr. Bundy had brought back from Saigon the views of the country team there. These views have been discussed with the President's advisers and an agreed recommendation had been made to the President." Bundy added that "A rolling consensus as to the proper course of action had developed after he returned to

Washington from Saigon." To Ford's question of "whether all we intended to do was to react to Viet Cong provocations," the president replied that "all Viet-Cong actions did call for a response but we did not intend to limit our actions to retaliating against Viet Cong attacks."

50. Cable from the President for Ambassador Taylor, February 8, 1965.

51. For Johnson's endorsement, see *PP* (Gravel), 3:321; see also Johnson, *Vantage Point,* p. 130.

XI. The Decision for Sustained Bombing

1. On the Qui Nhon incident, see Admiral U. S. G. Sharp and General W. C. Westmoreland, *Report on the War in Vietnam (as of June 30, 1968),* (U.S. Government Printing Office, 1969), p. 15; *New York Times,* February 11, 1965. JCS recommendation is in their cable to CINCPAC, "Courses of Action in SEAsia—1st 8 weeks," February 12, 1965. This JCS proposal also included the dispatch of an army brigade to Thailand for the purpose of deterring retaliation by Hanoi and Peking against these air strikes. The United States had by this time established several of its major air bases in Thailand. On the reprisal Johnson ordered, see Summary Record of National Security Council Meeting No. 548, February 10, 1965.

2. Nixon quotes are in *New York Times,* January 27, February 11, 12, 1965.

3. Fishel statements are in Department of State, INR Briefing, February 11, 1965. Public policy statement is in *New York Times,* February 23, 1965.

4. In 1965 this endorsement included fifty senators and more than half the membership of the House. Quote is from a mailing sent by the committee to its own membership and many other Americans on September 13, 1965, but the committee had made the China-Vietnam linkage long before this.

5. The figures were reported to the president by Bill Moyers on February 16, 1965, with the notation "Attached are the results

of the polls I mentioned to you last night. Lou Harris asks that we not let anyone know he did it for us."

6. On the Gallup poll, see *New York Times*, February 16, 1965.

7. On Viet Cong military gains, see CIA, Monthly Report, Annex, "Situation in South Vietnam," February 17, 1965. Quoted cable is from Taylor to RUEHCR/SECSTATE, February 9, 1965.

8. See *New York Times*, February 11, 13, 24, 26, 1965; United Nations Press Service, n. 3075, February 24, 1965. Additional details can be found in George McT. Kahin and John W. Lewis, *The United States in Vietnam*, 2nd ed. rev. & enl. (Delta, 1969), pp. 170–71. On February 13, U Thant informed Charles Yost, deputy to Stevenson at the U.N., that he was still awaiting the U.S. response to Hanoi's "very affirmative reaction to his initiative for talks between it and the U.S." See also cable from Ball to Rusk, (Amembassy Rio de Janeiro), November 18, 1965.

9. Thomson's complaint is in his Memorandum for Mr. Bundy, "The Vietnam Crisis—One Dove's Lament," February 19, 1965. McGeorge Bundy's advice was in his Memorandum for the President "Comments on Vietnam for Your Newspaper Editor," February 19, 1965. Frankel quote is from *New York Times*, February 18, 1965.

10. *Department of State Bulletin*, March 1, 1965, p. 293.

11. On Rusk's press conference, see *New York Times*, February 26, 1965. His elaborations occurred in discussion with the author, Washington, D.C., June 30, 1965.

12. The Harris poll is the same as was reported on p. 287. If the figure of 75 percent seems incongruous in view of the poll's reporting that 60 percent supported the president's Vietnam policies, it should be noted that 53 percent agreed with the proposition that "stepped-up bombing in North Vietnam could lead to a negotiated settlement." "A reconciliation" quote is in *PP* (Gravel), 3:255. "Sec def" quote is from cable from Assistant Secretary McNaughton for General Westmoreland, February 9, 1965. "Re the White Paper" quote is from Memoran-

dum from Chet Cooper for Mr. Bundy, February 9, 1965.

13. For Liechty's account, see Michael Getler, Washington *Post*, March 20, 1982. The White Paper appeared as Department of State Publication 7839 (U.S. Government Printing Office, 1965). A cable under Rusk's name responded to Taylor's February 20 cable: "In your exploitation captured boat hope you can get clear evidence boat dispatched from DRV prior February 7." (Outgoing telegram, Department of State, February 20, 1965.) Whatever Taylor's response may have been, this requirement appears to have been met with the incorporation into the White Paper of the statement "A newspaper in the cabin was from Haiphong and was dated January 23, 1965." Frankel quote is from *New York Times*, February 27, 1965. Mohr quote is from *ibid.*, February 8, 1965.

14. John Finney, *New York Times*, February 28, 1965. This issue also ran the text of the White Paper.

15. The full text of Johnson's February 13 cable can be found in *PP* (Gravel), 3:321–22. It also called for an intensification "by all available means of the program of pacification in South Vietnam," and for a pre-emptive approach to the U.N., "to avoid being faced by really damaging initiatives by the USSR or perhaps by such powers as India, France, or even the UN." The United States would go to the U.N. Security Council "to make clear case that aggressor is Hanoi" and "make it plain that we are ready for 'talks' to bring aggression to an end." But Taylor was to explain to the Saigon government that Washington was "determined to continue with military actions regardless of Security Council deliberations and any 'talks' or negotiations that might ensue, unless and until" Hanoi brought "its aggression to an end." Herbert Schandler quote is from *The Unmaking of a President* (Princeton University Press, 1977), p. 15.

16. Memorandum from McG. B[undy] for the President, "Vietnam Decisions," February 16, 1965.

17. Memorandum from McGeorge Bundy for the President, "Telegram to Am-

bassador Taylor," February 16, 1965. The changes, in Johnson's handwriting, are written into Bundy's typed text.

18. McGeorge Bundy, McNamara, and Generals Wheeler and Goodpaster also attended the meeting with Eisenhower. See Memorandum by Lt. General A. J. Goodpaster of Meeting with the President, February 17, 1965. Eisenhower also appears to have suggested (part of this section of the document has been sanitized) that if China or Soviet Russia threatened to intervene they should be threatened with nuclear reprisal: "He said that if they threaten to intervene we should pass the word back to them to take care lest dire results occur to them. He commented on how the armistice was brought about in Korea."

19. The analyst in the *Pentagon Papers* concludes that timing of the first strike under Phase II was "evidently" made by the president on February 18, inferring this from a cable sent on that date to nine U.S. posts in the Far East. Not only would this have been an unlikely step at the time in view of the need for absolute security, but the cable in fact mentions (as the Pentagon analyst acknowledges) no date and is simply a condensation of the president's cable to Taylor of February 13, outlining his general decision of earlier that day. (*PP* [Gravel], 3:324–25.) This mistake is repeated in the outline presented on p. 277 of this volume of the *Pentagon Papers*. Moreover, this analyst's reference to February 20 as the date for which the new program "was set" presumably should be clarified to indicate the day on which plans were to be ready—not the date for their implementation, or, in CINCPAC's terms, "a planning readiness date." (Sharp and Westmoreland, *Report on the War in the Pacific*, p. 16.)

20. McNaughton quote is from his cable to McNamara and Vance, from Saigon, February 7, 1965. Concerning Bundy's views on the Buddhists, see his Memorandum for the President, February 7, 1965, p. 5. Taylor quotes are in *PP* (Gravel), 3:323.

21. On Khanh's acquiescence and permission from Oanh, see cable from Taylor to Department of State, February 7, 1965. Khanh maintains that he was not consulted about the bombing plans, merely informed of them by McGeorge Bundy and Westmoreland after they had invited him aboard their plane "to discuss a question which they said was very important." There, he says, they told him that they had decided to recommend bombing of North Vietnam to President Johnson. He took no part in making the decision, he emphasizes. (Seminar, Cornell University, Ithaca, N.Y., December 6, 1973.) The apt "lame duck" phraseology is that of one of the *Pentagon Papers* analysts, in *PP* (Gravel), 3:323; see also *ibid.*, 2:353. Khanh himself informed the Armed Forces Council that Oanh would not be acceptable as prime minister except on an interim basis, because he was "too closely associated with the Americans." (CIA Information Cable, February 6, 1965.) After studying in Japan from 1939 to 1945, Oanh had worked for six years with U.S. occupation forces there, after which he had been given a U.S. government fellowship for study in the United States and finally received a Ph.D. in economics at Harvard. From 1955 to 1959 he taught at Trinity College, and in 1960 joined the IMF's staff in Washington. He did not return to Vietnam until after the overthrow of the Diem government. (CIA, Office of Central Reference, *Biographic Register*, January 28, 1965.) "Jack Owen" quote is from Cable from Taylor to Secstate (sec. II of II), September 2, 1964.

22. Incoming cable ("Priority") from Taylor to Department of State, February 11, 1965.

23. On Khanh's need to align himself with the Buddhists, see CIA, Memorandum for the United States Intelligence Board, "Subject: SNIE 53–65, 'Short-Term Prospects in South Vietnam,'" February 2, 1965. The conclusion as to the Buddhist perception of common ground with the NLF, which is shared by others who developed close contacts with the Buddhist leadership, is in part based on my own extensive discussions with Thien Minh, Tri Quang, and sev-

eral other senior Buddhist leaders in 1966, 1967, and 1970. In view of the attitudes of U.S. officials and most of the South Vietnamese military officers, the Buddhist leaders were afraid to speak openly about these objectives to them or in public statements and felt constrained to mask their views under a rhetoric emphasizing nationalism, representative government, and peace.

24. Robert Shaplen, one of the few American correspondents with a long-standing acquaintance with Vietnamese politics, had written as early as December 20 warning of the consequences of Khanh's "secret alliance" with the Buddhists and signs that they "might be ready and willing to negotiate a neutralist deal with the Communists." Observers who had been following the political situation closely, he said, were convinced that Tri Quang, as the paramount Buddhist leader in South Vietnam, was willing if not eager to do so, with the expectation that this would make possible the establishment of a Buddhist state like Ceylon or Burma where he, though not assuming power directly, would serve as *éminence grise* behind the government. (Robert Shaplen, "Plotting to Neutralize Vietnam," New York *Herald Tribune,* December 20, 1964.)

25. Alexis Johnson quotes are from his cable to Department of State, January 26, 1965. Taylor followed up this cable a week later with a report that among "Khanh's military colleagues" the conviction has developed that once he was in control of the government he would "follow the neutralist route attempting to become [the] Sihanouk of SVN in alliance with the Buddhist Institute." (Cable ["Pass Exclusive to McGeorge Bundy"] from Taylor to Secretary of State, February 3, 1965.) A CIA Intelligence Memorandum of February 3 reported that remnants of the old-guard Dai Viet and Catholic elements of the armed forces were convinced of this, and a cable from Taylor to Bundy later that day stated that General Huynh Van Cao reported that he was convinced that if Khanh succeeded in making himself chief of state, he planned "to lead [the] country toward negotiation with [the] Liberation

Front [NLF] and a neutralist solution," with "Khanh envisaging himself as the 'Sihanouk' of South Vietnam." (Cable from Taylor to State, "CINCPAC for Bundy.") "Khanh is plotting" quote is from CIA, Weekly Report, "The Situation in South Vietnam," February 3, 1965.

26. Khanh acknowledged his efforts vis-à-vis the NLF to me (December 6, 1973) as well as in a statement to the press in Paris (January 26, 1975). Tran Van Don quote is from his *Our Endless War Inside Vietnam* (Presidio Press, 1978), p. 167. This account is consistent with statements previously made to me by General Don and other South Vietnamese officers.

27. On Khanh's indirect feelers in France, see CIA, Intelligence Information Cable, December 30, 1964 [sanitized], which reported rumors that Khanh's emissaries in Paris were working "to prepare the way for neutralization of South Vietnam," but cautioned that these were based on "little fact and much speculation." Contacts with Phat and release of his wife emerged in my interviews with Tran Van Don and Nguyen Khanh. In his book Tran Van Don writes that Khanh "ordered the release of the wife of Huynh Tan Phat, the number one Communist leader of the predominantly non-Communist NLF. Khanh then sent Phat a secret letter, proposing his collaboration." (*Our Endless War,* p. 139.)

28. Khanh made this letter, a copy of which is in my possession, public on January 26, 1975, in a press conference in Paris, and I do not doubt its authenticity. Nearly fourteen months before, he had shown me a letter dated January 28, 1965, written in Vietnamese and signed by Phat, and his rough, off-the-cuff translation was consistent with the full translation he later mimeographed for the press. Tran Van Don also earlier saw the letter, and believed it to be genuine and its subsequent translation into English accurate.

29. The change in Washington's attitude toward Khanh was sudden. Even the day after his January 27 re-coup, McGeorge Bundy had cabled Taylor, "It looks to us as

if General Khanh for better or for worse is
the principal present power" and that as
long as he gave "a firm statement of determination to carry on with the war," as Bundy
expected he would, "we think you should
certainly respond that U.S. is equally determined to go on supporting Vietnamese government and people." A U.S. public statement to this effect would be made, Bundy
said, "just as soon as Khanh has made right
noise to you." (Outgoing telegram, Department of State, January 28, 1965.)

30. On Khanh's statement on U.S. aid,
see cable from Taylor to Department of
State, December 22, 1964; CIA Intelligence
Information Cable, "Alleged Concern of
Majority of General Officers That Trend of
Relations with the United States May Lead
to Withdrawal of U.S. Aid," December 31,
1964. On efforts to exploit Khanh's state-
ment, see CIA cable, "Nguyen Khanh's
Wish to Settle Existing Problems with the
U.S.," December 30, 1964. Thi quote is from
interview with the author, Washington,
D.C., October 5, 1966. By January 2, 1965,
Chester Cooper reported to McGeorge
Bundy that the embassy's contacts with the
Young Turks were loosening up and that
their relations with Khanh appeared to be
hardening. (Handwritten Memorandum,
"Quick Roundup of F E in Event President
Wants Latest from You," January 2, 1965.)
Taylor quote is from his cable to State,
March 8, 1965.

31. On this plot and Alexis Johnson's
assessment, see cable from Taylor to State,
January 23, 1965. A second plot—or perhaps
a variant of the one just described—was reported to be led by Colonel Pham Ngoc
Thao, with General Tran Van Don to replace Khanh. (Cable from Taylor to State,
January 24, 1965.) General Don states that
Pham Ngoc Thao offered him the positions
of defense minister and chief of staff, not
prime minister. (Interview, Ithaca, N.Y.,
October 31, 1979.)

32. It was this February 3 cable that
warned, "You may be arriving just in time
to witness some very important governmental developments." Suggesting that these

might have an effect on Bundy's visit, he
observed, "We may give you an interesting
time." Copies were sent to the CIA, the Defense Department, and CINCPAC, as well
as to the White House. Taylor quotes are
from his cable ("Pass Exclusive to
McGeorge Bundy"), via Department of
State, February 3, 1965. It is possible that
this second cable did not arrive until just
after Bundy had departed.

33. "His colleagues" and "In no way"
quote are from incoming telegram, Department of State, sent from Saigon 7 P.M., February 3, 1965. Remaining quotes are from
incoming telegram, Department of State,
dispatched from Saigon, 8 P.M., February 4,
1965. A Defense Department assessment
found Admiral Cang to be "a good leader
. . . anti-communist; friendly towards U.S.,"
and General Nguyen Huu Co to be an "outstanding officer . . . friendly to Americans."
(CIA, Intelligence Summary, Supplement,
"Vietnamese Coup Personalities," February
20, 1965.) At the end of January 1965, the
CIA reported that General Co had announced he would no longer attend meetings
of the Armed Forces Council, because
Khanh had accused him of "having been
bought off by the Americans." (CIA, Office
of Central Reference, Biographic Register,
January 29, 1965.) This same CIA source
reported, "A U.S. official described Thieu in
late 1963 as intelligent, highly ambitious, and
likely to remain a coup plotter with the aim
of personal advancement."

34. Regarding Quat as a candidate, the
CIA had as early as December 2, 1964, reported that he was Tri Quang's preference
for replacing Prime Minister Huong. (CIA,
Weekly Report, "The Situation in South
Vietnam," December 2, 1964.) Formerly a
distinguished doctor of medicine, Quat was
regarded as a leader and chief theorist of the
Northern faction of the Dai Viet party. He
served as education minister and later defense minister under Bao Dai, and was one
of the Caravelle group of critics jailed by
Diem. From February to October 1964, he
had served as Khanh's minister of foreign
affairs. For further detail, see CIA, Office of

Central Reference, *Biographic Register,* January 29, 1965. For CIA speculations about Quat, see CIA, Office of Current Intelligence, Intelligence Memorandum, "Individuals and Cliques in South Vietnam," February 25, 1965. Four out of the new Cabinet's twenty-four members were Catholic. Phan Khac Suu had previously been elected chief of state by Khanh's appointed and short-lived High National Council on October 24, 1964. After receiving a degree in agricultural engineering in France in 1930, he had served for ten years as director of the colonial government's Economic and Agricultural Research Service and was arrested and imprisoned from 1941 to 1945 for anti-French activities. After serving in Bao Dai's Ministry of Agriculture, he was appointed minister of agriculture by Diem in 1954 but was soon removed for allegedly having been involved in a Binh Xuyen plot against him. He was imprisoned by Diem in 1960 (for having signed the Caravelle Manifesto and allegedly supported the November 1960 coup attempt against him) and not released until Diem was overthrown.

35. Regarding the Young Turks' not being ready, on February 14, the commander of the marine brigade, General Le Nguyen Khang, while informing American officials for the first time that he was actively engaged in a plot to remove Khanh, had stated that the time was not yet ripe to do so because the military was not united enough to form a solid front against him. He said that his own officers had agreed to wait until Khanh could be eased out without any undue repercussions. "There was only one fly in the ointment: Colonel Pham Ngoc Thao," who he understood had linked up with several former generals. He advised that he could keep his own officers from being influenced by Thao only as long as they were confident that their own generals would stick to their plan to remove Khanh. (CIA Information Cable, "Khang's Statement That the Military Is Giving Thought to Removing Khanh," February 15, 1965; Supplement to a Defense Intelligence Agency Summary, "Vietnamese Coup Per-

sonalities," February 20, 1965. "Left little doubt" quote is from CIA, Office of Current Intelligence, Intelligence Memorandum, "Colonel Pham Ngoc Thao," February 19, 1965. "Thao acted first" quote is from Le Tu Hung, *Nhung cai chet trong cach mang 1-11-63* [*The Deaths in the November 1, 1963, Revolution*] (Saigon: Dinh Minh Ngoc, 1971), pp. 160–61. (Translated for the author by Mai Elliott.) A CIA Intelligence Memorandum reported that Pham Ngoc Thao appeared to be working in collusion with Ambassador Khiem, who the CIA thought might be the real power behind the coup. (CIA, Office of Current Intelligence, "Colonel Pham Ngoc Thao," February 20, 1965.)

36. "Primarily" quote is from CIA, Vietnam Working Group, "Implications of the Saigon Coup Events," February 20, 1965. The ties of the dissident Catholic officers were with the southern branch of the Dai Viet party, a rival of Quat's northern faction. (CIA, Office of Current Intelligence, "The Situation in South Vietnam," February 19, 1965.) Regarding the National Defense Force, see CIA Intelligence Information Cable, January 22, 1965. Nguyen Bao Kiem is assigned an important role in the coup planning by both Tran Van Don (interview with the author, March 24, 1981) and Le Tu Hung, *Nhung cai chet trong cach mang 1-11-63,* p. 132. See also CIA Intelligence and Reporting Subcommittee of the Interagency Vietnam Coordinating Committee, Weekly Report, "The Situation in South Vietnam," February 24, 1965; Memorandum for the President from McB[undy], February 19, 1965.

37. According to a contemporary CIA assessment, "Although a Buddhist, [General] Khiem is suspicious and critical of the Buddhist hierarchy, and enjoys Catholic support; there are reports that he was a 'rice-bowl' convert under Diem." It also noted that he was close to Thieu. (CIA, Office of Current Intelligence, "Individuals and Cliques in South Vietnam," February 25, 1965.) As early as December 16, 1964, the CIA cited reports that General Khiem,

while ambassador, and Colonel Thao were "continuing their intrigues abroad," and Khiem was charging that "both Khanh and the Buddhists were working for a neutralist solution." (CIA, Weekly Report, "The War in Vietnam," December 16, 1964, p. 4. "Khanh was leading" quote is from Defense Intelligence Agency, Intelligence Summary Supplement, "Vietnamese Coup Personalities," February 20, 1965. Initially U.S. intelligence believed General Don to be one of the two top coup leaders, but soon dropped this view when it became clear he was remaining in Dalat and the coup leaders were announcing that Khiem was their man. Don apparently did take part in its early planning, and has informed me that he had indeed remained the candidate of Pham Ngoc Thao for the post of minister of defense or chief of staff of the armed forces, but that the coup's Dai Viet supporters and Professor Kiem insisted that General Khiem be appointed to these positions. (Interview, October 29, 1965.) *The New York Times* printed its conclusion on February 20, 1965. Later, upon hearing of Khanh's overthrow, Khiem was reported to be jubilant, stating, "For me I am very happy. I think my objective has been realized." (*Ibid.,* February 22, 1965.) General Thi, among other officers who were not involved in at least this particular effort, informed me he was certain that the coup had been instigated by pro-Diemist elements abroad. See also his letter to Chief of the Military Council and to all Comrades-in-arms of the Republic of Vietnam Armed Forces, February 26, 1965.

38. Details of Khanh's escape are from an interview with the author, Cornell University, Ithaca, N.Y., December 6, 1973. The narrowness of his escape is corroborated by Takashi Oka, who has written the most comprehensive published account of these events. He states, "Colonel Thao has told intimates that the coupists very nearly caught Khanh . . . at the JGS [Joint General Staff], where all Friday morning top Vietnamese and American officials had been conferring. Khanh left the JGS at 12:30, minutes before the coupists' arrival. A col-

laborator inside JGS who had been assigned to close the gates failed to do so, thus letting the general slip through." (Takashi Oka, "The February 19 Coup," Institute of Current World Affairs, March 29, 1965, p. 8.) For a somewhat similar account of Khanh's escape, see Robert Shaplen, *The Lost Revolution* (Harper and Row, 1965), p. 310. On Westmoreland's intercession, see Department of Defense, Message Center, National Command Center, incoming cable from MACV, February 19, 1965; cable from Taylor to State, February 19, 1965.

39. On these broadcasts, see Department of Defense, Message Center, National Military Command Center, incoming cable from MACV (Saigon), February 19, 1965; incoming cable, "19 February Coup d'Etat Wrap Up of Situation as of 19:1601"; CIA Office of Current Intelligence, "The Situation in South Vietnam as of 0600 EST," February 19, 1965. See also Oka, "February 19 Coup," p. 8. An early CIA report of the coup stated, "Judging from the name of the group broadcasting over the rebel controlled radio, the coup is organized and led by the National Defense Force, a Catholic oriented group whose prime objective is stated to be the removal of Nguyen Khanh who they claim is a neutralist." (CIA, Intelligence Information Cable, "Sitrep as of 1700 Hours Local Time, February 19, 1965.")

40. On the Buddhist reaction, see Le Tu Hung, *Nhung cai chet trong cach mang 1-11-63,* pp. 157–58. Tam Chau was the recognized leader among the monks who had left North Vietnam in 1954–55, and he had approximately the same stature in the Mekong Delta that Thich Tri Quang had in Hué, Danang, and other parts of northern South Vietnam. Generally, but not always, the two monks worked on political matters in reasonable harmony.

41. On ousting Quat, see Memorandum for the President (apparently from the White House Situation Room), February 19, 1965. This memo bears the notation "Sent to the President per Bundy," and is prefaced "This is the latest information from General Westmoreland." According to Takashi Oka,

who talked with Thao during his coup attempt, this Catholic colonel mistrusted Quat, regarding him as "too susceptible to Buddhist peacemongering." ("February 19 Coup," p. 9.)

42. Regarding call for a standstill and denial of U.S. knowledge, see Department of Defense, incoming cable from MACV to Message Center, National Military Command Center, February 19, 1965; Memo for the President, February 19, 1965, cited above.

43. A CIA report of December 2, 1964, stated that Ky had told Westmoreland "that there was considerable dissatisfaction with Khanh and that, if conditions continued to deteriorate, he might lead an effort to oust Khanh." (CIA, Weekly Report, "The Situation in South Vietnam [26 November–2 December, 1964]," December 2, 1964, p. 4.) On February 3, 1965, the CIA reported that Ky had said Khanh was "on his way out," that "Americans need not be concerned over possibilities of bloodshed over serious problems in Khanh's removal," and that General Thieu might well be the replacement for Khanh as commander in chief. (CIA, Information Cable, "General Ky's Views on Present Power Position and Intentions of General Nguyen Khanh," February 3, 1965.) On February 19, Taylor cabled State, "Ky has no use for Phat but seems willing to see Khanh ousted." The retrospective assessment is CIA, Office of Current Intelligence, "Individuals and Cliques in South Vietnam," February 25, 1965. For Ky's marching orders, see cable from Taylor to State, February 19, 8 PM; incoming telecom from Department of Defense Message Center, to National Military Command Center, received 2:19 EST, February 19, 1965. The Defense Intelligence Agency rated Nguyen Bao Tri "anti-Communist and pro-US." (CIA, Intelligence Summary, "Vietnamese Coup Personalities," February 20, 1965.) General Tri had left Mytho for Saigon with a regiment-sized task force. (Department of Defense Message Center, National Military Command Center, incoming from MACV, 13.42 EST, February 19, 1965.) For Gruen-

ther's instructions, see flash from MACV to [Message Center] National Military Command Center and CINCPAC, February 19, 1965. For report about General Tri, see Department of Defense Message Center, National Military Command Center, incoming from MACV, 18.20, February 19, 1965.

44. On the Capital Liberation Force and Thi's flight to Saigon, see above cited DOD message. On the agreement of the morning of the 20th, see Department of Defense Message Center, National Military Command Center, 16.27 EST, February 19, 1965; cables from Taylor to State, February 19, 1965. On entry of the anti-coup forces and Thao's broadcast and departure, see Department of Defense Message Center, National Military Command Center, 16.27 EST, February 19, 1965; cables from Taylor to State, February 19, 1965.

45. On the first rump session and the U.S.'s supplying transport, see cable from MACV to National Military Command Center, February 20, 1965. On the second rump session, see Department of Defense Message Center, National Military Command Center, incoming cable from MACV, February 21, 1965. Attending the second session were Generals Cao, Co, Dong, Khang, Ky, Thi, Thieu, and Tran Van Minh. The phrases quoted are from General Cao's subsequent account, which accords with Westmoreland's reporting. See Cao's interview in *Hoa Binh,* February 4, 5, 1972. In the *New York Times* account of this second rump meeting, its Saigon correspondent, Jack Langguth, observed, "Brig. Gen. Robert R. Rowland, the Air Force Officer that advises Marshal Ky, went in and out of the Armed Forces Meeting." (*New York Times,* February 22, 1965.)

46. On Khanh's capitulation, see Department of Defense Message Center, Military Command Center, from Gen. Westmoreland, received 10. PM, February 21, 1965. EST. Rusk quote is from cable to Amembassy, Saigon, February 23, 1965.

47. Regarding the delay in the bombing program, Westmoreland had cabled on February 19 that the "political atmosphere was

not ripe for Rolling Thunder tomorrow."
(Department of Defense Message Center,
National Military Command Center, February 19, 1965.) Rowan quote is from his Memorandum for the President, February 23,
1965.

48. "Moving towards" quote is from
"Individuals and Cliques in South Vietnam," February 25, 1965, p. 6, NSF, Vietnam, vol. 29. Taylor quotes are from incoming telegram to Department of State,
February 26, 1965.

49. The text of the resolution and details concerning the Peace Movement Committee may be found in Thich Nhat Hanh,
Vietnam: The Lotus in the Sea of Fire (London: SCM Press, 1967), pp. 89–90.

50. On the Cabinet discussion, see CIA
Office of Current Intelligence, "The Situation in South Vietnam as of 0600 EST," February 28, 1965, and *New York Times* of the
same date. On the arrests, see Nhat Hanh,
Lotus in the Sea of Fire, p. 90, and *New York
Times,* March 3, 4, 1965. For quote from
staff correspondent, see *New York Times* of
March 2, and for Quat's announcement and
Ky's statement, see *ibid.,* March 2, 3, and 4,
1965.

XII. The Call
for U.S. Ground Forces

1. Total infiltration 1959–64 reported by
MACV was 39,517, broken down as follows:

1959–60	4,556
1961	5,443
1962	12,475
1963	7,713
1964	8,130
1965 (reported as of 21 April)	1,200

(CIA, Directorate of Intelligence, "The Situation in South Vietnam [15–21 April 1965],"
p. 9.) This estimate appears close to that in
the "recent study of infiltration" referred to
by Taylor in his January 6, 1965, cable to
Secstate marked "For the President," where

the total infiltration since February 1960 is
estimated at 34,000.

Positioning PAVN troops in Laos in
preparation for exercising the option of introducing them into Vietnam—whether in
case of or regardless of an escalation in U.S.
military input—might have taken place before the introduction of American combat
forces in March. References to PAVN units'
having "departed the North" in certain
months does not itself mean that they entered the South, whatever their ultimate des-
tination; and, of course, some troops were
destined for Laos itself.

2. Westmoreland's report was forwarded to Johnson by McGeorge Bundy
(NSF, Vietnam vol. 6). For the April 21 date,
see *PP* (Gravel), 3:392, 438. In his retrospective *The Vantage Point* (Weidenfeld and
Nicolson, 1972), Lyndon Johnson states that
"by April at least one full regiment" of
North Vietnamese troops was in the South
(p. 138). A CIA briefing of the CIA Subcommittee of the Senate Armed Services Committee of April 9, 1965 (a copy of which the
CIA's director, John McCone, sent to President Johnson), refers to an enemy build-up
in the northernmost provinces of South
Vietnam, "which probably includes regular
formations of the *North* Vietnamese army
for the first time." (Special Briefing for Senator Stennis, April 9, 1965.) The CIA's Office
of National Estimates, "Current Trends in
Vietnam," April 30, 1965, reported, "MACV
has recently confirmed the presence of a battalion of regular PAVN troops with the Viet
Cong, and we believe that there are two
more."

3. Incoming telegrams, Department of
State, from Taylor, May 5, 27, 1967, NSF,
Vietnam, vol. 34.

4. Quote is from Memorandum from
Earle G. Wheeler for Secretary of Defense,
"US/Allied Troop Deployments to South
Vietnam (SVN)," June 11, 1965. Subsequent
cable ("Immediate") was from Taylor to
Secstate, July 11, 1965.

5. Figures are in JCS Study Group Report, July 14, 1965; *PP* (Gravel) 4:295; 3:706.
For the number of U.S. troops in Vietnam at

this time, see Memorandum for the President from McGeorge Bundy, "The History of Recommendations for Increased U.S. Forces in Vietnam," July 26, 1965; National Security Council, "Chronology of Presidential Decisions: Deployment of Major U.S. Forces to Vietnam," July 29, 1965. The dispatch of an additional 49,000 U.S. troops was authorized on April 21, with the main body of the 173rd Airborne Brigade arriving in Vietnam on May 5. *(Ibid.)* For U.S. troop strength as of June 30, 1965, see Herbert Schandler, *The Unmaking of a President* (Princeton University Press, 1977), p. 352 (compiled from DOD statistics). For the figures on troop strength as of March 5, 1966, see General Wheeler's report of March 11, 1966, "Meeting in Cabinet Room."

6. For Westmoreland's February 25 assessment, see *PP* (Gravel), 3:337. The quote represents the summation of the Pentagon analyst; for his subsequent prediction, see *PP (NYT)*, p. 399.

7. In discussions with me, Tuyen said that he and others had developed plans for arriving at a settlement with both the NLF and Hanoi. These called for setting up joint committees with the NLF to work on problems relating to a settlement and political integration. They hoped to achieve a "normalization of relations" with Hanoi that would provide for commerce and cultural exchange, and after a considerable period they would consider reunification. (Saigon, January 16, 1970.) On April 16, 1965, *Le Monde* carried an account of an interview with Tuyen by Jean Lacouture and Jacques Decornoy, that had apparently been held no more than a few days before, in which Tuyen stated that it was necessary to end the war and proposed that the Saigon government be broadened to incorporate the democratic-socialist left, so that a national front could be created capable of negotiating with "the adversary" on an equal footing. According to a CIA Intelligence Memorandum, "The Quat government" was "the target of apparently unfounded rumours, probably stemming from Catholic sources, that it was secretly negotiating with the Viet Cong. . . .

Quat's deputy premier, Tran Van Tuyen, was also under suspicion for alleged contacts in Paris . . . with pro–Viet Cong or pro-neutralist Vietnamese exiles. [sanitized] the latter strongly denied any such contacts or any remarks favouring negotiations with the Viet Cong. It remains possible, however, that he did meet the exiles in question." ("South Vietnamese Government Contacts with the Viet Cong and Liberation Front," November 26, 1965.)

Quat clearly went along with the decision to launch the bombing campaign against North Vietnam. He may not have known of President Johnson's March authorization of the use of napalm on these bombing runs or its actual employment, which began on the 14th. However, he was aware of and acquiesced in the landing of U.S. marines on March 8 to protect the Danang air base. He went along with the decision four weeks later that these Americans be employed in counterinsurgency combat, though he seems to have been misled as to the extent of this, having been assured that these operations would be restricted to the vicinity of the marine bases at Danang and Phu Bai. (Cable from Ball to U.S. Saigon Embassy, April 5, 1965.)

Quote is from cable from Taylor to State, March 9, 1965. Quat acknowledged, Taylor observed, that it was far from certain that the Vietnamese generals would accept a joint military command, and Westmoreland responded negatively to the idea. Observing that there was "no longer an effective ARVN chain of command because of the irresponsible game of musical chairs among the top leadership," he cautioned that "the Vietnamese generals would accept integrated command only to the extent that the United States contributed troops" and he then "advised against U.S. commitment to any rigid arrangement" because the Saigon government and its armed forces "had not achieved sufficient political and military maturity." (*PP* [Gravel], 2:357.)

8. For the Military Council's orders, see Jack Langguth, *New York Times,* February 28, 1965. Taylor quotes are from his Weekly

Report to the President, March 2, 1965, NSF, Vietnam, vol. 30. Cooper's advice is in his Memorandum for Mr. Bundy, "Vietnam," March 1, 1965, pp. 1, 5.

9. CIA, Office of Current Intelligence, "The Situation in Vietnam as of 0600 EST," March 11, 1965. This report noted that Co's stance may have been in part a rationalization of his command's inability to concentrate forces for offensive actions because of a "preoccupation with defense against Viet Cong actions." General Co, a Buddhist, was regarded by the U.S. Military as "friendly to Americans." (Defense Intelligence Agency, "Vietnamese Coup Personalities.")

10. On these arrests of Cao Dai and expulsion of Huyen, see CIA, Directorate of Intelligence, "The Situation in South Vietnam (18 March–24 March 1965)," March 24, 1965, and cable from Taylor to State, March 12, 1965. (Dr. Pham Van Huyen later became a minister in the Hanoi government.) For the fullest treatment of the views and ouster of Quang Lien, see Takashi Oka, "Thich Quang Lien's Peace Movement," Institute of Current World Affairs, April 20, 1965. In a cable of March 4, Taylor said the Buddhist Institute (led by Tam Chau and Tri Quang) "seems to be smiling benignly on Quang Lien's program without any formal responsibility for it." Quang Lien's somewhat muddled and internally inconsistent proposal called not only for all U.S. troops to be withdrawn from the South and all Russian and Chinese advisers and troops from the North, but also for all NLF forces to be sent to the North or disarmed. Although with respect to foreign troops this might at first blush have struck some as a balanced proposal, its thrust was regarded as impinging heavily on the United States: no Russian troops were ever introduced into North Vietnam, and not until later, after the introduction of U.S. ground combat troops was further advanced in South Vietnam, did the Chinese send troops—engineering and antiaircraft units —into the North.

11. See Takashi Oka, "Thich Quang Lien's Peace Movement," pp. 7–8. The lack of greater aggressiveness at this time may

have been partly based on a division among the senior leaders. Though Thich Tam Chau appears to have been eclipsed by Thich Tri Quang while the latter was in the forefront of the effort to oust Prime Minister Huong, by early March Tam Chau had regained considerable ground, with Tri Quang and his powerful associate, Thich Thien Minh, now appearing relatively restrained. See cable from Taylor to State, March 12, 1965.

12. Memorandum for Chester Cooper, "Courses of Action in South Vietnam," March 22, 1965, White House Files: NSF, Vietnam, vol. 31.

13. Recommendation of three divisions is in Memorandum for the President from McG. B[undy], "The History of Recommendations for Increased U.S. Forces in Vietnam," July 24, 1965.

14. Memorandum from Office of Assistant Secretary of Defense, by John McNaughton, March 10, 1965. This was apparently the first draft of his memorandum "Plan for Action for South Vietnam," of which a later draft (March 24) is reproduced in *PP (NYT)*, pp. 432–40. (The authors of the *NYT* account are clearly incorrect in believing that the draft they cite was the first. The March 10 draft, from which I quote, bears the handwritten note on the cover page "Mac—A preliminary shot at an outline.") McNaughton held the post of assistant secretary of defense until July 19, 1967, when he died in an air crash in the United States.

15. In this version of March 24, 1965, the third option was subsumed within a section headed "Exit by Negotiations." (*PP [NYT]*, pp. 437–38.)

16. *Ibid.*, p. 278; *PP* (Gravel), 3:499–500.

17. This difficulty in distinguishing personal from U.S. prestige was emphasized by George Ball in a discussion with the author, January 1965, and by James Thomson, who during this period served as senior White House aide. (Seminar, Cornell University, November 5, 1979. See also his "How Could Vietnam Happen?," *Atlantic Monthly,* April 1968.)

18. As early as February 23, 1965, Rusk called for the immediate stationing of a marine-battalion combat team in Danang, "to be reinforced promptly to a brigade if the security situation calls for it." (Memorandum, "Vietnam.") Cooper quote is from his Memorandum for Bundy, "Vietnam" March 1, 1965, p. 3.

19. "Integrity" and anti-American demonstrations is from message from CINCPAC to JCS, National Command Center, February 21, 1965.

20. Westmoreland's assessment is in cable ("For the President") from Taylor to Department of State, January 6, 1965. Westmoreland estimated that to protect any one of the three large jet-capable airfields would require "up to 6 battalions of U.S. ground forces."

21. Taylor quote and personnel total is from his cable to Department of State, February 28, 1965.

22. Westmoreland quote is in cable ("For the President") from Taylor to Department of State, January 6, 1965. Thomson comment was in discussion with the author, Ithaca, N.Y., November 5, 1979.

23. Taylor quotes are from his Weekly Report to the President, March 2, 1965. CIA quote is from CIA, Office of National Estimates, "Current Trends in Vietnam," Special Memorandum No. 12–65, April 30, 1965.

24. Cable from Taylor to Secstate, March 8, 1965.

25. For General Johnson's report, McNamara's concurrence, and preference for second option, see *PP* (Gravel), 3:428–29. For Taylor's response, see Memorandum from McGeorge Bundy, July 24, 1965.

26. Figures are from CIA, Directorate of Intelligence, "The Situation in South Vietnam (31 March–7 April, 1965)," p. 4. Much smaller figures were released to the press; see *New York Times*, March 30, 31, 1965.

27. On the two-division request, see *PP* (Gravel), 3:406–7. In this cable to the Department of State of February 28, Taylor stated that in discussions with Quat and top ARVN officers, he and Westmoreland

"would emphasize the limited mission of the Marines and their non-involvement in pacification."

28. On three-division proposal and Rusk request for postponement, and on filling out existing units, see Memorandum from McGeorge Bundy, July 24, 1965; NSC Chronology, Departure of Major U.S. forces, July 29, 1965. With respect to the dispatch of the next two marine battalions, see outgoing cable from Department of State (Ball) to Amembassy, April 5, 1965. This message reads, "In discussions with Quat it is considered more desireable to describe the mission of the Marines as engaging initially in counterinsurgency combat operations in the vicinity of the Marine bases (Danang and Phu Bai)." It had, in fact, already been decided that the mission of these marines would not be confined to base protection. For Bundy's proposal on removal of restrictions, see *PP* (Gravel), 3:280; see also the White House Memorandum of April 1, 1965, prepared as a basis for discussion with the president that day, "Key Elements for Discussion, Thursday, April 1, 1965." Memorandum from McCone to Rusk, McNamara, Bundy, and Taylor, April 2, 1965, is in *PP* (Gravel), 3:364–65. In conveying his memorandum to the president, McCone added a covering letter that summarized it and indicated he was aware that his memorandum might never have reached Johnson. (Letter [undated], NSC Vietnam, vol. 32.)

29. NSC Action Memorandum No. 328, April 6, 1965, in *PP (NYT)*, pp. 442–43.

30. Quote is in *PP (NYT)*, pp. 403–4; *PP* (Gravel), 3:409. The president's endorsement is to be inferred from cable from the JCS to CINCPAC, April 14, 1965.

31. On Taylor's being bypassed and his reaction, see Cable from Taylor to State, April 14, 1965. See also *PP* (Gravel), 3:451; *PP (NYT)*, pp. 404, 444. Bundy's advice is in his memorandum to the President of April 14, 1965.

32. "No present requirement" quote is from cable from Taylor to RUEHCR/SECSTATE, March 26, 1965. Concerning Quat, see also CIA, Monthly Report, "The Situa-

tion in South Vietnam," April 2, 1965, p. 17.

33. Quotes are from cable from Taylor to Secstate (with copy to the White House for the attention of McGeorge Bundy), April 17, 1965, in both *PP (NYT)*, pp. 443–46, and *PP* (Gravel), 3:704–5.

34. For Johnson's postponement of the decision, see cable from McGeorge Bundy to Taylor, April 18, 1965. "Unanimous recommendation" is in Memorandum for the President from Robert S. McNamara, April 21, 1965.

35. See Johnson, *Vantage Point*, p. 140; William Bundy, Oral History, tape 5, pp. 9, 21–22. (For fuller discussion of this point see the next chapter.)

36. For Johnson's approval of this recommendation, see Memorandum from McGeorge Bundy, July 24, 1965.

37. Ball quotes are from his *The Past Has Another Pattern* (W. W. Norton, 1982), pp. 330–31. William Bundy quotes are from his Oral History, May 29, 1969, tape 2, p. 27.

38. Quote is in *New York Times*, May 5, 1965. A number of those who felt obliged to vote in favor of this appropriation, including Albert Gore of Tennessee and Jacob Javits of New York, took a line similar to that of George D. Aiken of Vermont; this did not mean "endorsement of the costly mistakes of the past" or "blanket approval of waging undeclared war anywhere."

39. For an indication of the administration's concern with the influence of what is termed "a vocal minority of students and professors" critical of its Vietnam policy and its efforts to organize countervailing efforts on the campuses, see the Joint Cable from State-AID-DOD-USIA (over Rusk's signature) of May 8, 1965, to American Embassy in Saigon. For substantial excerpts of the Washington teach-in debates, see *New York Times*, May 17, 1965.

40. Paul Warnke, "The Search for Peace," in *The Legacy of Vietnam*, ed. Anthony Lake (Council on Foreign Relations–New York University Press, 1976), pp. 318–19. Warnke was general counsel for the Department of Defense, 1966–67, and assistant secretary, 1967–69.

41. Rusk and Warnke quotes are in *ibid.*, pp. 319, 315.

42. Taylor quote is from "Waging Negotiations—A Vietnam Study," in *Legacy of Vietnam*, ed. Lake, p. 298. For South Vietnamese leaders on the NLF, see CIA, Office of Current Intelligence, "South Vietnamese Government Contacts with the Viet Cong Liberation Front," November 26, 1965.

43. Cooper quotes are from *The Lost Crusade: America in Vietnam* (Dodd, Mead, 1970), pp. 271–72.

44. These same distinctions between "discussions" and "negotiations" and between "parties" (which would include the NLF) and "governments" were made in the administration's response to an appeal by seventeen nonaligned nations on April 8. See *ibid.*, p. 272. For Saigon's public explanation, see George McT. Kahin and John W. Lewis, *The United States in Vietnam*, 2nd ed. rev. & enl. (Delta, 1969), pp. 554–55.

45. The proposal to work with Cornell was soon dropped.

46. The full text of the manifesto was carried by Liberation Radio, March 23, 1965, and is reproduced in Raskin and Fall, eds., *The Vietnam Reader*, pp. 232–49. Appended in the Raskin-Fall text (pp. 249–52) are the discrepancies between the Hanoi and the NLF radio-intercept versions. See also Kahin and Lewis, *United States in Vietnam*, pp. 208–9; *Jen-Min Jih-pao (People's Daily)*, March 25 and 29 and April 11, 1965.

47. This embassy assessment is carried in the April 7 report of the CIA's Directorate of Intelligence, "The Situation in South Vietnam (31 March–7 April, 1965)," pp. 13–14.

48. Quote and speculations about Trinh is in *ibid.*, p. 12. The other focus of the April 7 meeting (and of the DRV's Council of Ministers' Meeting on April 4) was "self-reliance" while making full use of the support of socialist allies.

49. From report of Premier Pham Van Dong, April 8, 1965, as given on Hanoi Radio, April 13, 1965.

50. "If we choose" quote is from "The DRV Terms and Possible U.S. Counter Proposals," April 24, 1965, p. 3 (probably written by Chester Cooper). Bundy quotes are from his Memorandum for the President, "The Demonologists Look at the Noise from Hanoi, Peking and Moscow," April 20, 1965.

51. Memorandum for the President from George Ball, April 21, 1965. Ball clarified the ideas contained in this during a discussion with me in January 1985. Quotes that follow are from his memorandum.

52. McGeorge Bundy, "Notes on Political Objectives," April 25, 1965.

53. Memorandum for the President from Dick Goodwin, April 27, 1965.

54. Quotes are from CIA, Directorate of Intelligence, "The Situation in South Vietnam (15–21 April 1965)," p. 17.

55. Quote is from Cooper, *Lost Crusade,* pp. 274–75.

56. *New York Times,* May 19, 1965.

57. Wallace J. Thies, *When Governments Collide: Coercion and Diplomacy in the Vietnam Conflict* (University of California Press, 1980), p. 95.

58. William Bundy, Oral History, tape 2, May 29, 1969, p. 28.

59. Even then Washington, while acknowledging the veracity of this report, stated it had no plans for releasing the text of Rusk's message. (*New York Times,* December 12, 1965.)

60. Ball, *The Past Has Another Pattern,* p. 404.

XIII. Constraints on U.S. Policy

1. On the nine countries, see "Free World Aid to Vietnam," May 26, 1965. The nine countries that had made contributions were Australia, Canada, nationalist China, France, Germany, Japan, Malaysia, New Zealand, and the United Kingdom. Quotes are from Memorandum for Mr. Bundy, "The Week in Asia," July 31, 1965 (probably from Chester Cooper and James Thomson);

cable ("Priority") from Ambassador, for Bundy, Taipei, July 7, 1964.

2. On the Chinat participation in a covert program in North Vietnam, see Memorandum for Messrs. Sullivan, McNaughton, Yarmolinsky, "Attached Draft Memorandum for the President from William P. Bundy," March 3, 1964, pp. 3, 15.

3. On the Chinat contingent, its origins, and composition, see Memorandum of Conversation, by Deputy Ambassador Johnson and Edgar C. Sovik, U.S. Embassy [Saigon] April 23, 1965; CIA, Monthly Report, "The Situation in South Vietnam," June 4, 1965, p. 12. For brief references to what appear to have been small increases resulting from initiatives taken by Nguyen Cao Ky in 1966 and 1967, see *PP* (Gravel), 2:290, 365, 402. For Kennedy's attitude, see the anonymous article (by "An American Officer"), "The Report the President Wanted Published," *Saturday Evening Post,* May 20, 1961. On Father Hoa and the Sea Swallows, see also Don Schanche, "Father Hoa's Little War," *ibid.,* February 17, 1962; *Life,* March 16, 1962; Dickey Chappelle, "The Fighting Priest of South Vietnam," *Reader's Digest,* July 1963. For Taylor's concern and "first step," see cable from Taylor to RUEHCR/SECSTATE, September 5, 1964.

4. In a British Gallup poll taken during the week of March 25–30, 1965, 45 percent of the respondents disapproved of "the recent American armed action in Vietnam," with only 30 percent approving and 25 percent answering "don't-know." To the question "If the U.S. Government asks Britain to help in the war in South Viet-Nam what should we do?" only 10 percent said "send troops," with 19 percent answering "send war materials only," 56 percent answering "take no part at all," and 15 percent answering "don't know." In France, Carl Rowan informed Senator Fulbright in March, even before adverse publicity there on the U.S. use of nonlethal gas in Vietnam, 41 percent of the public disapproved of American policies in Vietnam and only 10 percent approved. (Carl T. Rowan [Director of USIS] to J. W. Fulbright, "Foreign Opinion on the

U.S. and Vietnam," April 19, 1965. This memorandum also incorporates the British Gallup poll.)

5. The initial Australian contingent included some 1,400 infantry plus 100 military advisers and a 73-man air force. It is not clear whether the Philippine and Thai governments passed on to their soldiers all the supplemental U.S. allowance to which they were entitled. An attempt by the U.S. General Accounting Office to ascertain this with respect to Philippine soldiers was unsuccessful. (*New York Times,* March 26, 1970.)

6. Figures and quote are in General W. C. Westmoreland, "Report on Operations in South Vietnam," January 1964–June 1968, pp. 223–26.

7. On negotiations and bargaining with Manila, see Memorandum for Mr. Bundy, "The Week That Was," December 31, 1964, from Chester Cooper and James C. Thomson, Jr. "Free World Aid to Viet-Nam," May 26, 1965, p. 6. Chester L. Cooper, *The Lost Crusade: America in Vietnam* (Dodd, Mead, 1970), p. 267. Washington's offer to Manila of March 24, 1965, included, in addition to the overseas allowances for these troops ($2.5 million annually), "pay and allowances for the replacement troops needed for internal security within the Philippines (cost $1.9 million annually)," re-equipping the new troops ($3 million annually), and $1.75 million for operations, administration, and training. ("Free World Aid to Viet-Nam," p. 6.) On Symington's observation, see U.S. Congress, Senate, Committee on Foreign Relations, Subcommittee on United States Security Agreements and Commitments Abroad, 91st Cong., 1st sess., *Hearings: United States Security Agreements and Commitments Abroad,* held September 30–November 17, 1969 (hereafter cited as *Hearings: 1969*), pp. 265, 271.

8. For Marcos' exactions, see *Hearings: 1969,* pp. 255, 285; for his state visit, see *New York Times,* September 16, 1966; for quote see *New York Times,* October 13, 1969.

9. For payments to Thai government and its troops in Vietnam, see Cooper, *Lost*

Crusade, p. 267; Roland A. Paul, *American Military Commitments Abroad* (Rutgers University Press, 1973), pp. 109–14. (Paul had been chief counsel to Senator Stuart Symington's subcommittee of the Committee on Foreign Relations that in 1969–70 conducted hearings on U.S. commitments abroad.) *Hearings: 1969,* p. 842; for payment to Thai troops in Laos, see Symington Committee Staff Report, "Thailand, Laos and Cambodia, January 1972," May 8, 1973, p. 20. By the end of 1965 there were about 200 U.S. aircraft based in Thailand and over 9,000 U.S. air-force personnel; by December 1966 there were about 400 planes and 25,000 U.S. personnel; by 1968 the number had grown to 589 planes and 33,500 U.S. air-force personnel (in addition to 11,494 U.S. army personnel). Among the many air bases built by the United States in Thailand was the enormous complex at U Tapao where B-52s were stationed beginning in 1967.

10. On remuneration to South Korean soldiers in Vietnam, see Craig Whitney, *New York Times,* November 9, 1972; Leonard Santorelli (Reuters), Washington *Post,* August 11, 1969; Frank Baldwin, "The American Utilization of South Korean Troops in Vietnam," in *America's Rented Troops: South Koreans in Vietnam* (American Friends Service Committee, 1975[?]). Baldwin, who has produced the most comprehensive study on this subject, calculated (p. 11) that given a monthly salary for Korean privates of $1.60, the daily U.S.-paid overseas allowance of $1.25 (per day) meant that these soldiers were receiving twenty-three times their normal base pay.

11. For dollar remittances and other foreign exchange earnings, see U.S. Agency for International Development, Monthly Progress Report, "Korean Foreign Exchange Earnings from Vietnam," Korea, March 21, 1969; Tad Szulc, *New York Times,* January 25, 1970; Cooper, *Lost Crusade,* p. 266.

12. Quote is from Roland A. Paul, *American Military Commitments Abroad,* pp. 103–4. Fuller data can be found in *Symington Hearings: 1969,* p. 1545.

13. For total Korean earnings, see *ibid;*

Baldwin, "American Utilization of South Korean Troops," p. 7.

14. Wicker quote is from *New York Times,* November 25, 1969. "Use as a SEATO commitment" comes from Senator J. W. Fulbright, in *Hearings: 1969,* p. 261. Regarding the Philippine obligation under the Mutual Defense Treaty, the State Department representative at the hearings, stated that "Article V of the U.S.-Philippine Mutual Defense Treaty makes it clear that an armed attack in the 'Pacific Area' on either party engages the commitments of the other party under that Article. The Treaty itself contains no definition of 'Pacific Area.' The available legislative history . . . suggests that Vietnam and Korea are included as well [as Japan] in the term 'Pacific Area' as it is used in this treaty." (*Ibid.,* p. 36.)

15. As of June 11, the U.S. JCS reported, "Only two of nine V.C. regiments have been engaged and probably only a similar proportion of their separate battalions have been committed." (Memorandum for the Secretary of Defense, June 11, 1965.) The estimate of a single North Vietnamese battalion by mid-May was Westmoreland's and was conveyed by McGeorge Bundy to the president, May 13, 1965 (NSF, Vietnam, vol. 6); see also n. 2 to ch. XII.

16. William Bundy quote is from his Memorandum for Messrs. Sullivan, McNaughton, and Yarmolinsky, "Attached Draft Memorandum for the President," March 2, 1964, p. 18.

17. To the Secretary from Thomas L. Hughes [Director], "The Effects of the Bombings of North Vietnam," June 29, 1965 (NSF, Vietnam, vol. 35.) Napalm was first authorized with the bombing runs of March 14–15. (*PP* [Gravel], 3:284.)

18. A Defense Intelligence Agency "Strike Damage Estimate" appended to the Hughes report had estimated that through June 24, 1965, these attacks had destroyed 17.4 percent of North Vietnam's "national capacity" in ammunition depots, 13.1 percent of petroleum storage facilities, 9 percent of its power plants, 75 percent of its naval bases, 2.2 percent of its supply depots, and

2 percent of its barracks. In most cases much higher percentages were reported as having been hit—53.1 percent of ammunition depots, 14.2 percent of barracks, and 7.1 percent of supply depots. (NSF, Vietnam, vol. 35.)

19. Memorandum prepared by Daniel Ellsberg, April 6, 1965, for McGeorge Bundy, "Analysis of Mining or Blockade at D.R.V. Ports," conveyed by John McNaughton, April 8, 1965. I made an on-the-spot study of the effects of Nixon's bombing and port mining in October 1972. For further details, see my "Visit to a Heavily Bombed Area," Washington *Star,* October 22, 1972.

20. Memorandum for the President from Robert S. McNamara, "Recommendations of Additional Deployments to Vietnam," July 20, 1965.

21. Quotes are in Allen S. Whiting, *The Chinese Calculus of Deterrence* (University of Michigan Press, 1975), pp. 184–85.

22. Quotes are from CIA, Office of Current Intelligence, "Chinese Communist Military Presence in North Vietnam," October 20, 1965. In late June the U.S. Intelligence Board had reported that the headquarters of China's Second Railway Engineer Division had been deployed inside the DRV and concluded that "most if not all, of the Chinese Communist military entities deployed in the northeast region of North Vietnam are engaged in logistic activities." It also noted that "Since our last report the number of Chinese Communist [deleted] in the Sino/DRV border area has continued to increase. (Excerpt from the Combined Watch Report of the United States Intelligence Board, July 30, 1965.) See also CIA, Office of Current Intelligence, "Possible Change in Chinese Communist Military Posture Vis-à-vis Vietnam," October 17, 1965, which also gives mid-June as the date Chinese communist units began to appear in North Vietnam.

23. All quotes are from Whiting, *Chinese Calculus,* pp. 186–87.

24. *Ibid.,* pp. 188, 193.

25. *Ibid.,* pp. 187–88. Whiting notes that

"the fullest public summary" of the pertinent intelligence reports appeared in *New York Times,* December 1, 1965. An examination of that report discloses how very Spartan its coverage was.

26. CIA, Office of Current Intelligence, "South Vietnamese Government Contacts with the Viet Cong and Liberation Front," November 26, 1965; CIA, Directorate of Intelligence, "The Situation in South Vietnam (6 May–12 May 1965)," May 12, 1965.

27. As early as April 3, McGeorge Bundy's two Vietnam aides noted that there had already been "rumblings" that the Buddhists might withdraw their support from Quat. (Memorandum from Chester L. Cooper and James C. Thomson, Jr., for Mr. Bundy.) Taylor writes, "We Americans . . . suspected him [Quat] of being under the thumb of Tri Quang" and his government "sure to be sensitive to the vicissitudes of military-Buddhist relations." (Maxwell Taylor, *Swords and Ploughshares* [W.W. Norton, 1972], p. 336.)

28. Taylor's sense of Quat's opposition to more deployments is in his Cable to RUEHCR/SECSTATE, March 26, 1965, and Memorandum for the President from McG.B[undy], "The History of Recommendations for Increased U.S. Forces in Vietnam," July 24, 1965. "Quat is queasy" is from *PP (NYT),* p. 433. Taylor's May 19 warning is in his Cable to Secstate, May 19, 1965.

29. Tran Van Tuyen quote is from interview with the author, Saigon, January 16, 1970. Taylor quote is from his Cable ("For the President") to Secstate, May 25, 1965. Indicative of Quat's sensitivity on this charge was his defensiveness and felt need to give assurances to the contrary before the National Legislative Council—a largely powerless appointed body, but one in which sat several Buddhists close to Thich Tri Quang and Thich Tam Chau. There, according to Taylor, "Quat emphasized that [the] GVN must be master of its house in the conduct of war and in eventual negotiation of a political settlement." (Cable from Taylor to Secstate, May 29, 1965.)

30. For Harold K. Johnson's views, see his Memorandum for Chairman JCS, Chief of Naval Operations, Chief of U.S. Air Force, Commandant of the Marine Corps, April 12, 1965. Johnson characterized Quat's government as unstable and one that "lacks an appreciation of the responsibilities of a central government and has no identifiable power center to direct government operations or to attract unreserved or uninhibited support of fragmented Vietnamese leadership." On the mission's view of Quat, see cable from Taylor to State, March 5, 1965; see also *New York Times,* May 22, June 6, 8, 9, 1965. Lodge quotes are from Memorandum of Conversation, "Advice to Quat," Meeting with Ambassador Henry Cabot Lodge, April 28, 1965.

31. On Thi and Lieu, see CIA Weekly Report, "The Situation in South Vietnam," March 10, 1965. The marine commander, General Le Nguyen Khanh, reported to U.S. officials that he believed Thi and Lieu were planning a military takeover whereby General Thieu would be a figurehead leader and real control would be exercised by Thi and Lieu. (CIA, Intelligence Cable, May 29, 1965.)

32. For these developments, see especially CIA's "The Situation in Vietnam," reports for April 8–14, 1965; April 15–21; April 22–28; May 6–12; CIA Monthly Report, June 4, 1965; CIA, Information Cables, May 4, May 16, May 20, June 11, 1965.

The mutiny by a group of fleet commanders against navy chief Rear Admiral Chung Tang Cang resulted in his suspension by the armed forces commander, General Tran Van Minh. The CIA observed that opportunism by Cang's subordinates, who took advantage of his loyalty to Khanh, may have been a factor.

A partly sanitized CIA cable of June 11 reported that three of Quat's Cabinet members alleged that "the U.S. was behind the coup attempt of Pham Ngoc Thao," charging that U.S. involvement was linked to the recent visit to Saigon of Henry Cabot Lodge, whom they said they suspected of meeting with anti-Quat elements and "inciting them

to take action against the government."
(CIA, Intelligence Cable, June 11, 1965.) It is
possible that Pham Ngoc Thao's alleged
coup was Quat's fabrication—a stratagem to
provide an excuse for the arrests that followed. Among those sanitized documents
that bear on the coup and its planning are
CIA Intelligence Information Cables from
Saigon of May 4, 14, and 20 (two) and a CIA
cable of May 20. See also CIA, Monthly
Report, "The Situation in South Vietnam,"
June 4, 1965; cable from Taylor to Secstate,
May 25, 1965; Le Tu Hung, *Nhung cai chet
trong cach mang 1-11-63* (Saigon: Dinh Minh
Ngoc, 1971), pp. 140–42, 172.

33. "Apparently" quote is from CIA,
Directorate of Intelligence, "The Situation
in South Vietnam (May 20–26)," p. iii; see
also p. 2. Charges against Quat and a call for
his replacement are in cable from Taylor to
RUEHCR/SECSTATE, May 29, 1965.

34. "Had not" and "we will" quotes are
from cable (to be passed "eyes only to Secretary McNamara, McGeorge Bundy, Admiral Raborn, and Admiral Sharp") from Taylor to State, June 5, 1965, pp. 3, 5. (This
report had been drafted by the U.S. mission's intelligence committee and concurred
in by Taylor, Alexis Johnson, and General
Westmoreland). Langguth quote is from
New York Times, June 2, 1965.

35. Taylor reported Quat believed that
Suu was "deliberately being used by opposition elements to create crisis situation in
order to undermine Quat Government and
force Quat's resignation." (Cable from Taylor to RUEHCR/SECSTATE, May 26, 1965.)
On Quat and Thi, see cable from Taylor to
State, June 17, 1965; on the erosion of Quat's
position and his ouster see *New York Times,*
June 10, 11, 12, 1965.

As the Defense Department analyst
puts it, "Taylor easily acquiesced to the return to direct military rule." (*P.P.* [Gravel],
2:362.) One of Quat's deputy prime ministers, Tran Van Tuyen, charged that U.S. officials urged the generals to overthrow Quat's
government. (Interview with the author,
Saigon, January 16, 1970.)

A CIA report had characterized Gen-

eral Thi as "an erratic and unpredictable
officer of some political talent. He is widely
distrusted because of his obvious efforts to
link himself with Buddhist power in the
northern provinces which I Corps [of which
he was commander] controls and because of
his opportunism." (CIA Intelligence Memorandum, "Individuals and Cliques in South
Vietnam," February 25, 1965. An earlier report stated that U.S. military observers in
1960 had characterized Thi as "tough, un-
scrupulous, and fearless, but dumb," and
that he was then considered to be "both anti-
Communist and somewhat anti-United
States." (CIA Office of Central Reference,
Biographic Register, January 29, 1965.)

36. For Taylor's reservations, see his
cable to State, June 21, 1965.

37. Once Ky had abandoned Khanh
and agreed to work for his removal, he had
been much more favorably regarded by the
U.S. military. Co, a Buddhist, was commander of II Corps and was regarded by U.S.
military intelligence as an "outstanding
officer" and "friendly to Americans." (See
DIA, "Vietnamese Coup Personalities,"
February 20, 1965.)

38. On Ky and the new regime, see *New
York Times,* June 14, 20, 25, 27, July 1, 1965.
According to Vu Van Thai, the Vietnamese
ambassador to Washington, Ky later tried to
explain his remark about Hitler by stating
that his intention had been "to infuse in our
youth the same fanaticism, the same dedication, the same fighting spirit as Hitler in-
fused in his people." (Lecture, Cornell University, Ithaca, N.Y., March 3, 1966.) On
Ky's requests for troops, see cable from Taylor to Secretary of State, June 28, 1965; cable
from Taylor to Secstate—For the President,
June 30, 1965; airgram from American Embassy, Saigon, to State, "Secretary
McNamara's Visit: Meeting with G.V.N.
(July 16, 1965)," July 27, 1965; *PP* (Gravel),
2:363.

39. Mansfield quote is from his letter to
the President, June 9, 1965. On Ky and
Thieu's admission, see CIA, Office of Current Intelligence, Intelligence Memorandum, November 26, 1965; Memorandum

from Leonard Unger to Secretary McNamara, "Additional Deployments to Viet-Nam and Subsequent Developments," July 20, 1965.

40. Quotes are from airgram from American Embassy, Saigon, to Department of State, "Secretary McNamara's Visit: [July 16] Meeting with G.V.N.," July 27, 1965.

XIV. The Decision on Major U.S. Ground Forces: Phase I

1. Clark Clifford wrote the president on May 17, 1965, urging that U.S. ground forces be "kept to a minimum, consistent with the protection of our installations and property" in Vietnam. A substantial build-up "could be a quagmire," and "turn into an open end commitment."

2. For Viet Cong strengths and ARVN's declines, see cable from Westmoreland to White House, JCS, and CINCPAC, June 7, 1965; text of cable from Westmoreland (COMUSMAC 20055), June 14, 1965.

3. For Westmoreland and JCS troop requests, see cables cited above and Memorandum from Earle G. Wheeler, Chairman, JCS, for the Secretary of Defense, "U.S./Allied Troop Deployments to South Vietnam," June 11, 1965. (The JCS approval provided for a slightly different package from Westmoreland's, but its essentials were the same.) See also McGeorge Bundy, "The History of Recommendations for Increased U.S. Forces in Vietnam," July 24, 1965, and PP (Gravel) 3:470–71. Johnson statement is in Summary Notes of 552nd NSC Meeting, June 11, 1965, by Bromley Smith, p. 3. NSC, "Chronology of Presidential Decisions," p. 5.

4. On the June 19 approval, JCS ten-battalion addition, and Westmoreland comment, see McGeorge Bundy, "The History of Recommendations for Increased U.S. Forces in Vietnam," and PP (Gravel) 3:471. The JCS hoped that nine or ten of these battalions could be supplied by "third countries"—primarily South Korea.

5. Expectation of Taylor's replacement is clear in Mansfield's letter to the president of June 9, arguing that Alexis Johnson rather than Lodge should replace Taylor. On July 3, Rusk cabled Taylor that Lodge would be his replacement.

Bundy quote is from Memorandum to the President, June 5, 1965. Bundy stated that he was more attracted to this course than either McNamara or Rusk. Taylor was not willing to go that far, having just cabled, "We would avoid the sensitive area of Hanoi/Haiphong except for an occasional well selected target within the area to show that we can penetrate and that there is no sanctuary." Abiding by this limitation, he felt, would be unlikely to provoke a Chinese reaction. (Cable from Taylor to Secstate [Priority], June 3, 1965.)

6. Summary Notes of 552nd NSC Meeting, July 11, 1965.

7. Memorandum to the President from Mike Mansfield, "Vietnam," June 9, 1965.

8. George W. Ball, The Past Has Another Pattern (W. W. Norton, 1982), p. 396.

9. Quoted in ibid.

10. "United States Commitments Regarding the Defense of South Vietnam," June 23, 1965; a second memorandum of the same date (of which the first two pages have not been declassified), which argued in part that costs involved in a compromise settlement had been exaggerated; a third, dated June 28 and captioned "Cutting Our Losses in South Vietnam," partly reproduced in Ball's Past Has Another Pattern, pp. 396–97; and a fourth, on July 1, referred to below.

11. For Lansdale's role, see Memorandum from D. W. Ropa and Chester Cooper for Mr. Bundy, "The Weeks That Were: Vietnam," October 11, 1965, p. 3.

12. Memorandum for the President from McG.B[undy], July 1, 1965, 8:20 P.M.

13. The quoted material and a somewhat longer extract can be found in Ball's book, Past Has Another Pattern, p. 398.

14. Memorandum for the President from Robert McNamara, "Program of Expanded Military and Political Moves with Respect to Vietnam," June 26, 1965 (revised July 1).

15. On the lack of such material in the files made available, see PP (Gravel), 3:473.

16. McNaughton's draft is "Analysis and Options for South Vietnam," July 13, 1965.

17. Memorandum for the Secretary of Defense, June 30, 1965. (It is evident that Bundy had seen the June 26 draft of McNamara's July 1 memorandum.)

18. The account of this meeting is based on the comprehensive notes taken by William Bundy, which are reproduced in part, with his commentary, in his unpublished 1972 Vietnam study, ch. 27, pp. 15–21.

19. National Security Council, "Deployment of Major U.S. Forces Abroad: Chronology of Presidential Decisions," July 29, 1965, p. 4.

20. Airgram from American Embassy, Saigon, "Secretary McNamara's Visit: Meeting with GVN," July 27, 1965 pp. 7–9. In addition to Lodge and Wheeler, McNamara's party included John McNaughton, Chester Cooper, General Andrew Goodpaster, and Arthur Sylvester.

21. See, for instance, Rusk's highly confidential memorandum of July 15 to the director of the CIA [copy received in McGeorge Bundy's office the next day], which he begins with the sentence "In order to assist us in making contingency plans for possible increases in US forces in South Viet-Nam, I should appreciate it if you could provide an assessment of major reactions to a substantial increase in our force structure in South Viet-Nam."

As to whether the president had made up his mind two days later, the paraphrasing of the *Pentagon Papers* analyst for this period of a July 17 message from Cyrus Vance to McNamara in Saigon (*PP* [Gravel], 3:416, 475–76) is ambiguous (the actual text of the cable is not cited, nor is it supplied anywhere in the *Papers,* and the LBJ Library has not been able to find a copy—either classified or declassified). This has led the analyst to infer —incorrectly—that the president had already approved the deployment of thirty-four U.S. battalions. Since this was the number called for in the original, June 7 Westmoreland request, whereas the JCS proposal had stipulated forty-four, Vance may have meant that the president was favoring the

original Westmoreland request over the JCS plan. But, more to the point, it is not clear from the paraphrasing whether Vance is saying the president has decided to go ahead with an actual deployment (as the Pentagon analyst concludes) or simply with developing a plan for such deployment. Subsequently declassified documents—evidently not available to the analyst—now point to the latter interpretation, with Johnson at this point doing no more than the necessary antecedent planning for a proposed escalation he had not yet approved. The Pentagon analyst's paraphrasing of the Vance cable is roughly the same as that in the NSC's "Deployment of Major U.S. Forces Abroad: Chronology of Presidential Decisions" (from which it is presumably drawn), which states, "Vance told McNamara that the president had decided to go ahead with the plan to deploy 34 U.S. battalions and that he was favourably disposed to the call-up of reserves and extension of tours of active duty personnel." McGeorge Bundy finds the Pentagon analyst's interpretation puzzling, for though he believes Johnson already in his own mind had probably concluded that additional U.S. ground forces were necessary, he certainly had not decided how many, nor had he agreed to the JCS request for a call-up of reserves (discussion with the author, December 1984)—and, in fact, he never did. William Bundy, who earlier concluded that Vance's July 17 cable signified that Johnson had actually made a substantive decision, now believes that he probably had not yet done so, and that if he had, then he evidently pulled back from that position and did not commit himself before July 24 (discussion with the author, January 1985).

22. Memorandum for the President, "The History of Recommendations for Increased U.S. Forces in Vietnam," July 24, 1965, 8.15 P.M., p. 2.

23. Memorandum for the President from Robert S. McNamara, "Recommendations of Additional Deployments to Vietnam," July 20, 1965.

24. Cable from Taylor to Secstate, July 11, 1965. Taylor also reported that in June alone the Saigon government had lost con-

trol of 240 hamlets out of 1,500 to the Viet Cong in I Corps and 289 out of 2,061 in II Corps (p. 2 of sec. 7 of this long July 11 cable). The order of battle posited by U.S. sources for July 21, 1965, credited the Viet Cong with 53,000 regular troops (up from 37,000 attributed to it on March 17) and approximately 100,000 irregulars and guerrillas. Saigon was then credited with a total of 570,000 (including regular, regional, and popular forces), this incorporating 133 "infantry-type" battalions as against 72 for the Viet Cong. *PP* (Gravel), 3:441.

25. The nine-point outcome, McNamara stated, "could include also arrangements regarding elections, relations between North and South Vietnam, participation in peace-keeping by international forces, membership for North and South Vietnam in the UN and so on."

XV. The Decision on Major U.S. Ground Forces: Phase II

1. *PP (NYT)*, p. 415.

2. Opinions of McGeorge Bundy, William Bundy, and George Ball emerged in discussions with the author, December 1984 and January 1985. Before his extensive 1971–72 reconstruction of events during the week of July 21, 1965 (recorded in his unpublished 1972 Vietnam study), William Bundy had come to a conclusion close to that expressed by Cooper. For Bundy's earlier view, see his Oral History, tape for May 29, 1969, pp. 41–42.

3. Chester L. Cooper, *The Lost Crusade: America in Vietnam* (Dodd, Mead, 1970), pp. 284–85.

4. NSC, "Cabinet Room, Wednesday, July 21, 1965"; Jack Valenti, *A Very Human President* (W.W. Norton, 1975), pp. 319–56; Memorandum for the Record by C[hester].S.C.[ooper], "Meetings on Vietnam, July 21, 1965."

5. Valenti adds: "meaning, of course, the intrusion of Russian or Chinese troops into the fray." The context here and in the NSC and Cooper accounts, however, indi-

cates that the concern is with the introduction of large numbers of *North Vietnamese* forces.

6. Leonard Unger's memorandum to McNamara of July 20, 1965, "Additional Deployments to Vietnam and Subsequent Developments," reported that "several GVN leaders . . . appear quite persuaded that in the political combat that would come with peace, they would be the weaker adversary and that the Communists would win." William Bundy states that he had not been given a copy of Unger's memorandum (discussion with the author, January 1985). With respect to Ky and Thieu specifically, see the retrospective CIA Intelligence Memorandum (Office of Current Intelligence), "South Vietnamese Government Contacts with the Viet Cong and Liberation Front," November 26, 1965. This inability to compete successfully with the NLF politically was subsequently expressed to me in the clearest terms by the chief political adviser to Ky and Thieu, General Pham Xuan Chieu, in an extensive discussion in Saigon.

7. The Cooper account of Bundy's response to Ball is much fuller (even in its condensed version more than twice as long as Valenti's clearly attenuated account). The same is true of the immediately following comments by Rusk. (Valenti has here too missed much that is important.)

8. For Clifford's views see his letter to the President, May 17, 1965, NSF, Vietnam, List IV. Ball quote is in *The Past Has Another Pattern* (W. W. Norton, 1982), p. 402. For brief mention of the meeting, see also Lyndon B. Johnson, *The Vantage Point,* (Weidenfeld and Nicolson, 1972), p. 148.

9. Quoted in Ball, *Past Has Another Pattern,* p. 403.

10. Clark Clifford, Oral History, LBJ Library, tape 2, p. 16.

11. Memoranda for the President from McGeorge Bundy, "Timing of Decisions and Actions in Vietnam," July 21, 1965, 8 P.M.; "Reasons for Avoiding a Big Military Appropriation in Vietnam," July 23, 1965.

12. Memorandum for the President, "The History of Recommendations for In-

creased US Forces in Vietnam," July 24, 1965, 8:15 P.M., p. 3.

13. On July 25, the president informed the Australian government of a likely increase of U.S. armed forces in Vietnam, apparently having ordered Bundy to give such notification the previous evening after getting his recommendation that the McNamara/JCS proposal be accepted. This is implicit in Bundy's Memorandum for the President of July 26, 1965 (concerning Johnson's dinner with the Australian ambassador), and his handwritten note appended to it. The memorandum refers to a circular, presumably sent to governments that were contributing troops in Vietnam in support of the U.S. effort and were now being asked to increase their assistance, with Bundy's annotation reading, "I attach also the circular we sent in your name on the basis of your Saturday orders to me."

14. For details of Westmoreland's "Concept of Operations," see *PP* (Gravel), 3:481–82; 4:296.

15. "Camp David–Aspen Lodge," July 25, 1965 (NSC files); "Views of Clark Clifford on Vietnam," taken down by Jack Valenti, Camp David, July 25, 5 P.M. The account of Goldberg's role is from his letter to the writer of May 13, 1985.

16. "Camp David–Aspen Lodge," July 25, 1965. This record is from the National Security Files and is p. 24 of what is apparently a comprehensive record (possibly one prepared for Johnson when he wrote *The Vantage Point*), only a few pages of which have been released. The second sentence has been sanitized. Clifford states that the letter read by Johnson "could very well have come from Senator Mansfield" and "would certainly be consistent with his views." (Letter to the writer, June 24, 1985.) Mansfield thinks this could have been his letter, but is not sure. (Letter to the writer from Ambassador Mansfield, June 15, 1985.)

17. Letter to the writer from Arthur J. Goldberg, May 13, 1985.

18. William Bundy quote from his unpublished 1972 Vietnam study, ch. 30, pp. 10–11.

19. Present at the meetings on July 26, 1965, were the president, vice-president, McNamara, Rusk, Ball, Bundy, Lodge, Wheeler, Valenti, Busby, and Moyers, with Clifford, Helms, and Raborn joining the group thirty minutes after the meeting got under way. Before the last three arrived, the discussion centered on the bombing of SAM sites, but it presumably focused on the ground-troop decision afterward. It is that part of the record, following the initial discussion of SAM sites, which has still not been declassified. ("Cabinet Room, Monday, July 26, 1965, Subject: Vietnam.")

20. Memorandum to the President, from Mike Mansfield, "Meeting on Vietnam," July 27, 1965. The president that same day had his secretary of defense prepare answers to the senators' first eighteen points (with confidential copies sent to Aiken, Cooper, Fulbright, Russell, and Sparkman) and himself wrote Mansfield a note (apparently drafted by Joseph A. Califano, Jr.) assuring him of his confidence in McNamara, as "the best Secretary of Defense in the history of this country." (Memorandum for the President from Robert S. McNamara, July 28, 1965; letter from L.B.J. to Mike Mansfield, same day; Memorandum for the President from Joseph A. Califano, Jr., July 28, 1965.) Mansfield confirms that his own representations to Johnson were considerably stronger than the consensus reached by the six senators. (Notes attached to his letter of June 15, 1985, to the writer.)

21. Summary Notes of 553rd NSC Meeting, July 27, 1965—5:40–6:20 P.M., by Bromley Smith; McGeorge Bundy, Memorandum Prepared on November 2 from Notes Dated July 27, 1965 at 6 P.M. This bears his annotation "The memorandum is strictly limited to what the notes themselves contain; there is no reliance on memory." Attending this NSC meeting were Rusk, Ball, the two Bundys, McNamara, McNaughton, Wheeler, Raborn, Helms, Ambassadors Lodge and Llewellyn Thompson, Clifford, Rowan, Leonard Marks, Attorney General Nicholas Katzenbach, Treasury Secretary Henry Fowler, and White

House staff members Busby, Douglas Cater, Richard Goodwin, Moyers, Valenti, and Bromley Smith.

22. In this second declassification, the part of the document under paragraph b of Rusk's statement remained sanitized (on the grounds that this was "foreign government information").

23. Congressional Leadership Meeting, Tuesday, July 27, 1965 (NSC Files). Present were McGeorge Bundy, Busby, Califano, Cater, Lodge, Goodwin, McNamara, Moyers, Raborn, Rusk, and Wheeler, plus Senators Everett Dirksen, Bourke Hickenlooper, Thomas Kuchel, Russell Long, Mike Mansfield, and George Smathers; and Representatives Carl Albert, Les Arends, Hale Boggs, Gerald Ford, and Speaker John McCormack.

24. *New York Times,* July 29 and 30, 1965. During the first hour of the poll by Sindlinger and Company (which usually specialized in market analyses), 54.23 percent agreed with the president's actions, 23.55 percent disagreed, and 22.22 percent were in the "don't know" category. In the sixth and final hour of the poll, those in agreement had dropped to 46.97 percent, but with only 9.77 percent disagreeing and the "don't know" category climbing to 43.26 percent. (*Ibid.,* July 30, 1965.)

25. Johnson, *Vantage Point,* p. 152.

26. Doris Kearns, *Lyndon Johnson and the American Dream* (Harper & Row, 1971), pp. 295–96.

27. For a tabulation of U.S. forces in Vietnam based on official Department of Defense sources, see Herbert Y. Schandler, *The Unmaking of a President* (Princeton University Press, 1977), p. 352. The peak strength for U.S. forces, reached under Nixon in April 1969, was 543,000. For McNamara's memorandum of October 14, 1966, and for Westmoreland's request of March 18, 1967 (and its amended version of March 28), see *PP (NYT),* pp. 542–52, 556–65.

28. Maxwell Taylor, *Swords and Ploughshares* (Norton, 1972), p. 401.

29. See chapter XIII. Doris Kearns

writes: "Johnson operated on the fundamental premise that he could bomb only up to a certain point. To move beyond that point—for example, to mine Haiphong Harbor or bomb the Red River dikes—might risk war with Russia or China. Suspicious that North Vietnam had entered into secret treaties with the Communist superpowers, Johnson lived in constant fear of triggering some imaginary provision of some imaginary treaty." (*Lyndon Johnson and the American Dream,* p. 282.) For Johnson's view of LeMay, see Hugh Sidey, *A Very Personal Presidency: Lyndon Johnson in the White House* (Atheneum, 1965), p. 203.

XVI. The Final Polarization

1. Quote is from Memorandum from James Thomson, Jr., and D. W. Ropa for McGeorge Bundy, "The New Year in Asia," January 7, 1966, which goes on to observe, "There is some danger that prolonged and more intensive fighting will generate resentment against the U.S. or the Saigon government, and pressure for peace-at-any-price by pacifist elements such as the Buddhists."

2. *New York Times,* March 17, 1966.

3. Cable from Lodge to Department of State, March 30, 1966.

4. Michael Krepon, "Blanket Coverage: Two Case Studies of Area Weapons in Indochina," in *The World Military Order* ed. Mary Kaldor and Asbjorn Eide (Praeger, 1979), p. 54. Napalm's use in Vietnam had been authorized by President Kennedy by at least 1962.

Most of the civilian wounded who were lucky enough to get to the few Vietnamese hospitals attributed their wounds to the bombs and artillery shells so lavishly loosed into rural areas by American, South Korean, and South Vietnamese forces, or to air-delivered napalm.

In December 1966 and January 1967 I made a survey of civilian casualties in hospitals in Hué, Quang Ngai, and Saigon. A report compiled by medical staff at the Hué hospital indicated that almost 90 percent of the civilian war casualties were caused by American and South Vietnamese air bombardment and artillery; at Quang Ngai, an American staff member at the hospital reckoned that this was the case for about 70 percent of such civilian casualties, with the remaining 30 percent stemming from Viet Cong and North Vietnamese military action —mostly from land mines. The only information I could secure at Saigon's Central Hospital was that "most of the civilian casualties" there were from aerial and artillery bombardment. I presented these findings to an informal meeting of the U.S. Senate Foreign Relations Committee on March 20, 1967.

5. Authorization is in cable from CINCPAC to COMUSMACV [Westmoreland], Advance to Secretary of Defense, National Military Command Center, Message Center, September 26, 1964. (NSF: Vietnam, vol. 18,).

It is sobering to note that the Department of Defense saw Vietnam as something of a weapons laboratory for technological advances in the U.S. arsenal. Thus, the last paragraph of this cable reads: "Introduction of these weapons into combat environment for first time provides unique opportunity to monitor and record weapon effectiveness, develop optimum delivery techniques and tactics and to gather associated data which would prove invaluable in later use or to discover possible weakness or improvements in weapons. It can be anticipated that various DOD [Department of Defense], RDT, and E agencies will request such data shortly after commencement of employment. Without detracting from operational capability, request data cited above be documented for possible report to be submitted when sufficient experience has been gained and significant amount of munitions expended."

A cable from JCS to CINCPAC of January 22, 1965 (NSF: Vietnam, vol. 26), stated: "Currently, the CBU-2/A and the CBU-14, which used the same BLU-3 bomblet, are unclassified munitions and there are no special restrictions on their use. You are authorized and encouraged to employ these munitions in your area of responsibility, against suitable targets as indicated by operational considerations. . . . It is important that no publicity be given to the use of these weapons. . . . It is important to monitor and record weapon effectiveness, develop optimum tactics and delivery techniques, and gather associated data which may uncover possible weaknesses leading to improvements in munitions, tactics, and delivery techniques. Without detracting from operational capability, request the data cited above be documented to the extent feasible, and brief report be submitted to the JCS when sufficient data have been obtained."

6. Krepon, "Blanket Coverage," pp. 56, 60–61. For a vivid example of the lack of precision in bombing operations, see Jonathan Schell, *The Military Half* (Alfred A. Knopf, 1968), pp. 172–75.

7. Statistics and quotes are drawn from Raphael Littauer and Norman Uphoff, eds., *The Air War in Indochina* (Beacon Press, 1972).

8. David Marr, "The Technological Imperative in U.S. War Strategy in Vietnam," in *The World Military Order,* ed. Mary Kaldor and Asbjorn Eide (Praeger, 1979), p. 31. After five years in the marines, Marr became a severe critic of the American role in Vietnam and later emerged as one of the leading scholars of Vietnamese history in the West.

9. With respect to the early use of B-52s in close air support missions, see Cable from Taylor to President, July 20, 1965 (NSF: Vietnam, 1965). Quote is from Guenter Lewy, *America in Vietnam* (Oxford, 1978), p. 99 and rest of sentence is from *ibid.*, p. 101.

10. Jack Shulemson and Major Charles M. Johnson, USMC, *US Marines in Vietnam: The Landing and the Buildup, 1965* (History and Museums Division, Headquarters U.S. Marine Corps, 1978), pp. 47–48.

11. Schell, *Military Half,* pp. 200–201, 206–7. May had delivered pretty much the same talk to me impromptu some eight months earlier, when I spent a night in his heavily sandbagged house, and he was accoutered in the same large Mexican sombrero, bushy mustache, and Western-style

leather boots he wore with Schell—but Schell's account is fuller than my notes.

12. For a very different view, see the knowledgeable account of another Marine lieutenant colonel who found himself at odds with a number of aspects of Westmoreland's strategy, William Corson, *The Betrayal* (W. W. Norton, 1968).

13. Quote and Komer statement are from *Newsweek,* June 19, 1972. It is my understanding that Neil Sheehan is completing a major study of Vann's role in Vietnam.

14. John Paul Vann, "Harnessing the Revolution in South Vietnam," USOM, Saigon, September 10, 1965 (mimeo).

15. As of March 11, 1966, total crops destroyed by the use of herbicides was 39,794 hectares (or approximately 98,000 acres). The total for 1962–63 had been 379 hectares; for 1964, 5,690 hectares; for 1965, 27,300 hectares; and from January 1 to March 11, 1966, 6,425 hectares. (Cable from Lodge to RUHLC/SECSTATE, March 11, 1966.) For the three-year period 1965–67 a total of 391,120 acres of crop land and 1,383,000 acres of forest land were sprayed with herbicides. (E. W. Pfeiffer and Gordon H. Orians, "The Military Uses of Herbicides in Vietnam," in *Harvest of Death* [Free Press, 1972], p. 120.)

On reduction of land under cultivation in 1967, see William Corson, *Betrayal,* p. 124. Quote is from U.S. Congress, Senate, Subcommittee to Investigate Problems Connected with Refugees and Escapees, Committee on the Judiciary, 94th Cong., 1st Sess., January 27, 1975 (U.S. Government Printing Office, 1975), p. 39. Official figures on refugees were provided me by the Saigon government's Central Refugee Office (previously known as the Commissariat for Refugees). Figures for July–December 1965 are from Memorandum from Thomson and Ropa to Bundy, "New Year in Asia," January 7, 1966.

16. It should be noted that a subsidiary—though minor—cause of the drop in rice production was the fact that U.S. rice imported under the PL 480 program was sold at lower prices than locally grown rice. Export and import figures are from "Annual Report: FY 1970," National Bank of Vietnam, Saigon, p. 17.

17. Quote is from Memorandum from Thomson and Ropa for Bundy, "New Year in Asia," January 7, 1966, p. 6. In 1966–67 and on subsequent trips to Vietnam, I visited some of these camps.

18. Devaluation of the South Vietnamese currency in mid-1966 from sixty to 118 piasters to the dollar achieved only partial and temporary relief from inflationary pressures. Despite the devaluation and the lifting of quotas on foreign-exchange spending, the money supply more than doubled between 1965 and 1967. There was an inflation rate of 55 percent in 1965 and 59 percent in 1966. (U.S. Congress, Senate, Committee on Foreign Relations, Hearings: "Supplemental Foreign Assistance FY 1966, Vietnam," January 1966, pp. 219–20; "Improper Practices, Commodity Import Program. U.S. Foreign Aid, Vietnam," Permanent Subcommittee on Investigations of the Committee on Government Operations, *Hearings:* April 1967 [Part I].)

19. The massive increase in U.S. forces during the eighteen months after his memorandum first appeared in September 1965 reinforced this judgment and led him to conclude that the NLF had been losing support. (Note added to the April 1, 1967, reproduction of his memorandum.) But he acknowledged that this did not mean that defectors went over to the GVN side.

20. The trip was through Long An province, January 1967. Though this rich province abutted on the southern perimeter of Saigon, at least half of it was then controlled by the Viet Cong, requiring us to use a helicopter for most of the distance we traveled.

Despite his many criticisms of U.S. policies in Vietnam, Vann remained an ardent proponent of American intervention and saw the United States' global position as dependent on its performance in Vietnam. As he put it in his 1965–67 memorandum, Vietnam occupied "the center of a world stage in a drama potentially affecting the destiny of all mankind."

Some nine months before I took this

trip with Vann, Lodge had acknowledged that "land reform is a delicate problem. . . . Evidence is that many measures under consideration would adversely affect vested interests within or close to gov't." He observed that the steps then being taken by Saigon were "slow and hesitant" but were the "first steps taken by any gov't since Diem abandoned his ambitious program about 1959." (Cable from Lodge to State Department, March 21, 1966.)

21. Memorandum from James C. Thomson and Ropa for Mr. Bundy, "New Year in Asia," January 7, 1966.

22. General Chieu's remarks are in transcript of discussion with the author, Saigon, December 1966. General Chieu was the officer "in charge of its [the Directorate's] plans in the political field." (CIA Weekly Report, "The Situation in South Vietnam," January 12, 1966, NSF, NSC History, Honolulu Conference, vol. 3.) The U.S. mission in Saigon regarded him as the "most politically astute of its members," a view shared by the State Department and a number of the general's ARVN colleagues, who so informed me.

23. He stated that while he had served as Saigon's ambassador to Taipei, Chiang had "several times offered troops for Vietnam." (U.S. officials, however, continued to oppose any large-scale introduction of Chiang's soldiers, fearing to trigger a major response from Peking; as was noted earlier, the small number of Chiang's troops that were in fact in South Vietnam was a tightly held secret.)

24. The Buddhist position outlined here is a common denominator of views held in the spring of 1966, as expressed to me shortly afterward by several leaders of the Buddhist Institute, including Thich Thien Minh, Thich Thien Hoa, Thich Phap Tri, and Thich Nhat Hanh in 1966 and early 1967, and Thich Tri Quang somewhat later.

In a discussion and a subsequent exchange of letters with me during August 1965, William Bundy, then assistant secretary of state for Far Eastern affairs, strongly opposed elections' being held in South Vietnam either for a government or simply for a negotiating authority, even if Ky remained in office. Among the objections he cited was "the obvious consequences in terms of the South Vietnamese will to resist."

25. Komer quote is from Memorandum for Mr. Valenti, The White House, March 29, 1966. Oka quote is from "The Anatomy of a Crisis: Part II—The Buddhist Background," Institute of Current World Affairs, May 31, 1966, p. 8.

26. Thich Thien Minh's statements came in discussions with the author, Saigon, December 1966, January 1967.

27. For these immediate Buddhist objectives, see Takashi Oka, "Buddhism as a Political Force: Danang and After," and "The Anatomy of a Crisis, Part III—Maneuver and Counter-Maneuver," Institute of Current World Affairs, May 29, 1966, p. 4, and June 4, 1966, pp. 8–10. The provincial councilors had been elected in relatively free elections on May 30, 1965; the merely consultative nature of their role undoubtedly reduced any inclination in Saigon to influence the election results.

28. For Lodge's view of Tri Quang, see PP (Gravel), 2:376. Many U.S. officials disagreed with this assessment and, though worried that Tri Quang might be willing to negotiate with the NLF, did not regard him as procommunist. It is not certain that Lodge actually believed his own allegation. A CIA report of January 29, 1965, had stated, "U.S. embassy officials concluded on the basis of their extensive talks with Quang . . . that he was an anti-Communist, Vietnamese nationalist." (National Security Files: International Meetings and Travel Trip, McGeorge Bundy—Saigon 2465, vol. 5, JFK Library). For the Hughes article, see Newsweek, May 30, 1966, p. 23.

29. New York Times, April 9, 1965, p. 2.

30. "Personal satrapies" was the term still used in a National Intelligence Estimate written even after Ky and Thieu had been able to remove General Thi and a series of his successors. (CIA, NIE 53–66, "Problems of Political Development in South Vietnam over the Next Year or So," December 15, 1966, p. 5.)

31. Lodge's comments on a "Special Report Regarding General Thi," which had been passed to Walt Rostow—who had just replaced McGeorge Bundy as special assistant to the president for national security affairs—on April 5, with a covering note from Desmond FitzGerald, the CIA's deputy director for plans. (NSF: Vietnam, vol. 50.) McGeorge Bundy had left his White House post on March 1, 1966, to head the Ford Foundation. For about a month thereafter, Robert Komer occupied his position on a temporary basis, until it was filled by Walt W. Rostow, the nominee of Jack Valenti.

32. On reactions to Johnson's embrace of Ky, see *PP* (Gravel), 2:369. As the Pentagon chroniclers observe, the major thrust of this February 6–8 Honolulu conference was to stimulate what were termed "non-military pacification efforts." *Ibid.*

33. On the attitudes of senior U.S. officials toward Thi, see Memorandum for the President from Bromley Smith, March 9, 1966; cables from Lodge to State, March 25, 1966, and Rusk to Saigon, March 29, 1966; meeting of the president with most of his senior advisers, Cabinet Room, March 11, 1965. For Walt's opinion of Thi, see Lewis W. Walt, *Strange War, Strange Strategy* (Funk and Wagnalls, 1970).

34. On reactions in I Corps to news of Thi's removal, see CIA cable to White House Situation Room, "The Situation in Vietnam," March 11, 1966. Oka, "Anatomy of a Crisis," May 31, 1966, p. 3; Cabinet meeting cited above; cable from Lodge to State, March 16, 1966.

35. On Chuan's actions, see CIA cable to White House Situation Room, March 14, 1966; *Hoa Binh,* January 20, 1972. General Chuan as commander of the Fifth Division had taken part in defeating the coup against Diem in 1960 in which Thi was involved, and this record of opposition to Thi was apparently regarded as making it unlikely that he would cooperate with Thi's supporters during this new assignment. The CIA observed that "Chuan stands to benefit personally from supporting the government, but he has in the past been unwilling to deal harshly

with Buddhist unrest." Lodge quote and other opinions are in his cables to State, March 16, 28, 1966. In referring to Thi, Rusk, in a cable to Lodge of March 23, observed, "Whatever he has been saying publicly, we cannot help but feel that his private actions must have fed Buddhist fires, although we recognize that Tri Quang is heart of difficulty." Regarding Thi's future, a CIA report of March 14 observed that "there have been some indications of distrust toward Thi by some Buddhist leaders in I Corps suggesting that they have not been looking to Thi as an alternative to the present Saigon regime." (From CIA [Saigon] to White House, March 14, 1966.)

36. Cable from Secretary Rusk to Lodge, Martch 16, 1966.

37. Memorandum for the President from Bromley Smith, "Ky Plans to Steal Buddhist Thunder," March 17, 1966. In meetings with the Buddhist leaders, Lodge urged that the Ky government's program was the best way to move from military to civilian government. For more on meetings between Buddhist leaders, Ky, Thieu, and Lodge, see Takashi Oka, "The Anatomy of a Crisis, Part III," June 4, 1966, pp. 5, 6; Charles Mohr, *New York Times,* March 21, 1966; cable from Lodge to Secretary of State, March 17, 1964; and Memorandum for the President from Bromley Smith, March 17, 1966.

38. Lodge quotes are in *PP* (Gravel), 2:371. Frankel quote is in *New York Times,* May 19, 1966; see also *ibid.,* April 10, 1966.

39. On Ky's reneging, see Charles Mohr, *New York Times,* March 29, 1966. Oka, "Anatomy of a Crisis, Part III," p. 9.

40. On Lodge-Rusk interchange, see Cable from Lodge to Secretary of State, March 31, 1966; on efforts to split Struggle Movement, see Memorandum for the President from Dean Rusk, "Political Situation in South Vietnam," April 2, 1966.

41. For reactions to the betrayal, see *New York Times,* April 3, 4, March 30, April 1, 1966; *PP* (Gravel), 2:372, and Cables from Rusk to Amembassy Saigon, March 29 and 30, 1966. Quotes are in Memorandum

for the President from Rusk, "Political Agitation in Saigon," March 25, 1966.

42. Advice to Johnson is in Memorandum for the President from Dean Rusk, "Political Situation in South Vietnam," April 2, 1966. "Almost total absence" quote is from Daniel Ellsberg, Memorandum for the Record, "Ky's Candidacy and U.S. Stakes in the Coming Election," Saigon, May 4, 1967, p. 20.

43. For Lodge's urging and plans, see his cables to State, March 31, April 1, 1966. General Chuan states that while he was I Corps commander "a secret radio station had been set up in the Danang Air Base, at the headquarters of the 41st Air Squadron [under Ky's command], disguising itself as the radio of the Struggle Movement." (*Hoa Binh*, September 27, 1971.) This was confirmed to me by some members of the U.S. Foreign Service then serving in Vietnam, who were themselves outraged by this ploy. It is possible that this was the "airborne radio transmitter" Lodge had mentioned in a cable to Washington (3549) and about which Rusk had queried him in a cable of March 29, 1966. For Ky's April 3 announcement, see *New York Times*, April 4, 1966; and Chuan, *Hoa Binh*, October 19, 1971.

On Lodge's agreement to Ky's use of force, see *PP* (Gravel), 2:372. Lodge had cabled Washington of the plan to send troops to Danang and Hué three days before. (Cable to Secstate, March 31, 1966, NSF: Vietnam, vol. 49.)

44. Greene quote is in *New York Times*, April 4, 1966. Westmoreland subsequently credited Chuan with having "tried hard to ameliorate differences and convince Premier Ky that he should keep troops out of the cities" in I Corps. (General William C. Westmoreland, *A Soldier Reports* [Doubleday, 1976], p. 171.) For General Chuan's views, see the account of his trial in *Hoa Binh*, January 20, 1972, and the interview with him in its issue of November 29, 1971. Both Vietnamese and U.S. officials with whom I discussed these events were convinced that Walt was cut out of the planning. See also *Hoa Binh*, November 28, 1971. Philip Habib, head of the political section of

the embassy, and some other U.S. officials in Saigon with whom I spoke in January 1967 were highly critical of Walt's conduct during the period of the Buddhist Struggle Movement, alleging that he had encouraged Tri Quang to believe that the U.S. government was sympathetic to him.

45. Cable from Lodge to Secretary of State, April 4, 1966.

46. Meeting in the Cabinet Room, April 4, 1966, 7:10 P.M. Present were the vice-president, Rusk, McNamara, Taylor, William Bundy, Valenti, and the president's close friend the hawkish Supreme Court justice Abe Fortas.

47. For Rusk's admonition, see Cable from Rusk to Amembassy Saigon, March 29, 1966. On the use of U.S. transport and the troops and equipment carried, see Memoranda for the President from Arthur McCafferty, White House Situation Room, April 4, 5, 6, 1966; and Cable from COMUSMACV to National Military Command Center and CINCPAC, April 5, 1966. Weighing twenty-six tons each, the M-41 tanks were too heavy for U.S. aircraft based in Southeast Asia to carry. (Department of Defense, Report of May 24, 1966, Papers of LBJ, Pres. 1963–1969, Confidential file, Agencies Reports, Department of Defense, May 3–10, 1966.) The base facilities of the U.S. and Vietnamese air forces were commingled in the huge Danang complex, and the South Vietnamese Forty-first Air Squadron base was well inside the perimeter the U.S. marines were assigned to defend.

48. On the First Division and Ky's response, see *PP* (Gravel), 2:373, *New York Times*, April 6, 1966. Though the First Division was headquartered in Hué, it had some troops in the Danang area.

49. On the collapse of the blitzkrieg, Ky's apology and promise of withdrawal, and the junta's decision to seek accommodation, see cable from COMUSMACV to Department of Defense, April 4, 1966; Memorandum for the President from Arthur McCafferty, April 5, 1966; Charles Mohr, *New York Times*, April 6, 1966. See also *ibid.*, April 7 and 8, 1966. Lodge quotes are in his cable to State, April 8, 1966.

50. Westmoreland and McNamara quotes are in Meeting of the President and his top advisers, Cabinet Room, April 6, 1966, 5:20 P.M. William Bundy quote is in his Oral History, May 26, 1969, tape I, pp. 31–32.

51. Sketchy references to this review may be found in *PP*, pp. 82–91, but the full memoranda referred to and drawn on here were not declassified until September 9, 1985. They are all from John McNaughton Files, McNTN II, Papers of Paul C. Warnke, LBJ Library. (McNamara's position is reflected in the abbreviated handwritten notes made by McNaughton at a White House meeting on April 9.)

52. On this two-pronged strategy, see *New York Times,* April 7, 9, 10, 1966; *PP* (Gravel), 4:85. An effort to split the Buddhist leadership was also urged on the president by Jack Valenti in a memorandum of April 4. (Jack Valenti, *A Very Human President,* p. 195.) Valenti also resurrected Ambassador Taylor's earlier suggestion that the Dalai Lama be brought to Vietnam. Support for Tri Quang was greatest in Hué and Danang and the surrounding areas, but was also significant in Saigon, where his chief lieutenant, Thien Minh, had organized and led a large Buddhist youth organization. Tam Chau's major political base lay with Buddhists in the Saigon area who, like him, had come down from the North in 1954. For Rostow's strategy, *PP* (Gravel), 4:85. Sheehan quote is from *New York Times,* April 11, 1966.

53. On the junta's concessions, the National Political Congress, and Ky's promise not to retaliate, see *New York Times,* April 14, 15, 16 (Neil Sheehan) and May 17 (Charles Mohr, 1966; Cable from Department of State (Ball) to Paris, April 14, 1966.

54. This is based on discussions in 1966, 1967, and 1971 with several of the top Buddhist leaders, including Tri Quang, Thien Minh, and Tran Quang Thuan. For Tri Quang's appeal from Hué, see Saigon Radio, April 18, 1966; *Vietnam Press,* April 19, 21, 1966.

55. *Hoa Binh,* July 27, 1972.

56. Dinh's account is from discussions with the author. General Chuan stated that he too had found that Walt opposed the use of force to settle the dispute and had wanted to play the role of mediator. (*Hoa Binh,* November 28, 1971.) See also Neil Sheehan, *New York Times,* May 21, 1966. Regarding the original distribution of arms from depots of the First Division, see *Hoa Binh,* November 9, 1971.

Ton That Dinh, one of the most senior generals in the army, was a native of Hué and distantly connected with the former imperial family. He had supported the coup against Diem and Nhu, which, it was generally conceded, could not otherwise have succeeded. Consequently, he was popular with the Buddhists, and this was an important reason for his being appointed to replace General Chuan, whom Ky and Thieu had tricked into returning for consultations to Saigon, where he was then relieved of his command. See the report on Chuan's trial in *Hoa Binh,* October 25, 1971. (Translated for me by Mai Elliott.)

57. See Oka, "Buddhism as a Political Force," May 29, 1967, p. 3. As Oka notes, Loan combined his new position with his previous appointment as chief of military security. Lieu, who had been close to Thi, had apparently tried to remain neutral in the face of the dispute in I Corps and in any case had been unwilling to use as much force against demonstrators in Saigon as Ky had wanted.

58. *New York Times,* May 5, 7, and 11, 1966.

59. Quote is from Agenda, National Security Council Meeting, "Vietnam: Key Issues," May 9, 1966, p. 40. Efforts to secure the declassification of U.S. internal documents bearing on this split within the U.S. government have not been successful, but its severity was evident to me in talks with U.S. embassy officials. *The New York Times* for May 16, 19, and 21, 1966, discusses differences among U.S. officials, especially between Lodge and Rusk. Westmoreland's account of the struggle movement and the operation against Danang in *A Soldier Reports* is in several places seriously misleading. It takes liberties with sequence and chronology, omits or distorts some important events, and

collapses the April 5 and May 15 attacks into one.

60. Ky quote is from transcript of Dinh's trial (July 1966) as reported in *Hoa Binh,* November 23, 1971. Sheehan quote is from *New York Times,* May 21, 1966.

61. On the launching of the attack and its unexpected nature see *New York Times,* May 15, 1966; discussions with Ton That Dinh in May and November 1979. See also *Hoa Binh,* May 11, 1972. *The New York Times* estimated that initially there were only three to five hundred local forces left in Danang to confront the invaders, and ultimately no more than seven hundred. *New York Times,* May 16, 21, 1966. (Note the parallel with the tactics of Westmoreland's U.S. military advisers in Hué as reported by *The New York Times,* June 6, 1966.)

62. Information on the delivery of U.S. equipment and arms is from *Hoa Binh,* August 9, 1972; discussions with Ton That Dinh. He says that the arrangements for the delivery of small arms were worked out by Ky's new national-police chief, General Loan. Dinh states that the forty new tanks were driven out of the port area by American military personnel. (*Hoa Binh,* May 9, 1972; discussions with Dinh.) He estimated it would take about four weeks to train crews of the smaller tanks already in I Corps to man this larger type. It should be noted that U.S. naval support activities at Danang were not under the command of General Walt, but under naval officers who reported to Westmoreland. (*New York Times,* May 15, 1966.) Regarding the arrival of the armored personnel carriers, see *New York Times,* May 23, 1966.

Dinh states he had been tricked into believing that the tanks had been brought to Danang to join the fight against the Viet Cong and North Vietnamese forces, and been told that they would be turned over to him at a ceremony that he had planned for the next evening. Ironically, as military commander of the First Corps area, he had earlier scheduled a large, well-advertised ceremonial "reconciliation dinner" for the evening of May 15, to which he had invited General Walt as well as Buddhist and Cath-

olic leaders and representatives of the Cao Dai, Hoa Hoa, Dai Viet, and VNQDD. The gathering was to represent a new solidarity both among the local groups and between them and Saigon—an increased harmony to which Dinh believed, with some justification, his own efforts had contributed. As he understood it, his command was to receive the tanks as the culminating episode in the solidarity ceremony. The only problem that he foresaw, he says, was his lack of soldiers trained to operate this new and larger type of tank. This, however, was not the major difficulty posed by the tanks, as he soon learned. For Dinh's efforts at restoring harmony, see Oka, "Buddhism as a Political Force, May 29, 1966; *Hoa Binh,* May 12, 1972. Oka credits Dinh with having "worked patiently, tactfully, to restore harmony between the region's divided communities and to dissolve hostility towards Saigon." On Walt's position, see his *Strange War,* p. 122. Walt, who appears to have been unaware of the impending attack, states that for several days before, "all appeared to be returning to normal."

63. On Walt's grant of asylum, see Walt, *Strange War,* p. 122; Oka, "Buddhism as a Political Force"; see also *New York Times,* May 16, 1966. On the call to McNamara, see *Hoa Binh,* May 18, 19, 21, 1972; corroborated in discussions with Ton That Dinh in Washington, D.C., and Ithaca, N.Y., in 1979.

Dinh says that McNamara told him that the operation would be limited to Danang, that since it would not extend to Hué it should not be regarded as a suppression of the Buddhists, and that its objectives were to restore Ky's control of Danang, remove the city's mayor, and discipline a number of officers such as Colonel Dam Quang Yeu and the command staff of his unit. He says he complained to McNamara that he should have been told in advance of the operation, that any disciplining of officers in I Corps should have been communicated to him as its commander, and charged that Americans were manning the tanks involved in the attack, implying that the suppression was being carried out with American participation. Habib's hostile attitude toward the Buddhist leaders was well known and was clearly evident to me (as well as others) in talking with him.

64. Habib's meeting with Dinh was reported in *Hoa Binh*, June 16, 18, 1972, corroborated in discussions with Dinh in 1979.

65. For Westmoreland's account, see his *A Soldier Reports*, p. 173.

66. This account was given me by U.S. officials stationed in the First Corps area at the time, but can also be drawn from a variety of other sources. See *New York Times*, May 21 and 22, 1966; Washington *Post*, May 19, 1966. Bernard Fall noted that, in addition to the marines' protection of the airlift, "American artillery kept vital communication points covered until A.R.V.N. troops could take them over." (*Last Reflections on a War* [Doubleday, 1967], p. 152.) Though the chronology is inaccurate, a vivid account of the U.S. tactics taken to intimidate Colonel Yeu—including circling helicopters and napalm-laden Phantom jets—is to be found in Jerrold Schechter, *The New Face of Buddha* (Coward-McCann, 1967), p. 219. With respect to U.S.-marine casualties, see Walt, *Strange War*, pp. 131–32.

67. Sheehan quotes are from *New York Times*, May 21, 22, 23, and 25, 1966. Westmoreland quotes are from *A Soldier Reports*, p. 175.

68. For the meeting between Ky and Thi at Chu Lai, see Lodge's cable to Secstate, May 27, 1966. A copy of the letter in which Westmoreland made his offer to Thi is in my possession. Thi informed me that he was physically fit and needed no such checkup, his only problem being "a little sinus trouble."

69. On Ky's moves against the Buddhists in Saigon, see *New York Times*, May 19 and 24, 1966; Saigon *Post*, May 19, 1966; Oka, "Buddhism as a Political Force," May 29, 1966, p. 7. For Ky and Thieu quotes, see *New York Times*, May 22, 1966; Saigon Radio, May 24, 1966.

70. On reactions in and the attack on Hué, see Charles Mohr, *New York Times*,

June 19; for Apple quote, see *ibid*, June 6, 1966. On the role of U.S. police advisers, see Monthly Report from Hue City and Thua Thien (May 16 through June 1966), June 24, 1966, from Robert M. French and Francis Barnett, PSA/Hué–Thua Thien, p. 7. ("PSA" stands for "Public Safety Advisor.") The term "act of retribution" was used by an American official then in Hué. The U.S. police advisers worked with Colonel Loan in Hué and in the expedition he mounted soon thereafter against the struggle movement in adjacent Quang Tri province, and, in cooperation with U.S. marines at Phu Bai, they provided food, gasoline, and radio transmitters to Loan's forces. (Monthly Report for Thua Thien, July 19, 1966, from Francis L. Barnett, PSA/ Thua Thien, pp. 1, 5.

71. This information was given me by students of an anti-Ky underground organization in Hué who had close contact with the NLF. Their assessment was shared by a U.S. consular official stationed in the First Corps area and other foreigners living there. See also Oka, "Buddhism as a Political Force."

72. Responsibility for the grenade attack on Thich Thien Minh was laid at Loan's door by a wide spectrum of Vietnamese opinion as well as by several well-informed U.S. embassy personnel with whom I discussed this matter. On the Vien Hoa Dao pagoda, see *New York Times*, June 19 and 23, 1966.

73. Lodge quote is in *New York Times*, June 25, 1966; see also *ibid.*, June 15 and 20, 1966; Kahin and Lewis, *United States in Vietnam*, p. 258.

74. This was evident in discussions I had with them.

75. *The New York Times* was a notable exception.

76. From the section "Why Viet-Nam" in the Department of State's widely distributed pamphlet *Vietnam in Brief*, released December 1966. (Department of State Publication 8173, Far Eastern Series 153, Office of Media Services, Bureau of Public Affairs.)

Index

A NOTE ABOUT THE AUTHOR

George McTurnan Kahin was graduated from Harvard in 1940, served in the U.S. Army during World War II, and received his master's and doctoral degrees in political science from Stanford and Johns Hopkins, respectively. Since 1951 he has taught at Cornell, where he is now Aaron L. Binenkorb Professor of International Studies; from 1961 to 1970 he served as director of the university's Southeast Asian Program. He has received fellowships from the Social Science Research Council, the Guggenheim and Luce foundations, and the National Endowment for the Humanities. During the 1960s and 1970s he conducted extensive field research in both North and South Vietnam, and in 1967–68 was a member of the U.S. State Department's East Asia Advisory Committee. Mr. Kahin is the author or editor of many books, including *The United States and Vietnam* (1967, with John W. Lewis). Since 1975 he has been general editor of the Cornell University Press series The Politics and International Relations of Southeast Asia.

A NOTE ON THE TYPE

The text of this book was set via computer-driven cathode-ray tube in a face called Times Roman, designed by Stanley Morison for *The Times* (London), and first introduced by that newspaper in 1932.

Among typographers and designers of the twentieth century, Stanley Morison was a strong forming influence, as typographical advisor to the English Monotype Corporation, as a director of two distinguished English publishing houses, and as a writer of sensibility, erudition, and keen practical sense.

Composed, printed, and bound by The Haddon Craftsmen, Inc.,
Scranton, Pennsylvania
Designed by Virginia Tan

(continued from front flap)

for neither moral nor high-minded reasons but simply because he saw no viable government to support in Saigon—yet eventually bowing to what he believed to be the greater expertise in foreign affairs of various top advisers; taking a stand, on their advice, that meant irreversible intervention. And by 1967, as Kahin makes clear, U.S. policy was locked into a course that would take the United States through eight more years of war.

Intervention is an insightful, fascinating book that sheds substantial new light on the lasting and complex argument over America's participation in the Vietnam War.